Four Practical Revolutions in Management

Systems for Creating Unique Organizational Capability

Four Practical Revolutions in Management

Systems for Creating Unique Organizational Capability

Shoji Shiba
David Walden

With Contributions by
Alan Graham, John Petrolini, and Many Others

PRODUCTIVITY PRESS
New York • New York

CENTER FOR QUALITY OF MANAGEMENT
Cambridge, Massachusetts

Productivity Press
444 Park Avenue South, Suite 604
New York, NY 10016
United States of America
Telephone: 212-686-5900
Telefax: 212-686-5411
E-mail: info@productivitypress.com

Managing Editor Michael Ryder
Cover design by Shad Lindo and Stephan Scates
Page design and composition by William H. Brunson Typography Services
Printed and bound by Malloy

Library of Congress Cataloging-in-Publication Data

Shiba, Shoji, 1933—
     Four practical revolutions in management : systems for creating unique organizational capability / Shoji Shiba, David Walden
          p. cm.
     Rev. ed. of : New American TQM, 1993
     Includes bibliographical references and index
     ISBN 1-56327-217-2
     1. Total quality management. 2. Total quality management—Case studies
3. Organizational change. 4. Organizational change—Case studies. I. Walden David,
1942—. II. Shiba, Shoji, 1933— New American TQM. III. Title

HD62.15 .S55   2001
658.4′013—dc21
                                                                                        00-068424

07 06 05   6 5 4 3 2

To Mieko and Sara
and
To the Memory of Our Dear Friend Tom Lee

Contents

List of Cases   xiii

Preface   xv

Acknowledgments   xxiii

Introduction: BUSINESS EVOLUTION   1

1   The Evolution of the Customer Satisfaction Concept   3
1.1 What Is Customer Satisfaction?   3
1.2 Evolution of Customer Satisfaction Methods   11
1.3 Evolution of Company Integration   13
1.4 Continuing Evolution   15

2   Survival in a Rapidly Changing World   19
2.1 Practice Systematic Development of Skill   22
2.2 Treat Management as a Coherent System   28
2.3 Focus on People and Their Purposes   30
2.4 Integrate Best Practices   35
2.5 Financial Benefit   36

3   Developing a Unique Organizational Capability   41
3.1 Four Practical Revolutions in Management   41
3.2 Evolution of Our Understanding   43
3.3 Four Levels of Practice   47

The First Revolution: CUSTOMER FOCUS   49

4   Change in the Work Concept   51
4.1 Market-In   51
4.2 Customers   55
4.3 Philosophy-In and Philosophy-Out   56

5   Evolution of Customer Focus and Its Challenges   59
5.1 Three Stages of Customer Focus   59
5.2 Customer Concerns   60
5.3 Integration of Concerns   66
5.4 Individualizing Customers   69

The Second Revolution: CONTINUOUS IMPROVEMENT   71

PART 2A—INTRODUCTION: FUNDAMENTALS AND VOCABULARY

6 Improvement as a Problem-Solving Process   73
6.1 Management by Process   73
6.2 WV Model of Continuous Improvement   74
6.3 Continuous Improvement of Processes for All Types of Work   84
6.4 Continuous Improvement and the Scientific Method   92

PART 2B—MANAGING EXISTING PROCESSES

7 Process Discovery and Management   95
7.1 Thinking in Terms of Process   95
7.2 Process Discovery   98

8 Process Control and Variation   107
8.1 A Typical Example of (Mishandling) Variation   108
8.2 Making the Most of Variation   109
8.3 Process Control and Process Improvement   117
8.4 Continuing the Typical Example of Variation   118

9 Reactive Improvement and the 7 Steps Method   123
9.1 Identifying the Problem   125
9.2 Standard Steps and Tools   131
9.3 The 7 Steps: A Case Study   133
9.4 The 7 QC Tools   145

10 Management Diagnosis of the 7 Steps of Reactive Improvement 149
10.1 General Guidelines for Managers Diagnosing a QI Story   149
10.2 Step-by-Step Guidelines for Managers Diagnosing a QI Story   152
10.3 Case Study for Diagnosis of the 7 Steps   163
10.4 Run PDCA and Develop Skill   173

11 Process Management Mobilization Case Study—Teradyne   175
11.1 Introduction to the Teradyne Mobilization Story   175
11.2 Introduction of the 7 Steps   175
11.3 Experience Using the 7 Steps   177
11.4 Improving Mobilization   178
11.5 Process Discovery and Process Control   181

PART 2C—ONE-TIME EFFORTS

12 Planning Projects or Tasks   183
12.1 The 9 Steps Compared with the 7 Steps   184
12.2 The 9 Steps Mobilization at Teradyne   185
12.3 A Teradyne Illustration of the 9 Steps Use   186
12.4 Relationship of the 9 Steps to Other Methods   196

PART 2D—FINDING NEW DIRECTIONS

13 Proactive Improvement 199
13.1 Collecting Data for Proactive Improvement 201
13.2 Language Data and Use of Semantics 204
13.3 Toward Standard Tools and Steps for Proactive Improvement 211
13.4 Customer Visitation as a Method of Collecting Proactive
    Improvement Data 221

14 Applying Proactive Improvement to Develop New Products 235
14.1 Stage 1: Develop Understanding of Customers' Needs
    and Environment 239
14.2 Stage 2: Convert Understanding into Requirements 248
14.3 Stage 3: Operationally Define Requirements for
    Downstream Development 260
14.4 Stages 4 and 5: Generating Concepts and Selecting the Concept 272
14.5 Expanding View of WV Model and Proactive Improvement 278

The Third Revolution: TOTAL PARTICIPATION 283

PART 3A—INTRODUCTION

15 Engagement and Alignment of Organization Members 285
15.1 Engaged Employees for a Rapidly Changing World 285
15.2 Explicit Joining of Improvement and Routine Work 287
15.3 Processes and People 291

PART 3B—INDIVIDUAL SKILL DEVELOPMENT

16 Coordinating Behavior 297
16.1 Societal Networking Case Study of the CQM Study Group
    on Conversation 299
16.2 Expansion of the Principles of Semantics 302
16.3 Some Types and Models of Conversations 305
16.4 Burchill Case Study from the Navy 323

17 Leading Change 329
17.1 Technical Skill 331
17.2 Human Skill 332
17.3 Conceptual Skill 333

18 Self-Development 341
18.1 Lessons from the Non-Business World 342
18.2 Local Improvement in Absence of a Supportive Environment 347
18.3 The Bottom Line 358

PART 3C—TEAM SKILL DEVELOPMENT

19 Teamwork Skill   361
19.1 Some Fundamentals   361
19.2 Some Types of Teams   367
19.3 Models for Team Development   396

PART 3D—ORGANIZATIONAL SKILL DEVELOPMENT

20 Initiation Strategies   405
20.1 CEO Involvement   405
20.2 Case Study: Teradyne Strategy for Introduction   415

21 Infrastructure for Mobilization   423
21.1 Create Explicit Structures for Mobilization   423
21.2 A General Model for Mobilization: The 7 Infrastructures   425
    1. Goal Setting (Vision/Mission)   427
    2. Organization Setting   431
    3. Training and Education   434
    4. Promotional Activities   441
    5. Diffusion of Success Stories   441
    6. Awards and Incentives   444
    7. Monitoring and Diagnosis   445

22 Phase-In   453
22.1 Orientation Phase   455
22.2 Empowerment Phase   456
22.3 Alignment Phase   458
22.4 Evolution of the Parallel Organization   459
22.5 Common Patterns of Phase-In   461

23 U.S. Focused Strategies for Phase-In   467
23.1 Benchmarking   468
23.2 Six Sigma   472
23.3 Cycle-Time Reduction   479

PART 3E—ORGANIZATIONAL UNIQUENESS

24 Hoshin Management   503
24.1 Hoshin Management and Its Parts   503
    Phase 1—Strategic Planning and Setting the Hoshin (Proactive)   508
    Phase 2—Hoshin Deployment   510
    Phase 3—Monitoring the Hoshin; Controlling with Metrics (Control)   518
    Phase 4—Check and Act (Reactive)   521
    Phase 5—President's Diagnosis   521

24.2 Management by Objectives and Conventional
    Business Planning 524
24.3 Hoshin Management at Analog Devices 531

25 Leading Process Improvement 547
25.1 Modeling Personal Improvement 547
25.2 Employee Development at NIMS 549
25.3 Company Strategies 555
25.4 Individual Practice of CAPD by Managers 569

26 Further Case Studies in Mobilization 577
26.1 Teradyne Story Continued 578
26.2 HP Story 588
26.3 Analog Devices Story 593
26.4 Tom Powell's Research 602

27 The Practice of Breakthrough 607
27.1 Process versus Business Breakthrough 607
27.2 Case Studies and a Model of Business Breakthrough 610
27.3 Biggest Obstacle to Business Breakthrough 626
27.4 Integration of Ideas 636

The Fourth Revolution: SOCIETAL NETWORKING 643

28 Networking and Societal Diffusion: Regional and National Networking 645
28.1 The Japanese Model 646
28.2 Taking a Lesson from Japan—CQM 654
28.3 Comparison of National Methods 662
28.4 Use of Indirect Influence 671

29 Ongoing Integration of Methods 675
29.1 Applying Idealized Design to Hoshin Management 676
29.2 Structural Process Improvement Case Study 681
29.3 SerVend Case Study 688

Afterword 699

About the Authors 705

References 707

Index 729

List of Cases

Process Discovery Example   103
Broken Pellicle 7 Steps at Analog   133
Errorbusters 7 Steps Diagnosis at Analog   163
Process Management Mobilization at Teradyne   175
9 Steps Mobilization at Teradyne   185
9 Steps Case Study at Teradyne   186
BBN Customer Visitation Program Case Study   221
Societal Networking for Concept Engineering Development   236
Contextual Inquiry at Digital   243
Stripping Basket Case Study of Concept Engineering Introduced   237
    Customer Interviews   245
    Customer Image LP   248
    Translation of Customer Voices to Customer Requirements   250
    Use of the Seven Translation Guidelines   250
    Developing a Requirements LP   258
    Kano Questionnaire, Matrix, and Diagram   263
    Generating Metrics   269
    Use of a Quality Table   270
    Benchmark Analysis   271
    Commercial Success   277
Societal Networking via CQM Study Group on Conversation   299
Coordinating Behavior in Gary Burchill's Management Team   323
Evolution of a Japanese QC Team   371
Cross-Functional CQM Design Team   379
Core Teams at Analog Devices   385
Self-Directed Work Teams at Analog Devices   388
CEO Involvement at Teradyne   410
Teradyne Strategy for Introduction   415
SerVend Example of Goals, Values, and Mission   429
Monitoring Improvement Teams at Teradyne   445
Benchmarking from Xerox   468
Six Sigma from Motorola   474
Six Sigma at AlliedSignal   477
AΔT Example   480
CQM Study Group on Cycle-Time Reduction   484

APC Model for Cycle-Time Reduction 492
Hoshin Management at Analog Devices 531
Modeling Personal Improvement 547
Product Development Skill at NIMS 549
Long-Term Mobilization at Teradyne 579
Long-Term Mobilization at Hewlett-Packard 588
Long-Term Mobilization Analog Devices 593
Breakthrough at Seiko 610
Breakthrough at Yokogawa HP 613
Breakthrough at Yokogawa Electric 618
Breakthrough at Fuji Xerox 619
Breakthrough at Meada Corporation 627
Breakthrough at Teradyne Aurora 630
Breakthrough at ASKUL 633
CQM—An Organization for Societal Networking 654
Operationalizing Idealized Design 680
Structural Process Improvement 681
SerVend Case Study 688

Preface

WHY THIS BOOK WAS ORIGINALLY WRITTEN

The first edition of this book, titled *A New American TQM—Four Practical Revolutions in Management*, was drafted in 1990–1992 and was published in 1993. We had several reasons for writing the book.

A variety of companies we knew needed practices, methods, and tools to provide increased customer satisfaction in a rapidly changing world. In particular, the seven founding member companies of the Center for Quality of Management (CQM) had such needs. Shoji Shiba had seen that companies that developed practices, methods, and tools to support *four revolutions in management*[1]—customer focus, continuous improvement, total participation, and societal networking—seemed better able to maintain and increase customer satisfaction in the face of rapid change. In particular, their capabilities were enhanced when they treated the various activities as part of a system (perhaps a system unique to their company) for which over time they could understand the interactions between the parts of the system and improve the way the overall system operated. The book was written to help companies and their top management teams develop their systems, practices, methods, and tools in the four areas.

The book was aimed at senior management because broad business improvement works best when it starts at the top and is taken down to the rest of management and employees by a committed top management team. In particular, the book focused on issues of general management and treated narrow issues such as quality control very lightly.

Many books have been written on methods for business improvement, but far fewer provide the mix of theory, case studies, and detailed step-by-step methods that our book provided. On the one hand, our book provided tried-and-true methods; on the other hand, it also provided methods that were a half-step ahead of common practice. Also, the book did not take the viewpoint of any particular institution or individual; rather, it *synthesized* successful practices used around the world. Thus, the book could be read by those seeking state-of-the-art management concepts or those seeking something closer to an implementation manual of the best available methods.

All of these reasons for writing the first edition of the book continued to drive us as we developed the second edition of the book, and we emphasize some of them even more in the second edition, as described in the next section.

WHY AND HOW THE SECOND EDITION OF THIS BOOK CAME TO BE WRITTEN, AND ITS TITLE

Since publication in 1993, the first edition has sold and continues to sell well. However, since the book's genesis in 1990, much has changed in the world—especially in the United States for whose readers the book was primarily written—that demands this update, which we now publish under the title *Four Practical Revolutions in Management: Systems for Creating Unique Organizational Capability.*

    Continuing evolution of business needs and business improvement methods. The first edition of our book in 1993 was nominally about the why and the how of Total Quality Management (TQM). TQM by then had developed over nearly 40 years, first in the United States, then in Japan, and then again in the United States. Historically, TQM was focused on improving the quality of products and services and doing so with maximum efficiency. In other words, it was focused on quality assurance—the *management of quality.* Neither the first edition of this book nor this second edition puts much emphasis on this traditional focus of TQM on quality assurance. There are many other books on TQM narrowly defined as quality assurance.

    By the time we drafted the first edition of this book the focus of the methods known as TQM was beginning to move from the *management of quality* to the *quality of management*—dealing with the ongoing improvement of the way an organization is managed in a rapidly changing world. Thus, the focus of our first edition was on management and not limited to product and service quality. In fact, shortly after the first edition was published in 1993, we began speaking and writing about TQM as Total Quality *of* Management rather than Total Quality Management; in the last several years, when we were trying to be precise, we began to speak of TQ*of*M rather than TQM.

    Nearly another decade has passed since we began to write the first edition, and the evolution of the problems organizations face has continued. Beyond assuring product and service quality and more generally continuing to improve the way they operate their business, many organizations find it necessary to redefine their business upon occasion. To these ends they need to create an appropriate management system or organization for their own situation. In fact, during the time since the first edition appeared, we have come to see the TQ*of*M methods we were teaching as being aimed at helping a company create its appropriate *unique organizational capability.*

    Also, over the past decade or two, organizations of every type have come to think of themselves more as businesses. Once upon a time only for-profit manufacturing and service companies were thought of as being *in business.* These days, at least in the United States, there is increasing pressure for government, the military, health care organizations, schools and colleges, charities, and even churches to operate in a more business-like fashion. There is loud complaint when the government of a state or a health care organization "does not operate like a business" or "is not accountable."

    In this new edition, we describe methods to address these new needs. In particular, we describe methods to address the needs of organizations (a) to have a dynamic (not static) implementation strategy, (b) to plan for ongoing exploration and discovery and not just for execution, and (c) to diffuse improved capability not just within teams or within organizations but in a reinforcing way *among* individuals, teams, organizations, and across society. Addressing this combination of needs is a unique aspect of our book.

New case studies. The widespread use by companies of the methods described in the first edition, and newer methods since the first edition, has resulted in many new case studies being available for use in the second edition.

Emphasis on integration with other methods. The United States has had to suffer through another decade of the business press and business gurus declaring that one important management advance after another was first the panacea and then was dead. When this book was first written, TQM was the panacea, and then it was declared dead. Then came Business Process Reengineering and then Systems Thinking and Lean Production. Astonishingly, as this book is being revised, Six Sigma is becoming all the rage, as if it hadn't been a key component in Motorola's award-winning TQM implementation in the late 1980s. It is entirely natural that new business ideas get put forward. However, it is counterproductive to see them (especially to promote them) as being in conflict with each other or to see each new method replacing the older methods. Once one reconciles vocabulary differences, there is usually considerable overlap among the supposedly competing methods; and progress in all fields of human endeavor typically depends on newer methods building on or being added to the best parts of older methods. We believe that from the sets of management methods available, managers of companies must select the parts of each set that apply to their company and integrate them into a system appropriate for their company. We call this *designing integrated management systems*, and it is a thread that runs through this revision.

Dodging the uninformed perception that "TQM is dead." Some managers and students of management believe that "TQM is dead." Of course, the methods of TQM are very much alive. Many of the best companies use the methods of TQM, although in some cases they may not talk about them as being TQM. In fact, many TQM methods (for example, ongoing process improvement, customer focus, and employee involvement) have become so accepted that they are merely viewed as part of modern management, and companies that don't use the methods will find themselves at a competitive disadvantage. And, as already mentioned, the methods continue to evolve and improve, often in synthesis with other "name methods."

Nonetheless, so we can quickly move to teaching the use of the methods and avoid some of the distraction and mind set around "TQM is dead," we decided to drop "TQM" from the book's title. Without the ability to use TQM in the title, we now use as our title the old subtitle of the book, *Four Practical Revolutions in Management*, which alludes to the four areas of skill development covered in the first edition and in this new edition and that make up TQM or TQ*of*M: customer focus, continuous improvement, total participation, and societal networking.

Changes in vocabulary. Therefore, TQM will be unavailable to us as an abbreviation for the principles, methods and practices contained in the four areas of skill development. Unfortunately, our newer version, TQ*of*M, seems a little awkward and might still be confused with TQM. Therefore, in this book we will use words such as *to make organizational change, to do organizational learning, to do organizational improvement,* and *to implement organizational change and improvement* rather than *to implement TQM* or *implement TQofM*; and we will refer to *methods* or *practices of organizational change*, etc. rather than *methods* or *practices of TQM* or *TQofM*.

We will use *organizational change* and *organizational change and improvement* (not TQM) to refer to changing the total quality of management to develop an organization's unique capability. These organizational changes may be incremental improvements, breakthroughs from existing business practice, or the entrance into entirely new businesses.

In phrases such as "organizational change" we mean organization as a synonym for any business or non-profit entity such as a corporation, company, university, or society that might use the methods of this book to improve its overall management system. (In fact, much of the time we use *business* rather casually to refer to any for-profit or not-for-profit organization.)

Removing "American" from the title. The first edition of this book has been translated formally into Spanish, French, and Portuguese and has been used as a textbook in courses in the rest of Western Europe (particularly Germany) and Scandinavia (including Finland), Latin America, and in several Asian countries (including Japan). The book is also being translated and used in courses in China. Since the content of the book is not limited to use in the U.S., including the word *American* in the title was an unnecessary limitation and confusion.

Increased emphasis on the theme of systematic development of skill. The first edition of this book had a clear theme of the described methods being for the systematic development of skill in managers, teams, individuals, and organizations. The new edition puts greater emphasis on this theme and on systems for combining the several areas of skill development.

Supporting materials. The first edition of this book was used as the textbook for a variety of college and company training courses. In support of these courses, a parallel set of teaching material has been created, including step-by-step manuals on specific methods, quick reference cards, homework assignments, and in-class exercises. Some of these ancillary materials are included in the second edition and some are referenced. In addition, the *Journal of the Center for Quality of Management*, which was started in parallel with the drafting of the first edition of this book, has been publishing for nine years and is now on-line on the World Wide Web. This edition references a number of the papers and case studies in that on-line archive. Finally, we plan to have a Web site (www.cqm.org/4prim) in support of this book—at minimum, a list of errors and corrections.

What we have not changed. While we have dropped some case studies from the first edition, we have kept other old case studies. Good case studies can remain useful, even some that are a decade old and describe a company that no longer exists or operates in the same way. In general, we see case studies primarily as a way to illustrate practical use. We do not use case studies to *prove* the validity of a method. Good methods can fail. Bad methods can succeed. What works at one time may fail at another time, for a variety of reasons.

Although we have dropped TQM from the title of this second edition, we still use *TQM* in some examples, when the people involved thought of themselves as implementing TQM.

Despite economic problems in Japan in the 1990s and the buoyant U.S. economy during the same period, we have also kept many of the comparisons between the Japanese approach to business improvement since the advent of TQM in Japan versus the traditional U.S. pre-TQM approach to business. The Japanese approach significantly informed the approach now used by many of the best U.S. companies, which continue to benefit from using the methods.

This second edition is *still* intended to be a textbook for college courses and courses outside of colleges aimed at executives and managers. It is also intended to be read and referenced by CEOs and other organizational change agents who are engaged in improving the way their organizations (however large or small) operate. We aim to provide more than motivation for change and pat answers for how to accomplish change. We are trying to provide enough theory, practical methods, and examples to enable readers to develop their own theories for the future structure and processes of their organizations, to try them in their organizations, and over time to make them work. To support the practical use of the content of our book, we include many references to related works, both to provide pointers to additional information and to acknowledge our sources.

What we have not added. The environmental changes that may be having the biggest effect on the way business is practiced involve the Internet, World Wide Web, microcomputers available everywhere, and other electronic technology and infrastructure. A book needs to be written called *Managing in the Information Age.* Unfortunately, we will not be able to address that need here.

Second edition authors. Since the first edition was published, Shoji Shiba and David Walden have remained actively involved in developing and teaching the content of this book, while our colleague and friend Alan Graham has gone on to other interests. Thus, it was natural that this second edition be authored by the two of us.

ORGANIZATION OF THE SECOND EDITION

As with the first edition, this edition is divided into five parts: an introductory section, followed by a section on each of the Four Practical Management Revolutions of the title, as shown in the following table.

Introduction: Business Evolution	3 chapters
The First Revolution: Customer Focus	2 chapters
The Second Revolution: Continuous Improvement	9 chapters
The Third Revolution: Total Participation	13 chapters
The Fourth Revolution: Societal Networking	2 chapters

The Four Practical Revolutions are:

1. Customer focus—the need and means to pay attention to customers to know what to improve
2. Continuous improvement—the need and means to continue to improve
3. Total participation—the need and means to engage appropriate people throughout the organization in improvement activities and to obtain their particular knowledge and capabilities so that peoples' efforts help rather than hinder
4. Societal networking—the benefit and means of sharing good management practices with others, so that all can improve more rapidly

Each of the five sections of the book has a somewhat expanded number of chapters from the first edition. Specific methods relating to each of the four practical revolutions are described.

As can be seen in the table above, the book has many more chapters on continuous improvement and total participation than on customer focus and on societal networking. Continuing to improve the organization and expanding participation in the improvement are what an organization can do for itself. The customers and other organizations are external influences that motivate and support continuous improvement and increased participation.

In the first edition of this book, we waited until the beginning of the section on total participation to begin to introduce the methods of mobilizing people in the organization to participate in improvement activities. In teaching the content of the book, waiting this long has proved problematic—people cannot concentrate on learning the content for customer focus and continuous improvement because of their concern that it will be impossible to mobilize use of the methods in their organizations. Thus, in this edition, we begin presenting case studies of mobilization from nearly the beginning of the book.

We wait until the part of the book on mobilization to present a *general model* for mobilization. There we also summarize the relevance to the general model of the case studies presented earlier in the book. Finally, we present additional case studies of mobilization, and some more theory.

Order of Reading

For consistency with the first edition of this book and to highlight early on the importance of customer focus we present the four revolutions in the order listed above.

However, reversing the first two revolutions might be a more appropriate order of presentation, since historically the methods of continuous improvement were used to discover the need for and methods of customer focus. On the other hand, if we introduced continuous improvement first, we would not want to cover all of the material in the seven chapters of the book (Chapters 6 to 12) on continuous improvement before introducing customer focus (Chapters 4 and 5). In fact, we often teach the content of this book in the following order:

Chapter 6: an introduction to continuous improvement
Chapter 4: an introduction to customer focus
Chapter 5: on some challenges of customer focus
Chapters 7 to 12: details of specific methods of continuous improvement, many of which include a customer focus component

That could also be a sensible order of reading.

Iconography

Throughout the book we use variations of the following figure to help readers keep track of which section of the book they are in.

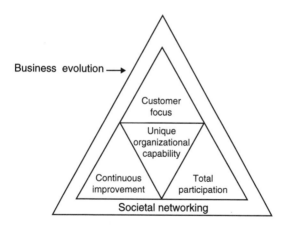

The meaning of the figure is that the evolution of business requires activity relating to each of the four revolutions—customer focus, continuous improvement, total participation, and societal networking (which accelerates efforts of the previous three revolutions). All of these activities taken together help a business develop its unique organizational capability.

Shoji Shiba
David Walden

NOTES

1. The phrase "revolutions in management" comes from Kaoru Ishikawa, in many ways a father of Japanese TQM, whose motivation for working at TQM was to "accomplish a revitalization of industry and effect a thought revolution in management" [147, Chapter 6].

Acknowledgments

SECOND EDITION CONTRIBUTIONS

A number of people have made contributions to this book. The contributions of Alan Graham, our co-author for the first edition of this book, are inseparable from the content of the second edition. John Petrolini, of Teradyne, has taught us much over the years about the Teradyne approach to management. In particular, he allowed us to use the set of Teradyne case studies that run throughout this book, including text and figures, even though he may include extended versions of this content in a monograph of his on the Teradyne TQM story. We have learned much from other individuals in many companies, but no one else has contributed as much to our understanding and to this edition.

The founding and current presidents of the Center for Quality of Management (CQM), Tom Lee and Gary Burchill, have been our collaborators in many activities we have drawn on for this book. They also were supportive of the writing of this book. We are privileged to be able to say that Tom and Gary are our colleagues and friends.

The first edition of this book has been used as the textbook of course 15.766 at MIT for a number of years. Business people who presented case studies for the MIT course that influenced this edition were Alex d'Arbelof, Rodger Dowdell, Warren Harkness, Brad Harrington, Brad Nelson, John Petrolini, Paul Snyder, Bob Stasey, Ray Stata, and Goodloe Suttler. Case studies from David Lowe and Fred Schwettmann were sketched for the MIT students by the authors of this book. Teaching assistants for the MIT course included Tonia Chu, Alvaro Cuervo-Cazurra, Martin Hahn, and Greg Scott. We also appreciate the participation and feedback of the 15.766 students from the Leaders in Manufacturing Program, the System Design Management Program, and other parts of Sloan School of Management and MIT.

We have also taught the content of this book in a variety of CQM courses, on two occasions at the ADL School of Management, and in other schools and programs. We appreciate the participation and feedback of the students of those courses.

Ira Moskowitz and Ken Bethea described to us their experience with self-directed work teams in their division at Analog Devices. Jeff Swift described to us his experience with core teams in his division at Analog Devices. Alex d'Arbelof told us about Teledyne Aurora. Bob Stasey provided a case study of hoshin management. Chris Mastro, Doug Mader, Marty Miller, Michael Carter, Yogesh Parikh, Trent Guerrero, Andrea Vlasak, Asoka Verravagu, and Rajesh Srinivasan provided insight, and pointers to people with insight, about the current state of Six Sigma practice.

Yogesh Parikh told us about the history of AΔT. Insight about the current state of the EFQM model was provided by Bob Barbour, Pat O'Neil, and George Wilson. Neil Rasumssen helped us understand APC's model of cycle-time reduction and co-authored a paper we drew on. Richard LeVitt updated us about HP's planning and management methods; Bob Grady described HP's use of software metrics. Greg Fischer told us the SerVend story. For the Self-Development chapter, David Walden talked either at length or briefly to golfers Ean Rankin and Jonathan Crane, tennis players Harry Kirsch and Mike Nacey, chess master Alex Cherniack, champion sailor Stewart Neff, sailing coach Ken Legler, violin teacher Ed Pearlman, management consultant Jack Reilly, and dancer Michael Grandfield. Shoji Shiba studied many companies mentioned in chapter 27.

Many people from the CQM staff past and present were drawn into helping us at one time or another: Gary Burchill encouraged us and provided personal case studies, Kevin M. Young helped prepare the manuscript; Eric Bergemann provided information systems support; Janice Hall answered software questions and did archive searches; Manfred Betz, Beth Hunter-Clark, Silja-Riitte Dandridge, Christine Duvivier, Steve LaPierre, Linda Pizzotti, Kathy Prasad, Jim Wahl and Toby Woll all were sent on quests for information of one sort or another; and the rest.

From Productivity Press, we greatly appreciate the encouragement and support of developmental editors Maura May and Steve Gstalder, and assistant Lia Rojales; production editors Michael Ryder and Lorraine Millard; then-president Steven Ott; Paul Obringer, formerly with the sales department; marketing specialist James Shea; Jessica Letney, former production editor; and also cover designers Shad Lindo and Stephen Scates. Robert Saigh, of Razorsharp Communications, Inc., both copy edited and indexed the book under contract to Productivity. Christina Lowman provided proofreading services to Productivity. Bill Brunson, of William H. Brunson Typography Services, was the compositor, also under contract to Productivity.

At the same time this book was being revised, the authors of this book, Shoji Shiba and David Walden, were simultaneously involved in the writing of another book [186]. In particular, David Walden provided draft text to the preface, a chapter and two appendices of that book that also served as draft text for this book. Some of that text came from a paper drafted in 1994 and 1995 by Thomas Lee and David Walden [187], which was heavily influenced by the thinking of Russ Ackoff. For this book, we also interviewed some of the same people interviewed for that book. While the vast majority of [186] (to which Chris Bergonzi also contributed) is different than this book, similar or the same figures and words, sentences or paragraphs may appear in the parallel sections of the two books.

We have included extensive footnotes and references, directing readers to original sources and attempting to properly acknowledge colleagues and authors from whom we have learned. However, as we have lectured over the years on the content of this book, some ideas and even phrases of others may have become so familiar that we now do not recognize them as other than our own. If you spot something that you think should be acknowledged to someone else and isn't, please let the second author know so we can consider making an appropriate correction in future printings.

FIRST EDITION CONTRIBUTORS

In creating the second edition, we are very grateful for the contributions to the first edition: they formed the basic structure and provide much continuing content of the second edition.

Most of all, we appreciate the great contributions of Alan Graham, our co-author for the first edition.

We are indebted to the Japanese and American companies that hosted CQM visits in 1990 and 1991. In alphabetical order they are: Florida Power & Light Co.; Fuji Xerox Co. Ltd.; Hitachi Ltd., Mito Works; Motorola; NEC Corporation; NEC IC Microcomputer Systems, Ltd.; NEC Shizuoka, Ltd.; Toto Ltd.; Xerox Corporation; and Yaesu Book Center. Senior executives and managers Akira Kuroiwa and Morio Katsuta from NEC Kansai, Ltd. and Mitsuru Nitta from Tokyo Electric Power Company were also extremely generous in visiting MIT and the CQM. The Japanese Union of Scientists and Engineers (JUSE) was invaluable in sharing its experience in societal networking.

We are likewise indebted to the practitioners who gave us the benefit of their experience: Mr. Jim Bakken (vice president, Ford Motor Company [retired]), Dr. George Fisher (former CEO of Motorola), Mr. Robert Galvin, (former chairman of Motorola), Professor Emeritus Masao Kogure, Dr. Yokio Mizuno (senior executive vice president, NEC Corporation), and Mr. Junji Noguchi (executive director of JUSE). We especially acknowledge Professor Emeritus Jiro Kawakita.

The CQM was founded by seven companies: Analog Devices, Inc.; Bolt Beranek and Newman Inc.; Bose Corporation; Digital Equipment Corporation; General Electric's division in Lynn, Massachusetts; Polaroid Corporation; and Teradyne, Inc. In March and April 1990, the following individuals from these companies and MIT participated in a full-time five-week project to study TQM and design how the CQM would function and the services it would provide: Ron Butler, Dave Darsney, Ralph Goldwasser, Steve Graves, Joe Junguzza, Tom Lee, John Petrolini, Ken Potashner, Art Schneiderman, Goodloe Suttler, and the three authors of this book (Shiba, Graham, and Walden). The initial outline of the course on which the book was based and many of the case studies were developed by many of these same individuals.

We hasten to acknowledge the remarkable ability of the MIT community to bring people and knowledge together. CQM co-founders Tom Lee, Ray Stata, and Shoji Shiba connected in one way or another through MIT. The preliminary content of the book was taught at MIT which influenced the final form of the book. There are other synergies with MIT too numerous to mention.

Many people helped directly or indirectly with the preparation of the book. Gary Burchill, Rich Lynch, Ira Moskowitz, Ron Santella, Diane Shen, and John Sheridan contributed to various instruction manuals to be used with this book and the CQM course based on this book. Ron Butler, Charlie Fine, Phil Gulley, Joe Junguzza, Mike LaVigna, Rich Lynch, Ira Moskowitz, Yogesh Parikh, John Petrolini, Owen Robbins, Art Schneiderman, and Del Thorndike presented case studies during the first two CQM courses. Gary Burchill provided a major case study for the book. Gary Burchill and Tom Heller were teaching assistants for MIT courses and in the CQM course upon which the book was based. Donna McGurk provided administrative support for the CQM course. Stella Tarnay transcribed the bulk of the notes taken on the first courses. Trish McKinnon typed redrafts of the material. Deborah Melone provided editorial assistance. Diane Asay and Karen Jones of Productivity Press edited the book. Gayle Joyce and Karla Tolbert of Productivity Press did important layout and graphics design.

Many people from the CQM and CQM companies were supportive of the book and the course on which it was initially based, especially Alex d'Arbeloff, Sherwin Greenblatt, Tom Lee, Steve Levy, and Ray Stata.

Introduction:
BUSINESS EVOLUTION

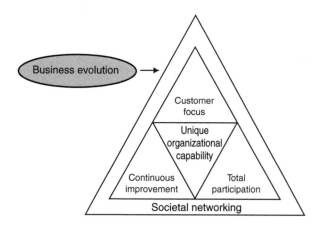

This introductory portion of the book provides motivation and background for the presentation of the methods of the Four Practical Revolutions of Management described in the rest of the book.

Chapter 1—The Evolution of the Customer Satisfaction Concept

- Sketches the evolution of expectations over the course of the twentieth century for customer satisfaction or quality, which has driven the driven the speed of business change and the need for more efficient methods of business improvement.
- Describes the evolution of methods needed to address the changing expectations for customer satisfaction or quality.

Chapter 2—Survival in a Rapidly Changing World

- Describes how rapid change in business requires changes in the way we think about management:
  - A systematic approach to developing individual and organizational skill
  - Treating management as a system
  - Dealing with people and their purposes
  - Integrating best practices

Chapter 3—Developing a Unique Organizational Capability

- Introduces the Four Practical Revolutions in Management and the rest of the book.

1

The Evolution of the Customer Satisfaction Concept

As we begin the third millennium, many people trying to manage organizations have a feeling that things are moving faster and faster and that it is more and more difficult to survive in business. Of course, this feeling is not new. Each generation feels things are moving faster, and each generation has been right. A major source of this increase in difficulty has come from an evolution in the meaning of customer satisfaction over the course of the twentieth century.

Customer satisfaction and quality can be thought of as two different names for the same thing. When customers are asked to define what quality means to them, in general what they mean is what it takes to satisfy them. Thus, in this chapter and the rest of the book we will use the words customer satisfaction and quality more or less interchangeably.

In this chapter, we relate a history of how customers and businesses have thought about customer satisfaction, focusing particularly on an explicit model, known as the *four fitnesses*, for how customer satisfaction has evolved.

1.1 WHAT IS CUSTOMER SATISFACTION?

What is customer satisfaction? (Or, what is quality?[1]) This is a multifaceted question, difficult to address in the abstract. It is easier to understand what is meant by customer satisfaction by considering the evolution of its meaning in leading companies. In the United States and Europe, quality control of one sort or another has been part of manufacturing for more than a hundred years, and the use of various quality concepts has come and gone and come again. By contrast, in Japan quality control was not significant until after World War II; since then, however, progress has been relatively rapid and uniform.

At the beginning of the evolutionary process, customer satisfaction or quality of any kind is not noticed or measured. Goods are produced and shipped. If customers want to send something back, they do so—end of story. This situation characterized Japanese companies in the early 1950s, when "made in Japan" meant shoddy, unreliable goods.

In the rest of this section we trace the evolution of company efforts to improve customer satisfaction by describing the *four fitnesses*—levels of quality or stages of evolution of customer satisfaction—and their weaknesses.

The four fitnesses are:

- Fitness to standard
- Fitness to use
- Fitness of cost
- Fitness to latent requirement[2]

Quality Concept 1: Fitness to Standard

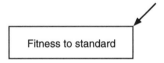

Fitness to standard evaluates whether a product built as described in the manual passes the standard. In other words, fitness to standard defines quality as the product that does what the designers intend it to do. Determining whether a product meets fitness to standard is mainly a question of inspection: does the product pass or not? To achieve fitness to standard, managers and engineers define each manufacturing task, record those tasks as standard practices in manuals, and define inspection procedures to enforce the standard practices. To evaluate fitness to standard, companies sometimes use the concept of statistical quality control (SQC), an approach the American quality expert W. E. Deming brought to Japan in the early 1950s.

When considered from a modern-day rather than a historical perspective, fitness to standard used alone as a definition of quality has two weaknesses.

The first is the notion that quality can be achieved through inspection. According to fitness to standard, you assure quality by inspecting the output of a manufacturing process and culling out and discarding the defective or low-quality items. In reality, however, this process often leads to an adversarial relationship between those who make a product and those who inspect it. Professor Shiba tells of a case in which the factory manager proudly described to him his factory's excellent inspection system, emphasizing that the inspection function was completely separate from the rest of the plant; indeed, the inspectors were government employees, not plant employees. When Professor Shiba talked to the workers, however, he learned that they considered the inspectors to be the enemy.

The second weakness of fitness to standard is its neglect of market needs. Creation of production standards and inspection geared to these standards orients people to the product and whether it does what it was designed to do, rather than to the needs of customers and whether the product fills those needs. Acting to correct this weakness brought leading Japanese companies to the next level of quality in the early 1960s.

Quality Concept 2: Fitness to Use

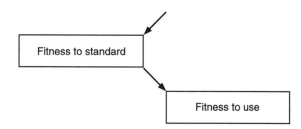

Fitness to use means to assure satisfaction of market needs. Can the product be used as the customers want to use it? For instance, a tool company makes screwdrivers to turn a certain size screw. For many users, their real need is to have the tool turn whatever size screw they have and also to open a can of paint. (The Sears Craftsman Tools no-questions-asked guarantee may have been an attempt to promise fitness to use.) It is not easy to forecast the diverse usage of the market, as the following amusing example from Japan illustrates.

A major appliance company made a new washing machine. However, there were many complaints about it from the customers living in rural areas. The company sent its engineers to the field to observe. They found that farmers were using the machines to wash the dirt off potatoes. Although such use wasn't prohibited by the manual, the machines weren't designed for such dense loads, and they would often break. When the manufacturer realized the use to which customers were actually putting the machines, the machine was redesigned to tolerate potato washing, and the machines returned to normal reliability. Fitness to use addresses the real needs or desires of the customer, not just the standards set by the producer.

As was the case with fitness to standard, fitness to use is achieved by inspection. Thus, a certain amount of conflict between inspectors and workers arises. Further, if the company wants products that can be absolutely counted on to perform as expected, that is, to have high fitness to use, then inspectors must rigorously reject products that deviate from the standard.

Any production process has variability from one unit to the next. Not all cars that come off an assembly line have exactly the same horsepower. Some bottles of soda will have caps too small, so that they don't quite stay on. Other bottles will have caps that leak because they are too large. Extremes on one or both sides of the standard must be rejected and reworked or thrown away.

Figure 1-1 illustrates this principle. The upper curve shows the statistical variation in some product characteristic such as horsepower, size of bottle cap, or amount of ice cream in the cone at an ice cream parlor. The products with characteristics beyond the acceptable tolerances must be rejected, which is a costly approach. As shown in the lower curve, if higher quality is desired, the inspection limits must be narrowed so that even more items are rejected, which is even more costly.

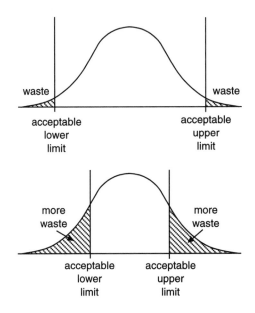

Figure 1-1. Statistical Variation in Product Characteristics

Another weakness of focusing on fitness to use is that use-based competitive advantage is tenuous. If a company has clearly understood fitness to use (meeting the needs of users), it may gain a monopoly position, so that it can charge prices high enough to compensate for the higher cost of higher quality through inspection. Competitors offering equally good products for cheaper prices quickly spring up, eliminating the monopoly position and the ability to offset costs incurred during the inspection process. For instance, from 1960 to 1970, a major Japanese camera company monopolized its market and charged high prices. But then the competition for cameras in Japan became fierce; sales of this camera company went down, and those of other brands went up. The camera company lost much of its market share in Japan.

Moving away from the high costs of "inspecting quality in" and toward "building quality in" brought leading Japanese companies during the early 1970s to the next level of quality.

Quality Concept 3: Fitness of Cost

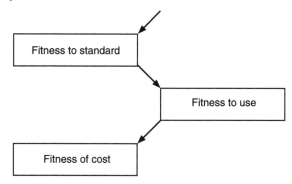

Fitness of cost means high quality *and* low cost. These are the two most universal requirements for virtually all customers, products, and services. To achieve cost reduction while maintaining high quality (with no products outside the bounds), a business must reduce the variability of the production process, so that all units produced are already within the inspection limits and none have to be discarded (see Figure 1-2).

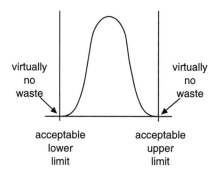

Figure 1-2. Reduced Variation Reduces Waste

A company seeking 100 percent quality without culling requires feedback and correction at each step rather than just at the end of the production process. To achieve this level of quality, it must completely change the production system. Worker focus must shift from controlling the output through inspection to controlling the process (see Figure 1-3).

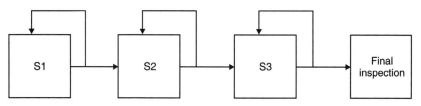

Figure 1-3. Feedback at Each Production Step

The modern methods to accomplish this shift are:

- Using statistical quality control
- Monitoring the process in addition to the output
- Providing for feedback at each step, whereby every line worker notices the work of his or her predecessor and can ensure that mistakes are corrected immediately
- Instituting line worker participation in the design and improvement of the production process to make it continuously more reliable

Workers are empowered to create this kind of continuous change through standardized, mass-taught tools and practices, such as the seven steps for quality control (7 QC steps, or 7 steps) and the seven tools for quality control (7 QC tools), which are described later (and are designated the 7 steps and 7 QC tools in this book).

However, a weakness remains. Companies that have achieved the quality level of fitness of cost are producing highly reliable, functional products at low cost. But competitors can create similarly reliable and inexpensive products. Newly industrialized countries can copy their skills of fitness to standard and fitness to use but have much cheaper labor, yielding low cost. This happened to Japan in the 1980s. Korea, Hong Kong, and Taiwan adopted Japanese technology, but had labor costs that were only one-half or two-thirds the Japanese cost.

For this weakness, the cure that leading Japanese companies began pursuing in a standardized way in the early 1980s was creating innovative products that would outsell competitors' products. This raised product quality to the next level (described after the following subsection).

Two Formulas That Help in Thinking about Cost versus Price

Fitness of cost aims simultaneously at an improved product and a lower price (cost to the customer). This is in contrast to a typical viewpoint that a better product can demand a higher price.

The traditional more-features-provide-higher-prices view may be represented by the following formula.

$$Cost + profit \longrightarrow price$$

According to this formula, we develop the product that has the features we think are desirable and, to the cost of producing the product, we add our needed profit level to derive the price.

However, in many fields today, price is dropping as the product is improving. An obvious example is the personal computer business, where capacity and speed continue to increase and prices continue to decrease.

The fitness-of-cost approach may be represented by the following formula.

$$Price - profit \longrightarrow cost$$

According to this formula, the market (for instance, competitive pricing) sets the price for the features the market demands. From that we subtract our needed profit level and thus derive the cost of producing the product, including all necessary features.[3]

Quality Concept 4: Fitness to Latent Requirement

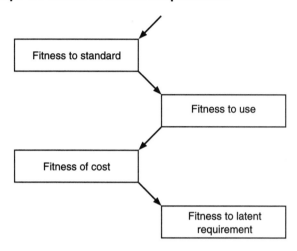

Fitness to latent requirement means meeting customer needs before customers are aware of those needs. If a company can find the latent requirement of the market, it may achieve a monopoly for a little while. The company can ask a higher price, which can be very profitable.

One of the most famous examples of a latent requirement occurred with the Polaroid Land camera. In 1944, while on vacation in Santa Fe, New Mexico, Edwin Land took a picture of his young daughter. She asked him why she had to wait to see the picture. On a solitary walk around Santa Fe, Land solved the puzzle implicit in her question, visualizing most of the requirements for a camera, film, and physical chemistry that permit what is now called instant photography.

A more recent example of a latent requirement is the Sony Walkman. This is a product we didn't know we needed, but as soon as it was available we found that our children couldn't walk or ride in the car without one, and the Walkman definitely improved the time we spent jogging and standing in grocery store lines.

The Great Leaps

The modern concept of how people thought about quality began with the shift to mass production and then evolved in three great leaps or revolutionary changes:

- To fitness to use—shift to mass production
- From fitness to standard to fitness to use—shift to the concept of market

- From fitness to use to fitness of cost—shift to the concept that the price is set in the market
- From fitness of cost to fitness to latent requirement—shift to the concepts of continuous change in market need and thus the continuous shortening of product development cycles

A Complete Example

Watches provide an example of all four levels of the quality concept:

- If a watch is put together with parts missing, it doesn't fit the standard. It must be thrown away or reworked.
- Watches must keep time to be fit for use. High-quality (accurate) chronometers of the eighteenth and nineteenth centuries were made of expensive components and were rigorously tested. Their cost was high, but they met the second quality standard. The classic mechanical Swiss watch of the twentieth century continued this tradition.
- Watches with electronics are both cheap and accurate, meeting the standard of fitness of cost. Many companies in many countries make such watches. Now watches can be had for under $10 that are more accurate than the finest mechanical watches of the pre-electronic era, but competition is brutal.
- Fashion and individuality were introduced into the low-end watch market by Swatch, a Swiss company. Meeting these latent requirements allowed the company to charge more and make a higher profit than for commodity watches.

Companies Must Be Aware of All Four Fitnesses

Above we described the evolution of the concept of quality, in response to societal pressure, through the four fitnesses. However, companies today can't evolve through the four fitnesses in the historical order—it would take so many years that the company would lose competitively to pressures of companies already skilled in all four fitnesses.

Companies may not have to implement all four fitnesses for every product, and some companies may decide to focus on just some of the fitnesses. In general, however, companies today have to be aware of and probably implement the four fitnesses in parallel.

Companies must also avoid the mistake of thinking that the later fitnesses are higher or better than the earlier fitnesses and are thus worthy of greater attention. For instance, some product development people become fixated on fitness to latent requirement. In product development, companies must always address fitness to standard and probably need to address fitness of use and fitness of cost. They need to address only a few latent requirements.

Weaknesses can remain even in companies that systematically meet their customers' latent requirements. These weaknesses arise not from the companies' current processes for product and production process design, but from the variable speed and appropriateness of improvement and change. Many companies are going out of business simply because they are not able to improve as quickly as their competitors. The tools and practices to address this weakness are discussed later in this book.

1.2 EVOLUTION OF CUSTOMER SATISFACTION METHODS

As the world changes, societal and economic forces drive the evolution of customer satisfaction or quality concepts *and* the tools and practices used to achieve them. Throughout the world people have intuitively understood and attempted to address the four fitnesses. Edwin Land's instant Polaroid photography, for example, addressed a latent requirement. His insight comprised both the concept and the means of its implementation.

However, intuition is often not sufficient. Therefore, we now describe the effort to create and diffuse a systematic quality improvement process. Standardized tools and practices were developed, deployed, and validated for each of the fitnesses and stages of the quality concept. These tools and practices were modified as corporations and their customers responded to the changes in the larger economy. We can expect to see further changes as competition develops along new dimensions and societal needs find new expression.

The evolution of methodology is summarized in Figure 1-4 and described in more detail in the following subsections.

Fitness to Standard $\longrightarrow$ Fitness to Use

Standardization, statistical process control, and inspection were the main tools used to achieve fitness to standard. The consumer revolution and fitness to use brought a new tool: market research to find out what the customer wanted and cross-functional involvement to deliver it.

Fitness to Use $\longrightarrow$ Fitness of Cost

At the next quality level, fitness of cost, the emphasis was on reducing costs while increasing quality (and, hence, on the need for low-variance production). Controlling and improving each production process, actively involving production workers, and developing the tools and practices suitable for a mass movement became necessary. Quality control circles (designated QC circles in this book) are described in Chapter 19. The 7 QC tools and the 7-step improvement process that uses them are listed in Table 1-1 and described in Chapter 9 (see also [181]).

Fitness of Cost $\longrightarrow$ Fitness to Latent Requirement

The next level in quality methods added design value, with products developed to satisfy latent needs. The standardized means for accomplishing this new kind of quality are quality function deployment (QFD) and the 7 management and planning tools

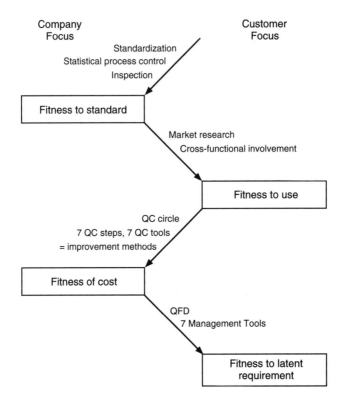

Figure 1-4. The Evolution of Methodology

(listed in Table 1-2 and described in Chapter 13). These tools help companies identify latent needs and translate those needs into plans for products and production processes. The term *management tools* is somewhat misleading because the tools are for engineers and staff people as well. Indeed, perhaps the most prominent and stan-

Table 1-1. The Tools and Steps of Quality Control

The 7 QC Tools	The 7 QC Steps
1. Check sheet*	1. Select theme
2. Pareto diagram	2. Collect and analyze data
3. Cause-and-effect diagram	3. Analyze causes
4. Graphs/Stratification	4. Plan and implement solution
5. Control charts	5. Evaluate effects
6. Histogram	6. Standardize solution
7. Scatter diagram	7. Reflect on process (and next problem)

*Some companies include stratification or process flowcharts as one of the 7 QC tools instead of check sheet.

Table 1-2. The Seven Management and Planning Tools

1. Affinity diagram (KJ method)
2. Relations diagram
3. Matrix diagram
4. Tree diagram
5. Arrow diagram
6. PDPC
7. Matrix data analysis

dardized application of these tools is quality function deployment, which specifically forges a common understanding among marketing people, engineers, and managers.

1.3 EVOLUTION OF COMPANY INTEGRATION

As industrialization increased during the first half of the twentieth century, companies evolved from craft shops, with the entire staff in one room, into highly compartmentalized organizations. Such companies were capable of producing a few standard products with great efficiency. In the second half of the twentieth century, however, compartmentalization left companies unable to address the changing definition of quality; thus, a reintegration process began.

The integration of various parts of companies and their environments occurred as a result of successive innovations in business improvement and organizational learning. As Figure 1-5 suggests, the pattern of integration has alternated between vertical integration (lower parts better connected with upper parts) and horizontal integration (better connection of different functions, such as marketing, customers, or development).

Fitness to standard and fitness of cost are related to where quality improvement takes place in the vertical hierarchy of the company.

With fitness to standard came the hierarchical integration of engineering in which specifications were provided for the production line and the quality assurance department assured that the production line met those specifications. However, improvement work (by management and engineering) and routine work (by workers on the production line) remained strictly separated.

With fitness of cost came the imperative to focus on cost goals and to move information for improvement activities up and down the hierarchy. QC circles not only improved the way line workers did their routine work, but they revealed ways for managers and engineers to reduce cost through process changes and product design. Thus, production and improvement work were integrated at all levels of the organization.

Fitness to use and fitness to latent requirement have to do with how quality improvement takes place across an organization, that is, with horizontal integration.

Fitness to use required integration of all functions so that the company could provide quality in the customer's terms. Functions became interdependent: market research data had to be taken, the design and planning people had to design a product based on those data, production had to work from the design to make a product, sales

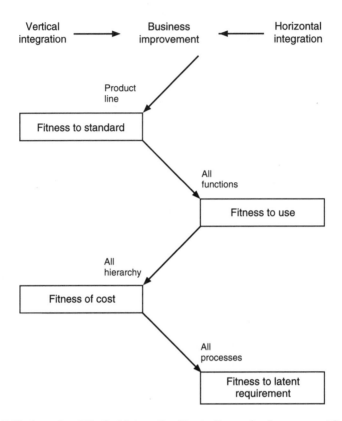

Figure 1-5. Horizontal and Vertical Integration Due to Successive Improvement Innovations

and support had to sell and deliver the product to the customer, and the cycle would be repeated (see Figure 1-6).[4]

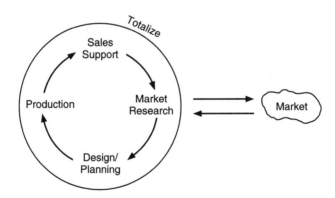

Figure 1-6. Total Integration of Company Functions

Fitness to latent requirement requires that processes be integrated. Integration of process has two meanings. First, it refers to integrating processes beyond the functional departments of the company (for example, customer processes used to identify anticipated needs) into the internal processes of the company. Second, it refers to extrapolating what is learned about processes in one area of the company to processes in other parts of the company so that the entire company may better anticipate customer needs.

Achieving fitness to latent requirement totalizes or systematically integrates quality practices across the customer's environment. Information about customer lifestyles and ways to improve them reach throughout the entire corporation.

1.4 CONTINUING EVOLUTION

Since the world is still rapidly changing, it is very likely that the concept of quality will continue to evolve and expand. In the 1993 edition, we suggested directions in which the definition of quality might evolve. Since 1993, we have seen signs of two new fitnesses becoming increasingly important, as shown in Figure 1-7.

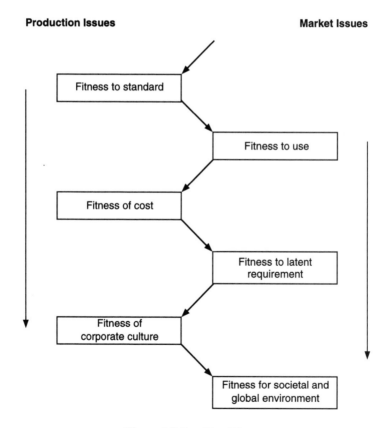

Figure 1-7. Two New Fitnesses

Fitness of corporate culture. Increasingly, companies are making decisions about products and promoting themselves on the basis of their corporate culture. For instance, NEC views itself as a company of computers and communications. We might call this fitness to corporate culture. Fitness to corporate culture fills out the stream of production from its starting point with the individual worker, through team efforts to address quality and cost simultaneously, to the product's place within the corporate strategy. This emphasis on corporate culture is needed for quick new product development in a rapidly changing business environment. We see this attitude in many Silicon Valley companies that emphasize the day-and-night schedules of their work, their living in "Internet time" (which purportedly runs several times faster than time in other industries), their entrepreneurial atmosphere, and so on.

Another example is from a Japanese maker of flexible panels for equipment which runs its business according to the "6-3-3-4 model": six months to develop a new product, three months to introduce the product to the market, three months of peak sales and production, and four months of product withdrawal from the market.

Fitness for societal and global environment. There is also increasing pressure for companies to improve the fitness of their work environment for employees and the fitness of their products and manufacturing processes for the surrounding environment, what might be called fitness for societal and global environment. This is a market-focused issue extending from fitness to latent requirement to include meeting the needs of the environment in which the customer lives. Note the increasing emphasis on the environmental standard known as ISO 1400.

Fitness for societal and global environment counter balances fitness to latent requirement. Fitness to latent requirement alone is not necessarily well suited to the long-term needs of society. For instance, many Information Systems managers in companies see frequent updates of computer software products by their vendors as too expensive and too disruptive. Planned obsolecence is now viewed as detrimental to the environment and the financial well-being of individual citizens.

A Consensus Next Fitness? More often than not when we ask our students what the next fitness will be, they say "fitness for all stakeholders in the organization"—moving beyond customers to include employees, owners, communities, and so on. Unfortunately, this proposed fitness does not fit neatly into our model of each new fitness alternating between production issues and market issues.

NOTES

1. For a thorough history of quality in the United States, see [110, Chapter 1].

2. The story of Japan's transformation from a situation where the term "made in Japan" meant shoddy goods to where it signified products of excellent quality is the story of the Japanese adoption and development of TQM. In fact, the four fitnesses characterize the four eras in the history of Japanese TQM through 1990. Since the different stages in the evolution of quality can be seen clearly in leading Japanese

companies more clearly than it can be seen in the U.S. or Europe, we frequently refer to the experience in Japan in describing the four fitnesses.

3. As with all models, these formulas are intended to be helpful but probably do not accurately deal with all possible situations. They do at least superficially apply to non-profit institutions if one sets profit to zero.

4. In fact, the *total* in *total quality management* originally meant integration of all company departments. Companies sought to "totalize" all divisions in order to unify efforts to satisfy customers.

2
Survival in a Rapidly Changing World

Most people in business, people in all walks of life for that matter, have the feeling that these days things are moving faster and faster. In business, only a decade or two ago, we brought out a new product and expected to sell it for a few years. Today, managers of many companies feel that they have to bring out new products at a relentless pace of every few months, or they will be overwhelmed by competitors' products.

Of course, business has always seemed to be moving fast, at least against the pace of its time. However, there is no denying that today information and things can travel faster than ever before. Satellites broadcast ads for new products and services around the world, new fads spread worldwide practically overnight, and we can order a product from a Web site across the world and have it by international air courier tomorrow or the day after tomorrow.

There is also near constant talk about globalization and the global markets and a perception by many that more companies are operating more globally than every before.

Furthermore, after the downsizing decade, even in the booming U.S. economy of the 1990s, many of these companies are operating globally with a relatively thin management superstructure.

In 1998, the Center for Quality of Management, a non-profit consortium of over 100 companies in the U.S. and Europe, did a series of interviews with 18 U.S. and 11 European CEOs. Their list of key issues that they saw facing their companies and themselves included:

- To deal with increasing speed and complexity—speed of change, complexity of products, and complexity of physical and organizational geography
- To achieve timely thoughtful action—decision making in the face of complexity and uncertainty

In the face of this feeling that things are moving more quickly and becoming more complicated (and that there is simply too much to do each day), many managers, and management thinkers, feel that the traditional management methods most companies used for much of the twentieth century are no longer adequate for the job.

We are all familiar with these traditional management systems: lots of hierarchy and organizational boundaries, lots of explicit policies and procedures, management by exception, and so on. Many companies used these methods to great effect for many years. What has gone wrong with them now?

It seems to us that the traditional management methods developed in a relatively stable world (compared with today) and were primarily an optimization system (see Figure 2-1). In a relatively unchanging world, what worked one day could be expected to work again the next day. Thus, the traditional management methods evolved so they provided a *company optimization system*—optimizing current practice for delivery to a relatively steady world what had worked well in the past and seeing to it that the same steps were followed in the future.

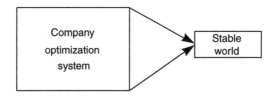

Figure 2-1. Traditional Methods Optimize Current Practice

In a more rapidly changing world, only optimizing what has worked in the past is insufficient—one needs a management system that is able to adapt to a changing environment. One needs an *organizational learning system* that is able to follow what is happening in a changing world environment and get feedback from it (see Figure 2-2).

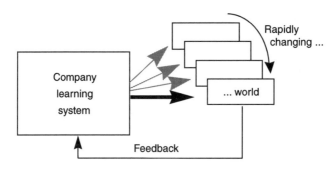

Figure 2-2. Need Methods to Adapt to Changing Environment

Unfortunately, obtaining such feedback is easier said than done. The traditional management systems—the company optimization systems—are aimed at doing the same thing repeatedly and thus tend not to dig for feedback on an ongoing basis. For instance, many of us may remember an instance when a customer did something "special" with a product we had sold to the customer (modified it or used it in a way we didn't expect it to be used) and that was under maintenance. And our company reacted not by trying to learn about the limitations of the current product line indicated by the customer's "special" actions; rather we canceled the warranty or maintenance contact on the product. In such instances, perhaps our customer maintenance management system was oriented to (and rewarded for) minimizing trouble calls rather than encouraging feedback about customer use of products. Many companies have such systems that don't encourage feedback that could help the organization to adjust to a changing environment.

Principles of Management Thinking for Today

To build a company learning system that adapts to a changing environment requires some different principles of management than the principles that appear to have supported the traditional management methods of a company optimization system. We can see a glimmer of four new underlying principles by reviewing the evolution of the concept and methods of customer satisfaction, as described in Chapter 1. There we saw:

- Companies put in place methods that enabled them to improve their skill.
- Companies began to integrate the various parts of their organizations into a system able to accomplish more demanding tasks.
- There was effort by companies to engage the intelligent, motivated participation of their employees.
- Companies adopted new methods from many sources.

From those glimmers and much observation of companies over the last ten years, we arrive at four explicit principles for thinking about management in today's rapidly changing world:

- Practice systematic development of skill
- Treat management as a coherent system
- Focus on people and their purposes
- Integrate best practices

We discuss each of these principles in some detail in the following four sections of this chapter. These principles are also highly relevant to the methods of the four revolutions in management thinking around which the main body of the book is organized, and they provide concepts and vocabulary we use in the rest of the book.

Note to reader. Some readers may prefer to skip directly to Chapter 3 and the main body of the book and to return to this chapter as necessary as they read the rest of the book. We make our students study this content now.

2.1 PRACTICE SYSTEMATIC DEVELOPMENT OF SKILL

Today's organizations need to improve their current performance and to evolve their means for future performance in response to changing business needs—they need to get better *and* get better at getting better. The question they must answer is *how* to get better and get better at getting better, in the most effective and efficient way—how to improve *systematically* rather than in a hit-and-miss fashion or in a fashion that is ineffective.

Before continuing to read, think for a moment what it means "systematically" (as opposed to "non-systematically") to develop skill either individually or in an organization. Think about how you would characterize someone who has achieved mastery in a field or how you would characterize the process by which people achieve mastery in a field.[1]

Note to reader: It might be useful for you to study a representative case study now. The case we recommend looking at first is that of the business known as NIMS. It is an old case study but an especially clear and compelling case study, and it begins on page 549. Over a multi-year period, NIMS systematically developed skill to meet the challenges of a rapidly changing world. NIMS developed a coherent system that met their specific needs drawing ideas from many sources.

Organizational Learning and Individual Learning

Though the goal of an organization is to improve the way it performs and to improve its ability to improve the way it performs, ultimately most improvement is individual: an organization cannot improve its ability to perform without the individuals in the organization improving the way they perform in their roles in the organization. Thus, individual learning is at the heart of organizational learning. Of course, individuals with improved skill also need to learn to perform better in the groups or teams that are required to carry out multi-person efforts. And at higher levels of the organization than the group or team—the department or division level—departments and divisions must learn better how to work together in the organization. This organizational learning may extend beyond the organization, to its suppliers, customers, strategic allies, and other business partners.

As we suggest in the prior paragraph and will describe in this book, organizational learning begins with personal learning and ultimately applies at all levels in the organization (individual, teams, divisions, whole organization, and partners beyond the organization) and to all people in the organization (individual contributors, first and middle level managers, and top managers and executives).

Phases of Skill Development

If we are going to study systematic skill development or organizational learning, it will be useful to consider the phases of skill development. In the next section we will describe a simple model of the phases of skill development that we will use throughout this book. In this section we will note some other models that may prove useful in thinking about the process of skill development.

We all know how hard it is to get people (or ourselves) to learn a new skill. There is a reason for that. As shown in Figure 2-3 , in any area of performance (physical or mental) in which we decide we need to improve, we may already perform with some degree of "skill" (by having "skill," we mean one can perform that task without thinking about it, however poor one's form may be). For instance, in a physical task such as swinging a golf club or tennis racket, through long repetition we may have really drilled an inefficient swing or stroke into our muscle memory so we can do it completely automatically. This is the stage of *unconscious incompetence* at the left bottom of the figure—our incompetent form is completely automatic to us.

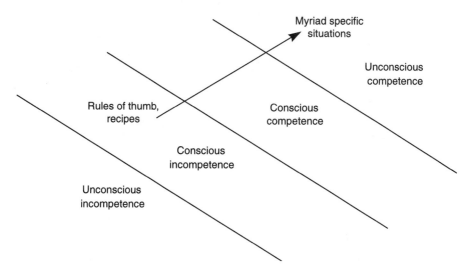

Figure 2-3. The Path to Skill

If we are going to improve, we typically move into a stage of *conscious incompetence*. An expert shows us the method of a new swing or stroke, and we have a hard time grasping it or a hard time doing it; in any case it feels awkward when we try to do it. "This doesn't work for me," is a typical first reaction.

If we persevere, over time we become better able to do the new swing or stroke and eventually it feels somewhat more comfortable. However, we are still very aware that this is a different way than we were used to, and maintaining proper form may require explicit concentration. It still feels awkward and uncomfortable, and we may still wonder if this is "right for me." This is the stage of *conscious competence*.

Finally, with lots of practice, the new form is drilled into our muscle memory and feels so completely natural that we forget we are using this new method. This is the stage of unconscious competence. In fact, for most significant tasks unless we can carry them out more or less unconsciously, we really aren't able to perform them usefully.[2]

With that model of skill development in mind, one can see why so many people resist improvement efforts. It requires going through the uncomfortable, awkward, and perhaps risky or scary phases of conscious incompetence and conscious competence. Figure 2-3 also illustrates another aspect of how we learn.[3] In learning any new domain, we start with simplistic steps that in effect are "rules of thumb." We learn a rule of thumb (literally) for holding a golf putter. We learn a rule of thumb doing simple subtraction. We use a rule of thumb for doing our first performance evaluation as a new manager. We learn rules of thumb as young engineers for writing what we hope will be maintainable software.

Of course, these rules of thumb are not sufficient for long-term success in the real, complex world. However, these rules of thumb do allow us to begin to perform at a rudimentary level. With experience at rudimentary performance and with further study (which may give us new, perhaps more complex rules of thumb), we have a chance to improve our level of skill. In time, with enough experience and study, we can learn exceptions to the rules of thumb, sets of rules of thumb to cover different situations, and (through even more experience) an unconscious intuitive feel for what needs to be done in particular situations.

In other words, skill development moves from conscious, usually awkward, application of rules of thumb, through conscious but increasingly fluid performance, and ultimately to an unconscious ability to handle myriad specific situations well.[4] (In fact, a definition that some people use for skill is the ability to do something unconsciously.)

The fundamental issue of skill development is "reflective practice"—practicing a new method, reflecting on what one learned, and practicing again.

A Setting for Learning

Our model of learning and skill acquisition that we teach in our courses has the following three parts:[5]

1. Information + commentary ⟶ knowledge

When people talk about something they have read, the words they use tend to come right out of the information source; this is knowledge. If the subject contains pure facts, this way of learning can be quite useful.

2. Knowledge + feedback ⟶ understanding

You deepen knowledge into understanding by speaking about the subject (putting it in your own words) with someone who already understands it and by attempting to use the knowledge in different ways. In turn, the person who already knows the subject can correct any misunderstandings the learners might have and thereby enable them to deepen their mastery of the subject.

3. Understanding + drive to use and schedule ⟶ skill

Ideas have to be used and practiced before they become skills. It is a rare discipline in which a person can jump immediately from talking about something to doing it at a fully professional skill level, in a real setting for real stakes. In practice, developing a skill useful in actual situations takes both motivation—a powerful reason to use new skills instead of playing it safe—and a commitment to use the skills, which often takes the form of a schedule. Once a skill is developed, benefit can be given to the customer and money can be made.

People in corporations have a straightforward charter: Get the information, work to understand it in the training context, and then use it on the job for real problems, following actual schedules, and with actual management oversight. An effective method for carrying out this charter has been the "cascade" method. First managers learn the skills and teach them to their direct reports, who then use the skills and teach them to their direct reports, and so on. Xerox Corporation calls this process LUTI: learn, use, teach, inspect.

In the corporate setting, and for that matter in a university classroom, reading the book is only the first step. Results come from skill. Gaining skill requires commitment to three things: openness to learning, serious application, and mutual learning.

Commitment to Openness to Learning

The first step in developing a new skill is willingness to learn, and even before that the willingness to admit you don't know.[6]

Several attitudes block openness to learning, and we ask students to commit themselves to giving these up. They are the following:

I Already Know It (IAKI). Knowing something is quite different both from having exposure to information and from possessing actual skill. IAKI must not become an excuse to tune out information and abandon the acquisition of skills.

Not Invented Here (NIH). It is easy to reject ideas and practices simply because they are new or foreign. Some practices are foreign to us in the sense that they are widely practiced in other countries, for instance, in Japan, and they are less used in the United States. Some practices seem foreign to people because they differ from their habitual styles of analysis and problem solving. Some practices may seem foreign because the examples given are from industries, functions, or situations other than the ones they work in. Many people proclaim their company's situation to be unique, but this assertion is seldom true. Students of organizational improvement must make a commitment either to avoid NIH or to abandon this attitude if they now hold it.[7]

Prove It to Me (PITM). In junior high school, students don't have a vote on whether to include essay writing and spelling in the English curriculum, although some students do question the teacher about the usefulness of these activities. No one can guarantee that all the skills we learn will be essential to us in the future, and indeed, some things we learn may never be used. But much of what we learn in the English curriculum turns out to be valuable and applicable later.

The same is true of organizational improvement practices. Before they become skills, it is difficult to see how they will be applicable. Therefore students of organizational change must forswear the use of PITM as an obstacle to full participation in or full comprehension of the subject being taught. In American education, we are often taught to listen critically. But this may have been poor advice. A better approach is to listen empathetically and later to think critically. If you listen critically from the start, you may be so busy finding flaws that full comprehension eludes you. To understand a lesson, you must assume temporarily that what is being said is correct, so you may fully hear about it and understand it. Only then are you in a position to form alternative opinions about the subject being taught.

Not My Job (NMJ); We Could Never Do That (WCNDT). There is undoubtedly an unending list of such attitudes that one could list that prevent openness to learning, such as these next two. All such attitudes must be guarded against, and it is probably best to address them explicitly.

Following the Process. One school of academic thought encourages instructors to give minimal guidance to students, so the students can practice the skill of discovering things on their own. This idea has become somewhat embedded in American culture, so people are commonly expected to experiment with variations and try out shortcuts to learning on their own. This approach can speed the conversion of knowledge into understanding. At the stage where understanding is turned into skills, however, it is less useful. Encouraging individual variation at the beginning of the learning process slows down progress considerably and may engender bad habits that have to be unlearned.

Many of us have seen the unfortunate results of not following the initial process shown to us by a golf or tennis pro ("hold your thumb like this"), the instructions on a paint can ("finish all sanding before applying any paint"), or a cooking recipe ("stir continuously to avoid sticking to the pan").

A general maxim in quality control for engineering or marketing is to standardize routine tasks and avoid routine defects, so you can focus on being creative. For business improvement methods, this means following the procedures closely at first and introducing variations only after the practices have become familiar to you. Trying to take shortcuts too early can undermine the learning process and interfere with getting useful results.

Commitment to Serious Application

Proficiency in organizational improvement skills cannot be achieved through study of the methods and examples in this book alone. Study must be accompanied by a well-organized sequence of applications to actual processes. For example, say a manager senses a problem and has some idea of what to do about it. Unless there is a common language for discussing improvement among the people who work for him, and unless the members of the group have some common experience of following the improvement process, it will be difficult for him to solve the problem or even to communicate its importance to his colleagues. Therefore, this book deals not only with concepts but with the applications for these concepts.

Aggressive Learning. Much of the material in this book concerns the development of skills. One skill often neglected in the training process is capturing and structuring information. Organizational change and business improvement cannot be practiced effectively with knowledge only. Understanding and skill are necessary, and these start with aggressive learning and listening. One example of aggressive listening is drawn from the section on management diagnoses of improvement activity: When improvement activities are being presented to management, at any point during the presentation, an aggressively listening manager will have a question or insightful observation. Simply listening passively to a presentation is not aggressive learning.

Another example is note-taking. Course materials in well-designed courses are closely linked to lectures and exercises. But reality doesn't come so neatly packaged, and neither does much new information. The material in this book may not always match that heard in a lecture course based on it, both because the written word is different from the spoken word and because the lectures are constantly being revised and improved.

Therefore, we ask participants in courses to develop the skill of copious, *verbatim note-taking*, in which they write down everything they hear. This activity will sharpen their focus on the information, preserve knowledge, and demonstrate interest and concern for the presenters. In addition, by disciplining themselves to take effective notes, the participants will acquire a useful skill.

Moving Forward. After we reviewed this list of commitments with the students in MIT's Leaders for Manufacturing program, we showed them a small ceremony, the "yo-one." The mechanics of the ceremony are simple: Once a task has been completed, everyone stands in a circle, so that they can all see each other. The leader starts by saying "yo-oh" (in two syllables). Other people join in, and then the group says the word "one" in a louder voice, and everyone claps their hands together once, simultaneously. The rhythm of this chant is approximately "one, two, THREE." A group needs only a couple of rehearsals to learn how to perform this ceremony.

The yo-one ceremony signifies completion and agreement. It is typically used when a phase of team activity is finished. Yo has no meaning, and one simply means one. The chanting of those words provides closure to an activity. The time just before the yo-one ceremony, when people are asking "are we ready to yo-one?" is explicitly designed to give people an opportunity to voice final doubts. If no one speaks up and the group goes ahead with the yo-one ceremony, everyone observes everyone else clearly and forcefully says yo-one and claps. Thus there is no doubt that all are unambiguously committed to making their work or their decision final. If someone attempts to reverse or rework a position, the group can remind that person firmly that he or she has "yo-oned" and is therefore violating a publicly made commitment. As an added value, a cheer at the end of hard work is invigorating and acknowledges a task successfully done. It makes people feel good.

The particular words used in the chant may differ according to corporate or national culture. One group of Chinese students used "Don't go BACK!" which worked equally well. What matters is that the ceremony is always used and is mutually understood by the group. Learning to perform the yo-one ceremony is the class's first work as a group; it is a micro-demonstration of commitment to move forward to real application.

Commitment to Mutual Learning

The traditional classroom learning environment, in which an instructor talks and students listen and then do homework, differs greatly from most learning environments on the job. In classrooms, students learn primarily from the instructor and from the teaching materials provided. Even much corporate training takes place in this manner. But the most common learning situation in work settings, and the one that the practices taught in this book support, is learning in groups in which no one is much more knowledgeable than the others. Therefore, this book emphasizes work in groups, whether on the job or in the classroom. In the approach we describe, reading is the only activity that each person undertakes alone from beginning to end.

2.2 TREAT MANAGEMENT AS A COHERENT SYSTEM

If you ask many managers what they do, they will tell you about the tasks they perform or functions they are involved in, such as going on sales calls, hiring and firing, and setting objectives. They will seldom tell you about how they have structured a management system for their company. In fact most companies have management structures that involve various functional organizations and various people performing their functional tasks, communicating around the organization in various ways, not because they have thought about the design of their management system but because they are replicating a set of functions, plans, reports and so on, that they (and all of us) are familiar with.

We believe that there is great power in taking the systems view of management, and many companies and managers we admire have done so.[8]

A good working definition of a system is that it has parts that are put together in some way (e.g., via organization and processes) to perform some function(s) to accomplish some more or less explicit purpose(s). It is probably pretty obvious to most of us that a system can be more than the sum of its parts, and this is the reason we create systems. For instance, a sales person, a development person, a manufacturing person, a support person, and a financial person, who individually only have the capabilities in their functional specialty can together create, sell, and deliver a product or service. It is just as obvious that a system can be less than the sum of its parts; this is why so many of us have such disdain for the organizations (systems) we are a part of. For instance, if we had ten machinists, each of whom could design and mill the parts of a machine and put them together into a working machine, we might hope that together they could make the machine ten times faster; however, together they might fail to agree on the design, trip over each other trying to get to the various tools and, in the end, take as long to build one machine as each of them would take individually (we have all seen situations like this).

The first difficulty in creating an effective and efficient system is that the parts may do more than do their own jobs (in which case we would hope their total effect would be additive)—they can affect each other in ways that may or may not be anticipated. Thus, it's hard to put the parts together in ways where we get more than the sum of the parts (or even to get close to the sum of the parts). In fact, the inter-part relationships may include a variety of time delays, including some that are very long, which make the inter-part effects doubly difficult to detect.

Thus, the job of someone designing or managing a system is to design and manage the interactions between the parts of the system. In particular, organizations need to plan how they deal with different rates of response in different parts of the system. However, this is easier said than done.

Of course, the first step in understanding what is happening in any situation is to look at the inputs and the outputs and to figure out the relationships between them, for instance, "If we do this, then that happens; or does it..." Some characteristics of a system are easy to observe or measure at the component level and from them calculate the overall characteristic of the system.[9] For instance, we can add up employee vacation time to approximate the temporary replacement person hours we need to pay for. Other characteristics of a system are harder to observe or measure because they are a function of interactions among components that may not be present in any individual component.[10] For instance, the developer may be able to create two new products a year, the support person may be able to release three new products per year while providing on-going support to 20 customers, the marketing person may be able to research the market and plan one new product per year, the sales person may be able to make 15 sales per year, the financial person may be able to arrange financing for two new product development efforts per year with ongoing support for 100 customers, and the manufacturing person may be able to produce 200 products per year. From that, we may be able to calculate how many new customers we can deliver to in a year but not be able to calculate how many highly satisfied new customers we will generate in a year. Customer satisfaction may have to do with a gestalt of activities within the company (and even may involve a significant component of luck), which can't be calculated from the characteristics of the parts alone and is difficult to calculate even when one can observe the interactions among the parts.

There is a lot to think about when trying to design a system. Many people find it useful to think about the purposes of the system, the functions of the system, the architecture (or organization) of the system, and the processes of the system.

However, designing the purposes, functions, architecture (organization), and processes of a system is not enough. We also have to design a measurement system to determine if the system is doing what we want to it do and to determine what the parts of the system or their interactions are doing, so we can change or improve the parts of the system or their interactions. In fact, often times the struggle to understand how to measure a system, its various parts, and their interactions leads us to better understand the system's purpose and function. Since complex systems (such as a business) initially never work as planned (remember the follow-on to Murphy's law about Murphy being an optimist), measuring the system in appropriate ways is critical to the experimentation with the system to understand how it inherently works, its function, and to change it until we align our desires for the system with the way the system performs.

This difficulty of observing and measuring, resulting from the interaction of the components, works in two directions. The first is that you often can't calculate the characteristics of the whole from the characteristics of the parts. The second is that from the characteristics one desires for the whole one can't often easily figure out what the characteristics of the parts should be, or how they should interact.

So, we need systems, but systems are difficult to design, measure, understand, and manage because of the interactions among the parts. The job of the manager is to manage these interactions. However, it's hard to figure out what's going on overall by measuring the parts; and it's hard to figure out from measuring the whole what the parts should be doing and how they should be made to interact. Unfortunately, creating an effective and efficient system tends to require a lot of experimentation, albeit starting with the best ideas available.[11]

2.3 FOCUS ON PEOPLE AND THEIR PURPOSES

The idea from the previous section of thinking about management as a system obviously isn't new. However, historically, managers have tried to treat their management systems as relatively simple entities. Looking back on management since the late nineteenth century, we[12] find it useful to retrospectively define and label three models for the practice of management which we think are quite representative.

Evolution of Management Practice

In presenting the three models, we do not intend to suggest that they are mutually exclusive. In the real world, things are not as distinct as the pure models suggest. In fact, as the evolution from mechanical to biological to social model has occurred, the later models have often maintained some aspects of the prior models.

The mechanical model. The mechanical model draws an analogy between an organization and a machine. In the model, the workers in the organization are the parts of the machine. The business situation is analyzed, and procedures are developed to turn inputs into outputs. Each worker is assigned a particular—typically independent—procedure and taught to follow it rigorously. As long as the workers follow their procedures correctly and the inputs are as expected, the machine will keep turning out the expected outputs. The top manager's jobs, therefore, consist of designing the appropriate machine and controlling the workers and inputs to minimize variation. The mechanical model assumes a static environment for which one can build a machine that does the same things over and over. In this model, as with the parts of a machine, the people in the organization have no purpose other than to function in the way the owner or boss directs.

Organizations based on variations of this model were common around 1900 and are still frequently seen today. We are all familiar, from literature, movies, or from personal experience, with companies operated according to the mechanical model. We have all heard some version of the "I don't pay you to think; I pay you to do what I tell you to do." The story is told of Henry Ford—definitely a controlling manager—going on a trip to Europe. After he left, some of his employees thought is was an opportunity to make some design improvements that they couldn't make while Ford was there. When Ford returned, the employees showed him their improved design. Ford jumped on the redesigned car, smashing it, saying, "Your job is not to make improvements; your job is to do what I tell you to do."

Managers practicing this model simplified the management system they were trying to design and control by treating it like a machine with the people as additional parts who would do their tasks according to standard processes which they could follow essentially without thinking. We noted earlier in this chapter that the job of designing a management system is to design or select the parts and manage their interactions. By thinking of the management system as a machine, with specified inputs and specified actions by the people involved, the managers were able to understand more easily how the parts of the system related to each other and the characteristics of the parts necessary to produce the desired characteristics of the whole system. There was minimal interaction about the parts to manage (if in fact they could get the parts, especially the human parts, to behave as predictably as they were assuming).

However, as businesses grew larger and more complex and became more distributed, the mechanical model ceased to be adequate as the design model for the entire business (although it was still practiced in parts of the system in many cases). This led to practices which we call the biological model of management.

The biological model. The biological model draws parallels between an organization and a biological organism. In this model, the workers are the arms, legs, and sensory and other organs, ultimately serving the needs of the organism as a whole. Unlike the mechanical model, the biological model assumes that the parts of the organism do their jobs according to their own program (including communication among themselves) much of the time rather than according to a program provided by the intellectual center. For instance, without conscious instructions from the head, the heart adapts on its own to calls from other parts of the body for blood to be pumped more or less rapidly. In the biological model, top management's job is to decide what the organism as a whole is supposed to accomplish, observe the functioning of the parts, and give feedback to the parts where the outputs aren't satisfactory. This monitoring of the outputs of the parts is necessary because the parts have the capability to operate to some extent without direct control of the top management.

Unlike the mechanical model, which assumed a static situation that could be handled by a machine, the biological model can be appropriate for situations where change needs to be dealt with, provided the change is either slow or predictable. If change is slow enough, an organism can gradually evolve to cope with it. If change is predictable (and if adapting is within the ultimate capabilities of the organism), top management can condition and train the parts to be able to handle the new situations. But, if the change exceeds the capabilities of the species to adjust, the species will become extinct, and its ecological niche will be taken by another species better adapted to the new environment; in some cases, this may be a species that evolved from the original species.

For much of the twentieth century, there has been an assumption that growth was the way to ensure survival of a company. Thus, an explicit purpose of the biological model has been business growth. In the mechanical model, the people in the organization had no purpose other than to function as parts of a machine as the owner or boss directed; in the biological model, the purpose of the people was assumed to be to support the growth of the organization as required by the top management, just as the hands or legs support the goals of the overall body as directed by the head.

Management methods consistent with the biological model (with some continuation of the mechanical model) have been what most companies in the U.S. used for much of the twentieth century—management methods such as traditional strategic planning, traditional cost accounting and control, functional organization structures, detailed job descriptions and standard procedures, a division of labor between those who do the work and those who improve the process, management by objectives, management by exception, and economic order quantities. Furthermore, typical measurements of performance such as return-on-sales and return-on-investment are output measures consistent with the biological model.

The biological model allows for clusters of parts of the system (functions, divisions, etc.) to have flexibility to address issues that come up which would not have been manageable unless designed into a mechanical model management system (which would be awfully complex if it anticipated and built in ways to handle every eventuality). Thus, in this case, a hierarchy of components exists with the managers at each higher level managing the interactions of the components below them. Presidents managed the interactions among functional VPs, functional VPs managed the interactions among their departments, and so on.

However, as businesses grew larger and more complex and also changed more rapidly, the biological model also proved to not be sufficient. The complexity of business and speed of change required the intelligent engaged participation of individuals throughout the organization, often working in dynamic arrangements across functional or divisional boundaries. And this individual interaction extends beyond the boundaries of the organization, to suppliers, customers, and other stakeholders. For instance, design teams can have people from every function in the organization along with suppliers, customers and even communities or special interest groups on them. Thus, management is required to manage (whatever that word means in this situation) a vastly increased (e.g., exponential growth) complex of interactions. The question is how to do this, and this brings us to what we call the social model of management.

The social model. The social model uses an analogy between an organization and a society of individual beings, where each individual has the ability to think and learn for himself or herself and have their own purposes. In this model, much interaction occurs among the individuals in the society, and the individuals depend on each other for their mutual adaptation and survival. This model is appropriate to situations in which change is unpredictable and to situations in which it is possible for the society to create its own future. In other words, the social model is the basis of a learning system: it is well suited to situations that require the continual development of new capabilities. The job of top management in the social model is to create a learning organization—to design a desirable future and to find ways to achieve it, particularly by managing the interactions among the individuals and organizational components in the society in a way that is compatible with (and builds on) the purposes of the individuals.

Because many mutually dependent individuals are in a social model organization, there can be many competing purposes within the organization; for example, the purposes of the employees, those of the company, and those of the larger society that contains the company. Sometimes these multiple purposes are in conflict with each other. Thus, the social model recognizes a multiplicity of purposes to be dealt with; however, the social model also assumes the possibility of a level of collective action that can offset problems caused by multiplicity of purposes.

Leadership versus Empowerment

When trying to develop a system for managing interactions, especially when many of the interactions are about interactions of people, it helps to have a theory of how humans behave. Implicitly, managers using the mechanical, biological, and social models have theories of human nature. The theory of human nature consistent with the mechanical model is that people need to be controlled.[13] The theory of human nature consistent with the biological model is that people are motivated to work if certain conditions are satisfied.[14] As we consider our experience, observation of organizations, and what has been learned about human nature in the era since MacGregor, it seems pretty clear that both theories are right, in some sense. Most people want to be led, and they want clear goals and security.[15] On the other hand, many people want to contribute, and some of them are interested in finding new ways to make these contributions; however, such contributions and innovation take initiative (going beyond what one has been told to do), and this is uncomfortable or insecure. Also, though people want to be led, they are also often suspicious of those who lead them. All in all, people in organizations often are in a state of at least partial ambivalence between wanting to be led and to make personal contributions and being paranoid about being led and being asked to make personal contributions.

A naive interpretation (we believe) of the evolution from the mechanical model, through the biological model, toward the social model is that as the employees (and other stakeholders) have become more empowered, management is required to become more laissez faire. Thus, many people think that the biological model is at the top left (point A) of Figure 2-4 and that the social model is at the bottom right (point C) of the figure,[16] and the biological model is somewhere in between (point B).

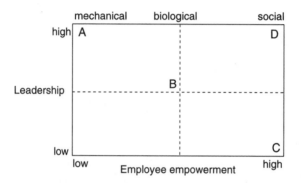

Figure 2-4. Leadership versus Empowerment

However, as we have already stated, people in general want to be led even though others are interested in innovating themselves. Also, for a large, complex organization (anything bigger than quite small and more complex than quite simple), laissez faire management doesn't provide sufficient leadership or management of all of the necessary interactions: we are likely to get something that is much less than the sum of its parts because people are not pulling together and others are not engaged or pulling at all.

Thus, to obtain a system's benefits in the face of the need for the social model, management has to learn how to design systems that function at the top right (point D) of Figure 2-4 —very strong leadership that provides alignment of empowered people (people with the skill, engagement, and authority to do what needs to be done) throughout the organization. Encouragement and alignment of participation is needed without exactly explicit enforcement of participation.[17]

Of course, developing a shared vision is important, and we will provide illustrations later in the book about how this was done. But that's not enough. As we noted in the last section, here again note that it's hard to figure out how to provide strong leadership, coordination, and alignment while simultaneously obtaining the engaged intelligent participation of the individuals. At this point, we know of no simple, widely applicable method of doing this (although various people have claimed such a method). Once again, creating an effective and efficient system tends to require much experimentation, albeit starting with the best ideas available.

2.4 INTEGRATE BEST PRACTICES

We don't see the methods that we describe in this book as being in competition with other methods. Rather, we see one of the jobs of the senior managers as integrating so-called "best practices" from all relevant sources into the organization's overall system.

The top management should select and integrate the components *apparently* relevant to the organization's culture and business. This will provide a system with which experience can be gained and lessons learned and which can be reflected upon and adjusted for increased relevance and efficiency. Without an explicit system or process, efficient improvement is unlikely (improving the intangible is very difficult, if not impossible); or, if one treats management as a collection of isolated tasks, improvements to one task may have detrimental unintended consequences for the other tasks.

The overall system might include components from lean production, systems thinking, interactive management, business process reengineering, system dynamics, total quality management, and others. There is no single right system. Companies need to integrate best practices from any relevant sources to create a system that, once created, provides a source of best practices for others to emulate or improve upon.[18]

Many people have a tendency to treat various management methods as separate and even in competition with each other. Business schools are typically organized into relatively isolated departments that specialize in particular management functions. Even disciplines such as system dynamics or systems thinking (which should take an integrated view), tend to see their discipline as the single true solution to all problems. Business consultants seek to differentiate their methods from other methods rather than to integrate them. Business managers often see the approach that has brought them success as a replacement for the methods of their predecessor in the organization. Business journalists delight in explaining which methods show startling promise and which previously promising methods are now discounted.

Of course, the real world does not work this way. A top manager cannot pay attention only to marketing or accounting, only to operations or strategy, or only to internal activities versus external activities. A top manager must be concerned with all phases of operation of the business. Similarly, a top manager cannot only be concerned with methods of human motivation, only with methods of process improvement, or only with organizational structure. A top manager must be concerned with having the appropriate amount of each of these in his or her organization.

From our perspective, one of the greatest losses of opportunity in business (not to mention causing the most possible damage) results from the tendency of managers, academics, consultants and everyday culture to see a system in terms of competing parts and methods rather than as a potentially integrated whole. One of the two most important contribution we hope this book makes is to get people talking about integrating management methods and perhaps to begin to cast doubt on the integrity of academics, consultants, the media, and managers who continue to promote destructive behavior of playing the methods against each other. The other most important point is to look at integrating the methods in to a system, which we discussed in an earlier section.

The integrative approach described in this section is the right one for at least the following reasons:

- The world is complex and it needs a variety of methods to deal with its different aspects.
- One is better off if one can build on what has gone before. This is the natural course of development in all fields of endeavor where one can tell if one is achieving increased predictability. The tendency in management to have various "schools" positioned against each other is more like the social sciences where various "schools" (or competing disciplines) are arguing who has the greater truth—this happens less frequently in the natural sciences, the performing arts, competitive sports, etc., where one form or another of the scientific method (e.g., what developmental psychologists might call "reflective practice") is used to determine what makes a predictable difference and the helpful methods kept and the unhelpful methods discarded.
- A method that works across disciplines may be more likely to be "true" (represent reality) than one which only appears to work in one discipline. We need to seek parallels between methods to be able to detect differences (which might help us in different ways) and to see what appears to be a more "universal truth."
- New innovations frequently result from cross-disciplinary interactions.

Throughout this book we will provide examples of companies that integrate best practices from a variety of sources.

In summary, each company must build and continue to improve its own system to address its situation, culture, and people's needs. A major purpose of this book is to summarize or generalize the methods that various companies and managers have successfully used to move their companies toward increased capacity to address today's business complexity and speed of change, so others may build on these experiences.

2.5 FINANCIAL BENEFIT

We cannot leave this introductory chapter without at least mentioning the issue of whether the results from business improvement are worth the effort, or the benefits worth the costs. In this book we will not address this issue thoroughly—we don't want to get involved in statistical debates. At this point, we only will make several summary points and sketch the results of some studies.

First, the tendency for companies that improve customer satisfaction (through better product and service quality) to do better financially has been extensively demonstrated.[19] We suspect that most people also intuitively believe this.

Second, studies of winners of and serious contenders for the U.S. Baldrige and other quality awards appear to indicate they do measurably better on various financial metrics than companies that haven't had this Baldrige success [134, 267, 280, 291].

Third, the majority of managers and workers we know assume that they must continue to improve how their companies operate if they are to remain competitive.[20]

Fourth, the top managers of many companies that we judge to have done excellent management improvement work give anecdotal evidence of the importance of their improvement efforts compared with where they might have been without the improvement efforts.

Another way of looking at the issue. It is always difficult to do an explicit quantitative benefit/cost tradeoff that shows the relative value of doing improvement work. The costs are often all too easy to capture, even though the benefits are hard to quantify and to correlate explicitly with the improvement work. However, there is another way of looking at this trade off—an informal way, but a way that may be more intuitively compelling. Rather than thinking of the benefit from an improvement versus the cost of the improvement, think about the cost of *not doing* the improvement versus the cost of doing it.

For instance, to do the "voice of the customer" project in order to understand the features needed in a new product line may cost a few person-months of labor, travel expenses, and so forth. Not to do the voice of the customer project will save tens of thousands or perhaps a hundred thousand dollars but may well leave a situation where insufficient motivation exists to undertake a needed new development with little knowledge of what the new development should provide customers. Without the project, the current product may grow old and lose market share with no new product to capture market share. Ultimately, a product generation may be missed with major financial consequences and perhaps failure of the business. The cost of doing the improvement may be insignificant compared with the cost of not doing it.

NOTES

1. We argue in this chapter that companies need systematically to develop skill to survive and flourish in the rapidly changing world. Therefore, we advocate treating management as a system or learning process and integrating into that management system relevant methods regardless of the source. How to do this is the subject of the rest of the book. In particular, we provide numerous case studies showing how various businesses and other institutions have proceeded in developing their unique organizational capability.

2. This four-stage model of skill development is frequently cited in the training establishment. The junior author believes he first heard it from Larry Raskin of

Analog Devices. We are not sure what the proper citation for this model is. A book that describes the model is [253, pages 11–12].

3. This model is described in detail in [86, Chapter 1, "Five Steps from Novice to Expert," pages 16–51].

4. In later chapters, we will demonstrate the benefit of beginning to learn a new skill by learning a step-by-step process (that is, a minimal sequence of rules of thumb), which gives one a way to practice performing in the new area and, through practice and reflection on the practice over time, to develop one's way to mastery.

5. We have derived this model of learning from [78].

6. Fernando Flores in [273] notes that any important idea typically receives one of two reactions. The first reaction often is "I already know it"; if perchance the people hearing the new idea are willing to admit they do not already know it, their other typical reaction is "It's trivial."

7. In 1992, we visited Japan with a group of CQM CEOs, quality officers, and development VPs. During this visit we heard a slogan encouraging learning from others. We were visiting the Software Quality Department of NEC, and they showed us a video that used the analogy of climbing Mt. Fuji, which is an important pilgrimage for many Japanese. Apparently there are two approaches to climbing Mt. Fuji. One is to attempt to walk all the way from the bottom. Another is to take a bus a substantial way up the mountain, to what is known as the Fifth Station, and to walk to the top from there. The former approach has the disadvantage that one may run out of energy before getting to the top of the mountain. The latter approach has the advantage that one conserves energy to make sure one has the energy to make the final push to the top of the mountain. The analogy the NEC software people were making is that in software development one should copy everything one possibly can from what has already been done by others—"take the bus to the Fifth Station"—so that an organization and its people have enough energy left to make the unique contribution that only they can make.

8. We see an important component of being a manager or leader as treating management or leadership not as just a collection of tasks but rather as a system or process that can be improved. Others support us in this view. For instance, Dr. Fred Schwettmann, a former senior manager at HP and former CEO of Read-Rite, in a 1998 presentation to a CEO Roundtable of the CQM West chapter, cautioned against treating leadership as just a collection of tasks and listed a nine-step "process of leadership" that included the following steps: choosing the top management team, statement of purpose, choosing the mission, declaration of values, five-year strategic plan, one-year tactical plan, implementation, review, and rewards and recognition.

9. Russell Ackoff calls these Type 1 properties.

10. Russell Ackoff calls these Type 2 properties.

11. For more detail in the topics of this section and the next, see [186, Appendix A] and [2, 114]

12. Taking a lesson from Ackoff.

13. The famous Theory X.

14. MacGregor's famous Theory Y.

15. Rapialle in a private session on leadership at the Center for Quality of Management, Cambridge, Mass., January 28, 1997, described how people (at least in the U.S.) want a leader to be someone who leads them. We also see this in everyday business life where people seem to want to create legends about the skills of appointed (and respected) leaders.

16. Bob Putnam of Action Design first showed us a figure of leadership versus empowerment, from which we derived our own version of the figure which we use here.

17. In some sense, this figure is representative of the overall purpose of modern management. It is not sufficient just to forcefully espouse a direction, and it is not sufficient just to have prepared people. A manager must develop people who can do what needs to be done and get them aligned to do it. All five traditional management functions (control, leadership, organization, planning, and staffing) are implicit in being at the top right of the figure.

18. For an expanded discussion of this topic, see [187].

19. The profit impact of market strategies (PIMS) study is one well-known example; see [251, 79].

20. The debate is only about how to undertake these improvements.

3

Developing a Unique
Organizational Capability

Broadly speaking, in the first two chapters of this introductory part of the book, we have told the following story:

- The practice of business has evolved over the past century, and it continues to evolve at an increasing pace.
- The evolution of business practice has been driven substantially by an evolution in the definition of quality or customer satisfaction and that, in turn, has driven an evolution of the methods used to assure quality and customer satisfaction. Customers have a greater variety of expectations and more options for satisfying their expectations than ever before.
- The evolution of business practice, to compete successfully in satisfying customers, has resulted in several important changes in management thinking. Businesses need systematic ways of developing skill. Management must be treated as a coherent system. Management must deal with people and their purposes and spend time creating "empowered" employees and aligning them. Ideological biases need to be swept aside and best practices from any relevant sources can be used as part of the management system.

We will now finish this story and introduce the rest of the book.

3.1 FOUR PRACTICAL REVOLUTIONS IN MANAGEMENT

The first edition of our book was nominally about the why and the how of total quality management or TQM. TQM had developed over nearly 40 years, first in the U.S., then in Japan, and then again in the U.S. Historically, TQM was focused on improving the quality of products and service and doing so with maximum efficiency.[1] Therefore, in our first edition we defined total quality management as an evolving system, *developed through success in industry*, for continuously improving products and services to increase customer satisfaction in a rapidly changing world.

41

TQM concepts and practices have been developed over many years by companies seeking practical methods to improve the quality of their products and services. TQM has never been an abstract philosophy, nor has there been a single correct way to implement TQM; it must be customized to each company's culture and history.

Although each company has had to find its own way to implement TQM, four areas of concepts and practices are common to most successful implementations, and these differ from practices in many non-TQM companies. They represent four revolutions in management thinking (see Figure 3-1).

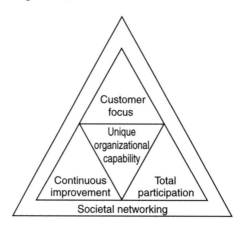

Figure 3-1. Four Revolutions of Management Thinking

1. Companies must *focus on customers* and on satisfying their needs. Therefore, they must be able to react fast to changing customer needs and to focus their limited resources on activities that satisfy customers. (This is in contrast to the common attitude that the "company knows best" what customers need.)
2. Companies must *seek continuous improvement* of the processes that lead to higher quality products and services. Continuous improvement involves using a scientific approach to make improvements (analyze facts, base actions on facts, test results empirically), doing step-by-step improvements to get to market quickly and acquire real experience, and doing iterative improvement to reach ever-higher levels of quality. (This is in contrast to the common attitude of "if it ain't broke, don't fix it.")
3. Companies must *seek total participation* of their employees. All capabilities of all company members must be used if companies are to make continuous improvement and to seek customer satisfaction. (This is in contrast to the common attitude that "some people think and some people do.")
4. Companies must *participate in societal networking* (that is, mutual learning with other companies) to avoid reinvention of methods, to implement quality practices more quickly, and to create a quality culture in which to do business. (This is in contrast to the common attitude of "only look out for 'number 1'.")

3.2 EVOLUTION OF OUR UNDERSTANDING

By the time we drafted the first edition of this book the focus of the methods known as TQM was beginning to move from the *management of quality to the quality of management*—the focus of the methods was moving to deal with the ongoing improvement of the way an organization is managed in a rapidly changing world. Thus our first edition was to some extent about improving the overall management of an organization and not limited to product and service quality.[2]

Nearly another decade has passed since we began to write the first edition, and the evolution of the problems organizations face has continued. For instance:

- Organizations must continue to improve and adapt within their existing businesses and general manner of operating—they must get better. They must also learn how to improve more quickly and efficiently—get better at getting better.
- Also, beyond continuing to improve the way they operate their business, many organizations find it necessary to redefine their business upon occasion. To these ends, they need to create an appropriate management system or organization for their current situation. In fact, we have come to see during the time since the first edition that the methods we were teaching were aimed at helping a company create its appropriate unique organization.
- Finally, over the past decade or two, organizations of every type have come to think of themselves more like businesses. Once upon a time only for-profit manufacturing and service companies were thought of as being in business. These days, at least in the U.S., there is increasing pressure for government, the military, health care organizations, schools and colleges, charities, and even churches to operate in a more business like fashion.[3] There is loud complaint when the government of a state or a health care organization "does not operate like a business" or "is not accountable."

The methods that fall in the categories we call the four revolutions in management thinking continue to apply to these expanding pressures on organizations; however, our understanding of the relationships among the four categories has changed, as has our understanding of the relative importance of the methods within the categories.

At the end of the day, the goal of each organization is to become the unique organization it wants and needs to be, however small or great a change this requires from the existing organization. Thus, each organization needs to transform itself and requires a process by which to accomplish the transformation (see Figure 3-2).

Obviously, there are two issues when one considers transforming an organization from its current state to a new state: what to do and how to do it (see Figure 3-3). In fact, there are two key problems that any business must deal with:

- Figuring out what the market wants and the intersection of that with what the company can provide
- Aligning and mobilizing itself to deliver what is needed

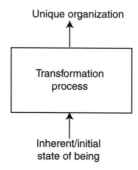

Figure 3-2. An Organization Needs a Transformation Process

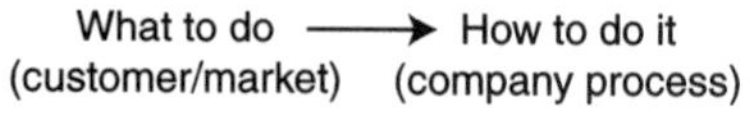

What to do ⟶ How to do it
(customer/market)   (company process)

Figure 3-3. Each Organization Has Two Fundamental Issues

The market provides input about what needs to be done. The methods of customer focus, one of our management revolutions, provide the means to hear and understand what the market is saying or will soon say. The how is what we have to do in our own organization, that is, to improve our processes (see Figure 3-4).

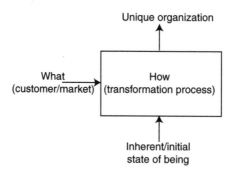

Figure 3-4. The What and How Drive the Transformation

Figuring out what the market needs is hard enough; unfortunately, getting an organization aligned and mobilized to provide what the market actually needs is often more difficult. Explicit methods are needed for alignment and mobilization. In particular, we need methods to undertake improvement efficiently and effectively—methods of continuous improvement, another of our management revolutions.

Organizations will be improving processes which involve material, information, or people. In any case, people (individuals, teams, the whole organization including perhaps outside allies) must be involved in changing the process. Thus, methods are also needed to assure participation of the appropriate individuals, teams, and parts of the organization in the improvement activities—methods of total participation, yet another of our management revolutions.

These two key components of how an organization transforms itself are shown in Figure 3-5.

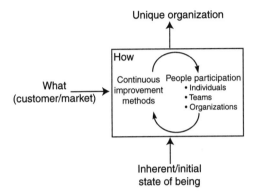

Figure 3-5. The components of the Transformation Process

Finally, all organizations live in a societal environment that affects and can support them in various ways. Thus, organizations need methods to understand and learn from their societal environment—methods of societal networking, our last management revolution. This is shown in Figure 3-6. The figure also illustrates that the unique organization that results from a transformation effort is the initial state for the next cycle of transformation.

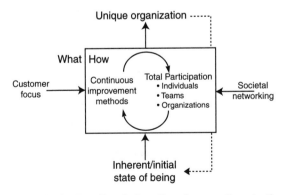

Figure 3-6. The Four Revolutions Transform an Organization

As can be seen in Figure 3-6, the methods of two of our four management revolutions take place primarily within an organization, and the methods of two of our four management revolutions provide the way that the organization collects information from the external world. While the methods in all four areas are needed, we see the methods of continuous improvement and total participation that deal with how the organization effects its transformation as more important; most of this book is about these two areas. The methods of customer focus and total participation provide the context for the methods of the other two revolutions. Thus, two chapters on customer focus begin the book and two chapters on societal networking end the book, bracketing the over 20 chapters on the other two revolutions that make up the bulk of the book.

In summary, the four management revolutions are the areas of practice for a company striving for business improvement and organizational learning. The goal of these methods is to create the appropriate unique organization (see Figure 3-7).

Figure 3-7. Four Revolutions for Creating Unique Organizational Capability

We describe these new needs and the improved methods in the rest of this book. In particular, the methods described address the following needs of organizations:

- To have a dynamic (not static) implementation strategy. The quality assurance mindset of TQM deals primarily with material and information processes that have static relationships between the inputs and outputs of the subcomponents of the processes. Our broader viewpoint emphasizes iterative cycles of development, phase-in, and maturity.
- To continue to investigate, explore, and study. The traditional TQM approach limits itself to interlocking cycles of routine operation[4] and improvement of the operation.[5] The goal is to plan for execution. Our broader approach recognizes that sometimes we don't know what to do next, and our goal must be to investigate, explore, and discover until we figure out what to do next—to plan for study.[6]

- To use diffusion in reinforcement itself. The typical TQM implementation focuses on mobilizing teams. Our broader approach is to diffuse the methods not just within teams but in a reinforcing way among individuals, teams, organizations, and across society.[7]

Addressing this combination of needs we believe is a unique aspect of our book.

3.3 FOUR LEVELS OF PRACTICE

Implicit in the four revolutions of management thinking is the need to practice business improvement and organizational learning at four levels: individual, work group, organization, and regional, industry and often global levels (see Figure 3-8).

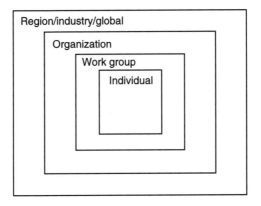

Figure 3-8. Four Levels of Practice

The purpose of the methods of the four revolutions in management is to appropriately transform the organization's capability. Ultimately, all transformation begins with individual action. Thus, the individual level of practice is necessary to shift the purpose of each employee's work from just doing the work assigned to satisfying the customer and to give the individual employee the tools necessary to accomplish this task. This practice level brings the idea of customer/supplier relationships to everyone in the company. If employees are to meet and satisfy the customer or next process, their skills must shift from just doing routine work to doing both routine work and improvement work. Effectively making such shifts requires a system.

However, individuals learn better and are better able to accomplish their desired improvements in the context of a supportive work group or team. At the work group level, you also want to unite routine work and improvement work (which requires a focus on process). You do this by encouraging mutual learning and teamwork, by providing a system that makes routine work and improvement clearly part of the job, and by taking the time for improvement.

In turn, work groups and teams learn more efficiently and are better able to accomplish their desired improvements in the context of a supportive organization. At the organizational level, you want to integrate innovative improvements with the corporate goals and mobilize the entire company in a systematic pursuit of the corporate goals.

Finally, organizations learn more efficiently and are better able to accomplish their desired improvements when they explicitly find those aspects of the external environment that motivate and support them. The industrywide, regional, or national level of business improvement practice should be directed toward a broader improvement culture that supports an individual company's business improvement or organizational learning efforts. This support can be through informal "networking," collaboration for mutual gain, and transfer of successful practices among companies and others interested in quality. The Center for Quality of Management (CQM) was established to provide such sharing of experiences and resources. This networking also motivates us to keep going when we are flagging. In Japan, successful practices are integrated into training materials from the Japanese Union of Scientists and Engineers and the Japanese Standards Association, which many companies use; the journals and seminars of national quality societies also serve this purpose. National quality awards, such as the Baldrige Award in the United States, encourage nationwide awareness of quality; Japan's Deming Prize is part of an extensive system of national quality awareness.

Chapters 4 through 29 describe the systems and methods you can put in place to implement the four practical revolutions in management and the four levels of practice.

NOTES

1. Thus, many people think of TQM as being focused on quality assurance, or the *management of quality*. Neither the first edition of this book nor this second edition puts much emphasis on this historic focus of TQM on quality assurance. There are many other books on quality assurance and this narrow focus of TQM.

2. In fact, shortly after the first edition was published in 1993, we began speaking and writing about TQM as total quality *of* management rather than total quality management. During the last several years, when trying to be precise, we have spoken of TQ*of*M rather than TQM.

3. See [186] for a number of case studies of the application of business improvement methods in non-traditional "industries."

4. The SDCA cycle.

5. The PDCA cycle.

6. This might be called the PSDA—plan, study, develop, act—cycle.

7. We will elaborate on this point in the following section.

The First Revolution:
CUSTOMER FOCUS

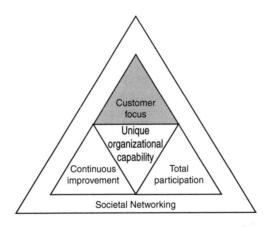

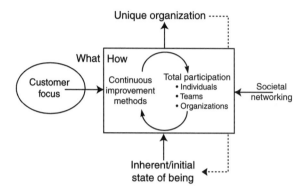

Customer Focus Drives What Needs to Be Done

This portion of the book describes the first of our management revolutions.

Chapter 4—Change in the Work Concept:

- Defines the concepts of product-out, market-in, philosophy-out, and philosophy-in and describes the relationships among them

Chapter 5—Evolution of Customer Focus and Its Challenges:

- Describes three stages in the development of the practice of customer focus
- Suggests a variety of perspectives from which to consider customer concerns
- Introduces the need to integrate across concerns
- Emphasizes that customers ultimately are individuals

4

Change in the Work Concept

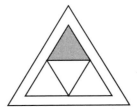

4.1 MARKET-IN

Understanding and fulfilling the expectations of customers is the best and only lasting means to business success.[1,2]

To this end, companies need to emphasize a concept called *market-in*, which focuses on customer satisfaction as the purpose of work, in contrast to the older concept of *product-out*, which focuses on the product as the purpose of work.

The traditional concept of work says that a job is done and done well if a product is produced according to the manual for making it and the product works up to its specification or standard. This is called the product-out concept because the focus is on the company's effort to output what it considers to be a good product (see Figure 4-1).

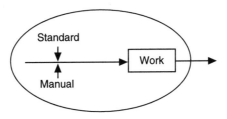

Figure 4-1. The Product-Out Concept

The product-out concept is often practiced in a fashion that suggests that the customers are stupid—that they don't understand their real needs. Often companies with a product-out orientation reject a customer's complaint about a product with the statement, "you are using it incorrectly," or "it's not meant to do that." Also, workers frequently believe that their job is just to do what is specified in their description, product standard, or production manual, and nothing more; managers may have this same "not my job" attitude.

But why do we work? Work is the means to the purpose of satisfying customers. The market-in concept focuses on input from the market and says that the job is not done well until the customer is satisfied (see Figure 4-2). The market-in concept says, "the customer is king" (or, queen—the Japanese translate their version of this saying as "the customer is god").

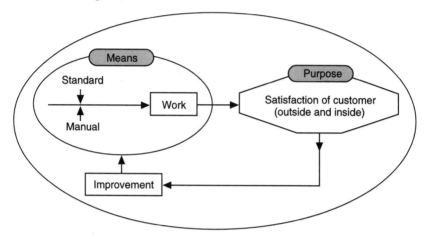

Figure 4-2. The Market-In Concept

The market-in concept says that every employee has customers. The company has outside customers, of course, and they must be satisfied; however, each person in the company, no matter how far from the external customers, also has customers. The now famous slogan, "The next process is your customer," means that each product or service step must satisfy or serve all subsequent processes. Therefore, internal customers (the next processes) have the same importance as external customers. Whoever uses the product of your work is your customer. In fact, each person may have many customers (and be a customer of many others). The market-in concept keeps your focus on customer satisfaction: the person you are talking to now is your customer, and you must try to satisfy that person.

The market-in concept ideal is to penetrate the entire company and reach all employees at all levels. Of course, customer requirements change, so you need feedback from the customer and processes to improve the product over time—its specifications, the way it works, and the way you produce it. The Japanese call this improvement process *kaizen*. The market-in concept includes the idea of an improvement process for adjusting the work and the product produced as dictated by changing customer needs.

Why Market-in Is Necessary

The product-out concept adheres to Taylor's theory of division of labor: some people follow standard processes, and others work on improvement [153]. Market-in tries to eliminate this concept of separation of labor. Instead, the market-in concept includes the dual function of work, that is, everyone works both on standard processes (routine work) and on improvement. The difficulty with Taylor's theory of division of labor is it does not allow for quick enough reactions to satisfy customers in today's fast-paced, rapidly changing world. The key phrase here is "rapidly changing"—of customer requirements, technology, staff requirements, the communities around you, the monetary system, and the international geopolitical situation—and such change is frequently unforeseeable. As shown in Figure 4-3, on-going business improvement can be thought of as synonymous with management in the face of rapid change.

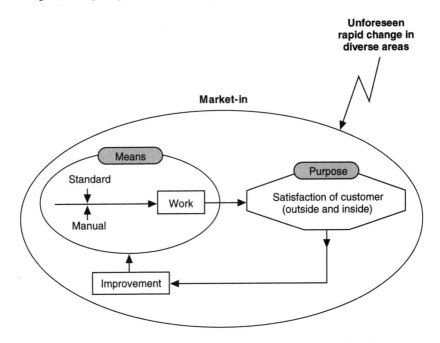

Figure 4-3. Market-In Enables Management in the Face of Rapid Change

Corning provided the following analogy to this increased pace and change in society and the need for business to keep up. For centuries, people believed running a four-minute mile was impossible. In the 1950s, Roger Bannister ran a mile in under four minutes for the first time. Today, running a four-minute mile is a basic requirement for any competitive miler. The business situation is similar. Companies that pioneered achieving total quality have raised the standard for competitive performance. Today, unless a company is achieving total quality, it is, or soon will be, uncompetitive.

The late Bill Smith of Motorola offered a related viewpoint summarized below:

You must be best in class in terms of people, product, marketing, manufacturing, technology, and service. Otherwise, you will not be competitive. Best in class means you do as well as L.L. Bean in order entry, as well as the Federal Reserve Bank in transaction processing, and so forth. Furthermore, once product quality is high, the customer will take it for granted and other factors (e.g., billing, order entry) will become more important to the customer.

These viewpoints suggest why many companies adopt methods of ongoing business improvement. In a fast-paced world they are under many pressures that threaten their survival—the threat of insolvency, poor staff morale, increased costs, and diminished market share or sales (the latter two are forms of market pressure).

The practitioner of market-in knows the customer is not concerned with a company's internal functional organization. The customer is interested in product quality, cost, and delivery (widely known as QCD). These require cross-functional effort—no one department or function can provide QCD by itself. This means you must have two overlaid organizational structures—a hierarchy for doing routine work and a cross-functional organization to ensure customer satisfaction. The cross-functional organization is needed to align the efforts of all parts of the company—divisions, departments, and individual employees—in a continuous effort to understand root issues (customer and internal) and improve and adapt to changing circumstances.

Traditional management structures are not typically well suited to working on total customer satisfaction. U.S. companies traditionally had functional management but not cross-functional management. They focused on results, not root causes, that is, they focused on the dependent variable and not the independent variable. They focused on trying to develop perfect standards and policies rather than viewing them as part of a continuous improvement process. They managed their workers rather than involving them in the improvement process.

Business improvement and organizational learning as we describe in much of this book needs to be a mass movement.[3] It is not a movement of the elite within a company. The leverage comes from getting everyone in the company to play the appropriate role skillfully—from focusing everyone on doing what he or she can do to satisfy the customer. It is the job of the manager to practice and teach market-in. As you look at companies that are practicing business improvement and organizational learning, you may sometimes wonder what it is that makes the focus on quality so effective. Several major *alignments* support the success of these companies.

First, the best way to satisfy customers is to deliver a high-quality product at a low price when the customer wants it. To reach these goals you must figure out what product the customer really wants, design and manufacture it so it works really well (removing all defects), and design and build it quickly (without any unnecessary cycle time). In addition to satisfying customers, all of these steps must save the company money by reducing wasted resources. The focus on customer-defined quality does double duty—it satisfies customers and it lets the company run as efficiently as possible.

Second, customers want many different things. Some focus exclusively on low cost, some are motivated by personal ambition, some want to avoid a controversial buying decision, and some enjoy dominating the supplier. However, the majority of customers are concerned with something else: probably some 70 to 80 percent of them want a quality product at a low price. Company staff members also want many different things. Some want profits above all else, some want to perform social good, some want to work with the highest technology, and some only want to seek personal promotion. Most, however, are striving primarily for excellence in their work. Quality is perhaps the only area where there is such great alignment between the goals of the customer and the goals of the staff. Achieving this alignment is another way in which a focus on quality does double duty.

Finally, achieving alignment between what the customers want and what the company is doing is hard. Customer focus helps:

- In these days of rapid change, a company constantly has to look to existing and potential customers so the company doesn't miss a signal of a change in the market.
- In companies, one hears that customers often don't know what they need. While this claim can be true,[4] a company is inevitably better off learning what the current and potential customers have to say and observe what they are doing to get greater insight than the company likely will have itself.[5] Then, people in the company can match their own knowledge about what is possible and intuition about what is needed with the external inputs to produce a more powerful understanding and innovation than the company would produce alone.
- Companies trying to address the market typically have two problems: one is their understanding the market, and the other is aligning themselves internally to effectively accomplish what they decide should be done. The second of these problems is frequently the more difficult. Hearing from and digesting what the market has to say not only brings in this very valuable external data; it also provides an enormous external energy and aligning force for the company.[6]

4.2 CUSTOMERS

Many companies we have observed over the years provide examples of a market-in approach to quality. Analog Devices states, "Analog Devices is committed to the establishment and continuous improvement of world class systems and processes aimed at satisfying our customers' evolving needs." Solectron, two-time winner of the Malcolm Baldrige National Quality Award and many other awards, says, "Solectron is committed to ... providing a full range of manufacturing and design solutions that exceed customers' expectations." NEC refers to, "Giving top priority to customer satisfaction through relentless efforts to provide better products and better services." NEC goes on to state, "In order to continue creating and providing products and services that are truly attractive to the customer, we must foster a corporate culture in which all employees think and act from the perspective of the customer."

Under the concept of market-in, for each piece of work you do, you must seek customer satisfaction. To achieve customer satisfaction, first determine who your customer is.

A customer is the person or group who receives the work you do. That work may be a product or it may be a service. The customer who receives your output may be either external or internal. An external customer is someone who does not work for the company but receives the company's products or services. Notice, these are not only the immediate customers of your company; they may also be anyone in the customer stream to which your products flow. An internal customer is someone who works for the company and depends on the work of other company employees to get work done. Everyone has customers for every valid business function: a secretary types a letter for a customer, an accountant produces a financial report for a customer, an engineer does a detailed design for a customer, and an employee submitting a trip report has a customer for that trip report. *A business function without a customer should not be performed.*

The market-in concept includes the idea of a process for improvement aimed at continuing customer satisfaction. Companies often have an explicit process or set of guidelines for dealing with customers (either external or internal). For instance, in its Total Quality Control Pocket Guide, Hewlett-Packard listed the following steps:

1. Who are my customers?
2. What are their needs?
3. What is my product or service?
4. What are my customers' measures or expectations?
5. What is my process for meeting their needs?
6. Does my product or service meet their needs and expectations?
7. What actions are needed to improve my process?

Motorola listed approximately the following steps:

1. Identify the work you do (i.e., the product).
2. Identify whom you do it for (i.e., the customer).
3. What do you need to do your work and from whom (i.e., the suppliers) do you need it?
4. Map the process.
5. Mistake-proof the process and eliminate delays (including non-value-added time).
6. Establish quality and cycle time measurement and improvement goals.

These are standard steps for executing and describing improvement. People are taught that the first step in identifying a problem is to see what customers want and aren't getting. Managers of improvement efforts therefore require this analysis. Market-in is not just a slogan but is built into the way things are done. Senior executives plan the sequence in which to institutionalize market-in.

4.3 PHILOSOPHY-IN AND PHILOSOPHY-OUT

It may not be sufficient *only* to listen to customers and to focus on their satisfaction. Customers may demand more or less than is beneficial to them in the longer run. The company must also be aware of the greater societal trends that may influence the needs of customers or what the company should do. We call this *philosophy-in*. This expansion on market-in (as shown in Figure 4-3) is shown in Figure 4-4.

Also, in some cases, the company may want to influence their customers or societal trends. For instance, the company may have less consumption-oriented packaging

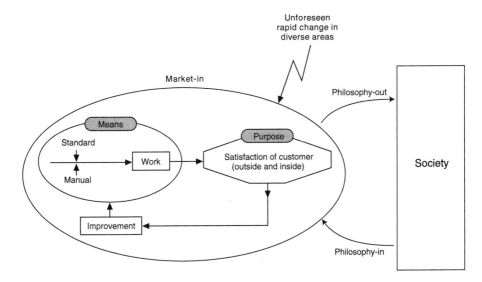

Figure 4-4. Philosophy-In and Philosophy-Out

ideas than the packaging methods customers are used to or think they want. It may be important for the company to put forth its vision for society. We call this *philosophy-out*. Concern for the environment, ethical behavior, public health concerns, and so on could be part of a company's philosophy-out approach.

Having described the potential need for philosophy-in and philosophy-out, we hasten to add that companies must not use them as an excuse to ignore their customers and the market-in approach. The companies must figure out how simultaneously to practice market-in and philosophy-in/-out. The company must integrate concerns between customers and itself.

The next chapter will deal further with the complications of customer focus.

NOTES

1. Furthermore, without someone to serve (a current customer or future customer), an organization has little reason for existing. Peter Drucker has succinctly stated (in more or less these words) that the purpose of business is to get and keep a customer. This also applies to non-profit businesses and other organizations that don't usually

think of themselves as businesses. The Red Cross, schools and colleges, state and local governments, and Girl Scouts all exist to serve their own sorts of "customers."

2. Focus on the customer is such an article of faith these days that we may forget how only a few years ago many if not most companies thought they knew best what their customers wanted. Even today, it is a widely held view among people in product development departments that they must educate customers about what they need. Furthermore, we all deal from time to time with companies (or other organizations) that seem unconcerned with our needs as customers; in most of these cases, we undoubtedly wish we had an alternative supplier that was more concerned with our concerns.

3. This statement is true for process improvement and process breakthrough. When we discuss business breakthrough in Chapter 27, we will introduce an explicit exception to the usefulness of a mass movement.

4. And even when they know what they want, customers often have a hard time articulating it.

5. Eric von Hippel in [296] reports that in 83 percent of the cases covered by his extensive research someone outside the company (e.g., a customer or user) created the innovative idea.

6. Jack Reilly, who retired a few years ago from the position of head of marketing for IBM U.S., makes the point that external, e.g., customer, demand for performance can overcome a lot of obstacles trying to get in the way of achieving significant performance challenges. In fact, Reilly says that without such external forces, we often don't have enough energy in our bodies to overcome the usual set of internal obstacles to collaboration.

5

Evolution of Customer Focus and Its Challenges

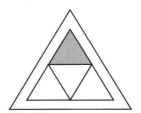

5.1 THREE STAGES OF CUSTOMER FOCUS

In the previous chapter we talked about the importance of customer focus. Unfortunately, as we began to suggest in Section 4.3, life is more complicated than just market-in, as we describe in this chapter. We begin by looking at some stages in the evolution of customer focus (see Table 5-1).

Table 5-1. Stages of Evolution of Customer Focus

0. No customer focus	Product-out
1. Expansion of idea of customers	Product businesses Service businesses Non-traditional businesses
2. Integration of concerns	Across customers Between customers and company
3. Satisfy each customer individually	Mass customization?

At least in years gone by, companies typically started by practicing product-out (stage 0 of Table 5-1)—they had little concept of customer focus. This is the situation in Figure 4-1 (page 51) illustrating the product-out concept.

In the first era of awakening to customers (stage 1 of Table 5-1), product companies discovered the benefits of customer focus (for reasons such as those considered in Chapter 4). This is the situation in Figure 4-2 (page 52) illustrating the market-in concept. Next, service companies realized it would also benefit them to focus on customers. Eventually, many other sorts of institutions (the Red Cross, schools and colleges, state and local governments, health care providers, National Public Radio, and so on) realized the benefit of thinking of those they serve as customers and adopted the methods of customer focus (or were forced to realize it by those they serve).

Today, organizations of all types speak in terms of having customers and use the methods of customer focus.[1]

Before we discuss stages 2 and 3 of Table 5-1, we need to consider customer concerns in some detail.

5.2 CUSTOMER CONCERNS

It is not sufficient just to identify that one has customers. One also has to be able to discover and understand what they care about. Customer concerns are often multifaceted, and the company often has a limited mindset about the value the company is providing to the customer.

Finding the Full Extent of Customer Concerns

The first step in understanding the full range of customer concerns is to be aware of them. To this end, practitioners and researchers have developed a number of different models of concern.

Four fitnesses. In Chapter 1 we introduced the *four fitnesses*: fitness to standard (the product or service works as it was designed to—according to the specification and manual), fitness to use (works the way the user wants or needs it to work), fitness of cost (has more capability and quality at the same or a lesser cost to the customer), and fitness to latent requirement (meeting customer needs before the customers are aware of those needs).

Quality, cost, and delivery (QCD). In Chapter 4 we also briefly mentioned QCD. In understanding the extent of customer and user concerns about a product or service, it helps to distinguish customer needs for quality (function and performance), for cost (tangible or intangible to the customer), and for delivery (where and when). We will elaborate further on QCD in Chapter 7.

Kano's requirements dimensions. Professor Noriaki Kano suggests that the quality of a product or service or customer satisfaction relating to it can be categorized and measured in terms of the different components shown in Figure 5-1.[2] The horizontal axis of the graph in the figure measures how fully functional to how dysfunctional a particular component or aspect of product or service is. The vertical axis of the graph measures how satisfied to dissatisfied the customer or user is. Three curves are plotted in the figure.

Some aspects of a product or service fall on the *must-be* curve in the figure. The brakes of a car are a typical example of a must-be requirement. If the brakes are fully functional, the customer or user will be neutral or indifferent, midway between satisfied nor dissatisfied in the figure; however, if the brakes are absent or dysfunctional, the customer will be very dissatisfied.

Other aspects of a product or service fall on the *one-dimensional* line in the figure. The gas mileage, price, or reliability of a car may fit in this category. The more fully functional each of these is, the more satisfied the customer is about it (and the more dysfunctional, the more dissatisfied).

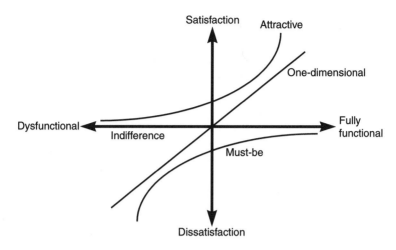

Figure 5-1. Kano's Dimensions of Product Quality

Still other aspects of the product or service may fall on the *attractive* curve in the figure. A built-in global positioning system (GPS) system for navigation in a new car in 1999 might fit in this category. If there is no GPS, the customer does not expect it and is indifferent to its absence; if a GPS is fully present, the customer is pleased.

Rapaille's cultural archetypes. Clautaire Rapaille, a French-born consultant who now lives in the U.S. and studies what he calls "cultural archetypes," has researched and reported how native-born people in various countries subconsciously think about issues [27, 233] such as quality [26], teamwork [28], loyalty [29], and leadership [234]. For instance, according to Dr. Rapaille [232], the U.S.-based cultural view of quality is that a product is a quality product *if it works*. In Germany, Dr. Rapaille reports that a quality product *is built according to standards and specifications*. In his native France, Dr. Rapaille reports with a smile, an item has high quality *if it is "useless,"* and he gives the example of an expensive silk scarf that a woman throws over her shoulder just for style and not for a utilitarian purpose.

As part of his consulting practice, Dr. Rapaille helps companies understand how customers and users subconsciously think about the different aspects of a product or service [136]. The Ritz-Carlton Hotel Company used Dr. Rapaille's survey and analysis methods to help discover that when U.S. clients think of clean bathrooms in their hotel rooms, they subconsciously mean white bathrooms. As Leonardo Inghilleri, VP of Human Resources for The Ritz-Carlton Hotel Company explained, "The customers said they wanted *cleanliness*, but what they meant was *immaculateness*. While we were busy redecorating with gray, green, or pink marble in the bathrooms, the customers really wanted white because white is more immaculate than these other colors" [143]. This allowed Ritz-Carlton to spend the large amount of money it spends outfitting bathrooms to buy white marble that the clients recognized as "clean" rather than with some other color that would cost as much and subconsciously be considered "unclean."

Inghilleri described another discovery: "Guests frequently use the word 'home,' which we took to mean that they want to feel at home when they are at the Ritz. But we found out that home is not what they want. They really want a home like their mother's, where everything is taken care of for them and where everything is clean and you don't have to pick up after yourself. This is the home they really want." Inghilleri stressed, "If a company wants to be successful, it must have a strong hold on its customers' needs. To have a strong hold on your customers' needs, you have to have a deep understanding of the words they use to communicate these needs."

Viewpoints

Unfortunately, while people are trying to hear about someone else's (for instance, a customer's) concerns, they have difficultly accepting what they hear—it doesn't match our own view of the situation. Conflicting viewpoints prevent them from accepting or perhaps from even hearing each other's points of view. Why is this?[3]

For any situation with any material amount of complexity, many of us don't think about the possibility of, or aren't concerned with, any other viewpoint than our own viewpoint of the situation. We call this a uniview. For instance, a circle indicating my[4] uniview about a situation is shown in the top left corner of Figure 5-2.[5]

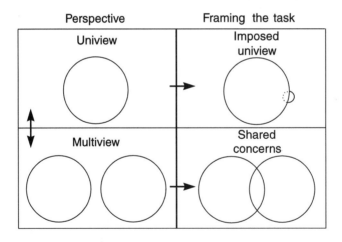

Figure 5-2. Uniview/Multiview Grid

There are a couple of ways one can move regarding one's uniview of a situation. One thing we frequently do is see the task ahead as arguing others into believing our uniview. We often do this in meetings or conversations; we spend a lot of time talking past each other, even to the point that we may be downright rude in our statements about each other's viewpoints.

For instance, in the top-right corner of Figure 5-2, I show a little circle indicating how little value I give to your uniview, and I blot out your viewpoint with mine, which I consider much more significant. We call this the imposed uniview.

Another direction I can go from my own uniview is down. In the bottom-left box I try to discover the multiview. This not only means recognizing that I have a uniview of my own, but also discovering the validity of your uniview from your point of view.

With this multiview—this understanding of my own uniview as well as yours, especially if you have been doing the same thing with regard to my viewpoint—each of us may see some overlap between the elements of the multiview and, therefore, be able to develop our shared concerns.

But where do our univiews about a given situation come from?

Reasoning Sequence

Let's look at a model in Figure 5-3[6] for how we reason through a situation. We have some facts available to us. We select some of these facts. We may make some inferences based on the facts we select. We probably will make some judgments. Finally, we will make some decisions. And based on these decisions we may take some actions.

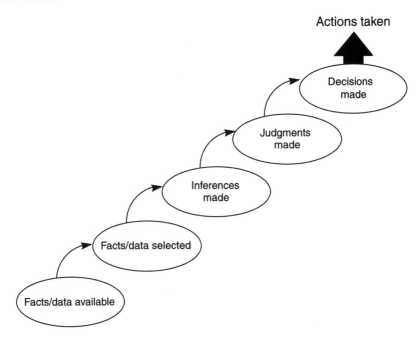

Figure 5-3. How We Reason

However, typically, we don't do these steps of reasoning slowly and thoughtfully.

Rather, we zip through the steps almost unconsciously at the speed of neurons. More quickly than we can explicitly think, we select some facts, make inferences, judgments and conclusions, and take actions. This rapid reaction is necessary most of the time. When we see a cardboard box in the road while driving at high speed, we don't have time to analyze the situation: whether the box is empty and we can safely drive over it, or whether it contains something that is dangerous to hit. We see the cardboard box and jerk the steering wheel to avoid it. If we reasoned everything out step-by-step in business, we'd never get anything done.

Our uniview about a situation comes from rapid-fire reasoning with almost unconsciously drawn conclusions resulting in actions.

Observer-That-One-Is

There is something behind this rapid-fire reasoning—the observer that each of us is (see Figure 5-4).

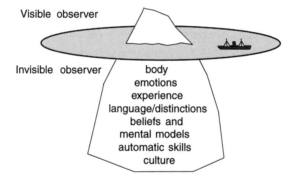

Figure 5-4. The Observer-That-One-Is

Each of us is able to see different things when we look at a situation: what we can physiologically observe; our emotional state; our experiences; the vocabulary we have and how we understand language; individual beliefs and mental models; automatic ways of reacting to things; and cultural background. Each of us makes assumptions that are so natural to us that, not only do we often fail to explain our assumptions to someone else, we are often not even conscious of them ourselves.

Some of the way we observe things is visible to others—above the tip of the iceberg. Another part may be visible to ourselves. However, much of the way we observe things is invisible to others and often partly invisible to ourselves as well. However, what we don't see, we still get. The observer-that-one-is is inside us all the time influencing how we reason.

An important consequence is each of us is a different observer of whatever there is to be seen: since *different* people see the *same* situation *differently, how people see something says more about the way they observe things than it says of the situation.*

Cycle of Reasoning

The observers-that-we-are influence the very facts we have available to us (see Figure 5-5). A marketing person typically can see different facts than a financial person does. The observers-that-we-are influence which facts we select, the inferences we make, the judgments we make, the conclusions we draw and the actions we take.

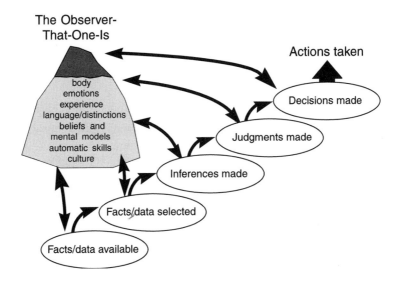

Figure 5-5. Complete Cycle of Reasoning

But it works the other way, too. Not only do the observers-that-we-are influence each step in our reasoning, each step in our reasoning tends to confirm the observers-that-we-are.

Humans have a wonderful capability to construct and reinforce internal coherence. We make a particular inference based on the way we look at things, and then the inference seems right to us and confirms to us that we really are thinking about things in the right way.

The cycle of reasoning shown in Figure 5-5 represents the entire combination of the reasoning steps and the observer-that-one-is.[7]

As already mentioned, the reasoning cycle operates at tremendous speed, almost without thinking.

Repeating ourselves: *different* observers see the *same* situation differently; therefore (logically), *how a person sees a situation says more about the person's way of observing and, thus, about the person than about the situation*. This is a key idea. If we are to understand the various concerns of people (for instance, customers), we must break out of the mindset that how we see something is how it is and that the other person's viewpoint or concern is wrong. We must try to validate the perspectives of others—to understand how they see the situation so we can understand them and their needs better. We must discover the multiview (bottom left of Figure 5-6).

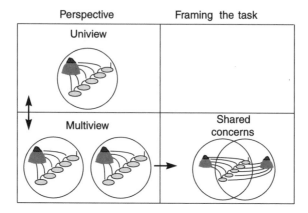

Figure 5-6. Uniview to Multiview to Shared Concerns

With a better understanding of how each of us observes the situation, we may be able to find an intersection in the way we reason about the situation allowing us to take action together usefully (bottom-right corner of Figure 5-6). For instance, the company producing a washing machine sees it as an appliance their customers use to wash clothes, but farmers also use it as a potato washer.[8] How the farmers see it says a lot about them that is useful for the company to know to allow the washing machine to serve both purposes.

Resolution of disagreement about what is wrong in all sorts of business and social situations[9] will be aided by validating the perspective of others and seeing the situations from a different point of view, understanding them better.

With these last two paragraphs, we have begun to slide into the next stage of evolution of customer focus.

5.3 INTEGRATION OF CONCERNS

The next stage of the evolution of customer focus, stage 2 of Table 5-1 (page 59), involves the integration of concerns—across customers, between what customers say and what they need, and between what the customer requires and what the company can provide.

Variations on Shared Concerns

Let's first discuss what can be meant by "shared concerns." The following figures illustrate variations on the idea.

Figure 5-7 Part A illustrates the obvious case where two people or entities approach each other more or less as equals (for instance, a company selling computer networking systems and a company wishing to buy a computer networking system), have different concerns (for instance, making a profit versus spending as little as pos-

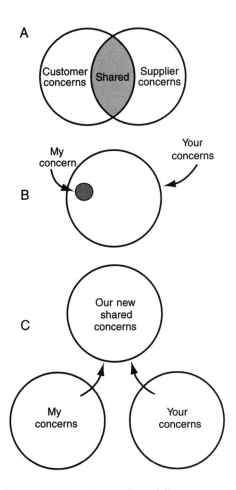

Figure 5-7. Variations on Shared Concerns

sible), and hopefully can find an intersection among them. The figure makes clear that mutual concerns don't have to overlap 100 percent. In fact, they don't have to overlap at all. For instance, your business may need to have a routine job done, and I may want an entry-level opportunity; this compatibility (if not sharedness) of concerns will be sufficient for us to succeed together.

Part B of Figure 5-7 illustrates the common situation where one party has a relatively big concern (such as becoming the world's largest bottler and distributor of soft drinks), and the other party (me) may just want to buy a soft drink at the closest neighborhood store. There is no specific give-and-take between the parties on this particular transaction. Nonetheless, the bottler and distributor need to be concerned for my (typical) concerns that the various flavors and diet/non-diet combinations of its soft drinks are available in every store I go into, at vending machines on the street, in the halls of my office building, and so on. Localized failures by the company to provide for the needs of the customers could damage the company's business in the larger region.

Part C of Figure 5-7 illustrates the situation where each party has different concerns to begin with. By talking with and observing each other, they may discover a new shared concern that neither had to begin with. For instance, one company has a customizable Web site design; it is trying to convince a lawyer (who practices admiralty law) to buy a Web site that it will customize to provide on-line advertising of the lawyer's service. As the two parties talk and get to know each other, a new possibility emerges: they will set up a new company in which they are partners that sells a monthly newsletter providing up-to-date world-wide information on admiralty law, using Internet distribution of electronic documents.

Listen, Observe, Interpret, and Integrate

Once a company has heard the breadth of customer concerns about a product or service and has sorted them out, merely to acknowledge that "the customer knows best" and to provide that is not sufficient. People within the company have heard different things and disagree on the proper course of action. Different customers have different needs. Furthermore, customers often do not really know what they want (even if they have spoken explicitly about it) or what they need. Additionally, what the company can currently provide may not match what the customers want.

A process is needed first to listen to what customers and potential customers have to say and to observe what they do (see Figure 5-8). The company must listen to what customers have to say because they may say useful things, they want to be listened to, and in any case the company needs the customers' vocabulary in order to speak back to them in words that are familiar to them. The company also must observe what users do because their words may be ambiguous, misleading, or shortsighted, and their actions will provide a context for understanding the real or, at least, a better meaning of their words. Then the company must analyze and interpret what the customer meant, in the context of the observed actions. Finally, the company must somehow find a useful intersection and integration of its own concerns and the concerns it has interpreted from various current and future customers. The company's concerns may include issues such as taking advantages of its core competencies/technologies or its distribution organization, or they may include social and philosophical issues (philosophy-in and philosophy-out) as illustrated in Figure 4-4 (page 57).

We will discuss at length in Chapters 13 and 14 how to follow a process such as that shown in Figure 5-8.

5.4 INDIVIDUALIZING CUSTOMERS

Integration of concerns across customers has made some companies and management thinkers realize that ways exist for companies to provide each customer with exactly what the customer wants (see stage 3 of Table 5-1, page 59); this is in lieu of a compromise. These companies attempt to practice one-to-one marketing [222, 188]. For instance, many retail companies now keep track of everything each customer buys from them, and try to provide new specifically tailored offers to each customer. Many U.S. grocery stores now track what each customer purchases and give discount coupons for future purchases they think the customer might be interested in based on previous purchases. On the Internet, separate companies exchange detailed information on everything someone looks at on the Web sites of any of the companies.

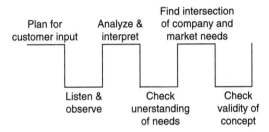

Figure 5-8. A Process for Seeking Customer Input

Other companies are moving to "mass customization" [225] to provide customers with exactly the product they want. For instance, a clothing manufacturer collecting size data on individual customers is then able to produce suits to an individual's own specifications. Also, numerous information services allow users to customize the topics covered and the format of delivered reports.

This one-to-one marketing and mass customization depends on information and manufacturing technology to collect the individualized data and to produce the individualized products and services.

As noted in Section 3.2 (page 43), any organization has two key problems:

1. Figuring out what its market wants and the intersection of that with what the company can provide
2. Aligning and mobilizing itself to deliver what is needed

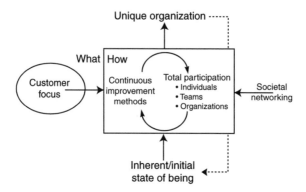

Customer focus, the topic of this and the prior chapter, drives what needs to be done. How to do it is the next issue and subject of the next two parts (and 23 chapters) of this book.

NOTES

1. Unless we make an explicit distinction, we mean "customer" generally—we do not distinguish among customer, user, purchaser, etc.

2. We will provide more detail in Chapter 14.

3. The content that follows on viewpoints and the cycle of reasoning provides a vocabulary that we will use throughout the rest of the book—we introduce it in the context of customer focus, but it is not limited to customer focus.

4. To avoid awkward linguistic constructions distinguishing between one person and another person, from here on in this chapter we will sometimes speak in our examples in terms of "you" and "me."

5. An initial version of the viewpoint diagrams was developed by Dave Walden, Gary Burchill, and Ted Walls; later Rafael Echeverria and Bob Putnam helped refine the figure.

6. Derived from [17].

7. The cycle of reasoning is a synthesis created by Action Design, the CQM, and Newfield Consulting.

8. Reusing an example from Chapter 1, page 5.

9. Examples: improving business productivity by focusing on revenue growth or cost cutting; dealing with the federal deficit by raising or lowering taxes; improving public schools by testing teachers or by providing vouchers that can be spent at private schools.

The Second Revolution:
CONTINUOUS IMPROVEMENT

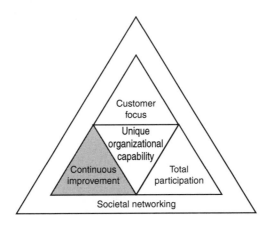

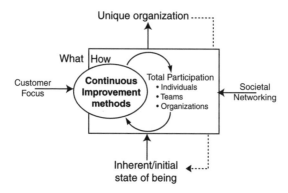

The How Begins with Continuous Improvement

This portion of the book, on continuous improvement, consists of four sections—an introductory chapter on the fundamentals and vocabulary of continuous improvement, five chapters on managing existing processes, a chapter on managing one-time efforts (projects or tasks), and two chapters on finding new directions. The following table summarizes this organization:

Introduction	Chapter 6 Improvement as a Problem-Solving Process
Managing Existing Processes	Chapters 7–11 Process Discovery and Management Process Control and Variation Reactive Improvement and the 7 Steps Method Management Diagnosis of the 7 Steps of Reactive Improvement Process Management Mobilization Case Study—Teradyne
One-time Efforts	Chapter 12 Planning Projects or Tasks
Finding New Directions	Chapters 13–14 Proactive Improvement Applying Proactive Improvement to Develop New Products

The first edition of this book had five chapters in this, the continuous improvement, part of the book. In this second edition we have added four chapters. Chapter 7 on Process Discovery and Management and Chapter 8 on Process Control and Variation are basic topics that have been added because many people do not know or practice these methods. Chapter 11 has been added to provide a case study of mobilizing process management and its methods. Chapter 12 on Planning Projects or Tasks has been added to extend the book's content on continuous improvement.

6

Improvement as a Problem-Solving Process

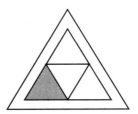

Chapter 4 introduced the concepts of market-in, continuous quality improvement, and customer satisfaction through an improvement process. Because every product or service is the outcome of a process, the effective way to improve quality is to improve the process used to build the product. The corollary of focusing on process is that the focus is not on the results—results are the dependent variable. The results come from whatever process is followed, i.e., process drives results.

This practice differs significantly from the methods used in many companies, where the emphasis is on objectives. However, objectives alone cannot produce sustainable results. The value of objectives is to help decide what process needs to be put in place to produce the desired results. That process (and the way you follow it) then determines the results.

6.1 MANAGEMENT BY PROCESS

We advise a form of focus on process that we call *management by process*. It consists of realizing that results come from process, building a process to produce the desired results, implementing the process so one can later figure out why it produced the results it did, and then feeding this insight back to improve the process next time it is used (see Figure 6-1).

Management by process works as follows. Set a goal and develop an implementation plan for accomplishing the goal, including assignment of the people necessary to accomplish the effort. Develop a system for measuring whether you are adhering to the plan and accomplishing the desired results. Then undertake the task, monitoring adherence to plan and results. With this information, analyze why you were unable to adhere to the implementation plan or why the plan didn't work, and use this analysis to revise the goal, implementation plan, and measurement plan. The emphasis is on changing the process and changing the inputs to accomplish the desired results. The outputs are important for the light they shed on how the process is working.

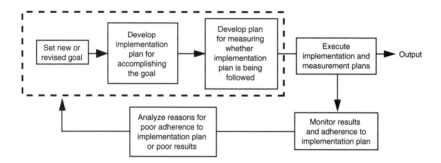

Figure 6-1. Management by Process

Implicit in the concept of focus on process is the idea that any activity can be improved if you systematically plan the improvement, understand the current practice, plan solutions and implement them, analyze the result and its causes, and cycle through these steps again. This scientific approach can be applied to improving a company's process for anticipating its customers' needs and also to improving the capabilities of individual staff members or groups of staff members. Throughout the rest of this book we will show examples of process as the means of making learning and improvement more efficient, simplifying communication, reducing variability of diverse results, building intuition and creativity, and improving ability to predict the future. Business improvement and organizational learning can be thought of as a process for helping a company to learn and improve—to change noncontrollable items into controlled or controllable items.

The theme of management by process, and more generally the process focus, recurs throughout the practice of business improvement and organizational learning. Managers need such a viewpoint to understand and improve their own daily work. And, as this chapter suggests, managers must be able to see improvement as a process in order to provide guidance and support to subordinates engaging in improvement activity. The manager's job is to treat improvement as a problem-solving process, as described in the rest of this chapter.

6.2 WV MODEL OF CONTINUOUS IMPROVEMENT

We use the phrase *continuous improvement* to stand for the idea of improvement as a problem-solving process. As shown in Figure 6-2, continuous improvement is based on two major ideas—systematic (or scientifically based) improvement and iterative improvement.

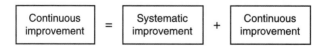

Figure 6-2. Two Components of Continuous Improvement

The WV model is used in this section to illustrate the key issues of continuous improvement.

Systematic Improvement

Improvements are derived from use of a scientific approach (and tools) and a structure for team or individual effort. A scientific approach considers a variety of possible solutions until the best—not just the most obvious—is identified factually. Structuring a team's efforts facilitates the participation of all members, eliciting information from even the more reticent of them. Having made a first step at improvement using these methods, the methods can be repeated to get continuous improvements.

We will use the WV model[1] to explain the concepts relating to improvement as a problem-solving process. The WV model is not a prescription for making specific improvements; it is too abstract for that. Rather, it is an aid to understanding and remembering generally used stages of quality improvement and quality maintenance. It also conveys the idea of moving systematically back and forth between abstract thought and empirical data during the process of solving a problem. Like all models, it is an abstraction and idealization, useful for figuring out where you are and where you need to go next.

The WV model depicts the overall form of problem solving as alternation between thought (ruminating, planning, and analyzing) and experience (getting information from the real world, e.g., through interviews, experiments, or numerical measurements). The path between these two levels over time forms the shape of a W and then a V (see Figure 6-3); hence, the name WV.

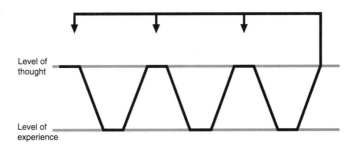

Figure 6-3. W and V Shapes in WV Model

For instance, as shown in Figure 6-4, you sense a problem and then collect data on where it might be; choose a specific improvement activity and then collect data on exactly what is wrong; plan a solution and then collect data to be sure it works; and then standardize on the new solution.

The WV model reminds you not to skip directly from sensing problem to standardizing solution—for example, from "sales are down" to "reorganize the company."

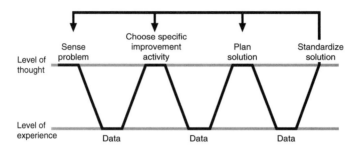

Figure 6-4. Using the WV Model for Problem Solving

Three Types of Improvement

In addition to illustrating the interplay between thought and experience, the WV model illustrates three basic types of problem solving, as shown in Figure 6-5.

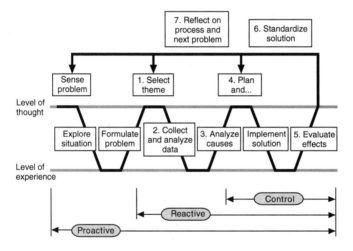

Figure 6-5. Three Types of Problem Solving

The three types of improvement are described below: process control, reactive improvement, and proactive improvement. Quality management started with process control in the United States in the 1930s and in Japan in the 1950s. Reactive improvement was added in the 1960s and 1970s, followed by proactive improvement in the 1980s.

Process control. Assume that you have an effective standard process to perform some business or manufacturing function. You must monitor the process to make sure it is working as intended and bring it back into proper operation if it gets out of alignment. Suppose a worker is charting her process with a control chart, such as the one shown below. In Figure 6-6, results of a process are plotted from left to right over time; the resulting chart highlights those results that exceed certain limits of acceptability.

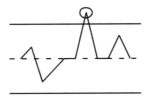

Figure 6-6. A Standard Process Goes Awry

If the process produces results that are out of its control limits, the worker takes corrective action as predetermined and described in the maintenance manual to correct the defect in the process. This cycle, known as the SDCA (standard, do, check, act) cycle, is shown in the rough shape of a V in Figure 6-7. For example, you have a standard bill-paying process (S); you use, or do, it (D) to decide which bills are valid to pay and when to pay them. You take data and evaluate or check (C) the results to make sure you are maximizing your cash position without paying so late that you incur payment penalties; and you act (A) to return to the standard process if it has gotten out of kilter and you are paying incorrectly, too soon, or too late.

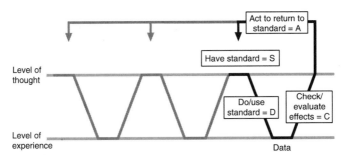

Figure 6-7. The SDCA Cycle

Thus, the method is to have a standard process, to use it to check whether the product meets the specification, and then to act to bring the process back to the standard. The concept is depicted as a cycle because one continues to apply the standard as long as the production procedure continues. This cycle to control or maintain the operation of a good process is known as process control. The monitoring system of process control includes use of inspection and some of the 7 QC tools.

Reactive improvement. The next stage of the WV model addresses the improvement of a weak process. Suppose you have a specific process that produces results that simply aren't good enough (Figure 6-8)—there are many points outside the control limits. Suppose, even if the worker corrects the process according to the process manual, the process repeatedly produces results that are out of its control limits. There is obviously something wrong with the process.

In this case, the worker must take data, analyze the data, find the root causes of the problem, and implement appropriate countermeasures. In other words, the worker

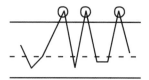

Figure 6-8. An Inadequate Process

reacts to a specific problem by using a problem-solving process to make the improvement, hence the title of this section (the WV Model of Continuous Improvement). For this case, a specific standard methodology exists. As shown in Figure 6-9, the steps of the methodology are as follows:

1. Select a theme (a specific improvement, such as "decrease after-shipment bugs reported in product X").
2. Collect and analyze data (to discover what types of bugs occur most often).
3. Analyze causes (to discover the root cause of the most frequent type of bug).
4. Plan and implement solution (to prevent the root cause from recurring).
5. Evaluate effects (to check the new data to make sure the solution worked).
6. Standardize solution (to replace the old process permanently with the improved process).
7. Reflect on process and the next problem (to consider how the problem-solving process could have been better executed and to decide which problem to work on next, such as the next most frequent type of bug from step 2).

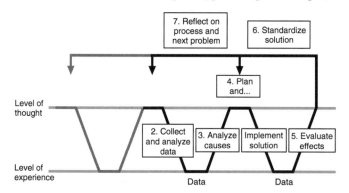

Figure 6-9. The 7 Steps for Reactive Improvement

These steps, designated the 7 steps in this book, are a standard methodology for improving weak processes. This approach is known as reactive improvement because it reacts to already existing weaknesses. Note that for a successful improvement, the last few steps become the SDCA cycle for maintaining the improvement. The 7 QC tools, and more sophisticated statistical tools such as multivariate analysis and experimental design, are also frequently used in reactive problem solving. Chapter 9 describes reactive problem solving in more detail.

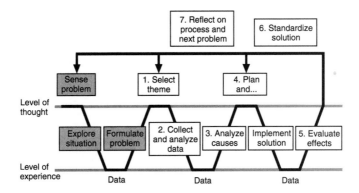

Figure 6-10. Proactive Improvement Steps

Proactive improvement. In many situations you do not start with a clear idea of a specific needed improvement. Rather, you have to choose a direction for the company before starting an improvement activity. For instance, you may need to decide what the customer wants, which product to develop, or which process needs improvement most. This situation is addressed by the final portion of the WV model, known as proactive improvement, as shown in Figure 6-10.

At first, you are only generally aware that there is a problem; you sense a problem. Then you explore the situation broadly to understand what is going on (what customers appear to want, what you are able to build, what processes need fixing). Having explored the situation broadly, you are in a position to formulate a problem, and then in many cases you can move into the 7 steps. The 7 management and planning tools (described in Chapter 13) and quality function deployment are useful for proactive improvement, especially in the initial steps. Other methods for proactive improvement in a variety of situations will be discussed throughout this book.

Task or Project Management. There is another common type of activity that is aimed at improving how the organization operates—the discrete or one-time project or task (see Figure 6-11). This is often a hybrid between the exploratory part of proactive improvement and the planning and implementation portion of reactive improvement. The 9 steps (described in Chapter 12) and other project management methods fit into this category.

Table 6-1 summarizes the various approaches to improvement that apply to various types of situations and methods to handle each.

Action Based on Facts

At each stage in the WV model, as you move between formulating problems or solutions and taking data, you move between the upper and lower lines on the WV model, or the level of thought and the level of experience. In the proactive stage, you have a feeling or image of a problem; you are at the level of thought. Next, take some data (for example, look at how the process or machine is actually operating); now, you are

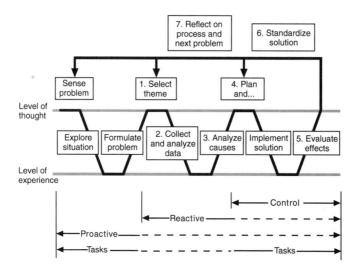

Figure 6-11. A Hybrid Form of Problem Solving

at the level of experience. Continue to move back and forth: formulating a theme (thought), taking data upon which to base root cause analysis (experience), planning a solution (thought), taking data to confirm that the solution works (experience), and

Table 6-1. Summary of Situations, Approaches, and Methods

Situation	Type of improvement	Goal	Methods
Existing process	Reactive control	More efficient process	7 Steps Standardization, SPC
One-time effort	Proactive control	New process or asset	9 Steps Standardization, SPC
New direction	Proactive	New product/ service	Concept engineering
		New strategy	Idealized design
		New capability	Hoshin management
		New business	Model, cycle, practices, and infrastructure of business breakthrough

standardizing successful solutions (thought). This alternation between thought and experience illustrates the important principle of basing actions on facts. *At no time do you use speculation or opinion as the basis of decision making.*

As shown in Figure 6-12, each of the three stages of the WV model uses a different kind of data. Data 1, the data of proactive improvement, is most often qualitative—in language, not numbers; its purpose may be unclear, the data is fuzzy and comes in many different forms, and you don't know in advance what kind of data you'll get. Jiro Kawakita's advice on how to collect data 1 is discussed in Chapter 10. Data 2, the data of reactive improvement, comes in both numbers and language, but you try to eliminate the language by defining a purpose (theme), which can be handled numerically. You must then define the data to solve the problem. Data 3, the data of process control, is typically accounting data and quality control data in specific formats, mainly numbers, and is defined to be used for a special purpose. The data of task of project management tends to be a combination of data 1 and data 2, rather than data 1 and data 3.

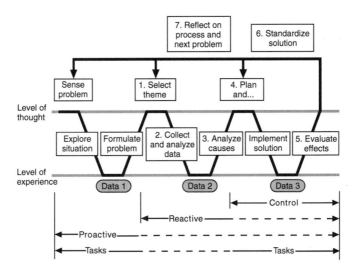

Figure 6-12. Three Kinds of Data for Problem Solving

Focus on the Vital Few

The WV model points toward another important aspect of systematic improvement: focusing on the "vital few" issues that will most affect your business if you improve them. At each state in the WV model and in each iteration, you will have many problems and improvements to choose from. Focus on the few vital things to improve, maximizing the impact of actions taken. Many opportunities exist for making improvements, but the resources for doing so are limited. Furthermore, experience has shown that only a few of the actions taken have significant effect. Therefore, work only on those improvements that are critical to a company's future (for example, those that improve customer satisfaction) and produce the biggest payback.

Current and future customer satisfaction should be guidelines in making key decisions about company products, practices, and systems, highlighting the few activities that will have the greatest impact on business success.

Iterative Improvement

Implicit in the WV model is the idea of iterative improvement—the cycling back to work on the next problem or the continued improvement of an already improved process. This is the famous PDCA (plan, do, check, act) cycle (see Figure 6-13). PDCA was contributed to Japanese quality control by W.E. Deming, who learned it from W.A. Shewhart.[2]

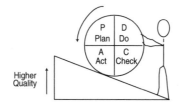

Figure 6-13. The PDCA Cycle

Plan: Determine analytically and quantitatively what the key problems are with an existing process or existing activities and how they might be corrected.

Do: Implement the plan.

Check: Confirm quantitatively and analytically that the plan works and results in improved performance.

Act: Modify the previous process appropriately, document the revised process, and use it.

PDCA symbolizes the principle of iteration in problem solving—making improvements in a step-by-step fashion and repeating the improvement cycle many times—doing the best job you can within relatively short improvement cycles. We recommend the *60 percent rule*: rather than trying for perfection the first time, shoot for 60 percent of the ideal, and build on that through successive iterations (as necessary) of the PDCA cycle (see Figure 6-14).[3] In that way, you can try an improvement of manageable size and get real feedback regarding the direction and distance to targets or goals.

It is important to get improved products or services rapidly to market or in the hands of the next process, in order to get this user feedback. If you are sailing a boat with the intent to intercept another boat, you periodically recalculate the course to the target. Each time, you make the best calculation you can. What you don't do is follow the initial course calculation without correction until the calculation indicates that you have reached the target and then look to see if you are near it. You realize that despite

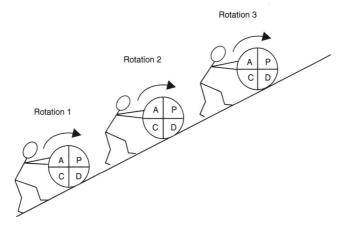

Figure 6-14. Stepwise Improvement: Successive Rotations through PDCA

your best initial efforts to calculate the course to the target, the target may be moving in unforeseen ways, and the currents and winds in which you are sailing may carry you off course. You follow the principle of seeking frequent feedback about your position and the target's position in relation to your course.

In business, however, people tend to think that they should be able to develop the correct plan or procedure for meeting business needs and execute it in one big step without trial and feedback. Unfortunately, experience shows that one big step is frequently an insurmountable task (see Figure 6-15). Even more frequently the target has moved by the time you get to it, if you ever had it accurately in your sights in the first place.

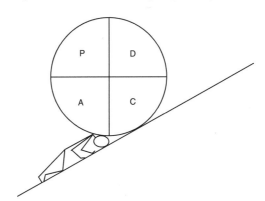

Figure 6-15. Tackling a Large Problem with a Single Effort

The PDCA cycle is always shown as a circle to indicate the continuous nature of improvement. All types of improvement and improvement maintenance require iteration. Compared with one big step, repeated PDCA cycles are a more efficient path to the current target and let you keep adapting as the target moves.

6.3 CONTINUOUS IMPROVEMENT OF PROCESSES FOR ALL TYPES OF WORK

When people introduce the methods of this book with their focus on management by process and continuous improvement to their companies, they often hear one of the following reactions: "Doing our work according to a process will stifle creativity and innovation," "My type of work cannot be turned into a process," or "Continuous improvement is incompatible with obtaining the breakthroughs we need." These negative first reactions to processes and continuous improvement can come from several possible confusions: a false dichotomy between no process and rigid process, an assumption that there is only one type of process, and a misunderstanding of the necessary context for innovation and breakthrough. A focus on continuous improvement of processes is a highly effective way to accomplish whatever a company needs, as we will show through many examples in this book.

The Right Amount of Process Increases Effectiveness

When people say "My type of work cannot be turned into a process," they are typically referring to (implicitly or explicitly) "a rigid process." They assume the bureaucratic worst case. They assume that if there is *any* process, then the requirement will be blind adherence to a rigid process. However, as shown in Figure 6-16, this is a false dichotomy. At the left end of the horizontal axis is the point of *no process* and at the right end is the point of *blind adherence to rigid process*—the extremes positions on a spectrum of process. Figure 6-16 suggests how effectiveness changes as a function of focus on process.

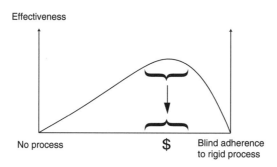

Figure 6-16. Optimum Balance between Too Little and Too Much Process

Without any process, effectiveness is limited. People don't work smoothly together, they don't learn from each other, they don't learn from past experience, and, in general, a company gains no leverage beyond individual capabilities. A certain amount of debilitating conflict will probably also be present. As companies begin to manage by process, efficiency goes up. However, at some point, the process ceases to be a tool to achieve improved results and becomes an end in itself. When process becomes an end in itself, the organization ossifies. Somewhere on the horizontal axis lies the balance point between too much and too little process. This is the point where companies will get substantial financial payoff from process, for example, learning how to get products to market faster. The job of managers is to use process sensibly and to teach its sensible use to gain maximum effectiveness. For most companies, to err in the direction of more process for a few years more is a safer bet.[4]

The problem described in the previous paragraphs undoubtedly comes partly from a misunderstanding that processes must always be completely standardized, as many manufacturing processes can be. This point is shown at the right (**M**) of Figure 6-17. However, as business improvement efforts expanded beyond manufacturing, the concept of process also expanded. In different applications, processes repeat less precisely from one time to the next as they deal with large numbers of variables or environmental changes that vary from one use of the process to the next. For instance, many administrative processes (and indeed some manufacturing processes) are a little less "standard" than traditional very standard manufacturing processes, and perhaps operate at point **A** of Figure 6-17. New product development processes perhaps operate at point **D**, and other applications perhaps reside between development and administration.

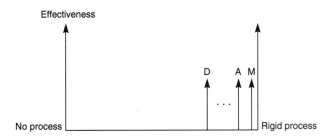

Figure 6-17. Different Applications Have Different Requirements for Standardization

Three Types of Processes

When we first talk about process, many people assume that their work cannot be reduced to a process. In particular, people in service organizations assume that their processes are different every time because they deal with a series of different customers or clients.

Part of the problem is when people talk about processes, they assume a step-by-step process, as one often finds in manufacturing or administrative transaction processing where the same process steps are executed over and over in a specific order (illustrated schematically in Figure 6-18).

In the mid-1990s, in reaction to concerns by member organizations in the service industries that TQM did not apply well to them, the CQM undertook a study of the

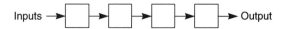

Inputs → ☐ → ☐ → ☐ → ☐ → Output

Figure 6-18. Step-by-step Process

relevance of processes to service [15]. Although the people from the service organizations went into this study with the presumption that a process orientation would be difficult or impossible for them, they came out of the study with the insight that all sorts of business have processes of each of three different types: operational, moment-of-truth, and innovative (or creative) processes [20].

Operational processes. Operational processes are defined to be step-by-step processes such as we often find in manufacturing and for administrative transactions (see Figure 6-18). Of course, every organization, no matter what its product or service orientation, has some operational processes, for example, the way it pays its bills.

Moment-of-truth processes. Moment-of-truth processes are those processes where a person from the company is dealing more or less directly with a customer. The interactions with the customer may take place in person, by phone, or by other means of communication (e.g., e-mail, traditional mail). Examples of people doing such moment-of-truth work are airline reservation clerks, sales people in general, customer support hot-line people, maintenance people who go to customer sites, and so on.[5] In a sense, moment-of-truth processes primarily deal with contingencies—branch points in interactions with customers where appropriate reactions are required, as illustrated in Figure 6-19. It seems clear that most organizations probably have some amount of this activity in their initial sales activity, in their later support activity, or as the core activity of a service business.

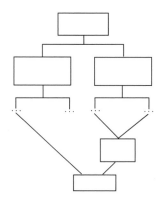

Figure 6-19. Schematic Diagram of Contingency Handling (à la PDPC)

Innovative processes. Innovative (or creative) processes are those where a person is inventing something more or less new, for example, in new product development or marketing. Such processes typically are trying to synthesize something new, often at the intersections of various types of activities. Some organizations may not have much of this sort of work (perhaps a fast food franchise does not). However, clearly many product or service organizations do have this sort or work.

Thus, many if not most businesses are involved with all three types of activities. The question then is to what extent moment-of-truth and innovative activities can be thought of as processes. Figure 6-20 will help answer this question. The goal of a moment-of-truth process, for instance the goal of the airline clerk, is to produce success with these moment-of-truth activities, as indicated at the right side of the figure. Consider then what factors are likely to lead to improved changes of success. As shown in Figure 6-20, some factors important to success are:

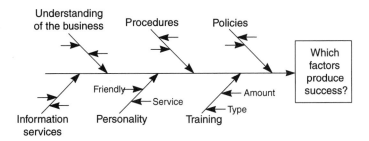

Figure 6-20. Service Process

- The tried-and-true procedures the clerk uses. Most customer interactions are quite similar. A clerk can try to follow a step-by-step process (as in Figure 6-18), for example, greet the customer cheerfully, ask what he or she can help the customer with, say "just a minute while I look up your records in my computer," do the look-up, etc.
- The amount and type of training the clerk has been given.
- The personality criteria used to hire airline clerks, such as friendliness and a service orientation.
- The information services the clerk has access to, such as alternative flight possibilities on this or other airlines
- The policies in place to allow clerks to make judgment calls that could recover the customer's satisfaction.
- The understanding the clerk has of the "value equation of the business" so, for instance, the clerk can factor in the short-term cost of helping the customer in some special way versus the long-term benefit or cost to the company.

There are undoubtedly many other factors. A company can study which factors and subfactors lead to success, and then create step-by-step processes to make sure those factors are in place, for example, a training process, personality testing as part of the hiring process, and so on.

The same reasoning works for innovative processes (imagine the appropriate variation on Figure 6-20). Product developers, building architects, and marketing people do not start each project from scratch without any process. Rather, even though no two buildings are the same, architects have a general process outline that they tend to fol-low for projects with similar purposes (an architect might tend to do one general sequence of things when doing residential design and another general sequence of things when designing large office buildings or schools). Architectural firms tend to hire people with the characteristics that fit their culture or needs or that suggest they will be first-rate designers.[6] There is probably a certain flow of documents that the firm uses, and the architectural office may have a standardized set of computer-aided design (CAD) tools. With increasing seniority in a firm, architects learn the guidelines of their craft and of the firm for bidding on a job. Certain specified structural analysis of designs is done. An architect who develops his or her process for interacting with a customer and ascertaining the customer's desires and needs will create designs that better satisfy customers. A given architect may even have "creativity methods" (per-haps learned from a mentor) that he or she explicity uses to stimulate creativity and synthesis.

In summary, we provide Table 6-2.

Table 6-2. Attributes of Different Types of Processes

	Extent of control	Process constraints	Data	Orientation
Operational	highly controlled	step-by-step process	pre-determined	to the expected
Moment-of-truth	bounded	according to guidelines	approx. real-time	to contin-gencies
Innovation (creative)	unbounded	statement of purpose	often intangible	to synthesis

Continuous Improvement versus Breakthrough

The first thing to note is that continuous improvement (PDCA) is a method for deal-ing with *repeated improvements of all sizes*, including some that may be beyond the scope of the 7 steps sketched earlier in this chapter. As will be discussed in more detail in Chapter 25, explicitly different methods are needed and available for incremental improvements and breakthrough improvements.[7] In Figure 6-21 [179], we call these $PDCA_1$ and $PDCA_2$. The words "continuous improvement" do not in and of them-selves preclude innovation, creativity, and breakthrough. We need continuous or repeated innovation, creativity, and breakthrough as well as continuous incremental improvement.

An easy way to demonstrate that incremental improvement is compatible with breakthrough is to remember that little things, the kind that incremental improvement might eliminate, can prevent breakthrough. Look at research and development for examples of such little things: accounting systems that make use of test equipment so expensive that it motivates minimizing testing, incompatibility between CAD systems

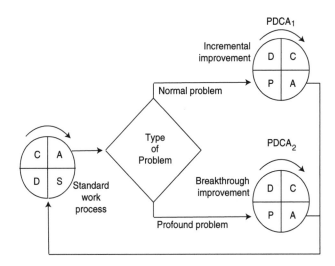

Figure 6-21. PDCA for Incremental and Breakthrough Improvements

in engineering and manufacturing, old or weak computer-based simulation and debugging tools, one component in a system whose design is bad, lack of colocation of the project team, ambiguous or changing product specifications, or no slack in the development schedule for unplanned eventualities. All sorts of process inefficiencies seem capable of delaying or preventing the breakthrough we are seeking.

Frequently, small things that can prevent breakthrough, such as those just given, are examples of weak process preventing breakthrough in the application area, as in the development of a new product. This suggests another way of looking at the compatibility of incremental improvement and breakthrough: incremental improvements in the process are compatible with breakthroughs in the application area. For instance, the 7 steps and quality function deployment processes provide guidelines for improvement that have been proven through experience to be efficient but that every team or person applies as appropriate to the problem being worked on. In other words, these tools require or bring out creativity on the part of those who use them.

Figure 6-22 [148, page 70] provides a further illustration of the idea. Many companies typically have a history of occasional innovation-based breakthroughs with periods of status quo in between. Smarter companies also have occasional breakthroughs, but they make continuous improvements in between. As shown in the figure, if the two approaches start at the same level on the left side of the figure, over time the combined approach results in a significant advantage. Since both approaches include breakthrough, the source of advantage is continuous improvement.[8]

The breakthrough-only approach loses to those who are using incremental improvement and breakthrough improvement together in synergistic ways.[9] In fact, some companies have used the extra profits gained through continuous improvement to invest in developing systematic methods of innovation and breakthrough [281, 314].

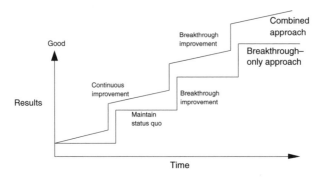

Figure 6-22. Incremental Improvement and Breakthrough Improvement

Companies that do not correct the imbalance between innovation and incremental improvement will fall further behind.

Finally, from decades of personal participation in and observation of high-technology research and development and study of many other fields, it appears that what people call a breakthrough is almost always a feeling of climax or appearance of great change that has resulted from extended incremental efforts. We have all read stories in the popular press about the "overnight" success of entertainers, performing artists, craftspeople, or athletes who in fact have worked hard and struggled for years before their popular "breakthrough."

Imagine a team of people boring through a thick concrete wall with a hammer and chisel (see Figure 6-23). Even though the team may have been boring through for a very long time, removing lots of little incremental chips from the wall, the moment of breakthrough is when someone finally begins to emerge through the wall. The same pattern holds in technology development, research and development, or other business

Figure 6-23. Breakthrough Is When the Result of the Work Becomes Apparent

areas requiring innovation. The breakthrough is usually the point where the results of extended effort (often by many people and groups) become apparent.

In [279], John Szarkowski describes the long and complicated prehistory of photography. The invention of photography is sometimes simplistically credited to Daguerre in about 1840 but, as Szarkowski shows, was really the result of the efforts of many people before and after Daguerre. As Szarkowski says:

> Inventions—the name by which we call devices that seem fundamentally new—are almost always born out of a process that is more like farming than magic. From a complex ecology of ideas and circumstances that includes the condition of the intellectual soil, the political climate, the state of technical competence, and the sophistication of the seed, the suggestion of new possibilities arises.
>
> Radical disruptions have long prior histories. After many incremental successes and nominal failures a new idea (which is generally not so new an idea) gains a measure of success that lifts it over the threshold into visibility, at which point it is given a name and begins its official history.
>
> In 1929 Abbott Payson Usher pointed out that it was futile to try to identify the inventor of mechanical printing, or the steam engine, or the airplane, since cultural achievement is a social accomplishment based on the accumulation of many small acts of insight by individuals [293]. Mr. Usher surely did not mean to suggest that each of these acts is of equal importance, but rather that the most imaginative and thrilling of them stood on the shoulders of a thousand earlier contributions.

We could give many similar examples of how contemporary companies are often credited and take credit for a breakthrough that in fact had a long history of incremental developments.

It is possible for breakthroughs to happen in a single act of brilliant insight with no incremental buildup. However, such occurrences are so rare and undependable as to be nearly irrelevant to our business needs.

The relationship between breakthrough and incremental improvement may vary with the maturity of a technology or industry.[10] The curves in Figure 6-24 illustrate how this works.

The curve starting at the top left of the figure shows a decline in the importance of breakthrough or size of discontinuities as industries or technologies mature. For instance, in the semiconductor industry, quantum mechanics, the band theory of semiconductors, and the silicon transistor represented giant intellectual changes. The integrated circuit and later the DRAM, EPROM, and microprocessor were great changes, but not so fundamental as quantum mechanics, the band theory, or the silicon transistor. In the 1980s and 1990s, many very significant improvements have occurred, but in many ways they were variations on what had gone before, such as denser packaging, RISC processors, and the multibus.

The curve starting at the bottom left of the figure shows how the importance of incremental improvement can increase as the size of breakthroughs decreases. Two

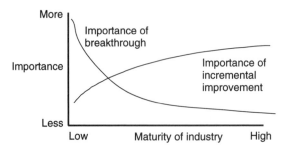

Figure 6-24. The Relationship between the Maturity of an Industry and the Importance of
Breakthrough versus Incremental Improvement

reasons exist for this increase in importance of incremental improvement. First, as
technology becomes more broadly applied, improvements in the production process
become a necessity and an important source of competitive advantage. Second, as the
technology becomes more mature, each improvement tends to be harder and more
complex to achieve and, thus, takes more process. For instance, it probably took only
a few people to develop the first DRAM. Now development of a 16-megabit DRAM
takes hundreds of people to do all the work and deal with all the little problems and
complexities. No one person can understand it all. In this situation, much process and
improvement of the process is necessary for success.

Other industries, such as the automobile industry, may be even more mature than
the semiconductor industry, while genetic engineering, by contrast, may be operating
at a point where breakthroughs are relatively more important and incremental
improvements are relatively less of a competitive advantage than in the maturer
industries.

6.4 CONTINUOUS IMPROVEMENT AND THE SCIENTIFIC METHOD

Basically continuous improvement is saying "apply the scientific method" to design
your organization's management system [38, 271]. While many companies don't practice continuous improvement (use the scientific method), the best companies already
do, whether they know it or not. (These companies typically adopt a common language of improvement or skill development, such as we have presented for the WV
model and PDCA cycle.)

The scientific method can be described in a way that will be intuitively familiar
to all of us: try something, digest what this tells you about how the world works, and
then try it again to confirm whether or not your presumption was right; or start with a
presumption rather than an experience and empirically test the presumption. Obviously, all of us have used this method, and have done so since we were babies; it's how
we learn about many practical things.[11] This method is the essence of pragmatism. It
is the way many of us have learned whatever we think we know about management.

Unfortunately, uncritical use of this method can lead to many suboptimal or incorrect explanations.[12] For instance, a young child who lives in a household with a

friendly family dog might presume from this experience that all dogs are friendly, and that presumption might be reinforced if the next door neighbor's dog is friendly and playful with small children, too. As a result of this overly simplistic theory, the child may attempt to pet an unfamiliar dog and get nipped. (Of course, with this nipping, the child will have to revise the theory that all dogs are friendly into a theory that better explains reality, and this is another intuitive use of the scientific method.) Let's take another instance, this time from business. As a young manager, a person might learn in a specific instance that by better utilizing some fixed resources (human or plant), a lower cost-per-unit-produced will be possible. As a result, the young manager may embark on widespread application of a theory of maximum utilization of all resources (in fact, traditional cost accounting is mostly about such optimizing). This will almost certainly lead the young manager astray at some point in his or her career, since maximum utilization of all resources is frequently (one is tempted to say almost always) incompatible with overall maximum throughput of a system, as Goldratt is fond of pointing out with his Theory of Constraints [116, 117].[13]

However, when used with a modicum of skill, the best approach to building a system to address a real life situation—the most pragmatic approach—is the scientific method. "The scientific method is the most effective method of learning about the real world," says renowned scientist Edward Wilson [311]; other authors say the same thing. The scientific method tests theory with experimentation and uses experimentation to get insights about possible new or improved theories. In fact, if you cannot test whether a theory is right or not, the theory likely is outside the realm of science and in the realm of philosophy, etc. Furthermore, if an experiment that purports to demonstrate the correctness of a theory cannot be repeated, then the theory is viewed as undemonstrated or incorrect. In general, the scientific method seeks to measure and understand cause and effect, including complex cause and effect with lots of things interacting.

Without theories that can be tested, measured, repeated, etc., we are left with the uncertainty of folklore and being wrong. Managers need to run experiments and find out what genuinely works in their situation. For an excellent example of a manager doing this, see the story of NIMS in Chapter 25 (page 549).

In the following chapters of this book, we will show numerous examples of organizations applying the principles of continuous improvement to create and evolve their management systems. In fact, many companies have used continuous improvement as the focus of their mobilization effort.

Finally, looking at history, the other three management revolutions certainly grew out of the continuous improvement management revolution. Like the scientific method itself, each of the other management revolutions is appropriate for one reason only—because it works well.

NOTES

1. Shoji Shiba modified Kawakita's W model [165, page 422] to create what Shiba calls the WV model.

2. W.A. Shewhart was a member of the Quality Assurance Department of Bell Telephone Laboratories. In 1931, he put the quality movement on a scientific footing when he published [259]. Kozo Koura described the history of the development of the PDCA cycle very nicely in [178].

3. Going 60 percent of the rest of the way on the second iteration gets you to 84 percent of the ideal and another 60 percent of the way in a third iteration would get you to almost 94 percent.

4. Albeit at a more global level, Professor Lester Thurow supports the point we make in this section in [283].

5. The name the study group gave to this second type of process is the name they were originally given by one-time CEO of SAS, Jan Carlzon, who defined moments-of-truth as those opportunities one has each day to explicitly anger a customer. He claimed that his company had hundreds of thousands of such opportunities each day. For a case study of moment-of-truth processes, see [186, pages 80–90].

6. Another example is given in [166].

7. In this chapter, when we talk about breakthrough, we have in mind breakthrough in processes, technologies, or in the way a business operates. Breakthrough into a new business area will be considered in Chapter 27.

8. We don't read any significance into breakthroughs in the latter approach (in Ishikawa's figure) occuring slightly to the left of the breakthroughs in the former approach, which we assume was for visual separation of the vertical lines.

9. See also [102].

10. This relationship was pointed out to us by Dr. Dennis Buss, then of Analog Devices, Inc.

11. Robin Dunbar has pointed out in his wonderful book on the scientific method [87] that use of a crude form of the scientific method is inherent in humans and many other species.

12. Dunbar spoke on this, too. Ibid.

13. See also [237].

7

Process Discovery and Management

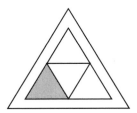

As suggested in the previous chapter, in this part of the book we will cover three different time spans continuous improvement can deal with: existing processes, one-time tasks, and finding new directions. This and the next four chapters will consider how to manage existing processes.

7.1 THINKING IN TERMS OF PROCESS

Many people do not think of themselves as participating in processes. They merely think of themselves as coming to work each day and doing their jobs. Nevertheless, everyone does follow processes, however explicit or documented or however vague or unwritten. Human beings are creatures of habit. Few go to work each day and handle situations or tasks in completely different ways than on previous days. Rather, we handle various tasks and situations in similar ways from day to day—we more or less follow processes, albeit not identically from instance to instance and not necessarily standardized or written. The first job in improving an existing process is to realize that one (perhaps in collaboration with one's co-workers) has processes.

Even when one realizes that one has processes, improving them is difficult if they are implicit. A fundamental aspect of the scientific method is that one has to make explicit what is happening if one is going to understand it and improve it; after all, the intangible is hard to improve. We all know this from our personal lives when we make vows, for instance, to do a better job of home maintenance.[1] Then, the next torrential downpour finds us once again on the top of a ladder, with lightning cracking all around, cleaning out the roof gutters and downspouts. Unless we put in place a system (process), for instance, a checklist of what routine tasks are done first thing in the morning or on the first Saturday of each month, our vow is more wishful thinking than an improvement method. Similarly, at work one might vow to spend more time doing "management by wandering around." Yet, unless a system one puts in place such as telling his or her assistant to leave a significant portion of each week unbooked with scheduled meetings, no time for walking around and having informal contact with employees can occur.

Thus, having realized that we have processes, the next step is to make them explicit. Then, we will have something to improve. Making our process explicit to ourselves is "process discovery," as shown at the top of Figure 7-1.

Once we know what our process is in a particular domain, then we can either monitor it (process control in the figure) to see if the process performs well enough, or we can intuitively understand without process control that the process needs improvement and move into reactive improvement (improvement of the existing process). As suggested in the figure, we recommend a step-by-step method for reactive improvement known as the 7 steps. We describe the 7 steps at length in Chapters 9 and 10.

As shown in the figure, once a process undergoes reactive improvement, it becomes necessary to monitor it (process control) to ensure it continues to work well. Any time, if the process ceases to be good enough, either because it begins to fail to meet specifications or because specifications become more demanding, then it is necessary to do more reactive improvement.[2]

Getting Better at Getting Better

Just as one needs explicit business processes to improve if one is to get better at various business functions, one also needs explicit processes for how to improve the business processes. We need not only to get better in our business, we need to get better at getting better. Thus, we encourage the use of explicit specific methods (as hinted at in Figure 7-1 and detailed in what follows) for process discovery, process control, and reactive improvement.

However, experience has shown that trying to mobilize the specific methods of process discovery, process control, and reactive improvement does not reliably take place without a system for mobilizing and managing teams of people using the methods. Thus, Figure 7-2 on page 98 shows the components of process management as being supported by a system for managing quality improvement teams.

Quality improvement team is the name we use to designate a team undertaking any improvement approach described in Chapter 6 (proactive, reactive, process control, or one-time task). (Quality improvement teams are also known as QI teams or QITs.) Quality improvement teams are introduced in depth in Chapters 9 and 10, and a variety of methods of mobilizing quality improvement teams are described in the part of the book on the third management revolution—total participation.

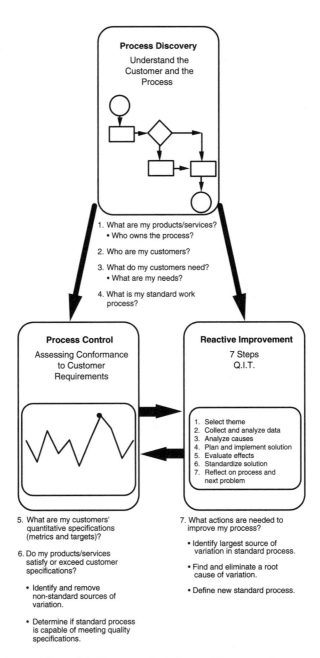

Figure 7-1. Components of Process Management

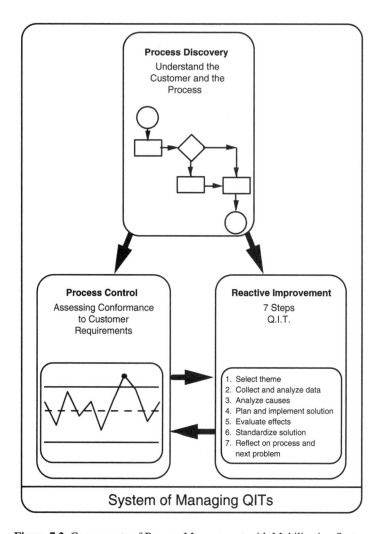

Figure 7-2. Components of Process Management with Mobilization System

7.2 PROCESS DISCOVERY

We will start with some common sense ideas about what a process is.

First, a process is a set of steps (perhaps with options and branch points) that we generally follow to perform some task. For instance, the process for reading e-mail might be to turn on the computer if it's not already on, connect to the Internet if not already connected, start the e-mail application if not already started, give the Check Mail command, wait until the e-mail application either says "Sorry, no mail" or "You have mail," read the first message if you have mail, reply if desired, give the command to file the message in an appropriate folder or the trash, and repeat the last three steps as long as you still have unread messages. Then give the "Send mail" command, exit the e-mail program, disconnect from the Internet, and shut down the computer if done using it. Obviously, other variations for this sequence exist; however, most of us would recognize it as a more or a less step-by-step process. Over time, we can improve this process: for instance, connect to the Internet, download new mail, and disconnect from the Internet; read the new message, reply to some or all of them, reconnect to the Internet, send the messages, and disconnect again from the Internet. This improved process could save connection charges to the phone company and from the Internet Service Provider. Also, one could further improve the process, for instance, by printing out requests to delegate to an assistant, or by preparing standard response messages for common queries.

Second, we think of processes as serving customers, although these may be non-paying customers and we may be providing a non-business service (such as a volunteer worker in a soup kitchen might provide).[3] We also think of processes as having suppliers, although again these may not be suppliers in the sense of a traditional business. In Figure 7-3,[4] we show the participants in the steps of a process (a team of people often is involved) between the customer(s) and supplier(s). The participants in the process receive requirements from the customer ("Can you sell me a chocolate soda?"), produce outputs for the customer ("Here it is."), and get feedback on performance from the customer ("Tastes good!"). To accomplish the process, the participants in the process give requirements to their suppliers ("I'll need four quarts of chocolate syrup this week."), receive inputs from them ("Here are the cans of chocolate you ordered; I'll be back again in three days."), and give them appropriate feedback ("It wasn't as rich tasting as I expected.").

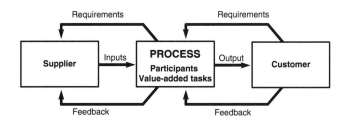

Figure 7-3. All Work Is a Process

Steps for Process Discovery

Clearly all tasks can inevitably be described as processes, still, many people have never thought explicitly about the steps they do to perform various tasks as being processes. In the case of processes involving more than one person, the participants are often unaware of the details of what the others are doing. Finding many important opportunities for improving a process becomes more difficult. Therefore, we recommend a process for discovering the processes of teams and individuals.

We recommend the following steps, each of which we will describe in turn:[5]

1. Who are our customers?
2. What products and services do we provide?
3. What are the customers' requirements?
4. What measures and targets apply to their requirements?
5. What is our process?
6. What do we require to deliver the product or service successfully?
7. Do our products and services meet or exceed their requirements?

Who are our customers? Typically, people doing tasks don't think about having customers. They just do their assigned task as they are told to do it. However, why do the task if someone doesn't use it eventually,[6] and we call this user the customer. The first step in discovering your process is to understand who your customers are. Since each person or group tends to have several different types of customers, one should identify the different types of customers. Since one will want explicit input from customers about their requirements, one should identify at least a few types of specific typical customers.

Note well: The user of one's output does not have to be a paying customer outside the company; the user can be the next person or group in a series of processes. This inside person or process is a customer. Remember the famous slogan, "The next process is your customer." For instance, the Information Services department provides computing facilities that the manufacturing department uses to build products sold to outside customers. The manufacturing department, in this example, is the customer of the IS department. Because your customer has its own customer which may have its own customers, try to identify the customer chain stretching out from you to better understand the requirements of your customers by understanding the customer environment they see.

What products and services do we provide? Think in terms of what products and services are provided to each customer identified in step one. Having considered what one's products and services are, typically one should focus improvement effort first on the products and services that are most important to key customers.

Each product or service should have a customer. If a product or service does not have a clear customer, then the function is probably not needed and certainly this would not be the place to focus upon for process improvement.

As the natural order of business, we recommend first identifying the customers and then the products and services relevant to them. However, in some cases where people may never have thought of having customers, first think about what the products and services are and from that derive the users of these products and customers who are, therefore, the customers.

What are the customers' requirements? Typically, groups or individuals assume that they know best what customers need. This is a mistake because without asking the customer about the customer's requirements, one cannot be sure the products and services one is producing are the right ones.

To aid in this discovery of the detailed customer requirements, we recommend thinking in terms of quality, cost, and delivery (QCD). By quality, we mean the functionality provided to the customer. By cost, we mean the total cost to the customer (both the tangible price and other charges, and any less tangible costs such as cost of negotiating the contract under which the product or service is delivered, downtime during installation, cost of learning to use the new product or service, and so forth). By delivery we mean the place, the time, and the method of delivery. By thinking in terms of QCD, companies may be able to break out of their mindsets that the function of the product or service is what *really* matters to the customer. In fact, intangibles, like ease of doing business, are often the deciding factor in a customer's buying decision.

The different customer requirements should be easily described in a few well-chosen words that capture the essence of the need. For example, a customer need for Internet communications switches might be "small physical size."

What measures and targets apply to their requirements? By determining the measures and targets relating to the customer requirements, one is likely to learn more about what the requirements really mean. For instance, "small physical size" is a vague requirement for an Internet communications switch. Once one understands the customer's measure is "number of Local Area Network (LAN) jacks in a three-inch high unit mounted in a 19-inch relay rack," one knows that the real requirement has to do with clever packing of the maximum number of network jacks on the unit's back panel rather than making the unit smaller than 19 inches wide.

However, in many cases, investigating the details of one's own process may be useful (the next two steps of process discovery) before focusing on the details of the customer requirements. Alternating between what the external world needs and what we are doing can be beneficial.

For each customer requirement under consideration, one needs to discover how the customers measure whether their need is being met. Pay attention to specific metrics (with their units of measure) and, for each metric, define a specification target value and any specification limits that further define the customer's requirements. If the requirement for a briefcase was a small physical size, two measures of customer satisfaction might be "weight in ounces" and "width in inches"; in this case, the targets and specification limits might be "seven ounces target but not more than 10 ounces" and "12 inches wide—not less than 11.5 inches and not more than 12.5 inches."

Eventually we will also need to understand how we are going to take the relevant measurements of the outputs of our process. In some cases, this will require special equipment, such as for measuring the requirement "car door shuts firmly."

What is our process? Is your process clearly related to the customer and product or service under consideration? We need to explicitly understand everything we are doing, and we need to make explicit the order we are doing it in. We need to write it down so we can look at it and analyze it; in other words, we need to draw some sort of flowchart. This flowchart can use traditional flowcharting symbols such as the circles, rectangles, and triangles illustrated in the Process Discovery box in Figure 7-1. Circles mean the beginning and ending of a part of a bigger process and connections to other parts of the process, rectangles stand for substeps in this part of the process, and diamonds indicate decision points.[7] This type of flowcharting has the advantage that anyone can do it with paper and pencil or a magic marker and flip chart. It is also supported by various computer graphics packages.[8]

As one flowcharts one's process for the first time, one inevitably sees unnecessary and inefficiently ordered steps. One has two choices: to document the process now and wait to fix it or to make obvious improvements in the process now. It is hard to resist the latter option, and often silly to do so; however, one must also be wary of changing the process before one fully understands it because changing it may have detrimental unintended consequences. Which of the two choices to make must be judged on a case-by-case basis, probably erring on the side of conservatism. Whichever option is chosen, the resulting process needs to be explicitly documented. Once the documentation is done, many opportunities for eliminating inefficiency and ineffectiveness will be visible, such as subtasks without any customer, long delays while documents sit in someone's inbox, approvals that neither add value nor reduce risk, and checks that could be skipped with better controlled production. The documented process may also provide insight that could lead to completely restructuring the way the task is done.

What do we require to deliver the product or service successfully? We need to think of ourselves as customers of others and how we specify our needs, measures, and targets to our suppliers (remember QCD). As in any chain of customers and suppliers, we must consider both suppliers to whom we give explicit purchase orders and suppliers whom we depend upon but may seldom think of in terms of purchasing services (for instance, the internal group that provides the phone and networking services to our desktops).

Do our products and services meet or exceed their requirements? Several ways exist to answer this question. We may be able to directly compare quantitative versions of customer requirements (metrics and specifications) with quantitative measures of our products and services. In more subjective situations, we may have to ask customers in one way or another if we are satisfying them. In fact, good practice is to explicitly and periodically check with customers in case we do not detect their dissatisfaction with our quantitative comparisons.

Another important issue is how we can tell if our process is *reliably* producing outputs within customer specifications, and this will be the subject of Chapter 8.

Benefits of Process Discovery

Discovering your process in the dimensions just outlined will prevent working on problems unimportant to your customers. It will deter you from tampering with your process (see pages 113–114 for a definition of tampering). It will enable you to identify "non-value-added" activities, which we define to be activities not of value to the ultimate paying customer and which, therefore, may not need to be done. Finally, process discovery helps provide focus on the few vital improvements you must do and for which there are resources.

Example of Process Discovery

Much of the information collected during the steps of process discovery can be tabulated in a worksheet as in Figure 7-4. We will consider an example of collecting this information for the first several steps of process discovery for a service function such as a payroll department.

Customers	Products/Services	Requirements	Metrics/Targets	Meet/Exceed?

Figure 7-4. Sample Process Discovery Worksheet

Who are our customers of the payroll department? Some possibilities (to be listed in the first column of the Process Discovery Worksheet are):

- the *employees* who get paid
- various government *tax agencies* that must be notified of amounts paid to each employee
- *payroll service bureau* that takes a pay list from the payroll department and prints the checks
- perhaps a separate *mailing service bureau* that posts the printed checks
- *banks* to which the payroll department sends direct deposits to employee accounts
- the subset of *employees who get paid in cash*
- *insurance companies* to which a portion of an employee's pay along with an employer contribution are sent
- *retirement trusts* to which a portion of an employee's pay along with an employer contribution are sent
- *unions* to which a portion of some employee's pay is sent for union dues
- *divorced spouses* of employees to whom a court has directed payment of a portion of an employee's pay
- others who are *lienholders* on an employee's pay
- company *cash management department* which must be kept up to date on the company's cash needs
- the *human resources department* which needs payroll information to do its job
- the *controller's office* which needs various reports to monitor the function of the payroll department

Suppose we decide to concentrate on the employees as the customer.

What are the products and services provided? The worksheet in Figure 7-5 indicates (in bold) the selection of the employees as the customer to be considered. In the second column of the worksheet are possibilities of products and services of interest to the employees. Notice that one of the potential services of the payroll department is answering other people's questions that will help the employee (seventh item in the second column), such as landlords or mortgage companies calling to make sure the employee can make rent or mortgage payments on a residence the employee seeks. This suggests a new type of customer that should be added to the first column.

Customers	Products and Services
employees	pay in hand or at bank
payroll service bureau	W2 or other employee tax forms
mailing service bureau	distributions to insurance, etc.
banks	changes in distribution amounts
employees who get cash	pay stub with summary info.
insurance companies	answers to employee questions
retirement trusts	answers to others to help employee
divorced spouses	pay advances in emergencies
lienholders etc.	
cash management dept.	
HR depart.	
controller's office	

Figure 7-5. Payroll Dept. Products and Services for Employees

What are the employees requirements? Suppose that the payroll department decides to focus first on the products and services specifically related to the paycheck and check stub. They need to consider what the employee requirements are, keeping QCD in mind. The best way to find out about employee requirements is to ask the employees. Some of their answers are tabulated in the worksheet in Figure 7-6. Regarding quality or function, the employees obviously want the check to be for an accurate amount with accurate distributions for the insurance company, retirement

Quality	Cost	Delivery
accurate amount	local currency	on time
accurate distributions		to right address
to the right bank		to special location
easy to understand check stub, etc.		
vacation day total on stub		

Figure 7-6. Employee Requirements for Paycheck and Check Stub

trust, union, tax withholding, and so on. They also want it sent to the correct bank. Next the employees thought about the check stub and of course want its information to be easy to understand. However, thinking about the check stub information makes them realize additional information would be nice to have on each pay stub, such as the number of unused vacation days accrued (this is probably trivial for payroll to provide and would be attractive to the employees). Regarding cost, employees assigned temporarily to other countries would like to be paid in the local currency, so they don't incur exchange costs. Finally, the employees would like the pay to be delivered on time, to the correct address or, in some instances, to special locations such as where the employee is vacationing on pay day. Whether or not the payroll department decides to address all these requirements is a separate step from trying to enumerate the large number of possible requirements.

Notice the similarity of the "to the right bank" entry in the Quality column of the table and the "to right address" entry in the Delivery column: the QCD categories are not necessarily mutually exclusive and help broaden the customer requirements investigation.

What measures and targets apply to their requirements? For each requirement, the payroll department can generate one or more metrics to measure the requirement, and then derive or seek from the customer appropriate targets. Suppose the payroll department chooses the on-time delivery requirements. An appropriate metric in these days of wire transfers and on-line banking might be *minutes after midnight at the end of payday by which the pay is available in the employee's bank account.* The target might be five minutes after midnight (to allow a little safety factor in not making the deposit "a day" early, and no later than 30 minutes after midnight so the employee has the money available essentially at the beginning of the next day. A different metric is required for employees who don't use direct desposit.

We will cover the last three steps of process discovery at other points in the book:

- What is our process? (Section 23.3)
- What do we require to deliver the product or service successfully? (Section 23.3)
- Do our products and services meet or exceed their requirements? (Chapter 8)

NOTES

1. Or, to get more exercise, etc.

2. Some organizations begin improvement activities with the 7 steps of reactive improvement rather than with process discovery. This is all right since the first step of the 7 steps includes process discovery if it has not already been done.

3. Even in the case where one is doing something for oneself, one can think of oneself as the customer of one's own process.

4. George Murray introduced us to this particular representation that CQM founding member Polaroid Corporation used.

5. As we remember, we basically got this list of questions from a six sigma presentation from Motorola. We reordered their questions because it's useful to investigate metrics to understand need.

6. Without a customer, it's not necessary to do the function. We again recall Peter Drucker's statement that the purpose of a business is to create and serve a customer. When we say this, some people argue instead that the purpose of business is to make a profit. Drucker has also made a compelling argument that profit is a *necessary* expense of being in business, not the purpose of business.

7. For a slightly more extensive description of flowcharting, see [309, Chapter 2, "Visualize your process"]. We recommend this book for your library.

8. Alternatively, one might use another form of flowchart, such as Design Structure Matrices discussed in Section 23.3 or Atoms of Work discussed in Section 16.3.

8

Process Control and Variation

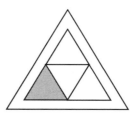

This chapter contains a brief sketch of some of the principles of the control portion of the WV Model. The control portion of the WV Model (see Figure 8-1) basically follows the SDCA cycle:

- Standardize the process; use process discovery (Section 7.2) if necessary to discover what the process is
- Do, that is, use the standard process and collect data on its operation
- Check what happens, that is, analyze the data
- Act appropriately based on the data.

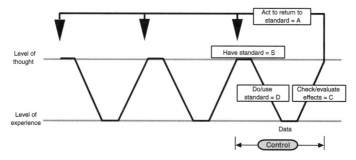

Figure 8-1. Process Control in the WV Model

All of the ideas in this section have been expressed by Shewhart, Deming, Ishikawa, and the other practitioners of statistical process control.[1] An enormous literature exists on the subject.[2] In fact, these concepts are so fundamental that in the first edition we assumed everyone already understood process control and barely touched on it, which is why we barely touched on it.

However, many senior managers—especially if they did not rise through the manufacturing side of the organization—are not familiar with the basic concepts of process control. If they know process control exists, they don't imagine that it could apply outside the manufacturing area. In fact, process control can be applied to processes as varied as order entry, training course delivery, billing, recruiting, daily cash forecasting, the monthly financial close, servicing service requests, forecasting telecommunications capacity needs, developing products, and corporate budgeting. *Process control can be applied to any repetitive and measurable process.* In other words, process control applies to practically all of the diverse tasks we have in business. No matter what length the process cycle or how complex the task, process control can be applied to it.

The fundamental issue of process control is variation. A basic understanding of the principles of process control and understanding variation will improve anyone's understanding of PDCA and of the benefits of systematic and iterative improvement in every aspect of business, including those that many people think of as innovative or creative. Creativity is often based on disciplined application of methods that are known to work.

8.1 A TYPICAL EXAMPLE OF (MISHANDLING) VARIATION

Looking at Figure 8-2, assume that we are in the marketing department and we are responsible for generating leads.[3] Here is a sketch of an all too typical way people in an organization deal with variation:

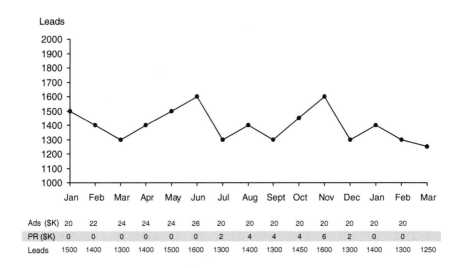

	Jan	Feb	Mar	Apr	May	Jun	Jul	Aug	Sept	Oct	Nov	Dec	Jan	Feb	Mar
Ads ($K)	20	22	24	24	24	26	20	20	20	20	20	20	20	20	
PR ($K)	0	0	0	0	0	0	2	4	4	4	6	2	0	0	
Leads	1500	1400	1300	1400	1500	1600	1300	1400	1300	1450	1600	1300	1400	1300	1250

Figure 8-2. Typical Struggle with Variation

- In January we get 1500 leads. On the last day of January, we commit $20K for advertisements and $0 to public relations to generate February leads.
- Only 1400 leads arrive in February, so on the last day of February we commit to spend $2K more on ads ($22K total) to generate leads in March.

- March leads slip further, so we commit to spend $24K on ads to generate leads in April.
- Leads go up in April. It looks as if we have found the right expenditure level, so we stay with it.
- Leads go up again in May, so we again stay with this expenditure level.
- Leads go up again in June, and we decide we'll give ad expenditures a little boost and perhaps generate even more leads.
- Oops, leads go down in July. Maybe we haven't quite got the right mix after all, so we change our mix of expenditures to $20K for ads and $2K for PR.
- Leads go up in August. It looks like PR really helps, so we add a little to PR expenditures.
- Leads go down in September, but we don't change expenditures. Maybe it was just an unlucky month.
- And leads go up in October. This is good. We must now have the right levels and mix, so we don't change expenditures.
- Leads go up in November. This PR really seems to be helping. We'll spend more there.
- Leads drop in December. This is getting confusing. We had better cut back on PR in case it didn't actually help as much as we thought it did.
- But leads go up in January. What's going on? Maybe PR really doesn't help, so we drop it.
- And leads go down a little in February. So confusing ... Don't know what to change. Do nothing.
- Leads go down again in March. This is awful.

Does this sound familiar? The results are varying, and we are varying inputs trying to make things better. However, we do not understand how these variations relate to each other.

We will return to this example later, in Section 8.4, after we sketch in the next sections the basics of process control and understanding variation.

8.2 MAKING THE MOST OF VARIATION

The essence of process control is making the most of variation. There is variation in everything we do, and the pattern of this variation is a key source of information. By appropriately stratifying the data, we can understand and make use of the data; translated, we can make the right decisions to improve the performance of people and their tools.

We do not have space in this book to develop the principles of process control fully and provide a theoretical or intuitive basis for them. Therefore, we will state the principles as efficiently as we can.[4]

Here are several basic principles that every manager should understand:

- Process control can be applied to a wide range of business process (discussed above).
- Customer needs determine the desired output.

- The process actually used determines the actual output.
- Inspection is a poor primary control method.
- To meet the desired output specification, reduce the variance of the actual output by finding and removing the sources of variation in the process.
- The actual process output inevitably has variance.
- To reduce successfully the variation, the variation and its general stability or lack of stability needs to be understood.
- Some variation is stable and some variation is unstable.
- The process behavior chart provides a tool to distinguish stable and unstable of variation.
- Process outputs and a process behavior chart indicate the proper course of action.
- Much of the effort and anxiety we put into making things better is wasted when we don't use the methods of process control (see Section 8.4).

These principles are described in more detail below.

Customer needs determine the desired output. The goal of business processes should be to satisfy an external or internal customer. Therefore, customer needs must determine the desired outputs of the processes of companies—you need to know what customers care about, and you need valid quantitative measures to track what they care about. For instance, continuing the payroll department example from the last section of Chapter 7, the employees may tell the payroll department that they want a "quick response to questions they ask" of the payroll department. This is typical of the qualitative statements customers make about their desires. The payroll department improvement team needs more specific and quantitative statements of need, such as, does "quick response" mean minutes before someone in payroll phones back to acknowledge a voice mail query, or hours until the query response is completed. The chosen quantitative measure, targets, and specification limits must be confirmed by customers.[5]

Figure 8-3, shows voice-of-the-customer-determined upper and lower specification limits (USL and LSL) for the results produced; results outside of these limits are defects that must be discarded or reworked.[6] Notice in the figure that the voice of the customer is outside the process and, in fact, is independent of it. We will return to this point.

The process actually used determines the actual output. As Figure 8-3 shows, the actual results produced, indicated by the output distribution, come from the process and its inputs and not from the voice of the customer or specification limits. If you have a process that produces outputs within a certain range, the outputs will be within that range regardless of the outputs customers desire. Suppose, for instance, your cash management department's process is only good enough to maintain cash balances of no more than plus or minus $3 million as a weekly target (see Figure 8-4). If the system cannot perform any more accurately than this, simply wishing it would improve or having a narrower specification from the customer will not make it do so.

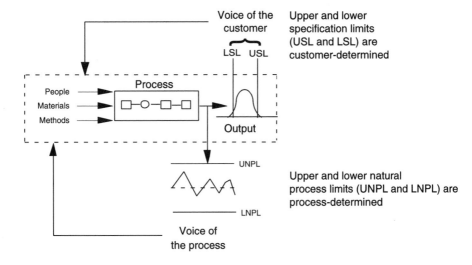

Figure 8-3. A Model for Process Control

Historically, people have tried two methods for producing results within specification—inspection and reduction of variance.[7]

Inspection is a poor primary control method. Inspection is a reactive method. With some processes you can avoid shipping defective products by inspecting the outputs and discarding those outside specification or sending them back for rework. Likewise, if the numbers in a departmental budget are not justified satisfactorily, the budget can be redone. Of course, this produces waste, extra expense, and perhaps delay.

In a case such as the cash management example, inspection will show that you are producing results outside of specification but that doesn't stop the results from happening in the first place. You can tell the people involved to produce better results

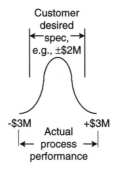

Figure 8-4. Specifications Come from Customers; Results Come from the Process

next time, another form of reaction, but this still doesn't assure that the process will produce better results next time. The point is that inspection and reaction are ineffective for controlling a process.

Shewhart, Deming, and those who followed them, teach that by focusing on meeting specification, one is unlikely to meet specification reliably. As long as inspection is used as the method of meeting specification, waste and extra expense will continue, some bad products will slip through inspection, results that were acceptably good will become unacceptably bad without warning, and in general continued good performance is tenuous.

To meet the desired output specification, reduce the variance of the actual output by finding and removing the sources of variation in the process. The second method of producing results within specification is reducing the variance in the process until the average and virtually all the output measurements are within specification (as in Figure 8-5); the results are inspected and the process or the way it is followed is modified to reduce the variance in the results. Poor results may still have to be discarded until the variance is so small that the products outside of specification are no longer produced.

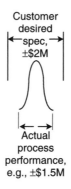

Figure 8-5. Meeting Specifications by Reducing Variation

Shewhart, Deming, and others teach that focusing on reducing variation is the best approach to meeting specification reliably. Low variation indicates expertise; just meeting specification may be luck. With sufficiently small variation, no bad products slip through inspection, and the system is stable and will provide warning of impending failure. However, as Shewhart explained, reduced variation can only be achieved through careful study of the sources of variation in the process and through action to reduce or eliminate sources of extraneous or excessive variation.

The actual process output inevitably has variance. Any process has some variability in its results. For instance, in the cash management system example, the cash balance at the end of each week will vary from the target for the week. Some of these variations will be acceptable (fall within specification), and some results will vary so widely that they fall outside of specifications.

This variability of response is typically described in terms of two characteristics that can be learned from the statistics on the output: a central tendency (average response), and natural variability (distribution of responses over the range of responses). The variation in the outputs may obscure what is happening with the process, and thus the variation must be understood so the process can be improved.

Some variation is stable and some variation is unstable. A process may have two types of variation, as shown in Figure 8-6 ; variation that has a stable and consistent pattern over time[8] (due to what Deming called common causes) and variation that has an unstable pattern over time[9] (due to what Deming called special causes). (Here we will call such stable and unstable variation, respectively, routine and exceptional variation.[10])

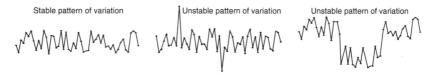

Figure 8-6. Stable and Unstable Patterns of Variation

Routine variation (the left example in Figure 8-6} is the variation inherent in the process—natural variation imposed by the physical limits of the process. Routine variation is statistically the same, as the process is run from one time to the next or from one day to the next. Exceptional variation (the big jumps seen in the middle example and the big shifts in the right example in Figure 8-6} typically results from not following the process reliably. That is, each time the process is run, it is run differently. This can happen because of poor operator training, problems with equipment, poor process documentation, unreliable supplier performance, or many other factors that can change over time.

Since routine variation is inherent in the process, it cannot be reduced except through a change in the process. Demanding that workers do a better job will not reduce the routine variation inherent in the process; demanding that specifications be met will have no effect on the variation of a process. Many managers don't realize this. They think that by setting objectives they automatically can affect the results of a process. However, whether the results of a process are within specification depends on the natural variation of the process, not the specification.

This is not to say that setting objectives is not useful; setting an objective is useful because without it no one will know what process to develop to produce the desired result. However, the process then produces the result it is capable of producing and not the result demanded by the objective.

On the other hand, you can remove exceptional variation by controlling the inputs and following the process accurately. Larger exceptional variation often masks the smaller routine variation, so that it is not possible to find and eliminate the sources of routine variation until the sources of exceptional variation have been eliminated. Deming argues that until the sources of variation have been understood, changes to a process are likely to make it perform worse than before; his term for this is tampering. Reorganizing in response to poor performance without understanding the causes of poor performance is a form of frequently practiced management tampering. Therefore, the scenario to follow in reducing process variation is, first, to make the process behave in a stable fashion by finding and removing the sources of the exceptional variation and, second, to find the sources of routine variation and change the process to remove them, thereby decreasing the variation until virtually all results are within specification.

The process behavior chart provides a tool to distinguish the two kinds of variation. The process behavior chart[11] and other tools of process control enable results of a process to be plotted over time and clearly show whether the process is behaving in a stable fashion or in an unstable fashion. For instance, a control chart plotting the difference between forecast and actual revenue will show whether one has an effective and stable process for achieving and forecasting revenues.

As shown in Figure 8-7, the process behavior chart includes a plot over time of the data from a process (for instance, the month-by-month or week-by-week difference between forecast and actual revenue). The mean of the results is plotted on the chart, as are the UNPL and LNPL (see Figure 8-3 on page 111).[12] The UNPL and LNPL are calculated from the data (they have nothing to do with the specification),[13] and they show whether or not exceptional variation occurs in the plotted data. In Figure 8-7, there are several points outside the natural process limits, indicating exceptional variation. The process is unstable. We cannot have confidence how it will behave next. It is necessary to find the source of the instability and remove it.

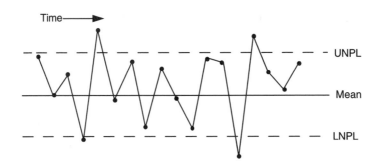

Figure 8-7. Process Behavior Chart Showing Unstable Variation

If the process behavior plot has no points outside the natural process limits, as in Figure 8-8,[14] then the process behavior is very likely stable.

The process behavior chart combined with a distribution of the process outputs compared with the specifications show whether a process is capable of reliably achieving the desired results, as shown in Figure 8-9.[15]

An aside to the reader: In many cases in the literature and in business operations, process behavior charts and distributions of results are shown side by side on the same

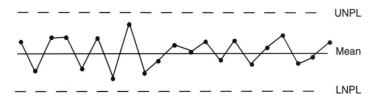

Figure 8-8. Process Behavior Chart Showing Stable Variation

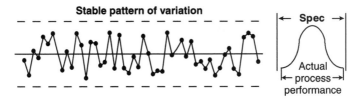

Figure 8-9. Graphs of a Process that is Stable and In Spec

scale as in Figure 8-10. Technically, this can be appropriate for some kinds of process behavior charts, e.g., X+MR. However, many process behavior charts plot a statistic that has different units than those of the results distribution, and in these cases it is inappropriate to compare the two kinds of graphs directly. Furthermore, routinely when we hear a top manager explain a process behavior chart (e.g., during a tour of a factory floor), the top manager describes the UNPLs and LNPLs on the process behavior chart as the specification limits. All managers need to distinguish clearly natural process limits which are part of the voice of the process from specification limits which are the voice of the customer, and they will do well to avoid confusing themselves by not plotting the two kinds of graphs side by side.

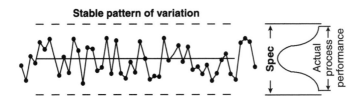

Figure 8-10. Side-by-side Graphs

Process outputs and a process behavior chart indicate the proper course of action. Ford Motor Company likes to say that process control provides the "voice of the process"—it enables you to learn what the process wants to say to you (see Figure 8-3). Once you can hear the voice of the process, you should be able to change the process so it can meet customer specifications, revealed through the "voice of the customer."

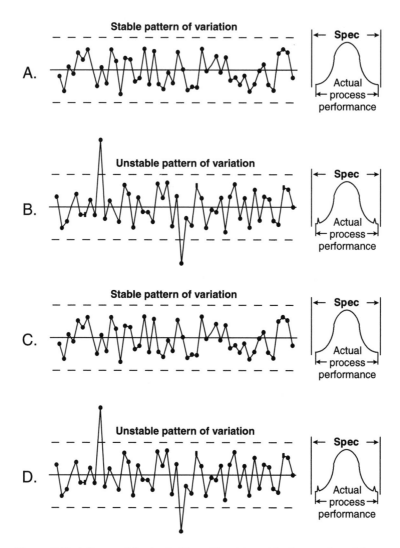

Figure 8-11. A Process May be Stable or Unstable and In Spec or Out of Spec)

As shown in Figure 8-11, a process may have stable or unstable variation independent of whether it is producing results that are in spec or not:

A. The graphs indicate this process is behaving in a stable fashion and is meeting specs. All is well, unless we would like to improve the specification, in which case the process will need to be improved so there is less routine variation.

B. The process is meeting spec but is not stable. Eliminate the sources of exceptional variation until the process becomes stable, so that good results continue.

C. The process is behaving in a stable fashion but is not meeting specs. Improve the process to eliminate sources of routine variation until the process produces results in spec.

D. The indicated process is out of spec and behaving erratically. First, eliminate sources of exceptional variation until the process produces stable outputs, and then improve the process by eliminating sources of routine variation until the process meets the specifications.

The next section elaborates the patterns suggested here.

8.3 PROCESS CONTROL AND PROCESS IMPROVEMENT

As noted at the beginning of this chapter, the basic cycle of process control is often called the SDCA cycle. In the SDCA cycle, there is a standard (S), and it is used to do the process (D). Then the results of the process are checked (C), and appropriate action is taken (A). If the results are within specification, the appropriate action is to continue to use the standard and repeat the cycle. If the results are beginning to drift or are actually out of specification (i.e., not meeting customer needs), take standard corrective actions.

However, from time to time you may decide that the specifications are not stringent enough and that you must improve the process (reduce the variance) so that tighter specifications can be met. When this happens, use a form of PDCA, the method of reactive improvement (described in Chapter 9), to find the source of the greatest routine variation and to improve the process by eliminating it. This interaction between the SDCA cycle of process control and the reactive improvement cycle is illustrated in Figure 8-12 on the next page. This alternation of SDCA and PDCA cycles also can be shown graphically, as in Figure 8-13 on page 119.

A scenario of interaction between the two cycles is illustrated from left to right in Figure 8-14[16] on page 119 and might go something like this:

SDCA Run an existing process for a while.
      Compute the natural variation limits, thus highlighting exceptional variation.

PDCA Find and eliminate the sources of exceptional variation.

SDCA Continue running and monitoring the new or now accurately followed process, using methods of process control.
      Eliminate the source of any unstable condition (exceptional variation) that begins to occur.

PDCA If it is desirable to reduce the natural variation of the process, for instance, to meet customer demands for narrower specification limits, use reactive improvement methods, e.g., the 7 steps, to find and reduce the largest source of routine variation.

SDCA Continue running and monitoring the new process, using the methods of process control.
      Eliminate the source of any unstable condition that begins to occur.

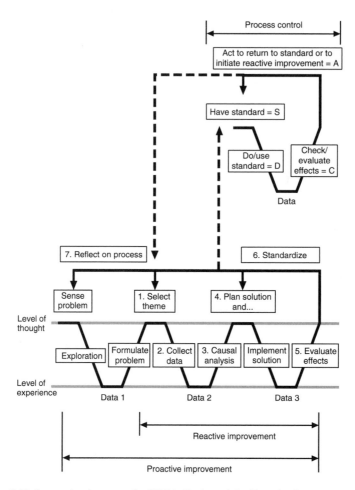

Figure 8-12. Interaction between the SDCA Cycle and the Reactive Improvement Cycle

8.4 CONTINUING THE TYPICAL EXAMPLE OF VARIATION

The previous two sections have shown the importance of using process behavior charts to highlight exceptional variation so it can be removed. However, another reason for highlighting exceptional variation is to see if improvement efforts are having any effect.

Returning to the example from the beginning of this chapter, Figure 8-15 on page 120 shows the process natural limits plotted based on the 15 months of data (through March of the second year) shown in Figure 8-2 (page 108); ignore the data for the last three months in Figure 8-15 for the moment. From the UNPL and LNPL we see that over the first 15 months the process was behaving in a stable fashion despite all of the changes we made in the mix of advertising and PR. In other words, the process was stable in a way that was incapable of producing more than about 1700 leads, and all our efforts and anguish were wasted.

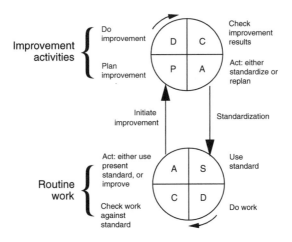

Figure 8-13. Alternation of SDCA and PDCA Cycles

In the absence of using process behavior charts, this is a very common result. We make changes to trying the improvement things, but we have no way to tell whether our process is behaving in a stable fashion or not. When our goal is minimizing variation, we do not know if the variation we will inevitably see in process outputs is routine variation or if it also contains exceptional variation indicating process instability. When our goal is to change our process results significantly, we do not know if the variation we will see in process outputs is routine variation indicating we are having no effect or exceptional variation indicating we have made a difference.

We now finish the example as shown in Figure 8-15: at the end of March, April, and May of the second year we increased PR efforts by a factor of four, and at last some results were produced that were beyond those expected from routine variation of the process as it operated over the first 15 months.

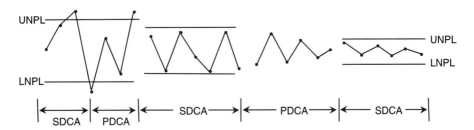

Figure 8-14. An SDCA/PDCA Scenario

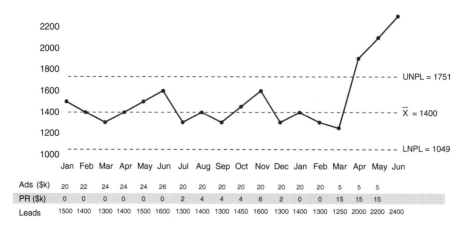

	Jan	Feb	Mar	Apr	May	Jun	Jul	Aug	Sep	Oct	Nov	Dec	Jan	Feb	Mar	Apr	May	Jun
Ads ($k)	20	22	24	24	24	26	20	20	20	20	20	20	20	20	5	5	5	
PR ($k)	0	0	0	0	0	0	2	4	4	4	6	2	0	0	15	15	15	
Leads	1500	1400	1300	1400	1500	1600	1300	1400	1300	1450	1600	1300	1400	1300	1250	2000	2200	2400

Figure 8-15. A Process Behavior Chart for the Earlier Example

NOTES

1. Our view of process control includes statistical process control.

2. Our favorite texts on process control include [8, 21, 22, 84, 122, 148, 210, 297, 308, 306, 307, 309].

3. For simplicity in describing this example, we assume the unrealistic situation that the leads generated in one month are a result of the ad and PR expenditures at the end of the previous month.

4. Managers who doubt the validity of these principles should immediately sign up for one of the numerous three-day seminars on statistical process control, view the tapes in the Deming Library (particularly seven, eight, and nine), arrange to participate in a simulation of Just-In-Time (JIT) manufacturing (Coopers & Lybrand has something called "the JIT wheel game," and other institutions offer similar simulations), have a long discussion with the company's quality control staff, or read a book on process control. Books particularly recommended for their ease of understanding are [22, 84, 306, 309].

5. In Chapters 13 and 14 we consider at length how to hear, interpret, and quantitatively specify the voice of the customer.

6. The voice of the process concept and elements of Figure 8-3 were presented by James Bakken (formerly of Ford Motor Co.) at [23]; [22] also provides an excellent discussion of how to find out what customers care about and how to decide on the appropriate measures.

7. We draw here on Wheeler's and Chambers' excellent discussion of this topic in [308].

8. Called variously routine, predictable, or controlled variation.

9. Called variously exceptional, unpredictable, or uncontrolled variation.

10. We are following Wheeler's and Poling's example in using the terms routine and exceptional variation.

11. Traditionally called a control chart or Shewhart chart; we follow Wheeler and Poling's notation in calling it a process behavior chart.

12. Again we use the notation of Wheeler and Poling rather than the traditional notation of Upper Control Limit and Lower Control Limit.

13. The UNPL and LNPL are calculated differently depending on the kind of data one has. We will not explain how to do such calculations here. The reader who wants to know more would do well to start by reading about the X+MR calculation in [309].

14. And otherwise produces output that does not have visible patterns to them, such as a repeated pattern of three outputs above the mean and three below the mean.

15. This figure and Figures 8-10 and 8-11 are schematic diagrams for illustrative purposes only; the run chart and distribution chart don't actually match numerically.

16. This figure is not completely original with us, but we don't remember where we first saw a version of it.

9

Reactive Improvement and the 7 Steps Method

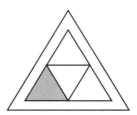

In Chapter 6 we introduced two components of improvement skill—reactive improvement and proactive improvement. Proactive improvement is what we need to design new products, choose new directions for our companies, and design new systems. Chapter 13 contains a detailed discussion of this approach. Reactive improvement (the subject of this chapter) deals with correcting or improving existing processes—reacting to flaws such as defects, delays, and waste. The WV model (introduced in Chapter 6) shows the connections among proactive and reactive improvement and process control (see Figure 9-1). We described process control in detail in Chapters 6 and 8. Proactive improvement will be discussed in detail in Chapters 13 and 14, and we'll touch on it briefly in Section 9.1 as part of identifying the problem for reactive improvement.

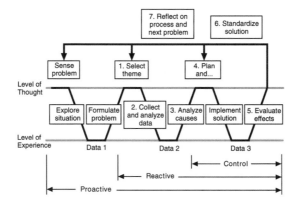

Figure 9-1. Proactive Improvement, Reactive Improvement, and Process Control

Our model of reactive improvement is shown in the right two-thirds of Figure 9-1. The model is as follows:

- First, select the specific problem to work on—select theme
- Second, collect appropriate data related to the selected theme and analyze it—collect and analyze data
- Third, based on the data, consider what the root cause of the problem may be—analyze causes
- Fourth, plan a change to the process that looks as if it will reverse the root cause and correct the problem, and try the change—plan and implement solution
- Fifth, collect more data and analyze it to see if the trial solution worked—evaluate effects
- Sixth, if the trial solution worked, standardize it—standardize solution
- Seventh, reflect on what was learned and what to work on next—reflect on process and next problem

The essence of the reactive approach is standardization of the problem-solving process, using, for example, the 7 steps and 7 QC tools.[1] The idea of a problem-solving process has been known since the Greeks but has typically been practiced only by a gifted few. In our own time, the inventor Thomas Edison, well known for his creative genius, used and required his assistants to use an explicit standard problem-solving process.[2] In this era of rapid change, everyone needs the benefit of standardized problem solving.

Reactive improvement as a standardized practice became common in the 1970s as the process used by QC circles in Japan. In the 1980s, the use of reactive improvement spread throughout the corporate hierarchy. For much of this time, the methods have been taught as part of quality improvement in the U.S. This use of reactive improvement by top and middle management is discussed further in Chapter 25.

Figure 9-2 shows a model for *mobilizing* reactive problem solving in an organization. Having sensed some sort of problem, the situation is explored and a specific problem to work on is identified. Then standard steps and tools are used, most often

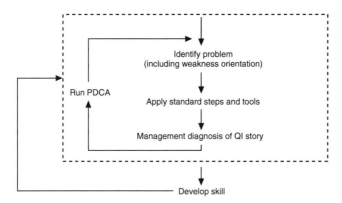

Figure 9-2. Model of Mobilization of Reactive Improvement and Learning

by an appropriate team of people known as a quality improvement team to isolate the source of the problem and to provide an improved process that corrects the problem. Once the problem has been corrected, the team is encouraged to describe its work in a standard format known as a quality improvement story (designated a QI story in this book), that is presented to members of management who "diagnose" what was done well and what was not in the team's improvement effort and application of the standard steps and tools. Through repeated use of this model, the quality improvement teams and management gain skill with reactive improvement. The rest of this chapter describes problem identification and the standard steps and tools in detail. The next chapter describes management diagnosis and considers skill development.

9.1 IDENTIFYING THE PROBLEM

How does one identify the area of the problem for a reactive problem-solving effort? The 7 steps do not explicitly include the proactive part of the WV model at the left third of Figure 9-1 concerning sensing a problem, exploring the situation, and formulating the problem to be solved. But these proactive steps are important. Therefore, it falls to managers to guide a quality improvement team in identifying an appropriate problem. Otherwise, teams may take a very long time to complete the improvement, fail to solve the problem, or perhaps waste effort on a problem that is not worth working on. Most failures of quality improvement teams occur because managers don't know how to guide the process, especially step 1 for identifying the problem (called theme selection).

Identification of the problem is the most important aspect of reactive problem solving. The process of identifying the problem may be divided into four parts:

- Weakness orientation
- Problem exploration
- Careful selection of the theme
- Clear statement of the theme

Weakness Orientation

For reactive problem solving, the first aspect of problem identification is using a weakness orientation.

From a process improvement perspective, weakness can be defined as the difference between the current situation and the target. For instance, in Figure 9-3, the target is changing as time moves from left to right, and the actual performance starts weak and becomes weaker over time. The goal is to eliminate the weakness, so you can move from the current level of performance to the target rate of performance. The weakness orientation focuses on closing the gap between the current situation and the target, that is, eliminating weakness as the basis of improvement. "Decrease delayed delivery rate from 25 percent to 15 percent" is a weakness orientation. Why is a weakness orientation preferable to a strength orientation? If instead of a weakness orientation you used

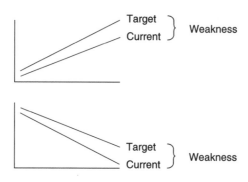

Figure 9-3. Identifying Weakness

a strength orientation, your goal would be to "increase on-time delivery rate from 75 percent to 85 percent."

The weakness orientation has several characteristics that are less likely to be present with a strength orientation:

- Focus on facts—base actions on facts, not opinion
- Focus on process, not results—results are the driven (effect) variable and you must focus on the drive (cause) variable
- Focus on root causes, not solutions—encourages objective analysis of causes ("What caused the delays?"), not jumping first to solutions ("What can we do to improve?")

The weakness orientation is the most important component of problem identification for improvement. For this approach to work, however, management (e.g., middle managers) must be supportive. Workers want to reveal weakness to improve quality; they may say, "Let's discuss last week's problem." However, managers may say, "Our factory is perfect," "Why not choose another problem?" or "When we have problems, they are small and we can easily solve them." Also, senior managers see reality through the middle managers. Thus, if a middle manager does not encourage and support workers who want to reveal weakness, the weakness will remain hidden from senior management. Senior management, in turn, must encourage a weakness orientation. If a senior manager blames the middle manager for revealing a problem ("Why was that allowed to happen?" or "Why wasn't that fixed sooner?"), the middle manager will never show another problem.

The key point is that workers should be encouraged by all levels to reveal problems. CEOs must be patient and refrain from blaming people about problems; they must encourage exposure of weakness. If CEOs don't encourage exposure of weakness, everyone will hide problems.

Many companies fail to implement methods of business improvement and organizational learning because they don't encourage revelation of weakness. For instance, if the CEO gets angry at a presentation of QITs, then the next time at QITs can easily create a story and data to make the CEO happy. If they do this, specific efforts at improvement and overall efforts for business improvement and organizational learning will fail.

In Japan, when a weakness is discovered, they say, "This is very good." Say it again and again; constantly encourage a weakness orientation. To get permanent good results, you have to define the problem in terms of weakness when selecting a theme.

Problem Exploration

The second step in identifying the problem is to explore the problem thoroughly. You could work on many problems. The question is how to select which problem to work on from among the many that could be worked on. The answer is to follow the chain of cause and result (see Figure 9-4). For instance, suppose you find a situation where a process or machine is poorly adjusted. You could work on that problem, but instead you trace the chain of cause and result until you reach the immediate cause of customer dissatisfaction or excessive cost, for example, a defective product. Choose that immediate cause as the theme. You must choose a theme directly related to the customer or the next process. If you do not, you risk working on nonvital problems that don't improve the company's ability to satisfy customers, or reduce costs; you can't afford to spend time on such problems.

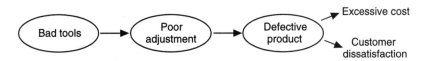

Figure 9-4. A Cause and Result Chain

The 5 *evils*—defects, mistakes, delay, waste, and accident/injury—is a device to focus attention on a theme directly related to basic satisfaction of the customer or next process—to focus on a market-in approach. Defects, mistakes, delay, waste, and accident/injury always cause customer dissatisfaction or excessive cost.

Thus, if you develop an initial theme, such as poor adjustment, you should try to trace it *forward* to a consequence that is one of the 5 evils, in this case, defective product that causes excess cost and customer dissatisfaction. Then, you can use the rest of the problem-solving process to work your way *back* along the chain of result and cause to a find a root cause that is really related to customers and costs; in this example, we tracked backward from defective product to poor adjustment to the root cause of bad tools. You must make sure that people tackle these 5 evils, not other problems, to get a good result from quality improvement activities. The 5 evils are a shorthand method to help in the mass movement approach to improvement we recommend. They are a good first approach to reactive improvement. People more experienced with reactive improvement may sometimes use the Language Processing method as well as the 5 evils to find problems that affect customer satisfaction or cause excessive cost (see Chapter 14).

Careful Selection of the Theme

The problem exploration step is likely to produce several themes to work on. The third step in identifying the problem is careful selection of the particular theme to use as an explicit statement of the improvement effort.

For continuous improvement it is necessary to repeat the problem-solving process. Thus, you don't have to select the most important or difficult problem at first. Select one theme at first and then another later, both building problem-solving skill, and find a manageable path to solution of a large, difficult problem.

If you are to experience the achievement of problem solving, you must tackle a problem that can be solved with current levels of skill and that is important to solve. Often there is a trade-off to be made. In selecting the theme, consider these issues:

- Sense of achievement to be gained
- Difficulty of situation
- Urgency/effect
- Quickness of potential solutions

First, look at the difficulty of the situation as shown in Table 9-1.

Table 9-1. Evaluating Problem-Solving Difficulty

		Area of problem		
		Equipment	Methods	Human behavior
	Yourself	1	1	3
Data collection or Potential solution implementation	Yourself and others	2	2	4
	Others	3	3	4

There are two dimensions in Table 9-1: Can you collect the data and implement the potential solutions by yourself, or do others have to do it? Is the problem area equipment, methods, or human behavior? The areas marked 1 are easiest for the beginner to work on. The second and third least difficult areas are also shown. Working on the human behavior of others is most difficult, as shown. You can use Table 9-1 to evaluate the difficulty of the situation in terms of both difficulty of data collection and difficulty of potential solution.

Next, having understood the difficulty of the situation, you might construct a *theme selection matrix*, which prioritizes problems for solution in terms of difficulty of the situation (data collection and potential implementation), urgency or impact, and speed of solution (see Table 9-2). Regarding speed of solution, three or four months is good; one to two years is too long.

Table 9-2. Determining Problem-Solving Priorities

Rank 1-3 (1 is best)	Ease of data collection	Ease of potential implementation	Urgency/ impact	Speed of solution	Priority (lowest total is highest)
Prob. 1					
Prob. 2					
Prob. 3					
Prob. 4					

Fill in the matrix in Table 9-2 for each problem being considered. Vote 1 (high), 2 (medium), or 3 (low) in each box. Add across the rows and put the total in the priority column to pick the first problem to work on, that is, the problem with the lowest total.

Clear Statement of the Theme

The fourth step in identifying the problem is making a clear statement of the theme. The following examples use this process of refinement to illustrate various ways in which themes are clarified.

Example 1

"Increase on-time delivery" is an initial attempt to state a theme. *"Decrease late delivery"* is better. The key point is that because of its weakness orientation, the second statement does a better job of directing the team toward the facts and causes of the problem.

Writing a clear statement of theme is difficult. First write the obvious theme, *"Increase on-time delivery,"* and then iteratively refine it until you reach an effective statement of theme. The following examples show this process of refinement.

Example 2

"Understand customer delivery, quality, and pricing requirement."

First, convert the above statement of partial solution to a statement of weakness, for example:

"We do not meet requirements of the customer in delivery, quality, and pricing."

But delivery, quality, and pricing are too much to tackle at one time, so let's focus on the delivery:

"We do not meet requirements of the customer for delivery."

Example 3 (for a Sales Group)

Start by exploring the problem. The first version of the theme is,

"Define the method to identify long-term opportunity customers."

You have already imposed the solution. What is the weakness?

"We don't know the long-term opportunity customer."

Suppose, in your company, there is already agreement on the following definitions: long-term = three to four years; opportunity = increasing sales; and customer = big-volume customer. Therefore, rewrite the theme as:

"We don't have a good forecast of three-year to five-year sales to big-volume customers."

This is not a theme, however, it is a problem. To convert this problem to a weakness orientation theme, write:

"Decrease misforecast of three-year to five-year sales to big-volume customers."

The past may not predict the future, but the past is all the data you have, so you have to use it.

Example 4

"Optimize face-to-face selling time."

This is not a weakness orientation. It anticipates a solution. Suppose experience tells you that you meet with the purchasing person 90 percent of the time and the user of your product only ten percent of the time. What does "optimize face-to-face selling time" mean; in other words, with whom do you want to meet in person? Suppose you believe that it is important to change the mix of face-to-face selling time so that you spend more time with the user. A better theme, then, would be:

"Decrease time spent with other than the end user."

That is an improvement, but now look for further improvement. What is the purpose of decreasing time spent with other than the end user?

"To sell more."

Time spent yields an order, which yields dollars. Decreasing time spent with other than the end user is one of the means to achieve the order. This leads us to think about what the real problem is. The real problem is to get an order. Thus, the theme should be (using a weakness orientation):

"Decrease orders lost."

You should select a theme directly related to the customer or money. Spending time with people other than the end user and not getting an order is an example of one of the 5 evils—waste.

Example 5

"Decrease delay between the committed and actual date of shipment."

This initial theme statement is product-out; delay is not defined. Before the senior manager suggests a better statement of the theme, however, he or she should first encourage the quality team: "Very good. Your theme is stated in terms of weakness.

But there is a way to improve it. Have you thought about it from a market-in point of view?" This leads to:

"Decrease the disparity between customer-demanded and actual date of shipment."

In addition to illustrating iterative refinement of a theme, the above examples suggest some of the characteristics of an effective theme:

- Weakness orientation
- Market-in orientation
- A problem, not a solution
- Results, not a solution
- A single problem, not several
- Every word well defined

Some managers worry that a weakness orientation will undermine morale. A correctly handled weakness orientation can coexist with high morale, for the weaknesses addressed are weaknesses of the system rather than weaknesses of the people who work within the system. Weakness is a means to an uplifting and positive end—continuous improvement.

The manager needs to guide the team or provide facilitation or training to enable the team to select an effective theme. Having a carefully selected, clearly stated theme is essential to successful application of the 7 steps. Application of the 7 steps is the key to empowering teams to solve problems on their own without requiring constant oversight and management intervention.

9.2 STANDARD STEPS AND TOOLS

Business improvement and organizational learning need to be a mass movement. Without the participation of all the people with impact on or interest in a given situation, improvement efforts will be suboptimal or fail altogether. Thus, the process of reactive problem solving must be:

- Easy to understand and learn
- Easy to use
- Easy to monitor
- Effective

Therefore, you need standard steps for reactive problem solving. One well-known and well-proven set of standard tools is the 7 steps, previously sketched in the description of the WV model in Figure 9-1. However, the individual steps and substeps require specific methods, for example, for collecting facts. This leads us to the need for tools, of which there are many, even for collecting data and analyzing facts. Therefore, many companies have focused on the most effective and most frequently used tools, based on experience of real problem solving in real companies. The 7 QC tools listed below (and in Table 1-1) are described in more detail at the end of this chapter:[3]

- Check sheet/stratification
- Pareto diagram
- Cause-and-effect diagram (also called an Ishikawa diagram or fishbone diagram)
- Graphs
- Control charts
- Histogram
- Scatter diagram

Section 9.1 described how to identify a problem and select an effective theme. The essence of the 7 steps and 7 tools is *standardized reactive improvement*. The steps are easy to understand, learn, and monitor; and, perhaps most important, they enable everyone in the organization, whether on the plant floor or in the executives offices, to practice a scientific approach to problem solving using graphical tools that approximate the analysis achievable with basic statistical methods.

The arbitrary number in the 7 steps and 7 QC tools is a strategy for mass movement—easy to become familiar with, to learn, to use, and to monitor. The only thing important about the number is that there are not too many steps or tools to learn. In fact, some companies have six or eight steps in their standard reactive problem-solving process, and variation exists among the seven standard tools themselves. Sometimes *stratification* is included as one of the 7 tools, for example, in place of check sheet. A process flowchart is also sometimes included in place of check sheet. Within each company, each tool is well standardized, both in the process of application and the process of teaching the tool and its use.

In Japan, most companies that undertake business improvement using quality improvement teams or QC circles choose a coherent set of standard steps and tools for use in their reactive improvement process. Even companies that use a standard set of tools are weaker without standard steps to connect them.

Table 9-3 shows the way the 7 steps and 7 QC tools are typically used together. The 7 steps define and clarify the problem-solving process. The 7 QC tools provide the methods to help execute the steps.

Table 9-3. How the 7 Steps and 7 QC Tools Work Together

PDCA	9 Steps	Tools
Plan	1. Describe the project 2. Explore the essentials and narrow the focus 3. Establish the metrics and constraints 4. Identify possible alternatives 5. Develop an optimistic plan with obstacles and countermeasures	LP Relation diagram Flowchart Block diagram Graphs Tree diagram Selection matrix
Do	6. Develop, implement and monitor the detailed plan	Arrow diagram 4W, 1H chart
Check	7. Evaluate the results	Graphs
Act	8. Standardize 9. Reflect on the process and select the next project	4W, 1H, 1C chart Flowchart

Most problems can be solved with use of only a few tools. For instance, graphs, Pareto diagrams, and cause-and-effect diagrams make up 60 to 70 percent of the tools used in Japanese QC circle activities. In the beginning, a company can focus on teaching and using these tools. It is not useful to teach a comprehensive tool set to beginners; they won't be able to make effective use of so much training before they have experience working on real problems. Teach the standard 7 steps and these three tools, and teach your teams how to apply them to their own problems and selections of themes. Following the 7 steps case study in the following section is a brief description (in Section 9.4) of each of the 7 QC tools.

9.3 THE 7 STEPS: A CASE STUDY

The following case study by the Broken Pellicle QI Team at Analog Devices illustrates the use of the 7 steps and the most commonly used three of the 7 QC tools. It also implicitly introduces a standard presentation format called a quality improvement story, or QI story.[4]

The case study quotes the text that accompanied a presentation of the QI story created by the Broken Pellicle Quality Improvement Team to summarize its work at its conclusion using the 7 steps to address the problem of "broken pellicles." This is a real story by a real team describing its use of the 7 steps and several of the 7 QC tools, with all the strengths and weaknesses of the the team's process.[5]

> Good morning. I would like to present to you the efforts of our quality improvement team, which we call the Broken Pellicle Team. Here are the members of our team. [See Slide 9-1.] Improvement teams at Analog Devices have specific members, usually cross-functional and chosen according to the nature of the problem being solved. Members are requested, but not required, to participate, and can be anyone with insight into the problem. Members remain on the team throughout the problem-solving cycle. There are two production operators, one production supervisor, one production trainer, one engineer, one technician, and a facilitator on this team.

Step 1: Select Theme

> Step 1 of the seven-step problem-solving process is theme selection. Each improvement team at Analog has a written theme—a specific, measurable goal. Here is the theme our team selected: *Reduce the number of broken and scratched pellicles in wafer fab by 50 percent by the end of 2Q91.* I will now explain the theme.
>
> Some of you may not be familiar with wafer fabs or the steps used in producing our product, an integrated circuit or "chip." This slide shows the major steps in making a chip. [See Slide 9-2.]

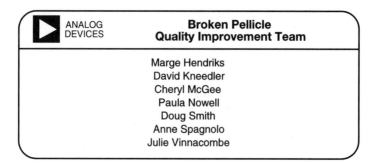

Slide 9-1

In wafer fabrication—wafer fab—a flat slab or wafer of silicon, a few inches in diameter, is used. Through a complex sequence of hundreds of photolithographic and chemical process steps within a clean room environment, individual integrated circuits are etched or imprinted into the silicon wafer. This is a cyclic process, through which a multilevel circuit is built up within the silicon. After wafer fab, certain parameters of the circuits are tested for functionality; good chips are taken out in the separate step, are assembled into packages, and are sent through a final test.

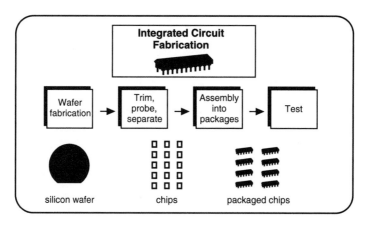

Slide 9-2

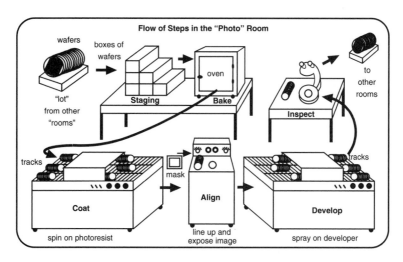

Slide 9-3

This team's theme addressed the photo area within wafer fab. [See Slide 9-3.] This room imprints images of the multiple levels onto the wafers in a process similar to taking and developing a photograph. In the photo area, wafers from other rooms are staged on a table. Some of these are baked in an oven before further processing. All wafers are then sent to the coat station, where a photosensitive polymer is spun on the wafers. The wafers are then sent to align, where previous processing levels are lined up with a mask pattern containing the current level; the image of this pattern is exposed onto the polymer film on the wafers. The image is then developed, inspected, and sent on to the next step in another room.

Continuing with an explanation of our theme, this figure shows a drawing of a photolithographic mask. [See Slide 9-4.] A mask is a clear glass plate, held by a plastic holder, and contains an image of the circuit being exposed at the current process level. The pellicle is a thin plastic film stretched across the glass plate to protect it from dirt and scratches. As shown in the figure, the image on the glass mask would be in the center of the mask holder, in the large circular area. The operator slides the mask holder into a groove on the loader arm, which protrudes from the aligner machine. The mask holder is held onto the arm via the groove at the bottom finger as well as by the mask holder slot on the side. The loader arm is then retracted into the machine and drops the mask into the proper position.

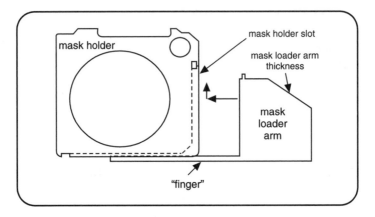

Slide 9-4

Teams are always asked to try to verify why their theme is important, so that they understand it better and have a feeling for its importance to the company. This team's verification is in terms of two of the 5 evils: waste (cost of repairs) and delay (increase in cycle time). [See Slide 9-5.]

Why is this theme important?

New vendor will replace ADS Mask fab:

• Cost to replace pellicle will be $400/mask, or $50,000 to $100,000 annually

• Delay will be 4 days/mask, or 500 to 1,000 additional days of cycle time per year

---

Slide 9-5

Step 2: Collect and Analyze Data

Step 2 of the seven-step problem-solving process is to collect and analyze data. Teams at Analog are encouraged to examine existing data collection systems carefully; to design a new system is better specifically for your problem-solving efforts than to struggle with the flaws and assumptions built into someone else's system. Our team examined the old data system (mask repair logbook) used when a pellicle was found broken and decided that insufficient information existed as to causes and types of holders, and our technicians had no ability to give more information and to form check sheets and Paretos more easily. The new data collection system devised by our team answers the questions: Who? Where? How? [See Slide 9-6.]

- Team member fills out logsheet with aligner operator
- Technician adds input
- Material control files logsheet
- QIP team analyzes/plots data

**Broken and Scratched Pellicle
Data Collection Check Sheet**

Date: _____

Operator ID# _____

Machine # _____

Time SL/PA notified _____ SL/PA initial _____

Serial # _____

Operator inputs: _____

_____

Circle one: scratched   broken

Circle one: machine   handling

Time given to tech. _____ Tech initial _____

Tech input: _____

_____

_____

Location of scratch: _____

Corrective action: _____

_____

Holder condition: _____

Holder type (circle):   black   white

Please return to Material Control upon completion

Slide 9-6

After collecting data for two months, we plotted our data with the use of a Pareto. Here is the data sorted by machine causes, handling (human) causes, and other (unknown; found broken) causes. [See Slide 9-7.] Our conclusion was that over 70 percent of the broken pellicles were caused by the aligner machine, so we focused on machine causes.

In studying machine causes, we found three categories. [See Slide 9-8.] The highest category included cases where the pellicle broke while the aligner was unloading the mask from the machine (over 70 percent); the next highest was when the aligner was loading the mask into the machine (20 percent of

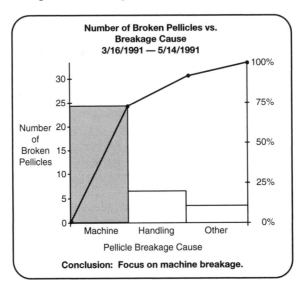

Slide 9-7

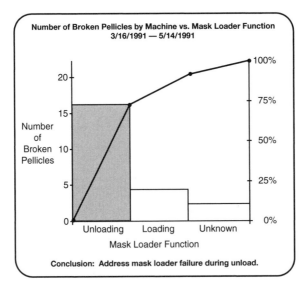

Slide 9-8

occurrences), and the rest of the causes could not be determined exactly. Thus, our conclusion was to study why the pellicles broke during unloading.

Step 3: Analyze Causes

We now felt we had sufficient data to move to step three. This figure shows our Ishikawa, or cause-and-effect, diagram, answering the question, "Why does the mask unloader arm break or scratch pellicles during unloading?" [See Slide 9-9.] We addressed causes due to machine, materials, and people. We decided that the root causes were of two types: The finger on the loading arm was out of alignment with the mask holder, and the tolerance of the groove on the side of the mask holder did not ensure consistent linkage with the loading arm. Thus, as the mask was withdrawn from the machine, it could shake or wobble, and the pellicle could be scratched or broken.

Teams at Analog Devices are asked to verify root causes discovered with the Ishikawa diagram. This team verified its conclusions by observing the

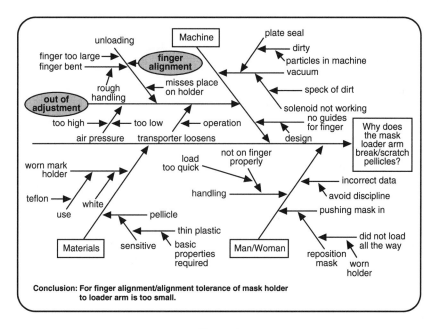

Slide 9-9

machine in operation, examining the motion of the arm each time a mask was unloaded. They found that the next six times a pellicle broke, the finger was observed to be out of alignment. They repeated the breakage under controlled conditions to verify the alignment problem and the tolerance problem. Thus, the team was confident that it had found the root causes.

The team also sorted the data for breakage during unloading into different types of mask holders. We were using two different types (made by different vendors), a white holder and a black holder. The figure shows that the white holders were in use for over 80 percent of the breakages. [See Slide 9-10.] The team measured the grooves on the two holders and found that the white holders had slightly less tolerance than the black holders.

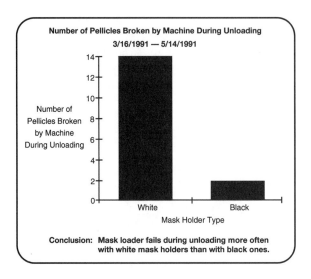

Slide 9-10

Step 4: Plan and Implement Solution

The team used a solution matrix to decide the effectiveness of various solution options. [See Slide 9-11.] The most effective solutions were to design and install a guide on the loader arms of each aligner machine, and to convert all the mask holders to the black type. The other factors making this an attractive solution were that the guide could be fabricated and installed by our own technicians. This team decided to design, install, and test guides on the machines with the most occurrences of breakage. In addition, all mask holders would be converted to the black type, since the data was so conclusive that this was a major cause.

These figures demonstrate the action of the guide, which is screwed to the mask loader arm and catches either side of the mask holder as it is inserted into the loader arm. [See Slide 9-12 and Slide 9-13.] The guide holds the mask holder firmly so that it remains in alignment with the arm, tolerance is improved, and the mask does not shake when the mask is unloaded.

Solution Matrix

Solutions	Finger Alignment	Mask Holder Alignment Tolerance	Other Factors
1. To design and install a guide	3	3	Fabricate in-house by our technicians. Cost minimal. Equipment down for 1 shift. Need resources outside of QIP but within department.
2. Ensure carriage is home	2	1	Requires 100% operator attention.
3. Hit run/reset if mask starts to come out wrong	1	1	Depends on operator being there 100%. After-the-fact "fix."
4. Designate mask holders	2	2	Requires transfer of plates 100% of the time (increases handling).
5. Convert to all black push-button-type holders	1	3	Limits vendor? May increase price.

Ranking system: 3 Very effective
2 Somewhat effective
1 Low effectiveness

Slide 9-11

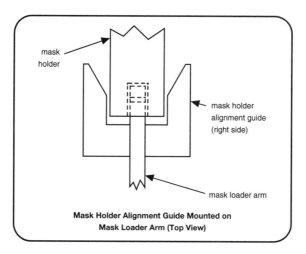

Mask Holder Alignment Guide Mounted on Mask Loader Arm (Top View)

Slide 9-12

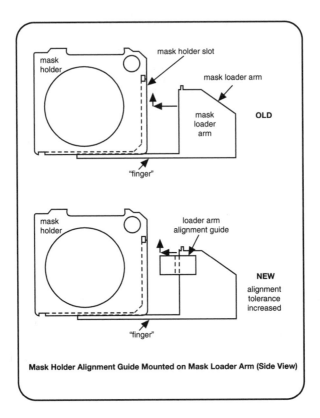

Slide 9-13

Step 4 of the seven-step problem-solving process continues with solution implementation. [See Slide 9-14.] The team used a matrix to indicate what needed to be done, who would do it, by when, and how the action would be performed.

Step 5: Evaluate Effects

In evaluating the effects of implemented solutions, the team plotted the data following solution implementation. [See Slide 9-15 on page 144.] The solution worked! Pellicle breakage caused by machines was reduced from 24 cases to two cases. In addition, handling breakage was eliminated because of increased operator awareness of the issue.

Solution Implementation			
Who	**What**	**When**	**How**
Dave Kneedler	Get first guide made.	5/22/91	Get commitment from Sonny and George.
Doug Smith	Install first guide as pilot on PE #5.	5/29/91	Doug/George to install. Anne will get priority on system.
Anne Spagnolo/ Doug Smith	Inform all shifts of pilot program.	5/29/91	Anne will inform the other supervisors and send a PROMIS message to Photo Mail. Doug will inform all Photo technicians.
Anne Spagnolo	Determine similiar amount of work thru PE #5 during data collection.	5/29/91	Via daily reports.
Anne Spagnolo	Ensure similar work load on PE#5 after installation.	5/29/91	Via daily reports.
Anne Spagnolo Julie Vinnacombe	Designate all black holders on PE #5 and PE #8.	5/29/91	Julie will inform all shifts and post a sign on PE's.

Slide 9-14

The team also evaluated the savings in terms of two evils, waste and delay, and demonstrated to management the significant reduction in costs as well as cycle time from their solution, as follows.

- Cost invested:
  - Mask aligner brackets $380.00
  - Black mask holders $31,620.00
  - Total invested $32,000.00
- Estimated annual cost to replace pellicles:
  - Before $52,800.00
  - After $3,200.00
  - Savings $49,600.00
- Estimated annual cycle time lost:
  - Before   528 days
  - After   32 days
  - Days saved   496 days

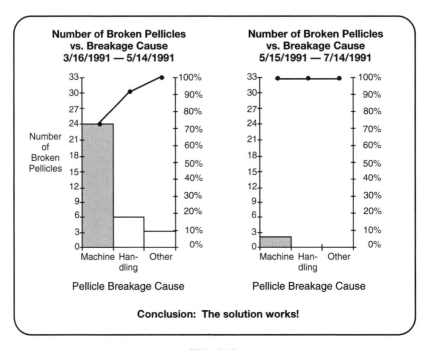

Slide 9-15

Step 6: Standardize Solution

The team again used a matrix to indicate what was to be done to standardize the solutions, who would do it, by when, and how it would be done. [See Slide 9-16.]

The team decided to reset its specs for mask holders so that all would be of the black type in the future, and to install guides on all remaining aligner machines.

Step 7: Reflect on Process (and Next Problem)

The PDCA cycle for this team's efforts would not be complete without step 7, reflection on process and choice of the next problem. Upon reflection, we decided that we wasted the first few weeks of our problem-solving process by trying to utilize the old data system; we should have recognized its weaknesses immediately and designed a new one. We recommend that teams always consider designing their own data system very early in the process. Secondly, we did not coordinate well with the other two shifts. Third, someone knowledgeable in mask fabrication should have been recruited to help from the beginning. For our next problem, we are considering working on the breakage caused during loading of the mask. Loading failure is now our most

Install Black Holders and Guides on All Machines

Who	What	By When	How
C. McGee	Reset spec black holders	6/30/91	Paperwork
C. McGee	Convert high runners to black holders	6/30/91	Order and install
C. McGee	Convert rest of holders	8/31/91	Order and install
A. Spagnolo	Continue monitoring "intangible effect"	perm.	Use same data system
D. Kneedler/ D. Smith/ T. Clark	Order and install remaining guides	8/31/91	Contract out

Slide 9-16

important pellicle breakage problem. Before we attack this problem, however, we will examine other problems within wafer fab to see if there is a more important topic to address with our team.

9.4 THE 7 QC TOOLS

In this section we say just a few words about each of the 7 QC tools, to clarify how each is used. In addition to these tools, other statistical tools, such as multivariate analysis and experimental design, are sometimes taught as part of reactive problem solving.

Check Sheet

```
A | x x
B | x x x x
C | x x x
D | x x
E | x
```

To analyze problems, you must collect data that represent the facts. Forms used for easy collection of data are called check sheets. Use *check sheets* to take data systematically regarding the frequency of various effects. They are much like a set of tally marks on the back of an envelope. However, they are usually marked on forms prepared in advance, according to expected effects. Also, they are calibrated so that when you take the data, you have a running plot of frequency of effects; the check marks create a histogram.

Pareto Diagram

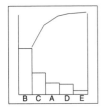

At any given time there are many kinds of problems around you. It is not practical to attack all these problems at the same time. Therefore, arrange the problems in order of importance and attack the bigger problems first. A bar graph that shows the biggest problem on the left followed by the lesser problems is called a *Pareto diagram*. Pareto diagrams help one focus on the vital few effects or causes. The absolute totals of effects are always shown on the left side, and the cumulative percentages are always shown on the right side.

Cause-and-Effect Diagram

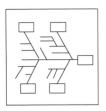

To solve a problem, it is important to know the real causes and the interrelations among causes. You can then identify the major causes to solve the problem. Use a *cause-and-effect diagram* to guide data collection and analysis to find the root cause of a problem. A cause-and-effect diagram shows an effect at the right and the main causes of that effect off the horizontal axis. These main causes are in turn effects that have subcauses, and so on, down many levels. This is not basically a statistical tool; it enumerates the variety of causes rather than the frequency of events. However, it is a useful tool for noting the frequency of events, once you have the data.

Graphs

Graphs display data. There are many kinds of graphs: bar graphs, line graphs, circle graphs, and radar graphs are some of them. Most people are familiar with the first three types of graphs.

The fourth type, a *radar graph*, compares several items on multiple dimensions. Suppose that for three competitive products, *E1* is performance, *E2* is cost, *E3* is reliability, and *E4* is delivery; in all four dimensions, the good direction is out from the center. The above example shows that one of the products is inferior in all dimensions. Of the other two products, one wins slightly in performance and delivery, and the other wins slightly in cost and reliability.

Stratification

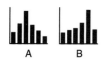

One of the practical ways to determine the specific cause is *stratification*. For example, when the diameter of the shaft of a rotor has too much dispersion, and it is made from two machines, you have to stratify or segregate the data corresponding to each machine. Thus, you can find the difference between machine A and B and easily make adjustments.

Control Chart

A *control chart* is a graph that shows the variations in process performance. It helps in spotting abnormal situations in standard manufacturing or other processes. Control charts are used to plot over time (left to right) the observed values of a process variable or output variable around the mean and between upper and lower control limits.[6] In the figure, the circled dot is outside the control limits.

Histogram

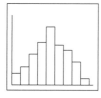

We produce a large quantity of products with a great number of parts and materials. Each of these products and parts cannot have the same quality but always has some amount of dispersion. A *histogram* is a graph that shows dispersion of the data. From this graph, we can analyze the characteristics of the data and the cause of dispersion. Typically, a histogram is a bar graph showing the statistical distribution over equal intervals of some measure of quality, such as defects. Histograms are used in analysis for stratification to create hypotheses for the reason defects are occurring.

Scatter Diagram

The relationship between cause and effect (for example, between illumination level and inspection mistakes) may be drawn on a graph called a *scatter diagram*. A scatter diagram plots many data points, typically with a measure of quality on one axis and a variable hypothesized to influence quality on the other axis. Used in analysis to test hypotheses on cause-and-effect relations, a scatter diagram is a visual representation of a two-dimensional correlation. A diagram such as this is often very useful because it illustrates patterns of data that are not otherwise obvious.

NOTES

1. Complete descriptions of the 7 QC tools are found in many books, for example, [145, 146, 181, 19]. Detailed descriptions of the 7 steps may be found in [181, 51].

2. Unreferenced statement by Peter Drucker quoted in [139, page 293].

3. The 7 QC tools are also often used as part of process control or even in parts of proactive improvement. They form a part of the common language of organizations working on business improvement and organizational learning. However, the 7 QC tools are probably more frequently used in reactive improvement than anywhere else.

4. As mentioned in the introduction to this chapter (see the description of Figure 9-2), quality improvement teams are encouraged to conclude their use of the 7 steps by describing their effort in the standard format of a QI story. The benefits of creating a QI story discussed in Chapter 21, and management diagnosis of a QI story presentation is described in the next chapter.

5. The case was prepared by Ira Moskowitz, then Production Manager, Wilmington Wafer-fab, Analog Devices. His references to a seven-step problem-solving process means the 7 steps, and his reference to a QIP team means a quality improvement team.

6. Called natural process limits in Chapter 8.

10

Management Diagnosis
of the 7 Steps of
Reactive Improvement

As mentioned in the introduction to the last chapter, QI (quality improvement) stories are the standard presentation format for the 7 steps reactive improvement activities. (The Broken Pellicle case study of the last chapter—Section 9.3—was presented in the format of a QI story.) The QI stories are presented to management, and managers have a standard way of responding, called management diagnosis [54], to the 7 steps QI story. There are several reasons for presenting and diagnosing the QI stories. Such a process does the following:

- Diffuses good improvement practices throughout the organization by example
- Acknowledges team accomplishment
- Increases improvement skills of the team through management review and comment ("diagnosis")
- Creates management buy-in to standardize the solution
- Ensures legitimacy of conclusions[1]

Ensuring legitimacy of conclusions is deliberately listed last. Employees following anything like the proper process will have acceptable results; reactive quality improvement at its most basic levels is not supposed to be difficult. It's a "mass movement," and everyone can use the 7 steps to create permanent improvement.

This diagnosis is an important way to help employees increase their problem-solving and improvement skills over time. Although ideally such coaching happens continuously, the one time when coaching is formally expected is when a team presents its results to management in the form of a QI story.

10.1 GENERAL GUIDELINES FOR MANAGERS DIAGNOSING A QI STORY
Senior Management Attends

Presentations of QI stories are not just for the managers who supervise the team members; they are for management at higher levels. At a variety of companies, we have

149

seen the senior management, starting from the plant manager or division director on down, attend the QI story presentation. The QI stories help these senior managers obtain intimate knowledge of what goes on in their plants and divisions.

Comments Highlight Positive Lessons and Areas for Further Improvement

It is more important to highlight key positive lessons than to identify and eliminate weakness. People learn more from good examples than from being told what not to do. Therefore, 70 percent of management comments during a QI story presentation should address the positive aspects of the work, and 30 percent should be on the most important areas for improvement next time; we call this the *70/30 rule*. The developmental status of the team should also temper diagnosis. A quality improvement team may be just beginning to use the 7 steps and related tools. Managers should praise such a team's use of tools rather than criticize the way those tools are used.

Furthermore, managers should restrict comments on both positive and negative QI stories to the vital few. A barrage of helpful or critical comments doesn't provide focus. Comments should be specific; rather than saying, "good theme," for example, say what specifically was good about the theme selection. Again, the goal is to provide focus. To highlight the appropriate lessons, the senior manager diagnosing a QI story might prepare a matrix, such as the one shown in Table 10-1, listing the key strengths of the QI story the manager is about to see and improvements that need to be made next time. A few of these would be mentioned to the team after the presentation, and others might be mentioned to the team facilitator at a later time.

Nonverbal Signs Show Management Interest

Because a major part of the function of QI story presentations is to diffuse positive lessons, the senior managers attending the presentation should give every sign that the work is important. Simple attendance is not as effective as visibly attentive listening. Holding conversations on the side, reading unrelated materials, or slouching and looking around the room send the message that the presentation is unimportant and uninteresting to the senior manager. On the other hand, facing the presenter, taking notes, and asking questions at the end of the presentation send the message that the work is significant and interesting. This evidence of enthusiasm and support is necessary to motivate further improvement activities.

Following are some specific examples of nonverbal ways to show interest, typical of Japanese practice.

- Senior managers are expected to attend these quality improvement team and QC circle presentations.
- Executives sit in the front row, with the CEO in the center, visible to the presenter in front of them and to the audience behind them. Senior managers have to show constant interest through their nonverbal behavior.

Table 10-1. QI Story Diagnostic Matrix

Step number	Step name and comment	Strengths	Weaknesses
1	Select theme		
2	Collect data		
3	Analyze causes		
4	Plan and implement solutions		
5	Evaluate effects		
6	Standardize solutions		
7	Reflect on process		

- During a QI story presentation, the senior manager must be present at all times.
- Senior managers must sit on the edge of their chairs and lean forward, expressing interest by behavior instead of words.
- In response to good points, they should nod their heads and say, "Very good."
- They should be seen taking notes; they should not interrupt the presenters.
- They should show attentiveness by asking questions at the end of the presentation.

Employees don't know what managers are thinking, just what they see them do. Sixty percent of communication is nonverbal; 40 percent is verbal. During QI story presentations, senior managers must be actors, in the sense of conveying interest through behavior.

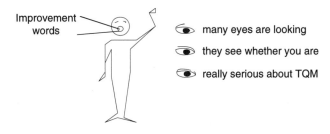

Don't Suggest Going Back

Diagnoses should be oriented toward doing better on the next turn of the PDCA cycle. While it is tempting to request redoing data collection, analysis, and so on, it is important for team morale to keep moving forward. If redoing something is important, due process of theme selection will shortly return the team to it on a subsequent cycle.

The process being followed in the QI story presentation is more important than the results. You have to teach this process to everyone. Ask people to follow the 7 steps process, and they produce better results.

The QI Story Should Follow the 7 Steps Format

For improvement skills to diffuse through the organization, there must be a common language. QI stories in particular must use a standard format because they are the medium for so much diffusion within a company.

The step number and name of each step should be on the first slide of each step. The first slide should give the name of the team and the team members to identify who undertook this improvement effort.

Each department says, "We are different, and we need our own version of Pareto diagrams." However, a common language throughout the company is needed; the mass movement approach we recommend requires discipline.

10.2 STEP-BY-STEP GUIDELINES FOR MANAGERS DIAGNOSING A QI STORY

Diagnosing Step 1: Select Theme

Guidance from Management

Since the 7 steps start after problem exploration (left side of WV model, see Figure 9-1, page 123), teams using the 7 steps need guidance from managers on problem selection. It is useful for the presentation to indicate how the team involved its management in theme selection.

Weakness Orientation

The theme should have a weakness orientation. Does it focus on the 5 evils (defects, mistakes, delay, waste, accident)? Beware of solutions masquerading as problems, such as decrease lapses in worker discipline. Also avoid phrases like "improve," "upgrade," "create a better...," which indicate a strength orientation.

Working on an Ongoing Process

The 7 steps and 7 QC tools are best applied to an ongoing process, a process in which the problem repeats. If the problem will not repeat, there is little benefit in undertaking a reactive improvement process. If the process has not repeated in the past, it is difficult to use the 7 QC tools to collect adequate data. If the problem does not repeat, it will be difficult to check whether the solution works.

If the problem doesn't repeat, it may make more sense to use processes and tools other than the 7 steps and 7 QC tools, such as proactive improvement, the 7 management and planning tools, or statistical analysis tools such as design of experiments and multivariate analysis.[2]

A problem stated in terms of future performance risks turning into a strength-oriented theme that focuses too quickly on solutions without first dwelling on data and causation.

It is difficult to forecast the effect of a solution. Implementing the solution produces usable feedback. This is possible with an ongoing process.

Market-in and Results, Not Causes

Does the theme have a market-in concept (focused on customers or the next process)?

State problems in terms of results, not causes: customers dissatisfied, next process hurt, dollars lost, and so on. Problem statements cast in terms of causes short-circuit the process of gathering data and identifying causes.

Demonstration of a market-in theme should include the facts. These might be a comparison of the company's error rates with those of a competitor, a plot over time showing a competitively important variable getting worse, or a customer survey showing that the problem area is a significant area of complaints. The more factual the ties to customer-related performance, the stronger the theme.

"My boss told me to do it" does not demonstrate understanding of the company's business or of customer satisfaction. Explaining the theme is a good way for employees to think about why they do what they do and who their customers are. The philosophy of the dual function of work[3] demands that the theme both makes improvements and follows standard processes. Doing improvements simply because you were told to is just another form of following standard processes; it is not real improvement work.

Explanation of Theme for Audience

QI stories are an opportunity to teach the market-in orientation in two ways. One is the customer orientation discussed above. The other is the recognition that the presentation is a product and the listeners are customers. A product-out orientation results in presentations that plunge ahead without regard for who its listeners are and what they know about the technical terms, processes involved, people and responsibilities involved, and so on. A market-in presentation, on the other hand, starts from terms the audience knows, giving its listeners the context they need to understand the theme. It dispenses with details that fall outside the main theme. Making such a presentation requires discipline.

Good explanations are essential: Listeners must understand the situation and learn something new, and quality improvement teams must understand their themes.

They must know the real reason for making the improvement; it should not be just something they are told to do. The presentation process is a learning process for the quality improvement team. The presentation should not include nonessential explanations of what the team did. The transparencies or handouts for a QI story should be self-contained, conveying their message without the absolute need for a presenter. Also, draw the relationship between data and conclusion clearly. Only show thematically relevant information, for example, details of trial and error. That is indicative of a product-out orientation. The customer (the audience for the QI story) doesn't need to spend precious time and attention on nonessential issues. If you must show such details, leave them for step seven.

Good explanations have benefits that go beyond the involved team. They promote good improvement practices throughout the organization. If people from other teams can't understand the problem, they won't understand how the steps and tools might apply to their own themes. As Professor Shiba says, "One success story gives more effect than 100 lectures."

Finally, explanation of context is important for acknowledgment. How can team members be acknowledged if the presentation doesn't say who they are?

"Middle Ground" in Narrowness of Focus

Themes stated too broadly can cause a team to flounder, while themes stated too narrowly almost presuppose causes and, therefore, solutions. An overly broad theme might be stated as "reduce manufacturing losses." Such a theme puts few bounds on the scope of the data collection and analysis. Should manufacturing losses include those whose root cause lies in product design? Should the team be addressing losses over all plants? All production lines? All processes? A narrower theme statement like "reduce scrap and rework on the B line" constrains a problem to the point where the analysis and solution are within the ability of a well-trained team.

Very narrowly stated themes fundamentally take responsibility away from the team and give it back to their managers. "Reduce tubing scrap generation at point 3 on line B" presupposes (correctly or not) that someone has done data collection and causal analysis to determine that point 3 tubing scrap is one of the vital few rather than the trivial many. But if the team doesn't get to make that determination, they won't learn to do it. Such themes are throwbacks to the division of labor, that organizational structure in which one set of people does analysis and another set of people executes. A theme should take the middle ground of focus, neither so broad that the theme becomes diffuse or undoable, nor so narrow that it involves no creativity or skill development.

Schedule Included

A Gantt chart to show the planned schedule should be included. Leave space to compare the planned with the actual.

Diagnosing Step 2: Collect and Analyze Data

Data Collection Process Described

Quality improvement uses the scientific approach, which requires that work be reproducible and reviewable and, particularly, that the specifics of data collection be described: Where and when was data collected? How often was it sampled? What are the definitions of counting? Without such descriptions, "data" is not much different from opinion.

Data Collected and Stratified

You must collect and analyze data to understand the cause of the problem. For this there are three important techniques: stratification, graphing, and focus on deviation. For instance, graph the data in many ways—according to time sequence, type of product, location in the process, and so on. Then, stratify the data according to the 4Ws (who, when, where, what). At each point along the way, focus on deviation. For instance, suppose a given product costs too much to produce on average. You might graph the distribution of costs for making this product (for example, see Figure 10-1). In this way, you see the distribution more easily.

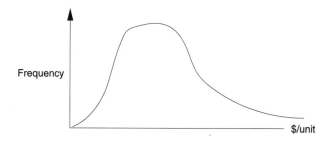

Figure 10-1. Graph

Next, stratify and graph the data in various ways (e.g., by plant that makes the product or by month in which the product is made) and continue to focus on the deviation (see Figure 10-2).

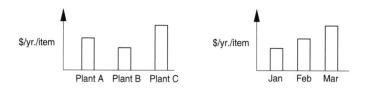

Figure 10-2. Graphs of Stratified Data

The graphs in these two figures show that average cost over the year didn't deviate significantly by plant but did deviate significantly at midyear, perhaps because of a midyear change in materials or process. Histograms, Pareto diagrams, scatter diagrams, and graphs are useful for highlighting deviation. A cause-and-effect diagram may be useful for considering possibilities. A Pareto diagram (see Figure 10-3 summarizing the relevant amount of problem by category) is almost always a part of step two of the 7 steps.

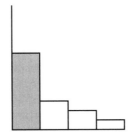

Figure 10-3. Pareto Diagram

Data Appropriate to Process

Did you collect data so that unusual factors don't cause misleading conclusions? Are an adequate number of samples taken? Are the samples taken far enough apart in time to represent independent samples (in the statistical sense)? Was anything unusual going on while the data was being taken (e.g., recovery from a fire)?

Appropriateness of data is a significant issue for improvement activities. Be careful about using data collected for process control purposes (data 3 in Figure 9-1), because it may not be appropriate for reactive improvement (data 2 in the figure). Definitions can be skewed, and errors in collecting data continue for long periods of time if no one actively tries to make use of it. Data taken before the improvement activity started is suspect—not necessarily wrong, just suspect.

Logic and Logical Consistency

There should always be a conclusion of the analysis. A flowchart of the logic leading to the conclusion is useful. In particular, make clear how conclusions follow from the facts. In cases where there were several rounds of data collection, for example, the QI story should visually show the logic by which the team progressed from one stage to the next, i.e., how it focused its investigation.

Standard Format of Tools

For the widespread diffusion of the 7 steps, use the tools in their standard forms. Here are some examples of standard forms to look for:

- Pareto diagram: no gaps between bars, a curve showing cumulative totals, scales on left and right, units labeled legibly, and conclusion written underneath.
- Ishikawa (cause-and-effect) diagram: effect is a why question, in a box on right, cause to effect flows left to right, major cause categories in boxes above and below horizontal line, and ideally, five levels of why.

Diagnosing Step 3: Analyze Causes

For managers, it is more important to diagnose the process than the solution of the theme. Senior managers should not ask too much of a beginning team; the team will improve through repeated use of the 7 steps.

Cause-and-Effect (Ishikawa) Diagram Derived from Pareto

For analysis of causes to be a teachable, diffusible process there must be an explicit process by which you can consider possible causes of a given problem. That process revolves around construction of a cause-and-effect diagram (or possibly a relations diagram). Without such a diagram, there is no way to know how well or poorly the team considered the possible causes of a problem. The effect of the cause-and-effect diagram should be related to an important bar in the Pareto diagram of step two (see Figure 10-4).

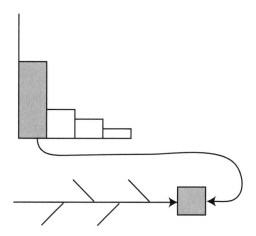

Figure 10-4. From Pareto to Cause-and-Effect Diagram

The head (right side) of the cause-and-effect diagram should be a result (effect), not a solution (cause). It usually takes the form of a why result, as in Figure 10-5.

Causes Investigated Thoroughly

The situation should be thoroughly investigated. Show the 4 Ms (man, machine, method, material), the 4 Ps (people, plant, policies, procedures), or other relevant categories (see Figure 10-5).

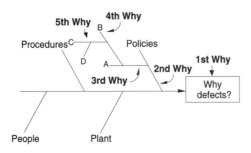

Figure 10-5. Cause-and-Effect Diagram

The cause-and-effect diagram reflects how thoroughly the team considered possible root causes for the problem. Superficial consideration usually yields a diagram with only one or two levels of branches. A thorough consideration, however, usually produces a diagram that traces back to potential root causes by answering "Why this result?" down five levels as shown in Table 10-2.

Table 10-2. "5 Whys" to Uncover Root Cause

Why?	Answer
Why defects?	Policies
Why policies?	A
Why A?	B
Why B?	C
Why C?	D

Managers can diagnose thoroughness just by seeing how many levels of branches the cause-and-effect diagram has. Having listed many possible causes on the diagram, you must find the root causes. This is done by eliminating improbable causes and by focusing on the causes that data show as most influential. Potential causes may be eliminated because they prove to be irrelevant, are disproven by prior knowledge, or are disproven through newly collected data. The remaining probable causes are hypotheses that should be tested against data to find the dominant root cause.

Understandable Conclusions

Make it clear how conclusions were reached and verified. This means that graphs should illustrate only one concept. Use separate graphs to illustrate separate concepts, each with its own conclusion at the bottom. The team may construct very complicated graphs while exploring the data. But the audience needs a simple, logically solid transition from the facts to a conclusion.

Diagnosing Step 4: Plan and Implement Solution

Solution that Reverses the Root Cause

Steps one through three are designed to make planning the solution straightforward. If the root cause has been found, the solution should be clear—reverse the root cause.

It is tempting to solve problems by redesigning the entire system. That approach is dangerous, however, for the team may not know why the rest of the process was designed the way it was. Redesigning the process, therefore, creates the risk of introducing new problems. It is safer to design very local solutions, sharply focused on eliminating the root cause, while leaving most of the system intact.

However, there may be several ways to reverse the root cause. The team should consider alternative methods and pick the solution that removes the root cause quickly for little cost.

Solutions Consistent with Causal Analysis

Surprisingly, teams often identify a major problem area, find the root cause, and then implement solutions that don't address the root cause, perhaps because of preconceived notions about the solutions.

In some cases, the team may think that the solution to the most important root cause is too difficult or beyond its authority to implement. In such cases, it makes sense to choose the root cause next in importance, gearing the solution toward that. Still, however, the most important root cause and its potential solution should be reported to the appropriate part of the organization.

Don't Try to Fix Everything at Once

Causal analysis may reveal many weaknesses of the present processes; fixing only the largest item on the Pareto chart is fine. Getting through the cycle does the following:

- Brings quick improvement to the organization
- Gets quick recognition and accomplishment for the team
- Brings analysis and better planning to the next PDCA cycle

This is continuous improvement, not only of performance but, more important, of improvement skills.

Also, if more than one change at a time is made, understanding the effects of each change may be difficult.

Solution Implementation Explained to the Audience

If other teams are to learn from an example of quality improvement and apply the knowledge to their own situations, they must be able to understand how the problem was solved. Diagrams and graphics are helpful.

Implementation Facts Shown

As with data collection, a conclusion statement like "we implemented our solution" is little better than opinion unless accompanied by verifiable facts. The standard format for presentation of facts about implementation is a matrix as shown in Table 10-3.

Use the following important checkpoints when implementing a solution:

- Were the people who will use the solution involved in planning the solution?
- Was there a pilot test of the solution?
- Was quick feedback obtained?
- Do undesirable side effects outweigh the advantages of the proposed solution?

Table 10-3. A Matrix of Implementation Facts

	Task	Who	When	Where	What	How
1						
2						
3						
4						
5						
6						

Management Acceptance of Solution

If a team has proposed a solution and its managers have accepted it, implementation becomes a responsibility of the managers as well as the team. If an accepted solution hasn't been implemented, senior management must take up the matter later with the team's supervisors or managers.

Diagnosing Step 5: Evaluate Effects

Resisting Temptation to Advance to Next Topic

The term *solution* connotes an ending point, which creates the temptation to turn to another topic. But a closer look at the facts suggests otherwise. Do you know the problem is solved? What have you done to ensure that it stays solved? Have you extracted the maximum amount of learning and improvement benefit from the work done thus far? The following steps should be taken after a "solution."

Confirmation of Improvement

Having proposed and implemented a solution (step four), you must find out if the solution actually solved the problem. A graph showing the decrease in defects over time indicates improvement. Before-and-after Pareto diagrams confirm actual reversal of the root cause, as in Figure 10-6, where an improvement has clearly been made to problem A.

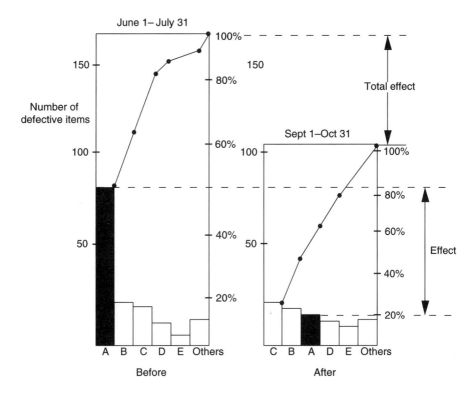

Conclusion: **Problem A has been reduced to less than one-quarter of its previous value; overall defects have been reduced 40 percent.**

Figure 10-6. Before-and-After Pareto Diagrams

Evaluation of Consequent Effects

Do not evaluate only the direct effects of the solution. More important, evaluate the consequent effects, such as more satisfied customers or increased staff morale. The process of selecting a quality improvement theme is based on the assumption that solving the specific problem would have consequent effects; the team will be frustrated if these effects are not noted.

Emphasis on Improvement Process

Improvement work is more like an investment than an expense: sometimes it pays off over time rather than immediately and perhaps non-financially, e.g., through the increase of problem-solving skills throughout the organization. Therefore, diagnosis should focus on following good practice as the path to good results. Teams that jump to solutions without defining a problem or collecting or analyzing data do not improve their problem-solving skills because they cannot identify and reuse a repeatable process. Even if the solution is very good, without due process, it is difficult to learn from the example, leaving good solutions in the province of genius and inspiration rather than making them easily accessible to anyone.

Diagnosing Step 6: Standardize Solution

Facts of Standardization

Standardization goes well beyond getting everyone to agree to do things in a certain way. To make clear a standard solution to the audience that the solution has been standardized, the presentation must give the facts about what creates and maintains the new way of doing things. Specifically, it should answer the following questions:

- What manual or document describes the new procedure?
- Who trains people?
- How often do people meet to review?
- What happens to minutes of review meetings?
- Who is in charge of scheduling meetings?
- What is the standard reporting for the new procedures, and to whom do reports go, and for what action?

Acid Test: If the People Go, Do the Procedures Stay?

An improvement must endure beyond the people who created it. One helpful heuristic for seeing whether something is standardized is to imagine what would happen if a key person got sick or promoted. Would the new procedures still be followed? Are there sufficient materials or knowledge in place for a newcomer to learn? What if two or three people got sick or left—will the system survive?

Process to Detect Future Problems

Does the improved process include check and act steps so that corrective action can be initiated if the process slips out of alignment or doesn't work as well as expected?

Diagnosing Step 7: Reflect on Process (and Next Problem)

A Focus on Most Important Lessons Learned

The reflection step allows the team to do self-diagnosis, with the same criteria senior managers use for diagnosis. The senior manager assesses the reflection step by checking the following:

- What were the difficulties during process, steps, and use of tools; does the team clearly understand the difficulties or not?

- Do team members clearly understand what they have learned and what the benefit was?
- Does the team understand what part of its process it is going to improve in the next improvement effort?
- Did the team leader keep the team motivated?
- Did the facilitator teach the 7 steps and the 7 QC tools?

Even if the team did a poor job on steps one through six, it may learn enough through step seven to do a better job next time.

10.3 CASE STUDY FOR DIAGNOSIS OF THE 7 STEPS

Read the following case study to practice the diagnostic process just described.[4] Construct a 7 steps diagnostic matrix as shown in Table 10-1. Read the case study and note, step-by-step, its strengths and weaknesses. Then, highlight the vital few strengths and weaknesses (remember the 70/30 rule). A filled-out matrix follows the case study (Table 10-4).

Improvement teams at Analog Devices have specific members, chosen according to the nature of the problem being solved and usually cross-functional. Members are requested, but not required, to participate and can be anyone with insight into the problem. Members remain on the team throughout the problem-solving cycle. Teams often choose a fanciful name (in this case, the Errorbusters, since they were to "bust" errors in wafer fab). [See Slide 10-1.] Teams sometimes have buttons, T-shirts, and other articles printed with their team's logo.

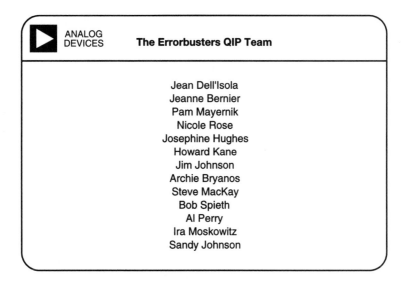

Slide 10-1

Step 1: Select Theme

Each improvement team at Analog has a written theme, with a specific, measurable goal, a metric, and a timeframe by which it intends to reach its goal. In this theme, the goal is to "reduce occurrences of incorrectly processed wafers in the photo area by a factor of two," the metric is "misprocessed wafers per million processed," and the time frame is nine months. [See Slide 10-2.] Note that the team avoided the use of the word errors, which suggests that human error is the cause of the problem. Instead, it used "incorrectly processed wafers."

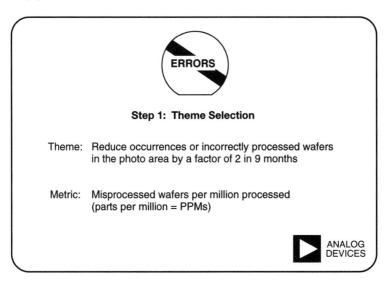

Slide 10-2

Teams are often asked to try to verify why their theme is important, so they have a better understanding and have a feeling for its importance to the company. This team showed, with a Pareto diagram, that of all the areas in the wafer fab, the photo room had the highest incidence of incorrectly processed wafers. [See Slide 10-3.] Since this affected yield and thus cost, the team demonstrated the photo room was the right theme to work on.

Step 2: Collect and Analyze Data

When the team first began to collect data, it found the existing forms used to report mistakes in wafer fab were not useful. Moreover, operators were reluctant to provide information out of fear the data would be used against them. The forms were traditionally completed by their immediate supervisor. As can be seen on this actual form [recopied for clarity on Slide 10-4 on page 166], the operator stated that the form is unfair and intimidating; the engineer's suggestion was to just "follow the spec."

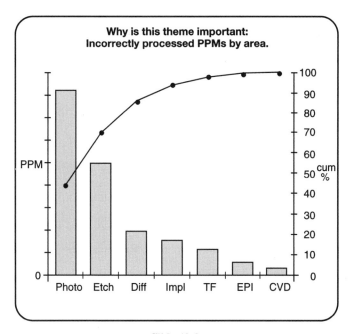

Slide 10-3

The team decided to collect its own data and make the form more useful and friendly. [See Slide 10-5 on page 167.] In addition, it obtained a commitment from management that errors would not be held against operators unless the error rate was excessive. When filling out the new form, an operator on the team sat down with the other operators involved in the incident, discussed the incident, and jointly wrote comments. The form was then sent directly and in confidence to the production manager (that is, around the direct supervisor), so the operators would not have to fear recrimination for their comments.

With data from their new forms successfully coming in, the team was able to focus on leading types of problems. One cut of the data [Slide 10-6 on page 168] shows the team found that wafers getting on the wrong track at the coat step and wafers receiving incorrect alignment at the align step were leading causes of incorrectly processed wafers in the room. The team moved on to step three.

Step 3: Analyze Causes

Slide 10-7 on page 169 shows one of the early Ishikawa, or cause-and-effect, diagrams the team created to determine the root cause of incorrectly processed wafers during the coat and align steps. Later diagrams focused on the people, investigating why too many machines were run at once, and on the environment, investigating why there was a lack of space.

Date: 12-12-88

Product Type: C841, C846,   Lot Number(s):   5685, 5994
    A848, A568 (CB's)   6031, 5683

Process: Step: M-NCONT   Quantity Affected: 10, 10, 10, 10

Supervisor: J. R.   Originator: J. R.

Operator(s)   9352   Date
Shift: 3rd   Misprocessed: 12-9-88

Disposition: Waived: ___ Reworked: ✓ Rejected: ___ MRB: ___

Nature and Results of Misprocess:

These lots were passed through pre-etch inspection with no

pattern due to a developer problem.

Supervisor's Corrective Action to Avoid Future Misprocessing:

Operator will be contacted.

Operator Comments:

From now on I'll have the engineer check CB lots. I do not want to sign

this form because the lots could be reworked. If they were scrapped —

that's different. Should allow for human error which can be reworked —

I don't think it's fair. This is very intimidating.

Engineering Recommendation:

Follow the spec . . . please!

Sign Off

Area Supervisor: J. R.   Operator: _____

Area Engineer: P. M.   Production
    Manager: _____
Engineering
Manager: _____

Slide 10-4

After further discussion and data collection, the team agreed on the root causes shown in Slide 10-8 on page 169, all dealing with either poor room setup and organ-

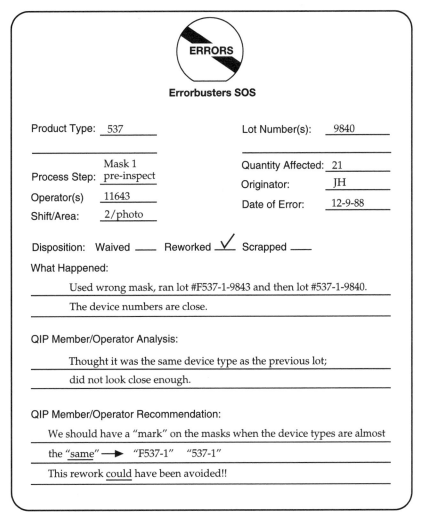

Slide 10-5

ization or poor task assignment. The team verified these conclusions by surveying all operators in the room.

Step 4: Plan and Implement Solution

The team moved on to step four, solution planning and implementation, as shown in Slide 10-9 on page 170. In their solution, the team borrowed concepts from just-in-time (JIT) methodologies, focusing on the use of kanbans to address the root causes

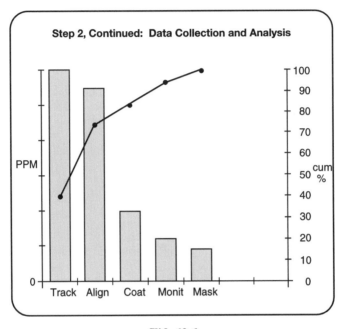

Slide 10-6

found in step three. The team also assigned responsibilities for each aspect of the implementation, and a timeframe for completion (not shown).

Step 5: Evaluate Effects

Slide 10-10 on page 171 shows the team's evaluation of effects.

The team was formed in March 1989, and implemented its solution during August 1989. Two special cases of incorrectly processed wafers were not related to the root causes at hand, as shown by the peaks at July and December of 1989 and February 1990. However, the team continued to implement and improve its solution, driving down the rate of incorrectly processed wafers until the problem virtually disappeared by March 1990.

As shown in Slide 10-11 on page 171, the room also reaped benefits from JIT methods in the form of queue time reduction.

Step 6: Standardize Solutions

The team recognized that the use of the JIT principles could decay over time unless the team performed step six—standardization. As shown in Slide 10-12 on page 172, the team instituted JIT meetings every shift to discuss problems or improvements for the system, with minutes of these meetings published daily.

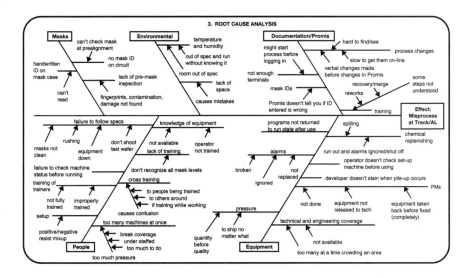

Slide 10-7

It also handed over the system to the supervisors and operators in the room to run, and agreed to meet only once per month as the Errorbusters to monitor progress and ensure that the gains were being held.

Step 7: Reflect on Process (and Next Problem)

In step seven, the team agreed that the main thing it did incorrectly was to focus on too many Pareto items during step two and, thus, on too many root causes in step three. [See Slide 10-13 on page 172.] Had it focused more closely when taking data, it would have solved the root causes one at a time and would have moved faster because its attention would not have been spread too thin. The team also decided to attack the

```
                     3. ROOT CAUSES

Work space too tight              Sharing of tracking, loading, etc.

Coater had too many tasks         Rushing

Incoming work piled up            Masks/work piled up

Lack of clear responsibility
```

Slide 10-8

---

4. PLANNING AND IMPLEMENTING SOLUTION
Kanbans

- "KANBAN" (signal)
  - squares with labels (bake, coat, develop) — OR —
  - racks numbered (inspect)

- Chain of steps (bake, coat, align, develop, inspect) analyzed for capacities, throughput, bottlenecks

- Quantities of kanbans chosen for each station

- "Incoming" racks moved out of room; coater controls incoming work via kanbans

- Coat, develop tracks:
  - "IN" kanbans: Full boxes waiting to start
  - "OUT" kanbans: Empty boxes waiting for wafers

- "Drybox" kanbans for align (coated lots)

- **Everything in room assigned a space**
  - taped areas for work being logged in to terminals
  - taped areas for tech tool boxes
  - taped areas for empty boxes waiting for wafers

Slide 10-9

next largest bar in the Pareto created during step one and, thus, work on incorrectly processed wafers in the etch room.

Sample Diagnosis of the Errorbusters QI Story

The matrix in Table 10-4 on page 173 shows notes that a manager might have taken while observing a 7 steps QI story presentation. The manager noted, step-by-step, the strong and weak aspects of the presentation. The "vital few" are highlighted. Such notes will provide good preparation for a diagnostic statement at the end of the presentation, in which the manager can highlight strong points of the presentation and also key weaknesses.

Many groups ask why they must follow the 7 steps closely. The diagnostic matrix suggests an answer to this question. Assume that the team being diagnosed in this case, like most, was well intentioned and serious about its improvement efforts. Assume the team followed the 7 steps to the extent that members understood it. From this perspective consider the diagnostic comments in the matrix.

- Because the team did not know or follow the 7 steps completely, it did not get as good tangible and standardized improvement as it might have. Improvement skill is not automatic; it must be developed through practice and emulation of past successful methods. Even a well-intentioned, thoughtful team is unlikely to achieve excellent results with ad hoc methods.

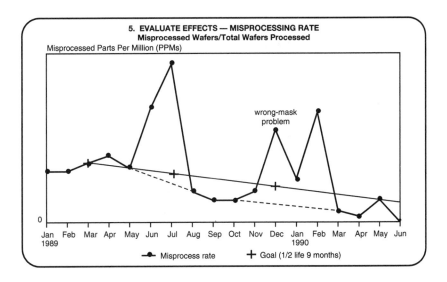

Slide 10-10

- Even partial use of the 7 steps produced some useful results. However new a team is to the process, using it will provide insight into its value and also produce some good results.
- In diagnosing a 7 steps QI story, management must be careful to provide the necessary amount of encouragement for the team's level of expertise with the 7 steps and to minimize criticism.

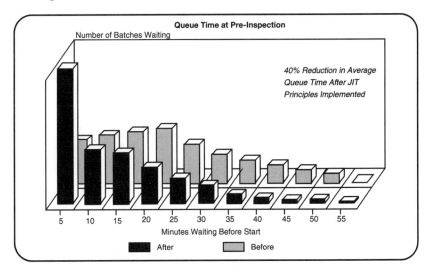

Slide 10-11

6. STANDARDIZING THE PROCESS

- JIT meetings held during each shift.

- JIT minutes published daily.

- Supervisors and operators given ownership for improvements.

- Errorbusters meet once/month to monitor misprocesses.

Slide 10-12

7. REVIEW PROCESS AND PLAN FUTURE WORK

- **Review of Process:**

  Team focused on too many Pareto items at the same time during Step 2. If team had focused on problems one at a time, the solution of each one would have been faster.

- **Future Work:**

  Attack next largest bar on Pareto of occurrences of incorrectly processed lots (the etch room).

Slide 10-13

Table 10-4. Errorbusters QI Story Diagnostic Matrix

Step	Strengths	Weaknesses
0.		• All the steps are not numbered with 7 steps number.
1. Select theme	• A weakness theme is used • The process steps are shown • The importance of working on a theme in the photo area is shown	• It would have been better to use specific figures, e.g., decrease from 2500 ppm to 1250 ppm.
2. Collect data	• **The decision to collect their own data is the best point of this QI Story [you want to collect your own data and the diagnosing manager should make a point of this].** • A Pareto diagram is used.	• The first slides of step two are not numbered. • The Pareto diagram in slide 8 has spaces between its bars and the cumulative distribution curve is not to the same scale as the bars.
3. Analyze causes	• An Ishikawa diagram is used • The head of the Ishikawa diagram is connected to the bars of the Pareto diagram in step two. • There are five levels of "why?" at many points in the Ishikawa diagram.	• Only one Ishikawa diagram is used for two characteristics (alignment and tracking); there should be a separate Ishikawa diagram for each. • The important root causes are not circled in the Ishikawa diagram. • **There was not focus on a single root cause.**
4. Plan and implement solution	• The team showed knowledge of the Kanbans.	• Too many solutions are attempted simultaneously. • It is not shown how the solutions are logically tied to the root causes.
5. Evaluate effects	• A run chart is included showing improvement.	• The run chart is not convincing. • "Before" and "after" Pareto diagrams are not shown. • A pilot test may not have been run.
6. Standardize solution	• The team has worked hard to standardize the improvement. • They have used nice graphics to show the various parts of the solution.	• The solutions are based on changing human behavior and will be hard to maintain.
7. Reflect on process and next problem	• **The team understood that it was not focused enough.**	

10.4 RUN PDCA AND DEVELOP SKILL

Sometimes, when you undertake an improvement effort you will get a poor or incomplete result. In such cases, you must simply try again. The concept of PDCA provides for such repetition.

PDCA teaches you to start again from step one of the 7 steps rather than going back to redo the last few steps of the previous PDCA cycle. You must build on what you did and learned during the previous iteration of the 7 steps. If during the previous iteration of the 7 steps the theme has not been completely addressed, the facts of the situation will lead to the same theme (from a new perspective) for the next iteration.

If the theme has been completely addressed, the facts will lead to the next most prominent and tractable theme to address.

In any case, iteration of the 7 steps or PDCA cycle will build a variety of skills: insight into the problem area, skill with the 7 steps improvement method, skill in working as a team, and skill at diagnosing the 7 steps process.

Table 10-5. Relationship of PDCA to the 7 Steps and 7 QC Tools

7 Steps	7 QC Tools	PDCA
1. Select theme 2. Collect data 3. Analyze causes	Checksheet, graph, Pareto diagram, histogram, scattergram, cause and effect diagram.	Plan
4. Plan and implement solutions		Do
5. Evaluate effects.	Checksheet, graph, Pareto diagram, histogram, scattergram, cause and effect diagram, control chart.	Check
6. Standardize solutions 7. Reflect on process		Act

Table 10-5 adds a column to Table 9-3, showing the relationship of PDCA to the 7 steps and the 7 QC tools.

NOTES

1. See pages 442–444 for more on the benefits of a QI story presentation system.

2. See, for example, [39, 91].

3. Defined on page 288.

4. The case study was provided by Ira Moskowitz, then Production Manager, Wilmington Wafer-fab, Analog Devices.

11

Process Management Mobilization Case Study—Teradyne

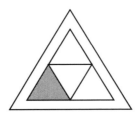

11.1 INTRODUCTION TO THE TERADYNE MOBILIZATION STORY

We use the case study of Teradyne to illustrate the mobilization and use over a number of years of several methods presented in this book.[1] Teradyne is a highly regarded $1.3 billion firm (in 1999) that manufactures semiconductor test equipment and operates in the U.S., Europe, and Asia. It is one of the founding members of the Center for Quality of Management.

The Teradyne mobilization began its current era of implementation at the beginning of the 1990s while Alex d'Arbeloff was CEO. That mobilization has continued under the current leadership of CEO George Chamilard.

Without apology, Teradyne calls its business improvement activities TQM, and in 1990, a TQM office was set up under the Companywide Quality Council (CQC).[2] Line manager Mike Bradley was installed as the first leader of this tiny office, expecting to serve for up to a couple of years and then rotate back to another line management assignment.[3] Throughout the Teradyne mobilization, John Petrolini, a contributor to this book, has served as corporate TQM manager, the key permanent position in the corporate TQM office. He has provided us with his perspective on the Teradyne mobilization story.

We will use various aspects of the Teradyne mobilization story at different times in the evolution of their mobilization to illustrate points throughout the book. In fact, this first instance from the Teradyne story is out of order and chronologically follows the story of the Teradyne initiation strategy in Chapter 20. We list the chronological order in which to read the whole story in Chapter 26, page 578.

11.2 INTRODUCTION OF THE 7 STEPS

By October 1990,[4] CEO d'Arbeloff and the Teradyne top management team decided that TQM would initially encompass the 7 steps and market-in, as implemented by quality improvement teams (which Teradyne calls QITs as we will also for this case study). Their version of TQM would address three goals: increase in market share, reduction in cost, and reduction in cycle time (see Figure 11-1). Each division business plan for the year had to address these issues with action plans.[5]

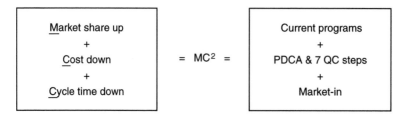

Figure 11-1. Teradyne's 1991 Goals and TQM Initiatives

The Teradyne 7 steps training did not begin with formal courses for a lot of teams. Rather, at workshops (see example agenda in Figure 11-2), 30 to 60 *senior* managers were each given a page or two sketching the 7 steps and told to apply the method personally to some business problem or at least retrofit a prior problem into the 7 steps outline. In some cases, they tried to do this by themselves, and in other cases they involved other people in a team. In either case, they attempted to work on real problems and, regardless of their limited knowledge about the 7 steps method, carried out the improvement project.

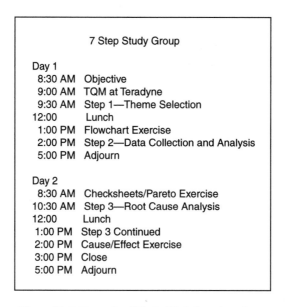

Figure 11-2. Example of Early Workshop Agenda

Then another set of follow-up workshops was held at which the managers reported in groups of 24 on their 7 steps efforts. From these post-attempt workshops, Teradyne discovered what each step meant, for instance, that step 1 should produce a theme that does not include a solution or an anticipated cause and that is measurable. These insights were organized on flipcharts during the workshop. From this input the TQM office drafted Teradyne's first 7 Steps Manual.

The content of the closing section of day two on the workshop agenda (Figure 11-2) is informative. It confirmed that all participants had the follow-up workshop on their calendar at which they would learn more, including about steps four through seven, from each other. It also included action items such as distributing the guidelines developed during the two days. Finally, it included a strengths and weaknesses analysis of the two-day workshop to improve those days for other groups' senior managers and to make the follow-up workshop more effective.

The above is a typical approach for Teradyne for learning something new. They find out a little bit about it, and then senior people try it. Some things work and some things don't. However, when something doesn't work, the person trying it does something to get by the obstacle. Some of these work-arounds may not be very good ideas and have no lasting value. However, other work-arounds turn out to have a lot of insight in them and become part of the documented guidelines for how to operate the method or process.[6]

At this point Teradyne scheduled a series of "TQM Day" sessions for June 10–13, 1991, during which a number of 7 steps QITs were to be ready to report. Scheduling the day for presentation of the results was in keeping with the "deadline effect" concept that Shoji Shiba promoted throughout the CQM—a behavior changing device that makes scheduling a public presentation or other immovable (and highly embarrassing to miss) deadline part of planning any activity to be accomplished—to strongly motivate completion of the task.

11.3 EXPERIENCE USING THE 7 STEPS

Many 7 steps QITs were initiated and a number of them had reasonably good results. At the first TQM Day in June, the 30 to 35 teams that had finished one cycle through the 7 steps presented their use of the 7 steps process and their process improvement results. A total of nearly 200 teams had been initiated by that time, or participation of about 14 percent of the workforce. Superficially, mobilization appeared to be going well.

However, Bradley and Petrolini reported some problems [41].[7]

Management was concerned ... that the deadline effect of TQM Days had artificially inflated the number of QITs completing their work in May and June, and that a dramatic drop-off in QIT activity would follow. To determine whether this was the case, the TQM Office ... coordinated some data-gathering on teams active in the company's [then] five major operating groups. They found evidence of slow progress. Moreover, a sharp drop-off was seen in QIT completions in July [immediately after the TQM Day].

Analysis showed that the average time being spent on each step in the 7 step process was high. . . . Anecdotal evidence from . . . teams also suggested that many were "bogging down."

11.4 IMPROVING MOBILIZATION

To address these problems, in August 1991, the CQC and division TQM managers organized themselves into what was effectively another 7 steps QIT.

Step 1. They picked the theme "What are the problems slowing QIT progress?"—not a particularly well-stated theme according to the guidelines of Chapters 9 and 10, but they were learning, too.

Step 2. The company's TQM managers collected data by posing the theme question to team leaders, team sponsors, and team members, as well as the division TQM managers themselves. They used the LP method (see Chapter 13, page 217) to group, organize, and summarize the answers to the question. Then, the interviewees were asked to vote on which elements of the summary were most important, with the following three items being the top vote-getters:

1. QIT sponsors and leaders are not performing their roles . . . the team sponsor is not reviewing the QIT's work.
2. QIT work is not done on time . . . daily work disrupts planned QIT work.
3. We are trying to do too much . . . themes are too broad.

Step 3. Three managers used interviews of QIT members to gather more data on the slow pace of progress, classified the answers into a few categories, and stratified the data into Pareto diagrams. They also used an Ishikawa diagram to analyze the interrelations among the various factors.[8] The analysis led to three proposed root causes for the slow pace of QIT work:

- Teradyne had no process for managing QIT teams.
- It had weak metrics for managing QIT progress.
- There was no clear linkage of QIT work to business goals.

The main team focused on the first root cause, and separate teams were established to work on the second and third root causes.

Step 4. To eliminate the root cause (no process for managing teams), the company's TQM managers in the fourth quarter of 1991 conducted a series of workshops on how to manage teams, in which participants shared their own experiences on the problems of and solutions to managing teams. The participants were primarily team sponsors and included many of the company's most experienced managers. The workshops were organized around investigation of a model QIT cycle as shown in Figure 11-3 [41, p. 12]. Eight experimental workshops were held in different Teradyne locations. Each participant was asked to bring to the workshop one problem encountered in each phase of the model with a case study of how he or she *solved* one of the three problems. At the workshop, corporate and divisional managers led the participants through a modified version of the LP method to understand and capture each group's understanding of the key weaknesses in each phase of the QIT process model. From this understanding, each workshop decided on its own standards that participating managers could use in managing their own teams. Each workshop after the first could critique and build on the insights of the previous workshops—a mini-PDCA improvement process.

Phase I	Phase II	Phase III
- QIT formation - Theme selection - Registration with GQC - Leader selection - Facilitator - Schedule/deadline	- Meetings discipline - Attendence - Methods & tools - Progress reporting - Participation - Technical expertise - Solution standardization - Roadblocks	- Reflection - QI reporting - Strengths/ weaknesses - Next cycle - Recognize/reward - Presentations - Process diagnosis

Figure 11-3. Three Phases of the QIT Process

Next, a standardized workshop and draft manual were developed to teach the lessons from the experimental workshops. The initial version of the manual was drafted in December 1991 and January 1992.

It included 128 points to be implemented in team management—from selecting a leader who has experience in the 7 steps process to using a standard format for reviewing the team's work with the sponsor at the completion of each step. Most of the points were originally provided by participants in the experimental workshops [41, p. 12].

Starting in February 1992, the standardized workshop was taught to managers of QITs.

Step 5. Analysis of numbers and rates of QIT completion, as well as feedback from team sponsors, leaders, and members indicated that the manual and workshop on managing teams substantially helped teams complete 7 steps projects faster and on time.

Step 6. The Managing Teams manual and the Managing Teams workshop were the primary tools at Teradyne for standardizing their improved process in managing 7 steps QITs.

In addition, this manual was made available to CQM member companies [56] and became the standard method for managing teams in many organizations throughout the CQM—an example of societal networking. This CQM-wide example of a societal network was built on top of the two internal examples of societal networking within Teradyne: the senior managers sharing their experiences of initial use of the 7 steps which resulted in the Teradyne 7 steps process, and the experimental workshops through which managers shared insights about managing teams and which resulted in the Teradyne team management process.

Step 7. Bradley and Petrolini's paper includes the following reflection on Teradyne's process of improving the way it managed 7 steps QITs [41, pp. 16–17]:

- The participants uncovered weaknesses early and began to apply this new knowledge immediately.
- The experimental workshops amounted to a series of rapid spins of the PDCA cycle, allowing more rapid development of a successful team management process, workshop, and manual than could have been accomplished with traditional methods.
- The team achieved good cross-divisional input through the experimental workshop process and the participation of TQM managers from all divisions.
- The workshop process helped team leaders and sponsors understand the ways in which management of QITs should utilize the skills the leaders have developed from managing other kinds of projects, whether or not those other projects have been called TQM.

Other Key Results

In addition to teaching more constructive involvement of team sponsors and managers in QIT efforts, through the Managing Teams manual and standard workshop, Teradyne made two other key changes relating to QIT mobilization.

First, going forward, QITs at Teradyne needed to have a problem area that was strongly connected to a significant business problem—not so hard as to be impossible and discouraging, but important enough so that the QIT work can compete effectively against other "real work" in the constant struggle of having too much to do and not enough time to do it in. Managers don't give much time to activities that don't clearly help them meet their business goals. In Chapters 9 and 10, we recommended that QIT members just being introduced to the 7 steps choose a first problem that is not too hard. This advice must be balanced against having it still be a significant business issue. Such balance is possible.

Second, Teradyne adopted a set of metrics for its QIT mobilization process. This set included:

- Average time from start to finish of a QIT
- Percentage participation of employees on completed QITs
- Number of active teams
- Percentage of employees trained in the 7 steps and other tools

This may seem somewhat artificial, and some people might ask, "How can you produce high metrics scores that indicate results instead of numbers of teams being started?" Teradyne was already aware of this issue in 1991, and the Managing Teams manual and workshop for managers and the necessity of a connection to real work substantially address this concern. Each team is required to "register" with division management, which enables divisions to monitor improvement activity.[9] Furthermore, Teradyne's CEO and top management believe that the way their business operates will continue to improve through *repeated* application of 7 steps QITs to a large number of business problems. Also, management believes that skill is acquired through repetition (just as an athlete or performing artist might believe that his or her performance will continue to improve through repetition of certain exercises). Thus, the above metrics were intended to force repetition—senior management believes that ensuring repetitions of improvement projects will develop skill and lead to increased business performance.[10]

11.5 PROCESS DISCOVERY AND PROCESS CONTROL

Earlier in this part of the book we presented process discovery, process control, and reactive improvement using the 7 steps as the logical sequence. Teradyne, however, started with the 7 steps for reactive improvement.

Teradyne does not have an explicit separate discovery process. However, it insists that step one of the 7 steps include a flowchart or other high-level description of the process and include a statement of who the customers are, what they require, and so on. In other words, they include a form of process discovery in the 7 steps. After a while, Teradyne also broadened its initial focus on PDCA and the 7 steps (see Figure 11-1) to include SDCA and process control.[11]

There is an interesting pragmatic issue relating to Teradyne's initial focus on PDCA and 7 steps. When Shoji Shiba was working with Teradyne in the early days of their TQM program, he advised that improvement activity (PDCA) could be more motivational and of earlier practical use than SDCA activity (process documentation and control). Teradyne's experience bore out this insight. By focusing on improvement activity, the company developed an improvement culture and, as part of this activity, also documented its processes (in steps one and six of the 7 steps) and controlled them (by adding process control methods), thus initiating an SDCA activity to fit with the PDCA activity.

Many companies have started by focusing on process documentation (SDCA), which can become boring and result in a rejection reaction before employees get to improving their processes.

Basically, two possible common places to start are: standardizing processes first (SDCA), or first finding the weakness in a process and then fixing the process and standardizing on the fixed process. Companies have succeeded starting with SDCA (or ISO 9000, for example), and companies have succeeded starting with PDCA. However, the successful experience at Teradyne supports our impression from observing many companies that doing PDCA first tends to work better in practice.

NOTES

1. In fact, we learned some of the methods from Teradyne.
2. The CQC is the Teradyne top management forum for planning and guiding their mobilization efforts. We'll talk more about the CQC in Chapter 20 on page 419.

3. Mike was a successful line manager who had been responsible for one of the most successful products Teraydne ever launched. Since serving as leader of the TQM office, he has served in several other line management positions, including VP of Worldwide Sales, and today he is one of the top management of the company serving as chief financial officer and chief of other general and administrative functions.

4. The company was considerably smaller then.

5. Teradyne's TQM efforts and QIT activities built on the company's previous study and implementation of Crosby's methods. Teradyne changed vocabulary over time and let teams evolve how they worked rather than disbanding them.

6. John Petrolini has explained that Teradyne does *not* add *theories* for work-arounds to their documented guidelines. Only work-arounds that have worked well *in practice* and thus include rich experiential learning are added to documented guidelines.

7. The following paragraphs paraphrase extensively from the Bradley and Petrolini paper.

8. This analytic work is described in detail, with figures, on [41, pp. 10–11].

9. Every team registers with its division quality council, usually through the division TQM manager. The team's management sponsor will already have reviewed the team's intended area of work for alignment with division objectives, having the right mix of team members, etc., Teradyne has found this review to be "very helpful."

10. Teradyne also uses these metrics to monitor and diagnose their mobilization infrastructure, which will be discussed in Chapter 21 and Chapter 26.

11. SDCA activity is counted in the metrics mentioned in the previous section. Whether the participation is PDCA oriented or SDCA oriented, it is included in the participation percentage.

12

Planning Projects or Tasks

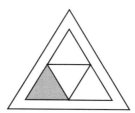

The preceding chapters, 7–11, described discovery, management, and improvement of existing processes. Chapters 13–14 will describe using proactive improvement methods to find new directions (for example, a new product and processes to produce it). This chapter deals with planning and executing tasks or projects that have not been done before and typically are one-time efforts. Such activity spans both ends of the WV Model as shown in Figure 12-1 and logically seems to fit here between the preceding chapters and the following chapters.

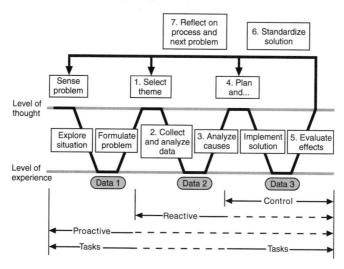

Figure 12-1. The WV Model

The primary tool described in this chapter for task or project planning and execution is the 9 steps method [52].

Note to readers: While this may be the logical location for this chapter, some readers may want a more complete understanding of proactive improvement before considering something between managing existing process and proactive improvement. If so, you might read chapters 13–14, and then return to read this chapter.

12.1 THE 9 STEPS COMPARED WITH THE 7 STEPS

The 7 steps is a standard method for improving performance of existing processes. It assumes previous experience with a process. Its Plan phase (of PDCA) goes as follows: in step one we select a theme (where there is weakness that needs improvement) for the existing process, in step two we collect data and analyze it, and in step three we hypothesize the root cause of the problem we are investigating which, if reversed, we believe will eliminate or substantially reduce the problem. This pattern is shown in the right column of Table 12-1.

Table 12-1. 9 Steps Compared with 7 Steps

PDCA	9 steps (project planning)	7 steps (reactive)
Plan	1. Describe project 2. Explore essentials/narrow focus 3. Establish metrics 4. Identify alternatives 5. Develop optimistic plan with obstacles and countermeasures	1. Select theme 2. Collect/analyze data 3. Analyze causes
Do	6. Develop, implement and monitor detailed plan	4. Plan/implement solution
Check	7. Evaluate results	5. Evaluate effects
Act	8. Standardize 9. Reflect	6. Standardize solution 7. Reflect

The 9 steps is a standard method for improving performance of new projects or tasks. It assumes little prior experience with a particular process. Thus, the 9 steps also start with deriving a plan for what must be done. The steps for deriving this plan are shown in the middle column (steps one through five) of Table 12-1—read these now. Where steps one through three of the seven steps investigate an existing process, steps one through five of the 9 steps plan a new project.

Also in the figure, both methods in their Do phase develop and execute a detailed implementation plan. They also have the same last three steps in common (Check and Act)—evaluate the results, standardize on what worked, and reflect on use of the method and what to do next.

The 7 steps assume repetition. Their goal is to prevent recurrence of problems already seen. Typically, problems are found relating to the 5 evils (defects, mistakes, delay, waste, accident/injury). When a defect or another of the 5 evils occurs, we seek to prevent the problem that *already happened* from happening again, using the 7 steps.

The 9 steps assume a new task or situation. Often, the situation is complex or uncertain. The goal in using the 9 steps is to avoid future problems that might occur during implementation of the task or project. The premise is that good planning will lead to better projects.

12.2 THE 9 STEPS MOBILIZATION AT TERADYNE

Chapter 11 described the beginning of Teradyne's mobilization of business improvement, focusing initially in 1990-91 on the 7 steps.

By the beginning of 1992, it was becoming clear at Teradyne that only having one tool—7 steps—was not enough. To some extent, they were having the problem that when the only tool is a hammer, everything begins to look like a nail. Also, people in engineering and marketing had been having a hard time seeing the relevance of the 7 steps in their areas, where projects were either long and collecting data quickly was hard or projects were seen as not being repetitive processes—where each new customer or development project requires unique handling.[1] Also, some teams in Teradyne were missing project due dates for a variety of different types of projects. Therefore, Teradyne sought a new tool perceived as better addressing processes like those in marketing and engineering that operate less consistently from one cycle to the next.

With Shoji Shiba's help, the tool Teradyne chose was the 9 steps for planning projects and tasks. There were two sets of reasons why they adopted the 9 steps.

First, the 9 steps were relevant to Teradyne's situation. The 9 steps, with its project and task orientation, seemed relevant to engineering and marketing, with their project and task orientation. Also, Teradyne was missing project dates on all sorts of projects throughout the company, and this often happened because a team hadn't anticipated potential problems. Thus, the 9 steps' emphasis on understanding potential obstacles and undertaking countermeasures to avoid the obstacles was relevant to Teradyne's situation.

Second, the 9 steps was another method (in addition to the 7 steps) that had specific steps and involved specific tools. Alex d'Arbeloff preferred methods that had explicit steps. John Petrolini's experience was that the powerful 7 QC tools didn't get significant use at Teradyne until they were presented to employees embedded in the 7 steps. The 7 management and planning tools were another set of powerful tools, relevant to task and project planning, that could be brought into use at Teradyne if embedded in a multistep process.

John Petrolini's perception is that Shoji Shiba and Teradyne were inventing much of the 9 steps as they were teaching it to the Teradyne people. In this sense, the roll-out of the 9 steps at Teradyne was parallel to the way the 7 steps were rolled out. They learned a little bit about the method, in this case from Shoji Shiba,[2] and they began to use it. In time they gathered the insights of managers, facilitators, and team members and created a manual and standard course for the 9 steps.

As use of the 9 steps spread in Teradyne, 9 steps activities were managed and monitored similarly to 7 steps activities. Teams finishing 9 steps projects presented their improvement stories to division management, which diagnosed the team's use of the 9 steps process using the 70/30 rule of 70 percent comments to reinforce and encourage good process practice and 30 percent mention of areas for improvement.[3] Nine steps activities were included in the overall QIT metrics of the number of active teams, average time from start to finish of a QIT, percentage participation of employees, and so on. Nine steps teams were sponsored and managed in the same way that Teradyne had learned to sponsor and manage 7 steps teams. By 1996–97, nearly 35 percent of Teradyne improvement teams were 9 steps teams.[4]

In time, the Teradyne developed a 9 steps manual [52] and course which were passed on to the CQM for sharing with other CQM member companies. John Petrolini and Shoji Shiba taught the first course to other CQM members interested in learning the method and how to teach the method. Once again we see an example of societal networking within a company (with Shoji Shiba bringing ideas from outside the company) to develop an improved method, followed by an example of societal networking where the newly codified method was passed on to other organizations.

12.3 A TERADYNE ILLUSTRATION OF THE 9 STEPS USE

John Petrolini, Teradyne's corporate TQM manager, provided us with a description of some of the details of the 9 steps method as used at Teradyne.[5] He includes an example of the use of the method, in early 1994, to plan and execute the annual TQM at Teradyne presentation/update to all employees. This 1994 example is part of the overall chronology of the Teradyne story which we are relating at various points throughout this book.

Step 1: Describe the project

As with a 7 steps theme, you want to state clearly in one sentence the objective of the project at hand. Teradyne's experience is that this statement should be positive and action oriented. An example is: *Deploy the TQM at Teradyne presentation to all employees by March 1, 1994.* This first statement is a generalization of the problem and may be revised as more is learned about the issue.

Step 2: Explore the essentials, and narrow the focus

Step 2 has two parts.

Step 2.1—Explore the essentials. The purpose of step 2.1 is to get a broader perspective of the project described in step one. You need to understand and grasp the essential issues, and confirm the real purpose of the project. To do this, you must *jump up*

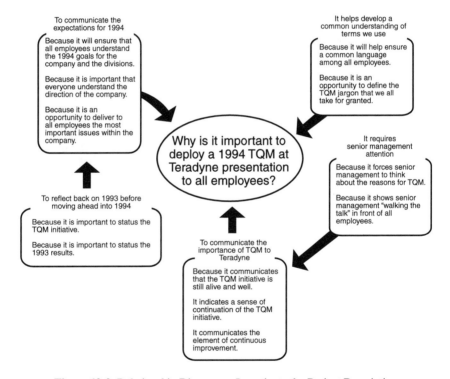

to see a bigger picture, using both language data and numeric data (see Figure 12-1).

The Teradyne team created the relationship diagram shown in Figure 12-2 to help them jump up and see the bigger picture. Relationship diagrams are one of the 7 management and planning tools for processing qualitative data (see page 172). It is a form of cause-and-effect diagram for use when loops can occur in the network of causes and effects.

Figure 12-2. Relationship Diagram to Investigate the Project Description

The Teradyne team followed the typical process for constructing a relationship diagram. The project description from step one was placed in the center of a large sheet of paper in a Why format. Then the team brainstormed answers to the question of why Teradyne must deploy a "TQM at Teradyne" presentation to all employees. The brainstormed answers were organized in a succession of cause-and-effect relationships.

After creating this diagram and studying it jointly to gain broader understanding of the stated project, the team concluded that *To communicate the importance of TQM to Teradyne* was the highest priority reason for addressing the stated project.

Jumping up is very important. Often the specification for a problem comes from above, and the team needs to find a point of view one level above the system it has to improve to ensure it is working on the right problem. Shoji Shiba emphasizes the importance of jumping up with a story of when he was a young consultant and was doing consulting work for a ship building company. The company had two businesses: building ships to a schedule, and repairing ships. Both of these functions were performed out of a single factory, as in the left of Figure 12-3.

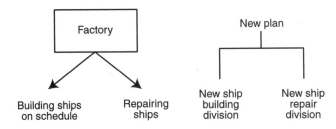

Figure 12-3. Alternative Approaches for a Ship Building Company

The CEO of the company told Shoji Shiba that they had decided to split the company into two divisions, each of which would handle one of the two businesses, as in the right of the figure. The CEO asked Shoji Shiba to analyze how many people would need to be employed in each of the new divisions. This analysis required forecasting the future business of the divisions, understanding the skills of the employees, and so on. Shoji Shiba first worked on a plan for the new repair division, and when done presented it to the company. No one, especially the CEO, paid any attention to his proposed plan. Therefore, Shoji Shiba studied the situation from a broader perspective, and he discovered that the company wanted to decide *whether* to split the company into two divisions or to continue to run the two businesses out of a single factory. The CEO had said they had decided to have two divisions, but this was not so. This early business experience drove home to Shoji Shiba the need to jump up to see the problem one level above the system and to grasp the essence of the problem.

Step 2.2—Narrow the focus. Having understood the problem, the Teradyne team needed to understand the proposed details of what they were undertaking, which detailed elements could be done relatively routinely, and key problems' locations.

To investigate the details, the Teradyne team started with the end points of their proposed project, with dates, as shown on the left side of Figure 12-4. Then, as shown on the right side of the figure, they filled in the substeps they felt they had to accomplish to reach the end point, again with desired dates. They felt they needed to analyze the strengths and weaknesses of the previous year's "TQM at Teradyne" presentation, determine the goals of the current year's presentation, determine the core message of

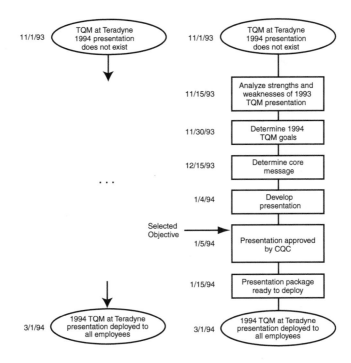

Figure 12-4. Understanding the Details of the Project

the presentation, develop the presentation, get the presentation approved by the company's top management (called the Companywide Quality Council, or CQC, when considering matters relating to TQM), and finally prepare the presentation package for deployment throughout the organization.

Some of these substeps were relatively straightforward, while one of the substeps (Presentation approved by CQC) seemed the most problematic. Therefore, Presentation approved by CQC was chosen as a more narrow focus for the project, completing step 2.2.

Step 3: Establish Metrics and Determine Constraints

In steps one and two, the overall project was described and a specific objective was chosen. The team's next step was to establish metrics by which they could tell if they accomplished their objective or not and to make explicit to themselves any other constraints the team and project would have to live within.

Step 3.1—Establish Metrics. At Teradyne, teams looked at four areas to help themselves consider what appropriate results metrics might be: Quality, Cost, and Delivery (as described in Chapter 7), and Amount. In the case of the selected objective, Presentation approved by CQC, it made sense to the team to develop metrics for two of these four categories, as shown in Table 12-2.[6]

Table 12-2. Metrics for the Presentation approved by CQC Objective

	Metric	Value
Quality	Consensus of senior management	At least 80 percent with core message and package
Cost		
Delivery	Number of days beyond 1/5 before review is approved	Plus or minus one day
Amount		

Step 3.2—Determine Constraints. The specific objective often is not the only goal a team must work toward. Frequently, a team also must live within (or desires to live within) other constraints.

At Teradyne, teams check whether there is a due date or time frame that they must live within, and they also find it useful to review the 4Ms (manpower, machine, method, material) or the 4Ws (who, when, where, what) for other possible constraints.

In this particular case, the Teradyne team developed the additional constraints shown in Table 12-3. As per Figure 12-4, the team desired CQC approval by 1/5/94. The team was also aware that the people available to develop the presentation package were themselves (the divisional TQM managers and the couple of people in the corporate TQM office). The team also wanted the presentation to be delivered by senior managers (see Methods in the table), because they believed in the importance of senior management leading by example or "walking the talk." They wanted the presentation process to illustrate the use of PDCA, by looking back at the weaknesses from the previous years and fixing them.

Table 12-3. Constraints for the Teradyne Project

Time frame	Approved by 1/5/94
Manpower	TQM Managers and TQM Office primarily
Methods	Delivered by senior managers Include reflection and then a look forward Communicate/exhibit PDCA being user

Step 4: Identify Possible Alternatives and Select the Best Alternative

Step four involves identifying alternative approaches of accomplishing the milestones and objectives and selecting the best alternatives for each.

In this step, the Teradyne team reviewed the milestones from step two (see the right side of Figure 12-4) and considered different approaches that could be used to accomplish each. Their lists of alternatives are shown in Table 12-4.

Only one alternative for determining 1994 TQM Goals existed; since this was the job of the CQC, only they could do it.

Table 12-4. Alternative Approaches to Meeting the Milestones

Analyze strengths/weaknesses of 1993 TQM Presentation
0   - Form subcomittee to analyze
7   - TQM office to analyze *
Determine 1994 TQM goals
7   - CQC to finalize at 12/3 meeting *
Determine core message
2   - Ask Alex to formulate message
5   - TQM office gains CQC consensus *
0   - TQM office formulates
Develop presentation
2   - Ask Alex to develop
5   - TQM office gains CQC consensus *
Presentation approved
0   - TQM office conducts one on ones
0   - TQM office presents at CQC meeting
7   - TQM office briefs each individual and then presents at CQC *
* indicates selected alternative

For the other milestones leading to presentation approval by the CQC, the team had alternatives. For instance, for the first milestone, a subcommittee could have been formed to analyze the strengths and weaknesses of the 1993 TQM presentation, or the TQM office personnel could do it. The team unanimously (7-0) believed the latter approach was better and selected it (indicated by the asterisk). For the third and fourth milestones, some members of the team believed that it would be best for the core message and the presentation to come from CEO Alex d'Arbeloff; however, a majority of the team felt that having the TQM office work to gain consensus would be more constructive in the long run. For the last milestone, again unanimity decided the best approach—the TQM office would brief people individually (to be able to answer questions and get feedback) and then would brief the entire CQC about the presentation at the CQC meeting.

Step 5: Develop an Optimistic Plan with Obstacles and Countermeasures

Step 5.1—Develop an Optimistic Plan. In step four, more specific approaches were selected for the milestones developed in step 2.2. This transformation of milestones to specific tasks is shown in Figure 12-5.

Next, the team needed to make this detailed set of specific tasks—this plan—be optimistic (aggressive). They decided on optimistic dates for the specific tasks on the right side of the figure. By creating an optimistic plan (but not impossibly optimistic) for achieving the milestones, the team in fact had a better chance of meeting the milestones.

Step 5.2—Forecast Obstacles. However, it is never sufficient to simply make a plan, especially an optimistic plan because much can go wrong. Therefore step 5.2 requires the team to forecast the obstacles that might derail each element of the optimistic plan. The aim of this substep is to anticipate what might go wrong with the optimistic plan—forecasting as many obstacles as possible for each element of the plan (without becoming unrealistic) based on the team's knowledge—and then focusing on the vital few obstacles.[7]

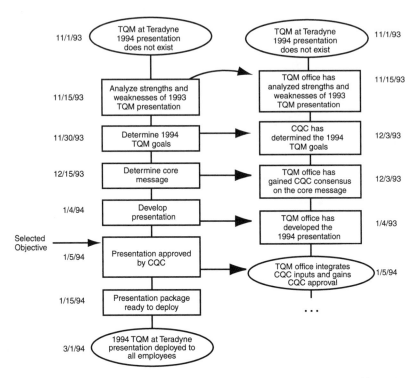

Figure 12-5. Transformation of Milestones to the Most Appropriate Specific Tasks

The Teradyne team did this for each element in the right column of Figure 12-5. For instance, for the second element on the right side of the figure (The TQM office has analyzed the strengths and weaknesses of the 1993 TQM presentation), the team forecast possible obstacles as shown in Figure 12-6.

As shown in the first row of boxes on the right side of the figure, obstacles to analyzing the strengths and weaknesses of the 1993 TQM presentation by 11/15 might include not being able to locate the prior year data which was supposedly collected centrally, not getting done on time, and finding the data is not meaningful.

Step 5.3—Develop Countermeasures. For each possible obstacle, the Teradyne team then developed a countermeasure, as shown in the second row of boxes on the right side of Figure 12-6. If the data could not be located at the supposed central repository, then perhaps the data could be obtained again from the divisional TQM managers and reaggregated. To counter the possibility of not getting done on time, a meeting could be scheduled a few days before the due date to review the current findings and, if necessary, assistance could be obtained. If the prior year data turned out to be meaningless, new data could be gathered by interviewing selected people.

Forecasting obstacles and developing countermeasures is one of the most important parts of the 9 steps. With good scenarios for what might happen and what can be done to prevent these things from happening, *future problems can be prevented.*

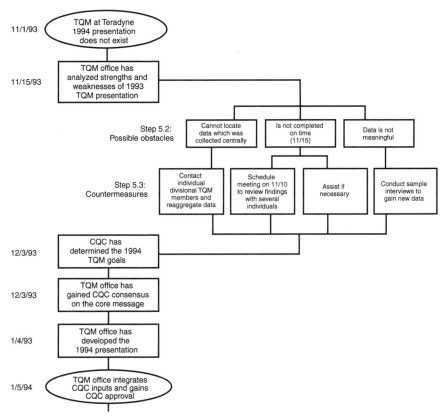

Figure 12-6. Obstacles and Countermeasures

According to John Petrolini of Teradyne, doing this well depends on the skill of the team members to propose real obstacles.

Step 6: Develop, Implement and Monitor the Detailed Plan

Steps one through five of the 9 steps state and refine the objective of the project, lay out the project milestones, select the best detailed approach to accomplishing each, and consider the obstacles and countermeasures to each detailed step. Next, the detailed plan needs to be developed, implemented, and monitored.

At Teradyne, they use traditional project planning tools such as arrow diagrams, flow charts, and Gantt charts to diagram the detailed plan. Any of these tools provides a chart against which to monitor project progress. At Teradyne, they also use the 4Ws and 1H (who, when, where, what, how) to clarify the ownership of tasks and the means of accomplishing them.

Figure 12-7 shows an example of the 4Ws and 1H for the same element of the Teradyne project that we have been considering in the last several steps and

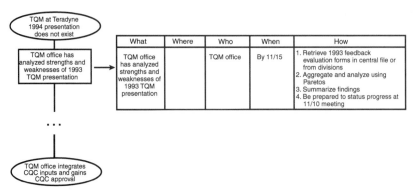

Figure 12-7. Teradyne Example 4Ws and 1H

substeps. Figure 12-8 shows an example of a Gantt chart for the same element of the project.

Having both the 4Ws and 1H and a Gantt chart available for project planning might seem to be overkill, but Teradyne finds that each tool has its own strength. The Gantt chart is better for monitoring progress against plan, and the 4Ws and 1H chart is better for understanding who is doing what.

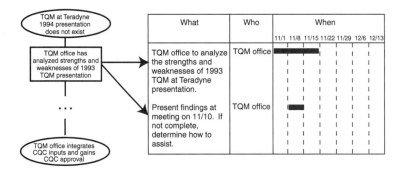

Figure 12-8. Teradyne Example Gantt Chart

Steps 7, 8 and 9

Steps five through seven of the 9 steps parallel the same numbered steps of the 7 steps.

In step seven the team uses the metrics developed in step three to confirm whether (or not) objectives are met. Table 12-5 shows an example from the Teradyne project.

Since the task at hand has not been done before (otherwise the 7 steps for reactive improvement would have been a more appropriate tool), use of the 9 steps results in a new process for performing the task defined in step one. In step eight, the team standardizes that process so the new process is repeatable as needed. For instance, in the Teradyne example we have been following, the process they developed in late 1993

Table 12-5. Target versus Actual for Metrics

Type	Metric	Target value	Actual	Conclusion
Quality	CQC score on planned evaluation	>80% agree on each question	Q1: 90.9% Q2: 81.89% Q3: 81.8%	CQC members agreed that TQM at Teradyne package delivers desired message.
Delivery	Number of days beyond 1/5/94 before the package is approved	+ one day	Completed 1/5/94	Intermediate milestone measure helped enure final date success.

and early 1994 could be the basis for developing the process for the TQM presentation that is updated and deployed every year.

In step nine, the team reflects on their just finished use of the 9 steps so they may improve the next time they use the 9 steps. The team also determines its next activity. Once the Teradyne team got approval from the CQC for the 1994 "TQM at Teradyne" presentation (the selected objective in Figure 12-4), the *next* 9 steps cycle was to return to step 2.2 and to use steps three through nine of the 9 steps to plan and execute the last two tasks from the figure, as shown in Figure 12-9.

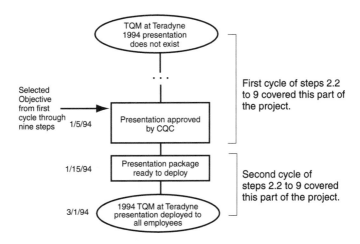

Figure 12-9. Second Cycle through the 9 Steps

Other Uses of the 9 Steps at Teradyne

The detailed illustration of the use of the 9 steps of the previous section was one of the earliest 9 steps projects at Teradyne. In addition to addressing a real problem, that 9 steps project also helped Teradyne learn about the 9 steps. Since then the 9 steps tool has been used for a variety of other projects, many in the mainstream of the company's business. Some example uses are:

- Breaking into new customer accounts
- Preparing for audits to remain qualified as suppliers to major customers
- Moving groups from one building to another
- Installing new equipment[8]

12.4 RELATIONSHIP OF THE 9 STEPS TO OTHER METHODS

People use many methods to plan and execute projects and tasks systematically. The 9 steps process is one of many. However, the 9 steps does have several beneficial components that people planning projects and tasks would do well to look for and use in whatever specific planning tool they are using.

According to John Petrolini, some strong benefits of the 9 steps include:

- Step 2.1 jumps up and explores the potential project from one level above the system under consideration. This significantly increases the probability of working on the right problem.
- In step 5.2, team members use their knowledge and experience to forecast obstacles that may interfere with project tasks. This allows countermeasures to be developed which may prevent the future problem from ever happening and thus increases the probability of successfully carrying out the project.
- Step six provides mechanisms that allow constructive attention to and support of the project by management. Without such management attention and support, the probability of any complex project succeeding decreases significantly.

The 9 steps is a scientific problem-solving method. It attacks problems by collecting data and hypothesizing a solution, planning and carrying out implementation of the solution, checking whether the solution works, and taking appropriate follow-up action to standardize a successful solution and to go on to the next appropriate task. The 9 steps also systematically lead to skill development in using the method, by applying it to real problems, finding weaknesses in using the method, and using it again.

In addition to the parallels between the 7 steps and the 9 steps noted in Table 12-1 (page 184), the two processes may also be combined in useful ways. For instance, the 9 steps could be used as step four (plan and implement solution) of the 7 steps, and the methods of the 7 steps can be used to help with the analysis for the Plan and Do phases of the 9 steps.

The 9 steps also use many of the tools that are part of reactive and proactive improvement (tools for the former have been described in preceding chapters and tools for the latter will be described in the following chapters). These tools encourage systematic and scientific problem investigation and hypothesis testing as well as a graphical form of statistical data analysis that non-statisticians can use. Table 12-6 lists many of these tools in the right column (compare this with Table 9-3, page 132).

Every business function (sales, marketing, development, manufacturing, support, administration, etc.) has repetitive projects and new projects. By using the 7 steps for improving repetitive tasks and the 9 steps for new projects, a company will be using

Table 12-6. PDCA Using the 9 Steps and Tools

PDCA	9 steps	Tools
Plan	1. Describe project 2. Explore essentials/narrow focus 3. Establish metrics 4. Identify alternatives 5. Develop optimistic plan with obstacles and countermeasures	LP Relation Diagram Block Diagram Flowchart Graphs Tree Dagram Selection Matrix
Do	6. Develop, implement and monitor the detailed plan	Arrow Diagram 4W, 1H Chart
Check	7. Evaluate the results	Graphs
Act	8. Standardize 9. Reflect on the process and select the next project	4W, 1H, 1C Chart Flowchart

scientific improvement in both situations. If people in marketing or development believe that their projects are always different (even if some people might think they are wrong in this assessment), then use of the 9 steps will still lead them along a path of increasing skill in scientific improvement. Furthermore, the last two steps of the 9 steps will encourage a transition from this new project to use of a repetitive process (which can therefore be further improvement over time using the 7 steps). And functions such as manufacturing and administration which mostly have repetitive processes (and where the employees are familiar with the 7 steps) will be able to move easily to a similar method—the 9 steps—when they do have a new project requiring a new solution.

NOTES

1. As described in Chapter 6, even though each time a new product is produced through a development process, that does not mean a repeatable development process cannot exist (or at least a repeatable way of developing resources that can reliably produce new products). However, at Teradyne as at so many other companies, people in some functions did not see it this way.

2. Shoji Shiba did know of earlier rudimentary methods used in the QC Circle movement.

3. The Teradyne system for having teams present their work for management diagnosis (whether 7 steps or 7 steps work) includes self-diagnosis by the team of its own efforts prior to management diagnosis. This eases the difficulty of management

providing 30 percent corrective comments—the team has often recognized the problems themselves.

4. Today at Teradyne, four different types of team activity are treated similarly: 7 steps, 9 steps, SDCA (process control), and VOC (voice of the customer; see Chapter 13 which describes customer visitation to collect the voice of the customer).

5. See [262, tape 4, "Reactive Improvement II"] and [52]; the CQM manual includes detailed instructions, guidelines, and tips for using the method.

6. If metrics were being developed for another objective, such as "Presentation package ready to deploy" (as in Figure 12-4), then metrics for all four metrics could make sense. For example: Q—package for each site crosschecked for completeness; C—less than $500 per site; D—at least three business days before the meeting scheduled at the site; A—copies to each of 11 sites.

7. Seeing the obstacles in step 5.2 seems to be enhanced if the milestones of the plan from step 5.1 are stated in the past tense. Stating the milestones as if they have already happened somehow enables a point of view in which the obstacles stand out.

8. Example areas of use of the 9 steps at Analog Devices may be found in the subsection on Self-directed Work Teams at Analog Devices' Cambridge Fab in Chapter 19, beginning on page 388.

13

Proactive Improvement

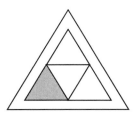

In this part of the book on continuous improvement, we have been moving through the components of the WV model (Figure 13-1). The WV model shows the problem solving moving between the level of thought and the level of experience. You sense a problem, explore the situation broadly, formulate a problem to work on, state a specific improvement theme, collect data and analyze the situation, find the root causes, plan a solution, implement it, evaluate the effects of the solution, standardize the process to include the new solution if it is good, and then take on the next problem.

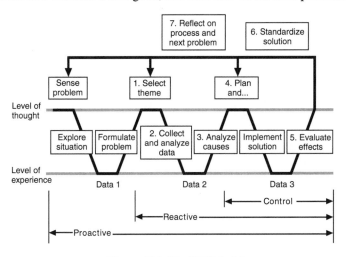

Figure 13-1. The WV Model

Sometimes a defect occurs during process control (right side of the WV model). You must eliminate it, following the manual for the process, to make the process work within specification again. Standard operating procedures are used to address the problem. This was described in Chapter 6. The key methods of process control are standardization, statistical process control, and inspection.

Moving from the right to the middle of the WV model, if you have a process but are not satisfying the customer, you must improve the standard and manual, using reactive improvement. In reactive improvement, there is a plan and an actual result, and the difference between them is weakness. The 5 evils (defects, mistakes, delay, waste, and accident) are examples of weakness. The reactive approach is to eliminate the weakness through a structured problem-solving process, described in Chapters 9 and 10. The 7 steps and 7 QC tools are key elements and methods of the reactive approach.

Instead of improving an existing process, you may also need to do a new or one-time project, as indicated at the bottom of Figure 12-1 (page 183).

However, what criteria aid you in deciding what to improve? How do you understand what customers perceive as weaknesses? How do you decide which process to improve or which task to undertake? This is the subject of this chapter, proactive improvement, shown at the left side of Figure 13-1, dealing with situations in which companies, having headed in one direction, now face several directions that could be followed but don't know which one to take.

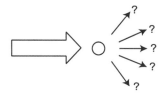

The proactive approach is used to find the upstream criteria upon which the rest of your improvement efforts are based.

An important component of proactive methods is to identify what the customer wants and what changes in society create those wants. Therefore, while moving through the proactive improvement parts of the WV model, with its broad-based exploration of essentials and alternation between the levels of thought and experience that defines key issues in ever-finer detail, you should also keep the market-in model in mind (see Figure 4-2, page 52) to focus on satisfying the customers' explicit and latent requirements.

Although proactive improvement, like reactive improvement, is well described by the context of the WV diagram and the market-in concept, the details differ substantially from the reactive practices described in Chapter 9. Proactive methods are also newer and probably less familiar to some people than reactive methods. Therefore, this chapter covers considerable ground to orient the reader to the practice of proactive improvement, with a section on each of the following:

1. Collecting quantitative or language data that is primarily what is available for proactive improvement, including Kawakita's 5 principles
2. Understanding the facts underlying that quantitative or language data, including the methods of semantics

3. Standard tools and steps to support the analysis of proactive improvement data, including the LP method
4. Customer visitation as an approach to collecting proactive improvement data that gets around preconceived notions and finds requirements customers themselves don't comprehend

And the next chapter describes step-by-step processes for collecting and analyzing proactive improvement data for several different purposes.

13.1 COLLECTING DATA FOR PROACTIVE IMPROVEMENT

As explained in Chapter 6 and shown in Figure 13-2, the WV model refers to three kinds of data:

- Data 1 is qualitative data used to design a product or to make other business direction choices. Data 1 is typically image or language data.
- Data 3 is quantitative data used to control processes. In order to control something, data 3 must be in the form of numbers and figures.
- Data 2 is used for reactive improvement activities. Data 2 falls between data 1 and data 3—it uses both numbers and language. The aim is to move toward data consisting only of numbers, but sometimes this isn't possible and an Ishikawa (cause-and-effect) diagram, for example, must be used.

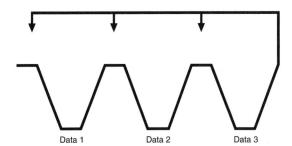

Data 1   Data 2   Data 3

Figure 13-2. The WV Model and the Three Kinds of Data

At the first data collection stage, look for qualitative intuition. As you move across the WV model, you increasingly seek quantitative data, focusing entirely on quantitative data by the last stage. Much theory and experience and many tools exist for collecting the numeric data 3. A different approach is needed for collecting qualitative data 1.[1]

Kawakita's 5 Principles

Jiro Kawakita, the inventor of the KJ method, has evolved five principles for collecting data 1 [163, pages 49–70]. These are summarized in the left column of Table 13-1 and described in the following text. The right column of the table contrasts these five principles with more structured approaches of traditional market research.

Table 13-1. Comparison of Kawakita's 5 Principles with Traditional Market Research Method

	Principles for collecting type 1 data, e.g., to design a new product	Traditional market research method
1	360-degree view: no hypothesis—walk all around reality—you want to find something new—forget your biased opinion	Focus: have hypothesis —look at reality through hypothesis testing
2	Stepping stones: leave a flexible schedule— be able to step from one person/place to the next as the opportunity arises during the day	Rigid schedule: scheduled hours for customer focus groups
3	By chance: utilize chances—if you are sensitive about a problem, you can see details you couldn't see before; concentrate on the problem to increase and amplify sensitivity.	Structured predetermined research plan which must be followed
4	Intuitive capability: logic may tell you certain data are unimportant, but if intuition says otherwise, then they are important—human intuition has great capability to find something new, for instance, something the customer is doing may be logically irrelevant, but may actually be the key to something new	Objective processes, e.g., statistical summaries
5	Qualitative data: numbers are not so important—cases and personal experience are important, e.g., different types of defects are more important than numbers of defects	Quantitative data

1. 360-degree View

Shoji Shiba recalls: "I have a friend who is a journalist. He says there are two kinds of journalists. One kind goes around and around the issue and looks at it from all different points of view. The other kind has a strong personal point of view and writes from that point of view." The latter is an approach for data 3, but not for data 1.

To create a new product you cannot believe your own ideas so strongly that you become blind to customers' needs. You cannot simply test a hypothesis. Starting with a predetermined hypothesis may prevent you from comprehending the customer's view. Like the first kind of journalist, you must look at the situation from all 360 degrees.

2. Stepping Stones

When crossing a river by means of stepping stones, you step on one and then decide where to step next (see Figure 13-3).

Figure 13-3. Stepping Stones

A customer visit often demands the same approach. One person you see may say, "I don't know how to answer your question. Why not see Mr. A?" Therefore, you can't have a rigid schedule or agenda when gathering type 1 data.

Keep a flexible schedule to pursue unanticipated opportunities; when you have no predetermined hypothesis, you have no way to know in advance all the people to see and things to be done.

Don't make a rigid schedule. Go from point to point, person to person to get data as people become more available. Be flexible enough to go anywhere at anytime to get data.

3. By Chance

When Professor Shiba was at a semiconductor company and counseled how to make customer visits, the question came up of which companies to visit. He puzzled over the question for several days. During this period he was invited to dinner by MIT professor Eric von Hippel, who spoke about his concept of lead user. Professor von Hippel studies user innovativeness, with categories ranging from active innovators to late adopters. This conversation enabled Professor Shiba to advise the semiconductor company on whom to visit. The opportunity was not totally by chance. By concentrating his attention and sensitivity, Professor Shiba recognized an opportunity to learn when it came along.

If you focus your interest, you will find the information you need. This is the *by chance* principle. Sensitivity to a problem, the result of concentrating on the issues surrounding it, enables you to notice and capitalize on obscure but valuable opportunities. Louis Pasteur said, "In the field of observation chance favors only those minds which are prepared."[2] There is also the old saw, "I believe in luck—the harder I work, the more of it I have."

4. Intuitive Capability

Professor Shiba tells the following story:

> I had an opportunity to work in ten countries (from one month to six months), working and living with workers. The data which I collected was logical, including such information as hourly output, etc. However, I had an intuition about style of eating. Different groups of people ate together, and although it

wasn't originally planned, I collected this data. The data later proved very useful. In India, hierarchy dictates completely who eats together. In Japan, it was mixed.

Believe your intuition. Experience provides a wealth of knowledge, much of which is unconscious—when the intuition alarm rings, pay attention to it. As Poincaré said: "It is by logic we prove, but it is by intuition we discover." Even before logic proves something, one's intuition may understand part of it. Therefore, don't collect only the data that logic dictates is "needed" for the problem. Also, collect information that intuition flags as important.

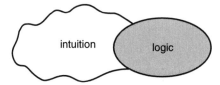

5. Qualitative Data

Collect qualitative data, not quantitative data. Collect real cases and personal experiences. The customer may try to generalize, but you must ask for specific personal experience and history. Data 1 establishes the *dimensions* of a problem; later, data 2 will measure *along* such dimensions. For type 1 data, the diversity or spectrum of data is much more important than the amount of data about any one point. The number of "data points" isn't important yet.

13.2 LANGUAGE DATA AND USE OF SEMANTICS

Business improvement by senior executives requires direction setting and proactive methods, which in turn depend primarily on qualitative or language data, data 1 from the left side of Figure 13-2. For instance, most of the data used in business, including that relating to proactive improvement, is image data ("I like the feeling of speed") or at best linguistic data ("I want a fast, inexpensive car"). Users and customers seldom specify in quantitative terms what companies need to do to satisfy their needs (you seldom hear, for example, "I want three liters of compression in the engine and 280 foot pounds of torque at the rear wheels"). Furthermore, each person asked sees a situation differently and jumps to different conclusions about it (recall the cycle of reasoning—Figure 5-5). Indeed, the use of Kawakita's 5 principles for collecting qualitative (type 1) data (see Table 13-1, page 202) result in just such a diverse collection of language data. Thus, business people need methods of understanding what such data actually means.

Just as statistical methods root out the underlying facts from numerical data for reactive improvement and process control, so are semantics methods the basis for discovering the underlying facts from language data [133]. Semantics is the scientific study of the relation between language and reality. Semantics provides a set of tools

Table 13-2. Comparison of Affective and Report Language

Affective Language and Leading Question for Translation	Report Language
Accountants aren't concerned with the important aspects of our business. [What makes you feel that way?]	Accountants give us the accounting rules that must be followed, and these prevent us from doing some things we want to do.
Salespeople lie to customers to get orders. [What evidence do you have of this?]	Salespeople promise delivery to get firm orders, even though they know the product cannot be delivered on time.
Engineers live in ivory towers. [What makes you feel that way?]	Product designs often omit features customers want.

that helps clarify linguistic data. The concepts of semantics are used in many ways; they even clarify numeric data. Semantics is a key tool for leaders.

Semantics for Bridging the Dual Function of Language

The field of semantics distinguishes between two kinds of language: affective language and report language. Affective language conveys emotional information ("We've just begun to fight!"). Report language conveys information that can be validated ("We shipped five computers before noon today"). Both functions of language are important.

Affective language is important for conveying enthusiasm and encouraging the staff ("Leadership through quality"); for getting along with colleagues ("Your idea is very good, but I have another suggestion"); for marketing ("Oh! What you do for me!"); or for achieving personal happiness ("I would enjoy spending more time with you"). However, to understand what is going on in a complex business or operational situation, you need logical, not emotional information. This is the language of reports.

Avoiding the "garbage in, garbage out" phenomenon requires realizing that much of the information available is initially in affective language ("I hate operating this machine"). Similarly, affective language is often used to express latent requirements ("I hate forgetting my car keys"). You must convert affective language into report language if you are to understand the situation sufficiently to improve it ("The control lever is on the right and I am left-handed"). Table 13-2 compares several examples of affective and report language.

The translations on the right side of Table 13-2 can still be improved (as will be seen shortly), but the first large step has been taken: translating emotionally charged affective language to the more objective report language. Making a legitimate translation requires the collaboration of the person making the statement. No mechanical translation will suffice; a mutual learning process takes place when one person translates the words of another. Especially when affective language is being removed, the refinement of language data is like a game of finding the hidden fact. A rich body of experiences is revealed even in the restricted domain of a person's statement. The mutual learning process involves discovering how to express parts of that experience in a simple and purely informational way.

For example, to design a product to satisfy a customer, first get the person to verbally describe his or her image of the product. This verbal expression is likely to be in emotional or affective language ("I like fast red cars"). Next, this verbal language must be converted into measurable parameters that can be used in designing and building a tangible product. That is, the customer's verbal data must be converted into detailed specifications of components that the customer wants. These specifications are written in report language.

Similarly, if a machine operator remarks that "this machine is awful to operate," or if an executive says, "I'm uncomfortable with the competitive analysis portion of this year's strategy document," you would use semantics concepts to convert this emotional language into report language. Only then could you improve the machine design or operating process. Use semantics concepts to convert affective data into data that precisely represents reality, and describe reality in report language.

Semantics concepts can also act as a bridge from report language to clear images in affective language. If the language of reports says that "we must decrease defects by 68 percent per year from 1988 to 1992 to catch up with our competitor," then you can say to the staff in affective language, "Six Sigma by 1992."[3] If the detailed design of a new car is expressed in the language of reports, it can be converted to affective language or to an image that can be used in marketing the new car (a sleek red car streaking, top down, across the plain under a clear sky with a beautiful couple sitting in the front seat, their hair blowing in the wind).

Figure 13-4 summarizes the way we use language in organizations and business. Daily language consists of a mix of affective language and report language which is available for our use. We must distinguish the affective language from report language and use the methods of semantics (see next section) to find the report data in the affective language. This report language can then be processed by tools such as the 7 management and planning tools (see the description beginning on page 213), particularly the LP method (see the description beginning on page 217). From this analysis, decisions can be made, which produce report language statements of the decisions. This report language can be joined with the affective language originally collected to produce action and motivational statements that get added to our daily language.

Keys to Clear Expression

Opinion versus Fact

Reports differ from one another in how verifiable they are. Some statements are couched in terms of who, what, when, where, and how.[4] In principle, such statements can be (or could have been) corroborated by an observer; they are verifiable reports. Some statements represent assertions of facts not directly observed but deduced from

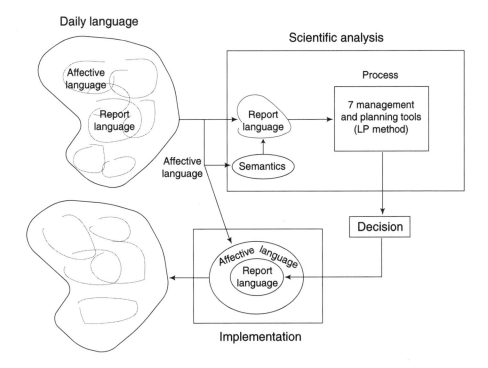

Figure 13-4. Use of Language

closely related observed facts; these are *inferences*. Finally, some statements represent opinion, approval, or disapproval, loosely, if at all, based on observed fact; these are *judgments*.

Refinement of language data replaces judgments with inferences and inferences with reports. It means eliminating judgment (approval/disapproval) and moving toward fact ("He is not a good operator" might actually mean "He did not operate his machine according to the manual"). Judgments often use evaluative words such as *poor*, *only*, *good*, *bad*, or *acceptable*, which imply comparison with the speaker's implicit standards. More subtle judgments are conveyed in comparative words, such as *too little* and *too much*.

The only acid test for inference is to ask whether what was said was literally observed. If it wasn't observed, it may have been an inference. Statements about states of mind ("He was melancholy") or potential ("He wasn't able to understand the design") are often inferences. Any statement about the future can't be a verifiable observation, so is most likely an inference ("The car won't start when we try again tomorrow"). Statements about hypothetical conditions ("If I had said so, he would have blown his stack") are often inferences.

In the appropriate context, judgments and inferences are both useful, but initially facts are more important. Inference must be converted to fact. "He doesn't know how to operate his machine correctly" might actually mean, "He turned the valve left when the instructions said to turn it right."

Like minimization of affective language, minimization of judgment and inference requires the participation of the person who made the original statement. Notice that a single judgment or inference may translate into more than one reported fact. But it is important for us to focus on the vital few important or symbolic facts.[5]

Ladder of Abstraction

Understanding is very much a process of moving from low-level facts to higher-level concepts; well-understood concepts can be explained in terms of lower and lower levels of abstraction. If you speak at high levels of abstraction without having reasoned your way to them from lower levels, then what you say is unlikely to be founded in fact, or understood by others.

A semantics concept called the *ladder of abstraction* can help you find the appropriate level of abstraction. The ladder of abstraction is critical to clear thought. Hayakawa provides an example of the ladder of abstraction referring to a cow [133, page 85] (start reading this example from the bottom):[6]

Wealth =	Very abstract, omitting almost all reference to Bessie's characteristics
Asset =	Still more of Bessie's characteristics are left out
Farm assets =	What Bessie has in common with other salable farm items
Livestock =	The characteristics Bessie has in common with chickens, goats, and other farm animals
Cow =	The characteristics that stand for the things we recognize as cows
Bessie =	The name we gave to that particular object of our senses
Cow we perceive =	What our senses abstract when we see the process that is a cow
Cow known to science =	Atoms, electrons, and so on, i.e., the physical process that is the cow

Work at the appropriate level of abstraction. It is not useful to speak at too low a level of abstraction, saying, for example, "I am sitting on a geometric arrangement of sticks, each of which is made of certain chemical compounds" when you mean "I am sitting in a chair." It is also not useful to speak at too high a level of abstraction; for example, saying "I am sitting on a household asset" is unclear and ambiguous.

Controlling the level of abstraction is among the most difficult skills to acquire for effective use of the 7 management and planning tools. Without an explicit clarification process, statements like "We've empowered our employees" often create the illusion that the senior executives share a common understanding. But one executive may mean "90 percent of my people's suggestions are implemented," whereas another may mean "I've officially told my people that I want them to make suggestions, and that should be enough." In terms of implications for action, these two understandings are very different. Without facts at a low enough level of abstraction, one can understand very little about important topics, whether they are customer needs or what the competition is doing.

In the initial fact recording, start low on the ladder of abstraction; only in later steps, when low-level facts are understood, should you build up to more abstract statements. Thus the initial clarification, or *scrubbing*, process usually pushes facts down the ladder of abstraction. An example appears in Figure 13-5. The LPs in Chapter 14 provide many additional examples of statements at different levels of abstraction.

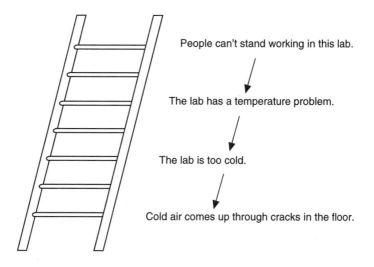

Figure 13-5. The Ladder of Abstraction

5 Ws and 1 H. The business improvement methods include the concept of the *5 Ws and 1 H*—who, what, where, when, why, and how.[7] One uses four of these Ws (who, what, where, when) and the one H to dig for detail, plow through emotion and dissect inference and judgment to get to the underlying facts and guide statements down the ladder of abstraction.[8] The following examples are taken from [142, page 235].

Who:	Who does it, who should do it, who else can do it?
What:	What to do, what is being done, what can be done?
Where:	Where to do it, where is it done, where else should it be done?
When:	When to do it, when is it done, when else should it be done?
How:	How to do it, how is it done, how should it be done, how can this method be used elsewhere?

By asking *why* five times, one can often get to the real facts of a problem.

Multi-valued versus Two-valued Thought

People have a strong tendency to use two-valued or 0-1 thinking ("It's a hot day," "Boston Harbor is polluted"). The two-valued scale is very gross, and it is unclear what the boundary between the two values means, as the top part of Figure 13-6 shows.

Hot/cold scale

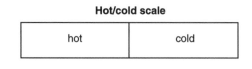

Fahrenheit degrees

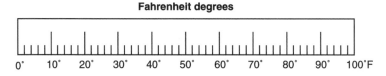

Figure 13-6. Two-valued versus Multi-valued Thinking

Two-valued thinking or speech, if used carelessly or deviously, can be a tool of rhetoric or demagoguery. It simplifies the situation to the point of nonreality, and people often use it for the purpose of dominating others or deluding themselves ("our product is the best on the market and doesn't need improvement").

Multi-valued thought and speech is the tool of those trying to understand a real situation and initiate effective corrective action ("our product has three features customers said they liked, two that they didn't like, and two to which they are indifferent"). Multi-valued thought uses a scale with fine gradations and precise locations of the values, as the bottom part of Figure 13-6 illustrates.

Table 13-3. Converting Two-valued Statements to Multi-valued Statements

Two-valued Statement	Refined, Multi-valued Statement
The day is hot.	It was 78˚F at noon.
Quality is acceptable.	3 percent of the units were returned under warranty last year.
We don't follow our standard development process.	75 percent of projects reaching stage 3 didn't get stage 2 sign-off by the VP R&D, as our process requires.

Converting two-valued statements to multi-valued statements is especially useful because two-valued statements often contain the germ of observable facts. For example, consider Table 13-3.

13.3 TOWARD STANDARD TOOLS AND STEPS FOR PROACTIVE IMPROVEMENT

A single standard process for reactive improvement (the 7 steps) was described in Chapter 9. The standard version of the WV model, Figure 13-1, shows the proactive process leading into reactive improvement. In this standard presentation of the WV model, proactive methods are used to explore the problem area thoroughly and to focus on a specific problem ("formulate problem") to which the 7 steps of reactive improvement and ultimately the methods of process control are applied.

The WV model can be redrawn in expanded form as in Figure 13-7 on page 213 to clarify the roles of the proactive, reactive, and process control activities.

The sequence from proactive to reactive improvement described in Chapter 9 is shown in the expanded WV model, starting at A, with a proactive investigation of the problem. Once the problem is formulated, ending with E, the 7 steps are executed, starting at B. (Benchmarking often has such steps to proactively discover a weakness and reactively correct it.) When a new standard is available, C, the SDCA cycle can be executed starting at D. From then on the SDCA and 7 steps cycles are interleaved, as shown in the top two rows of the expanded WV model.

However, in a typical planning or product development situation the early stage of proactive improvement from A to E does not usually lead immediately to the 7 steps and reactive improvement. A product or system must be developed before it can be improved. In this case, the flow goes from A to E and then continues across the bottom proactive portion to F, alternating all the way between thinking and experiencing.

Unlike reactive improvement where one standard step-by-step process is sufficient (e.g., the 7 steps), there are several proactive improvement processes that have standard steps. Thus, the "continue proactive improvement" portion at the bottom-right of Figure 13-7 does not list detailed steps as shown in the rest of the figure. Which proactive improvement process to choose depends on the particular proactive need:

- In Section 13.4, we describe a general method, known as customer visitation, for collecting data about what concerns customers, consciously or unconsciously.
- Chapter 14 explains in detail a 5-stage, 15-step process known as Concept Engineering [53] for operationally defining the voice of the customer in order to conceive a new product or service.
- The frequent follow-on to hearing the voice of the customer, quality function deployment (QFD), likewise has roughly standardized steps [4, 132, 168]. QFD is not explicitly covered in this book.
- Chapter 14 also introduces a step-by-step process known as FOCUS [47] that can be used to detect structural obstacles in business systems and reengineer them away.

Senior managers are unlikely to use the various methods and tools themselves to design products; even so, they need to become familiar with use of the methods for

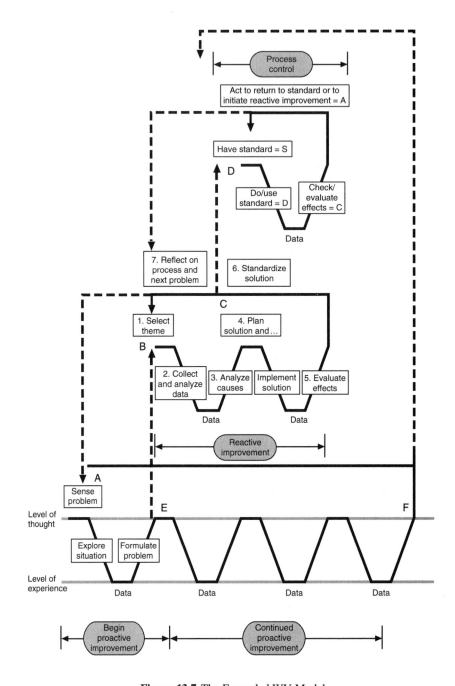

Figure 13-7. The Expanded WV Model

product design so that they can understand and diagnose the processes used by their design team. Senior managers *will* use customer visitation, parts of concept engineering and FOCUS, and the proactive management and planning tools described in the immediately following subsection to do business and strategic planning very much as they are used for product development.

The 7 Management and Planning Tools

The methodology of the proactive approach is not as well established as the 7 steps and 7 QC tools for the reactive approach or the standardization and statistical methods of process control. Several standard step-by-step *processes* for the proactive approach exist regardless of the situation. However, one widely known set of *tools* supports proactive improvement: the 7 management and planning tools developed by the Japanese Union of Scientists and Engineers Research Committee on the 7 Management and Planning Tools (chaired by Yoshinobu Nayatani) [208, 238, 42]. The 7 management and planning tools provide the means for understanding complex situations and making appropriate plans. The first six of these tools require an understanding of the concepts of semantics and type 1 data collection (discussed in earlier sections of this chapter).

Below we briefly describe the purpose of each of the 7 management and planning tools and hint at how they work. Beyond the references in the following paragraphs to further descriptions of each tool and its use, detailed definitions and discussions of the complete set of tools may be found in [208, 42].

Affinity diagram

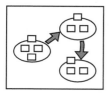

The affinity diagram is a tool that structures detailed data into more general categories.[9] It is used for providing initial structure in problem exploration, often for "what?" questions, e.g., "what is going on in a complex situation?" *Affinity diagrams* do their work by grouping similar data items and then abstracting the content of the group elements into group titles.

We recommend a richer and more precise tool known as the LP method [71] and describe it starting on page 217. We also illustrate the LP method in use in the case study in Section 13.4, in the concept engineering case study in the next chapter, and in the CQM Design Study in Chapter 19.

Relations diagram

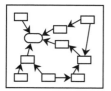

The *relations diagram* is a tool that shows a network of cause-and-effect relations. It is often used to trace through answers to "why?" questions, e.g., "why is 'what's happening' happening?"

For relationship diagrams, all the components of a situation are listed with arrows between pairs of components showing which components drive which other components.

Relations diagrams serve the same function as Ishikawa (or cause-and-effect) diagrams (see pages 139 and 157), for indicating cause and effect, but in situations where the tree structured format of Ishikawa diagrams is inadequate to indicate the complexity of the relationships.[10]

Matrix diagram

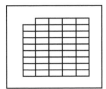

A *matrix diagram* is a tool for relating multiple alternatives to multiple consequences of each. It is often used to answer "which?" questions, e.g., "which things do we have to do to satisfy the customer's requirements?"

For matrix diagrams, columns are labeled with items in one dimension (for instance user requirements) and rows are labeled with items in another dimension (for instance means of achieving user requirements). Then, the intersections of the rows and columns are evaluated in terms of how relevant the item in the intersecting row is to the item in the intersecting column.

See the discussion of Figure 14-17 (page 270) for an illustration of constructing a matrix diagram. Examples of matrix diagram use are shown on the right side of Figure 13-8 (page 226) and in Table 14-6 (pages 272–273).

Tree diagram

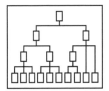

A *tree diagram* is a tool that is often used to relate a means to an end, which in turn is a means to a more general end. It is often used to structure answers to "how?" questions, e.g., "how do we do the things that we have chosen to do?"

Figure 14-13 (page 260) is an example of a tree diagram.[11] The overall purpose is shown as the root of the tree (left side in the figure). The middle column in the figure contains subitems that promote the overall purpose. In the right column of the tree, are subsubitems grouped by common purpose in promoting a particular subitem. Tree diagrams can be built by decomposing from the root to the branches or by aggregating from the outermost branches to the root. In effect the tree diagram illustrates the structure of a plan to accomplish an overall goal.

Another example of a tree diagram is shown in Figure 24-16 (page 517).

PDPC

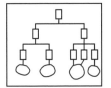

A *PDPC* (process decision program chart) is a tool to show the interleaving of alternative possibilities and countermeasures for each. It is often used to design responses to possible setbacks— answer to "what if?" questions.

For a PDPC, one typically starts with a plan showing a sequence or hierarchy of tasks and subtasks needed to accomplish an overall objective. (Such a plan is often represented by a tree diagram.) Then, each element of the plan is evaluated for whether something is likely to go wrong which would cause that task or subtask to be done incorrectly or late and, thus, interfere with the overall objective being met. Then, countermeasures are developed to prevent the anticipated problems, and the tree is expanded to include these new tasks or subtasks.

An example very much along the lines of a PDPC is shown in Figure 12-6 (page 193) and discussed in the descriptions of Steps 5.2 and 5.3 adjacent to the figure.

Arrow diagram

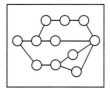

An *arrow diagram* is a simplified PERT chart, used for scheduling events and identifying bottlenecks ("critical paths"). An arrow diagram is primarily used to answer "when?" questions, e.g., "when do we have to do the things we have chosen to do?"

For an arrow diagram, the parts of a plan are listed from beginning to end with arrows showing which later tasks depend on which earlier tasks and the times to do each task shown on the arrow between each pair of tasks. Thus, the overall time to complete a project can be calculated.

Often an arrow diagram is constructed from a given end date back to a possible start date. In such cases the overall time of the project is constrained, and the scope of the tasks must be adjusted so they fit within the overall time constraint.

An arrow diagram is closely related to the well-known PERT, Gantt, or CPM charts, and may be used in conjunction with or can replace them.

Matrix data analysis

$$w_j = \sum_{i=1}^{p} [l_j \, x]_j$$

Unlike the other six management and planning tools, which are used to process language data, *matrix data analysis* is a tool to do mathematical analysis of data arranged as matrices, e.g., "where in the date do we find various patterns?"

With this tool, one frequently plots points on a two-dimensional graph. For instance, one axis may plot customer concern about an upset stomach from taking aspirin and the other axis may plot customer concern about relief of a headache from taking aspirin. Using such a graph, it might be possible to segment the market of aspirin users, for instance, into those who care more about relief than they care about the possible side effects of an upset stomach.

The methods of matrix data analysis are closely related to multivariate analysis, principle component analysis, cluster analysis, multiple regressions, and so forth.

Combinations of Methods and Tools

The management and planning tools are frequently used in combination. For example, one might apply them in the following sequence:

1. Use the LP method to get some initial insight into the key variables in a complex business situation
2. Use a relations diagram to show the relationships among the variables

3. Use a matrix diagram to show which corrective actions address which variables

4. Use matrix data analysis to quantify the overall benefit of each corrective action—from this and the first three steps, one may be able to choose the corrective action that has the largest potential leverage on the overall system

5. Use a tree diagram to plan how to accomplish the chosen correction action

6. Use a PDPC to make the plan more robust

7. Use an arrow diagram to schedule the plan

An example somewhat along these lines is shown in the case study beginning on page 665.

Table 13-4 shows how the 7 management and planning tools for proactive improvement are often used as part of PDCA in combination with the 7 steps and the 7 QC tools.

Table 13-4. The 7 Management and Planning Tools in Relation to PDCA, the 7 Steps, and the 7 QC Tools

PDCA	7 Steps	7 QC Tools	7 Proactive Tools
Plan	1. Select theme		KJ method Relations diagram Matrix diagram
	2. Collect and analyze data	Check sheet, graph, Pareto diagram, process flow diagram, histogram, scatter diagram, cause-and-effect diagram	
	3. Analyze causes		
Do	4. Plan and implement solution		Tree diagram Matrix diagram Arrow diagram PDPC diagram
Check	5. Evaluate effects	Check sheet, graph, Pareto diagram, histogram, scatter diagram, cause-and-effect diagram, control chart	
Act	6. Standardize solution		Arrow diagram PDPC diagram
	7. Reflect on process (and next problem)		KJ method
(Provides repetitions)	(Provides steps)	(Provides tools)	(Provides tools)

As the table suggests, a continuum exists between proactive and reactive methods. Even though initially teaching the 7 management and planning tools as part of a "mass movement" reactive improvement curriculum is probably inadvisable, the tools are useful in the reactive context. Matrix diagrams for theme selection, solution selection, and action planning may be the fourth most useful tool, after Paretos, cause-and-effect diagrams, and graphs. One way to select a 7 steps theme is through unstructured customer interviews and an LP diagram to analyze customer answers and understand what most concerns customers. Solutions that require coordination among several groups (e.g., redoing an administrative process) are natural applications for arrow diagramming and PDPC.

The preceding examples suggest that some reactive improvement activities (correcting currently existing, unambiguous defects) can in some steps have a distinctly proactive flavor (using richly available language data to help aim activities). Mechanically, this is revealed by the pattern of some of the 7 steps being well supported by the 7 QC tools (steps 2, 3, and 5), and the others (steps 1, 4, 6, and 7) having no QC tools but some management and planning tools.

Focus on the Vital Few

As shown in the rest of this chapter and the next, proactive improvement begins with a broad exploration of the situation (left side of the bottom row of Figure 13-7, page 212)—for example, with conversations with a diverse set of customers, open-ended questions, and other means of examining the situation from 360 degrees. Then, in the rest of the bottom row of the figure, the tools of proactive improvement are used to structure and focus the data toward specific plans. Finally, there is a check to make sure that the vital issues have been handled. Throughout the stages of proactive improvement, work repeatedly on detecting what is vital and focus on it.

Focusing on the *vital few* is a key principle of organizational change and improvement. At no time is focus on the vital few more necessary than in proactive problem solving, where there may be nearly unlimited directions from which to choose. It is not sufficient to focus just on a few; *vital* and *few* are the key components of the phrase. Proactive improvement provides tools for identifying the vital and selecting the few.

Sketch of the LP Method

As promised in the previous section, we will sketch the LP method, which we recommend instead of the affinity diagram for many situations. We describe this one management and planning tool for two reasons:

- The LP method is central to the case study in Section 13.4 of this chapter, to the extended case study of the next chapter, and to several other case studies in this book.
- The LP method is perhaps the most useful and powerful tool we know for analyzing complex situations—we use it day-in and day-out.[12]

The origin of the LP method exists in Jiro Kawakita's early work with students doing fieldwork in the 1950s. Methods developed for gathering and analyzing data evolved into the problem-solving approach now identified with his initials as the KJ method. A publication by Kawakita in 1964, *Partyship* (*Pati gaku*), described this early form of KJ, and it gained considerable recognition in the Japanese business community as well as the public sector. In 1967, Kawakita outlined this method in the publication, *Abduction* (*Hassoho*), and developed a training system detailed in the 1970 publication, *Abduction: Part Two* (*Zoku Hassoho*). Thousands of students from all sectors of Japanese society have since trained in the KJ method [165, 164].

The scope of Kawakita's KJ method included four aspects: 1. a problem-solving model (the W model); 2. qualitative data formulation and analysis tools (the KJ method, etc.); 3. a new type of field research concept and method (multipickup method, Kawakita's 5 Principles shown in Table 13-1, etc.); and, 4. teamwork concepts for creativity.

Later, JUSE developed a simplified version of the KJ method, which they call an affinity diagram [238, 42]. In 1990, Shoji Shiba began teaching a more step-by-step version of the KJ method which the CQM called the Language Processing or LP method [71].

The steps of Shoji Shiba's LP variation of the KJ method are described below as adapted for use in business improvement.

1. Agree on a topic.

Begin with careful consideration and team agreement on the appropriate topic to be considered. For a 7 step reactive improvement activity, the "theme" is much more sharply focused and usually calls for numeric data, for example, "Reduce the percentage of line items delivered after promise date by 30 percent in four months." The theme to formulate a problem using the LP method is fairly broad and calls for subjective language (rather than numerical) data, for example, "What do our customers dislike about our service?" In many other types of discussions or arguments, an entire meeting may be held without precise agreement on the topic being discussed.

2. Write and understand the data.

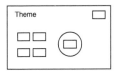

Next, all members of the team write down several facts they know about the theme (you can use ideas also). Each fact is written on a separate label. Writing the facts makes them explicit so they can be examined by all team members. Then, one by one, each fact or idea on its label is clarified (in writing), using the rules of semantics (discussed shortly), until all members of the team understand what is meant by each item written by the team members.

3. Group similar data.

The team then works together to group facts that intuition says are similar to each other. Writing high-quality facts is difficult, although people new to this tool often don't recognize the difficulty. Grouping facts is also difficult, since people new to the tool find it easier to group by logical classification. Such people ask, "Should grouping be done individually or collectively? What if people get in a loop, making and breaking the same groups?" The question indicates a two-valued mentality that needs to change to multi-valued thinking. The answer to the question is that each label has different distances from the others in the group of labels. Speaking is logical. Skilled users of the tool try to create an image in their heads. Intuition is image; they look at alternative grouping by physically moving the labels back and forth.

There is surprisingly little need for oral discussion, which in any case would be logical rather than intuitive. Shoji Shiba says, "Verbal statements such as 'I don't like this label to be part of this group' are counterproductive debate. Don't think with the brain; think with the hand. Listen to the facts because this is the voice of the customer. There is no methodology for hearing the facts. Skill must be gained through practice and experience." There is no right answer; there are just better ways. Consider how videos would show something: they would explain work by showing an image of a person sweeping a floor, a person standing at an assembly line, or a person sitting at a desk.

4. Title groups.

The groups of similar facts are then given titles that express the same meaning or image of the group of facts, but at the next higher level of abstraction. Again the principles of semantics are used to refine titles. Grouping and titling continues until a hierarchy of no more than five groups exists.

5. Lay out groups and show relationship among groups.

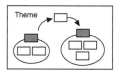

The group hierarchies are then laid out on the page to show clearly the internal structure of the groups and the relationship among the groups.

6. Vote on the most important low-level issues and draw conclusions.

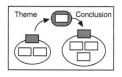

Once the team has reached a common understanding of the individual facts, their grouping and hierarchy, and the relationship among the groups, the team votes on the most important low-level facts (one must think of action in specific, not abstract, terms). From the important low-level facts a conclusion is drawn. Finally, the team decides what next steps are appropriate, given the outcome of the LP.[13]

MPM

Information often comes as language data from several sources: customer responses to surveys, transcribed notes from customer visits, or synthesized results from multiple LP diagrams. Any of these can result in dozens or hundreds of statements. The multipriority method (MPM), as we call it, is a methodology for winnowing these statements to a manageable number [57].[14]

There are two principles by which to reduce the number of data: emphasizing strength, and eliminating weaknesses. MPM follows the former principle, which is to focus on the importance or strength of the data in relation to the theme. The idea of MPM has some similarity to McGregor's Theory Y [201].

The statements to be winnowed typically are written on individual slips of paper. Table 13-5 outlines the MPM process. The first stage, *preparation*, includes a warmup, discussion of the theme, and selection of leaders.

Table 13-5. The MPM Process

Stage	Steps
Preparation	Warm up Discuss theme
Unconstrained pickup	Choose labels Count labels chosen
Focused pickup	Choose labels in turn

During the second stage, *unconstrained pickup*, team members mark the statements they consider likely candidates for final consideration. During each round of this stage, each team member marks all of the possibilities he or she thinks are important. If someone has already marked a statement, it is not marked again. At the end of each round, statements not marked during the round are removed from consideration. There are several rounds of unconstrained pickup, gradually reducing the number of choices. By repeatedly inspecting the list of statements at each round and marking them, team members reach a consensus on the most important issues, without taking time for discussion.

The third stage, *focused pickup*, represents the final focusing. About 20 to 30 percent of the statements chosen in the previous stage will be weeded from the final selection. Each team member is given a limited number of choices to designate final candidates. By this time, all team members have considered all the remaining statements several times, so they are ready to focus on the most important.

MPM is not just voting. Team members mark one statement at a time in a rotation. If there are six team members, the rotations continue until each person has chosen six statements. They may repeat this so that 12 statements will be selected.

After the MPM exercise, the labels are used for whatever purpose has been specified. For example, an LP diagram may summarize the findings for presentation to a management group, or a tree diagram may structure the results if the labels were selected as, for example, customer requirements.

13.4 CUSTOMER VISITATION AS A METHOD OF COLLECTING PROACTIVE IMPROVEMENT DATA

One of the most useful approaches to proactive improvement and hearing the voice of the customer was described by George Fisher, then CEO of Motorola [96]. He gave us five principles of customer visitation, a form of open-ended interview.

George Fisher's Five Principles of Customer Visitation

1. *Start with the CEO.* The customer visitation program must start with your CEO. It is an important, visible sign of respect to the customer. It is also a good signal for your employees.
2. *Don't sell.* Don't visit to sell, but to visit and listen to the customer.
3. *Ask key questions.* What does the customer like about doing business with your company? What does the customer not like about doing business with your company?
4. *Meet the toughest customer.* Motorola meets a certain demanding customer in Japan. If it can make this customer happy, it can satisfy any customer.
5. *Meet customers you want to understand.* If you want to see your product used, you need to see an end user. If you want to understand distribution channels, visit a dealer. If you want to understand the purchasing process, interview the participants in the decision to buy.[15]

BBN Customer Visitation Program Case Study

In late September 1990, BBN decided to undertake a customer visitation program.[16] A number of the senior executives of BBN had heard George Fisher's presentation on Motorola's executive customer visitation activities. His ideas about customer visitation were compelling. BBN was beginning to think about planning its TQM implementation, and visiting customers seemed an important part of BBN's TQM program as well as an excellent way to gain insight into what the rest of the TQM program should be. BBN had historically been a technology push or product-out company to a considerable extent. The customer visitation program is one of several important steps being taken to shift the balance toward market-in.

In addition to illustrating customer visitation, this case study also shows extensive use of the LP and MPM methods. Twelve MPMs and ten LPs are indicated by Figure 13-8, and another seven to nine LPs and seven to nine MPMs used in the actual case are not shown in the figure. The case study also shows use of matrix diagrams.

The BBN case study used Plan Do Check Act sequence, which our description follows.

Plan

The nine most senior managers of BBN, led by Chairman Steven Levy and guided by Shoji Shiba, spent about three-quarters of a day developing the customer visitation plan, using a variety of techniques and tools. At the planning session, they started by using the LP method to understand the purpose of customer visits. The executives concluded they had three purposes for their customer visitation program:

- To get better understanding of customers and to build long-term relationships
- To demonstrate the importance of customers to the BBN staff
- To find out how BBN compared with its competitors

The next issue was to determine what the output of the customer visitation program would be. After considerable debate the executives concluded that the output would be a customer focus day on November 27, 1990, to which several customers and 175 BBN managers would be invited and at which the findings of the customer visitation program would be presented. In retrospect, the nine senior executives felt that selection of the specific day for presentation, slightly less than two months in the future, was one of the most important aspects of the customer visitation program execution: by declaring this date to 175 other managers, the senior managers made a public commitment to the customer visitation program and simultaneously constrained the scope of the program to what could be accomplished in two months.

Next in their planning, the senior executives made lists of the minimum output they desired from the program, the specific output, which customers to visit and why, and which executive would visit each customer. Categories of customer considered for visitation were the following:

- Lost customers
- Customers with non-U.S. headquarters or focus
- U.S. government customers
- Customers who are key to BBN's future
- Companies who were targeted as future customers
- Unhappy customers
- Customers practicing TQM
- Good current customers
- Customers who buy multiple products or from multiple BBN divisions
- Distributors

According to Fisher's five principles of customer visitation, the goal in selecting nine customers to visit (one for each executive) was diversity—as much representation as was feasible from the categories shown in Table 13-6.

A senior executive was assigned to visit each of the selected companies, and a list was made of which part of BBN had the background information on the customer to be visited, as shown in Table 13-7.

To prepare for the visits each senior executive, with the help of the people in BBN who normally dealt with the customer to be visited, collected all of the available back-

Table 13-6. Diversity of Customer Representation

Company	Key/Target	Lost/Unhappy/Good	U.S. Government/Commercial	International (Non-U.S.)	Multidivision	TQM	Distributor
A	key	good	commercial			yes	
B	key	good	government		yes	yes	
C	key		government			yes	
D	key	good	commercial	yes			
E	key	good	government		yes	no	
F	key	lost	government		yes	yes	
G	key		government				
H		lost	commercial	yes			
I		lost	commercial	yes			

Table 13-7. Visit Assignments and Background Information

Company	Visit assigned to	Systems and Technologies Division	Commercial Division	Software Products Division	Advanced Computer
A	Levy		X		X
B	Walden		X	X	
C	Glabe		X	X	
D	Rampe			X	
E	Ide	X	X		X
F	Rankin		X		
G	LaVigna		X		
H	Barker	X	X	X	X
I	Goldwasser	X	X	X	X

ground information on the customer (trip reports, open trouble reports, recent annual report, and so on—everything in the customer file). A set of five questions and subquestions was developed. The five main questions were intended to be open-ended and to encourage wide-ranging response. The subquestions were prepared as handy follow-up questions in case the answers to the main questions failed to convey as much information as was desired. The list of questions follows:

1. What would be the most effective way for BBN to improve its visibility to your company?
   • What is the single dominant characteristic of BBN's culture?
2. What will your needs be in three to five years, and what must we do to be a strategic supplier?
   • What is your company vision?
   • What outside influence will affect your future?
   • What is the biggest challenge facing you today?

  • What is your expected market?
  • Who is your primary competitor?
3. Who should we benchmark our products against and what benchmarks should we use?
  • Who will/did you buy from if not us, and why?
  • Why did you buy from us originally?
  • What is the key reason you may decide to buy from us?
  • Who do you think our competitors are for your business?
  • What is it you like about other companies' goods and services?
  • What do our competitors say about us?
4. How do our product weaknesses and other weaknesses affect you?
  • What are the weaknesses of our products, services, and administration?
  • How do you use our product?
  • Is our product/service quality the best in the world?
5. What problems can we help you solve?
  • What aren't we doing that you'd like to have us do?

In some cases, the people who knew the customer best constructed an LP diagram of anticipated answers to the list of questions. This was done to further prepare the visiting senior executive, who in most cases was not deeply familiar with the customer's situation.[17]

The final planning steps consisted of the following three activities: development of an arrow diagram to create the schedule leading up to Customer Focus Day on November 27; two hours of instruction by Shoji Shiba for the senior executives on how to take notes and understand nonverbal communication (described as "Seven Key Points of Customer Visitation" on page 227 following this case study); and deciding who should go with each executive on the customer visitation to take notes and provide continuity with the customers.

Do

Seven of the nine senior executives were able to schedule and carry out their customer visits in the time allowed. In all cases, the customers were very receptive to the visitors from BBN. The BBN people felt they gained insight into the customers' feelings about BBN that they would not have been likely to obtain in the normal course of communication with the customers.

In each of the visits, the senior BBN executive and note-takers visited the customer without a time deadline for leaving (in keeping with the stepping-stone principle for collecting type 1 data). The open-ended questions were asked and active listening was practiced. Everything that the customer said was written down as close to verbatim as possible.

Check

Back at BBN after the visit, the verbatim notes were transcribed onto LP labels, with one thought per label. Typically this resulted in 50 to 200 labels. Then a group of people familiar with the customer (typically the relevant cross-functional customer support team) used MPM to pick out the most important voices from the large number of customer voices collected, and organize them into an LP diagram. This process of picking out the most important customer voices and structuring them into LP diagrams is shown at the left of Figure 13-8.

Two parallel courses of analysis were followed from here: dealing in the relevant division with specific issues brought up by customers, and finding the cross-customer, cross-company issues. Although it is not shown in the figure, dealing with customer-specific issues in a specific division typically entailed using MPM again on the LP diagram for the customer. This step enabled executives to find key problems, brainstorm to suggest possible solutions, and conduct feasibility and impact analysis to select the most powerful solutions.

As shown in the right two-thirds of Figure 13-8, the cross-customer, cross-company issues were analyzed in a two-day meeting of the nine senior executives. Each of the nine LP diagrams from a customer visit was presented to all of the executives. As shown in the figure, the MPM technique was used then to select 24 key facts learned about the customers, and these were organized into another LP diagram. The theme of this LP diagram was, "What are the most important voices of customers for us to listen to companywide?" The LP layout and evaluation process resulted in 11 key customer requirements. The general conclusion of the LP diagram was that BBN had an incomplete understanding of its customers' requirements, and BBN's processes for meeting those requirements needed substantial improvement.

Through a brainstorming process, executives proposed 154 possible means of satisfying the 11 key requirements, and reduced this list of 154 to 12 key means, using MPM twice, once for high-impact means and once for high-feasibility means. They then constructed a quality table (a particular use of a matrix diagram) that correlated the 11 key requirements with the 12 key means.

Act

From the quality table correlation, it was possible to pick three near-term activities that would have significant effect on customer satisfaction, as follows:

- Institutionalize customer visitation activities
- Implement a common product development process including core teams, phase review process, and product review board
- Create a monthly scorecard of defects delivered to customers

The customer visitation program, the analysis, and the above decisions were reported to 175 BBN managers at Customer Focus Day on November 27, 1990. After Customer Focus Day, senior management decided to appoint a cross-company team to plan how to implement each of the above decisions. These teams reported their implementation plans at BBN's second customer focus day, on May 1, 1991.

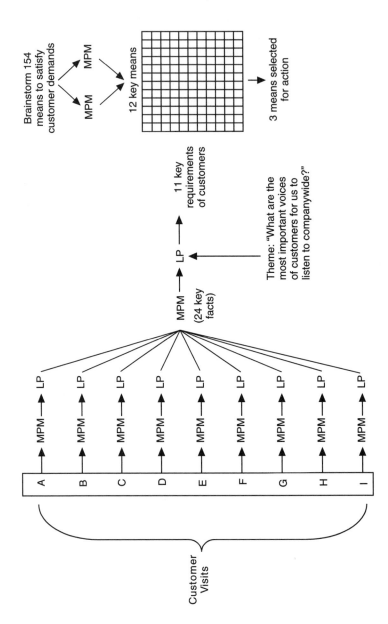

Figure 13-8. Using the MPM and LP Methods to Understand Key Customer Requirements and Meet Them

Seven Key Points of Customer Visitation

Seven key points of customer visitation emerged from BBN's customer visitation program. (In addition to being valuable guidelines generally, these principles strongly influenced the early steps of the concept engineering method described in the next chapter.)

1. Clarify the Purpose

The LP diagram constructed during the planning phase clarified the purpose of customer visitation and why BBN needed it. Three dimensions of the purpose are shown in Figure 13-9.

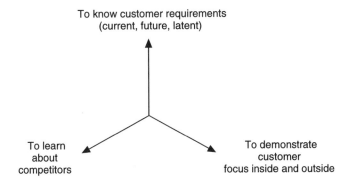

Figure 13-9. The Purpose of Customer Visitation

2. Set a Concrete Target

Always create a deadline and plan from the future to the present, instead of toward the future. This limits the scope of work and number of customers to visit and works as a mobilization strategy.

3. Train for Visits

Training the people who will visit the customers is necessary. The BBN executives were taught how to ask questions and take notes. Visiting an internal customer first is a useful exercise. Don't bring a structured questionnaire; questionnaires are useful for testing hypotheses and controlling the quality of existing processes. For example, traditional marketing research has a scale for the answers; this is a structured methodology. Use open-ended questions, briefly listed for the interviewer's use, not for the customer to read.

Asking for facts, facts, and more facts is not good. People want to talk in generalities, not specifics. Customers often don't know the facts; they only have opinions. They may get angry if you press for facts like an inquisitor.

Anthropologists and field social scientists have well-developed methods of drawing out information. Their technique is to develop the skill called triangulation. One finds the height of the mountain by triangulation, by looking at it from different viewpoints. Similarly, you have to ask in different ways and from different points of view to confirm facts. For instance, find ways of asking when, what, and where (without sounding like an inquisitor).

Keep the 5 Ws and 1H (who, what, where, when, why, and how) in mind when asking these questions, but don't ask them directly. The goal is to move iteratively from the customer's affective language to collecting report language, at the appropriate level of the ladder of abstraction; another goal is convert two-valued thinking into multi-valued thinking. The triangulation principle elicits this data and ensures it is interpreted correctly.

Professor Shiba does not recommend using tape recorders for customer visits. Sometimes these make customers uncomfortable. Also, mechanical problems may occur, transcribing tapes takes considerable time, and using a tape recorder does not increase one's note-taking skill for situations where taping is not possible.

The preferred alternative to tape recording is extensive note-taking. Two people should visit the customer. One should ask questions, focus on triangulation, and not take notes. The other should take notes full time, writing down everything that's said, exactly as said, without summarization. This may seem difficult. A helpful image in getting started is to think of what you see and hear going from your eye and ear directly to your hand, skipping your brain entirely. Trying to listen, interpret, summarize, and write all at once (eye to brain to hand) is more difficult and invites hasty interpretation.

When you take notes, write what the interviewee says, what you see, and what you think. Professor Shiba takes notes in Japanese. He writes the exact words of the customer, adding notes on what is intuitively interesting.

Training in semantics helps the questioner guide the inquiry. A customer's initial statements on a subject may be judgments ("it's good"), highly abstract, two-valued, or affective. Skill in gently clarifying meaning is needed to get factual data at a level of abstraction that can be acted on.

4. Respect the Customer

Demonstrating respect for the customer is not only an essential ingredient for information gathering, but is a fundamental purpose for visitation in its own right. Respect for the customer starts with deep study of the customer. Background information for a given customer is usually abundant. Annual reports, memos, and trip reports elucidate the background. In Japan, it is proper form to get information on senior executives and CEOs, such as their management style, job history, current stature, future in the organization, and role in decision making. Study of the customer's organization and decision makers allows perceptive questioning and greater understanding of the answers. But in addition, knowing the facts demonstrates a commitment to that customer.

Visitors also demonstrate respect by preparing the customer about what to expect: what will happen during the visit, how the results will be used, and what follow-up will be needed with the person being interviewed.

The next aspect of respect is nonverbal behavior during the visit. Training and practice of nonverbal behavior become especially important when you are visiting a different country. This is not a logical issue. There are many good books on nonverbal behavior, e.g., [212]. In Japan and the United States, arriving with an extra person to take notes signals the visit's importance and shows respect for what the customer says. By contrast, sprawling back in your chair indicates lack of interest. The most important nonverbal behavior is constant note-taking. It indicates that the company is paying close attention to the voice of the customer.

A final necessary aspect of showing respect for the customer, and the most difficult, is accepting what the customer says. Often, customers will say things about a product that are simply wrong. The first job of the visitor is not to attempt to correct or counter such misperceptions, but to receive them, acknowledge them, and triangulate on how such perceptions were formed and what they mean. BBN has found that telling visitors to "bite their tongue" isn't enough—people need to practice respectful listening. Eventually, customer misconceptions need to be resolved, but this can be done later, after the customer knows that the visitor has heard clearly. Make it clear that the visit's purpose is to hear the customer, and don't ruin it by going on the offense at the last minute.

One corollary of accepting customer input is keeping such informational visits strictly separate from direct-selling activities. Even employees who ordinarily sell to the customer on other visits need to refrain. Attempts to convince a customer of one's own point of view tend to stop the customer from giving his or her true views.

One way to show respect for customers is to do something unusual. One famous episode (although it did not occur on a customer visit) concerns the CEO of Asahi Brewery. Asahi is the second-place beer company in Japan (Kirin is the first). The CEO was attending a TQM meeting at a resort in the mountains. During a break in the meeting before dinner, some CEOs drank beer and cocktails and some walked around the garden. The Asahi CEO went around the nearby village unannounced to see small retail shops that sold his beer. At these shops, he said, "I am the CEO of Asahi Beer. Thank you for selling my products. Are there any problems? What are the reactions of your customers?" This behavior on the part of the Asahi CEO was unexpected and memorable. Such serious interest in hearing the voice of the customer becomes widely known very quickly.

5. Learn PDCA

There is no way to initiate a perfect customer visitation program. There is considerable variation in company cultures, customer cultures, and the skills of individual visitors. These issues will be only partly understood in advance. The only effective way to proceed is to use PDCA. Plan the first visit as well as is practical. Make the visit (perhaps with a very safe customer), and later check on the weaknesses of the visit by debriefing, perhaps even asking the customer. Act on the weaknesses by analyzing them for root causes. Then develop countermeasures that become part of the plan phase of the next visit's PDCA cycle. Do PDCA with each visit, and soon the visits will be effective and comfortable.

Senior executives can use explicit improvement methods to do PDCA on customer visitation, such as LP ("What were the weaknesses of the first customer visit?"). If done in a visible way, this PDCA is a fast, early opportunity for senior executives to lead the company's organizational change through visible personal practice.

Organizations also need a longer PDCA cycle. After completing the plan and do steps of a customer visitation program, check the results. Have the results been acted on, and do the customers say there has been improvement? Act on the results in two ways. First, analyze root causes of weaknesses to incorporate into next year's planning. Second, standardize on measurement of customer-validated issues for overall corporate quality control. If there is a full cycle where customers identify a weakness, the company improves it, and the customers say they are more satisfied, then the next step is to institutionalize measurement and response to this issue so that it never grows to be a problem again. This is creating the SDCA cycle from PDCA.

6. It Is Not Necessary to Meet Many Customers

Data 3 (numeric data control) is quite different from data 1 (language data for direction setting). With data 3, more data gives better results. MIT research shows that with data 1, after about 20 visits you reach a point of diminishing returns, where virtually all of the new concepts have been identified [125]. The MIT research showed that about 10 visits got 70 percent of the available data (see Figure 13-10).[18]

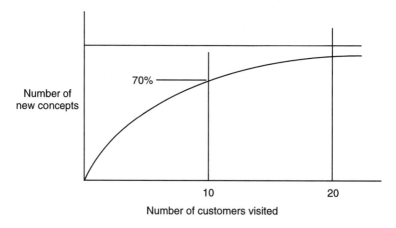

Figure 13-10. Diminishing Returns from Customer Visitation

7. Apply the Fishbowl Principle

Traditional market research starts from a hypothesis, which is tested through data gathering. Shoji Shiba says that this approach is like standing outside a fishbowl and from that vantage point measuring behavior inside the fishbowl (see Figure 13-11).[19]

Customer visitation, contextual inquiry, and other proactive improvement practices are all methods of jumping into the fishbowl (the market), swimming around and

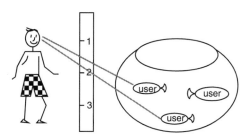

Figure 13-11. Looking from Outside the Fishbowl

seeing what is actually going on, and then jumping back out to reflect on what was seen and heard (see Figure 13-12). These practices define systematic processes for exploration prior to creation of a hypothesis.

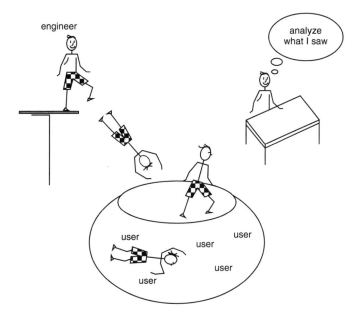

Figure 13-12. Jumping into the Fishbowl

The best method for using the fishbowl approach is observation: it shows the product in context, it shows you the customer's voice in context, and it increases your sensitivity to the customer's requirements. If you visit the customer, ask to see the product in use where the customer really uses it. Often it is difficult to believe customers' answers, but you must recognize their validity; you must see and understand what is actually happening.

Take unobtrusive measures. Take notes on what you saw in a company. Collect the "jargon" (i.e., conventional wisdom, pat sayings) of the company (e.g., "Company A is hard to work with"). These are also the facts of the product. For example, in Japan, when a machine does not do its job well, a circle is drawn on the floor near the machine and the engineer must stay in the circle, watching the use of the machine for a half day. This is another application of the fishbowl principle.

NOTES

1. U.S. researchers Barney G. Glazer and Anselm L. Strauss emphasized the need for methods of discovering new theories in addition to the orthodox methods for confirming theories in [115].

2. Inaugural lecture as professor and dean of the faculty of science, University of Lille, Douai, France, December 7, 1854 [223, page 473].

3. "Six Sigma by 1992" was Motorola's slogan, standing for its intention to reduce defects in all business functions to less than three parts in a million by 1992.

4. We exclude "why" from this list to highlight the frequent case in which causation, unlike other observable aspects of an event, is a matter of speculation or inference. Of course, apparent causation is sometimes directly observable and can, therefore, be described in terms of who, what, when, where, and how.

5. Symbolic facts (cases, examples, images, etc.) are described under the topic of Effective Leadership Principle 4 on page 275.

6. "Abstraction Ladder" adapted from *Language in Thought and Action*, Fifth Edition by S.I. Hayakawa and Alan R. Hayakawa, copyright © 1990 by Harcourt, Inc., reprinted by permission of the publisher.

7. Even though they are introduced here, the 5 Ws and 1 H are not strictly part of semantics; they are used extensively throughout business improvement activities to get the facts and to explore possibilities.

8. *Why* is used primarily for cause-and-effect analysis, which may or may not move statements down the ladder of abstraction.

9. The KJ method was developed by Jiro Kawakita before JUSE introduced the 7 management and planning tools. When JUSE introduced the 7 management and planning tools, they included the KJ method in a modified form as one of the tools and called it an affinity diagram.

10. Relationship diagrams are a simpler version of causal loops from system dynamics, shown in the case study from Gary Burchill beginning on page 564.

11. Tree diagrams are often drawn with the root at the top and the branches at the bottom instead of from left to right as in the figure; see, for instance, [59].

12. The LP method is much more powerful than an affinity diagram in terms of accurate understanding of a situation and creating new insight from a situation. We use the affinity diagram as a quick-and-dirty tool when the precision and richness of the LP method is not needed.

13. An analysis of how and why the LP method works is provided in [304, pages 29–37].

14. Along with his basic KJ method, Jiro Kawakita created what is essentially the multipriority method, although he called it the multipickup method [163, pages 152–162]. Like his KJ method (and our LP method), MPM uses facts or ideas.

15. While George Fisher was describing visitations with external customers, in our experience the same principles apply with internal customers. For instance, the information services department might do such visitations with its customers and users inside the organization.

16. This case study was prepared by Steven Levy and Michael LaVigna, then chairman and president, respectively, of Bolt Beranek and Newman Inc. (BBN), Cambridge, Massachusetts. In the mid-1990s, BBN was acquired by GTE and became part of GTE Internetworking. In 1999, GTE was acquired by Bell Atlantic, changed its name to Verizon, and spun out part of BBN as Genuity. Although this case study is nearly a decade old and from a company that no longer exists as an intact stand-alone corporation, the case study is a particularly clear example of using proactive tools to analyze customer visitation data; therefore, we have kept the case study in this edition of our book.

17. This is in keeping with the principle (discussed in the next section) of becoming deeply familiar with the customer's situation before the visit both as a sign of respect and to better understand what the customer says; in doing this, one must be careful to keep an open mind (remember the 360-degree rule).

18. Jiro Kawakita also pointed out this fact in his books.

19. Shiba's fishbowl principle is described in the cover story [207].

14

Applying Proactive Improvement to Develop New Products

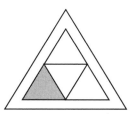

One of the most common uses of proactive improvement, and the one we will focus on in this chapter, is for product development. Proactive improvement clarifies vague customer requirements or unclear means for satisfying them. Customers often have only images of their needs and requirements. The proactive approach converts vague or invisible needs to physical specification for new products. The customer may also have clear requirements, but the path for converting them into a physical product may be unclear; you may not know how to solve the real problem. For example, a customer may want a low price, but you don't have the technology to deliver it. Thus, as Figure 14-1 shows, proactive improvement clarifies a customer's unclear image or finds a clear path to a desired physical product.

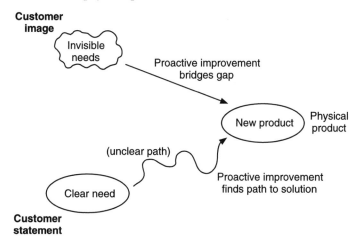

Figure 14-1. The Purpose of Proactive Improvement

Between the invisible needs of the customer and a new physical product there is a lot of work to be done.

There are common techniques for the latter stages of product development, including product and process development, and production, for example, [198, 199, 237, 269, 288, 310]. The earlier phases, which our colleagues in the Center for Quality Management (CQM) call "operationally defining the voice of the customer," "concept generation," and "concept selection" in many companies remain the weakest parts of the product development process, particularly making the vague customer requirements visible and explicit.[1] Therefore, this chapter will concentrate on "operationally defining the voice of the customer"—understanding in unambiguous terms what will satisfy and delight customers. The method we will describe for this is Concept Engineering.

Societal Networking and Concept Engineering

A thread runs through this book called societal networking—our fourth revolution. We described examples of societal networking, wherein different companies and parts of society share and exchange insights about methods and improvements so all may improve faster, in Chapters 9 and 10 relating to the development of the 7 steps and in Chapter 12 relating to the 9 steps. Concept Engineering, described in this chapter, also substantially came about through societal networking. Other examples of societal networking are given throughout the rest of this book, especially in Chapters 28 and 29.

Concept Engineering (CE) was initially developed in 1991–93 while Gary Burchill was on leave from the U.S. Navy where he served as a supply officer. He was pursuing a Ph.D. at the MIT Sloan School of Management. In the course of his studies, he brought together some ideas he heard from Shoji Shiba about how Japanese companies listened to the voice of the customer and analyzed it [3, 219], ideas from Deming about operational definitions [82, chapter 9], and some ideas of his own into an initial version of the multistage, multistep process that we will describe in this chapter.

Gary Burchill applied this initial version of the method to design a stripping basket, a device used in fly fishing, in a class on product development he took from Professor Karl Ulrich at MIT. The goal of Gary and his colleagues was to design a better stripping basket. They went to a major sporting goods retail chain and sought the names of "lead users" (defined on page 240) in the fly fishing community whom they could interview.

Eventually, Burchill decided that CE would be an important part of his doctoral dissertation work and the basis for field work for his dissertation [45]. He arranged with five CQM companies (Analog Devices, BBN, Bose, Genrad, and Polaroid) to try the method on product development projects, and he and company personnel worked to improve the method.

The basic method was described to company teams, which embarked on new product development projects. Members of teams visited each other in different companies. One or two people from other companies would attend team meetings in a particular company. A team or representatives of a team would present their results and representatives from teams in other companies would listen. Because one or another team would get a little ahead of other teams, slightly slower teams were able to learn of troubles one team had with a particular step and try improved methods when they got to the step a few days later. With each of these improvements, the interim documentation for the methods was updated. Thus, with several teams working more or less in parallel, it was possible to do very rapid PDCA cycles on various steps of the method and to rapidly PDCA the overall structure of the method.

Soon two results became clear to Burchill and the CQM companies: the fledgling CE method was making a big difference in the companies' abilities to see, hear, and understand their customers' worlds and needs, and the method improved the companies' abilities to successfully mobilize new product development projects.[2] Within a year or so after starting the activity, a draft CE manual was available through the CQM and it was possible to teach a course in the method. Burchill's professors at MIT began to draw on his method in the MIT course for which Gary originally conceived the method [290].

Soon a number of companies both inside and outside CQM were using CE (and a number of consultants essentially taught CE under alias names they use for the method). The method has been applied to new product and service development efforts (and redesign of organizational structure) with outstanding results (see, for example, [73]). Some specific examples where CE was used include:

- Creation of a commercial "loudspeaker" product [13]
- Redesign of the pharmacy capability of several hospitals that merged into one organization [47, pages 407–408]
- Design of outdoor apparel [109]
- Design of a new home heating controller
- Three related CE projects at one startup firm—design of a new Internet web product, design of the strategy for marketing it, and design of the tactics for selling it [138]

By mid-1998, over 100 companies had used the method and over 1,000 people had been trained in the method. A number of companies have undertaken multiple (in some cases many) CE projects. Perhaps 300–500 projects have been done in total using CE and the FOCUS variation (see page 280). Many companies have become self-sufficient in use of the method. A CE users group continues to meet periodically to exchange insights on how to better use and improve the method. Some companies have joined the CQM primarily to learn and get help with use of CE.

Concept Engineering and the Stripping Basket Case Study

In the following sections of this chapter, we describe the stages and steps of the CE method of operationalizing the voice of the customer [53]. Furthermore, in steps two through seven of our description we illustrate use of CE in conceiving a new design for an actual product, a stripping basket, Gary Burchill's commercial product development project done while he was still a doctoral student at MIT.

A stripping basket is a device used by saltwater fly fishermen (or fisherwomen) to collect their line before they cast it out. Typically it is a store-bought or home-constructed plastic container with four sides and a bottom, which is strapped to the chest or waist of the fisherman. While retrieving a cast, the fisherman lays the fishing line in the container so the line will pay out easily for the next cast. This process of placing the line in the container is called stripping. The goal of the class project was to design a better stripping basket.

Burchill's colleagues over the course of the design of the stripping basket were Ranjan Ramaswamy and Peter "Pip" Winslow. Ramaswamy at the time was a Ph.D. student in MIT's mechanical engineering department, and he added technical expertise to the team (today he is with HP in Barcelona, Spain). Winslow is an Orvis distributor in the New England states who specializes in salt water flyfishing. His fly fishing friends and associates were the survey subjects for stripping basket design.

Although space is limited, this case study contains enough examples of CE applied to the stripping basket to be realistic (it resulted in an actual product that sells well in Orvis stores and the Orvis catalogues). This multipart case study also illustrates the use of several of the 7 management and planning tools.

An Outline of the Concept Engineering Method

Defining customer requirements can be thought of as having three stages (as shown in Figure 14-2), which in turn can be divided into nine steps. These steps demonstrate the principle of alternating between thought and experience, or checking theory with reality, as shown across the bottom of the extended WV model (Figure 13-7, page 212). The steps (listed below) with asterisks are at the level of thought.

Stage 1: Develop an understanding of customers' needs and environment.

Step 1: Plan for exploration (decide how to explore broadly what customers may need).

*Step 2: Collect the voice and context of the customer (go hear what potential customers say they need and see what they are doing).

Step 3: Develop an image of the customers' environment (integrate and make explicit what you see customers doing).

Stage 2: Convert understanding into requirements.

Step 4: Transform the voice of the customer into customer requirements (on the basis of your understanding of what customers are doing, convert the possibly ambiguous statements of what customers need into unambiguous statements of customer requirements).

Step 5: Select the most significant customer requirements (from among all customers studied, select what requirements seem to be the most important).

*Step 6: Develop insight into the relationships between requirements (organize the most important requirements so you can see possible relationships between them).

Stage 3: Operationally define requirements for downstream development.
* Step 7: Investigate characteristics of customer requirements (ask the customers to help you categorize and prioritize the most important requirements).

Step 8: Generate metrics for customer requirements (consider possible quantitative metrics and measurement plans that can be used to measure whether the product meets customer requirements).

Step 9: Integrate understanding about customer requirements (select the metrics that will best measure whether customer requirements are met, select the appropriate targets for these metrics on the basis of customer data and competitive product data, and document the learning for downstream use).

The following sections describe these stages and steps in detail, interleaved with the stripping basket and other examples and concepts.

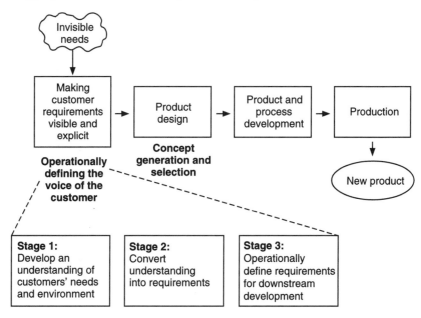

Figure 14-2. The Early Phases of Product Development

14.1 STAGE 1: DEVELOP UNDERSTANDING OF CUSTOMERS' NEEDS AND ENVIRONMENT

Step 1: Plan for Exploration

Purpose of the step: Decide how to explore broadly what customers may need.

Several issues must be considered as you plan how to explore broadly what customers may need.

Whom to visit. The first question is whom to visit. There are at least three dimensions to consider, as shown in Figure 14-3.

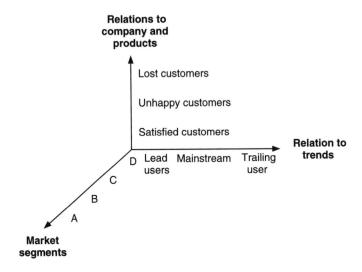

Figure 14-3. Dimensions for Considering Which Customer to Visit

Do not neglect any segments of customers. Understand why customers move from being happy to being unhappy, and how to position current offerings and predict future needs. The BBN customer visitation case study (pages 221–226) provided an example of listening to customers from a variety of market segments and in a variety of states of satisfaction. The stripping basket case study interleaved with the description of CE through this chapter provides an example of predicting future needs by listening to lead users.

The concept of lead users comes from Eric von Hippel of MIT who observes:

> Users selected to provide input data to consumer and industrial market analysis have an important limitation: Their insights into new product (process and service) needs and potential solutions are constrained by their real-world experience. Users steeped in the present are, thus, unlikely to generate novel product concepts that conflict with the familiar.[3]

He suggests seeking out a special class of users, which he calls lead users, from whom greater insight about future needs can be derived. He says [296, page 107] that lead users have two characteristics: They "face needs that will be general in the marketplace, but they face them months or years before the bulk of that marketplace encounters them," and "they are positioned to benefit significantly by obtaining a solution to those needs." Von Hippel goes on to say that, unlike users who are "steeped in the present," lead users often have the ability to perceive or express future needs as a function of their experience. Von Hippel's research shows that in a surprising number of cases, innovative product ideas come from these lead users rather than the company that produces the product.[4]

The idea of lead users is a powerful one. If you are trying to develop products today to meet the market's demands of tomorrow, it makes sense to interview the most innovative customers currently using your products or those of a competitor. These innovators represent a small percent of the entire market but constitute the leading-edge users. Their demands today are likely to be the mass market's demands tomorrow. Various researchers, including von Hippel, are working on how to identify lead users.

Who should collect the data. Von Hippel also provides insight into the important question of which staff member should visit the customer to collect data. The natural inclination is to have market research people make the visits and collect the data, and von Hippel's research confirms that they should participate because they are good at hearing what the customers have to say. However, his research findings also show that in a majority of cases lead users have already implemented something that will shed light on the requirements of the future market. Von Hippel therefore believes that people from the development organization must also participate in visits and help collect data since they are better at seeing what customers have already done to address their needs.

How to visit. The seven principles for customer visits (pages 227–232) provided some basic guidance on listening to customers. In this section, the theme is explored more broadly.

The voice of the customer is difficult to hear. Customers do not have the specific, quantitative data needed to design a product or make an improvement. Instead, they use vague images or affective language (Section 13.2, beginning on page 204). In the case of future customers, even their identity is vague. Nevertheless, companies must hear the actual voices of customers if they are to develop products or make improvements that will satisfy the customers. Therefore, all available methods must be used to hear the voice of the customer.

Of Kawakita's five principles (Table 13-1, page 202), two are "by chance" and "use intuitive capability." To capture the benefit of these principles, you must spend time with the customer. For example, you must have a 360-degree perspective of the actual environment in which the product or service is used to discover something new. There are three ways to explore the market:

- Through open-ended inquiry
- Through process observation
- Through participant observation

Figure 14-4 shows the degree of intervention with the user of each of the above methods and in what proximity to the user's actual environment the intervention takes place.

Open-ended inquiries are customer or user interviews in which open-ended questions are asked. They are not meetings in which a specific product hypothesis is being tested. Open-ended inquiries involve great interaction with the user and can take place near the user's environment or far from it.

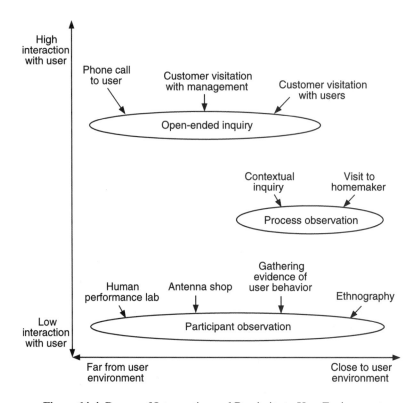

Figure 14-4. Degree of Intervention and Proximity to User Environment

Process participation involves watching users in their real environments and occasionally asking questions to clarify understanding.

Participant observation involves little explicit intervention with the user. It can take place in a human performance laboratory, where the product is real but the environment is not, in an antenna shop (a store where "interviewers" wait on customers to watch them make purchase decisions), or by watching the behavior of users in their own environment.

Step 2: Collect the Voice and Context of the Customer

Purpose of the step: Go hear what potential customers say they need and see what they are doing.

The BBN customer visitation case study (pages 221–226) provided one illustration of open-ended inquiry. The immediately following subsection describes a method invented at Digital for "living in" the customer's environment as a way of collecting the voice and context of the customer. The portion of the stripping basket case study beginning on page 245 provides an example of the method we teach as part of CE for hearing and observing the customer.

Contextual Inquiry at Digital

The method of hearing the voice of the customer known as contextual inquiry is a form of process participation. Following is a description of how Digital used contextual inquiry in the early 1990s.[5]

The voice of the customer is usually qualitative. To collect this type of data, use a questionnaire or do an interview. However, a particularly effective way to collect qualitative data is through process observation. Anthropologists have developed this technique to a high level. Digital used a technique called contextual inquiry to do process observations. It is a method of swimming in the fishbowl. It was only one part of Digital's overall voice-of-the-customer initiative. Following is a description of contextual inquiry as an input to quality function deployment.

The voice of the customer needs to include what customers don't say or can't say. Out-of-context inquiry methods such as surveys, focus groups, and human performance laboratories can miss such hidden sentiments or can change the meaning of the original voice. For instance:

1. Surveys ask about the customer's work and results, but
   - the customer tends to editorialize
   - the customer probably can't remember much—you get a three-line report for six months of experience
2. Focus groups give companies a chance to spend time with customers and discuss work and results; but
   - the information they provide differs from that given by surveys
   - you still only get what they remember, and you don't see them in their real work environment
3. Laboratory work (for example, watching users through a one-way mirror as they attempt to use a product) might seem a logical method of observing and discussing the user's work and end results, but
   - the work done in such performance laboratories is often not real user work, and
   - the work is not done in the users' real work environment

Figure 14-5 indicates some of the environmental and real work issues, such as interruptions and purpose, that typically are missing in the laboratory situation. When such environmental and real work issues are not present, companies are unlikely to understand the needs of the customer completely, especially the implicit or latent needs.

Contextual inquiry provides what is missing in the figure by investigating the context of the user's real work environment. In contextual inquiry, engineers sit with the customers as they work. This permits observation and discussion of both work and results. Contextual inquiry also provides these advantages:

- It provides an opportunity to intervene when the customer is having a problem. For instance, an engineer watching a user run a program on a terminal might ask, "Why did you use the complicated command instead of a simpler one?" or "Why did you save the file before you gave that command?"

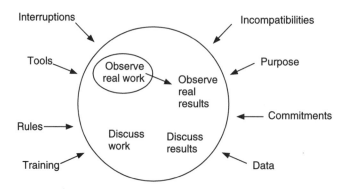

Figure 14-5. Issues Missing the Laboratory

- It places the observer in the context of the customers' actual work, thus revealing unavoidable distractions that can significantly affect how customers use a product and what they need the product to do. Say, for instance, that the user receives a phone call alerting him to family problems at home, the person from the next office asks what he is doing, and the boss stops by to tell him that his report must be done by 4 P.M.
- It permits the engineer to imagine and invent possible answers to the user's implicit requirements.

Contextual inquiry means living in the customers' environment and walking in customers' shoes to understand the customers' real situation. It requires time and travel to customer sites, so it should perhaps be done for only a few customers. From a few visits, a great deal of information can be gathered and qualified as follows:

- With each customer visited, the engineer records a large set of observations.
- From the recorded observations of several customers, you can begin to deduce potential customer needs.
- Then, using traditional market research, you can size the potential market related to these potential needs.
- The confirmed customer needs become the input to quality function deployment and product design.

Consider an example of the use of contextual inquiry. Suppose a systems manager responsible for a large computer center has multiple computers and many disk drives. The systems manager's task to manage and support such a system is complex, difficult, and critical (for instance, a large money-center bank has several billion dollars in transactions every hour; downtime, thus, costs the center hundreds of thousands of dollars per minute). The systems manager needs software tools (software products) to manage such a system.

To design tools or products with the features and functionality that users really need, the designers need to understand the users' real requirements in their real environment. Surveys and focus groups cannot convey the full complexity of the users' environment and needs to the product designers, and performance laboratories are impractical.

To learn to do contextual inquiry, the Digital design group attended a workshop, where they learned about the concepts and methods of contextual inquiry. The engineers then tried the method, first in familiar territory, with a customer inside Digital. Next, a group of engineers went to a few selected customers to hold a series of interviews. At the customers' sites they explained the purpose and context of their visits and then observed specific users in their own offices. They suggested that the users continue normal work (not proprietary work), and they observed all activities, taking notes. They also noted which artifacts define the work environment; for example, they noted Post-its notes on the wall beside a user's terminal. When it was necessary for their understanding of what was going on, they intervened in real time to ask the user clarifying questions, such as, "Why did you just do that?"

With prior permission, the engineers also recorded their conversation with the user. An example of one such recorded conversation follows:

"What'cha doing now?" "I'm running the payroll program." [The sequence of commands the inquirer sees the user execute would not be seen in a focus group.] [The user then walks to a separate console.] "Why did you walk over there?" "I'm starting another program which checks the configuration." [The inquirer keeps track of the physical environment, logs interruptions of the user, and keeps an eye open for things that would facilitate the user's process.]

After such a session, the design engineers transcribe the tape recordings, using the literal words of the user, and add annotations that only they, as observers, could make. Then, with the help of a facilitator, they transfer what they have learned during contextual inquiry to labels, which they post on the wall. These labels from contextual inquiry provide the input to quality function deployment, which is a rational process for translating the voice of the customer into a product definition.

At this stage, as they begin translating the voice of the customer, the design engineers have gained a profound understanding of implicit as well as explicit user needs, and they are better prepared to develop products that delight customers and provide the company with a competitive edge.

Stripping Basket Case Study of Concept Engineering—Customer Interviews

The stripping basket case study provides an example of the CE approach to open-ended inquiry. In this approach, customers and users are questioned from four perspectives, with questions woven into an interview script.

Four Open-ended Questions

Ofuji, Ono, and Akao suggest four open-ended questions as a highly effective way to glean important information from open-ended inquiry of such lead users [219].

1. "What images come to mind when you visualize this product or service?" This line of questioning warms up the participants for the remainder of the interview and provides the interviewer with the necessary inputs for the "image LP." From this question customer requirements can be developed in relation to actual use of the product.
2. "From your experience, what complaints, problems, or weaknesses would you like to mention about the product or service?" This line of questioning identifies factors that shape current expectations with respect to the product or service.
3. "What features do you think of when selecting the product or service?" This line of questioning determines factors that shape current perceptions.
4. "What new features might address your future needs?" This line of questioning identifies factors that can lead to increased customer satisfaction.[6]

Interview Script

Following is a sample script used to ask these four questions. Note that while the script appears to ask its questions in a straightforward manner, Burchill and his colleagues explicitly reviewed the principle of triangulation (pages 227–228). Thus, they attempted to approach the questions gently and from different directions in order not to appear too aggressive and to convert the affective language of the interviewees accurately into the language of reports.

> Hello, my name is _____, and I am part of a design team at MIT working with the ORVIS store in Boston on the redesign for stripping baskets. Pip Winslow gave me your name and number as a contact. Has he been in touch with you about this yet? We would like fifteen minutes of your time to ensure that our design criteria are the right ones. Is this a good time for us to talk? (If not, emphasize that we'd like to have a prototype by May.)
> Terrific! The discussion will consist of four sections:
>
> 1st: What scenes or images come to mind while you use a stripping basket?
> 2nd: From your experience, what complaints, problems, or weaknesses would you like to mention about stripping baskets?
> 3rd: What features do you think of when selecting a stripping basket?
> 4th: What new features might address your future needs?
>
> All right, let's begin. The first area concerns the scenes or images that come to mind while you use a stripping basket. For example: Pip mentioned moving down the beach to where the birds were working. What images come to your mind?
> That was terrific.
> The second area involves the complaints, problems, or weaknesses with current stripping baskets, for example, water problems once the water level gets above the bottom of the basket.

Great.

The third area concerns the features you think of when selecting a stripping basket, for example, durability in a salt water environment. What features would you look for?

This has been wonderful.

The final area addresses the features that might address your future needs, for example, collapsibility for packing. What would you like to see in the future?

_____, this information has been extremely valuable and will definitely contribute to a better set of design criteria.

Are there any additional comments or observations you'd like to share with us?

Finally, we'd appreciate the opportunity to follow up in a few days with a very quick and easy questionnaire. The purpose of the questionnaire is to separate the most important design criteria from the useful many that we will receive from our interviews. If possible, we would like to fax the survey to you.

Burchill and his colleagues interviewed 12 lead users; they were expert fishermen of the caliber seen on television sports shows. Altogether, Burchill and his colleagues collected about 200 individual statements ("customer voices") from these 12 lead users.

Following are a few examples of the customer voices that were collected during this interviewing process:

- Adjustable belt is important; sometimes I wear a sweater and raincoat and sometimes a t-shirt
- Quick-release basket so it doesn't get in the way when moving around the boat after a fish
- Bungee cord is tight so the basket stays horizontal, thereby keeping the line from bunching and tangling
- Fishermen don't like bright colors; any green or brown is OK
- It needs to wear like a good hat
- Belt must keep basket in front of you
- 4-inch to 6-inch depth so loops don't fall out
- How the water spills out of it, drainage
- All lightweight plastic, no possibility of rust
- Don't even feel it on your hip
- Canvas doesn't last
- Ease of carrying when not in use

Burchill and his colleagues followed the process described in the next subsection to interpret these voices of the customer.

Step 3: Develop an Image of the Customers' Environment

Purpose of the step: Integrate and make explicit what you see customers doing.
If the voice of the customer is difficult to hear, it is equally difficult to interpret. Yet, interpretation is essential to discovery of the specific design criteria for developing new products that customers will buy and to improvements that increase customer satisfaction. Thus, it is important to have a clear image of what the customer is doing and how the product will be used.

Stripping Basket Case Study—Customer Image LP

The key reason for developing the customer image LP is to tie the voice of the customer to the context of the product or service in actual use. The labels for the image LP are obtained from the answers to the first of the four questions and from actual observations of the customer's environment. If explicit effort is not made to maintain an image of actual operation, company preconceptions of product use may speak louder than the voice of the customer.

Constructing a customer image LP allows all the participants to have a common understanding or mental model of the product's use and environment as they collect the voice of the customer and discover the customer's specific needs. Interpretation of specific needs must be tied to the context of use if those interpretations are to provide any leverage for improving customer satisfaction. The customer image LP for the stripping basket case study is included in Figure 14-6.[7]

14.2 STAGE 2: CONVERT UNDERSTANDING INTO REQUIREMENTS

Step 4: Transform the Voice of the Customer into Customer Requirements

Purpose of the step: On the basis of your understanding of what customers are doing, convert the possibly ambiguous statements of what customers need into unambiguous statements of customer requirements.

Customer requirements (CRs) are detailed, unambiguous, qualitative statements of customer needs. Since the original voice of the customer statement may be far from precise, you need methods to accurately translate the original customer voices into CRs.

The method used for transforming each voice of the customer to a CR was developed by Ofuji, One, and Akao [219]. The process is shown in Figure 14-7.

When visiting the customer, collect both the customer voices and images of use, for instance, using Shiba's four questions. Link the voice to the context by referring to the image LP as you interpret the voices. Keeping the image in mind, for each voice of the customer identify one or two key items; from these key items, and using the seven translation guidelines given below, construct the customer requirements. Then go back and check the CR against the image LP and the original voice.

What scenes or images come to mind when you visualize saltwater fishing?

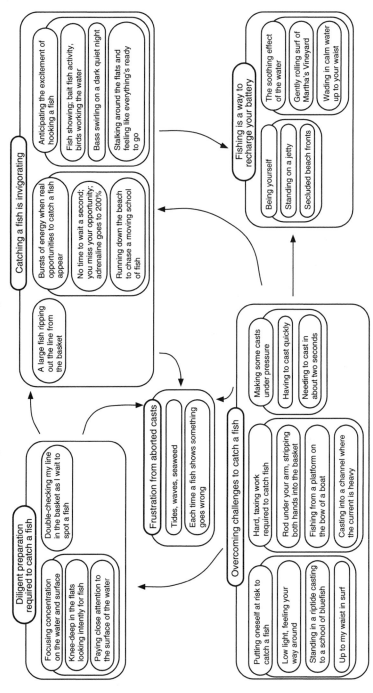

Figure 14-6. Stripping Basket Customer Image LP

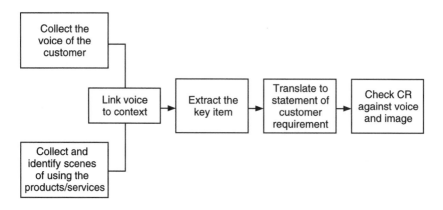

Figure 14-7. Transforming the Voice of the Customer into Customer Requirements

Stripping Basket Case Study—Translation of Customer Voices to Customer Requirements

Here is an example.

Voice: "Big enough so you don't think about putting the line in the basket; you do it unconsciously"

Image: Pressure to cast very quickly

Key item: Basket doesn't change fishing style for casting or stripping

Customer requirements:
• Basket is positioned at end of stripping motion
• Casting motion is the same with or without basket on

Seven Translation Guidelines

Professor Shiba summarizes Ofuji's, Ono's, and Akao's suggestions into seven translation guidelines for converting the verbatim voices of the customer into customer requirements, as follows.[8]

1. Avoid statement in a negative form
2. Avoid two-valued (0–1) concepts
3. Avoid abstract words
4. Avoid statement of "solution"
5. Avoid premature detail
6. Avoid the auxiliary verbs *should* or *must*
7. Avoid intangible concepts

Stripping Basket Case Study—Use of the Seven Translation Guidelines

Examples of use of each translation guideline are provided for the stripping basket case. Each example illustrates one guideline rather than a totally perfect customer requirement. In each case, both poor (–) and better (+) translation examples are given.

1. *Avoid statements in a negative form like "does not break when dropped."* Instead, write from an affirmative, or positive, perspective. It is better to design for strength rather than to avoid weakness.

   Voice: "All lightweight plastic, no possibility for rust"
   Image: Up to my waist in the surf
   Key item: No possibility for rust

   Translation:
   (–) The basket should not rust.
   (+) The basket is rustproof.

2. *Avoid two-valued (0–1) concepts* and use multivalued attributes. Use of the word not is a signal of two-valued thinking—avoid it. The world is not black and white but is mostly gray. Zero-one requirements inhibit the flexibility in addressing design trade-offs and conflicts in customer needs.

   Voice: "How the water spills out of it"
   Image: Up to my waist in the surf
   Key items: Drainage

   Translation:
   (–) Water does not accumulate in the basket.
   (+) Water drains quickly from the basket.

3. *Avoid abstract words* such as "reliable," "durable," and "appropriate to environment." Use words specific to the product and its use. Design requirements should be clear—the above words introduce ambiguity.

   Voice: "Durable—material made out of cane won't last; plastic will last longer than I will."
   Image: Each time a fish shows something goes wrong
   Key item: Basket must last

   Translation:
   (–) The basket is durable.
   (+) The basket is saltwater resistant.
   (+) The basket withstands exposure to the sun.

4. *Avoid statements of "solution"* that indicate the product's implementation or construction (e.g., "frame is made of steel"). If the requirement is strength, then describe some situation that indicates the desired aspect of strength (e.g., "frame supports a large man"). Customer requirements that are stated as solutions can prematurely limit design options.

   Voice: "Quick-release basket so it doesn't get in the way when moving around the boat after a fish"
   Image: Fishing from a platform on the bow of a boat
   Key item: Basket can be released easily

Translation:
(–) The basket has velcro fasteners.
(+) The basket fastener can be released with one hand.

5. *Avoid premature detail* such as "3 inches by 5 inches" before completing the customer requirements analysis. Customer requirements are neither abstract nor extremely specific (e.g., "power cord needs to run between unit and nearby plug"). Excessive detail can prematurely limit design options.

> *Voice*: "It needs to be designed as a truncated cone with a height-to-diameter ratio of one-third to one-half, so loops go to the outside of the basket; should be a parabolic dish"
> *Image*: Double-checking my line in the basket as I wait to spot a fish
> *Key item*: Bigger loops are better
>
> *Translation*:
> (–) Basket bottom is a parabolic dish with a height-to-width ratio of one-half.
> (+) Loops collect at the edges of the basket.

6. *Avoid the auxiliary verbs should* or *must*, which convey judgment. Instead, use present-tense forms of the verb to be, such as am, is, and are. Judgment-oriented statements draw premature conclusions about the necessity of those requirements. It is important to keep an open mind until all customer voices have been integrated. A later step will determine which requirements are necessary and which, optional.

> *Voice*: "The basket needs to be lightweight; you can walk for miles along the beach"
> *Image*: Running down the beach to chase a moving school of fish
> *Key item*: The basket must be light enough to carry easily
>
> Translation:
> (–) The basket should be easy to carry when transiting to the water.
> (+) The basket is easy to carry to the water.

7. *Avoid intangible concepts.* Use terms that are more concrete.

> *Voice*: "Comfort: to wear it for hours and forget it is there; like a good hat"
> *Image*: Hard, taxing work required to catch fish
> *Key items*:
> • Basket does not cause fatigue
> • Basket does not irritate the wearer
>
> *Translation*:
> (–) The basket is comfortable.
> (+) The inner edge conforms to the body.

Using the above techniques, Burchill and his colleagues translated the customer voices into customer requirements. Table 14-1 on pages 254 and 255 presents a selection of those translations.

Common Issues that Arise when Translating Customer Voices to Customer Requirements

During the conversion of customer voices to customer requirements, several issues commonly arise.

Successive refinement. The key item of the customer voice is often difficult to understand on the first attempt. A useful approach is to write down what appears to be the key item and customer requirement, and then compare the customer requirement to the voice and image. You then can improve on the key item and customer requirement through iteration (see Figure 14-8).

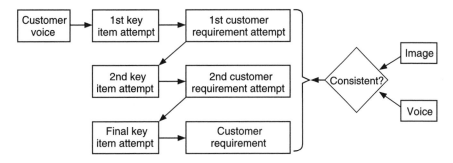

Figure 14-8. Refining the Key Item of the Customer Voice

Tip of the iceberg. Often the customers think they are being specific, when it is only the tip of the iceberg (see Figure 14-9). For instance, customers think and say they want a better manual for the appliance, when what they really want is an appliance simple enough to use without reading a manual.

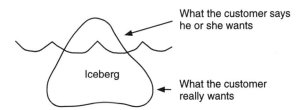

Figure 14-9. Tip of the Iceberg

A specific example of this phenomenon is given in one of the customer voices about the stripping basket: "stake or peg system to eliminate line shifting." The statement suggests that the customer is specifically asking for a stake or peg system. However, analysis revealed that the key item in this voice was "eliminate line shifting," which comprises two customer requirements—"line is stationary in the basket," and "line is tangle-free." The "peg or stake system" was only the tip of the iceberg. The

Table 14-1. Voice of the Customer Translation

Customer Voice	Key Item	Quality Requirement
most baskets are jury-rigged	no commercial products are good	not able to determine
I have an Orvis basket on a bungee cord. Adjustable belt is important; sometimes I wear a sweater and rain coat; sometimes a T-shirt	attachment device is adjustable	basket belt is adjustable
bungee cord is tight so the basket stays horizontal, thereby keeping the line from bunching and tangling	• basket does not tip • line does not bunch • line does not tangle	• basket stays perpendicular to body • line in basket is evenly distributed • line is tangle-free
fisherman don't like bright colors, army-green or brown is OK	natural, not neon, colors	color is natural/neutral
belt must keep basket in front of you	belt must fasten basket securely	basket is stationary after fastening
4"- to-6" depth so loops don't fall out	line put in the basket must stay there	line remains in the basket until cast
how the water spills out of it, drainage	water can not accumulate in the basket	water is free to drain
all lightweight plastic, no possibility of rust	no possibility of rust	basket is rust-proof
don't even feel it on your hip	basket is comfortable	basket conforms to the body
big enough so you don't think about putting line in the basket; you do it unconsciously	basket doesn't change fishing style for casting or stripping	• basket is positioned at end of stripping motion • casting motion is the same with or without basket
I want it 8" off my front leg/hip	position of basket is important	basket is positioned at end of stripping motion
somehow comfortable on your waist; not cumbersome	basket is comfortable	basket conforms to the body

would not get away from core product; functionality is key	basic functions first	• line is cast tangle-free • line is cast without drag
canvas doesn't last	material must be durable	basket is able to last through several seasons of use
if it only goes out 5 inches from front of stomach, feeding line into it becomes another step in the process	basket should not change fishing style	stripped line is placed into the basket at the end of the natural motion

What new features might address your future needs?

stake or peg system to eliminate line shifting	eliminate line shifting	• line is stationary in the basket • line is free
ease of carrying when not in use	easy to transport	basket is easy to carry when transiting to the water
ease of packing	easy to store	basket should conserve space when not in use
possible dual functions	device should do more than hold line	other fishing functions are satisfied by the basket

From your experience, what complaints, problems, or weaknesses would you like to mention about the product/service?

soft "sack-like" construction causes line shifts	line shifts	basket does not allow line to tangle
adaptivity to varying conditions/positioning	the basket position is changed to meet conditions	basket can be worn in different positions
fastening system	fastening	• basket is easy to fasten • basket is easy to detach • basket does not shift position after fastening
belt/rim connection	too vague to work with	

customer really wanted the line to be stationary in the basket to prevent tangles so the line wouldn't foul when cast (see Figure 14-10).

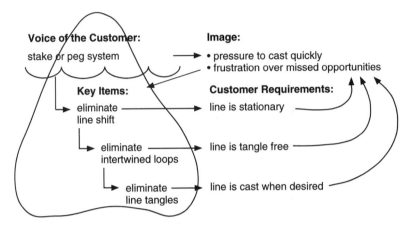

Figure 14-10. Iceberg Model for Stripping Basket Key Items [shibafig8-10]

This process of delving below the waterline of stated customer requirements necessarily involves much interpretation. To ensure that the interpretations are identifying true customer needs, one must continually refer back to the image LP.

Multiple thoughts. Another common situation is customer voices that have more than one thought in them. For example, one of the stripping basket customer voices was "Doesn't need to be deep. Only three or four inches. More depth is cumbersome. Only need 30 to 40 feet of line in the basket. Just deep enough so the line doesn't flop out." Although the customer apparently thinks he is addressing the issue of basket depth, there are really two key items in this voice: the line placed in the basket doesn't come out accidentally and a smaller depth is less cumbersome. These two key items lead to two customer requirements: the line placed in the basket stays there and the depth is less than four inches.

Multiple interpretations per voice. Statements made in one context can have entirely different meanings in another context. When developing customer requirements, determine if the voice might be able to fit more than one image. If so, create requirements for each image.

Step 5: Select the Most Significant Customer Requirements

Purpose of the step: From among all customers studied, select what requirements seem to be the most important.

Usually, there are too many customer requirements to be manageable. In this case, the vital few must be selected from the trivial many. The multi-priority method (MPM) is a tool to help with this.[9] Figure 14-11 shows how MPM may fit into the bigger picture.

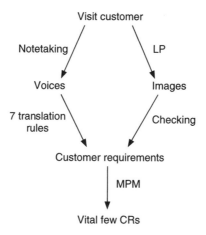

Figure 14-11. Selecting the Vital Few CRs

In the figure, note that MPM can be used after the voices of the customer have been converted to customer requirements. Alternatively, the MPM could have been done before the voices were converted. The first method is preferable because it pre-supposes an understanding of all customer voices before any are discarded as weak.

Understanding the key item in the customer voice depends on the context of the statement; similarly appearing voices from different customers may actually mean different things; this is the reason for using the image LP during the translation process and for converting the voices into customer requirements before eliminating apparently weak voices.

The second method, doing the MPM on raw voices, may be necessary if interpretation of all the voices is impractical. However, it is not necessary to meet a great many customers, as was explained in our discussion of the BBN case study (pages 221–226). After exploring what was learned in the initial few customer visits, seek complementary information from subsequent customers. By doing this successively, you should be able to gather enough information without visiting too many customers or getting too much duplicate information.

Step 6: Develop Insight into the Relationships between Requirements

Purpose of the step: Organize the most important requirements so you can see possible relationships between them.

Having understood the voices of the customer and selected the vital few customer requirements, you now need to organize the selected CRs and characterize their roles in satisfying the customer. The first step in organizing the CRs is to construct a CR LP diagram, which can have several uses:

- It facilitates group understanding of the integrated results to date. Until this point, visits and translations may have been done by individuals or subgroups.

Even if they have done all the visits and translations together, it is necessary to align everyone's understanding of what the group process has produced.

- The structure provided by the groupings in the LP diagram provides the basis for detecting glaring omissions. Omissions can easily occur, either because there was so much data to process that something was overlooked, or because no customer articulated a real need.

- The synthesis of CRs shown in the LP diagram may produce insight. For instance, the higher-level labels allow you to articulate the attractiveness of product features in the language of the customer.

- The LP diagram can be used as a tool for checking conclusions by showing it to customers to make sure they have been heard, by letting customers vote on the importance of the CRs on the LP, or by using the LP votes to check against later steps.

- The structure and grouping within the LP diagram may provide the basis for reducing the number of CRs to evaluate in later steps.

- Knowing the structure of CRs is useful for sorting out apparent inconsistencies among the means of addressing the CRs.

Stripping Basket Case Study—Developing a Requirements LP

Figure 14-12 is the CR LP diagram for the stripping basket case study. The votes on this LP were by the eight fishermen interviewed earlier, and their remarkable consistency reassured the design team that it had accurately heard and interpreted the voice of the customer. For instance, with 3-2-1 voting, "line comes out of the basket easily" got 23 points out of a possible 24 first place votes; "accommodates casting, stripping, and movement" got 13 of 16 possible second place votes; and "line moves only when desired" got 9 votes for third place.

The LP in Figure 14-12 shows a hierarchy of customer requirements. The evaluation of the LP diagram by lead users identified the following three groups of customer requirements as most important:

- When required, line comes out of the basket easily
- Basket accommodates casting, stripping, and movement
- Line moves only when desired

The LP diagram layout promotes understanding but is awkward for later use of the LP data. However, since the LP diagram is a hierarchy, converting portions of the LP diagram into a less awkward tree structure is easy, using the parts of the diagram deemed most important (see Figure 14-13).

This tree structure of a portion of the CR LP diagram is called a customer requirements table and will appear on the left-hand side of the quality table, which will be described in stage three, step nine.

The stripping basket case study started with a couple of hundred customer voices; then the MPM and LP tools were used to extract from these voices seven key customer

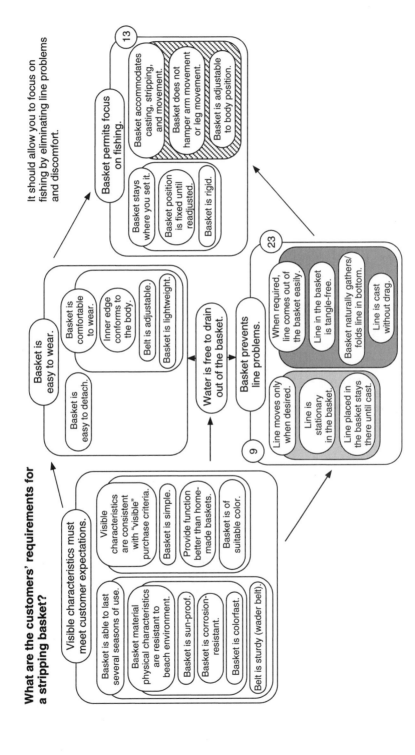

Figure 14-12. LP Diagram of Customer Requirements (Stripping Basket Case)

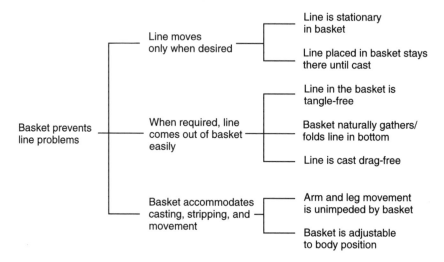

Figure 14-13. Customer Requirements Tree

requirements. As mentioned earlier, it is not feasible to address a large number of customer requirements—the ones most important to the customer must be selected.

14.3 STAGE 3: OPERATIONALLY DEFINE REQUIREMENTS FOR DOWNSTREAM DEVELOPMENT

Step 7: Investigate Characteristics of Customer Requirements

Purpose of the step: Ask the customers to help you categorize and prioritize the most important requirements.

There are many methods one can use to investigate the characteristics of the CRs that have been developed. One is to ask customers to rank order them. The particular method we will discuss here is based on the work of Professor Noriaki Kano of Tokyo Rika University.

Professor Kano and his colleagues developed a set of ideas [157, 158] that we summarize as follows.

Invisible ideas about quality can be made visible. Customer ideas about quality are often confused and difficult to see clearly, but they can be made clear. As the customer ideas of quality become clear, many requirements emerge; and they fall into several groups. These groups can be represented in a tree structure of customer requirements (as shown in Figure 14-13).

Customer satisfaction for some customer requirements is proportional to how fully functional the product is. The x-axis of Figure 14-14 indicates how fully functional a product is, and the y-axis indicates how satisfied the customer is. Traditional ideas about quality were that the customer satisfaction was proportional to how functional the product was, i.e., the less functional the product, the less satisfied the customer, and the more functional the product, the more satisfied the customer. The line going through the origin at 45 degrees graphs the correspondence between customer satisfaction and product functioning. The customer is more satisfied with a more fully functional product and less satisfied with a less functional product. Such customer requirements are known as "one-dimensional" CRs. For the stripping basket, the rate at which water drains out is most likely a one-dimensional CR—satisfaction is probably proportional to the drainage rate. Some companies use the word "satisfiers" instead of one-dimensional CR—that is, the more fulfilled this requirement is, the more satisfied the customer is.

Some customer requirements are not one-dimensional. These are indicated in Figure 14-14 by the curves labeled "must-be" and "attractive." The must-be curve indicates situations in which the customer is less satisfied when the product is less functional but is not more satisfied when the product is more functional. For instance, having a flimsy belt on the stripping basket causes the customer to be less satisfied; however, having a sturdy belt does not raise the level of the customer's satisfaction. Some companies call these must-be elements "dissatisfiers" because they can dissatisfy but they cannot increase satisfaction.

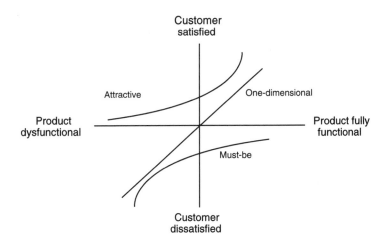

Figure 14-14. Identifying One-Dimensional, Attractive, and Must-be CRs

The attractive curve indicates the situation in which the customer is more satisfied when the product is more functional, but not less satisfied when the product is less functional. For instance, a customer is not unsatisfied when the basket is not adjustable to different body positions, i.e., stomach, hip, or thigh, but he is more satisfied when the basket has this feature. Some companies call these attractive elements "delighters" because they do not dissatisfy if absent but they can delight when present.

Customer requirements can be classified by questionnaire. Kano and his colleagues believe that the one-dimensional, attractive, and must-be CRs can be classified through a customer questionnaire. This questionnaire has the form of a list of questions, each having two parts: How would you feel if that feature were present in the product, and how would you feel if that feature were not present in the product? To each part of the question, the customer can answer in one of five different ways (see Table 14-2).

Table 14-2. A Customer Requirements Classification Questionnaire

If the water drains quickly out of the stripping basket, how do you feel?	1. I like it that way. 2. It must be that way. 3. I am neutral. 4. I can live with it that way 5. I dislike it that way.
If the water drains slowly out of the stripping basket, how do you feel?	1. I like it that way. 2. It must be that way. 3. I am neutral. 4. I can live with it that way 5. I dislike it that way.

The five choices in the table are those used in the stripping basket case study. The following alternatives, however, seem to differentiate better among the responses:

- I enjoy it that way.
- It is a basic necessity, or I expect it that way.
- I am neutral.
- I dislike it, but I can live with it that way.
- I dislike it, and I can't accept it.

Based on the responses to the two parts of the question, the product feature (how fast the water drains, in the above example) can be classified into one of six categories: A = attractive, M = must-be, O = one-dimensional, R = reverse, I = indifferent, and Q = questionable. The first three categories were defined above, and these are primarily what we are seeking in the Kano analysis. The other three categories indicate the following situations: there is a contradiction in the customer's answers to the questions (five questionable); the customer is indifferent to whether the product feature is there or not (five indifferent); or the surveyers' a priori judgment of functional and dysfunctional is reversed by what the customer feels (5 reverse).

You can determine categories of CRs by comparing customers' answers about functional and dysfunctional aspects of product features using a chart as shown in Table 14-3 [157, 158].

For example, if the customer answers "I like it that way" about "water drains quickly," and "I dislike it that way" about "water drains slowly," you look at the intersection of the first row and fifth column and find an O, indicating that the customer views speed of water drainage as a one-dimensional customer requirement.

In the following subsection, we illustrate in detail the use of Kano's methods for investigating the characteristics of CRs for the stripping basket. However, the use of Kano's methods has required, in practice, considerable insight, particularly to create

Table 14-3. Kano Evaluation Table

Customer Requirements →		Dysfunctional				
		1. Like	2. Must-be	3. Neutral	4. Live with	5. Dislike
	1. Like	Q	A	A	A	O
	2. Must-be	R	I	I	I	M
Functioning	3. Neutral	R	I	I	I	M
	4. Live with	R	I	I	I	M
	5. Dislike	R	R	R	R	Q

Customer Requirement is:

A: Attractive   O: One-dimensional
M: Must-be   Q: Questionable result
R: Reverse   I: Indifferent

effective Kano questionnaires and evaluate the resultant survey data. Therefore, a considerable exchange of insights about how to effectively use the method has occurred among users of the methods [72, 75, 103, 185].

Stripping Basket Case Study—Kano Questionnaire, Matrix, and Diagram

A portion of the Kano questionnaire for the stripping basket case study is reproduced in Table 14-4.

The results of the Kano survey of customers were then tabulated, as shown in Figure 14-15 [157, 158]. For the first customer, the classification of each customer requirement on the customer's questionnaire is determined on the Kano Evaluation Table.

Every customer's questionnaire is similarly classified, and all are tallied on a tabulation table. Table 14-5 shows the results for the stripping basket case study.

For each row of the tabulation—that is, for each customer requirement—the dominant customer view is indicated by the highest tally. If two or more categories are tied or close to tied, it is an indication that more information is needed: you may be dealing with two market segments, or you may need to ask more detailed questions about customer requirements.

From the tabulation of customer response to the Kano survey for the stripping basket case study, the Kano diagram was derived; it shows the must-be, one-dimensional, attractive, and indifferent qualities for the stripping basket (see Figure 14-16).

All CRs are not created equal. Improving performance on a must-be CR that is already at a satisfactory level is not productive compared with improving performance on a one-dimensional or attractive CR. Insight into which CRs fall into which quality dimensions can improve one's focus on the vital few. In general, must-be requirements must be adequately covered, the set of one-dimensional requirements must be competitive, and some attractive requirements are needed for competitive differentiation.

Table 14-4. Kano Questionnaire (Stripping Basket Case Study)

8a. If the line does not move around in the basket, how do you feel?	1. I like it that way. 2. It must be that way. 3. I am neutral. 4. I can live with it that way. 5. I dislike it
8b. If the line moves around in the basket, how do you feel?	1. I like it that way. 2. It must be that way. 3. I am neutral. 4. I can live with it that way. 5. I dislike it.
9a. If line placed in the basket stays there, how do you feel?	1. I like it that way. 2. It must be that way. 3. I am neutral. 4. I can live with it that way. 5. I dislike it.
9b. If line placed in the basket comes out, how do you feel?	1. I like it that way. 2. It must be that way. 3. I am neutral. 4. I can live with it that way. 5. I dislike it.
10a. If line in the basket is tangle-free, how do you feel?	1. I like it that way. 2. It must be that way. 3. I am neutral. 4. I can live with it that way. 5. I dislike it.
10b. If line in the basket is tangled, how do you feel?	1. I like it that way. 2. It must be that way. 3. I am neutral. 4. I can live with it that way. 5. I dislike it.
11a. If line gathers naturally in the bottom of the basket, how do you feel?	1. I like it that way. 2. It must be that way. 3. I am neutral. 4. I can live with it that way. 5. I dislike it.
11b. If line does not gather naturally in the bottom of the basket, how do you feel?	1. I like it that way. 2. It must be that way. 3. I am neutral. 4. I can live with it that way. 5. I dislike it.
12a. If the basket causes some drag on the line during casts, how do you feel?	1. I like it that way. 2. It must be that way. 3. I am neutral. 4. I can live with it that way. 5. I dislike it.
12b. If line casts from the basket without drag, how do you feel?	1. I like it that way. 2. It must be that way. 3. I am neutral. 4. I can live with it that way. 5. I dislike it.

Table 14-4. Kano Questionnaire (Stripping Basket Case Study) (*continued*)

19a. If the basket does not hamper arm or leg movement, how do you feel?	1. I like it that way. 2. It must be that way. 3. I am neutral. 4. I can live with it that way. 5. I dislike it.
19b. If the basket interferes with arm or leg movement, how do you feel?	1. I like it that way. 2. It must be that way. 3. I am neutral. 4. I can live with it that way. 5. I dislike it.
20a. If the basket is adjustable to different body positions, how do you feel?	1. I like it that way. 2. It must be that way. 3. I am neutral. 4. I can live with it that way. 5. I dislike it.
20b. If the basket is not easily adjusted to different body positions, how do you feel?	1. I like it that way. 2. It must be that way. 3. I am neutral. 4. I can live with it that way. 5. I dislike it.

The Phenomenon of Quality Satisfaction Decay

Kano's diagram showing the relationship among the attractive, one-dimensional, and must-be CRs is useful for illustrating another phenomenon.

Experience has shown that in many instances customer satisfaction with a given product attribute decays over time. For instance, the Sony Walkman was originally an attractive requirement. People were not unhappy without these portable radios, but they were delighted to have them. With time and widespread use, the Walkman ceased to be an attractive requirement and instead became a one-dimensional requirement. Not having one made people unhappy; getting one made them happy. The more features they had, the happier they were. It is arguable that the Walkman has now further decayed to the position of a must-be requirement. People get perfunctory appreciation for giving their children Walkmans; yet if those children don't have a Walkman, they tell their parents how deprived they are and compare their possessions with those of their friends. For many people having a Walkman is a given; they can't ride buses or jog without one.

In the computer industry, computer reliability was traditionally one-dimensional, and customers were willing to pay for higher reliability and fast field service. Today customers increasingly expect their computer to run without breaking. Computer reliability is a must-be CR, expected even of mail-order vendors.

The brakes on a car are always a must-be; having them does not make a customer happier, but not having them work at a specified level makes the customer unhappy.

Table 14-5. Evaluations of Customer Requirements (CR) for Stripping Basket Kano Questionnaire

C.R.	A	M	O	R	Q	I	Total	Grade
1.	3	6	**14**				23	O
2.	5	6	**11**			1	23	O
3.	2	5	**13**			3	23	O
4.	6	1	4	1		**11**	23	I
5.	1	**9**	6	1		6	23	M
6.	7		2	3	1	**10**	23	I
7.	1	2	**16**		1	3	23	O
8.	2	8	**11**	2			23	O
9.		10	**13**				23	O
10.		**13**	10				23	M
11.	3	4	**14**			1	22	O
12.		**12**	11				23	M
13.	9	1	2			**11**	23	I
14.	6	2	**11**			4	23	O
15.	6	4	**11**		1		22	O
16.	1	7	**13**			2	23	O
17.	1	3	**18**				23	O
18.		5	**14**	1		3	23	O
19.		8	**15**				23	O
20.	**9**	1	8			5	23	A

Customer Requirement is:

A: Attractive   O: One-dimensional
M: Must-be   Q: Questionable result
R: Reverse   I: Indifferent

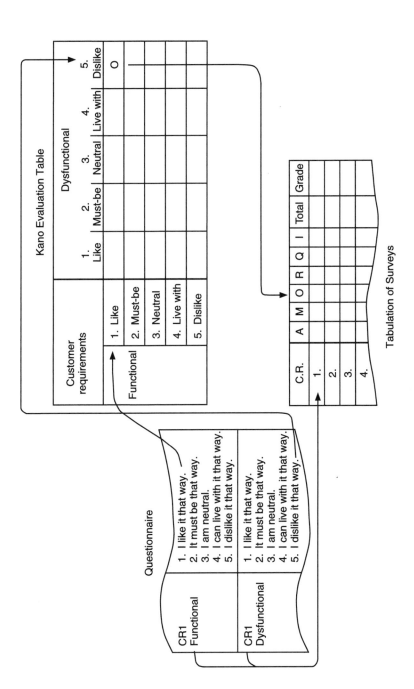

Figure 14-15. Tabulation of Kano Survey Results

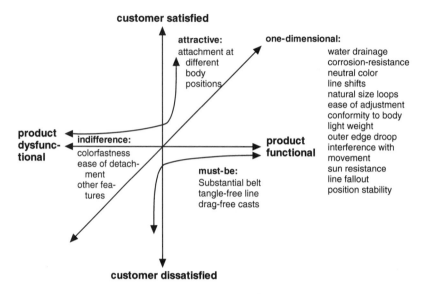

Figure 14-16. Kano Diagram of Customer Requirements

Notice the relationship between attractive, one-dimensional, and must-be and the four fitnesses described in Chapter 1.

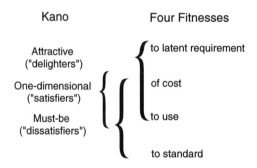

A product or service attribute that initially meets a latent requirement is a delighter. A product or service attribute that meets only fitness to standard is likely to be a dissatisfier; you get no points for meeting the standard, but you lose points for failing to meet it. Depending on the state of maturity of a product or service, meeting fitness to use could be one-dimensional or must-be, and meeting fitness of cost could be attractive, one-dimensional, or must-be.

This tendency of customer satisfaction to decay requires companies constantly to meet new latent requirements, decrease costs, increase usability and, of course, meet standards. In other words, to seek continuous improvement.

Step 8: Generate Metrics for Customer Requirements

Purpose of the step: Consider possible quantitative metrics and measurement plans that can be used to measure whether the product meets customer requirements.

Once you have characterized the CRs qualitatively and in the language of the customer, you must translate them into the quantitative language of the engineer. For example, if the CR is "line is cast without drag," the engineers need measurable physical targets for their design, such as "force needed to cast the line and fly a given number of feet." Such measured physical translations of CRs are called quality metrics (QMs). All of the vital few CRs must be mapped into such QMs.

The assumption is that if the measurement criteria and targets for each customer requirement are clearly identified, a good designer or engineer can find a way to implement the characteristic desired by the customer if implementation is in fact feasible. Thus, a clear specification is a key requirement for a satisfactory design.

Stripping Basket Case Study—Generating Metrics

There are several methods for deriving QMs. In the stripping basket case study, Burchill and his colleagues proposed QMs by brainstorming possible metrics for each CR, then using the tree diagram method for organizing them and checking for completeness [59]. All of the proposed QMs for each CR are evaluated for validity to the CR and for feasibility. Validity is given precedence over feasibility, on the assumption that further thought will reveal a feasible way to measure a valid QM. From the set of all proposed QMs, those that are most valid and feasible for each CR are selected, and these selections are organized into a quality metrics tree.

Some of the proposed QMs will be valid measures of multiple CRs, while many of them will not be particularly valid or feasible.

Specifically, some CRs may be more ambiguous than others and, thus, require multiple measures to quantify them. For instance, the requirement that water drains from the basket is relatively unambiguous, and a single measurement unit—time to drain two gallons of water—characterizes how well the CR is met. In contrast, "the basket is comfortable to wear" is more ambiguous. No one measurement unit captures the entire concept of "comfortable." Accordingly, it will take multiple QMs to assess comfort, e.g., body contour, the basket's inner edge, weight, force to secure.

Step 9: Integrate Understanding about Customer Requirements

Purpose of the step: Select the metrics that will best measure whether customer requirements are met, select the appropriate targets for these metrics on the basis of customer data and competitive product data, and document the learning for downstream use.

A process is needed for focusing and selecting a powerful set of QMs that fully spans the CRs without redundancy. The central element in this process is a matrix called the quality table. It has CRs on the left vertical axis and a QMs tree on the top horizontal axis, as shown in Figure 14-17.

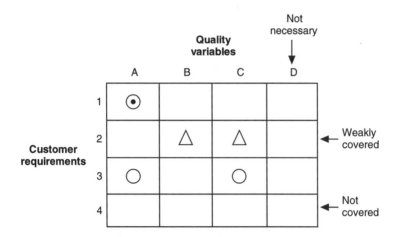

Figure 14-17. Quality Table

The quality table shown has four CRs, for which four QMs have been proposed. The circle with the dot means that QM A is an excellent measure of CR 1. The circles indicate that QMs A and C are only good measures of CR 3. The triangles indicate that QMs B and C are weak measures of CR 2. Where there is no symbol at the intersection of the requirement's row and the metric's column, there is no cause-and-effect relation between the CR and QM.

Thus, the quality table provides a tool to ensure that each CR is adequately measured by a QM and to eliminate redundant QMs.

In the above example, CR A is well measured by QM 1, and measurement of CR 3 requires a combination of the QMs A and C. CR 2 is poorly measured even by the combination of QMs B and C, and CR 4 is not measured at all by QMs A through D. Furthermore, QM B is not very useful, and QM D is not useful at all. In this example, we would do well to replace QMs B and D with QMs that effectively measure CRs 2 and 4.

We now return to the stripping basket case study to show step-by-step use of a quality table.

Stripping Basket Case Study—Use of a Quality Table

The quality table for the stripping basket case study is shown in Table 14-6.

At the middle of the left side is a CRs table, immediately to the left of the column of priorities 1-7. The CR table was derived from the CR LP diagram, as shown in Figure 14-18. The LP was converted to a tree and the tree converted to a table. The priorities were established from an evaluation of the LP by eight of the lead users.

Across the top of Table 14-6 is a QM table. In this case study, the QM table was derived by a brainstorming session that produced possible QMs for each item in the CR table. Then, a tree was constructed that classified the lowest level groups by common purpose. These groups were grouped by common purpose, and so on. Finally, the tree was converted to a table.

As described in the example above, after laying out the quality table, make an assessment of the relationship for each CR against each QM. In the stripping basket case study, an informal assessment process was used to determine the strength of the relationship using a four-level scale (see bottom-left of Table 14-6).

At this point, the quality table identifies a minimal, comprehensive set of QMs that capture the important features of CRs. The feasibility row indicates the feasibility of measuring each of the quality variables. But the translation may still be ambiguous because different people may understand how the metrics are to be measured in different ways. You need QMs that always give the same measurements regardless of who performs them. Thus, each QM requires a well-defined measurement plan. The measurement plan states what will be done when and by whom, and what will be observed in the process. The metric's measurement plans are indicated in the measurement plan row of the quality table. A QM with a measurement plan is said to be operationally defined.

Note the generality of the process of using a tree diagram to brainstorm metrics and a matrix to choose a set that will adequately measure multiple objectives. The same process can be used to define departmental or divisional nonfinancial performance measures, to define the needed capabilities of some process being redesigned, or to define internal corporate goals that assure satisfaction of external customers' needs (as in the BBN customer visitation case study described on pages 221–226). Using a visible process to define, refine, and choose metrics seems like a good way to reduce the consternation and conflict that the subject of metrics often engenders.

A quality table completed in this way provides an unambiguous way to communicate throughout an organization the most important CRs and how they will be measured; the quality table is a complete set of operational definitions for the design and development process. It specifies how to tell how good a product is. The next step is determining how good a product must be to provide customer satisfaction and to be competitive.

Stripping Basket Case Study—Benchmark Analysis

The customer benchmarking rating, on the far right side of the quality table (Table 14-6) is used to assess the customer's relative satisfaction with respect to each competitor for each requirement along the left side of the table. Table 14-7 shows the customer benchmark data for the stripping basket case study.

Design targets to meet or beat the competition are then established on the basis of technical benchmarking data, expressed in terms of operationally defining QMs. (See bottom of Table 14-6.)

Summary: Operationally Defining Customer Requirements

At this point we have unambiguous technical specifications of a product that will satisfy the customer and meet or beat the competition. We have operationally defined the voice of the customer in the language of the engineer—each CR derived from the

Table 14-6. Quality Table of Stripping Basket Case Study

Customer Requirements	Priority	Measure the bend radius of the inner edge	Measure length of inner edge body contact in four wear positions	Count the number of adjustable parameters	Measure the maximum belt length	Measure the maximum belt length	Measure height of upward step that can be made without impacting basket	Measure length of largest stride that can be made without impacting basket	Measure height of bottom above knee of wearer	Measure distance from stripping motion start point to outer edge	Measure distance from stripping motion start point to top of	Measure width of basket relative to width of wearer	Measure distance from top of basket to shoulder of
Line placed in the basket stays there until cast	4												
The line is stationary in the basket	6												
Line is cast without drag	1												
Basket naturally gathers folds line in the bottom	5												
Line in the basket is tangle free	3												
The basket does not hamper arm or leg	2						●	●	△	△	△	△	△
The basket is adjustable to body position	7	○	△	●	●	●							
Effectiveness		○	●	●	○	○	●	●	△	○	○	△	△
Feasibility		●	●	●	●	●	○	○	●	●	●	●	●
Measurement plan													
Technical Benchmarking Evaluation — Orvis													
Technical Benchmarking Evaluation — LL Bean													
Technical Benchmarking Evaluation — Surfcaster													
Technical Benchmarking Evaluation — Other													
Target value													

Column groupings:
- *1st level:* "Measures how well basket can be adjusted to fit the worker" (columns 1–5); "Test if basket facilitates body motions during fishing" (columns 6–12)
- *2nd level:* "Measure how well basket fits against body" (columns 1–2); "Measure how adjustable basket attachment is" (columns 3–5); "Measure how the basket affects walking" (columns 6–8); "Test if the basket accommodates stripping motion" (columns 9–12)

Customer Requirements left-side groupings:
- Basket prevents line problems
  - The line moves only when desired: "Line placed in the basket stays there until cast", "The line is stationary in the basket"
  - When required line comes out of the basket: "Line is cast without drag", "Basket naturally gathers folds line in the bottom", "Line in the basket is tangle free"
- Accommodates casting, striping, movement: "The basket does not hamper arm or leg", "The basket is adjustable to body position"

● = High   ○ = medium   △ = low   (blank) = none

voice of the customer is represented by at least one QM, and each QM has units of measure, a measurement plan, and a target. Figure 14-19 summarizes the process.

14.4 STAGES 4 AND 5: GENERATING CONCEPTS AND SELECTING THE CONCEPT

Once the customer's requirements have been understood and made operational in the form of QMs, targets, and measurement plans using the methods described above for stages one, two and three (see Figure 14-2, page 239), you are in a position to generate potential product concepts and select the concept (stages four and five as shown in Figure 14-20). Then you will do the detailed design for the selected concept in anticipation of product development and production.

Table 14-6. Quality Table of Stripping Basket Case Study (*continued*)

Check if basket prevents tangles/snags from occuring																			**Customer Benchmark Rating**	
Check if basket prevents line tangling				Check if basket prevents line movement in bottom of the basket				Measure how line covers the basket bottom		Check if line falls naturally into the bottom of basket				Measure the drag during casts						
Count the number of perpendicular loops	Count the number of overlapping loops	Count fouled casts due to line problems as percentage of total casts	Count snags during casts and drops	Count the number of loops over the top of cones / stakes	Measure height of loops from bottom of the basket	Measure how much line falls out of basket when placed in it	Measure outer edge droop in four wear positions	Measure the distribution of loops in the basket bottom	Count the number of loops in each section	Count the loops which are not circular	Assess the geometric shape of the loops	Measure size of loops	Measure loop radii	Measure the effort needed to cast a given distance	Measure length of excess line paid out on a drop after impact	Measure time for line payout after drop	Orvis	LL Bean	Surfcaster	Ours
				△		◉	○													
△				◉	○	◉	○	△	△											
△	◉													◉	○	◉				
○	△	△			△			△	○	△	◉	◉	◉							
◉	◉	◉	◉											○	△					
△	◉	◉	◉	◉	△	◉	○	◉	◉	○	◉	△	△	◉	○	○				
○	△	◉	◉	○	◉	○	◉	○	◉	△	△	○	△	◉	○					

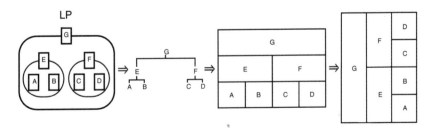

Figure 14-18. From LP to Tree to Quality Table

Table 14-7. Customer Benchmark Data (Stripping Basket Case Study)

Competitive Analysis			Customer Benchmark Rating				
		⊙ Better	Prod. A	Prod. B	Prod. C	Prod. D	Burchill Prod.
		○ Equal					
		△ Worse					
Demanded Customer Requirements	Must-be	Substantial Belt	○	○	△	△	○
		Tangle Free Line	○	△	△	△	⊙
		Drag Free Casts	○	○	○	○	⊙
	Attractive	Variable Attachment	○	⊙	△	△	⊙
	One-dimensional	Water Drainage	○	⊙	⊙	⊙	⊙
		Corrosion Resistance	○	△	○	△	○
		Line Shifts	○	△	△	△	○
		Loop Size	○	△	△	△	○
		Ease of Adjustment	○	⊙	△	△	○
		Outer Edge Droop	○	△	△	△	⊙
		Movement Interference	○	○	△	○	○
		Position Stability	○	○	△	△	○
		Conformity to Body	○	⊙	○	○	⊙
		Light Weight	○	⊙	△	⊙	⊙
		Line Fallout	○	△	⊙	△	○

The detailed methods of stages four and five are given in detail in [53, pages 71–98]. We will only sketch the steps in each stage, and make some observations about the stages and steps.

Stage 4: Generating concepts.

Step 10: Decompose design problems (look from different perspectives for subcomponents of the problem, to prepare to generate many different possible solution ideas).

Step 11: Generate ideas (using "creativity methods" and previously available data, generate ideas for solutions for each subcomponent of the problem).

Step 12: Generate solutions (create a number of more or less independent possible solutions to the overall problem).

Stage 5: Selecting the concept.

Step 13: Screen solutions (rank the possible solutions against the requirements or requirement metrics, and generate new solutions, possibly hybrids, that come to mind).

Step 14: Select the solution (again evaluate the alternative solutions against the requirements or requirement metrics weighted by the survey data from step seven).

Step 15: Reflection on the process (reflect on the solution concept that scores highest and other things you have learned to make sure that the selected concept will have support throughout the organization; reflect on what you have learned about the CE method so you will have more skill with it next time).

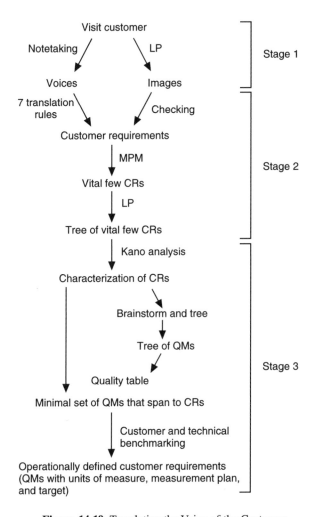

Figure 14-19. Translating the Voice of the Customer

Observations

Stages four and five provide a structured process for maximizing the possibility of a good (or great) solution, just as stages one through three provided a structured process for maximizing the possibility of really understanding customer environments and requirements.

Stages four and five (in which solutions are generated for requirements) are distinct from and follow stages one, two, and three (in which requirements are developed). This helps the team concentrate during stages one, two, and three on fully investigating customer environments and needs without jumping to a conclusion about what the solution is. This is important since there is a great tendency of team

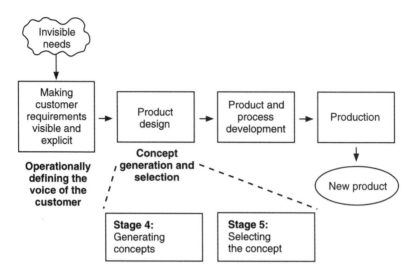

Figure 14-20. The Later Phases of Product Development

members to assume they already know what customers need. Since "solution time" (stages four and five) will follow "requirements time" (stages one, two, and three), find a place for solution ideas that team members see while investigating requirements, such as a large sheet of paper that will be the starting point for step 11.

Steps 1–4 of stages one and two generate a large number of possible requirements. Steps 5–9 of stages two and three narrow the focus to what the team feels are the key requirements and develop deep understanding of the key requirements. Similarly, steps 10–12 of stage four generate a large number of possible solutions, and steps 13-15 of stage five narrow the focus to a single solution which is deeply understood.

From the Operationally Defined Customer Requirements to a Product Concept to a Product

Once the customer's requirements have been understood and made operational (in the form of QMs, targets, and measurement plans) and a product concept has been selected that scores well against these requirements or metrics, you are in a position to deploy the operational CRs and selected concept through the detailed design, development, and production process. Quality function deployment may be the proper tool to provide an accurate deployment through the development process. Quality function deployment came to the United States from Japan in about 1984, and a number of U.S. companies have found it effective for translating the voice of the customer into high-quality products. The process we have described here of listening to the voice of the customer, understanding what customers are saying, identifying key requirements, and operationally defining them is an excellent addition to the front end of quality function deploymenet.

The goal of the entire product generation process is to move from the invisible or vague feeling of the customer to a physical product or tangible service that serves a real customer need. The three stages of operationally defining CRs convert the invisible or vague feeling into clear statements of CRs. These in turn are structured into measurable parameters against which potential product concepts can be evaluated and from which the engineering design process can proceed. The operational definitions of CRs provide a bridge between the qualitative needs of the customer and the necessary quantitative engineering process that realizes the physical product (see Figure 14-21).

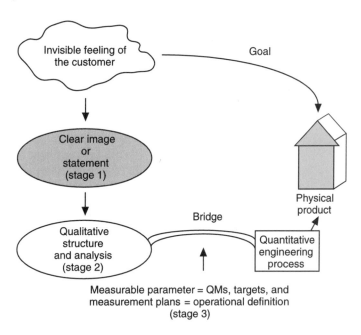

Figure 14-21. From Qualitative Customer Needs to Quantitative Engineering Process

Stripping Basket Case Study—Commercial Success

The newly designed and developed stripping basket was warmly received by sporting goods experts [44] and the fly fishing population. Sales have grown steadily over the years: 1998 sales were four times first year sales. In 1999, a third iteration of the product design entered production.

When we see a fly fishing person in a stream, lake or ocean, much of the time they are wearing or carrying the stripping basket Gary Burchill and his colleagues designed using the methods described in this chapter.

14.5 EXPANDING VIEW OF WV MODEL AND PROACTIVE IMPROVEMENT

In this section, we expand perspectives in two directions. First, now that you are familiar with the CE process overall, we make explicit how such a process fits into the WV Model. Second, we note that the methods of CE and the 7 management and planning tools can be applied to proactive improvement beyond conceiving new products.

Relating Proactive Product Development Process to the WV Model

In Figure 13-7 (page 212), we illustrated how the proactive portion of the WV model is extended to cover extensive planning and design processes. Let us work our way up to that version of the WV model again.

As shown in Figure 14-22, once upon a time it was possible to design a product, develop it, and then sell it. In the sense of alternating between thought and experience, this product-out approach first tested reality against theory when the company attempted to sell the product.

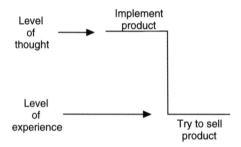

Figure 14-22. The Product-out Approach

Figure 14-23 shows that as customers became more demanding, companies learned to use the techniques of market research to listen to the market before they finalized the product design, developed it, and began to sell it.

The proactive methods described in this chapter increase the number of alternations between theory and the reality of the market before the product design is made final and the product developed (see Figure 14-24, which is a view of what the bottom row of Figure 13-7 on page 212 looks like in the case of CE).

One of the common objections when CE is described to people is, "we haven't got time for a multi-month project like that because we have to get a product to market as fast as possible." This is a short-sighted point of view:

• By repeatedly testing theory against reality, the company minimizes the work it wastes as a result of mistaken assumptions and maximizes its chance of bringing to market a product that customers will buy. Many of these reality checks can be done within days or weeks.

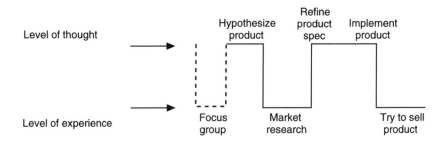

Figure 14-23. The Traditional Market Research Approach

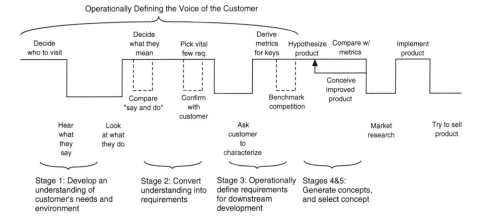

Figure 14-24. The Proactive Approach

- Burchill in his dissertation demonstrated that an early, thorough understanding of customer needs tends to reduce later changes and arguments that delay development. By thoroughly understanding customer environments and needs and arriving at a solution that scores well on objective measures of the requirements (as is done with the structured CE process), companies can get earlier success in the market than if, in the interests of getting to market quickly, they skip straight to implementing their ad hoc ideas about what customers need.
- Many companies have done CE in a couple of weeks of nearly full-time work rather than doing it for a few hours a week over several months. This works especially well if the company has a distribution network to its customers and users that allows user visits to be set up essentially overnight. Even without such a distribution network, visits can be planned in a couple of days of full-time work, then over the next few weeks the interviews can be arranged and carried out, and then there can be a few days of full-time data analysis, e-mail

distribution of the Kano surveys and requests for immediate response, and a final day of project selection. Whichever the case, we are speaking of perhaps two to six weeks, not months.

Curiously, in a number of cases when CE was tried in a company, people in marketing saw it as an invasion of their territory. This is unfortunate for two reasons: (1) CE teams are typically cross-functional and, thus, provide more insight and broader buy-in than work done by marketing alone; (2) CE and existing marketing methods are almost certainly complimentary.

Expanding the Range of Application of the Methods

Many people, when they first learn about CE, treat it as process that must be religiously followed. Of course, the method works when it is followed rigorously and the problem at hand matches the method well. However, having learned the CE method and the 7 management and planning tools, users will need to create their own versions of the process (and accurately follow the process they create) for some applications. We saw one example of such customization with the BBN case study (pages 221–226). We will see further examples of such customization in the CQM Design Study (pages 379–385) and in the structural improvement case study (starting on page 681).

Also, by 1995, it was clear that many people other than product development professionals could benefit from a standard process for collecting and analyzing latent customer needs that address more than just new product development. Therefore, Gary Burchill and Christina Hepner Brodie[10] (with the help of a project team from Joiner Associates) undertook to codify a variation of CE they called FOCUS. FOCUS stands for:

- Frame the project
- Organize resources
- Collect data
- Understand the voices
- Select action

One of the authors' ambitions for the FOCUS method was that, after collecting and processing data in ways similar to those used by CE, FOCUS allowed the user to choose one of three paths:

Targeted path: To answer a specific question, such as "What are the concerns of our customers?" or "What are the weaknesses in our auditing process?"
Requirements path: To develop a set of requirements, as CE does.
Systems path: To create a ground 360-degree perspective of the organizational issues that are resistant to improvement initiatives.

The authors' ambitions also included the following:

- Less rigorous steps than in CE ("60 percent is OK"), making it accessible to some people who might be turned off by the rigor of CE

- Many more explicit substeps so a person can learn the method from reading a book and following its recipes [47]

Thus, FOCUS extended the application of CE.

We also see FOCUS as combining and codifying the methods described in Chapters 13 and 14 of this book and making these ideas more widely accessible.

NOTES

1. This weakness remains despite a variety of work to call attention to and address these issues in some of the books cited above and, for example, in [292].

2. Also as part of his dissertation work, Burchill did academic analysis to validate the workings of the method.

3. From [296]; see particularly chapter 8. See also [295].

4. Lead users are a subset of early adopters from the well-known product life cycle of early adopters, early majority, late majority, and laggards.

5. This case study was presented in a 1990 session of a CQM course given by Yogesh Parikh, Digital Equipment Corporation, Maynard, Massachusetts. Karen Holtzblatt developed the contextual inquiry approach to gathering field data on product use in a post-doctoral internship with Digital's Software Usability Engineering group. Holtzblatt later described the approach in [137, 32, 31] and continues to teach the use of the method. In 1998, Digital became part of Compaq.

6. Useful alternative forms of this question are "what future needs might you have?" or "what changes are you starting to experience?"

7. In this case, the LP was prepared after the interviewers translated verbatim customer voices into quality requirements. However, during the translation and CR LP process, they had numerous discussions of context, and every selected quality requirement was tied to a commonly held image of the product's use and environment.

8. Burchill and the CE development team later consolidated the principles in these seven guidelines into three guidelines [53, pages 37–40]: (1) identify the customer's functional need, (2) make it as specific as possible, and (3) use multi-value language. These three guidelines focus on the most critical aspects of a good requirements statement, and three guidelines are easier to balance than seven. The team also adapted to writing product requirement statements according to the four admonitions from Strunk and White's classic style book [277]:
    - Be clear. When you say something, make sure you have said it.
    - Place emphatic words of a sentence at the end. The proper place in the sentence for the word or group of words that the writer desires to make most prominent is usually at the end.
    - Use the active voice. The active voice is more direct and vigorous than the passive.
    - Put statements in positive form. Make definite assertions.

9. MPM was briefly described on pages 220–221.

10. Christina Hepner Brodie was the Poloroid representative in the initial five-company project to create CE described above. From 1994 through 1999, she was the primary person who has taught and spread the CE method and later the FOCUS method. In the course of this work, she also helped refine the methods.

The Third Revolution:
TOTAL PARTICIPATION

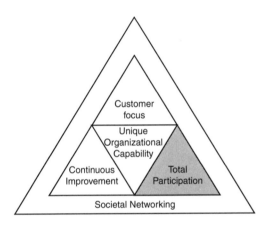

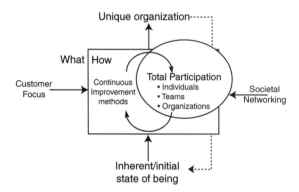

The How Continues with Total Participation

The first edition of this book had seven chapters on total participation. In this second edition, we have added six chapters: Chapter 15 explicitly emphasizes the importance of issues of human behavior, Chapter 16 introduces methods of making and keeping commitments, Chapter 17 introduces skills that help one lead change, Chapter 18 introduces methods of personal development, Chapter 26 adds additional case studies of mobilization of improvement in existing businesses, and Chapter 27 introduces a model for moving into new business areas.

Introduction	Chapter 15 Engagement and Alignment
Individual Learning	Chapters 16–18 Coordinating Behavior Leading Change Self-Development
Team Learning	Chapter 19 Teamwork Skill
Organizational Learning	Chapters 20–23 Initiation Strategies Infrastructure for Mobilization Phase-in U.S. Focused Strategies for Phase-in
Organizational Uniqueness	Chapters 24–27 Hoshin Management Leading Process Improvement Further Case Studies in Mobilization The Practice of Breakthrough

15

Engagement and Alignment of Organization Members

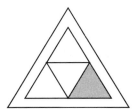

We now come to the part of this book on total participation (see the illustration on page 256). By total participation we do not mean everyone in the organization must participate from the first day or do the same thing or participate on improvement teams at the same time. Rather, we mean that there should be appropriate involvement and engagement of people throughout the organization in appropriate improvement efforts. Nonetheless, a strong bias to involving practically everyone relatively soon is in order. Much of the organizational improvement we are describing requires a mass movement.

15.1 ENGAGED EMPLOYEES FOR A RAPIDLY CHANGING WORLD

Companies need the engaged, intelligent participation of their employees to best compete in our rapidly changing world. The knowledge and skill necessary to take appropriate actions—what Michael Polanyi called tacit knowledge [226]—are spread throughout the company. In today's world, it is not sufficient to depend only on the few geniuses and highly effective people in a company. They can't hope to know everything they need to know. We need the collective genius of the individuals in the organization. Indeed, as people achieve greater mastery in specific domains of skill, it becomes difficult for them to articulate exactly how they accomplish the skill [86, chapter 2].

Furthermore, the active cooperation of the employees is needed to make use of this skill. Anyone in the organization can deny his or her knowledge and skill to the organization, for whatever reasons he or she may have. A few people in a company who are not involved or refuse involvement in customer satisfaction and continuous improvement activities can negate these activities for the company and everyone in it.

If some individuals are feeling particular animus toward the company, they may resort to what one company called malicious compliance: "I know this won't work for reasons that you, my manager, don't know, but since you told me to do it without asking for my viewpoint, I am going to do exactly what you ask without telling you why it won't work, and you will learn later why it's a big mistake." You will not even know they are effectively sabotaging business improvement activities until it is too late.

Obtaining appropriate total participation runs into the problem that for any situation of any consequence different people have different points of view based on their own experience, mental models, personality, professional cultures, and so on. (Remember the observer-that-one-is from Figure 5-4 (page 64) which leads to different reasoning as shown in Figure 5-5 (page 65) which leads to different univiews as shown in Figure 5-6 (page 66) and not necessarily to a multiview and shared concerns.) The top manager has a point of view, each lower level manager has a point of view, and each individual contributor has a point of view. The approach of any person, including the top manager, trying to impose his or her point of view on everyone else simply doesn't work most of the time. As already mentioned, anyone can stonewall anything or, worse yet, pretend to go along. Furthermore, the top manager often sees things in a way that doesn't resonate with the average employee in the company[1] and can't understand why the average employee "doesn't think about things correctly."

An approach that does work is for people with different points of view to understand what other people are saying or thinking and to understand why it is valid from their point of view. Seeing each other's point of view and why it is valid gives us new data about the situation to work from. It also gives us insight into individuals' concerns from which we may be able to see or develop a set of shared concerns that will allow us to get alignment around an action (as shown in Figure 5-6). We all know of the power that is unleashed when a set of individuals cooperate in trying to accomplish something rather than pulling in different directions.[2]

As is suggested in Figure 15-1 (which is a variation of Figure 2-4 on page 34), we need methods both to discover individual concerns and link them to the goals of the organization, and we need methods to align the activities of the individuals in pursuit of the common goals. In the following chapters, we will give examples of both of these. For instance, Brad Harrington has reported to us that parts of Hewlett-Packard (HP) used a bottom-up hierarchy of LP diagrams to inform the one or two key breakthrough goals the CEO set for the company each year, and Dr. G. Clotaire Rapaille [27, 234] has taught various companies methods to find the culturally derived subconscious obstacles and enablers to activity in a particular area. Also, many companies, including HP for many years, have used the hoshin management process for deploying an overall company goal throughout the organization, aligning every division, department, and work team as appropriate to participate in accomplishing the overall goal.

While many companies build their mobilization infrastructure around continuous improvement or around customer focus, some companies in fact build their mobilization infrastructure around engagement and alignment of activities and purposes across the organization, for instance, around hoshin management as in the NIMS case study (page 455).

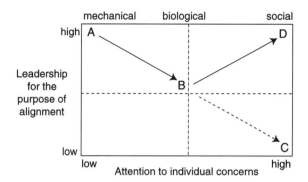

Figure 15-1. Leadership versus Empowerment

Today, whatever mobilization structure is chosen, all workers in the company must be mobilized to improve the way they do their jobs and satisfy customers. To mobilize everyone to achieve these goals, companies must change the way they think about and organize work.

15.2 EXPLICIT JOINING OF IMPROVEMENT AND ROUTINE WORK

All organizations have two functions: their routine function or work and their improvement function or work. The traditional method of organizing work within a company includes the division of labor between workers who do the routine work (R in Figure 15-2) and managers or improvement specialists (such as process engineers) who make improvements (I in the figure) in the way routine work is done.

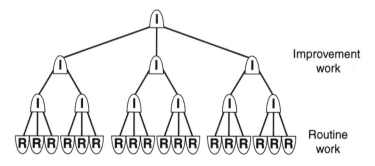

Figure 15-2. Traditional Division of Labor

However, this traditional organization does not react fast enough for the pace of change in today's world. Moreover, it kills human creativity. Many people are not satisfied doing the same thing every day according to standard. That is the job of machines, not human beings. Instead, total participation means developing the human capacity by uniting routine work and improvement work (review again Figure 15-1).

You should join the functions of routine and improvement work (I/R in Figure 15-3) at each level within the company and within each work unit so that quick and correct reaction to change may occur.

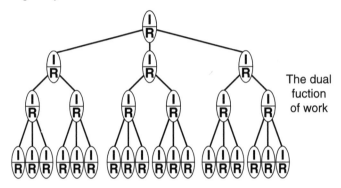

The dual fuction of work

Figure 15-3. Joining Routine Work and Improvement Work

We have a name for joining of routine work and improvement work: the *dual function of work*. The dual function of work is implicit in the market-in diagram (Figure 4-2, page 52): everyone in the company does two jobs, routine work and improvement work, in order to satisfy customers.

Routine work is any repeated activity, however long or short the period of repetition. Examples of routine work include running a machine, typing memos, supervising staff, preparing a monthly report, doing a quarterly forecast, and preparing the annual hiring plan. In many instances, the process for doing a routine work activity may not be explicit, especially for managers, but the process, however vague, repeats nonetheless.

Improvement work is aimed at improving processes for routine work and almost always involves discovering new things. Improvement work itself is more effectively done if a clear process is used.[3]

In general, people want creative jobs. Nevertheless, when the concept of the dual function of work is introduced, most people view the improvement work as an extra burden for which they have no time. An underlying reason may be a natural human avoidance of change. However, since a primary purpose for working on business improvement is to address the need for rapid change, it is important to put systems in place to facilitate systematic improvement and change and eliminate the "not my job" attitude.

The interlinking SDCA and PDCA cycles, first described in Chapter 8 (see page 117), provide a system for the evolutionary and continuous improvement of routine work. Organizational improvement practitioners commonly characterize routine work as following an SDCA cycle: Standard (know it), Do (the work as specified by the standard), Check (the work against standard), and Act (on any discrepancies between targeted and actual results, or return to Standard and do the work again). The SDCA cycle is shown in Figure 15-4.

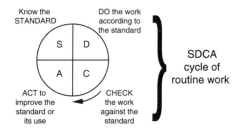

Figure 15-4. The SDCA Cycle

Reactive improvement—activities to improve qualities of conformance—arise from the SDCA cycle of routine work. Opportunities for improvement come from acting on non-conformance to standards in the Act portion of the SDCA cycle. When evidence clearly shows that something isn't working the way people want, improvement activities should begin, as Figure 15-5 shows. When improvement is verified, the remedies become new standards, which then become the new basis for the SDCA cycle of routine work.

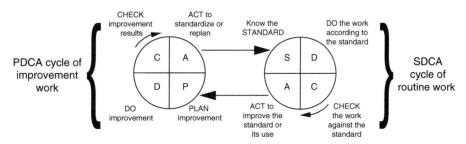

Figure 15-5. SDCA = Routine Work and PDCA = Improvement Work

Consider the application of the SDCA/PDCA model to a company just beginning to try to improve. In the SDCA cycle, the standard (S) is the current process for doing something. It may be invisible or virtually nonexistent, but it is still the current routine work process. Look at part a of Figure 15-6. Using the just mentioned perhaps weak or almost non-existent standard (S_0), you do (D) your work. You accept the result and continue using the current process (C and A).

Look at part b of the figure. Eventually during the check (C) stage of the SDCA cycle you may have some vague dissatisfaction with the results. Thus, you act (A) to initiate a PDCA improvement cycle.

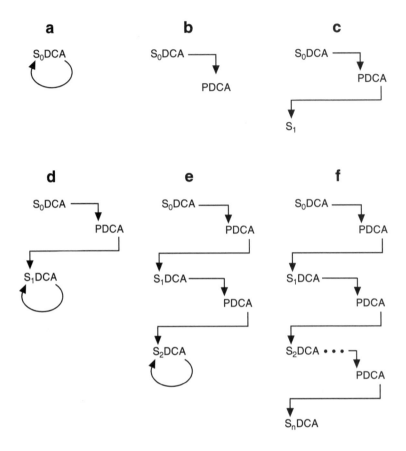

Figure 15-6. An Example of SDCA/PDCA Interaction

The PDCA improvement cycle is used to improve the routine work SDCA process. For instance, the first improvement (A) might be to document the current standard. As shown in part c of the figure, this in effect provides an improved standard, S_1.

As shown in part d of the figure, you use the new standard in the SDCA cycle for a while.

Eventually, at the check (C) stage (see part e of the figure) you are again (or still) dissatisfied with the result of the current process (S_1) and again you act (A) to initiate an improvement cycle, which again improves the standard process.

In this way, application of the principle of dual function of work successively improves the standard process (part f of the figure).

Improvement activities and routine activities are subprocesses of the larger process simply known as "the job" in a context of an organization working to improve itself. Indeed, some companies most impressively succeeding at total participation

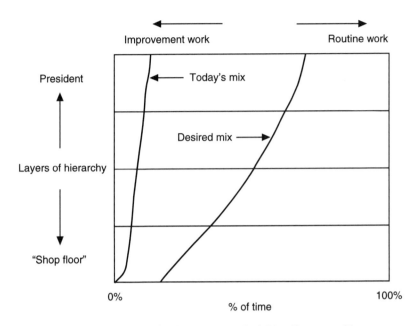

Figure 15-7. Increasing Improvement Activities Companywide

refuse to distinguish between improvement work and routine work and, thus, stress that improvement is part of everyone's job.

The balance between routine work and improvement varies, depending on where you stand in a company hierarchy. Higher ranking people get to do more improvement work than those lower down. The object of total participation is to increase everyone's improvement activities, as shown in Figure 15-7.[4]

15.3 PROCESSES AND PEOPLE

A simple way to think about improving our management methods is that we have to deal with: the processes we tend to follow as we do our daily activities and the people who are involved in these processes.

Over the past decades, many companies have made great productivity gains by concentrating on making their internal and customer-related processes tangible, analyzing them, and improving them. Some people think of work in this area as the hard side of business or organizational improvement.

However, this hasn't always gotten us all the improvement we would have liked. In many cases, people issues—issues of human behavior—have gotten in the way. People, for their own reasons, have not completely embraced the new methods. Furthermore, many of our interactions among people are seen as isolated or a one-shot deal—not as being part of repetitive processes that can be explicitly improved.

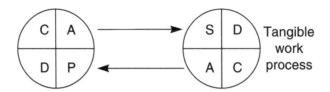

Figure 15-8. PDCAing a Tangible Work Process

Thus, increasingly, there is convergence of thought among practitioners that we must begin to address issues of human behavior and interactions, what we call soft side issues.

The previous section reiterated how the PDCA cycle is used to improve standard work processes (the SDCA cycle), as illustrated in Figure 15-8. When most people first think of moving from an SDCA cycle to a PDCA cycle, they have in mind the SDCA cycle for a tangible process such as we typically find in manufacturing, administration, and so on. They may even think about PDCAing a moment-of-truth process such as a customer hot-line or an innovative process such as new product development. Some people call such tangible processes "hard side" activities.

However, once an organization makes initial gains in improving such tangible processes, the dominant influence on its ability to improve the way the organization functions is typically such intangible issues as the way people in the organization relate to each other and converse with each other, the way people are motivated, perhaps by seeing a link between their individual concerns and the goals of the organization, and so on. These are all issues of engagement and alignment. Some people call such less tangible activities the "soft side." To continue improving our organizations, we need to improve soft side skills.

Unfortunately, the dominant soft side issues are harder to improve on than the hard side issues. Ray Stata, founder and chairman of Analog Devices and chairman of the CQM, likes to quote Roger Millikan (of Millikan): "The soft side is hard, the hard side is easy, and the soft side is more important."[5]

One important reason the soft side skills are more difficult to improve, i.e., we have trouble PDCAing them, is that we typically have nothing close to an explicit process for them (see Figure 15-9). At best people think of the way they talk to each other or motivate subordinates as style or some intangible leadership or behavior characteristic. Yet, one of the first principles of improvement is that you seldom can suc-

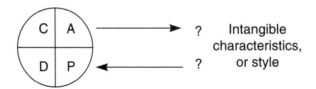

Figure 15-9. The Intangible is Difficult to Improve

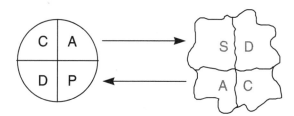

Figure 15-10. By Making the Soft Side Visible We Can Improve It

cessfully improve the intangible. That is why in reactive improvement we begin by discovering the process (making it explicit) and digging for data about the process.

Therefore, to increase the likelihood of improving such soft side skills, the first step is to try to make soft side activities more tangible. There may never be a fully explicit process, but you need some understanding of the repeated patterns of soft side behavior, however vague (see Figure 15-10). Rather than a relatively explicit process, you may be able to describe a model of what happens. We describe in Chapter 16, for instance, a four-stage model for making requests and keeping commitments, something people do all the time in business without thinking about how they do it.

Four Levels of Practice of Total Participation

The remaining chapters of this book, on total participation and societal networking, concentrate on developing tangible processes or models for soft side activities to enable these activities to be taught, explicitly practiced and improved.

As can be seen from the table on page 256, this portion of the book, on total participation, consists of five sections. The sections are ordered on the four levels of practice of skill development that we believe any management system needs to deal with, as originally described on page 39 and expanded upon in Figure 15-11. The goal of

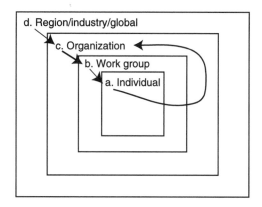

Figure 15-11. Four Levels of Practice

business is organizational change (c in the figure) for better organizational perform-ance. However, ultimately transformation comes down to individuals (a in the figure). Individual change works better in a supportive group work environment (b in the fig-ure). Mutual learning at the group level is made possible by a supportive organization-wide environment (c in the figure). And organizations learn faster in a supportive external environment (d in the figure).

Table 15-1. Learning Level vs. Type of Improvement

	Existing Business			Breakthrough into new business
	Control	Process/product improvement	Process/product/ capability breakthrough	
INDIVIDUAL				
16. Coordinating behavior	━━━━━	━━━━━	━━━━━	━━━━━
*25. Leading process improvement	━━━━━	━━━━━	■ ■ ■ ■ ■ ■	
17. Leading change	━━━━━	━━━━━	━━━━━	━━━━━
18. Self-development	■ ■ ■ ■	■ ■ ■ ■ ■	━━━━━	━━━━━
WORK GROUP				
19. Teamwork skill	━━━━━	━━━━━	━━━━━	━━━━━
ORGANIZATION				
20. Initiation strategies	━━━━━	━━━━━	━━━━━	
21. Infrastructure for mobilization	━━━━━	━━━━━	━━━━━	
22. Phase-in	━━━━━	━━━━━	━━━━━	
**23. U.S. strategies for phase-in	━━━━━	━━━━━	━━━━━	
**24. Hoshin management	━━━━━	━━━━━	━━━━━	
**26. Further case studies in mobilization	━━━━━	━━━━━	━━━━━	
**27. Practice of breakthrough				━━━━━

REGION/INDUSTRY
28. Societal networking ⎱
29. Ongoing integration of methods ⎰ In part 4, on the Fourth Revolution, Societal Networking

* Note non-sequential chapter number; see explanation in the following text.
**Creating unique organization

The chapters of this part of the book are ordered (with one exception) according to the four levels of practice. These are listed down the left side of Table 15-1. For each chapter, the table shows how the content of the practice levels and chapters generally apply to (across the top of the table):

- Control of existing processes
- Improving existing processes or products
- Breakthroughs within the existing business
- Breakthroughs into entirely new businesses.

While the first several chapters (at the organizational level) address how to get everyone in the organization to practice a standard system of business improvement and organizational learning, the rest of the chapters (at the organizational level) address how to make that system address the organization's unique needs.

Note to reader: Chapter 25, on leading process improvement, in some sense logically fits in the portion of the part of the book on the individual level of practice. However, many of the methods discussed and examples given depend on content of later chapters in this book. Therefore, we include this chapter among the chapters on organizational uniqueness at the point when we have the necessary context.

NOTES

1. Schein in [247] describes the different cultures of executives, operators, and developers.
2. Thomas provides in [282] a number of case studies illustrating conflicting social and political interactions among managers, engineers, and workers dominating the benefits of technological change in trying to improve the ways businesses function.
3. The *routine* work of improvement specialists—such as a process engineer or 7 steps facilitator—is improving processes or helping other people improve their processes. Their *improvement* work is improving the ways they improve processes or help others improve processes.
4. This figure is an adaptation and extension of Figures 1-3 and 1-4 in [141].
5. Thomas Powell's research [227] supports this assessment.

16

Coordinating Behavior

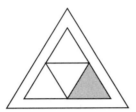

In this book we emphasize the importance of engaging employees and managing the interactions of everyone within the company. In particular, the social model (right side of Figure 15-1, page 287) requires people to understand each other, to coordinate actions with each other and ultimately to build trusting relationships.

Of course, there are many methods, formal and informal, for seeking understanding, coordinating actions, and building relationships. However, here we report a specific synthesis of methods that several CQM member companies have developed and that is evolving with experience. In particular, we will describe specific tangible models for a set of "soft side" activities that most people do more or less unconsciously and, thus, for which they are not well positioned to improve their skill.

Importance (and Difficulty) of Conversation

Conversation is the primary way we discover (observe) what is happening and how we create action in our organizations.

In fact, for almost all complex problems (or opportunities) most of the data we have is language data and most of the thinking, planning, and coordination of action we do is done through conversation or using language.

For instance, customers signal us that there is a problem using language. Using language we discuss and agree with each other within our organization that indeed a problem exists. Probably through conversations, we collect some more data to help us understand the problem. We plan a tentative solution using conversation. We coordinate carrying out the solution using conversation. And so forth. Even attempts to resist the solution (which sometimes happen in our organizations) typically involve language.

More particularly, the most frequent task or activity of many people in a business, especially managers, is attempting to communicate and coordinate with each other. In fact, if we think about what managers do, their primary tool is conversation. This also is the primary way they find out what's happening and the way they create action. We sometimes think of managers as being powerful people. This power results directly from their ability to create (or prevent) specific actions of others, and the tool that managers use as leaders, coaches, and initiators of action is conversation.

Ideally, communication and coordination is aimed at advancing the purpose of the business. However, much of the time we are confused and either do the wrong thing or do the right thing badly. If we investigate the source of this confusion and the resulting inefficiency, we discover that we frequently fail to make or keep the commitments necessary to take advantage of an opportunity, miss opportunities altogether, or generally operate in an environment of mistrust.

Effort = Useful Work + Waste

The formula shown is intended to indicate that the amount of effort we have to spend consists of effort spent on useful work—work we desire to have done—and effort spent on non-useful or wasted work.

If we ask the typical manager how much time he or she spends in meetings or other conversations, we typically get estimates of from 30 percent to 90 percent of their time. When we ask how much of the time spent in meetings or conversation is time spent on useful work, we typically get estimates ranging from 25 percent to 50 percent. In other words, 30 percent to 90 percent of our time we spend in meetings and conversations and 50 percent to 75 percent of that is wasted. We are probably wasting between 20 percent to 40 percent of all our time, and maybe more. And the time we waste results in things not getting done or not getting done correctly, which results in more waste in the form of rework or rebuilding of relationships. Finally, all this waste often causes subsequent damage in related areas, and we miss opportunities to be doing other productive things.

Two ubiquitous sources of waste are inefficiency (not doing things right) and ineffectiveness (not doing the right things). Inefficiency very often results from some form of missed commitment. People make certain commitments to do their part of a project and don't meet the commitments. People are assumed to have made commitments which they never actually made. People make the wrong commitments. Ineffectiveness very often results from missed opportunities. People don't seize an available opportunity. People don't discover an opportunity is available. People select the wrong opportunity. In either case, trust does not develop among the people involved, and in fact mistrust may develop. Without significant levels of trust, good communication and mutual support are not available, leading to increased inefficiency and ineffectiveness.

The point is that poor use of conversation and language can result in massive waste. It's hard to think of improving any single other activity that could have as much benefit as improving the way we use conversation and language.

Need Tangible Models for Important Classes of Business Conversations

The methods we typically use to seek and investigate opportunities and to make and keep the commitments necessary to pursue an opportunity successfully are methods of communication and coordination we have learned mostly unconsciously since our childhood and which let us down as much in private life as they do in business. The fact is that most of us have seldom or never worked effectively to improve these largely implicit and unconscious methods. Improved skill of some sort is needed to avoid such inefficiency and ineffectiveness.

As discussed elsewhere in this book (see, for instance, the section on Process and People, pages 291–293), one of the first lessons we learn about improving the way we manage is that it is difficult if not impossible to improve the intangible; we must begin an improvement effort by making the process or system visible to ourselves.

Thus, if we hope to improve the way we communicate and coordinate in business, we must seek to make more tangible what we are doing when we try to understand each other and coordinate action, as shown on the right side of Figure 16-1. From our point of view, this means we need improved models for such common human inter-actions as finding mutually satisfactory opportunies, making and keeping commit-ments, and in so doing building increased trust. This leads us to the CQM Study Group on Conversation, which is also an example of societal networking.

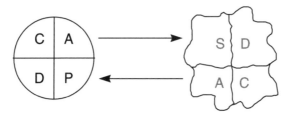

Figure 16-1. PDCA Cycle and SDCA Cycle for Soft Side Activities

16.1 SOCIETAL NETWORKING CASE STUDY OF THE CQM STUDY GROUP ON CONVERSATION

Since its founding, the CQM approach to improving management methods has been to identify common weaknesses in existing management systems and for member companies to work together to find management methods to address these weak-nesses. The participating companies then integrate the new skills into the existing methods, making the new methods as operational as possible so that they can be widely disseminated.

In the mid-1990s, Ray Stata (Analog Devices founder, chairman, and at the time CEO and CQM co-founder and chairman) began to see the "soft side" as the next area that needed improved methods if business improvement was to continue beyond the gains resulting from improving manufacturing, administrative, and other explicit business processes. Ray became aware of Fernando Flores and his "conversational turn" to thinking about business, Ray met with Flores, and Ray began to talk about "conversations" within Analog Devices [274]. Of course, CQM companies already knew the importance of language (see the discussion of Figure 6-12, page 81, and Section 13.2, beginning on page 204). In 1995, stimulated by Ray Stata's insight, several CQM member companies recognized skill in conversation as a critical void in the management methods they were applying. Having recognized the weakness in conversation, they could not find a single source for adequate tangible, operational methods that could be applied to improve the way we converse. Therefore, the CQM initiated a study group to investigate available methods relating to language and conversation. The group included participants from Analog Devices, Boston College School of Business, Intel, Keane Associates, the U.S. Navy, and W.R. Grace, and experienced business executives from the CQM central office staff.

Members of the study group read widely, listened to expert presentations, and wrote analytic notes to each other summarizing the connections they saw between available methods. Their first inclination was to study the concepts and methods of Fernando Flores. However, Flores himself was unavailable to the study group at the time, so the study group had to content itself with reading some of the available published writings of Flores [98, 312, 99, 100, 101] and getting presentations from some people who had studied with Flores:

- Jack Reilly introduced the study group to the ideas of speech acts (Section 16.2), shared concerns and the atom of work model for making and keeping commitments (Figure 16-6, page 309, and [236, 60]).
- Rafael Echeverria, then with the Newfield Group, introduced the group broadly to an "ontological philosophy" of business and methods [88], to the ideas of Umberto Maturana on how people observe things [196, 89], and to the elements of a request (pages 309–310).
- Beebe Nelson provided a useful illustration of three types of business conversations (Figure 16-3, page 306).
- Fred Cunningham provided much insight into the details of using the atom of work and the alternative "moves" to agreeing to a request and for when an agreement is not carried through.

To expand its perspective beyond the "Flores school," the study group also heard from:

- Robert Putnam of Action Design who introduced the group to the ideas of Chris Argyris and Action Science [17, 16, 230], to the ladder of inference (Figure 5-3, page 63), the left-hand and right-hand column device of Argyris (Figure 16-14, page 318), the action design model and its variations (Figure 16-15, page 319), and the distinction between advocacy and inquiry (Figure 16-16, page 320).

- Bill Isaacs who described the ideas of David Bohm on Dialog [35].

The study group members already knew well the language methods of S.I. Hayakawa (Section 13.2, pages 204–210, and [133]) and Jiro Kawakita (Section 13.3, pages 217–221, and [165]).

By the winter of 1996, the study group had created an initial synthesis model [76]. The model drew on, in approximate order of their influence, ideas from the business philosopher Fernando Flores and the codification related to the group by Rafael Echeverria, the psychologist Chris Argyris and his colleague Robert Putnam, the biologist Humberto Maturana, the general semanticist S.I. Hayakawa, the philosopher John Searle, the physicist David Bohm, and the anthropologist Jiro Kawakita, as well as many ideas from study group members themselves. We sketch this model in the following sections of this chapter.

The study group then recommended three major initiatives:

1. The synthesis approach was taught and tested in practice in CQM's TQM courses for senior executives, which covered the content of the first edition of this book.
2. A study was initiated to see how the methodology could be used to redesign complex business processes, specifically the new product development process.
3. New courses were designed to teach managers how to use the methodology in their roles as coaches and leaders.

The ways these initiatives were carried out further indicate the way a societal networking project evolves.

Gary Burchill and David Walden took the lead in codifying the initial synthesis by drafting, piloting, and refining the course for the first initiative [48, 298, 301]. As part of this activity, Gary did the original sketch of the trust loop (Figure 16-19, page 323), and Gary and David sketched initial versions of the cycle of reasoning and uniview/multiview grid (Figures 5-5, page 65, and 16-12, page 317).

Another study group including people from Bose, HP, and CQM was launched for the second initiative.

The third initiative was addressed in several ways. A subset of the original study group worked with Rafael Echeverria and Robert Putnam to develop a course (two and a half days) that Echeverria and Putnam delivered to senior executives. During this effort, the revised versions of Figures 5-5 and 16-12 were developed. David Walden, drawing heavily on Fred Cunningham's conversation course at Keane Associates, developed a one-day course for people who are not senior executives. Later, this course was revised by Burchill and Walden to deliver to intact company management teams. Also, Robert Putnam, Larry Raskin of Analog Devices, and Walden developed a two-day course suitable for intact work groups.

In May of 1997, the CQM was privileged to meet with Fernando Flores himself for two days, and he gave us his original slant on things and extended our awareness of the "conversational turn" into new domains [101, 273].

We have described a typical CQM societal networking effort. There is desire to explore a new subject area. People from member companies come together and learn from presentations and writings by experts, adding their own insights. A synthesis is created and tried, and it continues to evolve until it fits well with and supports the other methods member companies are using.

The rest of this chapter sketches the integrated model that was developed and has informally circulated since 1996 [301] and, since then, been taught to and practiced by people in a variety of types of organizations. Note that the purpose was to develop a model that could be made operational, that could be taught, and that could be improved based on experience. Thus, the study group sought explicit models and a "step-by-step" process—specific "rules-of-thumb," however simplistic—to let people begin to practice and gain actual experience and work their way toward the mastery that enables one to deal with complex, real-life situations.

There has been good progress in achieving this operationalization, and more must be done.

16.2 EXPANSION OF THE PRINCIPLES OF SEMANTICS

The operational models that resulted from the CQM Study Group on Conversation begin with an expansion of some of the ideas of semantics (pages 204–210), providing richer basic building blocks for dealing with language. Refer to Figure 16-2 while reading the following subsections.[1]

Statements of Fact

Some facts are of the natural world, and we use words to describe them. "There is snow on Mt. Everest," is a fact of the natural world. Some facts are created by people using words and create changes in the world.[2] The U.S. Declaration of Independence was such a fact. Distinguishing these two kinds of facts is important. In business, people mostly deal with facts created by people, and these kinds of facts *can be changed.* Unfortunately such changeable facts are often treated as if they are facts of the natural world. For instance, a certain report is prepared and distributed throughout the company every month by the MIS department even though the executive who originally demanded that the report be circulated is long gone from the company.

Two further examples of statements of facts are: "It snowed last winter in Boston" and "The customer canceled the order." The first is a natural fact, and the second was created by people.

The intention with facts should be to attempt accurately to describe the state of the world ("the word follows the world"). Thus, people have an implicit commitment to be able to provide evidence for the facts they state. They may not be asked for this evidence, but they should be able to provide it if asked. Consider how you would feel if someone told you "I have taught the course you are asking about five times before," and you later discovered the person never taught the course before; or, a colleague

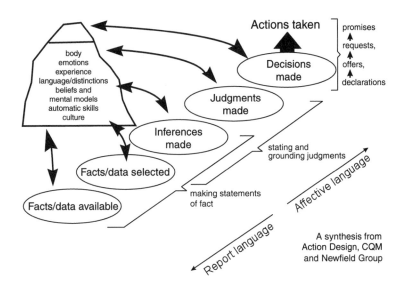

Figure 16-2. Elaboration on Semantics

tells you "the customer wants a better user interface on our product," when the colleague has never talked to the particular customer or otherwise learned about the customer's specific needs.

While statements of facts are intended to describe the state of the world, it is possible to be honestly mistaken. Thus, statements of (possible) fact can be true or false.

As a first step to improving understanding, each of us can easily volunteer a little evidence for our stated facts that will greatly improve the ability of the people listening to us to understand how solid our facts are. We only need say a few more words. For instance, instead of only saying, "It snowed in Boston around Christmas last year," one might include whatever additional evidence one has, such as:

- I think I remember snow last Christmas.
- My spouse was reminding me last week that we had a white Christmas last year.
- I remember digging my car out of the snow between Christmas and New Year's.
- I remember being out Christmas shopping for my wife at the last minute last Christmas Eve afternoon, and it was snowing so hard I had the streets to myself.
- I went on the Internet and looked up the snowfall for each day last year from Christmas Eve until New Year's Eve.

A few more words give the listener much more insight into exactly what facts you are stating and your certainty of them.

A good basic test for whether something is a fact or not is that facts have already happened. This is not always true, but be suspicious of statements of fact that are not in the past tense.

More about Judgments

Judgments are fundamentally different than statements of facts. Judgments evaluate or assess an object, person, or event. "This is a fine product," is a judgment. "Sales for the product in the first six months after introduction were $500,000," is a statement of fact.

Unfortunately, we constantly talk at the level of judgments as if we were stating facts. For example:

"This is a fine product."

"Yes, it is selling well."

"There is certainly no need to increase our advertising budget."

"Right, and we can spend the remaining budget on improving the product to make it even finer."

Whole meetings go on this way with judgment after judgment stated as facts.

Judgments are most constructive if they are used to evaluate a past or present situation for the purpose of choosing future actions. Judgments not for the purpose of future action are often just whining and complaining.

Judgments are not true or false, as are statements of fact. Rather, judgments are grounded or ungrounded. As with the implicit commitment to have evidence for statements of facts, there should be an implicit commitment to have grounding for judgments. Suppose someone says to you, "We don't need to increase the advertising budget." If you ask "Why do you say that?" and the person replies, "It's just a guess," you will probably not seek advice from that person again.

Once again, it is easy to add a few words to judgments that greatly help listeners qualify the level of grounding. Consider the following alternative forms of the same judgment:

- I feel as if this is true.
- I've looked at the data we have and from it I infer...
- I've got the following chain of logic that I followed...

Some statements are fairly clearly facts: "There are six people on our team." Some statements are fairly clearly judgments: "We have a good mix of skills on our team." Some statements are harder to distinguish: "We agreed to this at our last meeting." In this last instance, a few more words would help. Does the person mean, "I think everyone was in agreement as the team meeting suddenly broke up," or "It's in the meeting minutes that the five of us voted to buy the improved testing equipment, and Joey explicitly didn't vote no."

Declarations

Declarations are how new facts are created ("the world follows the word") and, thus, are very important. Companies are declared started, a minister declares a couple to be wed, a traffic policeman declares that cars can move north-south instead of east-west, or a certain type of piece of paper is declared to have purchasing power. Declarations are a key tool of leaders. True facts from the *past* and grounded judgments in the *present* let us make declarations that lead to powerful *future* actions.

The speaker of a declaration is implicitly committed to behave in a fashion consistent with the declaration. For instance, having declared purchase orders as the way a company places orders with suppliers, the company should accept and pay for materials arriving in response to a purchase order.

In business, we use declarations to set a context for future action. Since declarations are not based on existing facts, the validity (or non-validity) of declarations flows from the power or authority the declarer has or has been granted to make declarations in a particular topic area. Thus, another commitment implicitly associated with a declaration is that one has the power to make it. (Basing the declaration on true facts and grounded judgments also provides a certain sort of validation for the declaration.)

There are some declarations everyone must make for their own well-being and that of the organization, for instance:

- Yes—to be able to grab available opportunities
- No—to avoid the problems resulting from not being able to say "no"
- I don't know—to be able learn new things and to avoid spending lots of time spinning webs of excuses
- I'm sorry—to recover from inevitable missteps

A story of the three baseball umpires [14] illustrates the distinctions between a facts orientation, a judgment orientation, and a declaration orientation. The first umpire says, "I call 'em as they are"—this umpire sees the world in terms of facts. The second umpire says, "I call 'em as I see 'em"—this umpire is making a judgment. The third umpire says, "they ain't nothing until I call 'em"—this umpire understands declarations.

16. 3 SOME TYPES AND MODELS OF CONVERSATIONS

In the model the CQM study group developed, thinking in terms of four basic types of conversations, suggested by Flores and his students, proved useful:

- A conversation about which conversation to have
- A conversation to begin or build a relationship
- A conversation to discover possibilities (possible opportunities or actions)
- A conversation to coordinate action

NB: This chapter deals with interactions that are often between two people. To make the examples seem more immediate and to reduce the risk of seeming to lecture the reader on proper behavior, many examples are in the first person—what "I" might do or not do.

The first conversation we will discuss is a conversation to decide what type of conversation we should be having [274].

We have all had the experience of being in a difficult conversation because of differing frames of mind. For instance, if I am in development and you are in sales, you might ask if some special option for a product is possible, and I tell you it is. Later, you discover I have not assigned anyone to work on this special feature. After an acrimonious discussion, we discover that you thought we previously had a conversation for action and I thought we had a conversation about possibilities.

Taking time to understand which conversation we should be having can save much trouble.

Realize that some types of conversations may not be productive and are better avoided, such as, conversations of judgments and stories about who did what to whom.

Let's now talk about the other three types of conversation—conversations for relationships, possibilities, and coordinating action, as shown in Figure 16-3, where each oval and key word represents one of these three types of conversations.

Figure 16-3. Three Conversations upon Which Trusting Relationships Are Built

We begin with conversations for relationships (the outside oval). When we meet each other for the first time, we usually start by building a tentative relationship. We introduce ourselves, we say how nice the day is, we mention some current event in the news to find any commonality of interest, such as "How about those Red Sox; they don't usually begin their annual collapse so early in the season." We are looking for early signs of commonality. Basically, we are determining if being physically or emotionally near the other person is safe. Think about what happens when a stranger comes up to you on the street and begins a conversation: you are wary as you figure out if this person wants something benign (such as directions to a nearby location) or something you don't want to give (such as a handout). Or, imagine a situation where you board an airplane for a transoceanic flight and sit down in your seat. Then, the person next to you introduces himself with a hearty handshake and an enthusiastic greeting. If you are hoping to sleep most of the flight, wouldn't you carefully consider how responsive you want to be to this greeting?

Once we have decided having a tentative relationship with the other person is acceptable, we may explore if there are some mutually useful actions we can take together. In other words, we might begin a conversation for possible opportunities (the middle oval of the figure). This part of the model should feel familiar to anyone in sales. In the airplane example, we may discover we are involved in different aspects of the same business and can possibly learn something from each other.

If we discover a useful action, then we can move to a conversation for coordinating action (the smallest oval of the figure). For instance, before shutting off the overhead light to try to get some sleep on the rest of the flight, you may agree to send each other company information packages and then phone each other once home from the trip—simple actions but perhaps the start of something great.

Jumping to a conversation for coordinating action without having a conversation about possible actions or building a relationship can be counter-productive. We may not have sorted out enough about our relationship or individual concerns to develop sufficiently matched expectations to enable completed actions satisfying both parties. Obviously, when we meet someone for the first time, immediately asking if they want to buy our product doesn't work.

At any point in any of the conversations a mismatch in expectations can lead to a breakdown in the communication or action, requiring a "conversation about breakdown" as part of the recovery process.

To efficiently improve our abilities to discover shared concerns and coordinate accomplishing actions that address these concerns, we need explicit models or processes that can be taught, practiced, and improved. Thus, for each of the three types of conversations represented in Figure 16-3, the CQM study group selected an explicit model as shown in Figure 16-4.

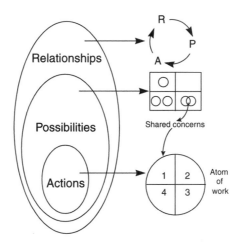

Figure 16-4. Improvable Models for Important Types of Business Conversations

Note to reader. In our courses, we sometimes introduce the models on the right side of Figure 16-4 from the top down and sometimes from the bottom up. Top down perhaps is more logical, and bottom up perhaps provides better motivation to the new students. Here we use the bottom up approach: we need to make keepable commitments (bottom right of figure); making keepable commitments requires broad exploration of possibilities and finding shared concerns (middle right); however, to broadly explore possibilities, we need trusting relationships (top right). If you prefer the top down approach, read the next three subsections (beginning on pages 308, 316, and 322) in reverse order.

Conversations for Action via the Atom of Work

Once we begin to coordinate actions, many problems can happen to defeat our intentions and leave a bad taste in our mouths. Often, we have made a request of someone else or have had a request made of us, thought a commitment was made, and someone ultimately was disappointed.

For example, I asked a clerical person to edit a document by a certain date and time, and the person said he would. However, the person's quantity of work was so great that he could not finish my work by the promised date, delaying my next step.

In another example, my performance missed expectations. I was asked to produce a document by a certain date and said I would. However, I had trouble figuring out how to do the project and didn't finish on time. Therefore, I could not supply the document to the person who needed it for a business trip.

Sometimes, people will do more than requested. I asked my secretary to ask the company library for any available information on a particular subject, hoping to get anything that was easy for the library to find. My secretary made the request of the library, and the library did an on-line search and charged my department hundreds of dollars. Because I was not clear that my interest was only casual, I had to pay much more for the information than it was worth to me.

Finally, all of us have given someone advice only to have the person say "who asked you?" In other words, we sometimes respond to requests that haven't been made, and people resent this.

To improve the quality of our conversations for action, consider the model or process called the atom of work (highlighted in Figure 16-5) that we use to hold conversations to coordinate action and that enables us to make more successful requests and commitments. This models aids in making and keeping commitments.

The atom of work (Figure 16-6) is a schematic representation of the possible paths of making a request or offer, agreeing to a promise, and carrying out the promise or reneging or otherwise failing somewhere along the way.

The atom of work involves four stages which are numbered 1, 2, 3, and 4 around the circle with a fifth element called "breakdowns" (not shown in the figure) and a sixth called "shared concerns." We'll describe each element in turn.

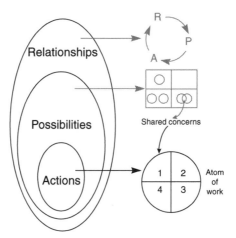

Figure 16-5. A Model for Conversations for Coordinating Action

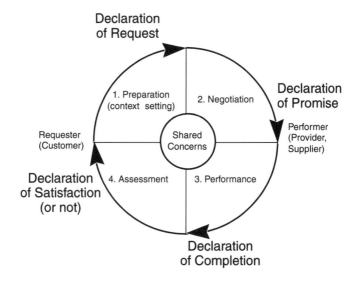

Figure 16-6. Atom of Work

Stage 1 (Preparation)

The atom of work typically starts with a requester or speaker making a request of a performer or listener. During this stage, the requester communicates context in which the request and promise are set. The stage ends with a request.

Unfortunately, while most of us can make requests facilely, they often are not very clear. To assure that things don't go wrong when we make requests, we need to think about many things.

For instance, there needs to be a speaker and hearer. Making requests to no one in particular is not sufficient: "Someone needs to fix the copier." Also, who at one time or another hasn't been disappointed or angry because someone else "should have known" to do something; how could the person have known to carry out the action if we never gave him or her an explicit request? And, we must be careful not to assume a request when no one is making one.

We need to be clear about what is missing. If I say, "I'm out of touch with the situation with customer X," am I worrying that I am not in control of the situation or am I concerned that I don't have information about the situation.

If I mean the latter, then we need to specify the future action to address what is missing. Do I want a report from our customer representative, a conversation in the hall next time you and I meet, or a meeting with the customer to get back up to speed on the situation?

Next, we need to be clear about the conditions of satisfaction, meaning what do I want and how.

We need to be clear about the time frame. The time frame could be listed as part of the conditions of satisfaction. We list it separately because it is so important and because it is often not specified. We just say we want something but don't specify the time.

We also need to be sure we have a shared background of obviousness. My background of obviousness is everything that is so obvious to me that I don't consider whether I need them to be clear to you. For instance, I may hate reports longer than one page, or my concerns about customers may always be strategic and I leave the tactical issues to the people in day-to-day contact with the customer account.

And you need to know if you can trust me when I make a request. Am I sincere and really need this information, or am I habitually making casual requests and then not really caring about the answers?

Stage 2 (Negotiation)

This stage should end with a promise (or, at least a clear statement of what will happen instead of a promise).

Unfortunately, as we often make unclear requests, we also often make non-specific promises. You ask me to do something, and I say, "sure," "as soon as I get a moment," or "why not?" I am not clear if I'm making a serious commitment and, as time passes, that I haven't made a serious commitment may become clearer. Or, if I made a serious commitment and carry out what I thought you wanted, I may discover later that I did the wrong thing.

During the negotiation phase of the atom of work, the requester and performer need to sort out any mismatches in expectations, and the potential performer must have the request straight.

Depending on how well the performer carries out the commitment, the requester will judge the performer and will decide whether to use this person another time. This is why getting clear requests, making good commitments, and carrying them out successfully are important. If we do not, we cast doubt on our capability for future opportunities.

Each of us is judging how much we trust each other every time we make a request. We can look at trust as consisting of three components: sincerity, competence, and reliability. If I make a request of you and you make a commitment to accomplish the request, then based on past experience I may judge you as reasonably sincere, competent, and reliable and decide to take a chance on you. Or I may judge you as exceptionally sincere, competent, and reliable in which case I won't be taking any chance at all. If I judged you as competent but neither sincere nor reliable, I might let you make the commitment but I certainly won't depend on it very much. Seeming to make commitments that we can't or won't live up to is a serious problem because we will be judged accordingly, limiting future opportunities.

Unfortunately, many of us don't feel we can decline a request, and as managers many of us make our people feel as if they must accept a request. For people to reliably live up to commitments, they need other options during the negotiation phase besides simple acceptance. People need to be able to negotiate, make counter offers, commit to commit later, and even decline. As managers, we need our people to use these alternative moves if we want to build a culture of making good requests and commitments. As your supervisor, if I only allow you to say "yes" when I make a request, I won't know if your answer means yes, no, or it's not possible. If I want to know what will happen, I must insist, when appropriate, that you use other options to "yes."

The best time to hear someone can't or won't succeed in a commitment is at request time, when a possibility exists of finding someone else who can and will accomplish the request.

Stage 3 (Performance)

During the performance phase, the person who makes the commitment carries it out. When done, the person declares the task complete.

Unfortunately, declaring performance complete is another thing not often done explicitly. Each of us has probably experienced a case when something we wanted had been completed but we didn't know about it. For instance, on Friday I left some work with the graphics department for a presentation I would be giving Tuesday. The graphics department personnel promised completion by Monday morning. However, on account of another job being canceled, they finished my work by the end of Friday; they sent it through inter-office mail to get to me Monday. Had they called me Friday and told me it was already done, I would have picked it up on my way home, checked it over on the weekend, and found any errors which could have been easily corrected before flying to the presentation site on Monday. However, by not getting the material until Monday morning and being very busy that day, I didn't get to look at it until I got on the airplane Monday evening; by then it was too late to correct an error I found.

We also often fail to declare at the earliest possible moment that we will be unable to perform according to the promised conditions of satisfaction or time frame.

From the point of view of the customer, we would all like suppliers to tell us at the earliest possible moment when they may not be able to deliver as agreed. For instance, the car repair shop personnel should call to tell me my car will not be finished and save me a trip on the subway.

Yet, when we are suppliers, we routinely don't give the earliest possible warning of a problem. This is the point of the fifth element of the atom of work—the declaration of breakdown. Part of the process is validation of the performer (or the requester in the event of a change in need) declaring, as soon as possible, that a problem exists while there is still time to do something about it. This would allow us to avoid making consequent commitments based on the commitment we thought we had.

Some of the time, we can complete a commitment we make by ourselves. However, much of the time we need help. Figure 16-7 shows how one atom of work can spin off consequent atoms of work. If, as a sales person from my company, I promise to deliver a product to you, I will probably make requests of and get commitments from others in my company to deliver the product to you.

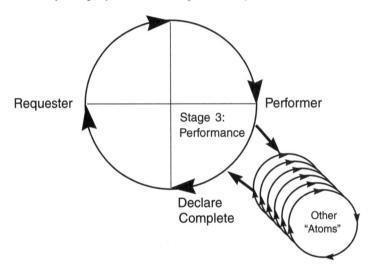

Figure 16-7. Atom of Work with Consequent Atoms

In fact, a whole network of atoms of work can be spun off from the first atom of work. Consider the situation in Figure 16-8. The branch office sales person makes a commitment to deliver a product to the client company. Then the branch office salesperson makes a request of the home office order entry/shipping person to enter the order and ship the product. The order entry/shipping person, in turn, requests an outside credit-check service to ensure the customer's credit worthiness and, finding that the customer's credit is good, ships the product. Then, the branch office salesperson requests the branch office installation person to install the product at the customer site. When this is done, the salesperson is finally in a position to declare the delivery commitment complete to the customer.

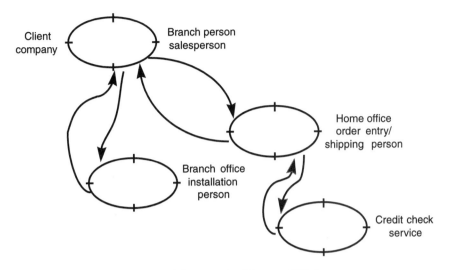

Figure 16-8. Network of Atoms of Work

Other atoms of work can be spun off of any stage of an atom of work. In the primary atom of work (in Figure 16-8), the branch office salesperson could have requested the company contracts department to help with the negotiation phase of the atom of work. This is shown in Figure 16-9.

Figure 16-9. Another Commitment May Be Required at Any Stage

Figures 16-8 and 16-9 illustrate that it is possible to think of the activities and processes we carry out in our organizations as being networks of requests and commitments. This is a powerful and flexible way to look at many of the things we do—more powerful in many cases than more traditional flowcharting and input-process-output models.

Stage 4 (Assessment)

During this stage, the customer assesses satisfaction with the job done by the performer.

Without a specific model, we typically don't execute the activities of this stage which means we don't learn how to do things better in the future. In fact, many people complain that they seldom know if their supervisor is satisfied with what they do. In many other cases, a performer assumes satisfaction that isn't there.

Two issues must be evaluated in stage four. More obviously, success or failure on the agreed-upon task must be judged. Less obviously, the requester and the promiser need to evaluate how well they applied the atom of work model. Did they declare breakdowns as soon as possible? Did the requester allow the requestee the possibility to decline the request? Were they really jointly commited to validating each other's concerns? However careful the request and commitment, sometimes circumstances overtake intentions and someone will not accomplish the agreed upon task, and this must be noted. Yet, even in the face of failure, a relationship may be saved and perhaps grow stronger if the parties behave with each other in accordance with the atom of work.

Stage 4 ends with a declaration of acceptance by the customer, or a declaration of non-satisfaction which means that the atom of work may have to be rerun.

Declaring breakdowns

Let's now ask ourselves, "where in the atom of work can there be a problem?" The answer, clearly, is everywhere. Problems can and do arise in every stage, which brings us again to the issue of breakdowns.

We have already mentioned the importance of declaring breakdowns as soon as we know we cannot complete a commitment.

We never would ride along in a car with a flat tire, blithely ignoring it, with smiles on our faces. However, we do this all the time in our organizations. We sit in meetings, smiling agreement with the boss's words, without stating we know the proposal is bad, won't work, and that we may not even intend to follow through as requested. Then, perhaps, after the meeting, we whisper to each other in the hall something like, "What a terrible idea; it will waste so much effort that could be spent more usefully."

We must encourage use of conversations about breakdown in our organizations. These can be needed in any stage of the atom of work or as part of any of the other conversations. We need to declare a breakdown and decide which conversation to have next. Do we go back and clarify a portion of the atom of work? Do we need to have a conversation for possibilities? Do we need to have a conversation for relationships?

Shared Concerns

We introduced the importance of finding shared concerns earlier (pages 62–66). The shared concerns in the center of Figure 16-6 (page 309) completes our sketch of the atom of work.

For the atom of work to work well, the parties to the atom of work need to understand what their underlying concerns are (their own and the other party's) and understand the compatibility between these concerns.

If your concern is reducing costs and my concern is I may be the cost you intend to reduce, I will probably carry out your requests poorly since my interest is not showing how my job might be done more efficiently. In fact, I once led an engineering group in a company that was downsizing, but where company viability was critically dependent on getting products to market faster. Still, some members of the development staff deliberately did their work more slowly than necessary because they assumed their jobs would be eliminated after they finished their current project. If we can find compatibility of concerns—we called them shared concerns in the figure—then the requester and performer can work toward compatible ends.

Offers

So far, we have described the atom of work in terms of requests and commitments. The model is also applicable to offers (see Figure 16-10). Stage 1 of the atom of work can begin with an offer from a potential supplier to a potential customer. The same elements for a request (conditions of satisfaction, time frame, shared background of obviousness, etc.) have to be sorted out. At the end of stage 1, both sides should understand the offer. Stage 2 may still involve negotiation that leads to a firm commitment for the supplier to provide something to the customer. Stages 3 and 4 are the same with the same need to declare breakdowns if they happen and to assess how well the agreed upon activity was performed and how well the atom of work was applied.

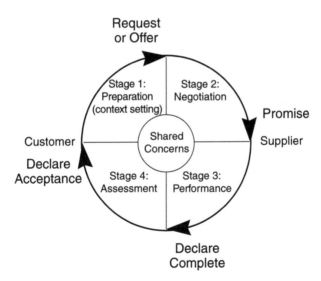

Figure 16-10. Requests and Offers

Offers are very important in business. Jack Reilly likes to say, "A business is defined by the offers it makes and the requests it accepts." This same may be said of individuals. We are defined in the eyes of others by the offers we make and the requests we accept and keep.

Conversations for Possibilities are Key to Discovering Shared Concerns

The idea of shared concerns begs the question of how do we discover our shared concerns, and this leads us back to our model of various types of conversations.

As shown in Figure 16-11, our conversation for possibilities may develop our shared concerns and these, in turn, will be available when we operate the atom of work as our tool for holding conversations for coordinating action.

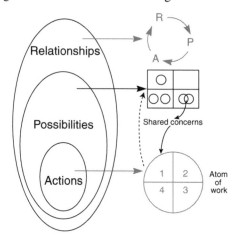

Figure 16-11. A Model for Discovering Possibilities

On the other hand, in some cases (see the dotted line in the figure), we may have started the atom of work without developing a sufficient understanding of our shared concerns; we may have to go back, have a conversation for possibilities to develop shared concerns, and feed these shared concerns into the atom of work.

However, our principle of developing explicit methods we can improve for soft side functions requires us to understand where our feelings about a situation and concerns come from and to create a model for developing those shared concerns, if possible. This model is based on the uniview and multiview grid and cycle of reasoning introduced in Chapter 5 (pages 62–66).[3]

How to create a multiview

Based on our cycle of reasoning, each of us has a uniview about every situation, as shown in Figure 16-12. The problem we need to solve is how to determine the other person's reasoning cycle (and make our own clear to ourselves) so we can discover the multiview (see Figure 16-13).

To find the multiview, we ourselves need to change the observers-that-we-are to become more *open observers*. We need to understand how others see things, and why their perspective on the situation makes sense given how they see the situation (remember our argument on the observer-that-one-is, on page 64, *that how a person sees something says more about the way he or she observes things than it says of the situation*).

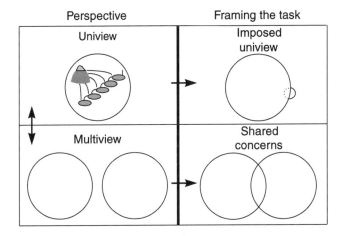

Figure 16-12. We Usually Start New Situations with Different Univiews

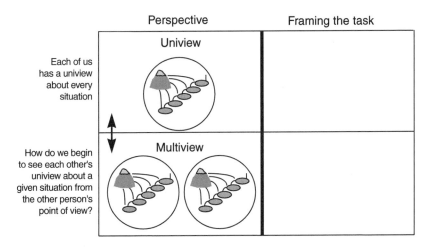

Figure 16-13. Steps to Find the Multiview

We need explicit methods to become more open observers and discover the multiview, such as the following "tools" and rules-of-thumb which we organize into a few categories.

First, we must defer assessments about the viewpoints of others; we must give ourselves a chance to understand the other person's point of view rather than focusing on convincing him or her of ours.[4]

Second, it helps to write down the entire two-way conversation or at least what the other person says. After a significant problem, give yourself a tangible artifact that you can study and learn from. See, for example, the right hand column (RHC) in Figure 16-14 (ignore the left hand column or LHC).

Context: Jane, John, and several colleagues are beginning the first meeting to plan a series of technology seminars around the country that will introduce attendees to a new technology concept and hopefully make them potential customers of a new product that takes advantage of the new technology. John is the key technology expert on the product development team, and Jane is a senior specialist in the companyís PR department who will be responsible for organizing and publicizing the seminar series. The meeting is just starting.

LHC = Thoughts/feelings (of John in this example)	RHC = What was actually said
Here I am having to listen to Jane again.	Jane: This time we have to put some sizzle in our seminar brochure.
With her fixation on image, she got the content wrong last time.	John: Weíve got to get the content right first.
I know. I know that's what you think. That's the problem.	Jane: The brochure has to excite people enough to get them to sign up for our seminars if we are going to find some potential customers for our product.
Why can't she understand this.	John: Of course. But we have to describe something I am able to able to deliver successfully.
Just like last time.	Jane: Hey, Iím a marketing person. It's my job to make the brochure be exciting.
This is hopeless.	John: (nods his head)
Blah, blah, blah.	Jane: Also, because of the date of the product release and the lead time required to publicize and hold this seminar series, weíll have to get the brochure to the printer by Friday of this week, so I'll need peopleís help quickly with copyediting. I'll be around with a draft later today.
When she finds me, I'll tear apart what she's done and make my point again.	John: OK. Find me when you need me.

Figure 16-14. A Meeting Dialog—RHC and LHC

Third, become aware that you are observing the situation from your own particular point of view—become aware of the observer-that-you-are and your own inner dialog. See, for example, the left hand column (LHC) in Figure 16-14.

Awareness of your own point of view (or, frame of reference) allows you to change your frame of reference. This is often the single most productive step in discovering the multiview—seeing how your own way of framing the situation might change. Figure 16-15, the action design model, helps illustrate this. On the left side of part A is the frame of reference from which a person sees a situation. In the middle of part A are the actions the person takes based on his or her frame of reference. On the right side of part A are the results of the actions. Depending on the results, one can either react and change the actions to produce better results, or one can move

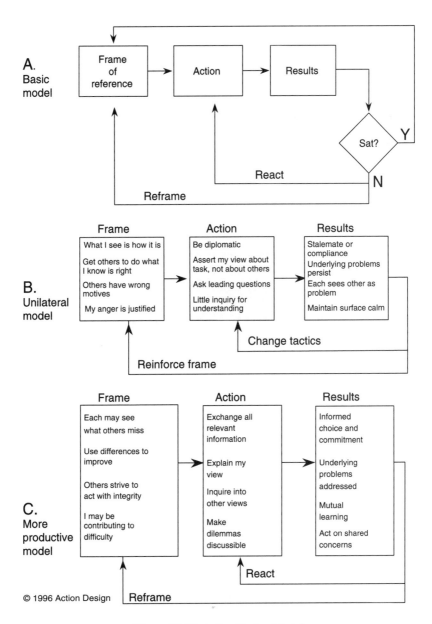

Figure 16-15. Action Design Model

to a different frame of reference which may lead to different actions which may lead to better results.

As in Figure 16-14 and in the unilateral version of the action design model (Figure 16-15, part B), the results are often persistent problems, perhaps disguised in an appearance of surface calm. In part B, without a change of frame, tactics change to "smoother" ways of cajoling compliance with the frame of reference a person "knows" to be right; the frame of reference (that the other person is "all messed up") is reinforced. This keeps one in the top right of Figure 16-12.

A more productive version of the model is shown in part C. Rather than reacting with a change of tactics for the same end, one reframes (changes one's point of view) to validate the other person's point of view: see yourself as possibly part of the problem and the other person's viewpoint possibly as part of the solution. This can lead to actions where we exchange points of view and understand each other's viewpoint rather than imposing our own viewpoints. This can lead to results based on mutual learning, informed choice, and actions based on shared concerns which in turn can lead to further improvements of frames of reference and actions.[5]

Fourth, an important distinction that helps us defer assessments is the distinction between inquiry and advocacy (see Figure 16-16). Advocacy often involves getting the other person to see our viewpoint (as in the top right of Figures 16-12 and 16-16. Inquiry usually has to do with putting ourselves in the other person's shoes and seeing their viewpoint. Too much business conversation takes place in the top right of the figure—high advocacy and low inquiry. From each person's own observations of a situation, the person tries to impose his or her uniview on the other. To find the multiview, one first needs to move to a position of high inquiry and low advocacy (bottom left).[6]

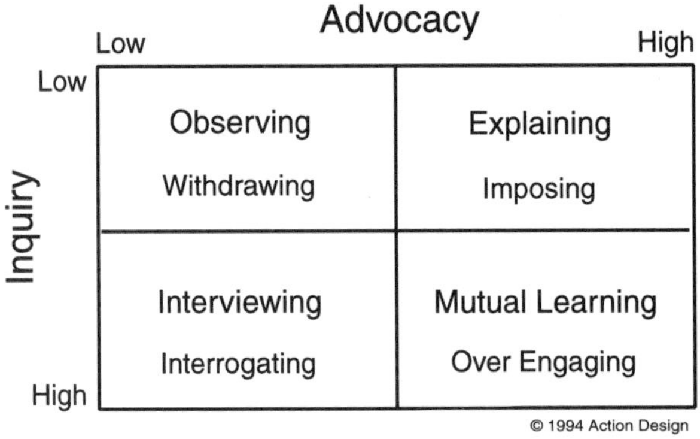

Figure 16-16. Advocacy and Inquiry

Explicit tools exist for each of the above mentioned guidelines. Also, a number of the tools in this book have methods of deferring assessment built into them and include a healthy dose of inquiry. For instance, during voice of the customer visits we ask open-ended questions, don't argue back, take verbatim notes, and use active listening to draw out and confirm that we understand what the customer is saying.

There are a number of other ideas that help one see the other person's point of view that we won't elaborate in this chapter beyond the following mention: listening for the other person's concerns, listening for the particular distinctions that the other person is making, observing and listening for the emotion in the situation, clarifying when the other person is making a declaration, judgment, or statement of fact, and listening for what commitments the other person is making in what they are saying.

How to find shared concerns

Once we have heard and understood what the other person is saying, we can move beyond finding the multiview and onto finding shared concerns. As seen, we can use a variety of tools to become a more open observer and to discover the multiview. We are left with the need for additional tools to find the shared concerns (to move horizontally in the bottom of Figure 16-17).

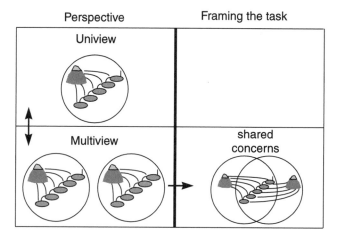

Figure 16-17. Steps for Finding Shared Concerns

The first presumption is that we are already working at becoming a more open observer, using the methods of the last subsection ("How to create a multiview").

Second, now is the time to use advocacy and inquiry together and to maintain them constantly in balance (bottom right of Figure 16-16). Each party will help if he or she takes full responsibility for understanding what the other person means and for making sure the other person understands what one means. There are many tools to help with this. For instance, important sets of tools for developing a multiview and finding shared concerns center around the pair of ideas of making language concrete and making reasoning explicit. Unless we make language concrete, it's hard to even know what we are saying and thinking, much less know it with any precision and convey it from one person to another. Unless we make reasoning explicit, we will not begin to understand the way each other reasons and backgrounds of obviousness about particular situations.

For instance, we can use Hayakawa's principles of semantics to move from affective language to more concrete report language. We can make reasoning explicit by looking at the reasoning cycle (included in Figure 16-2, page 303) and by asking ourselves questions such as what facts are and weren't available, what facts we did and did not select, what inferences we made, what judgments we made, and what conclusions we drew. We can also make various distinctions that let us see our backgrounds of obviousness more clearly. In other words, the reasoning cycle itself is a model for how to delve into each other's reasoning. We can dig down the reasoning cycle from ungrounded judgments and then build back up with better grounded reasoning of which we are both aware.[7]

In summary, we can use the techniques above for moving around the uniview/multiview grid to hold conversations for possibilities and thus leave ourselves a proper context for conversations for coordinating action.

Conversations for Relationships and Building Trusting Relationships

We turn to the third model, how relationships are built, highlighted in Figure 16-18.

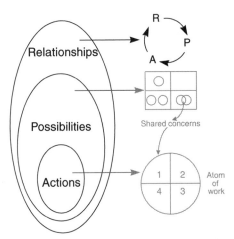

Figure 16-18. A Model for Conversations for Relationships

We call the model a trust loop. Shown in Figure 16-19, the model explores how conversations for relationships relate to conversations for possibilities and conversations for coordinating action and also explains how trust is built or lost.

As shown in the figure, we start with a tentative relationship. This builds a little trust. With a bit of trust, we may be willing to share enough about our own situation to look for some possibilities of working together. This sharing of possibilities may generate a bit more trust. The next step, in turn, could lead to coordination of action. If the action can be carried out successfully, this generates substantial trust, which leads to a stronger relationship because we see that we can actually accomplish things together through this relationship. With a stronger relationship, we may share with each other more about ourselves and the way we reason which could lead to more interesting possibilities. And, if we can successfully coordinate and carry out these actions, our relationship will improve more.

We now see the importance of setting up the proper context for action and carrying out the actions successfully and, thus, the importance of the atom of work. If we can act successfully, we can rise through a spiral of increasing power to perform together. However, if we cannot successfully coordinate action, either because we don't have tools like the atom of work or we don't properly set the context using techniques such as those to move from univiews to shared univiews, then trust and relationships are damaged and we will be less likely to look for possible actions together. If we fail again to carry out action successfully, our relationship may be completely fractured, and no further action may be possible.

Explicit Models for Aligning and Coordinating Shared Concerns

The social model requires that people understand each other's concerns and coordinate with each other (top right of Figure 15-1, page 287). Getting better at doing this requires continuous improvement. Doing continuous improvement requires making processes, models and systems explicit, so they are visible and can be improved.

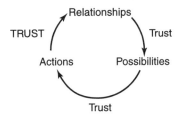

Figure 16-19. Trust Loop

By integrating methods from a variety of experts and areas, an explicit set of models and methods has been created to allow people to improve their understanding of each other and coordinating with each other. Since their creation, these methods have undergone several improvement iterations.

The methods include:

- A specific model—the atom of work—for making and keeping commitments
- A more general model—the uniview and multiview grid—and tools for investigating possibilities to find shared concerns which lead to the possibility of keepable commitments
- A still more general model—the trust loop—for how one builds trusting relationships through finding the right possibilities and effecting successful action

16.4 BURCHILL CASE STUDY FROM THE NAVY

In 1995, our colleague, Gary Burchill, participated in the CQM Study Group on Conversation. At the time, he was a Commander in the U.S. Navy managing a large procurement activity in the Supply Corps at the Naval Inventory Control Point (NAVICP).

Gary Burchill has shared with us his experience in applying the methods of this chapter with the people reporting to him at NAVICP.

First Learnings from the CQM Study Group

As described in Section 16.1, early in the deliberations of the CQM study group on conversation, Jack Reilly gave a presentation in which he described the atom of work. Gary reports that he was "blown away" by the simplicity and apparent power of the atom of work model for making and keeping commitments. Gary's style when he hears about something new is to determine how to apply it in his own situation. Therefore, he applied the atom of work model in a disciplined way to meetings he held at NAVICP.

A month of so later Gary presented his understanding of the atom of work model at a study group meeting. At the end of his presentation, Ray Stata, CQM chairman/co-founder and Analog Devices founder/CEO, told Gary that he was missing the boat—that conversations for possibilities were where all the power is, not conversations for coordinating action that Gary had been focusing on. At the time, Gary was unconvinced of Ray Stata's assessment because coordinating action is "where the rubber meets the road." However, in the following month it gradually dawned on Gary, and then hit him like a thunderbolt, that Ray Stata was right—Gary needed to move his focus from the conversations he was having to the ones he should be having, and those were conversations for possibilities.

At this point, six or eight weeks after the study group began, Gary Burchill gave the six or seven people directly reporting to him some initial training in the methods of conversation he had been learning in the CQM study group. He also provided the same training to several people who did not report to him but whose participation was critical to successful action for those who did report to him. Looking for a structured path among conversations about breakdowns, for possibilities, and for coordinating action, Gary introduced the people (he was training) to the personal quality checklist which he had learned about from Harry Roberts of the University of Chicago.

Personal Quality Checklists

Personal quality checklists are described in the book *Quality Is Personal* [240].[8] They keep track of what you want to improve (reduce defects for). You write improvement areas to concentrate on down the left side of a chart and in each row you keep a daily record of how many times you failed for the area listed in the left column.

The book suggests the following guidelines for personal quality checklists:

- Focus on processes you personally use to do your work
- Keep track of shortcomings in your processes—defects
- Use operational definitions[9]
- Keep it simple
- Recording defects makes you think and ask why

For instance, in his book, Harry Roberts decided he wanted to improve his "office practice" and listed six areas for improvement as shown in Figure 16-20. Each day he kept track of how many times he failed (had a defect) for each improvement area. At the bottom of the chart he totaled his daily defects in these areas. Thus, if on Monday he was late for two appointments, delayed returning one phone call, on two occasions didn't discard incoming junk promptly, and didn't have instances of the other three defects, his total for Monday would be five.

Harry Roberts' Personal Quality Checklist: Week of _____

Defect category	S	M	T	W	Th	F	Sat	Total
1. Late for meeting or appointment								
2. Searched for something misplaced or lost								
3. Delayed return of phone call or reply to letter								
4. Put a small task in a "hold pile"								
5. Failed to discard incoming junk promptly								
6. Missed a chance to clean up junk in office								
7. Unnecessary Inspection								
Total								

Figure 16-20. Harry Roberts' Personal Quality Checklist (Source: *Quality is Personal: A Foundation of Total Quality Management* by Harry V. Roberts and Bernard F. Sergesketter, Copyright © 1993 by Harry V. Roberts and Bernard F. Sergesketter. Adapted with permission of The Free Press, a Division of Simon & Schuster, Inc.)

Personal Use of the Methods

In a Managing Change course at MIT, Professor Edgar Schein required Gary and his fellow students to turn in weekly reports on their change activities, because Professor Schein said, "Without regular monitoring, there is no change." Thus, Gary required the people directly reporting to him to maintain personal quality checklists to diagnose and monitor their change as they learned to use new methods of conversation. They made entries on these checklists at the end of *every* meeting, regardless of whether it had been scheduled or someone just dropped in on someone else.

Gary also began to keep his own personal quality checklist because he wanted to show good "leadership" in use of the methods. However, when he began to monitor his own use of conversation, Gary was horrified to discover that he demonstrated more weakness than anyone. Figure 16-21 is an example of the third iteration of Gary's checklist. First notice that he kept it in a slightly different format than described in the

Roberts and Sergesketter book. Next notice that his checklist included items that Gary personally had trouble with. One such example is (item one on his checklist) expecting a commitment to action without having first ensured shared commitment to the action. Another such example is (item five on his checklist) not taking the time to legitimize the other person's frame of reference.

Date _____			
Missed Commitments	Yes	No	%Defects
1. Shared concern stated prior to commitment to action			
2. Deadline established prior to commitment to action			
3. Explicit assessment of satisfaction made upon acceptance/review of product			
Missed Opportunities			
4. Judgment of others frame of reference suspended			
5. Other's frame of reference legitimized			
6. Articulation of a shared concern			

Figure 16-21. Gary's Personal Quality Checklist

Team Use of the Methods

Because Gary and his team had the tangible personal quality checklists, it began to be their norm to share them at the end of meetings. Gary would ask to see the personal quality checklists of those who reported to him, and it would have been awkward for him not to share his own with them. Using the personal quality checklists, it became a good natured game to note breakdowns (including those of others) and to show that they were keeping track of their own on their personal quality checklist.

Gary and his team already had the tradition of having beer (or soda for the non-beer drinkers) after work on Friday, and the tradition was augmented so the person with the most defects for the week bought the first pitcher of beer. Since Gary directed the group and called the most meetings, he tended to have the most defects and often bought the first pitcher of beer. This game made it OK for junior officers and others who might have been hesitant to speak to declare the boss's breakdowns.

Personal quality checklists, the game of calling each other's breakdowns, and tracking of defects became the way that they got everyone engaged in pointing out defects and avoided future defects. In particular, Gary learned that he was his own worst enemy in this domain.

After four to six weeks of this activity and having improved themselves, Gary and the people reporting to him trained the next level of management. Having Gary and two levels of management practicing these methods resulted in what Gary calls "an enormous reduction in the time I had to invest in problems."

Collectively, they made the distinction between the conversations they were having and the conversations they should be having, for instance, when they should be having a conversation for opportunities rather than a conversation for coordinating action. Gary and his team also had fewer breakdowns in the execution phase. A significantly higher percentage of commitments were successfully completed by the planned delivery date. People were willing to declare breakdowns as soon as they became evident, allowing them to be addressed much sooner than had been typical.

When a person came to him with a story of some problem, Gary asked, "Are you making a request?" Often, the person would reply that he or she was "just venting"; in some cases, this was a person who historically had tried implicitly to transfer a problem to Gary.

Gary's personal bottom line was that without increasing the number of hours worked, the team was able to get its routine work done while spending Tuesday and Thursday afternoons on a large, high priority improvement project,[10] and Gary himself was able to leave work at 5 P.M. to coach his son's soccer team.

NOTES

1. Although we will talk about facts and judgments, the perspective we describe here derives from our study of the work of philosopher John Searle [255] and business consultant Fernando Flores [98, 99]. Searle and Flores (who was a student of Searle) use the terms *assertions* for what we call "facts" and *assessments* for what we call "judgments." People from CQM member companies are already familiar with judgments and facts and shifting over to assessments and assertions throughout all CQM materials is impractical.

2. Searle calls these "institutional facts" [256].

3. For a number of methods that complement and supplement this section, see [258, pages 233–293 on Mental Models].

4. To overcome the flight or fight reaction discussed by Goleman [118].

5. Regarding Figure 16-14, the basic action design model is an adaptation of Robert Putnam and his colleagues at Action Design of the model of double-loop and single-loop learning from [18] and the concept of framing from [254]. The unilateral and mutual learning versions are the Action Design adaptations of Argyris and Schön's model I and model II from [18].

6. To complete the explanation of the figure: Listening and observing (top left) can be a good way to learn while someone else explains (top right). However, imposing (top right) usually results in an attempt at reverse imposition (top right, too) or

in withdrawal (top left). Interviewing (bottom left) is constructive, but interrogating or leading the witness (bottom left) is not constructive. Ultimately, we need to learn from each other (mutual learning at the bottom right), but not just engaging for the sake of engagement.

7. For another tool for finding shared concerns, see [197, pages 125–127].

8. For a related story, see page 547.

9. Definitions that easily allow you to know whether you succeeded or failed.

10. See Chapter 29 (page 681) for that case study.

17

Leading Change

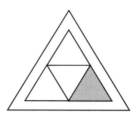

At a CEO roundtable on leadership at the CQM West chapter, chapter Chairman Fred Schwettmann made the following remarks:[1]

> Companies everywhere are dealing with increased complexity (size of organization and geographical dispersion of organization, as well as increased financial, governmental, legal, and regulatory issues). Companies everywhere are dealing with increased speed of change (shorter times between product introductions, increased demands for response from customers). Companies everywhere are dealing with unforeseeable shocks (such as, in 1998, the Asian financial crisis and the sudden drop of the price of a PC to under $1,000).
>
> With these sorts of challenges, companies need leadership more than ever, to declare needed changes in the organization, to provide a vision that the rest of the organization can align itself around, and to articulate that vision in a way that everyone can understand. But as the need for clear leadership increases, it also becomes increasingly evident that one person can't do everything anymore. Organizations are too complex, and the need for the right sort of involvement of people throughout the organization is essential. Highly skilled leadership is needed at all levels of the organization, leadership empowered to make high quality decisions. Thus, it is necessary to think of leadership as a system or process and a set of skills that can be seen and can be improved upon.

Over the past several years, Shoji Shiba has avidly studied the issue of leadership in companies. With his TQM background, he has naturally thought about leadership in terms of both incremental improvement (of leadership skill), discussed in this chapter, and breakthrough improvement (in the domain of the company's business), discussed in Chapter 27.

Over the decades there has been an evolution of the skills required by business leaders—from skill at incremental improvement within a business, to skill with breakthrough improvement within the same business, and finally to skill at breakthrough improvement into a new business area. Based on Shoji Shiba's studies with a number of organizations, he has summarized a set of skills for leading breakthrough and has derived a model for breakthrough that is described below. Another strong influence on Shiba's thinking about leadership has been his hobby of studying paintings, consistent with his own leadership principle of seeking new perspectives from novel sources. For context, we include below some of his thinking in that area.

Leadership generates almost unlimited discussion among people thinking about management. In this chapter, we focus on one way of looking at leadership.

Our perspective on leadership extends the methods on collecting and understanding qualitative data (Chapters 13–14) and is relevant to all situations of leadership where one is seeking new directions. Our perspective also complements the model of business breakthrough described in Chapter 27.

Among the many books and papers relevant to leadership, we frequently make use of [30, 101, 127, 162, 186, 253, 268].

Three Sets of Skills (and Five Effective Principles) of Leadership

Leaders require three sets of skills: technical, human, and conceptual. Each of these is shown as a region in Figure 17-1. As can be seen by the expanding areas of the regions in the figure, as one's management level increases, the requisite amount of each leadership skill also increases and the type of technical skill needed also changes.

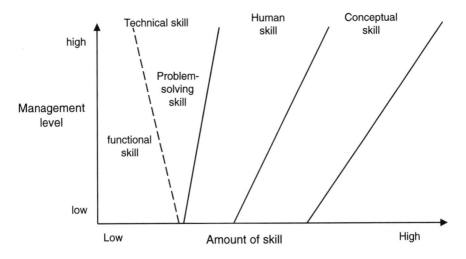

Figure 17-1. Skills for Leadership

The rest of this chapter has a section on each of the three areas of skill. In the course of the descriptions of the three types of leadership skill, we also emphasize *Five Principles of Effective Leadership* (Table 17-1).

Table 17-1. Five Principles of Effective Leadership

1. A leader's future skill for problem solving depends almost completely on skill with language.
2. Nothing can be done alone—create infrastructures to mobilize teams and the organization.
3. Don't be afraid to jump into the fishbowl.
4. Focus on qualitative data rather than quantitative data to achieve breakthrough.
5. Do not stick to surface phenomena; rather, jump-up (jump out of the fishbowl) to capture the structure beneath the surface.

17.1 TECHNICAL SKILL

Technical skill has two parts: pure technical knowledge (or functional skill) and skill to improve the efficiency of technology, that is, improvement skill or problem-solving skill.

As a leader rises the corporate ladder, he or she usually needs less pure technical skill and more improvement skill. Therefore, senior leaders need to focus on developing improvement skill. Since PDCA is the engine for improvement, PDCA is something every leader must understand.

However, a leader's concerns change over time, as does the data he or she can access. For instance, early in one's career, one is typically concerned with doing his or her job as reliably and efficiently as possible (what we call process control). Later, the concern is more with improving existing work processes or products (what we could call reactive improvement). As a leader rises further, he or she is seeking to understand future business and customer needs in order to reengineer processes or products to meet those needs (what we could call proactive improvement).

The kinds of data one typically sees in process control, reactive improvement, and proactive improvement are different (see Figure 6-12, page 81). Most important for senior managers, the data one inevitably must deal with when trying to improve something proactively are language or qualitative data (numerical data is typically supplementary). We hear from customers in the qualitative language of subjective likes and dislikes. We hear from investors in the qualitative language of subjective needs. We primarily hear from our employees and suppliers via subjective or qualitative language. This brings us to the first principle.

Effective Leadership Principle 1: A leader's future skill for problem solving depends almost completely on skill with language.

To make good decisions and take effective action one must ground opinions in concrete fact and one must abstract from concrete facts to new concepts. A primary tool for grounding is semantics (page 204) and a primary tool for abstraction is the Language Processing method (page 217).

Here is an example of grounding using semantics:[2] The leader hears someone initially state, "The operations manager would not listen to the engineers." By working to ground the statement, the leader discovers the more concrete fact that, "Process engineers analyzed forging deviations and presented the details for a process change, but the manager did not implement the changes." The second statement provides more information and might well help the leader avoid a wrong conclusion or decision.

Now here is an example of abstraction. Suppose the leader hears the following two statements:

- "Last year, top management <u>postponed a self-assessment workshop</u> two times giving the reason that there were higher priorities for the company."
- "Top management of X Company <u>did not show up</u> at the TQM <u>kickoff meeting</u> in May."

Both of these statements are concrete and factual, but what should the leader make of them taken together? Using his or her skill with the LP method, the leader underlines the "key items" (pages 248–256) and might form the following hypothesis of what the two key items mean together: to initiate new activities.

To recapitulate, the senior leader mostly deals with proactive improvement and mostly deals with language or qualitative data, which demands language skill on the part of the leader; the most powerfully useful language skills for the senior leader are grounding and abstraction.

17.2 HUMAN SKILL

Human skill, the second skill of leadership, is divided into three categories:

- Face-to-face human interaction skill
- Team communication skill[3]
- Skill to communicate with the entire organization

The higher one rises in the leadership of an organization, the more important the last of these three becomes. Unfortunately, the CEO cannot successfully communicate directly with all employees. It is difficult for the top leader or manager actually to access and *truly* communicate with more than a few employees in the organization, and then usually just the few nearest the top. The traditional idea of top-down communication throughout the entire organization doesn't work well. Thus, various infrastructures or systems are needed to effect communication from the top throughout the entire organization. This brings us to the second principle.

Effective Leadership Principle 2: Nothing can be done alone—create infrastructures to mobilize teams and the organization.

Three good examples of infrastructures to communicate with and mobilize the entire organization are the 7 infrastructures model (Figure 21-3, page 426), Disneyland, and books published external to the organization.

As will be discussed in Chapter 21, the 7 infrastructures is a strategy for communicating with the entire organization. Its seven components are:

1. Goal setting
2. A sub-organization that supports mobilization of the entire organization
3. Education and training
4. Promotion
5. Diffusion of success stories
6. Awards and incentive
7. Diagnosis and monitoring

Two of the seven are particularly important for senior leaders: goal setting and diagnosis and monitoring. However, all seven are used to communicate with the entire organization.

Disneyland has a superb infrastructure for communicating with the masses. All Disneylands are built on the same plan. There is one entrance so they can control the image people see going in. Once inside the entrance, people pass a happy policeman or a lovely young lady or Disney characters, all of which are intended to make people happier. Also as one goes down the main street, there is an open feeling in the space between the three-story rows of town buildings on each side: this openness occurs because the first story of the buildings is built to 9/10 scale, the second story to 8/10 scale, and the third story to 6/10 scale. The Disneyland infrastructure is aimed at giving the same image to everyone. Although the visitors follow a process designed to ensure an enjoyable visit, the process happens automatically and without explicit discipline.

Another tool to communicate to the entire organization is to speak publicly (well beyond one's own organization), so what one says is reflected by the outside world back to the people in the organization. For instance, Andy Grove has written the book [126] which describes his image of how the company has to deal with listening more to its customers. This book became famous and was widely read. Consequently, people inside the company undoubtedly were motivated to read the book and, thus, know much more about what Grove thought than they would ever learn from internal memos and presentations (imagine what would have happened had he sent a book length internal "memo" to all employees).

Some years ago, Dr. Koji Kobayashi at NEC[4] did the same thing when he was trying to promote the convergence of Computers and Communications. He wrote three books which were widely read (and translated into English as well); thus, everyone in his own company also read them and knew what he thought needed to happen.

More recently, we suspect that Bill Gates' book [112] and the second edition of [113] served a similar purpose—communicating Gates' vision of an Internet-based future to the employees within Microsoft at the same time it did to the world at large.

17.3 CONCEPTUAL SKILL

Conceptual skills, which comprise the third leadership skill set, are the source of creative thinking.

Conceptual skill begins with the exploration we call "the fishbowl principle." It has three parts (as shown in Figure 17-2, repeated from Chapter 13).

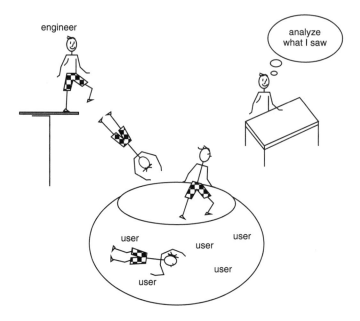

Figure 17-2. Fishbowl Principle

First, one needs to "jump into the fishbowl"—for instance, go visit users of your product or service in their own work and use environment. Second, one "swims with the fish"—experiences their environment. Third, one "jumps up" (page 187) to see the user environment in a broader context, after which one analyzes the actions in the fishbowl and the essence of the fish. One uses these three skills to create a new hypothesis.

The fishbowl principle is in contrast to standing outside the fishbowl looking in (see Figure 13-11 on page 231) and measuring how well what is going on in the fishbowl matches a preconceived hypothesis.

Professor Shiba derived the fishbowl principle from his hobby of studying the paintings of great artists. Consider these examples from the history of painting:

- Michelangelo used the perspective approach. If one looks at the painting of "The Last Supper," one can see it was done using perspective lines. The painter is using objective measurement to draw beauty from an outside perspective (something like standing outside the fishbowl and logically evaluating the hypothesis).[5]

- The impressionists, like Monet, jumped in and swam in nature and the industrial society. They left the studio and went outside into nature. Thus, their paintings show the steam of locomotives in the background of the scene, iron fences, and bridges, steam and iron being symbols of modernity in the time of the impressionists.

- The abstractionists, like Picasso, went further. They swam in nature, jumped out, and painted what they saw. The purpose of their paintings was not to copy nature but rather to show the viewer the sentiment, emotion, and concept the artist saw in nature.

This brings us to the third principle.

Effective Leadership Principle 3: Don't be afraid to jump into the fishbowl.

One aspect of jumping into the fishbowl is unlearning skill—little benefit is gained from seeing the fish's perspective if one cannot forget preconceptions, assumptions, and cultural constraints. On the subject of unlearning, Nobel Prize Winner Leo Esaki (who won the prize for his work with transistor tunnel effects) offered *Five Things Not To Do To Be a Nobel Prize Winner* (Table 17-2).[6]

Table 17-2. Five Things Not To Do To Be a Nobel Prize Winner

1. Do not allow yourself to be trapped by your past experiences
2. Do not allow yourself to be overly attached to any authority
3. Do not hold onto what you don't need
4. Do not avoid confrontation
5. Do not lose childhood curiosity in everyday life

A second aspect of jumping into the fishbowl is learning to take the time to do it. Everyone says they have no time. Alex d'Arbeloff is an example of a CEO who took the necessary time, for instance, during Teradyne's mobilization of TQM. D'Arbeloff says "the top person should spend one-fifth of his time on new tasks." He continues to do this even though he is now spending half his time as chairman of MIT.

As was already mentioned, the fishbowl principle is about creating a new concept rather than about validating an existing concept. Thus, it is not necessary to have large amounts of quantitative data to validate a concept statistically. Rather, one needs to seek inputs from all possible sources, and this means collecting qualitative data. This leads us to the fourth principle.

Effective Leadership Principle 4: Focus on qualitative data rather than quantitative data to achieve breakthrough.

Collecting qualitative data involves seeking real, specific, or personal cases. We want people to tell us their actual stories, rather than to give us their (frequently not well-founded) generalizations. Specific examples are typically rich in detail that can suggest many new possibilities.

In collecting qualitative data, diversity, not quantity, is key. During exploration we are not seeking statistically valid numbers of samples to verify a hypothesis. Rather, we are looking for as many different ideas as we can find, that can suggest new concepts to us.[7]

Finally, in collecting qualitative data, we do well to seek symbolic cases (images of real behavior). When we gather diverse real specific cases, we will hear lots of opinions and learn many facts. One must focus on that subset of cases that provides the most value in terms of providing graspable input (input images) and input that can be abstracted into useful concepts that can be conveyed to others (output images). Symbolic cases provide this value.

Symbolic cases/examples are specific, real, and represent an important class of situations. Some examples follow.

When Professor Shiba visited one company, someone was already waiting for him at the front door, and when he got to the meeting room people were on time for the meeting. From this and other symbolic cases Shiba created his hypothesis that a core value of the company was that time matters. This was his way of grasping the invisible culture of the company.

Another situation occurred at MIT's Leaders for Manufacturing (LFM) program, a joint graduate program of MIT's Engineering School and Sloan School of Management. One day, some executives and former LFM students now working at a company visited LFM to tell the current LFM students about their company. Professor Shiba's most important impression came from seeing all visitors dressed in dark blue jackets, white shirts, and dark red tie. For him, this was the key symbolic case. Standing there in their identical dress, their words touted the importance of diversity of products and markets. However, from their dress, Professor Shiba hypothesized that the company strongly needed diversity.

Of course, there is no single interpretation. Each person selects his or her own examples of symbolic behavior and creates his or her own hypotheses. Leaders must train themselves to be open to what images are telling them.

Professor Shiba suggests potential leaders can look at paintings to help them understand the use of symbolic image. Painters can be geniuses at showing symbolic images, such as "The Surrender of Breda," by Diego Velazquez. Nicknamed "The Lances,"[8] the painting depicts one army in disarray surrendering to the other army with all their lances standing tall and in a row. Other notable symbolic images can be seen in Edouard Manet's painting, "The Railway,"[9] showing a Paris scene with white vapor in the background (from steam locomotives, invisible in the painting) and an iron fence in the middle ground. For Manet, these images were symbolic of modernity in his age.

After exploration, a leader needs to formulate a new concept, and this leads to the fifth principle.

Effective Leadership Principle 5: Do not stick to surface phenomena; rather, jump-up (jump out of the fishbowl) to capture the structure beneath the surface.

After jumping out of the fishbowl, from above one can see many types of fishbowls and fish. The ability to shift your perspective and way of thinking intentionally allows you to conceptualize a coherent hypothesis about what is taking place in the overall environment. There are three different dimensions to this kind of thinking, as illustrated in Figure 17-3 and described below:

- One can change the time scale of observation. With a monthly or yearly time scale instead of daily one, one may see longer patterns. Alternatively, one might look at a minute-by-minute time scale instead of a daily one to see details that might otherwise be missed.

• One can change the space in which or from which one observes, for instance, doing benchmarking in another country, or getting down on one's knees on the floor to see how the product is used by children.

• One can change the human point of view, for instance, looking at things from the customer or market point of view rather than from the company point of view.

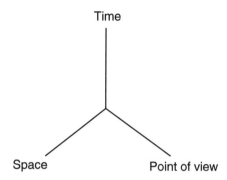

Figure 17-3. Different Dimensions of Thinking

A leader can use comparison to understand, structure, and create a hypothesis. Again, we look to art as an analogy. If one looks at a painting of a couple dancing (for instance, Pierre-August Renoir's "Dance in the City"[10]), one will see what it shows; and if one looks at another painting of another couple dancing (for instance Renoir's "Dance in the Country"[11]), one sees what it shows. However, if one compares the two paintings of couples dancing one sees and understands more than either painting shows alone; by looking at each painting, you can see what is (or is not) going on in the other painting.

Here is another example of comparison. Two companies visited and gave presentations to MIT's LFM program one summer. In each presentation, the company listed its core values. The first company, Intel, listed its core values as "results-oriented, risk taking, great place to work, quality, discipline, and customer orientation." The second company, General Motors, listed as its core values "customer enthusiasm, innovation, teamwork, integrity, and continuous improvement." We ask the reader to take a moment to think about and compare these two sets of core values and what hypothesis you would draw. Remember, each person needs to create his or her own hypothesis.

The concept Professor Shiba gets from these two different sets of core values is "different frequency of new product introduction." For instance, Intel has no time for continuous improvement: they must "copy exactly!"

Figure 17-4 graphically summarizes what has been said about conceptual thinking.

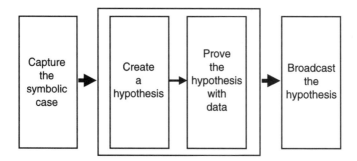

Figure 17-4. Elements of Conceptual Skill

Leaders will do well to develop skill in capturing an appropriate symbolic case, creating a hypothesis, proving the hypothesis with data (the hypothesis alone is just a hypothesis—one needs somehow to validate its plausibility), and finally broadcasting the hypothesis.

Sometimes a leader sees the need for breakthrough. This requires several stages of conceptual skill:

Stage A: Exploration and formulation of a new concept
Stage B: Moving from the past business to a the new business
Stage C: Recreating organizational integrity

Stage A has been covered in this section; stages B and C are handled in Chapter 27 on the Practice of Breakthrough.

NOTES

1. This CEO roundtable of CEOs took place in August 1998 at Hewlett-Packard's Palo Alto training center. Dr. Fred Schwettmann was general manager of a large division of HP before becoming CEO of ReadRite Corporation. He is now retired. This quotation is as close to verbatim as our notetaking allowed; it may be something of a paraphrase.

2. Remember the four key concepts of semantics: the dual function of language and distinguishing report language (to convey logic) and affective language (to convey emotion); differentiation between opinion and fact; movement up and down the ladder of abstraction; and usage of multi-valued rather than two-valued data.

3. For instance, you can have the skill using the LP method to have a team of people understand and organize a body of qualitative information. Or, you can have skill using the CE method to have a team of people gather and understand the qualitative voices of the market and from them derive and agree on new product and service concepts.

4. Koji Kobayashi was president and later chairman of Japan's NEC Corp. from the 1960s to the 1980s. He foresaw the convergence of computers and communications, and strongly promoted convergence as NEC's corporate mission and "C and C" (computers and communications) as NEC's corporate slogan. To this end, he wrote books which were published [171, 172].

5. Perhaps even more relevant to Figure 13-11, an Albrecht Durer work that shows a female model lying on a bed on the left side of a vertical gridwork of transparent small squares; and on the right side, looking through the grid work and using it to estimate relative relationships in the tableau of the model, an artist copies what he sees onto a large piece of canvas also marked off in a grid of squares. (The literal English translation of the Japanese translation of the title of this print is "Diagram of Drawing a Nude.")

6. The fourth guideline may be necessary in Japan; many people in U.S. companies may already have sufficient confrontational skill.

7. See Figure 13-10, page 230.

8. Museo del Prado, Madrid.

9. National Gallery of Art, Washington, DC.

10. Le Musee d'Orsay, Paris.

11. Le Musee d'Orsay, Paris.

18

Self-Development

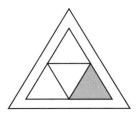

Ultimately organizational transformation of the kind we describe in this book comes down to individual transformation. The rest of the chapters of the book discuss organizational, team, and society-wide systems to engage the necessary individual participation. This chapter deals with individual transformation independent of existing systems for two reasons: even within an existing system, a person can do more individually to get additional benefit from the system, and an individual may want to do an improvement effort in the absence of an organizational system to encourage the effort.

When the organization doesn't support improvement

When we teach the methods in this book, inevitably we get the question, "How do I do this stuff if my organization or the management above me is not supportive of it?"

One possible response to ask the querying employee, "Do you genuinely want these methods and don't envision a supportive environment, or are you looking for an excuse not to employ the methods?" (We might ask this question in a slightly more gentle way.) Nonetheless, in our experience many people do not have an open mind about the methods and are looking for reasons why they cannot practice them, such as "my management doesn't support this." If this is the case, then trying to convince them that something is possible may not be worth the effort.

On the other hand, the person may be genuinely interested in attempting organizational change and improvement and genuinely doesn't see a supportive environment, either because higher level management is not on board or wants to do something but is not very good at it. Then we feel an obligation to try to help the person.

In Chapter 20, we point out that mobilization of the methods of organizational change and improvement *throughout* the organization is difficult if not impossible without the active support of the CEO or president. Also, if you ask any CEO who has successfully mobilized these methods in his or her organization, the CEO will undoubtedly tell you that mobilization is not possible without active CEO leadership. We have heard this from CEOs on many occasions. However, this is not satisfactory. We cannot simply ignore people who want to improve their own skills and skills of those working for them because they are in an unsupportive organization. So what are the possibilities?

Clearly a better situation is if you have competent support from management above you. However, without this, you can usually still learn and practice the methods locally or personally. You can substantially, if not completely, isolate yourself from negative influences elsewhere in the organization. Outside influences will somewhat affect you, but much of the time you will be able to minimize the impact of negative influences. Within your own group, you can learn and practice the methods without broadcasting to the rest of the organization that you are doing so. You can let the improved performance you will derive from the methods speak for you. Successful people have always found ways to get around bureaucratic obstacles and, in many organizations, are ultimately rewarded for their performance. Just as you can "do what must be done" to support a customer, you can do what must be done to use the methods of organizational change and improvement.

The good performance you will likely achieve by systematically developing your skill and that of your local organization can provide you with new opportunities:

- Those who succeed tend to get more opportunities on other important projects.
- In time you may move to a position in your company in which you have more influence and can remove some of the obstacles that blocked your path.
- You may be recruited to an opportunity with a more supportive company or with a company where you can have more influence.

All of these possibilities will increase if you ensure your own success and that of your people.

We will discuss improvement at a very personal level in the rest of the chapter.

18.1 LESSONS FROM THE NON-BUSINESS WORLD

We all know the methods of successful improvement for how we succeed or fail at things we attempt in our personal lives. We know that if we have a system for regular home maintenance, it gets done. We know if we decide to learn to play the guitar but miss lessons and don't practice, we don't learn. We just do not apply what we know to business (any more than we apply it to our personal lives much of the time). We do know what works, even though we may have insufficient discipline to use effective methods.

In 1994, David Walden reread the late Eric Twiname's classic book on sailboat racing [286], the best book we know on being your own coach, which stimulated him to undertake a sequence of interviews of experts in a variety of non-business fields to discover what they said about how people systematically develop skill outside the business world.[1] In the rest of this section, we relate some of the findings of that survey [300] and, in so doing, remind readers what they already know from their own life experiences but probably don't practice rigorously.

Successful Performance Depends on Personal Mastery

Performance at superior levels in any field depends upon individual mastery. This is certainly true in such areas as golf and other sports, chess and other games, instrumental music, ballet and other performing arts, physics, math, sailboat racing, airplane flying, and war fighting. It is also true for activities within businesses.

We can turn this idea around. We consider a person to be an expert in an activity—to have mastered it—when the person can reliably outperform all but a fraction of the population engaged in the activity.[2]

Superior performance has little to do with luck. Over the long haul, and perhaps in the short run as well, the non-master is simply no match for a master; neither is the less skilled person a match for the more skilled person on average.

Individual mastery is the key to competitive performance and is inevitably an acquired capability; for all practical purposes, even the person with the most natural talent is not born with mastery but rather has to acquire it through extended effort.

We are not talking about what is required to become world champion in a field, which some will argue requires natural talent.[3] Rather, we are talking about a level equivalent to shooting par on a golf course, to playing even with the teaching pro at a local tennis club, or to learning a new dance and performing it competently in the corps de ballet of a regional ballet company. Many people without so-called natural talent achieve this level of skill we call mastery.

Common Element of Achieving Mastery

As David Walden looked at various fields that people master, he noticed several characteristics of how people gain mastery, as shown in Figure 18-1.

First, typically, a prior tradition of skill is presumed for one to learn to become a master. Most fields have essentially conservative traditions, teaching what has worked before and changing only gradually over time.

a. Serious students typically study with masters, or at least study the methods of masters, to learn the prior tradition and best current practice. Accomplished musicians and dancers tell you who their teachers were and their teachers' teachers. Accomplished baseball and basketball players can explain whose swing or shot they copied. World champion sailboat racer Dennis Connor says to copy the methods of the fastest sailboat racers in your class and get going as fast as they can go before developing your own improvements [68].

b. Typically, a relatively common language and notation for the field (what one might call "technical jargon") allows practitioners to discuss their topic in detail and to communicate their thoughts to each other.

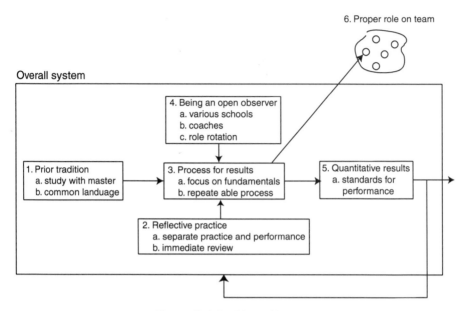

Figure 18-1. Enablers of Mastery

Second, reflective practice is the norm.

a. Activities are separated into performance and practice, and these two activities
have different purposes. Performance is directed toward accomplishing a job
or beating a competitor. Practice is directed toward learning new skills, honing
old skills, or correcting breaks in form.[4] Repetition through performance alone
is not an effective improvement method and, in fact, can solidify poor form.

b. After performance and frequently also after practice, there is an immediate
review for the purpose of understanding what worked and, particularly, what
didn't work and why not. This happens after bridge tournaments, chess games,
rounds of golf, musical rehearsals, war games, etc.

Third, the focus is on developing a process that produces the desired results.

a. A major purpose of all this practice and evaluation and modification of performance is to make the skills reliably repeatable—to turn them into a process
that can be successfully duplicated every time (and, thus, leave some physical or
mental capacity available to deal with exceptional situations or to observe the big
picture). Hall of fame basketball player Larry Bird shot hundreds of practice foul
shots the same way each day, enabling him to make his shot even after being
severely jolted and possibly a little dazed or a little injured from a flagrant foul.

b. In fact, emphasis on the mastery of a few fundamentals can move one past a
large percentage of participants, and the fundamentals are a necessary base for
reaching the highest levels of skill. Tennis teacher Vic Braden says learn to hit

reliably the "same old boring winner" deep down the center and you'll "be famous by Friday" [40]. Golf champion Jack Nicklaus says that he doesn't believe in systems—he believes in fundamentals [217].

Fourth, there are means of sampling and experiencing many sources of masterful technique and understanding the entire subject, related to what we call "becoming an open observer" (page 316).

    a. There are typically a variety of different methods or schools for teaching the same fundamental skills, or emphasizing different aspects of them. Note, for instance, the Horton, Graham, and Cunningham techniques in modern dance [61].

    b. Even at high levels of mastery (and certainly at lesser levels of skill), coaches are available who objectively watch for breaks in form or weak skills. If such coaching is not available, practitioners often develop methods of self-coaching whereby they objectively look at their own performance.[5]

    c. In the course of developing high skill levels, students frequently work their way through various positions, learning the skill from all perspectives and understanding the total picture, or they make significant changes in their game strategy as their skill improves. In sailboat racing, one may start by repacking sails in the bowels of the boat, get promoted to trimming a sail, increase ability to calling tactics, and finally end up skippering a boat.

Fifth, there is a serious effort to evaluate performance.

    a. In many fields, a quantitative result allows one to distinguish among levels of skill and between master and non-master, e.g., Martina Navratilova's win/loss record against Pam Shriver in tennis, or a 2200 rating versus a 1800 rating in chess. In cases where no quantitative result exists, an obvious qualitative result often exists, such as the difference in grace of movement we see between a professional ballet dancer and a less skilled amateur. In either case, accepted standards of performance allow us to see the difference between skill and the lack of skill.

Sixth, in fields requiring team effort, individual team members, in addition to being skilled in their roles, must be assigned complementary roles within the team. People must learn and take responsibility for different functional roles, some of which are less desirable than others. Some people on a team will have already achieved their full potential, others will be developing their skill, and still others may be slightly past their prime. Furthermore, people should develop secondary skills so as to back each other up where possible. Role playing often requires subordination of self to the good of the team. Only one person can lead a team. One team member may have to give up the position he or she is best at to someone who is even better. A team member occasionally may have to defer to less skilled performers to give people needed experience. In general, people must play the roles that the team needs most and subordinate their own preferences. The team leader typically must organize and motivate such role playing; having a leader who understands what needs to be done and can motivate teams members to play appropriate roles is key to successful team performance.

Room for Improvement

We all know the difficultly of putting forth sustained effort, e.g., to learn the piano, to improve our golf game, or to lose weight. We may be voluble about the challenges we have set for ourselves, and we often try new beginnings. But mostly we fail to reach and maintain any significant plateau. Even if we put in a year or two at the beginning to reach a level where we know what we're doing and can have some fun, after that we mostly just play at it and don't achieve real mastery. Thus, most people working in an area are performing at a level lower than the ultimate level they could reach if they applied themselves more diligently.

For instance, Figure 18-2 suggests the distribution of golf skill among all golfers.[6] Across the bottom we have the handicap or average number of shots a golfer shoots above par. Only about one to two percent of golfers actually shot par on a routine basis, i.e., qualify as expert golfers. A few additional percent of golfers come within five or ten shots of par on a regular basis. Most golfers shoot between 11 and 40 shots over par. And then a handful of golfers shoot even worse than this. To the right of par is the realm of most golfers. To the left of par is the realm of the touring pros and the very best amateurs. These players regularly shoot below par and have negative handicaps on normal courses. Therefore, this figure indicates most golfers have much room for improvement.

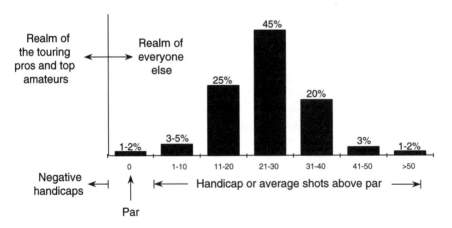

Figure 18-2. Typical Distribution of Golf Skill

Even though the parallel is not perfect (for most people, golf is not a full-time occupation), in business most people are also performing at a level lower than they could if they worked harder or smarter at self-improvement. Assume—because we went to good schools, were selected by companies known for choosing only excellent talent, and work full time at our jobs—that we have no one in our company with the equivalent of a handicap over 25, that is, we are all at least in the better half of the population. Even so, most of us would still have a lot of room for improvement.

How many of us would honestly say there is nothing we can do to improve our skills and performance?[7]

In golf, and most other fields of endeavor, so-called natural talent is not a limitation for most people. Most people with enough practice, coaching, and discipline could raise their average golf scores to within, let's say, ten shots of par. A certain degree of natural talent may be necessary to reach the realm of the touring pros and top amateurs, but that is not required for success by most people.

In fact, as in most fields of endeavor, what we think of as "process talents"—the talent of motivation, the talent of diligent self-application, the talent for finding the right instructor at the right time—are typically more important than what many people call natural talent. Not having sufficient natural talent is inevitably an excuse for not bothering or not having the time to learn the form of the masters.

In *The Boys of Summer*, the author, Roger Kahn, tells the story of meeting with retired Brooklyn Dodger ball player George Shuba and complimenting him on the "natural swing" he was known for during his playing days [155, chapter on George Shuba]. Shuba replied that Kahn could have had a natural swing, too, and he took Kahn to the basement of the house in which he'd lived while playing baseball. Hanging from the ceiling was a knot on the end of a rope on which Shuba practiced his swing by hitting the knot. Around the room were little pieces of paper with tally counts, ⊔⊔⊔⊔⊔⊔⊔, where each tally stood for 60 swings, 600 swings a night, 4200 swings a week, 45 to 50 thousand swings every winter.

Roger Tory Peterson, who invented the modern bird watching guide and in effect created bird watching as a spectator sport, drew all his own bird portraits for over 60 years. He said a year or two before his death that he was mastering his craft of painting: "If you want to be the best, you have to practice a lot" [7].

18.2 LOCAL IMPROVEMENT IN ABSENCE OF A SUPPORTIVE ENVIRONMENT

The techniques of achieving personal mastery are highly developed in many fields, for instance, dance, piano playing, basketball, plumbing, and all manner of topics studied in colleges and trade schools. In many cases, however, once people come into the business environment, all that is available is informal on-the-job training with no explicit process for systematic improvement.

What is needed most is scientific investigation—an attempt to use new methods and new metrics and to see what works—yet we live in a corporate context that doesn't particularly understand or value trial and error, effort spent learning rather than working, practice rather than performance, or time spent coaching. Neither the managers nor the individual workers (because of human nature and the way we teach them in school or the way we brainwash them in business) understand the tremendous value these activities.

Therefore, we now consider personal or informal ways to "do something" within a local organization so you and your people can at least improve even if no one else is. These methods are based partly on the simple idea of looking for ways of reproducing, in a business setting, the characteristics observed in the way people attain mastery in other fields. Some of these suggestions are for attitude changes and some are more tangible. Most of the ideas discussed below come from the world of R&D, a business function particularly prone to seeing an absence of supportive methods from the broader organization.

We tie the following discussion to a variation of Figure 18-1 shown in Figure 18-3. The six elements of Figure 18-1 have been augmented in Figure 18-3 by two elements (7 and 8) that will be discussed at the end of this section.

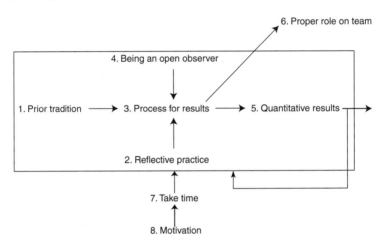

Figure 18-3. Practices for Achieving Mastery

1. Prior Tradition

In business, we often do not have an explicit prior traditional of systematic skill development. Therefore, the challenge is to discover the successful improvement methods we have. In addition to the search for fundamentals, discussed immediately below, the techniques described (under elements 3b, 3c, 3d, and 4c) are also relevant to discovering an appropriate "prior" tradition of skill development.

Search for fundamentals. We need more consensus on what the fundamental skills are for excellent performance in various functional areas. In many non-business fields, including highly complex ones like sailboat racing and war fighting, certain skills are generally accepted as necessary for mastery.

Many of us might agree on some fundamentals for the business function, such as hardware engineering, where we work. If so, do we delineate these skills to all concerned in recruiting, training, and performance? Do we clarify that we expect mastery of these skills, or that we expect a skill development program to be in place and functioning on an individual basis? In other areas where people do not agree on the definition of the fundamental skills, they need to talk and make some assessments about what the skills are.

2. Reflective Practice

2a. Take time for practice instead of performance. Simply performing a skill does not often result in adequate improvement. People can compete for years with the same level of golf, bridge, or sailboat racing, or work at the same level of VLSI design, sales, or management skill. To improve, people must set aside time for learning new skills and practicing them, or for whipping old skills back into shape through practice observed by a coach. The time spent in periodic practice will pay for itself many times over with the performance improvements.

In business, finding methods of "practicing"—ways to build or refine particular skills—will require a good bit of our intellect. It will be effort well spent.

One way to learn is to volunteer for other jobs. The more you can learn about the activities and methods of others, the better off all will be. Another method of learning new skills or practicing new ideas is what some computer people traditionally called "hacking." In the best tradition of hacking, computer software programmers, for instance, would stop working on the main job from time to time to code a new tool or simply something that interested them. The hacking went on simultaneously with or interrupted the main project and resulted in a tool that shortened the overall length of the main project or provided additional skill or experience. Hacking has a bad reputation in some quarters, and no doubt some hackers have behaved irresponsibly, but hacking is also a good way to try new techniques and perfect them. When hiring new people, managers might ask if they sometimes envision the need for a new tool that will make them more productive and hack it together if it doesn't exist. In the absence of having a good company system for providing time for improvement, organizations need people who will take initiative to make themselves more productive.

2b. Embrace trial and error. Trial and error or experimentation is, after all, the way people find out what works and what doesn't; it is particularly important to find out what doesn't work and eliminate this from our practices. Embracing trial and error is difficult, however, in many organizations. People don't feel as if they have the time in business to make any errors. People want assurances that the methods they try are going to work; therefore, organizations make it dangerous in some cases for people to try new methods and perhaps discover superior ones. Improvement often doesn't result in steadily increasing performance. Rather, performance may decrease at times as one breaks old habits and integrates new skills. This is especially true if one is searching for new methods rather than learning the next well-known technique.

Perhaps one of the reasons "skunk works" organizations work so well is they can test new things without letting anybody know. Some of the best people you know probably try new things and build new tools without asking anybody; if a new idea doesn't work, they quietly shelve it, but if it does work, they make it available to their colleagues or throughout the company.

2c. Find methods to test one's form regularly. Another major problem in much of business is that "project reviews" don't happen in productive ways. This is especially true in functions where projects can be long or where there is only ongoing work and no explicit projects. In the latter case, there may never be a project review at all.

With long projects, a single "lessons learned" meeting typically happens only at the end of the project, or perhaps a few of major management reviews occur during the project; in either case, months or years may pass between reviews that help us understand our performance level and what we might do to improve it. This contrasts with fields such as sports or the performing arts, where every day, after every practice, and after every match or public performance, those involved exhaustively review what did and didn't work. Everyone will benefit greatly if they provide some method of frequent (e.g., daily or weekly) "after-action review" to increase improvement.[8]

The NIMS case study (Chapter 25) describes reviews where a professional sits with a less senior engineer every three or four days and asks him to discuss what problems might arise and to evaluate the state of the design. Then, three or four days later, the engineer would come back and tell the master engineer whether the anticipated problems actually happened or not, and whether other problems he had not anticipated had happened; the less senior engineer would also get a review from the master engineer of the quality of his design over the past several days. In engineering, just as in chess or bridge, the non-master often does not even know whether or not he or she has a good position or design. The same is undoubtedly true for other business functions.

2d. Continuous improvement as a means of breakthrough. As we discussed in Chapter 6, people must get away from the idea of seeking breakthrough as an excuse for not doing continuous improvement. The breakthroughs involving a truly sharp break with the past seldom happen. Practically every breakthrough we talk about is the result of many experiments, many people working over time, and ideas that are in the air; finally, someone takes a step that seems like a very big step, perhaps looking at the problem in a different way, and the world calls it a breakthrough. All of the great scientists engaged in repeated, detailed investigations and experiments probably had many failures before they had their breakthroughs. Edison purportedly said "if you want more successes, you have to have more failures," Pasteur said "in the natural sciences, success only favors the well prepared," and more than one person has said "the harder I work, the luckier I get." Big breaks from past business practice may be required; people may have flashes of inspiration. However, persistence and organization will undoubtedly be required. Continuous improvement is a means of breakthrough. In fact, a most impressive characteristic of research scientists is dogged persistence, through routine and setbacks, until they finally succeed.

Donald Knuth, a computer scientist and mathematician whose research has changed the way people think about the mathematical analysis of computer algorithms and who was awarded computing's top prize, the Turing Award, tells a wonderful story.

> I was scared stiff that I wasn't going to make it in mathematics. My advisors in high school told me that I had done well so far, but they didn't think I could carry it on in college. They said college was really tough, and the Dean had told us that one out of three would fail in the first year ... At Case, I spent hours and hours studying the mathematics book we used—*Calculus and Analytic Geometry* by Thomas—and I worked every supplementary problem

in the book. We were assigned only the even-numbered problems, but I did every single one, together with the extras in the back of the book because I felt so scared. I thought I should do all of them. I found at first that it was very slow going, and I worked late at night to do it. I think the only reason I did this was because I was worried about passing. But then I found out that after a few months I could do all of the problems in the same amount of time that it took the other kids to do just the odd-numbered ones. I had learned enough about problem solving by that time that I could gain speed, so it turned out to be very lucky that I crashed into it real hard at the beginning. [6, pages 181–203]

3. Process for Results

3a. Focus on process goals to achieve results goals. As in every other field of endeavor, if people want to achieve results goals (e.g., zero software defects), they must concentrate attention on process metrics and targets (e.g., formal code inspections held) [299]. Sports psychologist Jerry May, while working for the U.S. Olympic Sailing Team, explained it clearly:

> I don't think people achieve just by serendipity. If you have visions of what you would like to focus on and accomplish, you have to come up with ways of getting there. I don't want to overstructure goals, but in sailing, if you want to be a great sailor, you need to be thinking about what you want to achieve. We call those "wish goals." The media, the public, and athletes tend to measure sports by those goals. They're okay, but they're overemphasized. Examples are: "I want to win a gold medal" or "I want to be in the top five in this next regatta." Although they may help motivate you, just sitting around wishing about those goals does nothing to achieve them. "Task goals" are the ones that need more attention. These are skill development goals. The sailing coaches and I met, and we came up with six areas where they'd like to see athletes focus on task goals: Sailing technique (such as boatspeed and boathandling), racing technique (starting and tactics), physical conditioning, mental skills (such as understanding your arousal level and proper focus), organization (like boat and equipment selection), and personal goals. The last one is a concept I discuss with anyone who is in top-level competition and a high-achiever, whether they are business people, medical students, or athletes. We must find time for personal relationships, education and other kinds of career goals, and recreations. [228]

3b. Make processes more explicit. People have to make their processes more explicit. It is impossible to improve a process reliably that isn't explicit. There are several ways of making process more explicit. First, you can document your existing processes. This is a simple way to make them more explicit and, therefore, more subject to improvement. Second, over time you can build tools or other bits of process technology. (Probably one of the greatest sources of potential payoff is investment in process technology.)

Of course, when some people hear about process they often fear that addition of process will stifle their creativity or be too rigid. These need not be true as was discussed at length in Chapter 6. We have all seen acts that appear to be supremely creative. In practically every instance, what we take for creativity is actually inspired application of hard-won skill. The renowned dancer/choreographer Martha Graham put it this way: "Technique is the craft which underlies creativity." In many fields— music, language study, debate, acting, dance—improvised performance is practiced until it comes easily, often through combinations of fragments of practiced routines.

Certainly, if you are documenting your own processes you should be able to avoid making them too inflexible.

3c. Teaching is a good way to discover one's own theory and process. A particularly good way to discover one's own processes is to try to teach it. Many of us think we have a theory or process, but in fact we don't have anything that is particularly concrete. However, we have to make it concrete in order to teach it to other people. This lets us sort out what we are actually doing, as well as perhaps suggesting things we might change.

If you haven't been asked to teach someone, volunteer help to those who seem to need it. They will benefit from your insight, and you will sort out in your own mind the scope of your insight.

3d. Develop explicit theories that can be tested. It is not sufficient simply to have processes. People also need theories about what processes should work. To be capable of the greatest improvement, they need to understand why things work. These theories can be derived either by a search of the empirical evidence or an intellectual process. In either case, by hypothesizing what might work and documenting it (however informally), people can put forward theories that can be tested. Notice that one of science's definitions is that it deals in testable theories. Putting forth a hypothesis which does not permit testing is the realm of religion rather than science.

Saying that individuals should put forth theories and test them is not the same as saying that everybody can do their own thing. That does not meet the improvement needs of an organization or of individual employees. Everybody on one team, in one division, or in one company must participate to test certain overall theories, and if there are differences in individual practices, those must be tested systematically to understand micro-theories.

Nonetheless, each person should be regularly thinking about what theories will explain successful (or unsuccessful) practice and, then, try the new theory in practice. This is the most efficient path to improvement.

4. Being an Open Observer

4a. Curiosity, an open mind, and real case studies. People should not underestimate the value of curiosity and the open mind. Learning new methods and improving weakness require an open mind and curiosity. The great scientists and engineers tell us this, and people who are experts in various other fields of endeavor tell us this. However, in many instances in business, as in many other endeavors, an open mind and curiosity are not available in great abundance. Many people have this attitude: I do my job, that is all I am responsible for, and then I go home. Others resist the idea that there could be a better method for them than the present one. Once again, employees will benefit most if they improve; therefore, if employees have closed minds and lack of curiosity, the company will be hurt and the employees will be hurting themselves more.

Everyone should read or learn about real case studies. Remember the traditional way people learn skills in most fields of endeavor is experiencing real cases, apprenticed to a master. Individuals need to seek out people who do work at high levels and inquire and study in detail what they did.

Furthermore, as people study these cases and read these methods, they need to accept and understand what they are reading and hearing before they evaluate. People have a strong tendency (especially people who are highly trained but perhaps not highly experienced) to evaluate a new idea as they are hearing it, and want to find problems with it or improve it. This means that if the problem is complex, they will not likely have completely understood what's being explained. Unless people who are listening give their all to absorb the idea, grasp it in its fullness, and look for all its best aspects, they may never completely hear or understand the method. We have plenty of time to reject methods after we have learned and understood them. On the other hand, if we reject ideas before we understand and try them, we will probably lose these improvement methods forever.

4b. Make contact with customers. People need to make contact with customers. Contact teaches what game they need to learn to play and which skills need improvement, such as speed, precision, skill in certain technical areas. They may discover they simply aren't delivering the products or services customers desire. Even if they cannot visit external customers, they can contact them by phone or e-mail—especially when the customers call the company—and take the opportunity to ask questions. Internally there should be plenty of opportunities to turn chance meetings in the hall or cafeteria into instances when they learn what the customer needs.

Customers can greatly focus and impel the individual and his or her group forward. Customers will also explain their true interest, which is often not what the people in the company think their primary product is.

4c. Rotate first-rate practitioners with passable pedagogic skills through a coaching role. Most functional organizations in business seldom have coaches. Some managers and some senior professionals or senior craftspeople coach a little. However, all too often the people we assign to lead our improvement efforts are not our best people, although they may have a sincere interest in the method's improvement.

In some fields, the performance phase of a career is relatively short. Thus, a person who has been very skilled is available for much of the rest of his or her life to teach and coach others. In other fields, such as sports or the performing arts, only the world's best performers can make a living performing; experts who aren't able to earn enough from performing but are still highly skilled, make their living teaching.

In business, our work life (our performing life) consumes most all of our career. Therefore, often our best performers aren't available to teach and coach.

We must find some alternative way in business organizations to make coaches available who are or were themselves first-rate practitioners. One way would be to rotate first-rate practitioners through a coaching role, spending a year or two teaching others what they do. This approach would have two benefits: first, the experts would pass on their knowledge because they would have a lot of time to do it and, second, they would come to understand their own methods better by making them explicit enough to teach to others. Such a period of teaching would improve everyone, those teaching and those being taught.

Another approach might make use of the geography of people's offices/cubicles and work assignments. We talk about providing mentors, but too often the mentor and the new person are not sitting close to each other. As a result, the mentor relationship becomes one of checking occasionally whether the new person has settled in, rather than the mentor taking responsibility for expanding the new person's skill. David Walden had the following experience:

> When I first got out of college and went to work at MIT Lincoln Laboratory, I was assigned not to a project but to a senior engineer who was assigned to the project. I was his to use and teach. Soon, offices were rearranged so that I shared half of a two-person office with my mentor. I went everywhere with him and did everything with him. He would break off little pieces of design or implementation (a day or two long) and give them to me to do. We talked through "our" design and implementation together, he answered my questions about why we were doing this or that, and he gently helped me see problems and improvements in what I had done. And he praised me for how quickly I did my little bits and how quickly I caught on (whether or not it was completely justified).
>
> After a month or two, I was doing bigger pieces, but because we shared an office, my mentor knew when I was struggling and would talk to me about what I was working on. Also, he would ask me to look over what he had done and give him comments. Since he was responsible for system integration in addition to developing some of the system modules, in time I became the second most knowledgeable person about the whole project. After a year or so, I began to receive more independent assignments, but we still shared the office and he never stopped being my teacher, though I had become his co-worker rather than trainee.

5. Quantitative Results

5a. Use quantitative data where possible. In 1883, Lord Kelvin William Thomson said,

> When you can measure what you are speaking about and express it in numbers, you know something about it; but when you cannot measure it, when

you cannot express it in numbers, your knowledge is of a meager and unsatisfactory kind: it may be the beginnings of knowledge, but you have scarcely, in your thoughts, advanced to the stage of science. [24]

People don't seek out or note quantitative data that is available. You don't have to start an explicit 7 steps quality improvement team to notice or collect some data. You don't need much effort to keep an informal check sheet on the back of an envelope recording various daily activities that seem interesting.

Most people have an intuitive capacity to develop some metrics that objectively measure their actions so they can determine if they are improving and if they are measuring relevant things. By beginning to keep run charts as well as check sheets, trends may appear.

Also, these days, with so many people spending so much time using information systems, you may discover that the information system already collects useful data that just needs to be printed and examined.

5b. Gather qualitative data. In some cases, quantitative data may be hard to collect. In these cases, people should gather qualitative data as the next best thing to quantitative data. For instance, everyone makes notes to themselves as they go about their jobs. In some cases, people maintain logs, for instance, of telephone messages. Saved over a period of time, such notes and logs might provide valuable information.

We told a story about Donald Knuth above. He has written a book called <<*Literate Programming*>> [170]. In two long chapters, Knuth presents and comments on the logs he kept for several years of all the bugs he found in his TEX math typesetting program and of how he corrected each bug. How many of us keep a log of our activities? Knuth has kept an exhaustive log; maybe Knuth is so much better than the rest of us in the software world because he consistently gathered this qualitative data, analyzed it, and thereby improved his skill.

Many people in the R&D function maintain a laboratory notebook. How many of these use it as a source of insight about potential ways to improve personal skill?

5c. Have accepted standards of performance. People need to create relevant standards of performance for their activities, standards that measure what people doing the job know to be relevant. In business, many people have few accepted standards of performance, and some of the ones they do have aren't very good. For instance, Goldratt dedicates an entire book to describing how the most common cost accounting data in manufacturing usually leads to suboptimal results [116]. Also, Capers Jones in [151] describes why the most often used measure of software programming performance, namely lines of code written, is at best irrelevant and at worst catastrophically misleading. Unlike golf, with its quantitative score, or ballet, where you can see if the dancers stumble when they pirouette, in many business functions we tend to work in little corners by ourselves, creating difficultly evaluating who is actually very good and who is only average. Undoubtedly some people we think of as experts are really not particularly more skilled than others whom we don't think of as experts.

6. Proper Role on Team

In team endeavors, careful manipulation of the participants' team roles are important for team mastery. People need to pay this area more attention.

First, in business, we need to find a parallel to the practice by many successful teams in other fields whereby the individual team members must be primarily committed to the team's success. The individual's success comes from being a member of a successful team from which to gain experience and new skills.

We also need to help team members understand the benefits to themselves and the team of "playing different positions" over time. For instance, in software development, test activities and development skills would be improved if developers worked in the testing function periodically and vice versa. However, developers often disdain the test function and resist spending time there, and test people are often uncomfortable rotating through development.

Some team members are a lot better than others and can personally make an enormous difference in team performance. If great team performance is needed quickly (for instance, because the product release date is coming fast), some participants may have to concentrate on helping the best players maximize their output rather than all participants working as equals. In other cases, one of the better people may temporarily take on a "lower" or support assignment for the good of the team.

A strong team leader needs to know how to arrange for people to play the roles best supporting the team as circumstances vary over time. Members who willingly perform, with all their energy, whatever role is most important to the team are always popular with team leaders and team members throughout an organization, and such people can have a great impact on team success.

7. Take Time

The most frequent objection to improvement efforts is "we don't have time." However, people must take time to do such things as have been mentioned here or find ways to do them without using extra time (such as the master and apprentice sharing an office). People must take time to visit customers. If they don't, they will waste time developing products that don't meet key customers' needs, and they will waste time discovering innovations that customers could have just given them. (An efficient way to do this might be to invite people from customer organizations to join our teams.) People must do frequent reviews of their results and methods. If they don't, they will waste more time using suboptimal methods. They must discover valid metrics for their results and methods. If they don't, they will waste time using poor or possibly counterproductive methods. Every bit of time people waste and every mistake they make because they haven't taken the time to improve their skills allow competitors who are more skilled or working harder at improvement to pass them.

If people can't find a way to undertake improvement activities without taking additional time, they simply have to find ways to take the time. The payback may be relatively immediate, or there may be evidence of eventual payback. For instance, taking a few extra weeks to understand the customers' needs, to create a specification document, and to develop a detailed project plan will payoff well for potential product success even if the scheduled release date is apparently delayed. The delay will continue to pay for itself with big multiplicative factors over the life of the product.

One of the problems people face is making time for team meetings to review improvement results and plan new improvement activities. People always have something more pressing to do, for example, responding to a customer complaint, or providing needed material to allow another person to do their job. Many times we have heard people say, "I'm already working infinitely hard; there's no time to add improvement work." Therefore, the proper time for team improvement work is Monday from 8:30 to 10:30 A.M. Then, the improvement meeting is done for the week, people can be trying new ideas, and they can still schedule nearly as much "real" work for the rest of the week.

Much improvement work is individual and doesn't require team meetings, however. Much improvement work can be done incrementally, without disturbing anyone, if people believe it is important. Mastery takes much time and effort. As the Zen master told the young student, "If it takes a long time to do, we must begin today."

8. Motivation

8a. Self-motivation is the first step. Improvement takes time and discipline. In other words, improvement is hard and will never happen if people aren't motivated to do it. A champion sailor listed all the systematic improvement methods essential to making him a champion, many along the lines we describe in this chapter. However, at the top of his list were the urgency he felt to improve and the importance he placed on winning. These gave him the motivation to do the practice and skill building necessary to win. Companies can provide some of this motivation (certainly they can work to resolve obstacles to motivation). Managers or leaders can provide more; in fact, we often define a good leader as one who can provide such motivation. However, over the long run, each person mostly does what he or she wants to do. If people aren't motivated to do improvement work, they will manage to avoid it. As Edgar Schein says, "You can't motivate change; you can only try to link existing motivation" [245, 246].[9] People can stymie improvement efforts in our business functions if they want, and then sit back and complain about the company, its management, and their lack of success.

Ultimately, what people define their jobs to be is the issue. If their definition includes self-improvement, then people will be noticed by and will gravitate to others who are also improving themselves, as well as to team leaders selecting people for competitively dominant teams. They can be part of the solution rather than part of the problem. The source of people's motivation is not important; it may be to win, become proficient, be a team member, be recognized, or be a desire for self-sacrifice. In every field of team endeavor, expert performers (winners) are looking for people willing to commit to the team goals and work enthusiastically to improve themselves to serve the team better.

8b. Take responsibility for own success. Individuals and teams must take responsibility for their own success. In companies, many people somehow have the idea that the company is responsible for making them successful. Of course, an enlightened company will do all it can to aid team or individual success. However, in the end no one cares about the team's success more than the members of the team do themselves, and no one cares more about an individual's success than the individual. A job applicant once came from another company looking for an engineering job. The interviewer asked him about the technical journals he read, and his response was, "I don't read any because my company doesn't buy them for me." Of course, it is a fairly unenlightened company that doesn't provide technical journals for its engineering staff. But it is a far more naive and even stupid person who does not understand that, as his skills erode and he becomes unmarketable, he is going to suffer most, not the company. In all the endeavors described in the prior section, the individual practitioner wants to succeed, for whatever reason. Our work groups will make a lot more progress if we determine, both individually and as a team member, that we are going to do what is necessary to improve our level of skill so we can compete successfully. Certainly, no team can perform outstandingly well if the team members haven't developed their individual skills.

18.3 THE BOTTOM LINE

Achieving mastery of one's field is the key to competitive success. In addition, mastery is gratifying in its own right; continued learning required to gain mastery is one of life's great joys. The best people don't quit jobs because there is too much work; they quit jobs and move on when they are not learning anything. Increasingly, mastery of one's field and lifelong learning are required for our companies' success and for our individual success in our careers.

We will be much better off if we take control of our own destiny and do the necessary improvement work in our work groups (or, if necessary, as individuals) than if we yield that responsibility to someone else, who perhaps doesn't understand scientific improvement methods. Helping employees improve their skills is certainly in the company's interest, but ultimately the individual is responsible to improve his or her own skills. No one else cares more about the employee's own development than the employee. This is particularly true as we move toward the world of the virtual corporation where an increasing number of people are essentially self-employed.

In this book, we describe a set of methods for the systematic development of skill at the individual, team, company, and societal level for business success in a rapidly changing world. Thus, use of these methods empowers people to improve their own skills. You are being asked to do what is necessary to improve the skills of your organization, of your team, and of yourselves. This is not the time to be reticent; it is the time to embrace that empowerment and get to work.

No one is more qualified than ourselves to figure out how to apply improvement methods to our situation. But this is going to take all of our intellect and enormous energy. We need to attack the issue of how to become more productive and more competitive, as individual workers, as teams, and as functional organizations systematically (using scientific methods). It will help our companies, and we owe it to ourselves. Somewhere a group of people are already working harder and more efficiently than we are to develop their skills, and we could be their target. To paraphrase Donald Wheeler, "People who understand scientific methods of improvement and don't use them will have no advantage over those who can't use them."

NOTES

1. Twiname's wonderful book may be more accessible in its second edition [287].

2. Ericsson and Charness, note that a plausible definition of an expert is someone who performs at a level more than two standard deviations better than the mean of the population of participants in a field of endeavor (i.e., top ≈ 2.25 percent) [90].

3. World champions (grand masters) play at a level significantly above experts (masters), i.e., more standard deviations above the mean.

4. According to [90], practice is for "restructuring of performance and acquisition of new methods and skills."

5. As Twiname says [286], they learn four things: to keep their own training plan and practice log; to follow a (perhaps mental) checklist that reminds them to maintain good practices in the heat of competition; to turn off their competitive juices during post-performance review and practice being brutally objective, analytical, and systematic in finding and eliminating their weaknesses; and to discipline themselves to work hardest on the parts of their game they like least which are probably therefore the weakest parts.

6. This information came orally from an expert golfer but not from an authenticated source. Still, it's not a surprising distribution, and intuition would probably suggest to most a similar distribution for performers in many other fields.

7. The NIMS case study presented in Chapter 25 provides an example where the full-time employees working for an eminent company were able to improve their skills. In addition to instituting a number of other development techniques, NIMS ended up with a program that works on the systematic development of engineering expertise with the goal, to use the golf analogy, of significantly reducing the handicap of every engineer in the organization and bringing everyone as close as possible to the level of a professional.

8. David Lowe, then CEO of ADAC which won the Baldrige Award, explained that weekly PDCA cycles were used, and "quarterly or monthly reviews just don't work." A report in [235, page 28] describes Cisco as "[monitoring] many new product development metrics on a weekly basis," often enough to operate their process effectively.

9. Some systems of training explicitly seek to discover who has this intrinsic motivation and to develop it and to excuse from participation those who don't have it. See,
   for instance, [85]. One of the ways people traditionally motivated themselves is to
   participate in study or practice groups for which commitments to one's study and
   practice partners are difficult to break.

19

Teamwork Skill

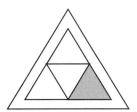

Everyone in a company must be involved effectively in customer satisfaction and continuous improvement activities. In today's world, depending on only a few geniuses and highly effective people in a company is not sufficient. A company must also avoid letting certain people be roadblocks to what the company needs to accomplish. Today, everyone in the company must be mobilized to improve how they do their jobs and satisfy customers. To mobilize everyone to achieve these goals, companies must change how they think about and organize work.

In addition to embracing the dual functions of work (defined on page 288), today's world requires a change in the way you organize work. It is no longer sufficient to assign individuals to all of the roles and positions that must be filled. Today, teams and teamwork must be a fundamental component of how organizations work.

19.1 SOME FUNDAMENTALS

Teams are entirely natural. For anything more difficult than one person can accomplish, people routinely (and naturally) form into groups to work together on a task. Minimally, people work together in a perfunctory manner, e.g., passing material or information around, only doing their individual jobs, and not trying to perform as a "team" in any higher sense.

However, to deal with the speed and complexity of business today, we need more than the sum of the perfunctory capabilities of the individuals. We need more than most individuals can give alone. We need the power that comes from pulling in the same direction and actively supporting each other. We need the collective genius of our employees. We need teamwork.

Here are some of the problems companies face today:

- Products are complex.
- Businesses are complex.
- We are competing on many fronts: product performance, process technology, time to market, reliability, eliminating non-value-added work, delivery, support, being first with new strategies.
- We are trying to deliver solutions (not just products), and solutions require knowledge of many subjects and the ability to see and hear many things.
- The world is moving toward more knowledge work, in which functional organizations are less important and knowledge workers have specialized skills which must be integrated.

Teams and teamwork activities help address such issues and are important to business improvement for several reasons:

- As discussed in Section 15.2 (page 287), companies must avoid division of labor. Everyone needs to focus on customers and do improvement work. Teamwork provides a mechanism to avoid this division.
- Cross-functional teams can often help address increased complexity and speed.
- In the face of this complexity, businesses need to find a future strategy; this requires great creativity. To compete in the global market, companies need the collective genius of all their employees. They must have teamwork to obtain the collective genius.
- Also, real-life knowledge workers are most likely specialists, and the performance of the whole depends on how we integrate them. Teams are a way to manage the integration among specialists.
- Group learning has a greater effect on the organization than individual learning.
- People who learn together motivate each other to continue; one person learning alone finds it easier to stop.
- When a group has learned something together, that learning becomes a group asset, as well as an individual one.

Of all the ways of addressing problems today, teams perhaps are the most compatible with existing organizational structures and thus will result in a lesser rejection reaction than more unusual changes. For instance,

- Teams are compatible with our current corporate hierarchies (in fact, many of the most effective teams are in highly hierarchical organizations).
- Teams naturally integrate performance and learning, and thus lead to improvement without major emphasis on the necessity for learning.

Therefore, for many companies, teams are the primary available way to increase performance.

Since teams and teamwork are a fundamental part of business improvement, the business improvement system must encourage practices that allow teams to function effectively. This is the subject of the rest of this chapter.

The Aspects of Teams and Teamwork on Which this Book Focuses

You can read many excellent books on teams and teamwork, for instance [252, 161, 239]. Those books, individually and in combination, give a comprehensive view of how to make teams work in an organization and what to avoid ([239] is especially good on what to avoid). We recommend you read them.

In this chapter, after recounting a few fundamentals that bear repeating or often get insufficient emphasis (the following subsections of this section), we concentrate on the issue of how teams and teamwork develop. We do this through:

- Case studies of some types of teams that provide several perspectives on how teams and teamwork develop (Section 19.2)
- Several models for how teams and teamwork develop (Section 19.3)

Our thrust on teams and teamwork is in keeping with our philosophy that practitioners need to study a number of approaches, choose those most appropriate for a particular situation, and to alternate between appropriate theory and practice as they develop systems that work for their environments.

Group Work and Individual Work

Many people misunderstand teamwork. Teamwork is not just work done in a group. Teamwork requires two kinds of effort: group work and individual work.

In group work, a consensus is sought on targets (tasks to be done) and the methods of accomplishing the tasks; then tasks are allocated to individuals or combinations of individuals for execution. Much of the work of the team is actually done as the work of individuals or combinations of individuals. Thus, teamwork combines group work and individual work, as shown in Figure 19-1.

For example, making a cause-and-effect diagram or an LP diagram can alternate individual work and group work. Writing the theme, warming up, and distributing labels are group work. Writing labels is individual work. Scrubbing (clarifying the labels so that everyone can understand them) is group work. Even within steps, individual work and group work can be alternated.

As stated earlier, the purpose of group work is to decide on the target (purpose), decide how to do it, and then to allocate jobs to individuals. Individuals do their assigned jobs, which constitute much of a team's work. Then, the group evaluates the results and decides on new targets, allocations, and so on. A typical quality improvement team follows this alternation. Such groups meet periodically for one or two hours; then, people separate to work for a few days. If people work only as a group, they can't get the job done even if they meet more often. Meeting too much often disturbs individual efforts, hinders creativity, and decreases team effectiveness.

Most of the creative work of teamwork is typically done in small subgroups or by individuals. The group work makes much of its creative contribution through its task selection efforts. Still, while much of what happens in the group setting is agreeing on directions (developing a shared sense of context, giving and reviewing assignments,

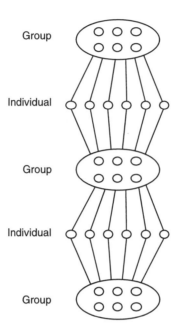

Figure 19-1. Group and Individual Components of Teamwork

etc.), creative work can happen in the groups as individuals stimulate each other and existing ideas are combined into new ideas. The most effective system balances individual creativity with group consensus and creativity.

In the U.S., an obstacle to teamwork is the cultural emphasis on individual heroes. Many people see the group aspects of business improvement and organizational learning as a hindrance to creativity. However, as we have just mentioned, creativity comes about with teamwork, from the individual and group components. Teamwork increases the possibilities for creativity.

An Environment for Efficient Teamwork

The most common symptom of dysfunctional teams is interpersonal conflict. A common approach to promoting effective teamwork is to provide methods of conflict resolution. Our approach is to provide methods that don't create conflict. It does this in three ways: by providing teams with a clear mission, requiring that plans be based on verifiable facts, and providing standard processes for analyzing the facts and reaching consensus. In addition, the team completes the PDCA cycle as a group of equals. This work of completion as a team creates an enhanced sense of achievement. Note, the methods we propose for fostering effective teamwork are not aimed at promoting collegiality, although that is useful. Indeed, collegiality is often the result of practicing the teamwork methods.

In the rest of this subsection, we mention a few methods of working together in groups that seem most important to us.

Setting up Meetings

In our experience, actually meeting is among the most difficult parts of teamwork activities. If you can get all the team members to all the meetings, you've had major success.

Scheduling is very important. Schedule for the same day every week or month. Consider having factory-wide or company-wide meetings at the same time (this can avoid the complaint from one function that people in another function are not available when needed because of their business improvement activities). Schedule a half year or year in advance.

Not postponing is a paramount principle! There are two elements to it: First, schedule the meeting to take place sooner rather than later because teams can't make good progress if meetings are delayed until times that are optimally convenient for everyone. Second, once a meeting is scheduled, never postpone it. Once you postpone, that time is irretrievably lost, and the team may not meet again.

Group Work Leader

At the group sessions, always appoint someone to the job of reminding the team members to keep focused on their group process and moving through the process. This can be the same or different person at each group session.

A Detailed Plan

Create an a priori detailed daily plan for any substantial team task. Too often, plans consist of a few milestones spread throughout the task. However, without a detailed plan, until you've reached a milestone you won't know you are behind, and then it may be too late to recover. Also, without a detailed plan for how to get to them, the milestone dates are often wishful thinking. With a detailed plan you have at least a plausible plan for success, you can track delays on a daily basis, and you can make necessary adjustments to stay on schedule (e.g., for the next step on the next day, only attempt half as good a job as you intended so you get back on schedule).

Physical Arrangement

The physical arrangement of people in a meeting can focus their attention on the meeting's activities. Consider, for example, the physical arrangement of people meeting to create an Ishikawa diagram, a tree diagram, or to use other tools. There are three things to note. First, the participants sit along a table facing a nearby wall on which paper is posted, as shown in part A of Figure 19-2. With this arrangement, they will be impelled to concentrate on the paper. No one should be allowed to sit between the table and the wall.

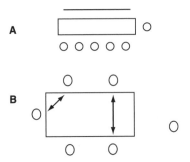

Figure 19-2. Alternative Physical Arrangements

Second, the physical arrangement includes writing the session theme in letters two inches high, so everyone in the group can continuiously see the theme. This prevents confusion and lack of concentration. The theme is always in sight; therefore, it should always be on their minds.

Third, the size of the table should force people to sit shoulder-to-shoulder facing the paper. This arrangement promotes participation in the group process and discourages side conversations.

If the participants sit as shown in part B of Figure 19-2, people will naturally talk across the table to each other, except for the one person who has distanced himself from the proceedings.

Delegation Is Only for Routine Work

For improvement work, neither delegate downward (team members must do the work themselves), nor delegate upward (team members are responsible for finding the solution). You must not delegate the job of improvement. The need to delegate is a symptom that the wrong people are on the team.

Everyone is equal within a team. The team members themselves have to gather supplies, take meeting minutes, and participate in the problem-solving processes of the team. Some people protest that "my job is making decisions, not doing detailed work." This attitude is incompatible with improvement work. Routine work implies standardized and, therefore, well-understood work. The purpose of improvement work, however, is to discover new ways of doing things; the issues surrounding improvement work are, therefore, not well understood beforehand and, therefore, not delegable.

PDCA

In all things where you want to develop skill, a good practice is to plan what you want to try, try it, reflect on what did and didn't work, and then decide what you want to try next. This obviously is the PDCA cycle. A team needs to make its process for working together explicit, at least as a list of bullets on a page. The PDCA cycle can be applied to the team's teamwork process many times over the course of a lengthy team project.

19.2 SOME TYPES OF TEAMS

Traditionally, in Japanese companies where methods of business improvement and organizational learning were first highly developed, the two types of work groups were formal taskforces and informal groups. These are shown in the top and bottom rows of Table 19-1.

Table 19-1. Types of Work Groups in Japanese Companies

	Setup	Members	Problem to solve	Duration of work
Task force	Ordered by superior	Selected by management	Work-related but given	Duration of the task
QC circle	Volunteers	All workers in same group	Work-related but self-selected	To work continuously as long as the work group exists
Informal	Volunteers	Volunteers	Not work-related and not given	To work continuously as long as the members exist

The quality control (QC) circle was invented in Japan to fill the position between the traditional, overly-rigid taskforce team and the traditional, overly-flexible informal group. The goal in creating the QC circle was to establish a work group that continuously works on work-related improvement, by bringing together all the members of a group on a voluntary basis (more about "voluntary" later) for individual and mutual development.

QC circles were never broadly successful in the U.S.; and after great success in Japan for many years, their popularity is declining. However, we will still introduce them here because their theory and practice provide a solid foundation for comparison with other types of teams. We see in QC circles the essence of the reasons for teamwork, as discussed at the beginning of this chapter: dealing with harder problems, integrating across greater collections of people, and improving learning. The other types of teams are mostly aimed at the same goals—on-going, engaged participation of a group for self-development and progress toward a common goal.

In the first edition of this book, we considered three kinds of teams, all explicitly oriented to business improvement:

a. Quality circle, or QC circle
b. Quality improvement team (also known as a QI team or QIT)
c. Cross-functional team (or cross-company team[1])

In this revised edition, we consider three additional kinds of teams:

d. Core teams
e. Self-directed work teams
f. Top management teams

Figure 19-3 compares various attributes of these six kinds of teams.

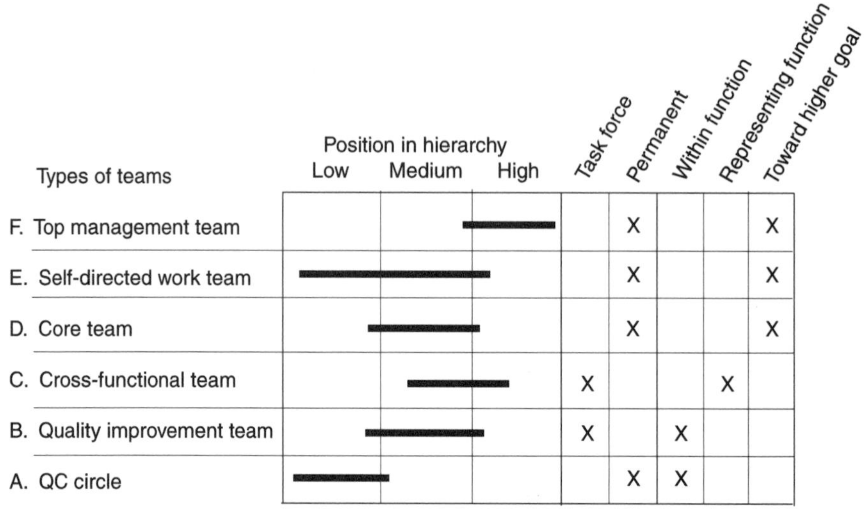

Types of teams	Position in hierarchy Low	Medium	High	Task force	Permanent	Within function	Representing function	Toward higher goal
F. Top management team			▬▬		X			X
E. Self-directed work team	▬▬▬▬				X			X
D. Core team		▬▬			X			X
C. Cross-functional team		▬▬		X			X	
B. Quality improvement team		▬▬		X		X		
A. QC circle	▬▬				X	X		

Figure 19-3. Attributes of Various Types of Teams

Regarding the first three types of teams (A, B, C), QC circles are at a low level, cross-functional teams are at a higher level, and quality improvement teams are roughly in the middle. QC circles are permanent; quality improvement teams and cross-functional teams exist only for the task's duration. QC circles and quality improvement teams function within a functional area; cross-functional or cross-company teams work across functional and other organizational boundaries.

QC circles often consist of individuals who spend most of their time doing work according to standard, for example, workers on a manufacturing line or people doing standard processing of paperwork. The QC circle is a continuing activity that allows the group to work regularly to improve its performance. QC circle activities regularly address the reactive portion of the WV model and occasionally the proactive portion.

Quality improvement teams are established most often to accomplish a reactive improvement task, although occasionally they address proactive tasks. We discussed examples of quality improvement teams in Chapter 9 on reactive problem solving. (Some companies also use standing quality improvement committees, permanently established to look for improvements in a particular area and direct quality improvement teams to specific issues.)

Cross-functional or cross-company teams are often established to accomplish a proactive improvement task, although they could also work on a reactive task. Cross-functional teams allow all functions to meet multiple requirements. Close relationships among functions in an organization yield greater efficiency and faster cycle time. Such teams can coordinate all functions to make market-driven changes.

Regarding the second three types of teams (D, E, F), core teams span roughly the same portion of the organizational hierarchy as quality improvement teams did; however, they are quasi-permanent (living for the life of a development project, for instance) and more operationally oriented, bringing the benefits of teamwork to everyday operations. Self-directed work teams [97] bring the benefits of teamwork to an even broader portion of the business—typically, the entire manufacturing plant—and span a greater portion of the organizational hierarchy. They are completely permanent in that the teams and their roles exist on an ongoing basis; however, people typically rotate among the roles within a team. Top management teams address the highest portion of the hierarchy and are also permanent. These three new kinds of teams all are intended to escape the functional mindset with team members dedicating their efforts to broad company goals.

Roughly speaking, the evolution of team types from A to F in Figure 19-3 has been aimed at: increasingly integrating routine work and improvement work; spanning ever larger portions of the business system; providing more autonomy to the team enabling action without lots of approvals; and making all of the above more permanent and ongoing.

The principles for teamwork are nearly the same regardless of the team type. Cross-functional membership teams perhaps have a larger inherent risk of conflict than other team types. Top management teams appear to have the hardest time functioning as real teams.

Mobilization of quality improvement teams have already been discussed in detail in the Teradyne case study in Chapter 11. We will discuss the other five types of teams in order from the bottom to the top of Figure 19-3.

Team Activities in a Functional Group—QC Circles

QC circle members are from a single functional group, which promotes long-term development of individual and team skill [146] and reduces much of the potential for conflicts cross-functional teams may suffer from and which we will describe below.

In Japan, a QC circle is a small group of about three to ten workers in whose activities all members participate. If seven employees work together in the same production line (i.e., form a natural work group), all seven participate in the circle activities; no one is left out. The circle has two work-related objectives: quality control to minimize the quality fluctuation in products and services, and improvement of quality in products and services. In achieving these objectives, the group hopes to work toward the development of the individual worker, which is its main goal. (Review Figure 19-4 in parallel with reading the next few paragraphs.)

Two principal features enable the QC circle to reach its goal. First, it applies appropriate process improvement methods, which its members have to learn and apply to the problems they tackle. Without this methodology, improving the quality of a product would be difficult. Second, QC circle activities are voluntary. The workers decide if they want to set up a circle.[2] If they do organize a circle, they choose the problem to focus on: they decide on the data gathering approach, on the countermeasure plans, etc.

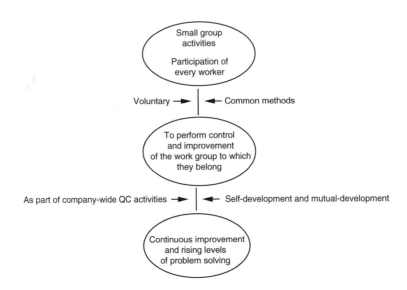

Figure 19-4. QC Circles

Every step of the way, it is they who decide. In a true QC circle, an order from above does not exist.

However, someone in management must remain responsible for a team's improvements. Otherwise, the organization could lose control of its activities and adversely affect customer satisfaction. A system for providing permission from a team's management is important, but maintaining control without disempowering a team is a delicate business. Several CQM companies have found it effective for management to suggest the initial problem areas (but not the theme) or to review the theme with the team. Management also may need to review the implementation plan, especially if it affects others. The trick is to maintain awareness of the team's activities without guiding the team too much, trusting good improvement process to produce useful results and then standing behind those results. Of course, if a team is at risk of going seriously astray, management must provide more guidance.

Problem solving in the QC circle is a continuous process. Often a group will begin by tackling simple problems—such as cleanliness in their workshop or miscommunication between workers—and move on to more complex ones, especially problems in product quality, productivity, and those that affect multiple groups. This continuity is possible because the company supports the group. The company gives permission for QC circle activities to be held during work hours and provides conference rooms for meetings. This support, without which the QC circle cannot function, provides the group with an institutional framework.

The QC circle also gives workers the opportunity for self-development—this is one of the most important aspects of QC circles. Through the problem-solving process and meetings, workers learn from each other's strengths; during QC circle conventions, circles share with one another the processes (not the results) they have discovered to be beneficial to their workshops. Finally, QC circles can expand the improvement scope by including suppliers, multiple circles, and the like.

From a company viewpoint, the most important function of QC circles is to institutionalize the dual function of work for the participants.

The invention of the QC circle was the invention of a new kind of teamwork. Ishikawa's original work with QC circles began in 1962. By 1993, there were five million participants in Japan and QC circles in 60 countries. Perhaps one-third of the companies in Japan with more than 30 employees had QC circles. Japan has enormous experience in establishing QC circles and using them for the long-term development of individual and team skill. Let us, therefore, study a famous example from Japan—the Ladybug Circle.

Teamwork Case Study: Evolution of a Japanese QC Team

The following description is excerpted from the translation of a paper and presentation by Yoshiko Fujino and Kimiko Kimura [105].

> Kobayashi Kosei is a leading cosmetic maker whose products are used throughout Japan. Our Sayama plant is located in Sayama City, Saitama Prefecture. At this plant, situated on a 110,000-square-meter site and surrounded by greenery and the fragrance of tea, 950 workers work, full of vigor. At the production headquarters to which we belong, 150 circles are energetically engaged in QC activities daily, under the overall headquarters policy of "building groups that learn and that struggle actively..." All the QC activity organizations are defined as parts of the TQC-promoting organization. Wider linkages to sustain the activities are provided by the leaders' meetings (for circle leaders) and instructors' meetings (for instructors who provide support "from the rear").
>
> At our specific workplace, our assigned work is the filling, packing, and finishing process for cosmetic products, which ranges from putting the cosmetic materials into containers to packing the products in boxes. The work force is divided into specialized squads, such as the Cream Squad, the Milky Lotion Squad, and so forth, but depending on the product, a squad may become short of personnel. Our squad's particular mission is to fill such personnel shortages, for we are the Relief and Reinforcement Squad ... Each morning after the chores (morning meeting), we disperse among the different squads; such has been our life and work as wandering workers.
>
> Our circle consists of seven middle-aged female part-timers whose average age is 45.[3] As soon as I joined the company in 1979, my life as a wandering worker started. As a trainee, I could barely handle half of the volume of an average worker, and regular employees young enough to be my children would shout out: "Old lady, don't be so slow! You are really more of a hindrance!" If there were some defective products, then it was always the

fault of us older part-timers: "It's your fault." I was getting rather dissatisfied with life as a wandering floater, and my footsteps were dragging as I commuted to work each day.

On top of all this, there was another large burden of QC circle activities. Our circle was formed on the recommendation of our superiors, but our feelings were that as part-timers who just worked slotted hours we could not have meetings delay our returning home. We took a stand of "didn't do it, don't know it, and can't do it," and so ours was a circle without even a shred of motivation or energy.

In 1981, there was a change in our squad leader, and we got a new woman chief who was full of motivation and energy toward her work and the work of the squad. Seeing that we were lacking in vitality and cheerfulness, she suggested that we have some interviews and social activities with her, in order to brighten our workplace. After we had interviews and meals together several times, it became much easier for us to talk about our families, discuss our problems at work, and so forth. Thus, these occasions served as opportunities for cleansing our hearts.

Next came the study sessions. Studying after work, when we were exhausted, was not always effective. Then she assigned material that we could not absorb as our homework, and she conducted tests on top of all that! It got to the point that we wanted to scream at her "You devilish chief!" On just such an occasion, the chief gave a notebook to each one of us, saying, "It's a present. If there is anything that you cannot understand, please write it down, okay?" When we wrote down things that we did not understand, she would write comments in response to them and would encourage us, "Please keep it up! A little more to go." We were moved by the chief's enthusiasm, and now it was our turn to show our true mettle. So we began to talk about the problems that existed in the different squads to which we were assigned, and as we made contributions in those squads, our work in those squads (with which we were also fed up) became that much more enjoyable. We, who had no motivation for work, began to desire to use what we were learning in our work.

In 1982, a large-scale production of small-sized products was planned for execution in a short time period. Since specialized squads alone were not sufficient to meet the delivery dates, it was decided that the people in the relief squad would also be assigned to production work. All members of our circle grasped onto "An Operation to Annihilate Shortcomings in Work Stages for Product A" as an ideal chance for us to apply what we had learned, together.

However, this production period was going to last for only one month. To be able to make improvements in this short period, we decided to collect information on shortcomings related to work stages from the specialized squads who had been engaged in production from an earlier period. From the data we gathered, it became clear that the preparatory work was very important, so we put this insight into practice with the motto, "Eight minutes to set up for work." As a result, we exceeded the goals we set and made significant improvements in a short period of time.

This QC theme was honored with an Award of Excellence at the Women's (QC) Meeting in the company, where it was decided that we would take part in the companywide quality control contest. We felt good that we had tried so hard. This feeling gave us additional motivation for further progress ...

Because of our meetings and our efforts to gather data, we were often late in getting home, which caused much inconvenience for our husbands and children. Dissatisfaction grew accordingly.

Around this time, the husband of one of our members was hospitalized, and the family was in distress because they could not harvest their crop of citrons. So we invited members of our families to join us in helping this family; it was a great success, and our support was greatly appreciated. With this as the ice-breaker, we began to have singing contests, with a karaoke (a music accompaniment tape player) and other events, and our family members gradually began to develop a better understanding of the good qualities of QC circle activities.

In this way, we prepared for, and participated in, the companywide quality control contest and won the Cattleya Gold Prize. We took turns taking the award certificate and the tape recording of our presentation home, and we shared the joys of receiving this award with our family members.

The presentation goes on to specify more of the specific improvements the Ladybug Circle created, and describes various appraisals of the successful improvement of the circle's activities from 1979 to 1984. Note the balance of various factors in the overall assessment of the circle's activities over the five years. The factors were the following:

- Extent of applications
- Study
- Recreational activities
- Extent of family cooperation
- Meeting conduct
- Themes completed
- Number of suggestions for improvements

At least two conclusions can be drawn from this list of criteria. First, team activities clearly support human values in the workplace. Teams that sacrifice all personal life for productivity will not win any awards or respect. Second, the process of improvement activities is valued more than the output of those activities, the improvements themselves. Evaluation of QC circle activities is detailed in the bible of QC circle activities, *QC Circle Koryo* [144], and its working manual, *How to Operate QC Circle Activities* [147].

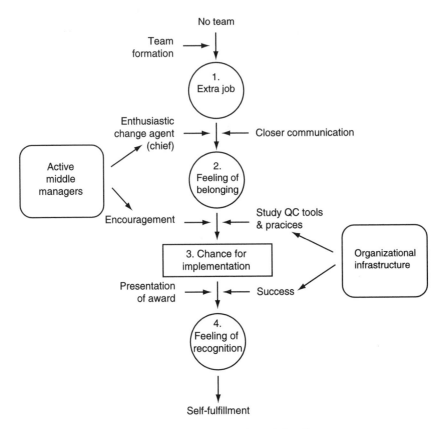

Figure 19-5. Evolution of the Ladybug Team

Small Group Dynamics: Evolution of Enthusiasm and Effectiveness

Let's analyze the development of the Ladybug Circle by examining Figure 19-5, start-ing from the top. In stage 1 a team is formed. The team views improvement as an extra job. The new chief, an enthusiastic change agent, begins encouraging the team and fos-tering closer communication. This gives the team some feeling of belonging (stage 2).

Additional encouragement is provided. Eating together is a basic methodology of starting teamwork in Japan (men often start with drinking). Eating together and hav-ing face-to-face conversations are standard management practice to encourage work-ers to feel good about QC circles. Focusing on socialization and having personal discussions is fine in this situation.

Study is encouraged, with notebooks distributed, and so on. Individual counsel-ing and encouragement are provided. Also, only a few tools are taught at first. These are used three to four times, studied or learned again, and then applied to three to four themes. Shiba's experience in European QC circles suggests that middle management support is lacking at this stage. The managers say "teaching is not my job" or "I taught them everything at the beginning." This isn't teaching, it is initialization.

Next comes an opportunity for implementation (stage 3) and being allowed to use improvement skills in one's real job.

Next, the team must have success. If the QC circle fails to solve a problem, it won't use the tool again. So, choosing the right theme is important. The rewards of success are the sense of accomplishment coming from solving a problem and the chance to present the team's story at a QI story meeting. The team is also given a tangible award or prize. Success and reward lead to a feeling of recognition (stage 4) and, eventually, to a sense of fulfillment. In the words of Yoshiko Fujino of the Ladybug Circle:

> Even though we started as wandering birds, with the cooperation of the circle members and consideration from others, we found out that even middle-aged "old ladies" can do a good job, and we have grown more self-confident as a result. In this process we have been able to get a tangible sense of the wonderful nature of QC activities as well. This year we are tackling with even greater energy the job of eliminating defective work processes and waste, and we have broadened the scope of our activities. As for the future, we are determined to polish our capabilities still further to create quality that will be appreciated, and to overcome all difficulties and obstacles through resolve and resistance. In this way, we firmly intend to continue to burn the light of our QC circle.

The organizational infrastructure to implement the above will be discussed next.

Triggers for Improvement

Shoji Shiba and his graduate students have studied winning QC circles that appear in the proceedings of the All-Japan QC Circle Conferences and polls of work unit supervisors and circle members [231]. Most teams performing at award-winning levels develop in the pattern described above. There is also a startling contrast between performance progress in daily work and performance progress in improvement activity. In daily work, performance improvement in both physical labor and engineering activity is closely related to the length of career, shown by the straight sloping line in Figure 19-6.

By sharp contrast, in QC circle activities, the development of the team is not a function of time but is a function of developmental triggers. QC circles rise through a series of plateaus, shown by the irregular steps in the figure. There are identifiable "triggers" that move teams to higher stages of performance [215]:

- Enthusiasm and communication
- Encouragement of study
- Opportunity for application
- Success and recognition

Just as managers diagnose QI stories to determine what skills a team needs to perform better next time, so must they diagnose teams to determine when they are ready

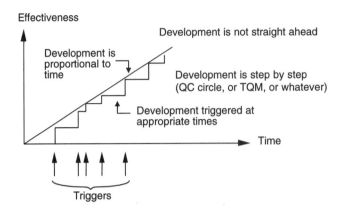

Figure 19-6. Pattern of Improvement in Daily Work

to move to the next development level. It is their responsibility to monitor the developmental status of teams and to see that these triggers are present at the right time for each team. One of a manager's most important jobs is to educate subordinates, providing proper levels of training at proper times.

Triggers are created by management (the arrival of the new chief, in the Ladybug case), teaching new advanced tools, and the chance to apply the tools and achieve success. The manager must stay aware of the team's stage of development and give necessary triggers and support.

Voluntarism and Motivation

If QC circle activities are to reap benefits, management must systematize all the necessary elements. It must provide the necessary infrastructure for encouragement, space, scheduling, training, team formations, facilitators, recognition, etc. In particular, it must deal with three key issues: participation, real results, and diagnosis.

Participation. The ideal is 100 percent voluntary participation. Why not just tell people to form QC circles? The answer is related to why QC circles are necessary at all. You need teamwork not only for improvement but also to develop human capacity. The idea is to develop staff abilities and facilitate innovation. However, enforcement means making improvement part of routine work—working to standard and not creating something new. Improvement work needs to be creative and motivating. Without significant participation of work groups in QC circles, QC circles won't work, and the company will lose major improvement possibilities.

Real Results. Management must ensure the success of QC circle activities. QC circles need to gain a sense of achievement. They need to work on something that affects the company financially. Remember the diagram of the dual function of work. Management must focus QC circles on the vital few activities directly increasing the customer's satisfaction (see Figure 19-7).

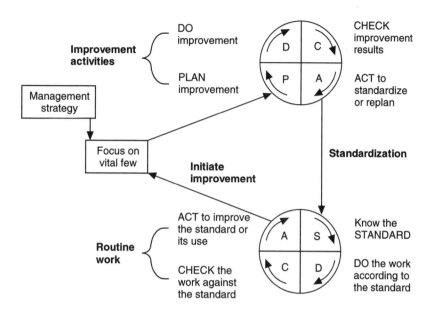

Figure 19-7. Focusing on the Vital Few for Successful QC Circle Activities

Next come the actual improvement activities: problem-solving steps, the weakness orientation, and the use of market-in concept.

Another team—a quality improvement team or cross-functional team—may be needed to pinpoint the vital few activities needing improvement. Management needs to articulate the vital few directly or to form teams that do. In fact, the extent of (voluntary) QC circle activities can be an indicator of a manager's ability to motivate his or her subordinates.

Diagnosis. The final key strategy is assessment and diagnosis. You must do assessment and diagnosis to find opportunities for further development and the way to future success.

Cross-Functional Teams

Quality improvement teams (team type B in Figure 19-3) were described in Chapter 9. Thus, we now move on to cross-functional teams.

The description of cross-functional teamwork focused on mechanisms for avoiding conflict and gave an example of how to develop a team quickly that needed to be effective over a task of limited duration.

At least three areas of potential difficulty with cross-functional teams exist:

1. Conflict among different functional business units
   • Different unit goals
   • Desire of each unit to run its own business

2. Conflicts among team members
   • Representing home unit interests
   • Different experience
   • Personal goals
   • Lack of respect for others on the team
   • Different ranks of people on the team
3. Conflicts between team effort and home unit effort
   • Insufficient time for cross-company efforts
   • Home units don't trust team to take into account real business issues

We reviewed the cross-functional teams we'd participated in, including the CQM design study described next, to consider ways of addressing the problems as shown in Figure 19-8 on page 380. We sorted these ways into three categories: setting up the team, during team activities, and the end of the team effort.

Setting up the Team

Select a team with sufficient breadth and experience to develop an appropriate solution. Also, consider adding one or two relatively inexperienced people to the team, primarily for their learning benefit rather than for their contribution. Avoid an overly limiting charter so the solution is not dictated by the charter. That way, the team will find the actual problem and an effective solution.

Ensure that team takes time to do its tasks. Set aside significant blocks of time for team effort—don't start if you can't get this commitment. Make team efforts the first priority (daily work will still get its share of time), and have an absolute near-in deadline that no one on the team can change.

During Team Activities

Reinforce the members' feeling that they are a team. Instruct them (explicitly or implicitly) that their obligation during team efforts is to the team (not to their home units) and its efforts to improve the company. Arrange to have the team members travel together at an early date—this is an excellent way to get them acquainted. You might even schedule some social meetings.

Design the process to avoid divisive debate. Steer away from topics that generate conflict during early team efforts or on the first revolution of PDCA. Start by focusing externally (on customers, success stories, and authorities). Focus on weaknesses contrasted with best industry practices, and benchmark to learn best practices so you can deal with goals and other divisive topics from the standpoint of fact rather than opinion.

Design how the team deals with facts to minimize conflict without stifling insight. Give introductory business improvement and problem-solving training (which also leads the team to root sources of problems and effective conclusions). Such an introduction enables all team members to speak the same language. Leave little time for unstructured discussion in meetings. Stick to discovering the facts and using improvement tools—don't leave time for personal agendas and competitive instincts to emerge.

Of course, for the team to come to a firm conclusion, members need to have the same experiences and study the same facts. Even if subteams or individuals do their own investigation, they need to report what they uncover in a factual and nonevaluative way.

The focus of the team should be on process. The team facilitator manages the process and revises it as necessary (if the team accepts leadership in the process, great progress can be made). If the managers who created the team ask for an interim report, report process and not results. The focus on process eliminates the possibility that upper management will dictate a solution halfway through the study effort.

End of the Team Effort

The team as a whole should report its process and results: the team needs management to acknowledge and confirm its receptivity to the team's efforts. Trust the team and its process—accept and implement its findings. Finally, use process diagnosis and PDCA to improve the process for the next time, and ask the team to include recommendations for improvement in its report. Demonstrating thoughtful analysis of possible weaknesses makes the recommendations more trustworthy and implementable. These techniques are illustrated in the following case study.

Teamwork Case Study: The CQM Design Team

The CQM design study took place in March and April 1990 and is an example of cross-functional and cross-company teamwork.[4]

The CQM has seven founding companies:

- Analog Devices
- Bolt Beranek and Newman
- Digital Equipment Corporation
- Polaroid Corporation
- Teradyne
- Bose
- GE Jet Engine Division

People from the first five companies plus MIT participated in the five-week design study. Shoji Shiba of Tsukuba University was our guiding advisor. Therefore, the CQM design study team was cross-functional, intercompany, and international. Although we did not realize it at the time, Shoji Shiba was guiding us through an example of PDCA, as defined in Table 19-2 on page 382. The following text and Figure 19-9 on page 383 describe the flow of our activities.

As part of the planning phase (Plan), we did team building, considered our goals, and were given basic TQM education.[5] We did an LP diagram on what we learned about TQM (see top left of Figure 19-9).

Expect high-quality team activity

Provide time to meet

Encourage team self-sufficiency

Set an absolute near-in deadline that can't be changed.

Enable team to meet.

Give team effort first priority.

Set aside significant blocks of time for team effort.

Avoid too limiting a charter for the team.

Provide the team with the resources to do its work

Select team with sufficient breadth and experience.

The team facilitator manages the process and revises as appropriate.

Appreciate and encourage team activities.

Have the entire team give its final report and recommendations.

Ask the team to include thoughts on improving its process in the final report.

Ask the team to report process, not results when early progress report is desired.

Bring team members together

Discourage divisive debate

Leave little time for unstructured discussion in the meeting.

Direct the team's attention away from private agendas.

Avoid topics likely to generate conflict in the early days of the effort.

Instruct the team that its first obligation is to the team's effort to help the company.

Provide time for team members to get to know each other.

Arrange to have team travel together at an early date.

Have some meetings just for being sociable.

Figure 19-8. Some Ways to Build Cross-Functional Teamwork

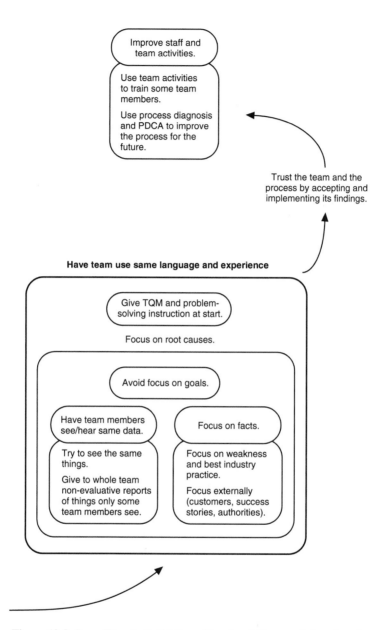

Figure 19-8. Some Ways to Build Cross-Functional Teamwork (*continued*)

In the visit stage (Do), we read about the companies we were to visit when reading materials were available. For each company we visited, we prepared an LP diagram of questions we wanted to ask. For the Japanese companies, Shoji Shiba translated our LP into Japanese and faxed it ahead so they would know what questions

Table 19-2. Activities in the PDCA Process

Stage	Activities	Week number
Plan	Team building Basic education in TQM Preparation for fact finding	1
Do	Fact finding through company site visits in Japan and the United States	2, 3
Check	Consolidate facts, identify requirements (test by Deming and Baldrige benchmark), identify means, and construct quality tables of requirements versus means and company weaknesses versus requirements	3, 4
Act	Prepare first-year plan; outline future plan	5

we had. Then, we visited the company. At the end of the visit, we checked our LP of questions to make sure all questions had been answered, and asked for further information on incompletely answered questions. After our visits, we prepared LPs of post-visit questions for each company. These would have been useful had we visited again, but we did not. However, it was helpful in thinking about questions for the next company. We also prepared an LP on the facts we learned and reduced this to a manageable group of facts using the MPM method (see top middle of Figure 19-9).

In the Check phase (bottom of figure), we studied what we had learned during our visits and from formal training in TQM as recorded on our LP diagrams. From these important facts, we constructed a tree of components of a TQM system, which we then checked against the Deming and Baldrige criteria. We also constructed a tree of means of implementing a company TQM system. We did a correlation of these components and means to find the most relevant means for each component. Then the individual participants of each of the five participating companies studied the needs of their own company and correlated these with the components of a company TQM system to find the most relevant components to each of their needs. We then identified the key components that met the common needs of all five companies. We used the key components to select the key means via the components/means correlation table (bottom of Figure 19-9).

In the Act (or standardization) phase, we sketched the process steps for implementing each of the key means and divided them into two categories: those each company had to do for itself and those the CQM could do for all the companies. The latter we divided into a group to be implemented in the first year and a group to be left to later years and future PDCA cycles (top right of Figure 19-9).

As we did our studies and analysis, Shoji Shiba taught us to use some of the QC tools, the LP method, relations diagrams, tree diagrams, matrix diagrams, and quality tables. He demonstrated that with an experienced facilitator, a cross-functional team without previous experience can simultaneously learn new problem-solving techniques and apply them usefully to an important and urgent problem. Figure 19-10 shows the principles by which we worked.

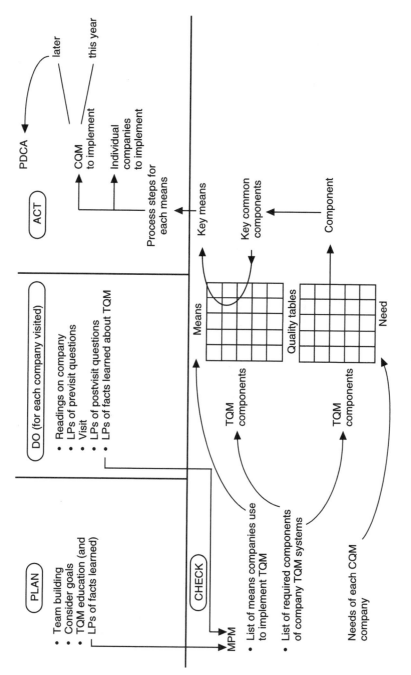

Figure 19-9. CQM Design Team's PDCA Process Activities

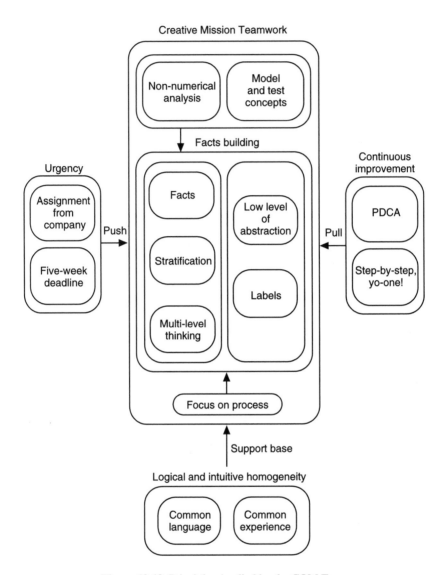

Figure 19-10. Principles Applied by the CQM Team

Inside the big rectangle of Figure 19-10 are the elements of our work process enabling us to do a thorough job: we focused on facts, data stratification, multi-valued thinking, working at a low abstraction level, and capturing words on labels; all of these enabled us to get the detailed facts. We obtained our raw data by focusing on process and using analytic tools to handle non-numeric (language) data from which we developed concepts and models we could test. These were our group norms. However, with these norms alone, we risked getting mired in detail.

Around the big rectangle are three elements that led to quick, high-quality work. First, we felt great urgency. We were on a high-level assignment from our respective companies, and we had a five-week deadline. The urgency required that we eliminate debilitating differences in perspective and language. Second, therefore, we made great efforts to learn and see the same things—we learned a common language and experienced the same things. This gave us logical and intuitive homogeneity, which enabled us to quickly build upon each other's ideas rather than spend time trying to understand what the others were saying. Third, we adhered to the continuous improvement concept. We didn't fix our mission concretely at the beginning of our study. Instead, we turned the PDCA cycle many times in the five-week period, moving step-by-step with plenty of opportunity for feedback and reflection. This enabled a reasonable five-week goal and solution to emerge. We resisted the impulse to seek a perfect answer or unattainable quality of answer, assuming more PDCA in the future.

The design study report concludes with the following observation from the team:

> The team worked in a very process-oriented way, following the tenets of TQM, and found these practices to provide a quantum leap in productivity of the planning and decision-making process. The team used the LP method of analyzing qualitative facts as a substitute for less structured discussion. By agreeing, as a team, on each process to follow before embarking on it, the team was able to work rapidly and achieve consensus on both substance and presentation of these complex issues within the five-week time frame [74].

Core Teams at Analog Devices

Throughout the 1990s, there was much discussion, especially in the high-tech industries, of the pressure for more rapid product development cycles so companies could bring products to market more quickly. In particular, many discussed the limitations of the traditional functional structure of the people involved in new product development—development teams drawing people from functional departments such as hardware development, software development, software test, system QA, etc., and serial handoffs from the development organization to manufacturing, to marketing and sales, and finally to the delivery and customer support organization. A major difficulty with this functional organization is that functional managers are under enormous pressure to provide human resources to many competing projects and often succumb to over scheduling their people. Thus, individual projects may have trouble accessing the people as needed, lengthening time to market.

An alternative organization promoted by many (see, for instance, [199]) was the so-called *core team* of people representing the various functions and who were essentially dedicated to the particular project. Development of the core team process within a company was typically an explicit improvement effort aimed at reducing time to market through use of core teams to carry out development projects.

In 1997, Jeff Swift, then Director of Engineering for Analog Devices Transportation and Industrial Products Division, told us the story of the division's use of core teams.[6]

The Transportation and Industrial Products Division (TIPD) focuses on automotive, automatic test equipment, motor control, and industrial control industries. Over the three previous years, TIPD had been implementing an increasingly team-based structure.

TIPD's work with teams arose from examining why their new product development activities took so long. In the past, they had addressed issues including new product processes, methodologies, standards, and skills; however, they were still short of the needed performance levels. They analyzed this situation and determined that the root cause lay in their personnel resourcing strategy for people working on projects.

TIPD had used the typical resourcing strategy that encouraged passing a project in a linear fashion to completion through marketing, design, layout, testing, and other functions. Though this strategy seemed fundamentally logical, it had flaws.

First, new projects started as soon as anyone was free. Since there's always someone free, a new program could begin any time (even though there may be 20 projects already backed up in queues throughout the process). Unfortunately, queues stretch out time to market.

Second, because people often were split among many projects (and, in fact, many projects had no full-timer on them), the division had difficultly coordinating availability of a person working on multiple projects with activities on a particular project. This also hurt time to market.

The resourcing strategy's third flaw emerged at the end of most programs. People involved later in a program naturally questioned fundamental assumptions made by others at the program's beginning. Changes often resulted. Again, these late changes lengthened time to market.

The Benefits of a Core Team

Through research, TIPD discovered that team-based resourcing strategies were more immune to these flaws. They concluded that the core team model of [199] had unique capabilities.

When core teams are used, some members (like designers or test engineers) can participate full time. They are with the team from start to finish. For this core team of people, their top priority is the team's goal. Other people (like CAD or layout people) can participate part time. These extended or part-time team members offer a service to the core team, or to multiple teams simultaneously, then move on to other duties.

With the core team approach, before a project can get going seriously, it has to have the bulk of the full-time team ready to be allocated full time. Also, with the core team approach, the success of the project on which the full-time member is participating (versus success of an individual's job) should be the individual's number one priority. Getting the necessary commitment of the full-time team members occurs through a negotiation process, which considers available resources, the project goal, and the time to do the project. At least one of these (resources, goal, or time) must be considered "negotiable" so a realistic plan is possible to which team members can commit.[7] Enough time is taken to get necessary commitment before the project begins.

The core team approach provides fast time to market within an environment that shares resources.

In the first year TIPD used this strategy, time decreased by 25 percent, and new product introductions increased by 30 percent. New product revenue doubled. These positive results and others convinced TIPD to pursue this strategy further.

After one year, TIPD reassessed the process and found that although team members had positive feelings, they were also confused. They had the following questions: the difference between a team leader and a manager; how individuals can really feel accountable to a team goal; how to measure and reward teams; and whether team meetings were really necessary.

Using the techniques of hoshin management (that we will describe in Chapter 24), TIPD chartered four hoshin teams to focus on how a resourcing strategy based on core teams could help Analog Devices meet its vital product development goals. These teams spent the next year addressing infrastructure issues. They defined the roles and responsibilities of sponsors, team leaders, and team members. They also created methods for assembling new core teams and processes whereby core teams could measure and assess their own performance. Lastly, the hoshin teams created reward systems. Analog Devices incorporated much of this new knowledge into a new course, "Succeeding with Teams," that they gave internally and made available to other CQM companies.

The recommendations of the hoshin teams were unanimously accepted within TIPD and implemented. For a second year, TIPD time to market dropped by 48 percent and new product revenue doubled.

Tackling Performance Management

After two years, TIPD again reassessed the process. Although normal metrics showed gangbuster performance, people were concerned. Teams were working, but something in the old functional structure had disappeared. People were asking new questions pertaining to promotion, career path, and mentorship. These concerns differed greatly from those of the previous year.

Again motivated by their new product success, four more hoshin teams tackled the new set of issues. Over the next year, these teams drew upon academia, industry experts, and TIPD itself and created some truly breakthrough solutions. They changed the review and performance processes, made mentorship more broadly available, established career paths focusing more on skills and competencies, and created functional forums enabling people from all teams to network and enhance their skills. Again, the division unanimously accepted the recommendations of the hoshin teams.

By this time, TIPD had grown to be Analog Devices' second largest and, at times, its fastest-growing division. TIPD became the dominant supplier in several marketplaces and created strategic partnerships with many of Analog Devices' "platinum accounts."

Ironically, when TIPD reassessed the process again, they found that even with three years of experience with the core team approach, they were back where they had started. They had major accounts whose demands grew faster than they could address them. Because of their success in the market, resources were again spread too thin!

They frantically created teams to deal with this situation. They hired people rapidly and stole from existing teams where possible. Simultaneously, they diverted people to assist with customer overdemand problems that their factories were experiencing. Lacking control over project proliferation, coupled with their inability to assimilate new talent quickly enough, time to market increased (rather than decreased) and new product revenue flattened for the first time in four years.

Next Steps

Tough problems require faith, desire, and discipline. TIPD incorporated more proactive hiring policies. It focused on a process crossing product lines that drew more skills and competencies into the front end of the system. They adopted required resourcing levels on teams and a multi-level management approach to deal with excess demand for new product creation.

They also initiated training (as described in Chapter 16) to help team members improve their communication skills. In a team-oriented environment, the heart of operating efficiently can be found through clear requests and promises, improved relationships, and constructively handling breakdowns.

At Analog Devices, the core teams concept worked. They created a mutual learning environment where team members are learned from and taught each other. They exceeded expectations for growth, profitability, and employee and customer satisfaction. Finally, they created a culture that enabled the constant change necessary to improve work and life.

Self-directed Work Teams at Analog Devices' Cambridge Fab

In 1996, one part of Analog Devices was under intense time pressure for a variety of business reasons to get a new wafer fab plant up and running in an empty building in Cambridge, MA.[8] In addition to the severe time constraint, competition for the equipment and other components needed to establish the new "wafer fab" (as the semi-conductor industry calls such plants) was intense. The wafer fab was for a new division and would be relatively small (as wafer fabs go).

Ira Moskowitz and a few colleagues were responsible for getting the wafer fab operational. They undertook a 9 steps activity (as described in Chapter 12) to determine what organization would be appropriate for the small plant with its aggressive time schedule. During an early step of the 9 steps, they realized they needed people who were very experienced, unusually flexible, highly cross-trained, and who had unusually effective and efficient communication mechanisms available for their use.

They were aware of the concept of self-directed work teams (SDWTs) from an earlier benchmarking project, and they came to see that the wafer fab's organizational needs would be met by self-directed work teams. In addition, Ira saw this small-scale, clean slate situation as an appropriate opportunity for him to try to use such teams. Therefore, the team made the decision that they would go down the path of the SDWT.

A Five Stage Model for Team Maturity

Although Ira had earlier benchmarked the concept, he and his people had no personal experience with SDWTs. Therefore, when it came time to hire a production manager, one of the selection criteria was that the prospective employee have expertise with SDWTs. They hired Ken Bethea who had the appropriate breadth of experience, having installed SDWTs in his previous job. In addition to Ken and Ira, the team that initiated the SDWT program included Craig Core (then Process Engineering Manager) and Rick Melvin (Director of Human Resources).

In early 2000 when Ira and Ken described their experience to us, they noted that although they were in their fourth year operating using SDWTs, the system for such teams was still a work in progress, undergoing regular PDCA and evolution, including major changes as recently as 1999. They emphasized that although in their experience SDWTs are very productive, managing an organization of such teams is very hard relative to managing a typical hierarchical organizational structure and, thus, takes considerable management commitment.

From his previous job, Ken brought with him a concept of five stages of development of maturity of SDWTs. The Cambridge plant of Analog Devices adopted and significantly elaborated the five stages concept. The five stages are shown in Figure 19-11, which Ira and his people call the "running chart." Each conceptual stage provides a template covering a maturity level relating to the "four-legged stool" of process, equipment, teamwork, and math and technology (also shown in the figure). The four-legged stool idea is that teams and team members need skills in each of the four areas, and without a balance of skill in all four areas, the stool will not be stable. *Process* has to do with the team and team members knowing how to process the work through the various process steps in the wafer fab. *Equipment* has to do with understanding the equipment in the wafer fab. *Teamwork* has to do with the dynamics of teams, particularly SDWTs. *Math and technology* have to do with the mathematics (e.g., statistical process control) and technology of semiconductor operation and fabrication (e.g., semi-conductor physics).

In the first of the conceptual stages, team members have beginning involvement and have bought into the concept of SDWTs. Each successive conceptual stage suggests levels of training, cross training, etc., appropriate for a team at that stage. At conceptual Stage 5, which might take two or three years to achieve, team members are fully certified semiconductor fabrication operators with the additional capability to do major preventive maintenance work and minor repair work, all of which requires formal certification.

STAGE 1	STAGE 2	STAGE 3	STAGE 4	STAGE 5
Attributes □ Mission statement □ Code of conduct □ Unanimous understanding, acceptance, and commitment to participate in SDWT □ Metrics understood—shift □ Participate in SDWT meetings □ Utilize communication system between shifts and teams (passdowns and logs)	**Attributes** □ Understand and follow safety program and protocol □ Accountable for adherence to housekeeping □ Know and understand cycle-time goals and yields; also where to find the data □ Following meeting rules (agenda, roles, conduct, etc.) □ Understand GCT metrics and goals □ Using SDWT process	**Attributes** □ Involved in TQM project performing root cause analysis of high-frequency problems □ Provide feedback for individual team development □ Team making own decisions and held accountable for decisions □ Housekeeping happening 100 percent of the time □ Team/individuals work together in a positive manner □ Self-facilitation skills emerging □ Demonstrating SDWT success	**Attributes** □ Using feedback to identify training gaps and team needs □ Evidence of success of problem solving and continuous improvement on goals □ TQM tools always used in all appropriate situations (automatic data-driven culture) □ Safety program accountable for □ Can openly disagree or, criticize without conflict □ Gaining experience in team roles	**Attributes** □ Full capability to apply knowledge and solve problems □ Independent of facilitators □ Teams own, run, and improve safety programs □ Team operates as one □ Team truly multi-skilled and multi-functional □ Recognizes other teams' great performance □ Full capability to determine root cause of the next highest frequency problem □ Strive for zero safety incidents □ Strive to exceed cycle time and yield goals □ Provide input to improve efficiency of work area □ Coordinate action items with other teams' involvement toward completion and resolution
Training **Process:** Manufacturing area certification 50 percent **Equipment:** PROMIS training, wafer handling, training **Team:** Introduction into SDWT **Math & Tech:** XL technical overview	**Training** **Process:** Manufacturing area certification 75 percent **Equipment:** Initial PM training **Team:** TQM training **Math & Tech:**	**Training** **Process:** Manufacturing area certification 100 percent **Equipment:** Area-specific PM training (ongoing) **Team:** Ongoing team skills, facilitation skills **Math & Tech:** SPC training	**Training** **Process:** Initial cross-training in other areas **Equipment:** Area specific PM training (ongoing) **Team:** Ongoing team-building skills **Math & Tech:** Semiconductor devices process training commences	**Training** **Process:** Full cross-training in other areas **Equipment:** Minor equipment repairs addressing breakdowns and provide analysis **Team:** Continual team training skills

Figure 19-11. Stage Development Chart ("Running Chart")

Team Operations

The Analog Devices Cambridge wafer fab runs 24 hours a day, seven days a week. Four separate teams handle a continuous operations schedule of shifts. During any one shift, the on duty team runs the plant. Each team must cover the areas of chemical vapor deposition, trim, diffusion, etch, implant, photolithography, and thin film. Each area includes several relevant functions, and it is desirable for team members to become certified for all functions within multiple areas.

These teams do not have supervisors on their shifts. In fact, all of the operators (called Manufacturing Technicians or "MTs" in the Cambridge operation) on all four teams report to Ken in his capacity of production manager. These supervisorless teams completely run the plant on a daily basis. The teams plan and decide everything that must be done.

Because specific people are needed to direct attention to various aspects of operation, each team rotates team members through roles: production representative, yield representative, safety representative, continuous improvement representative, and training representative. This rotation pushes cross-training.

Some of these roles need to coordinate with engineering and with the senior managers of the plant, and appropriate meetings are held. The people in the relevant roles are expected to attend these meetings, which may be scheduled when the people are not on shift. One team member is declared to be site manager (the person who speaks for the plant in case of some emergency); however, this person does not otherwise manage the site.

Ira and his people use Figure 19-12 when describing the roles of management and the four SDWTs (teams A, B, C, and D) and the overlap between the roles.

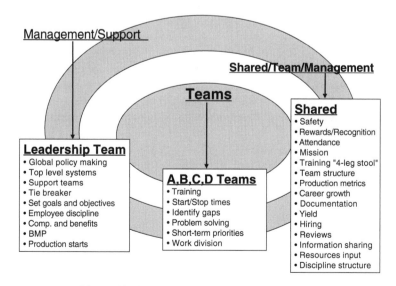

Figure 19-12. Cambridge Fab Boundary Structure

Much data is collected on a variety of aspects of plant operations, and each team is required to hold an hour meeting weekly for data review. For team meetings, team members rotate through another set of roles: team leader (for the meeting), time keeper, scribe, and facilitator. Teams produce written minutes of meetings. Teams are graded on both productivity and on attendance.

Management, Team Monitoring, and Improvement of the Team System

Within the wafer fab, Ira has three people reporting to him: production manager Ken, a wafer fab manager, and a site facilities manager. Ira himself reports to the general manager of the division as well as having a strong dotted line to the Vice President of Analog Devices' worldwide manufacturing. In a more conventional plant, Ken might well report to the wafer fab manager. However, in his particular situation in Ira's organization, Ken also is responsible for assembly and test production operations and so he reports directly to Ira.

Each week there is an "SDWT meeting" attended by the management team, at which strengths and weaknesses are analyzed.

Annually everyone in shift operations (on the SDWTs) and everyone on the five-day/week support staff are surveyed. Manufacturing top management carefully analyzes the survey data and proposes a list of ten top issues to the teams. The teams provide feedback that adjusts management's understanding of the important issues. Finally, the top three or so issues are selected, and improvement teams are formed involving appropriate people from across the four teams to address the issues. Typically, each improvement team undertakes a 9 step process, because the most important issues to date are more related to missing parts of an SDWT organization than with parts needing improvement. Examples of issues dealt with after the annual review have been accountability, communication, recognition, rewards and goal congruence.

One of these 9 step efforts dealt with the question of how team performance was measured and recognized. This, in turn, resulted in creation of an ongoing team known as the Goal Congruence Team, meeting every other week, to operationalize such issues. Another example was an issue about lack of responsiveness by management to team problems. Another 9 step team was formed; part of the solution was the creation of forms that could be filled out by the teams to request management response and tracked by management.

Every person on the manufacturing floor is given a performance review twice a year. Originally, Ira and his top management colleagues avoided the complications of having the members of SDWTs evaluate each other by having Ken do all the evaluations himself, which of course was a huge job. This also had the problem that, without a layer of supervisors in daily contact with the people on teams, team members felt that Ken wasn't fully aware of their performance. Eventually, this issue was assigned to a 9 step team that invented a process for performance evaluations being done by the SDWTs. The plan included training of facilitators on teams. This process is used during one of the two yearly performance review cycles. Five other team members of each person's team review that person. (They call this a 270-degree review process because it is less exhaustive than the well-known 360-degree review process, which also includes review by subordinates.) The resulting reviews go to the team's training representative who summarizes them in writing. The team training representative, the reviewee, and the facilitator then meet to discuss the review summary and finally the review is forwarded to Ken. This very important but time-consuming process is now actively being reworked through PDCA loops.

One problem that the SDWTs have struggled with is the minority of people who arrive late for work or leave early. They tried to make the self-directed teams responsible for this; however, the teams gave the problem back to management saying that having to deal with this issue would hurt team dynamics and relationships more than it would help the punctuality problem. Management responded by installing an electronic card-swipe system to monitor the team's adherence to shift start/stop times. This is an example of the constant vigilance required to understand and adjust team responsibilities versus management's responsibilities.

On the more positive side, at this point the SDWTs have matured to the point that they are doing their own interviewing of new team members.

Benefits and Problems

When asked about the benefits of SDWTs, Ira responds that originally he and his colleagues chose the SDWT plan to get their new plant up and running well with a small staff over a short time. And it worked: they did get the new plant up and running very quickly.

In addition, in the longer run, productivity has been higher than Ira imagined was possible. This productivity has two sources:

- Of course, some financial savings result from not having supervisors
- The more important productivity increase, however, comes from the fact that the SDWTs run the plant very effectively and efficiently

Ira also emphasizes that their operation is relatively small; to obtain this productivity in a larger operation would be more difficult.

Apparently the self-directed work team situation provides important motivation for the people. Ken says, "we can't seem to turn them off." For instance, before taking a vacation, a team member will recruit someone from another team willing to work overtime in his or her place.

Occasionally, a particular order has been declared "high priority"—has to be produced especially quickly—and was produced so fast that Ira and his top management team wondered if it was physically possible and carefully reviewed the component routing records to convince themselves it was. The SDWT structure, eliminating the need to communicate up and down hierarchical ladders, allows exceptionally effective communication between shifts.

Ira and Ken emphasize that SDWT structure is much harder to manage than conventional methods, requiring continuing improvement work to function well. It takes great management commitment. In particular, since no layer of supervisors exists,

Ken says that constant effort is required to stay in touch with people in the organization, including meeting with people on other shifts, coming in on an ongoing basis outside weekday work hours, and using various means of "networking" to stay in touch with the pulse of the organization.

Also, great team member commitment is needed because people must deal with personal interaction issues and take responsibility for things that they wouldn't do in a typical hierarchical structure. On the other hand, despite complaints about the difficulty and stress of SDWTs, they have low turnover. In their annual survey, most people answer that they like the system and would recommend the division to their friends.

Ira stresses that people with much bigger plants should be very careful about trying to institute SDWTs. He also thinks that converting an existing hierarchical system is more difficult than starting with a clean slate, although Harris Semiconductor in Melbourne, FL, made such a conversion, turning supervisors into facilitators who truly ceased to be supervisors. In other situations of so-called SDWTs, Ira has benchmarked or read about, there tends to be a mix of a hierarchical and self-directed situation, which Ira and Ken believe would be an easier approach.

Finally, in Analog's Cambridge plant, they basically only hire people with wafer fab experience and give them very high levels of training, which facilitates the ability of the teams to function autonomously.

Team Members Speak

After providing us with the above story, Ira Moskowitz and Ken Bethea suggested that hearing the point of view of the SDWT members would be useful, and they invited anonymous contributions from team members. The full text of the comments by four team members is included in [213]. Some excerpts follow.

Team Member 1. [SDWTs] provide a sense of worth that one usually doesn't feel in a normal work environment.

Team Member 2. ... the team is self-directed, not the individual. Think of the team as a baseball or football team. It takes many players in different positions to play the game. What kind of game would it be if everyone was the quarterback or the pitcher ... Forgive and forget—especially the forget part ... Give credit where credit is due. Sometimes the little personal successes are the greatest achievements ... It is important that everyone in the team has an equal voice and everyone's opinion is valued. It is okay to disagree—that is how we see through other people's eyes. Evaluate opinions or input based on logic rather than personal preference ... Honesty may be the best policy, but consider the feelings of others. There are many ways to get the point across, but it is not worth it if it is at someone's expense."

Team Member 3. Trust is an important factor for the SDWT to succeed. When one member of the team loses trust, the team breaks down causing animosity. Regaining the trust is essential to remain successful as an SDWT.

Team member 4. The key to a successful SDWT is people. A team of hard-working focused people can take levels of productivity and morale to new heights. A fully functional SDWT is an awesome thing to see in action. Without the burden of management breathing down your neck, people are free to do the job they are there for, and they do it with much pride and fervor ... Freedom to change the workplace to facilitate greater throughput and work ergonomics is available and self-contained in [a person's] team. People expand on their knowledge and talents with ease and share all related information accordingly ... The downfalls of this environment are minimal compared to the benefits, and over time the team grows stronger, relationships get tighter, work gets done faster, and self-esteem rises.

Top Management Teams

Everyone talks about "the top management team." However, in company after company, both the top management group and other people in the organization observing the top management group report that it is not really a *team*.

In [161, chapter 11], Katzenbach and Smith describe some of the difficulties top management groups have in really functioning as part of a team. Like teams everywhere, top management groups confuse working as a complete group with teamwork, have a hard time working together in the face of hierarchical relationships, and so on—only more so than lower level teams. In the same chapter, Katzenbach and Smith suggest methods of overcoming such problems in acting as a team. Focusing on specific tasks to be done, remembering our distinction between (whole) group work and individual (or small group) work (pages 363–364), assigning appropriate subsets of the top management team to various tasks, and remembering our admonition about not delegating (page 366) will go a long way toward enabling top management teamwork.

When a top management group is able to function as a team, its way of operating can be similar to any other team although the sorts of issues it addresses will differ. Greg Fischer, ex-CEO of SerVend and now involved in the start-up of a variety of new companies, has the following to say:

> While teamwork from top management teams does not typically take a different form, there are higher expectations for the business deliverables from top management teams. These teams have an obligation to demonstrate good teamwork and good team process if they expect other teams in the organization to produce valuable output.
>
> At SerVend, we started the teaming initiative with my staff so we would send a signal to the organization that teamwork is not something that is only expected from the "lower levels." Additionally, my staff needed to gain the experience with the teaming process so they could be value-added coaches to the other teams as they were being formed.

A final note, the top management teams tended to focus more on planning and setting direction versus the lower level of abstraction work (more "doing") from the lower level teams.

19.3 MODELS FOR TEAM DEVELOPMENT

In the discussion of Figure 19-5 (page 374), we described a model of team development derived from study of QC circles in Japan. In this section we introduce three additional models for team development. The first, the Tuckman model, is a better known model that, like the model of Figure 19-5 (page 374), describes the phases a team goes through to become fully functional. The second, the Katzenbach and Smith model, is central to the discussion of their excellent book [161] and defines a sequence of team levels in terms of ability to perform. The third model was sketched by Burchill and Walden and presented in CQM courses and describes a repetitive cycle of ever increasing team development.

The above four models give you a rich vocabulary with which to think about teamwork and give multiple perspectives from which to consider the teamwork case studies of this chapter, the rest of the book, your own examples of team development.

Tuckman Model

Almost everyone who talks and writes about teamwork seems to know the "forming, storming, norming, and performing" model for development of a team. We don't know where we first heard about it, but we first read about it in [252, pages 6-4 to 6-7], which attributes the article to Bruce W. Tuckman [285].

In this model, teams pass through four stages in order to become successful (we paraphrase the description of [239], which also acknowledges Tuckman):

- *Forming*: Members of a newly declared team begin to learn to deal with each other and not much work gets done.
- *Storming*: Team members strain and struggle to find a way to work together successfully.
- *Norming*: Workable roles and ways or working are accepted by team members and team feeling develops.
- *Performing*: The team is performing a high levels with an efficient and effective way of working together.

Katzenbach and Smith Model

Katzenbach and Smith in [161, chapter 5] present the model shown in Figure 19-13. As we read this figure, the vertical axis is how much the team accomplishes and the horizontal axis is how much the group behaves like a team. Katzenbach and Smith define what they call a "work group" and four levels of "teams."[9] (We paraphrase the following from Katzenbach and Smith's discussion.)

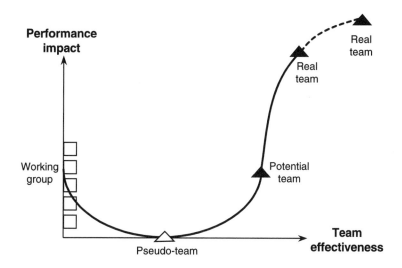

Figure 19-13. The Team Performance Curve

Work groups: Members interact to share information, best practices, etc., and to coordinate action and make decisions; however, there is no need or desire to increment performance significantly. Work groups can be effective enough in a number of situations, indicated by the broad range of little blocks on the vertical axis.

Sometimes, performance is needed beyond what can be provided by a work group. The purpose of a "team" is to get more performance than a work group can provide—better coordination, more from individuals, faster improvement, etc. (The purpose of a team is not to empower members, not to improve relationships, not to transfer responsibility to the team from management.) Since the purpose of teamwork is performance, we need clear definitions of team success.

Pseudo-team: A significant increment performance may be needed and the group may call itself a team, but the team is not focused on collective performance and is not trying to achieve it. The group may have the trappings of teams, e.g., attending team training, declaring empowerment, etc. There may also be forces on the "team" with personal agendas. Pseudo-teams cost more than they are worth and, therefore, are a net loss.

Potential team: A significant incremental performance is need, and the group is really trying to improve its performance.

Real team: A small group of people with complementary skills who are equally committed to a common purpose, goals, and working approach for which they hold themselves mutually accountable.

High-performance team: A real team whose members are also deeply committed to one another's personal growth and success. We are skipping this type of team and only dealing with real teams for the purposes of this day.

In their book, Katzenbach and Smith discuss their levels of teamwork in detail and give guidance on how to get to the higher levels.

Trust Loop Model

Many people, when they first think about teamwork, think about how to train people in teamwork and think about getting a group of people together who have "good chemistry." Of course, training and chemistry can be useful; however, as Katzenbach and Smith emphasize, teamwork comes from mission—training itself doesn't create teamwork and teamwork is different than friendship.

Significant performance challenges are the greatest force for teamwork. While many things that can prevent teamwork (e.g., poor team composition), significant performance challenges (such as a demanding customer) can often overcome such obstacles. It's often been demonstrated that you get what you expect from people. This leads to an entry point into Figure 19-14, another model of how a team develops.

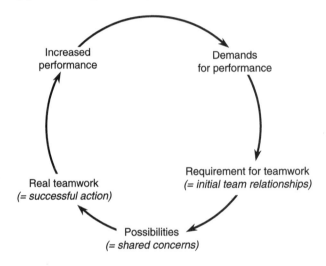

Figure 19-14. Developing Teamwork

As shown at the top right of the figure, a demand for performance (such as might come to the company from a customer) can produce the requirement for teamwork. For instance, people in various different internal functions, involved in internal squabbling, often suddenly pull together when faced with a customer crisis from outside. With the requirement for teamwork, a team relationship is formed. The fledgling team sorts out and integrates across possibilities—the various concerns that led to formation of the team and concerns from within the team. Hopefully, some real teamwork emerges. As teamwork improves, performance increases. The curious thing is that as performance increases, the demand for performance typically goes up further. Once customers see that you can produce a lot, they bring you their harder problems. Once a team is used to improved performance, the members tend to set higher standards for themselves. And they get into a success spiral. Of course, the possibility of succumbing to obstacles and having a downward spiral also exists. It should be clear that Figure 19-14 is a variation trust loop (Figure 16-19, page 323), for bonding together as a team by building trust by creating effective action.

It all starts with demand for performance. A strong performance ethic is a lot more effective for teamwork than anything else, e.g., than empowerment and training. The issue is not teamwork per se. That exists or will try to exist given sufficient challenge. The issue is effective and efficient teamwork.

Teamwork Must Come from Inside the Team

Teamwork is not something that can be imposed. A manager can try to order up teamwork, but we have all probably experienced where teamwork didn't really happen. Teamwork, by its very nature, is something that develops among a group of people—teamwork is of the team, as in Figure 19-14. Team members will develop rapport with each other and begin to function as parts of a team.

Outside forces can be used to provide impetus and support for teamwork, e.g., providing a worthy challenge, making people available with appropriate skills, and removing organizational and cultural obstacles to teamwork. (Outside forces definitely should not ignore obstacles or create new obstacles.)

Looking at things in reverse, a team cannot ignore outside forces but must explicitly deal with them if the team is to work effectively and efficiently [11, 10].

Teamwork Develops Incrementally (but Support Helps)

Teamwork is not something that develops instantaneously. Little steps are made, little successes happen, and these encourage improved teamwork. This is illustrated as a series of plateaus in Figure 19-6 (page 376), the accompanying discussion of some "triggers" that help a team move from one plateau to the next, and in the series of loops implicit in Figure 19-14.

Management must be sure someone sensitive to such plateaus and triggers is on a team or assigned to support it, if development of a team is to move ahead steadily rather than having a higher probability of foundering.

This is why we often assign successful team leaders or managers to future teams. We know or hope that they understand implicitly or explicitly how to trigger the team from plateau to plateau. It is why Teradyne developed a process for facilitating teams [56]. It is why authorities provide lists of methods for supporting teams [161, pages 119–127].

Leaders will emerge as part of the team. These may be people the organization appointed to lead the team, or it may be other people. The team may have rejection reactions to some proposed leaders.

Leaders, Coaches, and Managers

Many have talked about managers being coaches or leaders, but perhaps we have not had enough clarity about the differences between the functions of a manager, coach, and leader. One perspective is this: a leader points the team where it has to go and why and gets the team to follow him or her there; a coach helps figure out how to improve so the team can get there (coaches are people who help others see their blind spots); and a manager helps organize the necessary resources.

In some cases, more than one of these three functions can be resident in one person, but not always. In some cases, the people providing these functions are members of the team and sometimes not. These functions also can be provided by different people at different times and at different levels. Managers might be chosen by the company and given authority to manage. Coaches and leaders might also be chosen by the company, but authority to actually coach or lead is granted by the team, if it is granted at all.

Five Necessary Conditions for Teamwork

Personal experience and the various authorities (particularly the Flores school of thinking about business and leading teams) suggested five conditions are necessary for team performance. We don't claim that we have the only five conditions for team performance. Other experienced managers or authorities on teamwork may think of a few other important conditions. We do claim that these five are significant, and the first and fourth conditions are critical.

We say these are necessary conditions because we think effective teamwork is difficult, if not impossible, without them. However, these conditions are not sufficient; strong obstacles to teamwork may be more than a match for these necessary conditions.

In each case, explicit methods are needed to ensure the given condition is satisfied. You can find the subset of methods you use to satisfy the five conditions in the team case studies in Section 19.2 of this chapter, various methods described through this book, and in books such as [252, 161, 239].

1. Shared Commitment to Mission. Figure 19-15 shows the vectors from each participant and the resultant output in terms of effort accomplished and direction.

On the left side of the figure, we see that people are pulling in different directions—they don't have a shared commitment to the mission. In fact, the person represented by the bottom arrow is pretending to pull in the correct direction but is actually pushing in a contrary direction. In fact, such a person may sneak around to change the direction of the result after it is completed. We've all known people like that, who never quit pushing things to go in a certain direction.

On the right of the figure, we see the situation where everyone on the team shares a commitment to the mission, and the result is strong and straight from left to right, as desired.

The shared commitment to mission not only has to do with each member of the team having the same mission, it also has to do with the commitment to overcome any obstacle to accomplishing the mission. For instance, if someone tried to divert the result arrow, the team will either go around this obstacle or go right over it.

To develop a shared commitment to the mission, we need a way to develop a shared image of the situation, problem, and solution. Then, we don't really need to care

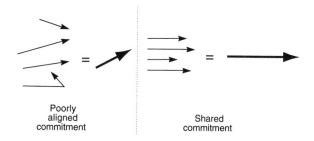

Figure 19-15. Weak versus Shared Commitment

why each team member develops a shared commitment to the mission, just that each has it. In fact, Ed Schein at MIT says, "You can't motivate people; you can only tap into the motivation they already have." People are motivated for their own reasons which can include desire for accomplishment, for affiliation, for learning, guilt, and so forth. From somewhere, each of us needs to develop a sense of importance and urgency for the mission.

2. Personal Responsibility and Accountability. This condition may be thought of as a corollary of shared commitment to the mission. When we talk of personal responsibility and accountability, we have two principles in mind:

- Making the team's mission one's own (i.e., committed to the team mission).
- Accepting accountability for one's own tasks and for not letting other members of the team fail in their tasks (i.e., personally accountable to fellow team members for fulfilling commitments).

The latter point is especially important: accountability is not just to the company and boss. Notice that this might be considered an extension of the idea of the dual function of work. Not only do we eliminate the separation between bosses and workers improvement work and daily work, but we eliminate the separation in responsibility for success between bosses and workers.

The following relevant definitions come from Mark Samuel [244, pages 6 and 193]:

- *Accountability*: People can "count on one another" to keep performance commitments and communication agreements.
- *Interlocking accountability*: Each team member is accountable to all affected team members for his or her relationships, performance, and agreements. Each team member is accountable for holding other team members accountable for either breaking an agreement or keeping an agreement . . . by making the person aware of the situation without judgement . . . and by asking how can I/we support you while you make the changes to address the situation.

3. Individual Skills. Effective teams also need team members with skills appropriate to the mission.

Some types of complementary individual skills that a team has to be concerned with are the following:

- Functional/technical—surprisingly often teams start without having a key technical skill or a plan for acquiring it
- Problem solving/decision making—people are needed with skill in both application problem solving and decision making and with skill regarding the team process itself (this and the following points on interpersonal skills and emotional skills tend to be the "process talents" as opposed to the "application talents" involved with functional/technical skills)
- Interpersonal—listening, speaking up, backing off, mutual support, etc.
- Emotional—willingness to work with other people, a can-do attitude, enthusiasm for the task, willingness to learn from others, enthusiasm for seeing the whole, etc.
- Training—including a person or two as a way of helping develop their skill, so we have more qualified people later

While each team will have some very critical skills it can't start without, no team ever starts with all the skills it needs. New skills will be developed and can be added as the team works.

4. Substantive Coordinated Action. Once we have some people with a way to develop shared commitment to the mission and people able to develop personal responsibility and accountability and who have a sufficient starting set of individual skills, we need a way to coordinate action within a team. For great success, coordination methods should be more substantial rather than less substantial, i.e., a lot more than a casual informal comment to each other now and then. We recommend the methods of Chapter 16.

5. A Problem-solving Process. This condition may be considered to be a corollary of substantive coordinated action. Team development is not an event or retreat. Team development is an ongoing process of measuring, reviewing, changing/optimizing, and practicing team/player functions in order to maximize team results. Team development is for improving and optimizing team performance against measurable results. The WV model and the 7 steps of reactive improvement are a highly effective place to start.

Interlocking accountability (part of the second of our five conditions) is also necessary. People need to help each other do what is necessary to recover from either individual failures or danger to the whole team from external sources.

NOTES

1. A cross-functional team often is within one division, e.g., within the development organization. By a cross-company team we mean either a team that crosses divisional boundaries or possibly a team that involves participants from different companies.
2. In Japan, a QC circle is officially organized when it is registered with QC Circle Headquarters (in the Japanese Union of Scientists and Engineers or JUSE). Com-

pany management is not involved directly; however, as will be seen shortly, management can nurture growth of QC circles in many ways.

3. Part-time employees work full time but are employed for one-year terms.

4. This case study was prepared by David Walden (Bolt Beranek and Newman Inc., Cambridge, MA), who participated in the study. We retain this case study in this edition because it is a good example of cross-functional work, it is another example of use of the voice of the "customer" and proactive improvement methods from Chapters 13 and 14, and it provides additional details relating to the CQM case study of Chapter 28. The design study is comprehensively documented in [74].

5. In 1990, Shoji Shiba and the CQM Design Team were thinking in terms of TQM, the first set of methods adopted by CQM member companies. Today's reader may mentally substitute "business improvement methods" for TQM.

6. Jeff's story is also documented in [278]. Today, Jeff is Director of Engineering for Analog's Micromachine Products Division (MPD).

7. This is parallel to an idea we heard is used in parts of Hewlett-Packard where new product development teams trade off project cost, project time, and product features: the team and management must agree on which one of these is fully required, which one is optimized to the extent it can be within other project constraints, and which of these is unconstrained. This approach came about after a long series of projects which failed to meet expectations because cost, time, and features were all fixed, which put too many constraints on projects for the projects to have realistic plans for successful completion.

8. This case study was told to us by Ira Moskowitz, Director of Manufacturing for Analog's Micromachined Products Division (MPD), and Ken Bethea, Production Manager for MPD.

9. From *Wisdom of Teams: Creating the High Performance Organization*, by Jon R. Katzenbach and Douglas K. Smith. Boston: Harvard Business School Press, 1993, pages 84, 91, and 92. The figure and paraphrase of its description are used with permission of the publisher.

20

Initiation Strategies

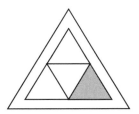

We see organizational improvement as a mass movement intended to reach everyone in the company. But such a broad improvement initiative is also new to many companies, and mobilizing everyone can be difficult. A mobilization strategy is needed. An effective strategy must have three parts: CEO involvement, strategies for introduction, and organizational infrastructure. The first two parts are the subject of this chapter; the last is the subject of Chapter 21.

20.1 CEO INVOLVEMENT

The most important aspect of a mobilization strategy is CEO involvement (see Figure 20-1 [260]). For instance, successful introductions in Japan, Europe, and the United States of TQM[1] as the method of organizational improvement start from involvement at the top. Later sections give fuller definition to "involvement."

The next most important criterion is the absence of strong opposition from the workers (e.g., trade union resistance). But opposition of the workers' organization can be slowly reduced by the efforts of the CEO to build trust and create a role for the union in organizational improvement.

The middle or upper management of a company may try to introduce company-wide improvement without the CEO's involvement (they may see the necessity for changing the way the business operates that the CEO is blind to). However, the long-term success of such an approach depends on a strong societal culture of quality and business improvement. Sufficiently strong societal knowledge of the necessity for and methods of organization improvement might provide the necessary impetus in the absence of CEO impetus. (Societal learning, described in Chapter 28, refers to the set of practices and institutions that allow companies to learn from other companies.) This approach sometimes works in Japan, but since societal learning may be weaker in Europe and the United States, organizational change is unlikely to succeed outside of Japan without strong CEO leadership.

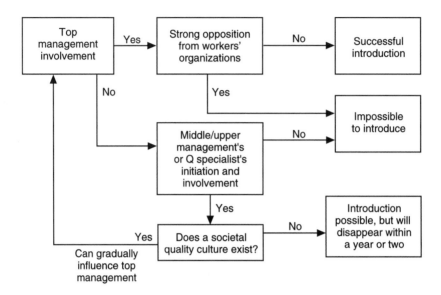

Figure 20-1. The Importance of CEO Involvement in TQM Mobilization

It is conceivable for a plant or division manager to create an island of change and improvement, if this manager is in effect the CEO of his or her operation. In such cases, a manager must control the operation and have no interference from above that negates divisional efforts. However, when the sponsor moves or departs, such islands tend to disappear.

A company should hesitate before trying to introduce companywide business improvement and organizational change activities without strong motivation on the part of the CEO. Without CEO involvement, there is a strong chance of failure. Once a company fails, success becomes more difficult; the initial failure creates a belief within the company that such change methods don't work, which will make the retry difficult.

Shoji Shiba has collected Japanese data indicating that if the CEO is involved in QC circle implementation, additional levels of management and workers can be involved in turn [176]. The CEO can bring on board the upper managers and facilitators (people who help with the detailed QC circle implementation planning). If the CEO can make upper managers and facilitators enthusiastic, then middle managers can be convinced. Finally, the middle managers and facilitators bring in workers from the shop or individual contributors. This might be called the domino theory (Figure 20-2).

The data supporting the domino theory are shown in Figure 20-3. Shiba measured levels of promotion of QC circles at various levels within many companies. He then sorted companies into groups according to how actively the CEO was involved.

In Japan, many companies are subsidiaries of parent companies, and these parent companies put pressure on their subsidiaries to implement QC circles. If the CEO is

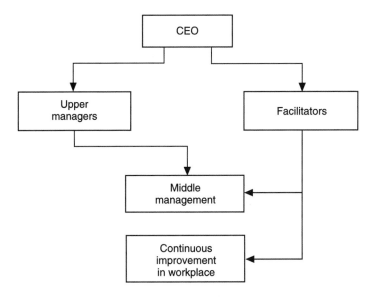

Figure 20-2. Domino Theory of Implementation

very involved, the facilitators can be highly effective and other functions (such as managers' involvement and education) can be high. If CEO involvement is low, the facilitators still may try to implement a circle, but quality activities will remain weak (as in the bottom curve). Empirically, the CEO's level of involvement is an upper limit on the other quality activities of the company.

What does CEO or top management involvement mean? In world-class companies the authors have visited, it means hands-on participation in organizational change, as is shown in Table 20-1. This table also characterizes unsuccessful cases; note that simply approving and delegating, which is standard management practice, didn't work.[2]

Table 20-1. CEO Activity in Successful and Unsuccessful Cases

Type of Activity	CEO Activity in Unsuccessful Cases	CEO Activity in Successful Cases
Decision to implement TQM	Approve decision	Make decision
Plan	Appoint those in charge, i.e., delegate to quality specialist	Initiate planning for implementation
Do		Participate in improvement activities
Check	Evaluate results	Evaluate process/results
Act		Initiate next phase

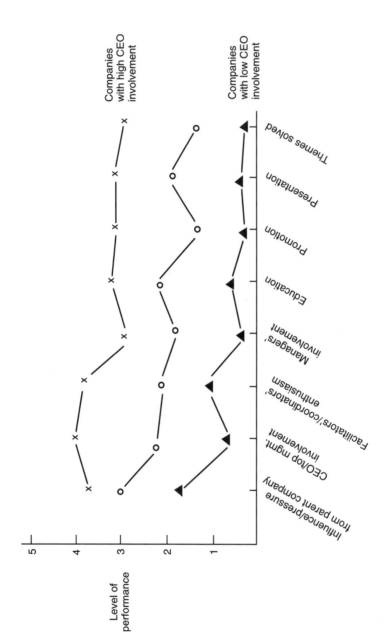

Figure 20-3. CEO Involvement: Domino Effect

We have provided empirical evidence of the necessity for CEO leadership of change in the way a business operates. Theoretical bases also exist for CEO leadership. First, as both military and business strategists observe, a two-front war is much more difficult to fight than a one-front war. Splitting CEO attention and resources is more difficult than focusing them. Leading simultaneous crusades for cost reduction, ubiquitous adherence to standards, faster design, and so on, is more difficult than leading a crusade for quality which can encompass all of these.

Second, because true charisma is rare, most leaders need a leadership style that depends on visible participation and articulation of values and strategies more than sheer force of personality.[3] The organizational change and improvement methods we describe have evolved many standardized opportunities for CEO involvement: from initial visits to other companies using the methods to involvement in planning and piloting, running the corporate quality committee, goal setting, taking and then teaching the first courses, diagnosing QI stories at events, and the presidential audit.

The next question, then, is what motivates the CEO to lead? The CEO's motivation has two parts. The first part is learning. Most of the CEO's learning comes from outside the company. Examples of external sources are seminars, pressure from the parent company, communication with other CEOs, and personal experience. Personal experience is particularly influential. For example, in the mid-1980s, the CEO of Xerox knew of Fuji Xerox's practices. In about 1990, Bose was introduced to a new perspective on manufacturing quality by its Japanese customers [123]. In the mid-1990s, the CEO of American Power Conversion was introduced to Teradyne's activities. At least in Europe, Shiba's surveys indicate that only about 20 percent of the information that motivates a CEO (to implement TQM) comes from inside the company [260].

However, learning alone is not enough to provide the necessary motivation to the CEO. Learning only creates interest in doing organizational change. Another trigger is needed. That trigger—the second motivator for a CEO—is fear, or crisis: increased costs, reduction of worker motivation, decreased sales or market share (market pressure for change), or even bankruptcy.[4]

That is not to say the crisis is the sole motivator. Actual crises are clear to everyone. But delaying action until a full-blown crisis occurs may be acting too late. The CEO's job is to focus on the latent crises that others in the company may not yet see. Bose Corporation president Sherwin Greenblatt drew Figure 20-4 to emphasize the idea of the latent crisis when he told the story of the crisis that led Bose to business improvement [123, pages 4–5].

In about half the cases in Japan, organizational improvement initiatives are started because of a latent crisis. The CEO must be able to visualize the latent crises and bring them to the company's attention.

Although now old, an example from Xerox bears repeating:

> In 1980 we were horrified to learn that the selling price of the small Japanese machines was our manufacturing cost," Kearns (the CEO) says. "We were not tracking the rate of speed of their improvement. We tended to put a peg in.

Figure 20-4. The Latent Crisis

By the time we thought we were up or thought we were close, we found ourselves still off the mark." Kearns began paying even more attention to Fuji
Xerox, the company's Japanese partner. There, total quality control was the
focus of its New Xerox movement, so the New Xerox movement became the
model for Xerox Corporation's own focus on quality [150, page 172].

Kearns used the rate of improvement information, the cost information, and one year's
poor profit to identify a latent crisis and create a powerful and lasting source of change
throughout the organization.[5]

Case Study: CEO Involvement at Teradyne

Alex d'Arbeloff, CEO of Teradyne, one of our CQM companies, provides a useful
case study of CEO involvement in a company's implementation of organization
change and improvement (called TQM at Teradyne, although Teradyne's TQM is its
own unique management system).

In 1990, Teradyne, which develops and sells electronic test equipment, had six
operating divisions, each with about 30 managers. As part of Teradyne's TQM kickoff, d'Arbeloff met personally with the 180 managers of the six divisions, in 12 groups
of 15. (A full description of Teradyne's TQM introduction strategy is given later in this
chapter.) In August 1990, before he spoke to each of these groups, he sent each manager a videotape entitled "Getting Ready for the '90s." In the videotape, d'Arbeloff
reflected on the need for Teradyne to implement TQM.

The videotape shows d'Arbeloff in his shirtsleeves, looking informal and down-
to-earth. The image is that of the man all company managers know—engineer, company founder, and concerned colleague.

D'Arbeloff begins his videotape presentation with a story about the company's receipt of an order from a new customer.[6] Following is a paraphrased version of d'Arbeloff's video statement to his managers.[7]

> I said something to the customer about being glad to have them as a new customer, and the customer said that the issue was not about there being a new customer but about there being a new Teradyne—a Teradyne that wanted to satisfy customers. Teradyne is changing, and the customers are seeing it. However, it takes a while for customers to see change; and until the customer sees the change, the change does not exist for the customer.
>
> Teradyne's business has been and will be a good business. However, in the last five years growth has slowed. This has resulted from the recession, the high dollar value, and the Japanese gain in market share. Teradyne has to do better, and I will explain how I think we can do much better.
>
> I predict that our market will grow in the next decade, and that our business will be global and highly competitive. We must find a way to win. There are good competitors, but we also lose some orders to rinky-dink companies. We need more business to support our programs and your ambitions. Some will come from growth of our industry, but we can also take orders from our competitors. We need to find a way to be a lot better in everything we do, so that there is no question in the customer's mind that we are the company to deal with. We must be better in everything we do—administration, sales, development, and so on.
>
> There is a method I have been studying and that we have used a bit, with spectacular results. I have been spending lots of time studying this. The method is TQM. I am not now training you in TQM. I am just telling you what we are thinking and why.
>
> TQM is focused on everyone's satisfaction. TQM is an unyielding, continuing, improving effort by everyone in the company to understand, meet, and exceed the expectations of customers. TQM is not just a quality control program. It is a different way to manage. I have visited Japan, and I thought their culture was different, but I now think I'd just given myself an excuse. Japan's good companies have found a new and better way to manage. In the United States, we believe "if it ain't broke, don't fix it" and in "management by exception." The Japanese have processes that they define; then they improve them to make them better and better. Event-driven management jumps around and sets our priorities. TQM is a different way to set priorities for what we see needs to change. There are many good things about Teradyne's culture:
>
> 1. We have open communications.
> 2. We have integrity: we are honest with customers and each other; we let our actions speak for us.
> 3. We have high respect for people.
> 4. We have participation of people in decisions (and sometimes consensus).

5. We are an informal company; we have the minimum structure to get the job done.
6. We focus on real values: what we add to make customers satisfied; actual business rather than formalities or mechanics of business.

What do we need to change? There are four things that we have to bring into the company. Everyone must be involved in each of these.

1. Work Is a Process

I'll give you an example of a sales manager and five salespeople who want to communicate better, so they have a meeting at 8 A.M. on Monday. At the first meeting, only three people showed up and no one was prepared. They worked hard so that on the next Monday everyone came, but they still weren't prepared. The next week they worked to make sure everyone was prepared, but the meeting wasn't very focused. The next week they scheduled one hour for management of the general sales situation and the other hour to focus on two accounts. For the next week, the sales manager provided further focus by making a list of what to discuss about the two accounts to be discussed that week. And so on. After six months of incremental improvements, they will have much better meetings.

2. Management by Fact

We must get real data; statistical process control fits here. The ineffective way is management by anecdote ("I feel...; I think..."). For example, the Japanese board-test market is a fraction of the U.S. market. Why? We have never found out the facts about this. Another example: from 1980 to 1985, testers shipped was four percent of semiconductors shipped; since 1985, it was two percent. Why? No one knows why. Is this important to us?

3. Teamwork

Typically, we glorify people who bail out failing projects, but we don't glorify groups that just do solid work and don't screw up. We have to reverse this behavior, to reward and recognize groups whose work is under control.

4. More Training

Our training is inadequate. In proportion to Texas Instruments, Teradyne would have to give 15,000 hours of training per year. We are far short of that today.

I'll review what I've been saying:

- Testing is good business.
- We must be better by a lot in everything we do.
- TQM is a method to make the 1990s the most exciting decade in the history of the company.

We have to win for the sake of our company and the sake of the electronics industry. The best of times is now!

Patterns of CEO Crusades

In 1990, Ron Butler of the CQM Design Team did a survey of U.S. approaches to CEO involvement and leadership of business improvement and organizational learning [264, pages 317–320]. The companies surveyed included six Baldrige Award winners and one Deming Prize winner. The investigation revealed that, in the U.S., the CEO crusade was a typical approach to CEO involvement and leadership. A common structure, shown in Figure 20-5, also appeared, involving seven common elements. The seven common elements retain validity today.

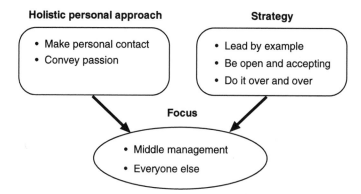

Figure 20-5. Common Structure of CEO Crusades

Make personal contact. The president or CEO must do the executive audits and site visits. Personal contact is required; 10 to 20 percent of the time should be spent in the field. The continuation of the Teradyne case study in the next section (Section 20.2) describes CEO Alex d'Arbeloff visiting with management groups throughout the company to introduce them to his plans for the company. Section 26.1 describes Teradyne's presidential diagnosis system.

Capture the imagination and convey passion through conviction. Symbolism and folklore can be important tools of leadership. Greg Fischer tells of burning the traditional, counterproductive performance review procedure at a company meeting when he was CEO of SerVend. Gary LeBlanc recounted in [184] a story of Hillenbrand Industries' CEO Gus Hillenbrand at an off-site meeting of key Hill-Rom managers where Hillenbrand was trying to make business improvement a permanent part of the Hill-Rom culture for the third time.

Then, CEO Gus Hillenbrand spoke with such emotion that his declamation has become known in Hill-Rom lore as the "significant emotional event."

He made clear his own commitment to permanent improvement saying, "I will not allow any of you not to do this again—you will do it or you will be gone."

The third time took.

Lead by example. Practice what you preach, "walk the talk," and become a quality expert. In Chapter 11 and in Section 12.2, we described how the CEO and top management team at Teradyne mobilized the 7 step and 9 step methods by personally practicing the methods and then promulgating the "Teradyne way" for the methods to the rest of the company.

Listen to people, work in teams, and open up. Methods like LP and cross-functional teamwork help executives break out of traditional power relationships. Chapter 19 included multiple case studies of using teams to open things up and get the contributions of everyone. Also, SerVend reported the following [124]:

> SerVend's real strength in ... human resources ... is our natural work teams. Each team member at SerVend is a member of a work team in his or her functional area. These teams are permanent entities that exist to allow rapid deployment of knowledge and skill, and to own constant improvement of their own systems and processes. In addition, we have a handful of cross-functional teams which are formed to resolve specific business-wide issues within the company. Our teaming system ... emphasizes the inherent worth and need to develop people within your organization....

At Milliken, President Tom Malone purportedly took down the fourth wall of his office to make "a structural change."

Repeat yourself, and use all communication channels available. Use all company channels—memos to the staff, speeches, newspapers, videos for company news, and training videos. Earlier in this section, we reported on Alex d'Arbeloff of Teradyne creating a videotape to circulate throughout the company. In the next section, we describe Alex's visits throughout the company. Teradyne also has posters, brochures, regular "improvement days" at which methods and results are reported, and so on.

Work with middle management. Organizational change is tough for top management and just as tough for middle management. Teach teamwork. Theory meets practice at the supervisor level. Openness is more than a feel-good principle—it is fundamental to successful change. At Milliken, "Since 1983, corporate leadership has charged every management associate to construct personal plans to obtain a minimum of 40 hours of formal continuing education each year" [206]. Removal of Tom Malone's fourth wall at Milliken also was on target for middle managers.

Educate everybody. Education develops a language for top-to-bottom and bottom-to-top communication. Education enables improvement. Milliken maintains a corporate university and offers over 250 courses "... to help each and every associate achieve their full potential. Only by each associate growing to their full potential can Milliken & Company move forward" [193].

20.2 CASE STUDY: TERADYNE STRATEGY FOR INTRODUCTION

"Introduction" is here used in a narrow sense as the phase coming after senior management learning and occurring during or after initial pilot improvement projects, goal setting, and establishment of governance and organization. Introduction happens before rolling out widespread education in improvement skills. The following is a case study of Teradyne's introduction strategy.[8]

Prior History of Quality Improvement

In the late 1970s and early 1980s, the semiconductor to which Teradyne supplies test equipment began to move to Japan. Nonetheless, until 1985, the industry grew well and the company prospered. Its company systems were predicated on continuing growth.

The move of the major part of the semiconductor industry to outside the U.S.[9] created a big problem for Teradyne since 70 percent of its business was with this industry.

Teradyne had quality programs before. George Chamilard, who had been heading Teradyne operations in California, which did a great deal of its business with the Japanese, returned to Boston to lead the central manufacturing activity. He initiated a quality improvement activity in 1984, and selected John Petrolini to be his quality improvement person for central manufacturing.[10]

They selected the Crosby 14-point process and followed it precisely. They trained approximately 2,000 people in Crosby programs. Additionally, the Teradyne staff had knowledge of statistical process control, and one division held a quarterly zero defects day. These programs continued up to 1989. Using the Crosby and other programs, Teradyne realized substantial payoffs—reductions in defects, late deliveries, and costs associated with rework and failures.

Teradyne CEO Alex d'Arbeloff had supported quality programs for some time; however, during the Crosby period, he was more of an observer and supporter than an active participant in Teradyne's quality programs. Procter and Gamble chairman Edwin Artz, a long-time practitioner of quality improvement, sat on Teradyne's board and was instrumental in steering d'Arbeloff and Teradyne toward TQM, including sending Earl Conway to Teradyne to describe TQM. And, like many CEOs in the electronics business, d'Arbeloff had traveled often to Japan and had seen the results of TQM firsthand. He was also close to Ray Stata, CEO of Analog Devices, another Boston-area company that had been contemplating implementation of TQM.

Companywide Introduction of TQM

In 1989, three things happened to move Teradyne to the next step in its quality journey:

- The central manufacturing group had picked most of the low-hanging fruit, but they still had problems with some percentage of their products.
- Teradyne received the famous letter that Motorola sent to its suppliers (after it won the Baldrige award) instructing each supplier to prepare itself to apply for the Baldrige award.

- CEO Alex d'Arbeloff met Shoji Shiba, who had come to the Boston area at the request of Tom Lee.[11] Shoji Shiba was able to describe a systematic approach to TQM implementation to d'Arbeloff.

Additionally, Teradyne faced a crisis. Its industry experienced excess capacity, difficult price competition, and difficult product and service competition. Teradyne itself was not growing, was having difficulty sustaining profitability, and was dealing with a geographic shift in its market: nearly 50 percent of its customers were now in Asia.[12]

An immediate impetus was the receipt of the Motorola letter. Following that, 11 of the senior people read and discussed six books at the same time and in the same order. The six books were:

- *The Deming Route to Quality*, Scherkenbach
- *Out of the Crisis*, Deming
- *What is TQC? The Japanese Way*, Ishikawa
- *Company-wide Total Quality Control*, Mizuno
- *Juran on Leadership for Total Quality*, Juran
- *Quality without Tears*, Crosby

When others in the company heard that the senior managers were reading these books, they also wanted to read them. Many read at least three of them.

The managers also attended three seminars—a four-day seminar by Deming, a one-day seminar at Texas Instruments, and a one-day seminar in-house from American Supplier Institute.

This activity began to give top management a flavor for TQM, but they still didn't really know what to do. However, when Shoji Shiba came on the scene, he was able to provide some insights that helped d'Arbeloff and his top management team choose a specific direction.

Teradyne has always had a top-down culture in which the top managers want to be involved in the details and know what is happening. Thus, it was natural for Teradyne's managers to start by trying themselves to learn about something new. Shoji Shiba encouraged this top-down attitude of d'Arbeloff and his top management team. Teradyne's approach was consistent with Ishikawa's famous dictum: "Quality begins and ends with education, and education starts at the top."

The basic strategy of TQM implementation at Teradyne has been to involve successively more people. CEO d'Arbeloff got involved and first spoke to his seven-member management committee (see Figure 20-6). Their objective was to have the management committee educated and poised to implement TQM starting in July 1990. Then, they involved the 42 upper managers from the company.

From their study, the Teradyne managers concluded that they would adopt a new management method based on three principles:

1. Process-driven versus event-driven
2. Continuous improvement versus "if it ain't broke don't fix it"
3. Customer satisfaction instead of assuming they know what the customer needs

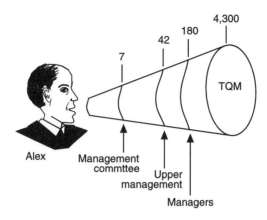

Create knowledge and consensus

Figure 20-6. Progressive Involvement of Management and Employees

Teradyne has a "Teradyne Values" book that reflects the "culture" of the company. The managers decided that this culture under TQM was going to change in four key ways:

1. While we still have a need for quick reactions to crisis situations, we will move toward organizing and managing our work as a process, whether in sales calls, service response, design, or order processing.
2. We will base our decisions on facts and move away from reactive or instinctive management, in which decisions are based on "I think" or "I feel."
3. We will structure our efforts to develop and take advantage of teamwork as well as rewarding team versus individual performance.
4. Training will become a more conscious part of how we run our business.

The time had come to talk to the next 180 managers. Between August 22 and September 6, Teradyne carried out its CEO crusade. It scheduled six sessions in which CEO Alex d'Arbeloff met with managers and supervisors from the divisions. Each session consisted of two two-hour meetings. Fifteen people from a division attended the first meeting in a session, and another 15 people attended the other meeting in a session.

The crusade was planned carefully:

1. *Homework was assigned before the meeting to create readiness.* People were invited by a letter from Alex and then asked to watch videos, read the old values book, preview the new values, and be prepared to speak out in the meetings. Participation in a meeting was required.
2. *The PDCA cycle was run after each meeting and session.* Teradyne managers sought feedback on weakness after the meetings (two labels from each participant—one thing learned and one weakness; see Figure 20-7). This involved

quick 15-minute spins of the PDCA cycle in the half hour between meetings, and larger (but still quick) spins of the PDCA cycle after each session. For instance, some of the weaknesses reported were

- Agenda/objectives—lack of structure
- Participation—not speaking out
- Lack of implementation plan

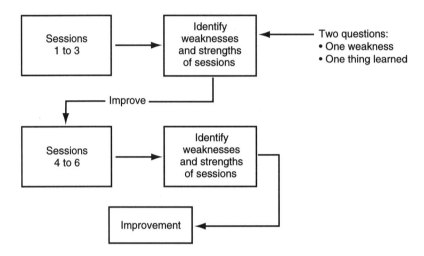

Figure 20-7. Post-meeting Feedback and Improvement

After the first meeting, Alex took corrective action for the next meeting based on the strength and weakness labels, including the following:

- Opened with an explanation of meeting's purpose
- Issued follow-up agenda
- Called on people who didn't speak out
- Removed the video camera, which was inhibiting response

John Petrolini observes that these quick improvement activities were the first instance of Alex doing PDCA, and John could see the light dawn for Alex as he saw for himself what PDCA really meant and could mean for the company.

After meetings four through six, the managers again made improvements, shifting their attention to later weaknesses as they corrected earlier weaknesses.

3. *They planned the diffusion of TQM beyond the 180 managers to all employees.* Each manager was asked to meet with his or her direct reports and send a written report on that meeting to Alex d'Arbeloff. The purpose of these meetings was to explain that it was right to change the company culture and that they would do so. Each manager was also being asked to do what Alex had done, which was to use meeting feedback in a PDCA cycle.

Teradyne decided it needed a parallel organizational structure for quality. Its Companywide Quality Council (CQC) is the same as its management committee (i.e., its highest-ranking management group). While the CQC and management committee have the same members, the agendas for the two parallel entities differ. The CQC sets TQM priorities and controls the company's TQM agenda. For instance, it deals with TQM implementation issues (e.g., training and deployment) and improvement issues. There is also a small companywide, or corporate, TQM office (two managers and an administrator). Each division has a similar structure, with its own quality council and TQM office (one full-time person as shown in Figure 20-8).

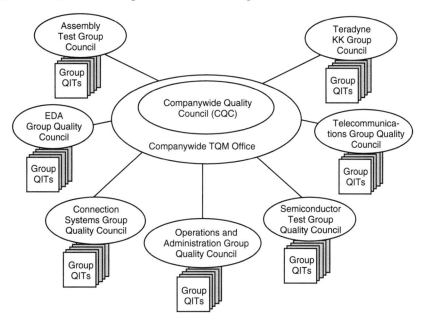

Figure 20-8. Teradyne Quality Organization

After listening to Shoji Shiba's explanation of how the 7 steps could be a method to get many people involved in business improvement, d'Arbeloff decided that for Teradyne TQM would initially be the 7 steps and market-in, implemented by quality improvement teams addressing three goals: increase in market share, reduction in cost, and reduction in cycle time (see Figure 20-9). Each division business plan for the year addressed these issues with action plans.[13] Teradyne was following this logic:

1. TQM is a mass movement.
2. The 7 steps can be applied by all.
3. Teradyne had many problems.
4. Teradyne could get everyone involved in TQM with the one tool of the 7 steps.

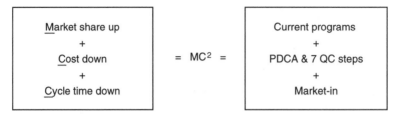

Figure 20-9. Teradyne's 1991 Goals and TQM Initiatives

Teradyne next undertook a program to take this message to its 4,300 people. The program included meetings for all employees and development of a TQM brochure. D'Arbeloff himself led doing an LP diagram to decide the content of the brochure, which included the following points:

- Explain why TQM is the method chosen.
- Jobs will change with the implementation of TQM.
- On-the-job examples are the basis for market-in.
- Explain market-in to the staff.

By 1992, Teradyne had 200 to 400 QITs, and Alex d'Arbeloff was deeply personally involved in Teradyne's quality activities.

In summary, Teradyne's strategy involved three phases:

1. Consensus among the 42 top managers
2. The CEO crusade strategy to reach the 180 supervisors
3. A strategy to reach 4,300 employees

To reach this many numbers and levels of people, a company needs a system and structure. It requires management. If a company totaled only 42 people, it would just need communications. With 4,300, a company requires strategy.

Teradyne's initial crusade was followed in a few months by cascading and expanding training in the 7 steps and 7 QC tools for teams already formed and working and then to other teams (as described in Chapter 11). Teradyne took this approach even though its top management was trained in the 7 management and planning tools and customer visitation. With established systems for forming quality improvement teams, measuring quality, and monitoring customer complaints, use of the 7 QC Steps was practical and sufficient for the initial wave of education.

NOTES

1. In this instance and others described in this chapter, Shoji Shiba specifically collected data on TQM implementations. Nonetheless, we and others have observed similar patterns no matter what the change program is called.

2. The chart derives from a three-year study of implementation described in more detail in [260].

3. For example, see [30] for typical strategies. Another study [214] classifies leadership style into charismatic, instrumental, and institutional. The latter two classifications can be thought of as the highly involved style of leadership of organizational change, which will be explored throughout this chapter.

4. Empirically, major organizational change of any kind seems almost always to be precipitated by clear crisis. This is demonstrated by studies of companywide organizational change in general, and for Deming Prize winners in a survey by Professor Noriaki Kano.

5. Kano and Koura's research [156, page 87] supports the model that visible or latent crises plus CEO leadership trigger implementation.

6. Professor Shiba, who has been active in video production, notes that video is particularly appropriate for a CEO presentation such as d'Arbeloff's. By contrast, video is not the medium for logical diffusion, or what takes place in a classroom lecture. You use video to convey affective language, to speak personally to individuals, not formally to a classroom. For instance, Alex d'Arbeloff momentarily fumbled with a couple of items he was holding at the beginning of the video, and this conveyed an informal feeling. Backlighting and close-ups would increase this feeling.

7. See [81] for a complete transcript of d'Arbeloff's videotape presentation.

8. This part of the Teradyne case study is a presentation prepared by Owen Robbins of Teradyne and presented in December 1990 at the CQM's first senior executive courses augmented with details supplied by John Petrolini.

9. A chart of the top ten semiconductor companies in the 1970s versus the 1980s shows the U.S. companies moving from the top to the bottom.

10. John Petrolini is our contributing author who has helped us prepare the Teradyne story that runs throughout this book, starting with Chapter 11. We'll return to George Chamilard's involvement with Teradyne's business improvement activities in Chapter 26.

11. Tom Lee was attempting to start the CQM. The CQM design team effort that took place in early 1990 (described in Chapter 19) reinforced Teradyne's quality efforts as did the mutual learning and friendly competition that developed between Alex d'Arbeloff, Ray Stata, and Steve Levy. All three were CEOs of founding member companies of the CQM, and Ray Stata along with Tom Lee and Shoji Shiba are recognized as the CQM co-founders.

12. Note that the Teradyne case study matches the model, in which the crisis plus information leads to CEO involvement in TQM. The crisis plus information about TQM prompted Teradyne's CEO to become directly involved in the company's quality activities.

13. Teradyne's initial TQM efforts and quality improvement team activities were built on the company's previous study and implementation of Crosby's methods. Teradyne changed vocabulary over time and let Crosby-style teams evolve how they worked rather than disbanding them.

21

Infrastructure for Mobilization

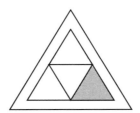

When a company has only a few dozen people, they can talk to each other, read the same books and, in general, communicate with each other about how to implement a change and improvement initiative. With thousands of people, however, a company needs a strategy and structure for introducing change.

First, the CEO can't do it alone. At best, the CEO can directly speak to only some of the people in an organization, for example, the people at the top and a small percentage of others that the CEO can occasionally seek out and speak to.

Second, articulating the vision is not enough, especially since the existing management system is likely to contain many obstacles to accomplishing the new vision. The leader needs to build a support infrastructure that broadcasts the leader's vision throughout the organization and mobilizes action in support of the leader's vision.[1]

21.1 CREATE EXPLICIT STRUCTURES FOR MOBILIZATION

We will start by recounting a lesson the CQM Design Team learned from Frank Voehl in 1990 and that we were reminded of by Goodloe Suttler.[2] Mr. Voehl described Culture Model #1, shown in the Figure 21-1. The top-down nature of this first culture model—that a corporation's culture drives everything—leads many managers to think about culture as being the overarching issue and that the way to change the company is to focus on changing the culture.

However, the behaviors that result from the culture reinforce and try to preserve it. Thus, Voehl went on to state that trying to change the culture directly seldom works. This is illustrated in Culture Model #2, shown in Figure 21-2. Based on his experience as a senior executive for many years at Analog Devices, Suttler concurs that the effective way to change an organization culture is to attack this hierarchy from the bottom up, that is to put in place structures and processes that define the roles and actions which in turn will enforce behaviors which ultimately will result in a changed culture.[3]

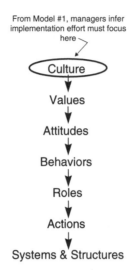

Figure 21-1. Culture Model #1: A Corporation's Culture Drives Everything

Of course, you don't ignore the cultural issues. First, you have to envision the new culture you want and articulate it to the entire organization ("talk the talk"). However, that is far from enough. Unless management also makes the necessary changes to the structures and processes to cause the desired new actions and roles—and ultimately behaviors, attitudes, values, and culture—to come into being (unless management "walks the talk" by actually changing things), the employees see hypocrisy where the management has good intentions. Frank Pipp, who was VP of Development and Manufacturing for Xerox says, "Employees can smell hypocrisy at one part in a million," and management has to demonstrate complete integrity between words and actions for a very long time before the employees will give management the benefits of the doubt and allow that management may have made an honest mistake but is still committed to the articulated culture change. Walking the talk must include putting in place the structures and processes that actually implement the talk; otherwise all you have is talking the talk. Some managers think walking the talk means setting a good example, but alone this is counterproductive; employees will know that the structures and processes aren't in alignment and will know management either isn't really serious or may be serious but doesn't really know what must be done.

In recounting the above lesson, we are not arguing that top-down or CEO leadership is not necessary in business (especially in the business of business improvement). It is necessary or an organization will not change and improve. However, a misconception is that such leadership is primarily about something intangible, such as the charismatic or by-force-of-personality aspect of leadership. Of course, a "leader's personality" helps the top person lead change, especially major change. But such personality-based skills are not sufficient for the two reasons given above: the

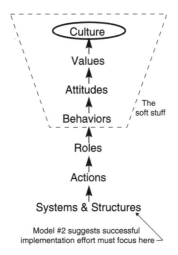

Figure 21-2. Culture Model #2: You Can't Change a Corporation's Culture by Working on Culture Directly

CEO can't directly speak to enough people, and speaking to them is not enough; they need to be "mobilized" more concretely.

Alex d'Arbeloff's CEO initiative at Teradyne[4] provides an example of a system that enables the CEO to speak to the entire organization. The CEO can also speak to society at large, as Andy Grove did in his book *Only the Paranoid Survive* about what he had learned about remaking Intel for the new business environment. This allows the CEO to use "reflected practices" from the rest of the industry or society to speak to his own organization. Because Grove's book became a best-seller, undoubtedly many people in Intel read Grove's words in more detail than they ever would have heard his words using conventional top-down communication mechanisms.[5]

21.2 A GENERAL MODEL FOR MOBILIZATION: THE 7 INFRASTRUCTURES

The following model was originally described as an organizational infrastructure for implementing TQM. Since then companies have used the model for mobilizing many kinds of organizational change. We now see it as a useful general model for mobilizing change.

There are seven elements of organizational infrastructure for implementing organizational change and improvement (see Figure 21-3):[6]

1. Goals must be set for the company's change implementation and for the company's business.
2. An organizational setting must be provided; people in corporate management and in the operating divisions must help plan and mobilize the company's implementation of change activities.

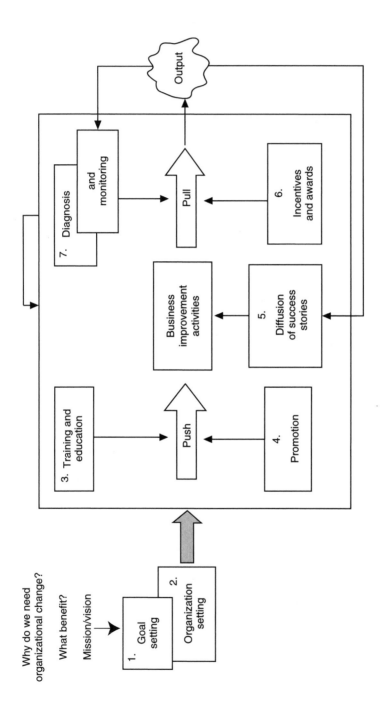

Figure 21-3. Organizational Infrastructure for Implementing Change

3. Training and education must be provided.
4. The change program must be promoted throughout the company.
5. Operational success stories resulting from the implementation of the organizational change and improvement methods must be diffused through the rest of the company (not stories about how well the change program is working).
6. There must be appropriate awards and incentives to mobilize use of the change methods.
7. The implementation effort must be monitored and diagnosed by top management.

Note that the description of infrastructure above applies to suborganizations as well as the larger organizations. Managers of suborganizations must support their people in the companywide mobilization of change by having clear goals and improvement organization, promoting and giving training for improvement activities, widely publicizing success stories, recognizing improvement achievements, and doing PDCA on the operation's improvement activities. For a small unit (or a small company, for that matter), these elements of infrastructure will be executed less elaborately and more informally and personally.

The following subsections detail the seven elements of infrastructure. A manual is available that goes into much more detail about how the 7 Infrastructures may be used to mobilize change [58].

Goal Setting (Vision/Mission)—Infrastructure Element 1

There are three types of goals: noble goals, intermediate goals, and annual goals.

Noble goals. Noble goals are abstract and are aimed outside the company; they include ideas such as "contribute to society" or "benefit the customers." Alex d'Arbeloff of Teradyne gave a noble goal in the videotape described in Chapter 20 (pages 410–413) when he said that the company must succeed for the sake of the electronics industry. NEC, in its positioning as a computer and communications company, also has a noble goal: to "advance societies worldwide toward deepened mutual understanding and the fulfillment of human potential." Noble goals motivate people; long-term goals of profit or growth are not noble goals.

Intermediate goals. A company also needs intermediate goals stated in a language common to everyone in the company. Noble goals motivate people but are too abstract to guide them on strategy for attaining the company's goals. In Japan, the intermediate goals are ideas such as "management by facts," "focus on the vital few," "PDCA," and so on. These goals encourage the processes necessary to accomplish the noble goals.

The authors found that American market performance-oriented intermediate goals, in many companies not aggressively trying to improve their business systems, are primarily longer-term quantitative goals, such as market share, sales, or profits. The intermediate goals in companies actively working on improvement of business systems vary. Some publicize Japanese-like customer focus goals and process goals (six sigma is an example of the latter). Some deploy quantitative longer-term goals, focused on quality and cycle time results.

Annual target and goals. A company also needs a specific annual target, for example, having cost down 10 percent (CD10) from the previous year. In Japan, a company might monitor several annual targets but focus on one target for mobilization purposes.

NEC Shizuoka provides good examples of all three types of goals [140]. Shizuoka has a noble goal in common with all of the NEC companies, as given above. A management philosophy and slogan provide intermediate goals. Shizuoka's management philosophy has three parts:

1. Management that places top priority on quality
2. The customer comes first
3. Creation of a workplace where individual potential can be realized to the fullest

Shizuoka's slogan is "immediate response when quality is at stake." If quality is at stake, the company pours in every resource. Finally, each manager has yearly targets for quality assurance, profit, and manufacturing lead time, which are selected on the basis of the prior year's results. Incidentally, when we asked Michio Ikawa, Shizuoka's president, the reasons for the company's good results, he cited having a process for systemizing improvement activities and other business processes, and lowering costs via factory automation.

U.S. Company Value and Mission Statements

In 1991, Joe Junguzza (of Polaroid Corporation) investigated and revealed some common threads of U.S. value and mission statements [264, pages 341–342]. He found three main threads in these value and mission statements:

1. Our goal is to attain global leadership as a best-managed company, to gain the respect and loyalty of our customers, and to provide a positive return to investors.
2. Our methods for doing this are the following:
   • To fully satisfy the customer's expectations
   • Through innovative products and services
   • By doing it right the first time
3. Quality improvement is a basic business principle and everyone's job.

Today, this general outline seems to remain fairly valid, although U.S. companies probably de-emphasize the third bullet of point two and the word "improvement" in point three.

For U.S. companies, the noble goals are perhaps a little less noble than in Japanese companies, but not so down-to-earth that they become intermediate goals. Japanese companies are process-oriented, and their intermediate goals are process-oriented: manage by facts, manage by process, focus on the vital few, and use the PDCA cycle (see Figure 21-4). In Japan, if the annual goals are not met, then they redoubled their attention to the intermediate goals the following year. Companywide business improvement needs these intermediate goals.

The typical U.S. company attempting organizational change and improvement is more results oriented than its Japanese counterpart; most of its goals, like annual

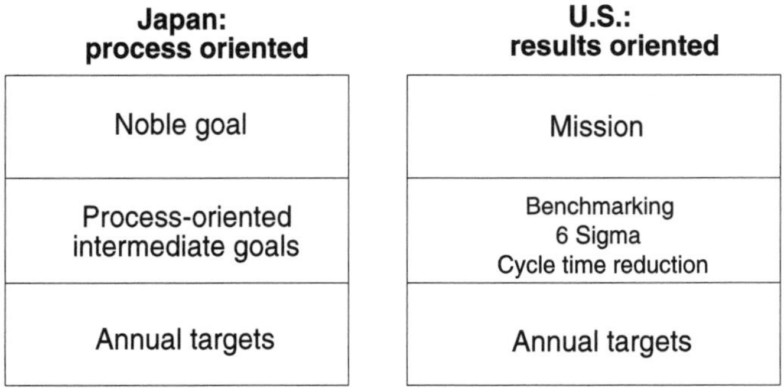

Japan: process oriented	U.S.: results oriented
Noble goal	Mission
Process-oriented intermediate goals	Benchmarking 6 Sigma Cycle time reduction
Annual targets	Annual targets

Figure 21-4. Japanese and U.S. Approaches to Goal Setting

goals, are short term and focused on dollars. However, a results orientation is not the best way to achieve improvements. Process-oriented intermediate goals of some form are needed. Since broad organizational improvement is a mass movement, its language must be geared to the company culture. Process-oriented intermediate goals are best, but a company must be realistic and find a compromise that includes as much process focus as is tolerable. The U.S. inventions of benchmarking, defect reduction (six sigma), and cycle-time reduction serve as a useful compromise (see Chapter 23, pages 468, 472, and 479, respectively). They provide process-related intermediate goals in a results-oriented environment.

Cycle-time reduction permits a simple focus on numeric improvement objectives (reduce cycle-time by x percent) that directs companies to analyze and to change process. Six sigma permits a focus on numeric improvement objectives, but the goal of extreme reduction of defects forces companies to significantly change the process. Benchmarking usually starts with a look at the numeric results of another company but then leads into a study of the processes by which they achieve those results.

Benchmarking is especially useful in the United States. In Japan, imitation is the first step for learning. In the United States, however, people don't like to imitate. Benchmarking is a way for U.S. companies to encourage intelligent imitation without incurring the stigma often attached to imitation.

Benchmarking is an intermediate concept (see Figure 21-5). It falls between the Japanese process-oriented intermediate goals and the U.S. inclination to results-oriented goals. By focusing on the results and methods of performance of the best companies, benchmarking provides the targets the United States likes so well along with processes to imitate to achieve these targets.

SerVend Example of Goals, Values, and Mission

SerVend International is a manufacturer of ice and beverage dispensers. Their set of goals, values, and mission provide an interesting example of contemporary U.S. practice.[7]

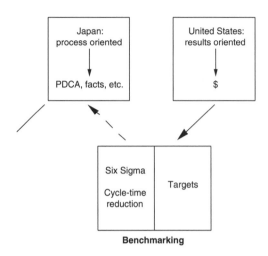

Figure 21-5. Benchmarking as Intermediate Goal Setting

SerVend didn't explicitly think in terms of the three levels of goals—noble, intermediate, and yearly. However, their mix of purpose, mission, values, what they call their "top five goal areas" (for 1996, in this example), and what they call "requirements" cover these three levels of goals.[8]

The SerVend purpose is clearly a noble goal: SerVend exists to create value and opportunities that change people's lives for the better. (This is in contrast to their mission statement which relates to a specific customer initiative.)

SerVend's "goal areas" for 1996 are the equivalent of intermediate goals:

- Reducing variation through process standardization (process quality)
- Decreasing cycle-time (product quality)
- Opportunities and rewards at SerVend (workplace excellence)
- Increasing yield and safety (lower cost)

Each of these goal areas sets an objective of developing capabilities—structures, processes, people—to achieve the noble goal and mission more easily. These goal areas continue from one year to the next and increasing levels of capability are achieved. Starting in 1993–94, SerVend's capability, i.e., intermediate, goals focused on natural work teams. Then, in 1995–97, the evolving goals drove implementing various elements of the four revolutions in management described in this book.

The fifth of the goal areas for 1996 was the equivalent of an annual goal, as we define them here: Set a record in 1996 for SerVend sales. In 1996, SerVend also had 10 "requirements" which clearly fit into our annual goal category, for example, specific dollar figures for revenue and cost reductions for the year, defect reduction percentage, and 7 steps improvement cycles completed in the year per team.

Organization Setting—Infrastructure Element 2

People are needed in a "change organization" to help corporate management and the operating divisions plan and mobilize the company's implementation of change activities. Two essential components comprise a change organization: the change committee and the change office. The corporate change committee (which goes by many names: change steering committee, quality committee, TQM committee, etc.) is the group responsible for leading, diffusing, and managing change; it is the management group of the organization, convening with organizational change and improvement as its agenda. The change office is a small office that assists the CEO and the change committee. These two components are typically used at the corporate level and the divisional level.

Over the years, we have looked into the organizational setting for change at many companies. In many cases, the company had a change organizational structure roughly similar to that shown in Figure 21-6.[9] The Teradyne example given in Chapter 20, Figure 20-8 (page 419), also follows the pattern.

The change office reports to the top manager or the CEO (see Figure 21-6). It helps the CEO, who will lead the implementation of the organizational change and improvement program but will not have time to do all the detailed planning.

No job description exists for the change office. The change vice president, like the president, has to create the job (see Figure 21-7). The primary role of the change office varies from company to company. In some, the primary role is teaching and coaching the senior management, or even just the CEO. In other companies, the VP of change is the "leading learner," and the change office mostly designs and starts courses. The job may be promoting and organizing events and courses. By analogy, VPs of finance in some companies drive financial planning, in others cost cutting or organizational change. Similarly, VPs of change (or, more generally, the head of the change office) address whatever needs the company has.

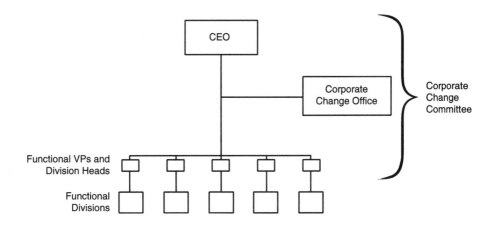

Figure 21-6. The Change Office

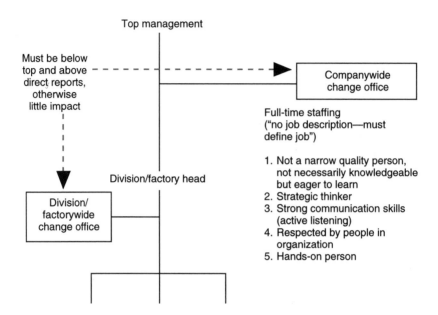

Figure 21-7. Structure of the Change Organization

The person in the change office has no formal authority over most of the organization; he or she relies on persuasiveness, the ability to articulate issues, and particularly active listening. The change VP needs the respect of the rest of the organization from the start; potential future presidents come out of the change office.

The person leading the change office typically is not a change or improvement specialist, particularly not in the companywide change office (e.g., Mike Bradley of Teradyne, page 175). These people don't have to know the methods of organizational change and improvement, but they must have strong motivation to learn about them. In Japan, sometimes a respected strategic planner takes responsibility for the change office, but more often it is a line person, not a change specialist. The person leading the change office is typically on assignment from a line management position and has five qualifications: a strategic thinker, respect throughout the company, a good communicator (particularly a good listener), hands-on capability (such as dealing with real data), and a strong personality.

There are several reasons for the leader of the change office being a line manager rotated into the assignment for a couple of years and then rotated back to line management a couple of years later. These include the following:

- The change officer must not have a narrow attitude focused on improvement as an end in itself, which might result in an improvement bureaucracy.
- The change officer needs broad perspective, to be able to adapt the change methods to fit real-world needs.

- A change officer with line management experience, who people in the company know will be rotated back to line management after the change officer assignment, will probably get more respect from people throughout the organization than a change specialist will. He or she will more easily influence people throughout the organization.
- The assignment is too important a learning experience to be spent on specialists. During this assignment, line managers can learn and think in ways that will have great value when they rotate back to line management.
- Rotation of a succession of line managers through this position will eventually result managers throughout the company having a deep understanding and experience with planning and implementing organizational change and improvement.

The above benefits will be further increased by rotating rising stars into the change officer position. It is very common in Japanese companies for presidents to have served a tour as change officer.

As said earlier, the change office should be relatively small. However, one person has a hard time doing things alone. Therefore, two or three people in the companywide change office is appropriate for a company of a few thousand people. A division of such a company would have one full-time person or a part-time person (depending on the size of the division) in a division change office. The full-time change office staff for a 100,000-person company might be 10 to 20 people. More people are needed for the initiation phase than later, when a stable organizational change system is in place.

The division change offices support the division VPs and division management teams in the same way the companywide change office supports the CEO and top management team. Basically, the division change office people need the same qualities as the person in the companywide change office: a strategic mind, good communication skills, the respect of others, broad-mindedness, and hands-on quality practice. It is also a position through which line managers can be rotated, for the same reasons people are rotated through the corporate position of change management officer.

The companywide and division change office people work together to diffuse the methods of organizational change and improvement. John Petrolini, who is corporate TQM manager at Teradyne, says the following about the divisional level change management people:[10]

> Each division has a full-time TQM manager who reports to the division manager. Their role is one of assisting the division management teams in TQM strategy and implementation/deployment.
>
> I conduct a monthly conference call and quarterly face-to-face meeting of the world-wide TQM managers to get us on the same page where appropriate, standardize where appropriate, share best practices, and increase skills. I view one of my roles as the training of these rotating TQM managers. This meeting is a great forum for doing that training and integration [224].

The form of a company's organizational structure for quality depends on the company size. Companies of a few thousand people can have the quality organization described immediately above. A company of 100,000 people needs its own internal "Center for Quality of Management" to oversee planning and sharing among divisions just as the CQM facilitates sharing among companies, through special events, networking, promotion, and development of improved methods (see Figure 21-8).

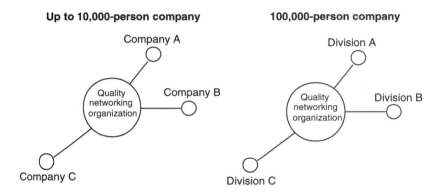

Figure 21-8. Intercompany and Internal Networking Organizations

Training and Education—Infrastructure Element 3

Ishikawa, in many ways the father of modern Japanese TQM, is widely quoted as saying "TQM begins with education and ends with education" [147, pages 37–39]. This remains true as the scope of organizational change and the improvement system expands beyond what traditionally has been thought of as TQM. That such education is important is now a widely espoused belief. We see many companies with explicit systems for training and educating the employees in the methods and systems of organizational change and improvement.

Less widely acknowledged are the differences between such education as practiced at a world-class level and the traditional classroom methods that are used in many companies. These differences can be illustrated in a simple model containing seven observations on world-class training and education (see Figure 21-9).[11]

At the left of the model are the inputs to education and training: the participants, contents, and teachers. At the center top and bottom of the model are the environmental issues affecting education and training: the learning-style environment and the institutional support systems. The learning-style environment refers to the environment in which learning is provided, e.g., in the classroom, on the job, through study groups, via one-on-one situations such as reviews, and through visiting other divisions or companies.

The institutional support system consists of the company's policies, funding, and administrative structure for education and training. Toward the top right of the model is the normal monitoring of effectiveness, which goes on within the education and training system; this feeds back to modify the inputs and environmental situation. Finally, at the far right of the model is the yearly diagnosis by senior management; its

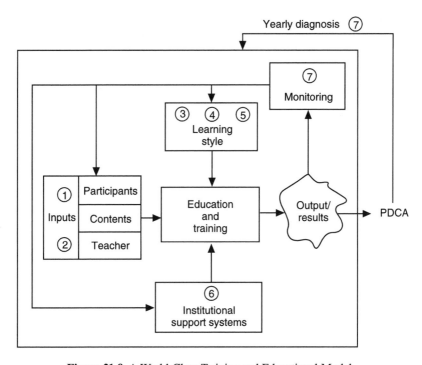

Figure 21-9. A World-Class Training and Educational Model

job is to create the education and training system and diagnose it, not to plan the course content. The components of the model are discussed below.

Seven Observations on World-Class Education

Our seven observations are offered merely as aids in designing an appropriate education system for one's own company. There is nothing magical about them.[12] As education in the methods of organizational change and improvement (and corporate education in general) advance, we hope some of the observations will become well known and will no longer have to be stressed. Furthermore, more commonalities will be discovered.[13] However, the ones offered here should be helpful in breaking through the traditional classroom mind-set. They are the following (numbers correspond to the circled numbers in Figure 21-9):

1. Plan the inputs to training to reduce variance of output.
2. Don't use education professionals to teach.
3. Use mutual learning, not the traditional teacher-student roles.
4. Create opportunity for learning in daily routine work.
5. Create environmental influences for learning.
6. Create institutional support structures.
7. Manage education with PDCA.

Plan the inputs to training to reduce variance of output. To reduce the variance of the output of a course, you must reduce the variance of the inputs. This is basic quality control. The inputs are the participants, the learning contents, and the teacher.

Stratify the participants by background and needs. For instance, give classes for specific function, management level, or prerequisite training. Stratification may involve giving separate sessions with "open enrollment" for interested individuals versus management-mandated training of entire teams together. Stratification means teaching serious learners and ejecting those who miss a class. Stratification allows adaptation of teaching (pace, nature of group work, types of examples and cases, and relative emphasis on subjects) to produce uniform learning.

Stratifying by needs often means organizing courses by some means other than topic. Companywide training is given for particular *roles* (e.g., QC for technical staff), and specialist training only is given for particular *subjects* (e.g., design of experiments).

Uniform learning of concepts of organizational change and improvement requires uniformity of teaching materials. Teachers must be taught what they can change (examples, emphasis, homework) and what they cannot change (the steps and formats for problem solving and tool use, the vocabulary, basic concepts such as *the four revolutions*).

In this book we have deliberately used a variety of terms to encourage liberal translation among different company organizational change and improvement programs. But within a company, a core body of practices and concepts must be standardized to facilitate communication between specialists and managers, superiors and subordinates, and one function and another. A company can enforce these standards naturally by supplying and mandating the use of materials (overheads, manuals, cases) that conform to the standards.

Uniform learning requires uniform quality of teachers, which in turn implies an effective process for recruiting, training, preparing, and diagnosing teachers. For managers rotated into quality offices as facilitators, consultants, or teachers, "train the trainer" courses are common.

Even in situations where much less structured preparatory work is possible, planning the inputs and the process can still yield uniformly good results. For instance, the CQM has had CEOs teach most days of its six-day course. The CEOs who are invited to teach have already taken the course and have personal experience in the general area being taught. The course design emphasizes real cases and group work. Only about a third of the course is lecture, and most of the lectures are accounts of diverse examples. CEOs are requested not to teach theory but rather to share personal experiences.

Leaders for each day (the CEOs are not called "teachers") are given videotapes and full classroom and analysis/diagnosis materials from previous offerings to support preparation.

The course format requires preparation of overheads, which ensures a certain amount of preparation. The overheads are checked to provide advance warning of major problems of pace or omission. Always in attendance in each course is an administrative support person and a course committee member (i.e., someone familiar with both organizational change and improvement methods and the course), over and above the people brought in by the leader to facilitate, present cases, and otherwise supplement instruction. The process ensures effective education without dictating how a CEO goes about preparing.

All of these strategies are designed to ensure the course's participants have learned what they need to know about organizational change and improvement. Contrast this with the typical "Darwinian model" of public education, where students who do poorly just get poor grades.

Don't use education professionals to teach. All but the most specialized topics in world-class companies practicing the methods described in this book are taught by managers. The CQM design study team, examining about a dozen world class companies, never met trainers whose professional training or job function was in education.

Xerox, in cascading its initial quality awareness course, had every manager teach his or her subordinates, as part of its learn, use, teach, and inspect (LUTI) cycle. David Lowe, CEO of ADAC at the time it won the Baldrige award, reported that his training department was one person handling course logistics. Company managers did the actual training. When asked, "What if the manager is not a very good teacher," David Lowe responded, "Then that person is not a very good manager because training is part of the job."

A misconception is that teachers must have professional qualifications in education. This further divides teacher and learner, professional teacher and consultant, teacher and doer, a division that has proven ineffective. All must teach and learn. As the Japanese say, "All teach." There are many advantages to designing a management system in which everyone teaches, especially busy line managers. The managers learn better by teaching. Subordinates learn better from a teacher with the authority of rank and personal practice in what is taught. Finally, having managers teach provides one more reality check on the curriculum: Is it necessary? Is it simple enough?

Consider the opposite strategy of selecting teachers who are not managers. Imagine the cost of hiring and training professional instructors to develop and deliver a curriculum tuned to the examples of every nook and cranny in the corporation. Imagine the difficulty of getting instructors to understand the issues of every particular function well enough to teach authoritatively and create understandable examples. The strategy of simply hiring instructors and buying fixed curriculum is ineffective. So, the only real question is which training and how far to cascade down from the top versus rotating managers into either part-time or full-time instruction.

Teaching is the best way to learn. For instance, in the year after the founding of the CQM, executives and senior managers from member companies helped teach a six-day business improvement course to the senior managers of the CQM companies. The executives and the senior managers all learned from this effort. Since then, many CEOs and vice presidents of CQM companies have taught many days of the six-day course and uniformly say they learned much from the experience. "I didn't know how much more I had to learn until I taught it," is a typical comment. In a number of cases, these executives have cascaded this approach into their own companies.

From the viewpoint of a professional educator, the "all teach" strategy represents a major role shift. Professional educators need to create, adapt, and perhaps buy curriculum materials.[14] More subtly, professional educators need to collaborate with the company change office in designing and executing the "delivery management system" that translates business strategy into educational strategy and then into curriculum development processes, trainer training, monitoring, diagnosis, and PDCA.

Use mutual learning, not the traditional teacher-student roles. The traditional image of the teacher is one of a "master" who imparts wisdom by talking to students. This image belies the kind of learning happening within modern organizations. No teacher comes anywhere close to "knowing it all." All students are functioning adults. A model of learning that recognizes these facts can be called mutual learning, in which a community or group of people share what each has learned and learn from others.

An environment for mutual learning is necessary even in the classroom, and many ways exist to create one. Homework can be posted on the wall so that the students can study each others' efforts, strong and weak. Another example is using a workshop to roll out initial 7 steps training: participants "retrofit" problems they've solved into the 7 steps format and present them in a workshop. The participants discuss each other's work and formulate guidelines to improve 7 steps problem solving. This mutual learning format eliminates the need for teacher omniscience.

Mutual learning extends learning beyond the classroom if work groups rather than individuals can be trained together. Such training promotes a common language and teamwork and makes it easier to implement the results. Don't send one person to a course; always send at least two. People in teams teach each other better practices. Indeed, one or two people are sometimes put on a team to learn, rather than because of special expertise or position.

Presentation meetings diffuse success stories. Exchange visits with other work groups, divisions, or companies (even competitors) provide opportunities for mutual learning and knowledge of the customer or new process. One need not be a world-class authority to provide learning to others. Being a practitioner of a specific good practice is sufficient. Indeed, much about world-class organizational change and improvement can be taught through the sharing of individual cases among CQM member companies, even though many have not yet achieved overall world-class performance. This is the great strength of mutual learning.

Create opportunity for learning in daily routine work. To quote Ishikawa,

> Formal education is less than one-third of the total educational effort. Education does not end with assembling workers to receive formal instruction. At best, this instruction can represent only a small portion of their total education. It is the responsibility of the boss to teach his subordinates through actual work [147, pages 37–39].

The concept "learn first and apply later" must be avoided. To really learn something most people need to apply it immediately after or as they learn it. An argument can be made, however, for "apply first and learn later." By trying to use a technique before learning it, students will better understand the issues involved when they do learn the technique. The idea that a new technique must be learned perfectly before it can be applied must be squelched.

Avoid one-shot learning. At the minimum, students should alternate learning with practice. For instance, before a course, participants can register a theme from their job that they have to solve during the course, and courses can be given in several sessions, with several weeks between sessions for using the new learning on the job. After all, the purpose of the training is to improve on the job. Students may also write their own monographs on what they have learned. In Japan, participants commonly take detailed notes they turn into a document on what they learned.

Avoid thinking that theory is above reality. The idea that the tool has to be applied in the theoretically correct way is mistaken. In fact, reality (daily job) is above theory; what is needed for the real situation is what should be learned. Do not "force-fit" a problem into either a purely reactive or purely proactive framework; instead, do whatever creates permanent improvement and learning. Reality is a teacher. A method can be applied, the weakness in the method found, and the method improved. In particular, real customers are the best teachers.

Managers can create numerous opportunities for learning as part of normal work outside class. Linking class work to the job as described above is a start. So is on-the-spot teaching or seeing improvement teams' work-in-progress. Any review processes, whether personnel reviews or budget reviews, are opportunities to show where improvement methods can be used.

Create environmental influences for learning. Education and training should not only be passed from the top. Education and training are available from many sources (see Figure 21-10). Presidential audits, QI story diagnosis, and customer visits are all part of an environment that teaches senior executives.

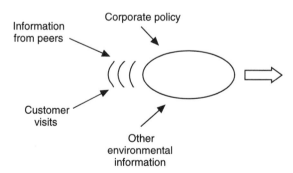

Figure 21-10. Environmental Influences for Learning

One indirect influence on learning is a teaching assignment. Monetary and non-monetary incentives are another indirect influence. A monetary incentive may be nothing more than footing the bill for refreshments at team meetings. Visits outside the company can be a good incentive.

Create institutional support structures. Just as most companies have institutionalized the process of planning, acquiring, and monitoring the use of capital equipment, so have companies with world-class organizational change and improvement systems institutionalized the process of planning, delivering, and monitoring the use of education for these methods.

Therefore, normal business planning would establish annual goals for training and education. Course content and the choice of participants must support annual corporate goals. Targets must be related to choice of company strategy and business goals. For example, if cost reduction is a target, course content should include training on reducing costs, and participants should be chosen for their ability to apply cost reduction techniques successfully.

Another support structure, we learned from Motorola, is a nonrefundable training and education budget. For instance, if a division does not spend the money on training and education, it loses the money—it cannot spend it for any other purpose.

Standards should be established and performance monitored and measured against the standards. The processes described in Chapter 14 (see page 269 and preceding pages) for translating the "voice of the customer" into metrics can be used to translate weaknesses and potential problems in education for organizational change and improvement into appropriate metrics.

Manage education with PDCA. As with many business processes, long-term success in the organizational change and improvement training process depends much less on where it starts than on how well it improves over time.[15]

The Plan phase happens at several levels in the organization. Senior management derives the design for courses directly from business needs. Planning deployment of courses is done by the change office and sometimes by professional educators, as is designing the actual curriculum materials. Similarly, the Check phase of PDCA happens at several levels and time horizons. Following the new standard training practice, participants give daily feedback; some aspects of courses can be improved overnight by instructors. The use of course content in improvement work is monitored by the change office or corporate education staff on a three-month to six-month time scale, and corrective actions are taken.

For example, in the 1990s, Teradyne's TQM office rapidly rolled out a 7 steps course. After several months, it discovered teams were going through the steps more slowly than expected. The primary cause was that the managers to whom team members reported (called sponsors in Teradyne terminology) didn't have clear ideas on how to monitor and encourage team progress or on what constituted appropriate progress. So, the TQM office instituted a short course for team sponsors, and teams accelerated their problem solving.[16]

Finally, on a yearly basis, senior managers diagnose (Check and Act on) strategic issues: determining whether business needs have changed and whether improvement goals are being met. Often changes or additions in courses or their deployment result from senior management diagnosis.

Promotional Activities—Infrastructure Element 4

Promotional activities create a fertile environment for organizational change and improvement. Figure 21-11 shows the three dimensions of promotion of these activities: logic, events, and image.

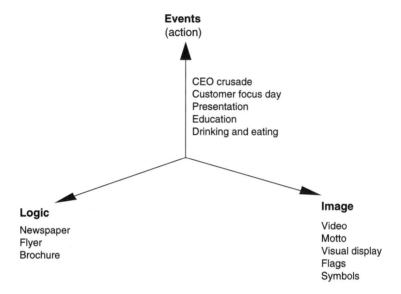

Figure 21-11. Three Dimensions of Promotion for Organizational Change and Improvement

Logical activities include newspapers, flyers, and other written material. However, people don't often read written material, which makes images more important.

Image activities include videos, visual displays (such as QI storyboards), quality flags, and symbols. The manager of one Japanese steel factory always greeted QC circle leaders with a hand sign that means "what is the progress of your QC circle?" At the Hitachi factory front gate, big thermometer charts indicated the progress of various quality activities.

Promotional events include events such as the CEO Crusade described at Teradyne, the customer focus day described at BBN, presentation ceremonies (of QI stories and to reward individual and team activities), educational events, and eating and drinking events used to build teamwork. Promotional activities often integrate with other activities.

Diffusion of Success Stories—Infrastructure Element 5

As we see it, organizational change and improvement is not a theory. It is a mass movement. There is much genius in the masses—collective genius. If someone has a good idea, it should be used, standardized, and diffused. Japanese practice of

TQM developed a system of regular presentations of QI stories to help with this diffusion. This diffusion system is useful whether or not a company calls its change and improvement effort TQM. QI stories are always like those described in Chapters 9 and 10, with a standard story format that shows process and tools. These stories teach the "how-to" of improvement by example and also promote improvement activities.

Japanese companies developed a nationwide presentation system in which the best QI stories from each region are presented. (The system for choosing quality improvement teams to present these stories is important and will be described later.) Tokyo Electric Power uses such a presentation system. Tokyo Electric has about 40,000 employees and 4,000 QC circles. Nine circles are selected for the company's annual presentation day at the largest auditorium in Tokyo. There is a long queue of executives waiting to get in to see it. Two thousand staff members come together to hear the presentations of the nine teams. Documents for each presentation are handed out to attendees. (These presentation days are also documented with videos that are distributed throughout the company.)

The CEO is involved in presentation day, sitting in the front row, attentive at all times. The presentations document success stories and detail how the 7 steps were used. The 7 steps format is strictly followed to ensure the diffusion of process skill. Teams use graphics, comics, and color to clarify the presentations. Each presentation is 15 minutes long and clearly organized, with a five-minute discussion session.

In Japan, separate presentation systems exist for workers, engineers, and managers. In general, there are two types of presentations: those on improvement processes and those on supporting processes. Workers mainly give presentations on improvement processes, while engineers and managers give presentations on improvement processes and on the processes they use to support workers in their improvement processes. When presenting improvement processes, workers, engineers, and managers all use the 7 steps format. The engineers and managers try to follow the 7 steps but don't necessarily limit themselves to them because there is no standard process for proactive problem solving. The separate presentations also allow people to hear their peers in language they can understand. Worker presentations are the easiest to give, so companies should start with these. Worker presentations tend to deal with actual improvements, while manager presentations deal with focusing workers' activities.

QI stories are judged by eight to 15 judges. The teams use a standard presentation format, and the judges use a check sheet, which lists several items to check for, to score each step.[17]

Many U.S. companies use a presentation system similar to the one the Japanese developed although usually not with such formal judging. The U.S. companies see similar benefits to those the Japanese companies see.

Seven Benefits of the Japanese Presentation System

We have mentioned that some Japanese companies have a highly developed system of QI stories presentation. More detail on this system and its seven benefits follow. Of the seven, the first three—diffusion of success stories, mobilization, and deadline effects—benefit the company. The fourth and fifth—reflection and motivation—benefit individuals, and the last two—real cases for societal learning and exchange and networking between companies—benefit society.

1. Diffusion of Success Stories. A thoroughly done QI story represents an appreciable amount of work for the team. Therefore, people should extract maximum benefit from their improvement activities. The presentations and written documents widely communicate the success stories. They communicate not just the idea that improvement can happen but the specific means by which it is accomplished.

2. Mobilization. Some Japanese companies have many branches or divisions; Tokyo Electric Power is an example. In October, each branch or division has its own presentation day, at which each QC circle in the branch presents its QI story. One QI presentation is selected from each branch or division for regional competition. All the circles in a branch or division are given modest awards, so that no one feels like a loser.

The QC circle selected from each branch or division attends a regional presentation day in November. From each division one is selected for a companywide presentation in December. This hierarchical presentation system is important, for it creates motivation for improvement activities at every location of the company. Indeed, the preliminary events in the branches are more important than the companywide event.

3. Deadline Effects. Everyone in the company knows a year in advance the days of the branch presentations in October, the regional presentations in November, and the companywide presentations in December.

These well-known dates provide pressure for all QC circles to finish their work by October. Without such a deadline, many reasons not to finish will occur.

4. Reflection. Quality improvement is a trial-and-error process. It doesn't go smoothly through the 7 steps. For instance, Figure 21-12 shows an unimpeded progression from step 1 through step 4. At that point, however (perhaps because the solution didn't work well enough), the team repeated steps 2, 3, and 4, before going on to step 5, at which point it had to return to step 3 before completing the process.

The presentation lets the team reflect on its trial-and-error process and on how to improve. Most serious weaknesses and failures of the 7 steps process, as well as the successes, are presented. However, the presentation should basically show forward progress and only hint at problems. The focus should be on the use of the 7 steps and improvement through use of the steps. The presentation also enables the team to reflect on how well the members worked together. The presentation should show the real process, acknowledging loops in the process but not showing so many that it confuses listeners.

5. Motivation. Many quality improvement team members have a fear of public speaking or simply don't like making public presentations. The presentation system motivates such people to overcome their resistance. Giving presentations often rewards workers with a sense of fulfillment and achievement. It also reveals hidden worker skills such as drawing, speaking, or data collection, which can be recognized and used.

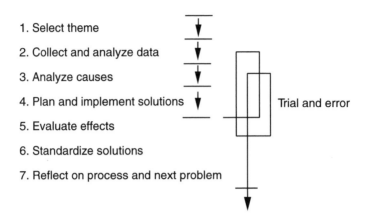

Figure 21-12. Quality Improvement through Trial and Error

6. Real Cases for Societal Learning. The sharing of real cases furthers societal learning. The presentation materials must be gathered in a document and distributed to nonattendees. These documents accumulate and in time create a body of standard methodology.

7. Exchange and Networking between Companies. Even at company events, other companies are invited to share their stories. Many companies invite listeners from subsidiary or sister companies, for example. In this way, the presentation system disseminates knowledge not only through documents (point 6: real cases for societal learning), but through live presentation and personal contact.

Awards and Incentives—Infrastructure Element 6

In 1991, Joe Junguzza of Polaroid examined how many U.S. companies used awards and incentives to mobilize organizational change and improvement [264, pages 365–368]. The companies studied had activities in two areas: recognizing and encouraging desired behavior. Awards can be thought of as recognizing desired behavior, and incentives can be thought of as encouraging desired behavior.

Companies use many forms for rewards and recognition to reinforce appropriate behavior. Such rewards may go to individuals, teams, or divisions, and they may be monetary or nonmonetary awards. The monetary awards range from tens of dollars to thousands of dollars. The nonmonetary awards include certificates, suitably decorated coffee mugs, tickets to sports and arts events, employee-of-the-month pictures on a public wall, skill development opportunities, and so on. The awards are presented in every forum from formal awards ceremonies to company picnics. Some awards are given yearly, but monthly or "as appropriate" awards are more common.

Most managers believe that nonmonetary awards are helpful or, at least, don't cause significant problems. Many managers believe that cash incentives (especially if they are more than token payments) are more trouble than they are worth, frequently leading to attempts to "game the system" or bitter disappointment when someone else wins the award.

No single answer exists. Companies must find what really works—beyond what seems as if it should work—for them.

This brings us to the issue of incentives, mechanisms to encourage people to change the way they behave. Perspectives on incentives are as numerous as on rewards. Perhaps the most important incentive, what people care about most, is their own personal development and advancement. You can give the best projects to people or promote people who are enthusiastic about and are developing skill in organizational change and improvement. (Eventually, many key positions will be filled by skilled, improvement-minded people.)

Monitoring and Diagnosis—Infrastructure Element 7

Monitoring and diagnosis represents the Check part of PDCA for a company's overall organizational change and improvment activities. In companies that have progressed to the Deming Prize or Baldrige Award level (or near that level), monitoring and diagnosis of change and improvement activities are fully integrated into the PDCA of all the company's business processes.

Monitoring Improvement Teams at Teradyne

In Chapter 11 (pages 177–181), we described Teradyne's discovery of the importance of managing their improvement teams. Teradyne manages and monitors their teams at several different levels:

- They monitor each division's performance against targets for numbers of teams, percentage of people on teams, cycle time of teams, and training of employees.
- Each team has a management sponsor. The sponsor prepares for and attends team kickoff meetings. The sponsor also attends team meetings at major milestones in the 7 steps process. The sponsor attends the final meetings of teams and provides diagnosis such as that described in Chapter 10 (pages 149–163). The sponsor and the team leader reflect on the activities of a team and develop plans for the next team (and the sponsor) to improve next time.
- Teams are also registered with division management to enable the bookkeeping on how many teams, percentage participation, and so on, to be captured (for more about this, see the section on "Other Key Results" beginning on page 180).
- They select their "best" quality improvement team efforts to present at an annual TQM Day, which is an implicit sort of monitoring and diagnosis.

Other companies use other methods. For instance, some companies maintain central databases of things that need improvement. Entries in these databases may come from alternative themes not selected as highest priority at the time by improvement teams. New teams may draw on "opportunities" in this registry.

Monitoring the 7 Infrastructures

The diagnosis element of the 7 infrastructures consists of both on-line and off-line diagnosis. The former kind of diagnosis should follow the 70/30 rule[18] and address the dimensions shown in Figure 21-13.

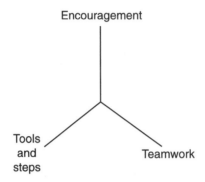

Figure 21-13. Components of Diagnosis

On-line diagnosis presents the tip of the iceberg. Off-line diagnosis addresses the volume below the surface of the water. This can be done using a system such as the 7 infrastructures to ensure their integrity of alignment activities.

The 7 infrastructures system itself needs to be monitored and diagnosed to improve the way the 7 infrastructures are used to mobilize organizational change and improvement.

The example we will use to illustrate monitoring and diagnosis of the 7 infrastructures will be part of the story of the Teradyne system that we are presenting throughout the book. However, we will defer presenting this example until Chapter 26 (page 577) after we've described (in Chapter 24) the related system of diagnosis and monitoring of hoshin management.

Diagnosis by External Assessment

Another way companies monitor and diagnose their business improvement activities is by assessment. Rather than checking against goals and process standards a company has created internally, assessments use generic categories applicable (somewhat more loosely) to a wide variety of companies.[19]

Deming Prize. The original external assessment standard is Japan's Deming Prize. Though it was originally intended as a national promotion device (see Chapter 28), Japanese companies uniformly "challenge the Deming" in order to get the insights and improvements that come out of the examination process.

Malcolm Baldrige National Quality Award. America's Malcolm Baldrige National Quality Award was likewise intended as a promotional and diffusion device. To make it less arduous and less open to the criticism of subjectivity, the Baldrige

Award examination process is done according to seven major categories, some thirty examination items, and approximately 100 areas to address.[20]

Self-assessment. However, a new use of the public award processes has appeared. Companies use the Baldrige categories to assess their business improvement and organizational learning programs, without any firm intention to apply for the award. Motorola publicly required all its suppliers to have plans for applying for the Baldrige Award. IBM only required some of its suppliers to have a "Baldrige-like" self-assessment system in place.[21]

One variation of self-assessment is normative phase-based, or maturity-based, assessment, which scores an organization relative to other organizations of comparable overall TQM maturity. An example of this is Hewlett-Packard's Quality Maturity System (QMS), which has been documented in [128, 209]. At HP, the reviewers of one division are general managers from other divisions who have been trained to do QMS reviews. The outcome of such assessments is a profile of weaknesses relative to comparable organizations. Of course, the usefulness of such a profile depends on the quality of the organizations being compared.

Another important category of monitoring and diagnosis is embedded in hoshin management (described in Chapter 24).

European Foundation for Quality Management (EFQM) Business Excellence Model. Within Europe, the most widely used framework for organizational assessment is the "EFQM Business Excellence Model," perhaps the most extensively used assessment model we know. It is used both for external assessment and for self-assessment, and the EFQM does much training of people in the EFQM assessment technique. The model is used by all sizes of organizations in the private, public and voluntary sectors. The majority of the National Quality Award processes in Europe have also adopted the EFQM Business Excellence Model.[22]

The essence of the EFQM Business Excellence Model, as shown in Figure 21-14, is that customer results, people results, and a good standing in the local community are achieved by leadership driving policy and strategy, partnerships and resources, and management of personnel through processes that will ultimately lead to excellence in planned key performance results.

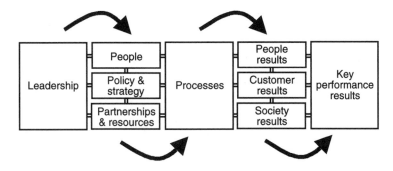

Figure 21-14. The Theory of the EFQM Model

The model has two discrete areas (see Figure 21-15):

- *The Enablers*—the approaches, activities, and methodologies used in making leadership, people management, policy and strategy, resources, and processes happen. The model looks at the approaches used and how well these have been put into practice and continuously improved.
- *The Results*—what has been achieved in terms of customer, people, society and key performance results through the deployment of the enabling activity. The model looks at the quality of these results, the ubiquitousness of the results across all relevant aspects of the product or service and organization, and how the data drives improvement through innovation and creativity.

During the process of assessment or self-assessment, the model enables the allocation of an overall score as well as scores for the individual criteria. These are useful to give a baseline and for measuring the progress of the improvement efforts.

Figure 21-15 shows the scoring associated with each of the nine criteria. A useful benchmark is that best practice organizations (typically winners of the European Quality Award) would be scoring between 750–800 points.

EFQM sees organizational assessment as a comprehensive, factual, and objective assessment of how the organization is managed. The process differs somewhat from

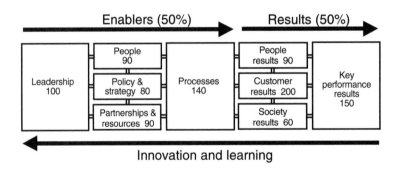

Figure 21-15. Relative Rankings of the Components of the EFQM Model

other audits and assessments in terms of the criteria used in the EFQM model. The assessment is designed to examine the following aspects of an organization:

- How the organization is led, in order to provide vision and direction
- How appropriate information is gathered and used to plan for the future
- How people's talents are developed and aligned with business objectives
- How the organization determines exactly what its customers need, and how it sets out to meet these needs
- How the flow of work is organized, to eliminate waste and error and, hence, improve products and services

- How the organization is performing, from various perspectives: employee morale and involvement, customer/marketplace, productivity, efficiency, and financial performance

The assessment process can be conducted in different ways, depending on the objectives set by the organization. However, EFQM believes all of the following benefits can be achieved by a properly designed and executed assessment:

- It builds commitment to change among key personnel
- It provides a reliable, dependable, and reputable method of preparing an improvement plan
- It helps management identify the vital few areas for improvement, which can have the most leverage in improving performance
- It provides a tool that can be built into the annual planning cycle as a way of driving yearly continuous improvement

The typical assessment process goes as shown in Figure 21-16. The first step is usually to provide an education, awareness, and planning session for the senior executives. The next step is to create an internal fact-finding team and provide them with training for their task. This team can then interview key individuals, documenting

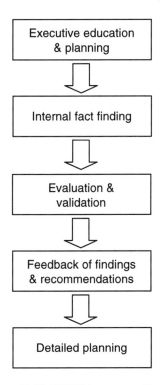

Figure 21-16. EFQM Assessment Process

what they discover and assembling supporting evidence and other documents. Their reports will delineate the facts without any comment on what is and isn't good. Evaluation and validation are then conducted internally or externally. The next step is to feed the findings back to the executives. Since the assessment is based on an objective review of the evidence provided, the subsequent feedback highlights deficiencies against the criteria and may challenge existing practices and views. The stage is now set for the development of an improvement plan, usually carried out in a detailed planning workshop shortly after the feedback has been received.

Many organizations decide that the assessment will need to be repeated, so that the effectiveness of the actions taken can be measured and identify the next steps. By building the assessment process into the annual planning cycle, the organization can create a reliable mechanism to drive the improvement process year on year.

NOTES

1. The subsection on Leadership versus Empowerment in Chapter 2, pages 33–35, is closely related to and has anticipated the principle we articulate here, as is the section on Engaged Employees for a Rapidly Changing World, in Chapter 15, pages 285–287.

2. See Chapter 19, pages 379–385, for the full story of the CQM Design Team.

3. Kelner [167] notes, "Mobilizing an organization has to do with getting specific behavior . . .You can attempt to control the people or you can attempt to control the situation. [People's] fundamental motives do not change much, or easily . . . it is easier to create a new situation than reinvent the people you have." Daniels [80] suggests going after the overall culture change you want by changing the behavior in meetings, a place people spend much of their organizational time.

4. Described in detail in Chapter 20, pages 410–413.

5. Koji Kobayashi, CEO of NEC, did the same thing to teach society and, thus, his own organization about the convergence of Computers and Communications. We previously mentioned these indirect strategies of Grove and Kobayashi in Chapter 17, page 319.

6. This model has come to be known informally as "the 7 infrastructures."

7. This system was explained to us by Greg Fischer, co-founder and retired CEO of SerVend. SerVend's business system will be described in greater detail in Chapter 29; see also [124].

8. Thus, the SerVend management, in one way or another, recognized the need for the different kinds of goals. Their hierarchy of goals also has parallels with the hierarchy of goals and means that characterize hoshin management, which we will describe in Chapter 24.

9. Joe Junguzza did research in 1991 that is summarized in the figure, and we have seen other examples since then.

10. Remember that Teradyne sticks with "TQM" as the name of their business improvement activities.

11. Created by Shoji Shiba and Alan Graham on the basis of the CQM design study of eight world-class TQM practitioners, Shiba's visits to Japanese and European companies, and observations of several noteworthy CQM companies.

12. For a perspective on such codifications, consider the history of Philip Crosby's "four absolutes of quality," as described in [77, pages 51–52]: "The Absolutes, as they now stand, were laid out as a teaching aid for the first Quality College course ... There had been five Absolutes originally. They were listed in *Quality Is Free*. I eliminated two and replaced them with one. The two were designed for quality professionals. Therefore, they did not mean much to managers. They are both still true, but we teach them in different ways."

13. Candidates for additional generalities: (1) Senior managers get longer classes in organizational change and improvement than junior people; (2) the first course is about organizational change and improvement awareness (what it is, its importance, its vocabulary) and the second course is basic problem-solving methods (7 steps or the equivalent). Bear in mind that these are observations of companies that have ascended rapidly (three to five years) in organizational change and improvement. Companies that have been practicing these since the inception of TQM, such as Toyota, may have different characteristics.

14. Purchased or licensed curriculum materials make PDCA and diffusion difficult. Typically, licensees may not alter materials, which makes continuous improvement difficult and education, therefore, less effective and more costly. Also, companies usually cannot share licensed materials with other companies. Without the ability to share successful practices, the evolution of business improvement practice regionally or nationally is impaired. Chapter 28 discusses such issues further.

15. The authors are aware of the sharp distinction often made by education professionals between education (broad and conceptual knowledge learning) and training (focused, results-oriented skill learning). We consider this to be unnecessary 0-1 thinking, and we advise against even speaking in ways that separate improvement skill from the surrounding conceptual context. Here, the terms are used interchangeably, to reinforce the notion that training and education are united and balanced.

16. This assessment of the 7 steps rollout was done formally as a 7 steps exercise, and is reported in [41]. The story also is sketched in Chapter 11, pages 177–181.

17. Masao Nemoto gives a useful discussion and examples of checklists for evaluating QI stories in [216, chapter 5].

18. Where 70 percent of the commentary is positive (about parts of the process that were relatively well done) and no more than 30 percent deals with (a selected few) problem areas—see page 150.

19. A comparative analysis of the assessment criteria that go with a number of quality awards may be found in [177].

20. The central document for the Baldrige Award is the "Application Guidelines" (including the application forms), which is available free of charge from the Malcolm Baldrige National Quality Award Office, National Institute of Standards and Technology (NIST), (formerly the National Bureau of Standards), Administration Building, Room A537, Gaithersburg, MD 20899. A good synopsis of the usefulness of the award and discussions surrounding it appear in Garvin's paper [111] and in [12] where several noted commentators respond to Garvin's article.

21. Other assessments, such as ISO-9000-1, may provide somewhat greater emphasis on quality maintenance than the Deming or Baldrige assessments do.

22. The explanation of the EFQM model in this subsection was given to us by Bob Barbour, Executive Director, Northern Ireland Quality Centre, Belfast. See also [220].

22

Phase-In

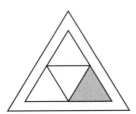

The discussion of initiation strategies in Chapter 20 broached the topic of how to mobilize everyone in a company to help with organizational change and improvement. We took an apparent detour in Chapter 21 through elements of infrastructure, because empirically, world-class companies tend to implement the methods of organizational change and improvement by emphasizing various elements of infrastructure in turn. Or, more accurately, they formulate the elements of infrastructure to reflect phase-in sequences found to be typical.

Shoji Shiba and Masanobu Abe created a general description of phase-in from research on Japanese quality circles activities and from a document of presentations from Deming Prize winners, which includes synopses of reports by companies that won the Deming Prize from 1982 to 1988 [263]. The CQM design team found the same sequence in American companies it visited in 1990.[1] Since then, many other companies have followed the phase-in model presented here.

Figure 22-1 reproduces the seven elements of infrastructure divided into the three most typical phases of phase-in.[2]

1. *Orientation.* When you introduce organizational change and improvement, setting goals and creating new organizational structures is necessary. Tell the company employees why change is necessary and your organizational change and improvement plans (infrastructure element 1 in the figure). Then create a new change planning and facilitation organization within the traditional organization (element 2).

2. *Empowerment.* You must create "pushing power" for organizational change and improvement activity. Employees must be given the tools to accomplish organizational change and improvement (element 3) and be encouraged to use the tools and get involved in the effort (element 4). This must be reinforced by diffusion of improvement success stories (element 5).

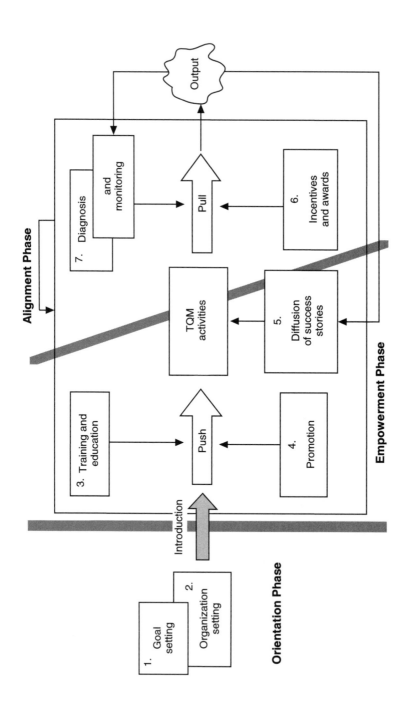

Figure 22-1. Three Typical Phases of Phase-in

3. *Alignment.* Once the organizational change and improvement effort has started and is moving ahead, you need "pulling power" to direct the activity—to synchronize and align the organizational change and improvement activities with business goals and practices of the company (elements 6 and 7).

These three phases are unlikely to be executed in a strict 1-2-3 order. Typically you start with orientation and then move on to empowerment. However, you usually can't wait for full empowerment within various functional areas before beginning cross-functional and intrahierarchy alignment. Thus, you cycle back and forth across the three phases, advancing in each phase as necessary to support the activities of the other phases. This may take four to five years.

"Implementation" of organizational change and improvement efforts such as we are describing always takes several years and several discrete stages that differ from company to company. However, avoid the overly simplistic and 0-1 term "implementation." It is too easy to speak of change and improvement as implemented at one company and not implemented at another. A more precise term is phase-in, as in "what phase the company is in on its ongoing journey toward organizational change and improvement." A discussion of each typical phase follows.

22.1 ORIENTATION PHASE

The orientation phase is where you make people in the organization aware of why you think the company has to change what it is doing and how you think you are going to get there. The orientation phase emphasizes goal setting and organization setting. The activities necessary to do these tasks effectively are senior management learning and middle management exploration and piloting.

Effective goals require articulation of latent or actual crises, which in turn requires that senior management acquire convincing facts. Alex d'Arbeloff's videotape presentation (pages 410–413) was part of Teradyne's orientation phase; in it d'Arbeloff set the context for the crises he saw and what he believed Teradyne needed to do about it. Some companies set goals by benchmarking; indeed, in the late 1980s Xerox practically invented the modern idea of benchmarking as it benchmarked competitors and others with best practices as a way to set its goals. Similarly, Motorola practically invented the formal version of what we call "customer visitation" when it had its executives start regular customer visits as a way of understanding what its goals needed to be.

Senior managers need to learn about organizational change and improvement more extensively than those below them, in order to design and lead the company's program. Senior executives in CQM member companies uniformly take longer courses than mid-level managers (e.g., six days versus two days). In 1997, David Lowe (then CEO of ADAC) described jump-starting ADAC's own business improvement activities with numerous visits by its senior management to other Silicon Valley companies, such as Solectron and ReadRite, practicing relevant methods. (See Chapter 28 for more discussion about learning from other companies.)

The orientation phase involves exploration and experimentation. As the late Bill Smith, VP for quality for Motorola's largest division, Communications Products, told us in 1990, "We tried everything, but what worked is six sigma." Entrepreneurial middle managers commonly attempt smaller-scale improvement activities, from which the company can learn what works and what doesn't work. Large companies may draw on successful experiments by entire divisions, as Hewlett-Packard did in drawing on the experience of YHP in Japan.

The role of the senior executive learning in the orientation phase motivated the order of presentation in this book. Step 1 of successful phase-in is always learning about the basics of improvement and the organizational systems needed to support them. Numerous choices are available for phase-in strategy. Without knowing what those choices are and how to fit them into the culture, strengths, and needs of a specific organization, discussing phase-in strategy makes little sense.

During the orientation phase, the other elements of infrastructure are likely to be informal, done primarily by senior executives and a few pioneering managers lower down. Training and education mixes classroom work with much visitation among peers from other companies, perhaps a half step ahead in phase-in. Promotion is likely to be from person to person, as is diffusion of success stories. Incentives and awards are personal satisfaction and the high regard of people engaged in orientation. Diagnosis and monitoring will likely consist of informal assessments of knowledge: Do we know enough to create an effective companywide program based on PDCA?

22.2 EMPOWERMENT PHASE

As we mentioned earlier, our definition of empowerment means having the capability to do the job, i.e., having the engagement, skill, and authority to do the job.

The empowerment phase is often marked by initiation of training and promotion unequivocally intended to reach everyone in the company. The training needs to cover what can be done and what must be done in terms of both technical skills and people issues. The training and the methods need to be promoted broadly.

This phase also often begins when training cascades from managers to their direct reports, when "train the trainer" graduates move to active teaching, and when widespread diffusion of successful stories begins. Empowerment is working when training creates more training and success creates more success. This can be called the "snowball model" of phase-in (see Figure 22-2). Having a system for diffusing success stories—publicizing the detailed methods by which workers create improvement—is the key to creating a snowball effect.[3]

By contrast, any strategy in which a limited group of people expends more money or effort to train and engage the larger organization might be called the "Sisyphus model" of phase-in, after the Greek mythological figure condemned to push a large rock uphill forever (see Figure 22-3). Examples include hiring outside trainers or sending all managers to an outside course. These strategies are expensive and don't build on success.

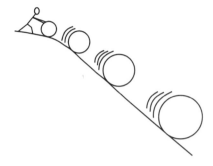

Figure 22-2. The Snowball Model of Phase-in

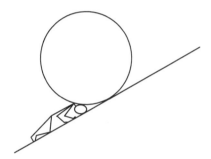

Figure 22-3. The Sisyphus Model of Phase-in

The empowerment phase, then, is a period when the new concepts and practices of organizational change and improvements are spreading throughout the organization.[4]

During the empowerment phase, the orientation phase activities of goal setting and organization setting change character as they penetrate the organization. Goals are deployed as managers figure out how their respective functions contribute to the overall corporate goals. The goals become a focus of promotional efforts both through regular communication channels and through the "why" questions posed in organizational change and improvement courses.

The choice of methods taught and how they are taught also embed goals into the training programs. For example, the 7 steps can be focused on specific company goals such as cycle-time reduction or reduction of product defects.

The change organization also extends further into the company during empowerment. Divisions and sites create their own change office and change steering committees. Early training goes to change officers, facilitators, or trainers, who may or may not be the same people. Also, cross-functional activities begin to happen more regularly.[5]

During the empowerment phase, the alignment activities of incentives and awards, monitoring, and diagnosis take place on a larger scale. The incentives and awards are likely to be recognition coupled with QI story diffusion.

22.3 ALIGNMENT PHASE

Orientation is where employees are made aware of what must happen, and empowerment is where the employees' capabilities expand so they can do what needs to be done. However, business improvement and organization learning on a large scale probably cannot happen until the employees are aligned and working together toward a common purpose.

On this point, Ray Stata, founder and chairman of Analog Devices, quotes what he calls Russell Ackoff's axiom:

> The performance of an organization depends more on the interaction of its parts than on the performance of the parts separately; that is, it's not the sum of the parts which counts, but the product of their interactions.
>
> The parts of a social system have a purpose of their own. The containing system has its own purpose. These purposes tend to come into conflict. The challenge is how to align the purpose of the parts with the purpose of the whole. [275]

Ray went on to note that the military, church, tribe and family, and many traditional machine age companies are examples or organizations that oftentimes deal with the alignment challenge through authoritarian leaders and the parts subordinating themselves to the whole. However, this no longer is a satisfactory approach in today's rapidly changing world.

The transition to the alignment phase is difficult to define sharply. However, there are general themes. Some form of improvement activity has spread to almost every part of the organization. With the ubiquity of standardized problem-solving methods, it becomes possible to incorporate PDCA into all planning processes, including practicing hoshin management (explained in Chapter 24). There is a new emphasis on the monitoring and diagnosis element of infrastructure.

With most of the "low hanging fruit" of early improvements already harvested, further improvement corresponds more closely to the quality of individual or team efforts, and to the methods they use in making the improvements. Therefore, awards, incentives, and recognition can more reliably reflect individual and team merit, which causes them to become more widespread. This is a new emphasis on the incentives and awards element of infrastructure.[6]

During alignment, the focus of organizational change and improvement activities undergo a transition. Dominated in the empowerment phase by the addition of more systems or activities, the focus now shifts to integration, standardization, and customization. As will be seen (Chapter 24), hoshin management can be thought of as managers integrating individual and team improvement activities throughout the company by working toward consistent goals and minimizing inconsistencies in means (such as excess resource demands) by planning. Means planning and control by measurement are standardized processes that managers use to carry out improvements. Integration and standardization capitalize on synergies among different processes. For example, hoshin management can yield information about which markets to target for product R&D. In even a medium-sized corporation, there are many opportunities to find synergy among processes. As John Petrolini of Teradyne has told us, "TQM isn't a separate activity anymore; it's the way we do business."

A final theme is customization. With several years of experience in organizational change and improvement, companies typically improve their methods (sometimes in ways that would not have been feasible earlier). The companies create unique change and improvement systems, what we call integrated management systems. For example, Akao's books on hoshin management and QFD reveal many different variations in these practices [5, 4]. Companies may de-emphasize some of the 7 QC tools and add others (often a process flowchart, for example). Chapters 26 and 29 provide additional examples of companies developing their own unique systems.[7]

22.4 EVOLUTION OF THE PARALLEL ORGANIZATION

The form of organization changes with phase-in of organizational change and improvement concepts and practices. Organizations begin with a standard formal organization, as shown in Figure 22-4.

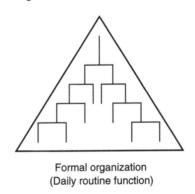

Formal organization
(Daily routine function)

Figure 22-4. Standard Formal Organization

A company goes from where it is to where it wants to be in a few years by applying the PDCA improvement cycle, as illustrated in Figure 22-5.

The improvement cycle is applied to the conventional or formal organization in two ways. First, it is applied within functional groups at every level, as shown in Figure 22-6.

Second, the improvement cycle is applied in a cross-functional way to cross-functional systems by a mutual learning network parallel to the formal organization for routine execution of work, as shown in Figure 22-7.

The formal organization evolves for control of routine work processes—divisionalized for some companies, functional for others, and so on. Likewise, a parallel organization evolves to support improvement activities. As part of the mutual learning network, a permanent committee structure may be developed to parallel (and often

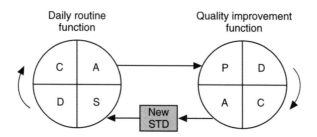

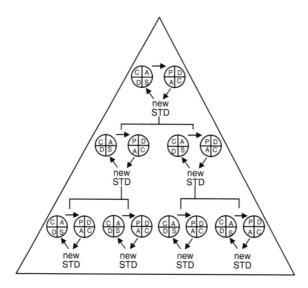

Figure 22-5. Using the Improvement Cycle to Create a New Standard

Figure 22-6. Applying the Improvement Cycle within Functional Groups

overlap) the organization for routine execution of work. There may be permanent cross-functional committees directed at long-standing goals like cost, quality, and delivery. Toyota used this approach. As of 1993, IBM had established permanent worldwide ownership by 14 committees, each assigned a single fundamental business process. In a recent case, Analog Devices founder and chairman Ray Stata reports [275] that in a division he was temporarily managing the leadership team included both his direct reports and many of the people that reported to them. In all cases, the permanent organization spawns initiatives for individuals and task teams.

A parallel mutual learning organization to organize improvement is essential.[8] The routine work organization, shown on the left of Figure 22-7, is constrained by job descriptions and operational pressure to do ad hoc and one-shot improvements. The routine work organization generates improvement problems. The parallel improve-

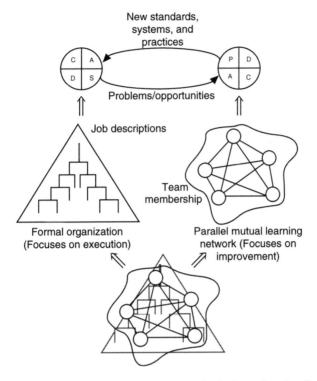

Figure 22-7. Applying the Improvement Cycle Cross-functionally

ment organization (quality improvement teams, the change office, and the change committee) has the flexibility to do what needs to be done to make permanent improvements. The parallel improvement organization develops new practices and standards for the hierarchical routine work organization.

The parallel organization also develops behavioral norms and practices for itself that differ from those for routine execution of work, even though the same people participate in both. Table 22-1 summarizes these ideas.

22.5 COMMON PATTERNS OF PHASE-IN

As emphasized earlier in this chapter, phase-in typically progresses through three phases: orientation (recognizing the need for change and improvement and to learn its basic principles), empowerment (learning the methods of change and improvement and developing skill in practicing them), and alignment (harmonizing the business and change and improvement goals and practices of the company). However, as was also mentioned, phase-in is unlikely to execute in strict 1-2-3 order. There are nearly as many different patterns of phase-in as companies. Nonetheless, we have seen two patterns of phase-in which particularly stand out, as described in the next

Table 22-1. Comparison of Organizational Principles

Functions	Elements of infrastructure	Principles of organization	
		Formal organization	Parallel organization
Orientation	Goal setting	Regulation	Philosophy
	Organization setting	Hierarchy	Networking
Empowerment	Training	Discipline	Mutual learning
	Promotional activities	Top-down exhortation	Permeation
	Presentation	Penalty	Praise
Alignment	Companywide mobilization	Mandate	Support
	Diagnosis	Supervision based on result	Diagnosis based on process

two subsections: a narrow initial focus and getting ahead of yourself. In the final subsection, we describe templates for alignment required in different situations.

A Narrow Initial Focus

Many companies initially concentrate on one area of activity as their phase-in strategy. They may even initially describe their organizational change and improvement activities as being limited to a narrowly focused area. For instance,

- Teradyne initially focused on quality improvement teams using the 7 steps (Chapter 11).[9]
- LaRosa's[10] and Webspective[11] initially focused on understanding what would satisfy customers (Chapters 4, 13, and 14).
- Motorola, Allied Signal,[12] and General Electric have focused on six sigma (Chapter 23).
- Xerox focused on (and practically invented modern) benchmarking (Chapter 23).
- High Voltage focused on cycle-time reduction (Chapter 23).
- SerVend focused on natural work teams (Chapters 19 and 29).
- NTT Data Corporation focused initially on hoshin management [106, chapter 3].

Each of these approaches focuses on a specific type of process as the way to get improved results. Each of these approaches balances process and results. In the following chapter, we will give company cases studying several activity areas.

After gaining skill in one area, companies often maintain the original activity while adding a new area of focus. Teradyne and SerVend provide examples described in this book (pages 578 and 688, respectively). Also, the first focus area leads companies to other areas. Wherever a company starts, sooner or later it must address other issues; nonetheless, a company usually will be more effective starting in only one area.

Getting Ahead of Yourself

The management of NIMS (for details, see Chapter 25, page 549) began with orientation, but it became captivated by the concept of hoshin management (to be described in Chapter 24) as a method of aligning activities companywide. Therefore, from the orientation phase, managers attempted to move directly to hoshin management and the alignment phase. However, NIMS discovered that it was trying to implement hoshin management (a tool normally used during the alignment phase) before its staff had gone through the empowerment phase (in which basic change and improvement capabilities are developed). In other words, it attempted to skip from the orientation phase of phase-in to the alignment phase. Finding that the NIMS staff did not have the necessary skill to work on companywide activities, the company was forced to go back to the empowerment phase to teach the basics of TQM. With a little empowerment, NIMS tried alignment again and was again forced to return for more empowering skills. This cycle repeated until NIMS had reached extraordinary levels of individual empowerment, after which the company finally succeeded in alignment.

In one sense, the NIMS management moved too quickly to the third phase of alignment and was repeatedly forced back to the empowerment phase. However, in the long run, things worked out well for NIMS. In effect, hoshin management became the tool NIMS used to deploy each year's improvement ideas and to systematize successful ideas; hoshin management became the tool they used to PDCA their system.[13]

Alignment Strategies

Ultimately, resources have to be aligned so they are working together toward a common goal. Without alignment, much of the effort of orientation and empowerment will be wasted as broad changes to business systems will be impossible. Different situations require different alignment strategies, as summarized in Figure 22-8.

Across the top of Figure 22-8 are the four levels of learning we consider in this book (see Figure 3-8, page 47), although in this section we only cover the first three (we deal with the fourth learning category in part 4 of this book). Down the left side of Figure 22-8 are three types of business activity: execution of daily operations, improving (either incrementally or with a breakthrough) the way an existing business operates, or breaking into a completely new business. Study the figure row by row.

Alignment for *execution of routine operations* is typically done through the hierarchical organization (as discussed in Section 22.4, page 459). The hierarchical organization typically focuses people in the organization on standard processes to achieve standard goals (SDCA). The standard process depends on the trained and skilled understanding of the individual worker (the individual observer).

When *improvement of the existing business* is needed, the company needs a network of appropriate people throughout the organization more than a set of people

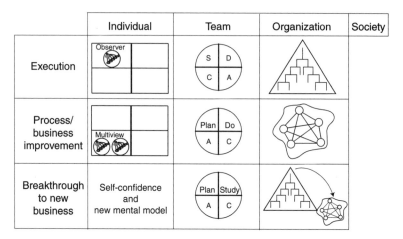

Figure 22-8. Alignment Strategies

from only one part of the organization (also discussed in Section 22.4). People networked from throughout the organization can bounce ideas and insights off each others (find the multiview). With this broader perspective in its collective mind, the improvement team can run the PDCA cycle, which can produce new approaches which the networked organization can feed back to the hierarchical organization for routine execution (as in Figure 22-7).

When the goal is *breaking into an entirely new business*, perhaps out of an existing business, a different strategy is needed. At the individual level, great self-confidence is needed by the leaders (either the official or unofficial leaders). They need to make a plan to Study the changing state of the world and the resulting opportunities (not yet a plan to Do something). This can provide a new mental model. However, fundamentally new ways of seeing things may not survive within the existing organization (even in a parallel networked organization). To nurture and develop the new mental model, a small team operating as a close-knit network has to be spun off of the existing organization (either formally or as some sort of skunkworks), a team that is capable of mutual learning in the world outside the existing organization. Because the existing organization will try to kill the new mental model, the new team should operate, from a formal point of view, relatively autonomously. We will discuss breaking out of the existing business in considerably more detail in Chapter 27.

NOTES

1. Shiba's sequence is consistent with empirical descriptions of implementation from Juran, Corning Glass, and other American companies of the time. Juran's "Quality Roadmap" as adapted by Digital Equipment has five phases: decide, prepare, start, expand, and integrate. Corning's implementation sequence is roughly described in [69, pages 15–17]. A description surprisingly similar to Shiba's appears in [65, pages 280–91]; for more detail, see [64].

2. The idea of push and pull, introduced in the figure, are derived from the ideas of [189].

3. No doubt our colleagues in the field of system dynamics would have us explain the same phenomenon as increasing the gain of a positive self-reinforcing feedback loop, as described qualitatively in [257].

4. Which functions start organizational change and improvement most aggressively differs from company to company. Japanese companies typically emphasize manufacturing and "move upstream" during empowerment phase to bring in R&D and marketing. (For instance, the NIMS division of NEC, a purely R&D operation, started "downstream" with design reviews and moved upstream with design plan reviews.) By contrast, Xerox's strategy for cost reduction focused as much, or more, on its product development process as it did on manufacturing.

5. Here, the American and Japanese practices may differ. In contrast to the Japanese QC-circle-like emphasis on forming work group improvement teams first, the CQM design team saw a general American tendency to encourage cross-functional improvement teams right from the start. And, unlike Japanese companies, which according to Shiba formed permanent cross-functional committees in the empowerment phase (like Toyota's committees on quality, cost, and delivery), the American companies we visited made no mention of such permanent committees; functions cross only high up, where they meet in the normal hierarchy.

6. W. Edwards Deming has been a vocal opponent of performance-based pay schemes, contending that most variations in individual performance are outside the individual's control and many are simply random. Certainly Deming's objections apply with a vengeance to rewards for improvement in the absence of ability to identify cause and effect. Until a Pareto diagram, in step 5, can demonstrate that observed improvement comes from the changes made, rewarding improvements is equivalent to flipping a coin. For awards to be motivating instead of becoming a source of contention, 7 steps or the equivalent should already be widely used.

7. See also the numerous case studies of developing unique management systems in [186].

8. The concept of a parallel organization originated in [159]; also [189, pages 112–116] develops the idea of the "hybrid parallel organization."

9. The chapters listed in parentheses are the places in this book where a description may be found for the particular method.

10. A chain of over 50 company owned and franchised Italian restaurants operating in the tri-state area around Cincinnati.

11. Since acquired by Inktomi.

12. Now merged with Honeywell to which it extended six sigma.

13. NTT Data Corporation also began with hoshin management, earlier than experts told them hoshin management was normally introduced. Despite this, the company was awarded the Deming Prize only a couple of years later.

23

U.S. Focused Strategies for Phase-In

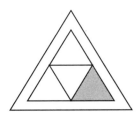

U.S. Invented Methods that Balance Process and Results

Organizations differ from one another in their organizational change and improvement needs because they differ from one another in their history, culture, and business needs. Each company must find an organizational change and improvement phase-in strategy (or strategies) that works for it. This often means focusing on a topic particularly relevant to the company's situation, as shown in the list on page 462. In an additional example not on that list, Alcoa Aluminum drove its program with safety as the primary focus, which not only embraced a noble goal explicitly but also highlighted shortcuts taken because of inefficient standard processes or inadequate tools for daily work [276]. Safety is a theme that company unions can embrace more readily than, say, cost cutting.

Table 23-1 summarizes a number of successful strategies for phase-in organized according to the three phases discussed in the previous chapter. U.S. and Japanese companies have used a variety of these strategies.

Table 23-1. Successful Strategies for Phase-in

Orientation phase (what must be done)	Customer satisfaction Benchmarking (best performance)
Empowerment phase (how to do it)	7 steps Benchmarking (best practice) Six sigma Cycle-time reduction
Alignment phase (getting everyone to do it)	Customer satisfaction Various teamwork methods, e.g., QIT, core, SDWT Hoshin management Assessments

In Japan, such concepts as market-in, fact-based problem solving, and focus on the vital few are used to orient the company to what must be done. QC circles, improvement activities, and managers teach people how to improve their processes to increase quality and customer satisfaction. Market-in provides alignment along the chain of suppliers and customers to the ultimate customer. Hoshin management and cross-functional quality assurance activities focus all of the managers in a company in an annual cycle aimed at realizing the vital few breakthrough improvements the company must make. Finally, challenging the Deming Prize is used in Japan to focus the company on achieving the highest levels of quality practice.

U.S. companies also use customer satisfaction to orient the company to what must be done (as in Japan, customer satisfaction aligns everyone in the chain of suppliers and customers). U.S. companies also use various improvement methods (e.g., 7 steps) and a variety of team types to help involve people. The Baldrige assessment (or other assessments) can focus the company on achieving superior levels of quality. A number of U.S. companies now employ some form of hoshin management.

In the rest of this chapter, we focus on three additional phase-in strategies that are important U.S. innovations: benchmarking, six sigma, and cycle-time reduction.[1]

All three of these methods emphasize the relationship between the processes of a business and business performance. Benchmarking formalizes the idea of learning from others by first measuring the performance level of best-in-class companies, which orients the company to what must be done to be competitive. Then, study of the processes used by best-in-class companies to achieve their superior levels of performance shows how to reach these competitive levels. Six sigma shows a company how to improve its processes to eliminate defects, and cycle-time reduction shows a company how to improve its processes to reduce the number of steps and amount of time for processes.

In the following sections, we describe benchmarking, briefly note the synergies it achieves (which often expand beyond the associated phase shown in Table 23-1), and follow a similar procedure for six sigma and cycle-time reduction. Then we will discuss cycle-time reduction in somewhat more detail. Our subsections on the positioning of six sigma compared to other methods (beginning on page 478) and on the APC model for cycle-time reduction (beginning on page 492) explicitly discuss the relationship between a business and its processes. All of this discussion is within the context of an existing business or organization.

23.1 BENCHMARKING

A place to start in any study of benchmarking is the book *Benchmarking: The Search for Industry Best Practices that Lead to Superior Performance*, by Robert C. Camp of Xerox Corporation [49].[2] Camp gives the following two definitions of benchmarking[49, pages 10 and 12]:

> Benchmarking is the continuous process of measuring products, services, and practices against the toughest competitors or those companies recognized as industry leaders.

Benchmarking is the search for industry best practices that lead to superior performance.

Various words in these definitions are significant. Benchmarking is a process (a process orientation is the way to learn and implement methods of lasting effectiveness), and it is *continuous* (because the environment keeps changing). Benchmarking includes *measurement*, both inside the company and outside the company (i.e., it is based on objectively defined, consistently collected facts). Benchmarking looks at *products*, *services*, and *practices* (it is not just aimed at competitive analysis). Benchmarking also looks at those *companies recognized as industry leaders* (not just competitors). Benchmarking is a *search for best industry practices*; in other words, the aim in benchmarking is to learn from others, whether or not they are within your own industry.

Camp's book describes Xerox's process (as the company defined it in the early 1990s) for carrying on benchmarking activities. The book contains a chapter on each of the following steps, with many implementation hints.

- Planning phase
    1. Identify what is to be benchmarked.
    2. Identify comparative companies.
    3. Determine data collection methods and collect data.
- Analysis phase
    4. Determine current performance "gap."
    5. Project future performance levels.
- Integration phase
    6. Communicate benchmark findings and gain acceptance.
    7. Establish functional goals.
- Action phase
    8. Develop action plans.
    9. Implement specific actions and monitor progress.
    10. Recalibrate benchmarks.
- Return to step 1

An alternative formulation of a benchmarking process was provided by one of the founding members of the CQM, Digital, which first studied the Motorola process. It was a four-step benchmarking process:

1. What to benchmark? What are the critical success factors for the function being benchmarked?
2. How do we do it? What is our process?
3. Who/what is best? Who performs our function at world-class levels?
4. How do they do it? What are the "enablers" that create world-class performance?[3]

Steps 1 and 2 are internally oriented, and steps 3 and 4 are externally oriented. Steps 2 and 3 focus on "enablers" for improvement; steps 1 and 4 focus on critical success factors.

Digital described benchmarking as, "a search for industry process and procedures leading to superior performance. Benchmarking is not a competitive analysis of products, but rather a driving force for continuous quantum improvements." For instance,

- Look for the best-in-class examples, e.g., for distribution look at L.L. Bean and Hallmark Cards.
- Don't focus on the financial numbers of the company you benchmark (they probably don't apply to your company). Look at the process it uses and the operationally defined numbers for the business process or function you are benchmarking.

In Japan, imitation is considered laudable. On a 1991 trip to a major Japanese company, we were given the analogy of climbing Mt. Fuji. Apparently, pilgrims climbing Mt. Fuji can either walk from the bottom in which case they risk not having the energy to reach the top, or they "can drive or take a bus to the fifth station" and conserve their energy so they can make the final walk to the top (Figure 23-1). "Our goal in developing our products is to build on what we or others have done before, and thus conserve our scarce resources to reach the top, rather than walking all the way from the foot of the mountain." In the United States, imitation is not admired. Benchmarking provides an acceptable guise for imitation, enabling U.S. companies to learn demonstrably useful practices from each other without losing face, and thereby preventing wasted efforts on rediscovering (or never discovering) the wheel.

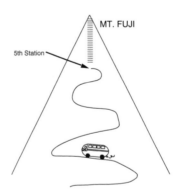

Figure 23-1. Take the Bus to the Fifth Station

In the years since those early formulations, benchmarking has become widely practiced, although not always as a formal improvement process. It is now routine to go visit other organizations to see what it is achievable and how they did it, i.e., to benchmark them.

Still, you must be careful not to benchmark things that shouldn't be done at all; you want to eliminate waste, not improve it. Also, Xerox noted (as have many other companies) that getting benchmarking data is easier from noncompetitors than competitors, but this is all right since the best-in-class organizations may not be competitors, such as the examples of L.L. Bean and Hallmark Cards above.

Benchmarking, as one focus for an organization's change and improvement activities, can fulfill several functions as is summarized by the matrix diagram in Figure 23-2.[4]

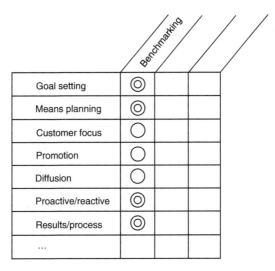

Figure 23-2. Matrix of Means for Organizational Change Requirements (Benchmarking Example)

Goal setting. Benchmarking establishes both the need for and the feasibility of aggressive goals.

Means planning. For small-scale problem solving by quality improvement teams, planning the means for improvement is straightforward: reverse whatever is the major cause of the defect being pursued. For larger-scale improvement efforts, such as automating production or speeding up product development, the means of accomplishing improvements are less straightforward. Benchmarking best-in-class examples often provides means to achieve difficult targets.

Customer focus. Companies need to find ways of putting a customer focus into operation. By focusing externally (beyond the local group or company), benchmarking encourages the outward focus that market-in requires.

Promotion. As opposed to pure goal setting, benchmarking provides a credible factual foundation on which to set goals—how competitors and best-in-class companies are outperforming your own. Such credibility helps promote organizational change.

Diffusion of success stories and learning from others. Benchmarking could be considered as an interesting variation on systems for sharing success stories. In particular, benchmarking is a way of defusing the "not invented here" (NIH) syndrome.

Proactive methods balanced with reactive methods. Benchmarking offers a middle path between reactive improvement and proactive improvement. It identifies problems (opportunities for improvement) before they would otherwise become obvious in a company's operations. Benchmarking asks for moderately demanding effort to identify customers and their needs, perhaps more demanding than the typical 7 steps reactive effort but less demanding than a purely proactive approach such as concept engineering.

Results focus balanced with process focus. Benchmarking highlights necessary new goals, but as part of the benchmarking process it discovers *how* the best-in-class performer achieves the best-in-class results.

As Figure 23-2 indicates, if the requirements profile was identical companywide, benchmarking would seem to be an effective focus because that single focus would accomplish a multiplicity of necessary functions.

Benchmarking requires considerable effort. As with any single organizational change and improvement practice, companies should decide whether benchmarking is a permanent, companywide focus, something that top management and quality specialists do to set goals, or something not necessary to get started.

23.2 SIX SIGMA

Six sigma and cycle-time reduction were the dual focus of the TQM program Motorola created in the late 1980s.[5] The purpose of cycle-time reduction is to do things faster and more efficiently throughout the organization; it will be discussed in detail in the following section. Six sigma focuses on defect reduction, and is the primary subject of the rest of this section.

One of Motorola's divisions had been working with statistical process control and reducing variation to be better able to manufacture components to specifications. Later the same techniques were promoted for a companywide push to reduce variation to better meet specs. Six sigma was a more popular name for what was essentially the idea of reducing variation.

Six sigma was meant to imply a statistical concept; however, it was also a slogan calling for a multi-year reduction in defects in all products and company processes to a remarkably low level.[6] In fact, the complete Motorola slogan was "Six Sigma by 1992" (i.e., within four years beginning in 1988). The specific 1992 goal was a defect rate of no more than three parts per million.

Motorola defines sigma levels in terms of defects per million *opportunities for defects or errors*. This mathematical normalization establishes a metric that applies uniformly across products and processes, from making bread to making pocket-pager networks. The following sigma levels are defined by Motorola (according to mathematics discussed in various Motorola publications):[7]

2σ	308,700 ppm
3σ	66,810 ppm
4σ	6,210 ppm
5σ	233 ppm
6σ	3.4 ppm

As Bill Smith told us, Motorola did extensive benchmarking while the six sigma concept and program were being conceived. Perhaps the most interesting finding was that once processes were normalized with the appropriate definition of sigma levels, most processes created errors or defects at around the four sigma level. Product manufacturing, payroll processing, airline baggage handling, doctors' prescriptions, orders written, journal vouchers, wire transfers, restaurant bills, and purchasing materials all tended to run around four sigma for processes not subject to world-class improvement efforts. Note that the list includes doctors' prescriptions, indicating that defect rate doesn't depend on intellect or level of education. Rather, it depends on process. The airline flight fatality rate is 6.4 sigma (.43 ppm) showing that, with correct training and procedures, six sigma is achievable. Conversely, IRS tax advice is worse than two sigma, perhaps indicating the difficulty of attaining quality when the underlying standard is ambiguous.

Motorola's best-in-class competitors tended to run processes around six sigma. So, "Six Sigma by 1992" became a matter of demonstrated competitive necessity.

Motorola created a "six steps to six sigma" improvement process that integrated these concepts into the mechanics of improvement:

1. Identify the work you do (i.e., the product).
2. Identify who you do it for (i.e., the customer).
3. Identify what you need to do your work and from whom you need it (i.e., the suppliers).
4. Map the process.
5. (a) Mistake-proof the process and (b) eliminate delays (including non-value-added time).
6. Establish quality and cycle-time measurement and improvement goals.

Steps 1 through 3 are the concept of market-in. Steps 4 and 5(a) are the defect reduction or six sigma concept. Steps 4 and 5(b) are the cycle-time reduction concept. Step 6 is the benchmarking concept.

Why It Is Called Six Sigma

The name six sigma came from the desire to have the specification limits of the items produced by a process be twice the natural variation ($\pm 3\sigma$) of the process outputs (or, to put it another way, the natural variation to be half the specification limits).

Suppose the outputs of an in-control process have some distribution with a natural variation $\pm 3\sigma$ as shown above the top dashed line in Figure 23-3. By the definition of $\pm 3\sigma$, 99.87 percent of the outputs are within $\pm 3\sigma$ and therefore only .27 percent are outside $\pm 3\sigma$. Thus, if the specification limits for the process *were* set equal to $\pm 3\sigma$ for the process, as shown between the dashed lines in the figure, we could expect .27 percent of the outputs to be out of specification. In other words, we could expect 2.7 unit per thousand or 2700 units or parts per million (ppm) to be out of specification.

What should be done if a rate of defects of 2700 ppm is too high? If the specification limits are kept at the same place and the process is improved so the output

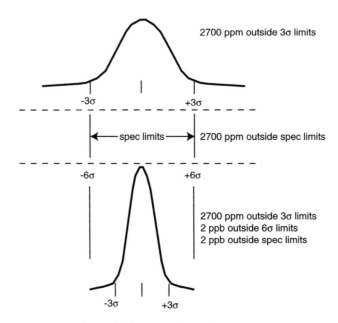

Figure 23-3. Derivation of Six Sigma

variation is much less, the probability of producing a unit out of specification will go down. This is shown below the bottom dashed line in the figure. In particular, suppose the process is improved to the point where the interval of natural variation (±3σ) of the process is half of the interval of the specification limits (which then by definition will be ±6σ for the process outputs). Then, the probability of producing a unit outside the ±3σ interval remains .0027 (by definition of ±3σ), but the probability of having a part produced out of the specification interval is much, much less—about two times in a billion (by the definition of ±6σ). In Motorola's definition of six sigma, it allowed for a shift of the mean of up to ±1.5σ, which increases the probability of producing an out of spec unit to 3.4 per million, which is the figure mentioned in the introduction to this section.

Application of Six Sigma

In 1991, George Fisher (then chairman of Motorola) told an audience of CQM members that perhaps 25 percent of the value of a good company's revenue is waste. His ambition was to eliminate much of that waste at Motorola. However, goals must be aggressive to get people energized and prepared to achieve the goals. A 10 percent improvement goal may attain a 10 percent improvement, but people may rationalize existing structures and only tweak them a little. Great improvements are unlikely with modest goals. A 50 percent improvement goal may attain 50 percent improvement. However, it may well require a substantial change of the existing process. The original six sigma goals at Motorola were a 68 percent reduction in defects each year for four years—a total of a 100-to-1 decrease in defects over a four year period. These original six sigma goals were intended to induce major changes at Motorola.[8]

Many companies report similar observations, that is, factors of five, 50, or 500 of waste in many company processes. It is obvious that the cost of rework, waste, and delay of processes working at the 3σ level (i.e., 6.7 percent defects according to the Motorola chart on page 472) could be many times the costs to make those six units, and many processes in companies operate at much worse than 3σ levels.[9] Both AlliedSignal and GE have claimed billions of dollars in savings from reducing defects in their processes through their six sigma programs.[10] Finally, when we checked in 1999, six sigma was still very much a part of the management process and culture of its inventor, Motorola.

Figure 23-4 summarizes the synergies created by the dual focus on six sigma and cycle-time reduction. We will discuss cycle-time reduction at greater length in the last section of this chapter, outside the context of Motorola and six sigma.

	Six sigma	Cycle time	...	
Primary driver for most business goals	◎	◎		
Applicability to diverse functions	◎	◎		
Simplicity of goal deployment	◎	◎		
Balance of process versus result orientation	◎	◎		
Balance of proactive versus reactive methods	◎	◎		
...				

Figure 23-4. Synergies from Dual Focus on Six Sigma and Cycle-time Reduction

Primary drivers for most business goals. As Bill Smith of Motorola put it in 1990, making large improvements in defect levels (six sigma) and cycle time will make large improvements in every single one of your business goals. Figure 23-5 uses another matrix diagram to suggest how this can be so.

Applicability to diverse functions. Defect levels and cycle-time are drivers not only for the most important business goals; these improvement methods are applicable to nearly any process.

Simplicity of goal deployment. Most companies have a planning process to deploy goals down to the individual group or worker. Sigma levels are relatively easy to deploy. For instance, if the defect goal for an assembled device is six sigma, the goal for each of the components and for the assembly process is likewise six sigma.

Balance of process versus results orientation. The essence of six sigma is to understand the process as a way of producing results.

Balance of proactive and reactive. Six sigma is far from a purely reactive method. It includes aspects of market-in, benchmarking, reactive improvement, and new process design.

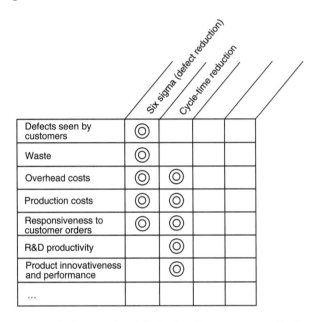

Figure 23-5. Impact of Defect Level and Cycle-time Improvement on Business Goals

The Spreading Practice of Six Sigma

A curious thing happened in the mid-1990s. The popular press printed story after story about the "death of TQM," while the keystone of Motorola's TQM activities (that had its roots deeply in Demings ideas of TQM and reducing variation) which Motorola called "six sigma," spread to a number of other high-profile companies. In some cases, six sigma augmented an existing TQM program (this was the case at AlliedSignal), and in some cases six sigma was touted as a new program that had great potential for improving business performance.

This spread of six sigma began with Motorola's efforts in the early 1990s to help IBM, Texas Instruments, Digital, Kodak, and ABB make use of six sigma. Perhaps the most visible of these was at IBM where it was promoted by the CEO. However, IBM's CEO changed and that visibility died down. In the same era, Mikel Harry and Rich Schroeder left Motorola to help ABB's efforts. In time Harry and Schroeder were involved in the formation of the Six Sigma Academy which took on AlliedSignal as a client, and eventually many other companies.[11]

The most visible path in the business press of the spread of six sigma was the implementation at AlliedSignal. AlliedSignal was the beginning of the current round of visibility for six sigma. From there, six sigma spread to GE and then to a high-profile position in the consciousness of CEOs throughout the world, including implementation at companies such as Dow, Poloroid, Kodak, and GM.

AlliedSignal

TQM was launched at AlliedSignal[12] in 1991 (the year Larry Bossidy became CEO).[13] Until that time, the corporate culture was one of "if it ain't broke, don't fix it" with change mostly being viewed negatively. Bossidy espoused the idea that change is expected. TQM changed the AlliedSignal culture by encouraging teamwork, establishing a standard nomenclature across the corporation, and teaching basic quality tools such as process mapping and control charts to all employees. TQM helped lay the foundation for six sigma deployment in 1995 under the highly visible sponsorship of CEO Larry Bossidy (visible within the company, to shareholders, and in the business press).

Six sigma built on TQM by giving AlliedSignal employees a more explicit project focus, a rigorous process improvement methodology (DMAIC) and advanced statistical tools such as gage studies, multivariate analysis, and design of experiments. The DMAIC methodology is shown in Figure 23-6.[14]

Figure 23-6. AlliedSignal DMAIC Framework

Within the DMAIC framework AlliedSignal uses many process improvement tools: process flowcharting, gauge capability studies, teamwork, benchmarking, histograms, Pareto diagrams, process control charts, capability studies, regression analysis, analysis of variance, cost of poor quality analysis, control plans, cause and effect diagrams, design of experiments (or Taguchi experiments), fault tree analysis, quality function deployment, and so forth. Overall, like Motorola, AlliedSignal's key metrics for process improvement are defect reduction and cycle-time reduction. Of course, all of this is driven by customer requirements.

AlliedSignal also has an explicit mobilization system for communicating the framework, goals, results, and future direction of its six sigma program to internal and external audiences. This includes top management leadership, use of highly trained experts known as "black belts"[15] (four weeks of training) and "master black belts" (nine weeks beyond the four weeks for black belts) and a goal of "green belt" level of training (1 week) for all salaried employees,[16] management sponsorship of improvement teams,[17] change management training to address the "soft stuff," alignment of improvement efforts with business unit goals, driven by the operating organization and not the quality specialists, registration of improvement teams, some standard metrics across all types of business activities, a common language for continuous improvement, and so on.[18]

In December 1999, AlliedSignal finalized an acquisition of Honeywell, and the combined business now operates under the Honeywell name. The merger of the two companies was substantially justified by the synergy created by leveraging AlliedSignal's six sigma culture and program across Honeywell while leveraging Honeywell's innovation and customer focus culture across AlliedSignal. Even before the acquisition was final, the spread of six sigma across Honeywell was begun and is being completed in a much shorter time than it originally took to spread six sigma across AlliedSignal. The combined Honeywell company is now calling their business improvement program Six Sigma Plus. They have added more tools and concepts such as a stronger voice of the customer focus, activity base management (ABM), total productive maintenance (TPM), and (from the original Honeywell) the Honeywell quality value (HQV) which is modeled after the Baldrige criteria.[19]

GE

According to accounts in the business press, Larry Bossidy told Jack Welsh of GE about the successes of six sigma at AlliedSignal, and GE launched six sigma across its organization in 1996.

GE uses the same DMAIC methodology as AlliedSignal did. However, unlike AlliedSignal, GE makes training in six sigma a requirement for promotion. Managers and those who want to become managers must meet black belt training standards. Executives who meet six sigma milestones receive bonuses, and are able to participate in the variable incentive compensation plan by master black-belt level quality professionals.[20]

Positioning Six Sigma versus Traditional TQM and Other Change Systems

Several advances are claimed by proponents of six sigma compared with the TQM implementations they are familiar with. For instance:

- Executives are involved in selecting improvement projects monitoring ROI of the program, and rigorous accounting mechanisms are implemented to track expenses, savings, and the creation of shareholder wealth.
- Six sigma focuses on specific aspects of operational excellence versus a general notion to "satisfy customers."
- Facilitators (the black belts) are assigned full-time to work on six sigma implementation.
- DMAIC (called MAIC in many places) provides a roadmap for application of the various traditional quality and more sophisticated statistical tools.

These claims are more true for some organizations than for others. While many TQM implementations have been quite unstructured, many other implementations of TQM are very structured (for instance, the Teradyne example extensively documented in this book). The business improvement and organizational learning systems in companies we admire include executive leadership of specific activities to improve business performance, trained facilitators are used and explicit problem-solving roadmaps are used. To give one example, Toyota's TQM program[21] combines explicit mobilization methods with sophisticated statistical tools (Toyota speaks of an "SQC renaissance"), a good textbook, and many instructors like the six sigma "belts." Also, Chris Mastro says,

> ... In my six sigma role I use [the] A New American TQM book and my TQM class notes as a reference. TQM and six sigma build on each other and DMAIC overlays almost identically on the 7 step TQM problem-solving method ... In my opinion, the key success factors (for successfully implementing TQM, six sigma, etc.) are having top leadership buy-in and visible support, driving continuous improvement through well-defined projects with quantifiable metrics and goals, and providing sufficient resources (training materials, time, manpower) to implement the change process throughout the organization.

Chris went on to suggest that having a total quality culture in place helps six sigma to grow and be effective.

The distinction appears to be the explicit nature of the emphasis in six sigma. Six sigma explicitly includes a structured deployment system that in particular focuses improvement efforts on areas that will provide tangible financial benefit. Also, part of the explicit emphasis of six sigma is using more sophisticated statistical tools than we describe in this book.[22] This is possible because of availability of highly trained "black belts." In these ways, six sigma seems to us to include important advances, and anyone thinking of how successfully to deploy TQM, Lean Production, etc., will do well to study the comprehensive six sigma system.

As with any other business improvement system, we remind the reader that six sigma is not the be-all, end-all. It includes important advances that can be useful to anyone doing business improvement and organizational change. Other organizational change and improvement needs, such as breaking through into a new business, may require additional concepts and processes. You have to create the integrated management system that is appropriate to your organization. This is what the combined AlliedSignal-Honeywell company now operating under the name of Honeywell appears to be doing as of late 1999, calling it Six Sigma *Plus*. We laud this approach regardless of the name given to the integrated management system.

23.3 CYCLE-TIME REDUCTION

Part of six sigma at Motorola, AlliedSignal, and probably others is cycle-time reduction. We choose to discuss cycle-time reduction separately because it has an interesting potential starting focus in its own right for a company's phase-in strategy. In particular, cycle-time reduction has potential to *make time available*. The first argument against any organizational change and improvement activity is, "there is no time to do more." Therefore, why not begin phase-in by doing something to make time available? Cycle-time reduction also has other potential advantages, such as:

- Customers like immediate response.
- There is pressure in many industries to introduce new products and services faster and faster.

- Reducing cycle time makes it necessary to predict less far into the future.
- There are usually lots of "low hanging fruit"—processes where a quick look will reveal many unnecessary or too long steps and delays that are easy to eliminate.
- Reducing cycle time typically results in simplifying a process and thus also helps with defect reduction. By eliminating steps, you eliminate places where mistakes might be made. Techniques such as design for manufacturing and design for assembly, or other mistake-proofing techniques, prevent defects from happening or uncover them earlier and in so doing reduce cycle-time.
- Reducing cycle time often also reduces costs because decreasing cycle-time can reduce costly mistakes/rework and shortening scheduled time tends to lessen effort expended.
- Reducing cycle time tends to draw a company and its people toward other important improvement areas and techniques, such as customer focus, defect reduction, benchmarking, and the like.

We are not claiming that cycle-time reduction is the best place to start phase-in. However, in the absence of reasons for focus in another areas (such as defect reduction, customer focus, or benchmarking), cycle-time reduction is an interesting place to seriously consider starting.

Cycle-time reduction is applicable in the factory and elsewhere:

- Shigeo Shingo, the Japanese guru of Just-In-Time manufacturing, converted setup activities in factories that used to take many hours into ones that take only a few minutes by eliminating unnecessary motion.[23] For instance, he eliminated the step of the mechanic going to the tool room to get the right wrench by permanently welding the wrench onto the nut.
- At the Indianapolis 500 car race, mechanics change four tires and refuel the car in 20 seconds. They achieve this speed by closely studying the process, eliminating waste, and improving what has to be done; they film themselves and look frame-by-frame for what they can cut out.
- In the following subsection, we give an example of the potential for a two orders of magnitude reduction in cycle time of an administrative process.

In this section, we mainly deal with cycle-time reduction for sets of processes running over relatively short time scales, with the possible exception of multi-year new product development processes. Another important set of issues has to do with speed of change within an industry, interlinking the cycle times throughout supplier chains, and so on. We recommend a book by our MIT colleague, Professor Charles Fine, as a place to start learning about these issues [92].

AΔT Example

We like the explanation of cycle-time reduction CQM founding member Digital gave us in the early 1990s: "a structured approach to review all implementation times against the theoretical optimum—the basis of elimination of all wasted time." This definition uses a fairly pragmatic meaning of the word "theoretical." It means the "calculated optimum" based on analysis of the current (or actual) situation. Digital had a cycle-time reduction process based on this definition called AΔT, standing for "actual-delta-theoretical."

The AΔT process came out of Digital's Colorado Springs manufacturing plant (we are unsure of the exact name of its original author). The method was later included as one of four components in Digital's TQM program. It also was taught by Digital to a number of other companies; in fact, Digital trademarked it. A Xerox facility in Rochester picked it up and in about 1990 was recognized as one of the top manufacturing facilities in the U.S. and gave credit to AΔT for part of its success.[24]

Digital's AΔT four-step process was:

1. Describe the actual process (A).
2. Identify the theoretical (T).
3. Analyze and eliminate the difference (Δ) between the actual and the theoretical.
4. Challenge the theoretical (that is cycle back to step 1 with the theoretical as the new actual).

Step 1 includes flowcharting the existing process, with each person analyzing his or her own job (and others looking from higher levels to make sure they eliminate unnecessary processes). At step 2, people think about which steps in the process are unnecessary and how long the remaining steps should take if everything goes smoothly. At step 3, they modify their processes. With their newfound experience, they begin again and reanalyze what the theoretical optimum should be.

An example of AΔT follows.

Suppose, for instance, a company is considering how it might reduce the cycle-time of its typical process for having employees get reimbursed for travel expenses.

As shown in Table 23-2, we first list the current *actual* process that is similar to what many companies use ("you" is the customer in this case). Second, we list the average *elapsed time* for each step of the current process. Notice that we are describing the real process that includes delays, having to talk to people personally, and so forth—not the process as stated succinctly in a policies and procedures manual. Take a minute or two to look at Table 23-2.

The steps in the table total something approaching 35 days, which is probably not completely atypical. Certainly 15 days would not be surprising for many businesses.

We now want to make note of the value-added steps from the point of view of the traveler.

To understand which steps are the value-added steps, one needs to understand what is meant by non-value-added steps. By "non-value-added" work, Digital meant work that is not of concern to the final user or customer. For instance, asking for reimbursement for travel expenses, the employee who traveled (the customer) just wants to submit a list of expenses and receive cash or a check. This is "value-added" work by the Digital definition. Digital did not mean to suggest that other steps in this process that people are doing are unimportant to the company or without value. For instance, a financial analyst often checks over expense reports and the travelers' supervisors often

Table 23-2. AΔT Example

1. You begin to enumerate what you spent, by organizing your receipts and expense notes for entry onto expense report flying home on the airplane Friday, form **[1 hour]**.
   - You sort the envelope of receipts into by expense report category.
   - You make handwritten notes on hotel receipts of which expenses are for lodging, meals, phone and fax, and other expense report categories.
   - You find currency conversion receipts for each currency conversion in each country visited, and do some sort of rough calculation of what the exchange rate is for cash expenses in each country visited (factoring in conversion fees, bits of change that couldn't be converted and were put Red Cross box in an airport departure lounge, etc.).
   - Using a pocket calculator, you convert all the cash charges in foreign currencies to dollars and note the dollar amounts on the receipts or notes about cash expenses.
   - You note which expenditures in foreign currency were charged to credit cards, and therefore the actual conversion rate will not be known until the charges get to the credit card company.
   - You carefully save all of the above sorting and notes for later use.
2. Get home **[4 hours]**.
3. Upon arriving home, you put the last receipt, for the taxi home, in the envelope with the rest **[3 seconds]**.
4. You wait for a week hoping the foreign charges will get to the credit card company **[7 days]**.
5. You phone AMEX and tell them the different charges that were made (giving them country, service establishment name, and amount in the foreign currency) **[2 minutes]**.
6. When asked, you try to remember whose name the company AMEX account is in before the AMEX representative will tell you anything about the account **[15 seconds]**.
7. AMEX tells you the exchange rate for all but one of the charges, which hasn't cleared yet **[3 minutes]**.
8. You wait three more days **[3 days]**.
9. You call AMEX again, and get the exchange rate this time for the remaining transaction **[5 minutes]**.
10. You get expense form from department forms rack **[1 minute]**.
11. You fill in the expense report by date, by expense category, and in dollars, add it up with pocket calculator, stable receipts to form, and sign form **[15 minutes]**.
12. Submit form, by putting it in inbox of department financial analyst **[1 minute]**.
13. Wait to hear from financial analyst **[3 days]**.
14. Analyst arrives in your office to question the detailed reasons for some of the charges, to be able to attribute them to expense codes; no other problems this time—no argument about expenses being too high. **[10 minutes]**
15. Financial analyst signs expense report and puts it in inbox of department manager **[2 minutes]**.
16. Wait for department manager get around to reviewing expense form, perhaps including coming back from a business trip **[2 days]**.
17. Department manager sits with assistant signs all the documents as fast as possible, including your form **[15 minutes]**.
18. The manager's assistant puts the expense report in the interoffice mail to the accounting department **[2 minutes]**.

Table 23-2. AΔT Example (*continued*)

19. Envelope travels through interoffice mail system and arrives in inbox of accounting secretary who delivers it later in the day to the inbox of the person now handling travel expense reports **[1 day]**.
20. Wait until the accounting clerk gets to processing this envelope from the inbox **[1 day]**.
21. Accounting clerk notes that the department financial analyst who signed the report is one who sometimes makes mistakes and rechecks the arithmetic **[10 minutes]**.
22. Accounting clerk initials the expense report and fills out an on-line check request form on the IS system coded to the correct department account and expense category **[2 minutes]**.
23. Electronic check request form sits in on-line database until twice monthly check run **[7 days]**.
24. IS system prints check **[1 second]**.
25. Check sits in a pile with other checks waiting to be stuffed into an envelope [2 hours].
26. Accounting clerk stuff the check in a envelope and put it in outbox **[10 seconds]**.
27. Envelope travels through interoffice mail system **[1 day]**
28. Envelope sits in inbox of department secretary **[2 hours]**.
29. Department secretary delivers envelope your office chair **[2 minutes]**.
30. You take check home and put it on your desk **[4 hours]**.
31. Check sits until Saturday morning you put the check in an envelope to your bank with a deposit slip, and you mail it Saturday afternoon **[2.5 days]**
32. Check travels through U.S. mail to bank which receives the envelope Monday **[2 days]**.
33. Tuesday the deposit is credited to your account **[1 day]**.

have to sign them. By Digital's definition (and for the purposes of the AΔT method), that is non-value-added work; however, the company values this work and an employee doing such assigned work should feel no decrease in self-worth.[25]

With the distinction between value-added and non-value-added firmly in mind, we can now "circle" the value-added steps in the table, for instance:

1. Enumerate what was spent, while flying home on the airplane Friday.
2. Get home.
3. Upon arriving home, include the final entry for the taxi fare home.
12. Submit for reimbursement to company.
33. Deposit is credited to your bank account.

Once we look at the process in terms of these steps that are of value to the end user (in fact, as one enumerates the steps of the existing process), opportunities for "reengineering" the process become apparent. For instance, the process could be reengineered so the above five value-added steps that the customer cares about can be done very quickly from the point of view of the customer:

- The company could put the expense form in a software package that could be installed in the laptop computer the traveler carries along on the plane. This on-line package accepts expense amounts in all common currencies. Thus, the traveler can just type the expenses into an on-line form on the airplane without worrying about currency conversions.

- The employee can dial up the company employee-only Web site from home (or the plane) and upload the trip report form.
- The IS system estimates the reimbursement amount in dollars and tells the on-line user it will be transferring that amount to the user's bank account immediately. From the point of view of the customer, the process is essentially over.
- After the fact, the following steps are carried out:
    1. The IS system types up a fully organized and categorized travel report and forwards it to the department financial analyst (for any further checks and coding the department desires).
    2. The traveler gives the division financial analyst an envelope full of receipts and notes.
    3. If the IS system or the financial analyst notices anything unusual, it is followed up on an exception basis.

Here then are the *theoretical* times the traveler cares about:

1. Enumerate what was spent to the trip report software, while flying home on the airplane Friday **[45 minutes]**.
2. Get home **[4 hours]**.
3. Upon arriving home, include the final on-line entry for the taxi fare home **[5 minutes]**.
12. Submit the on-line form for reimbursement to company IS system, including whatever dialog is necessary with the IS system **[10 minutes]**.
33. Deposit is credited to your bank account **[1 minute plus 1 day for bank to recognize it]**.

Total time is 1.25 days. Thus, the ratio of the actual for the current system shown in the table to the theoretically possible is 28, i.e., approximately 96 percent of the current activity is non-value-added activity and can *potentially* be removed.

Clearly, our typical manual systems and systems with checks and balances (included as the routine case instead of on an exception basis) have lots of room for acceleration. You may not get all that acceleration, and you may not convert much original time to other work. For instance, you may decide you want to keep some of the non-value-added steps, and you may not be able to coordinate actions so perfectly to eliminate all delays. Nonetheless, the reductions in cycle time you can make tend to have a disproportionate gain (since unnecessary steps and delays tend to have multiplicative repercussions as activities increasingly get in each others' way). The non-value-added work highlighted by the AΔT process is a good place to begin looking for activities and delays that might be eliminated.

CQM Study Group on Cycle-time Reduction

Since its inception, the Center for Quality of Management (CQM) has regularly undertaken study efforts to address an expressed interest in a particular area by CQM member companies. A 1997 survey of member companies and CEOs revealed that cycle-time reduction was a topic of great interest to CQM members. Thus, in 1997–98, the CQM undertook a study group on cycle-time reduction.[26]

Study group members met twice a month for four hours from September 1997 to June 1998. They heard presentations from experts and users of various methods (almost a dozen of them), did individual reading/study and reported back to the whole group (over a dozen significant reports), circulated other papers and book chapters to each other to read (about 100 altogether), and tried to synthesize a model for cycle-time reduction that could be tried and improved in CQM member companies. The work of several book authors [116, 117, 202, 237, 243, 269, 288, 314] was particularly important to the study group effort.

An extended report on this study effort can be found in [235]. In parallel with this effort, the CQM Cincinnati chapter's research committee visited a number of Cincinnati and Louisville companies to see the details of how they worked on reducing cycle time [241, 184, 124].

Cycle-time Reduction Process Wisdom

For study group members, the CQM study effort focused several important bits of "process wisdom" relating to cycle-time reduction. Common sense understanding is often misleading: ignorance of process wisdom specific to cycle-time reduction is likely to result in failure of efforts to reduce cycle-time.[27]

Complete utilization and high throughput are incompatible

Optimization of utilization of the components of a system is incompatible with overall system throughput (fast cycle times).

One of the most common business measures is resourse utilization, that is, cost per unit; many people try to reduce that as far as possible. This is shown in Figure 23-7.[28]

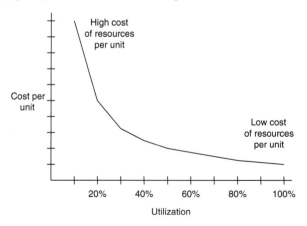

Figure 23-7. Cost per Unit Goes Down as Utilization Goes Up

However, queuing theory (and practical experience) tells us that as utilization goes to 100 percent, delay goes up rapidly. This is shown in Figure 23-8.[29] As the delay goes to infinity, the throughput goes to zero. The increase in delay toward infinity (and drop in throughput to zero) may begin with utilizations as low as 20 percent or as high as 65 percent to 80 percent, depending on the pattern of "arrivals" of work to be done, time distribution to do the work, ability to handle interruption, etc.

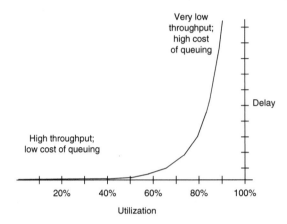

Figure 23-8. Delay Goes Up Non-linearly as Utilization Goes Up

It may be counterintuitive to some people upon first consideration that delay does not rise linearly with utilization (or, indeed, that delay grows large before a system is overutilized). Consider the schematic diagram shown in part A of Figure 23-9 of cars traveling on a three-lane (in each direction) highway and passing through an electronic tollbooth that does not require them to slow up to deposit the toll.[30]

Assume the road can be used at 65mph at 1/3 utilization. We illustrate this average utilization in part B of the figure by showing three cars in nine car lengths of roadway (three lanes times three car lengths).

Now suppose one lane at the toll booth closes, and the three cars in part B must fit into two lanes, as shown in part C of the figure. Utilization is now 1/2. However, even though 50 percent of the highway capacity is still unused, delay goes up, and throughput goes down. We can try to intuit by how much: perhaps car speeds drop to 55mph, maybe less.

Now suppose another lane closes, and the three cars must fit into one lane, as shown in part D of the figure. The utilization is now one. But what happens to delay? We all know the answer. Even though in some theoretical sense the system is not overutilized (utilization is one, not greater than one), delay becomes very long and we are likely to have a multi-mile backup at the toll booth. Throughput on the highway goes practically to zero. The issue at hand is variation: car arrivals and departures through the tollbooth cannot be synchronized closely enough to maintain full throughput (or anything close to it).

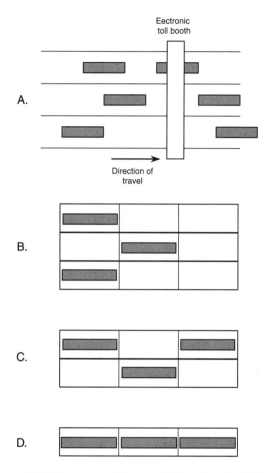

Figure 23-9. Illustration of Changing Utilization of a Highway

Figure 23-10 is derived by plotting our previous utilization and delay curves (Figure 23-7 of the cost per unit and Figure 23-8 of the cost in terms of delay) in a way that is somehow normalized and adding the two curves to produce a new total cost curve.[31] Figure 23-10 shows that as utilization rises, the per unit cost from plant capacity decreases. However, as utilization rises, the cost of delay or cost of queuing rises. In particular, full utilization is incompatible with high throughput and with low cost per unit processed. Therefore, the process designer needs to think about the best mix of cost and throughput for the particular situation, e.g., somewhere between 60 percent and 80 percent utilization.

Queues are not always visible, but they always have a cost. Local optimizations (e.g., full utilization of components of the system) damage the cycle-time performance of the overall system. Queues, not task performance, are the dominant factor

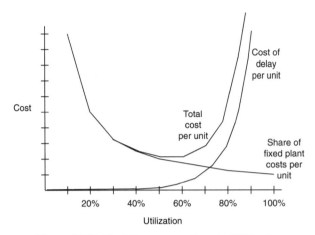

Figure 23-10. Total Cost versus Capacity Utilization

influencing cycle time in most slow cycle-time processes. Clearly, understanding queuing theory should be a requirement for those attempting cycle-time reduction.[32]

Focusing on queues also has the advantage that queue lengths are a leading indicator of cycles times, while direct measurement of throughput is a trailing indicator of cycle times.

Project tasks seem inevitably to come in later than planned

Projects (and sub-projects) never get done before their planned due date, no matter how far out the due date. This is shown in the pair of diagrams in Figure 23-11. The top diagram in the figure shows the dreams people have about the due date of project, i.e., that the distribution of possible finishing times surrounds the planned due date with some probability of finishing early and some probability of finishing late. However, we all know this is not reality. The bottom diagram in the figure is more realistic. There is little chance the project will be done early, and most of the distribution of finishing times is later than the due date. In fact, people usually put some slack time in their estimate of completion times for each component task to protect against trouble that will cause time delays, but that slack time is exhausted or worse.

The slack time we put into a project is exhausted for a variety of reasons: multi-tasking as discussed in the next subsection, waiting until the last minute to start, not telling anyone in those rare instances when something is getting done early, etc. The later-than-planned completion time provides justification for the slack time we put into the schedule to guard against a time overrun, and the next time we remember the later-than-planned completion time from last time and may add more slack to that. Pressure increases for the estimated completion dates of projects and their parts to lengthen.

The slack needed to protect against unexpected delays is usually part of each sub-task as shown in part A of Figure 23-12.

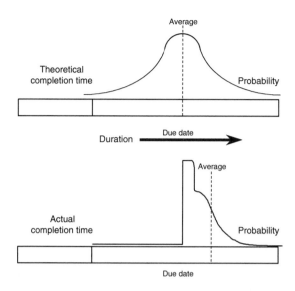

Figure 23-11. Task Completion Times—Theoretical versus Actual (Source: *Managing the Design Factory: A Product Developer's Toolkit*, by Donald G. Reinertsen, p. 18. Copyright © 1997 by Donald G. Reinertsen. Used with permission of The Free Press, a Division of Simon & Schuster, Inc.)

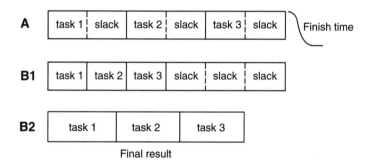

Figure 23-12. Usual and Better Approaches to Scheduling Slack Time

However, we have already pointed out that each bit of slack time usually gets used, so the actual finish time is longer than the total of all of the estimated subtask times and the slack time allowed for each. Slack needs to be eliminated for subtask planning and aggregated in a few key places, and then it must be allocated to subtasks only as needed, as shown in part B1 of Figure 23-12 (where the total of task time and slack time is identical to part A, but rearranged so the slack time is aggregated together). This might result in actual subtask times as shown in part B2 of the figure. Thus, we need mechanisms to help ourselves take slack out of subtask planning and to clump it where needed.

What we are discussing now is closely related to Goldratt's concepts of Theory of Constraints [116] where he shows that you maximize throughput in industrial processes by finding the process constraint, putting enough buffering (inventory) before that constraint to keep it from becoming a bottleneck, and eliminating other buffering from the process. A parallel set of examples can be given where time, not inventory, is what must be buffered against, and Goldratt describes this in [117]. We must eliminate slack time (i.e., time buffers) everywhere in the system (because such time typically is irrevocably lost) and only put slack time (time buffers) at the few constraints in the system. Then we can carefully control these time buffers.

Unfortunately, it is hard to find a politically and motivationally acceptable system to put all the needed slack time at the end or the few critical path points in the project where it doesn't inflate the time required for the subtasks but is still available if needed. To date each company (or division or department) that succeeds in doing this uses its own ad hoc methods.

Avoid multi-tasking

Time-sharing resources among projects—having the same resources work on multiple projects in parallel—is often incompatible with fast program cycle time. Consider Figure 23-13 which shows different orders for completing four projects, A, B, C, and D, each of which involves two months of effort.[33] In the figure's top sequence, the average finish time of the project is 6.5 months. In bottom sequence, the average finish time of the projects is four months. As the time slice becomes smaller, the limit of each of these metrics moves toward the total time to finish all four projects. This does not take into account the added and explosive inefficiency of switching among and coordinating across projects.[34]

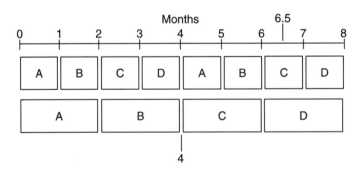

Figure 23-13. Effect of Multi-tasking on Cycle Time

Many companies multi-task and share their people among projects. In some companies many projects have no one working full-time on average (or maybe no full-time person at all). In most companies, people are scheduled well over full capacity. As a result, project time extend drastically and throughput (completion of projects) goes down, down, down.[35]

As many of the most successful managers will tell you, the first step in controlling an out-of-control project completion situation is to stop overscheduling people and stop sharing them among projects. Projects will get done, and overall project completion throughput will go up even though at any one time people are attempting less. The core teams case study from Analog Devices (page 385) provides an example of this.[36]

Practice Starts Control

"Starts control" is the system and criteria that allow a new project to be started—the system and criteria that limit project starts below a utilization level and avoid too much switching among projects which in turn will result in maximum throughput. In other words, starts control significantly addresses the previous points of process wisdom.

For example, if we improve our new product development process, then the improved process should include a way of controlling when instances of developing a new product get started. Without such starts control, gridlock is possible: too many projects get started, which have to share resources too much, and thus get in each other's way, delaying all of them.

Unfortunately, the natural human tendency is to start more projects than can be successfully done at the same time. We can't bring ourselves to make choices. We convince ourselves everything must be done, soon! We can't choose which projects are less important and can be delayed. We dream that time-sharing among the available resources will get all the projects done in the same time period (and, then, we frequently dramatically overschedule resources, e.g., to the 200 percent level).

In some domains (such as new product development), starts control can be the single most important issue. Without starts control, too many projects compete for available resources, switching among and coordination of resources increases, and throughput goes down.

Devices must be created for limiting starts. However, as soon as we say that, someone will say, "but in real life..." (implying that we are some sort of ivory tower theoreticians) "... we don't have the option of delaying key projects" (forgetting that more projects will be delayed by overscheduling than would be by not over utilizing resources). As John Goodhue from Cisco (who spoke to the study group) said, "It is emotionally hard to think about deliberately making someone unbusy some of the time. Also, [in new product development] scheduling an engineer at less than 100 percent could cause good ones to feel unchallenged and to move on."

To repeat, devices are needed for limiting starts and avoiding overutilization and counterproductive multi-tasking. Seven detailed real-life examples of methods of starts control may be read in [235, pages 21–27].

APC Model

Of all of the participants in the CQM study group, Neil Rasmussen (co-founder and chief technology officer of American Power Conversion Corporation, or APC) did the most work to synthesize a model he could test and use in his own business.

Rummler and Brache [243] make the point that one needs to know what one wants. One should not simply dive in and do cycle-time reduction. This advice is in contrast to some of the hype about cycle-time reduction that suggests that if one concentrates on cycle-time reduction, other improvements (such as quality, cost, and customer satisfaction) will be free. The fact of the matter is that cycle-time reduction may not be superior or even appropriate for every company. Different companies have different needs, and needs may change over time. Before embarking on a cycle-time initiative, a company should make sure this is what it needs most.

The model being used at APC for cycle-time reduction includes discovering the context for doing a potential cycle-time reduction project and confirming cycle-time reduction is the needed improvement. The APC model also includes a supportive environment for cycle-time reduction. This model is shown in Figure 23-14. Interleaved with the following description of the model from Rasmussen, we include a little more insight from the study group. A more detailed explanation can be found in [235].

Phase 1. Alignment and Orientation

An organization's top management needs to be sure Phase 1 elements are in place. Otherwise, cycle-time reduction efforts are likely to fail.

1A. BUSINESS OBJECTIVES

There needs to be a business reason for undertaking improvement efforts. There need to be more than the simple declaration "we need to do cycle-time reduction."

Improvement work to be undertaken must be aligned with business objectives, or else the improvement work will be starved for resources. Resources are not given to projects not addressing important business objectives.

Cycle-time reduction may or may not be a primary business priority. Defect reduction, cost reduction, or better understanding of customer needs are types of improvement work that might have higher priority than cycle-time reduction. Also, beware of improving a process that should instead be outsourced.

1B. CUSTOMER REQUIREMENTS

One also needs to have alignment with customer requirements. However, one must know the difference between what looks like a cycle-time reduction requirement and what actually is one. For instance, many companies commonly believe reduced cycle time is needed when a customer complains about late deliveries. However, examining a customer's situation often reveals the customer actually wants the promised delivery date to be met exactly and is less concerned whether the promised date is a little later or not. The customer often has other activities that have to be synchro-

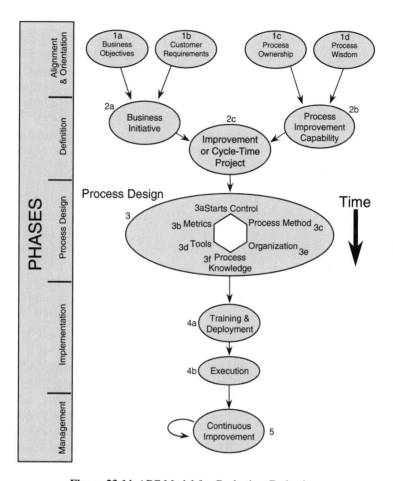

Figure 23-14. APC Model for Cycle-time Reduction

nized carefully with the promised delivery, including site preparation, hook-ups to related systems and equipment, scheduling downtime for normal activities, and so on.

1C. PROCESS OWNERSHIP

A company typically has somewhere between six and a dozen major business processes, such as product development, order acquisition, production, and customer support. Each of these spans various functional organizations and bits of organizational hierarchy. Thus, anyone trying to work on one of these typically is doomed to failure because no one owns the whole business process. The attempt to improve it runs into numerous political and structural roadblocks. A primary message from Michael Hammer (of Business Process Reengineering fame) is to have process owners for these key processes, so someone can make the necessary trade-offs.

1D. PROCESS WISDOM

Many people work full-time in an area and can execute their work reasonably well, but that doesn't mean they have process wisdom. For instance, each of us walks fluidly every day. However, do we understand the physiology and mechanics of walking and are we qualified to undertake a project to improve the efficiency of how we or someone else walks? Similarly, we spend much of our lives in queues, but that doesn't mean we understand queuing theory or are qualified to try to change a process to accelerate throughput through a network of queues. Wisdom is needed beyond conventional or commonsense wisdom, which is often flawed or completely wrong.

Wisdom comes in two forms:

- About improvement processes in general, for example, making processes visible, having metrics with which to measure what is happening in a process and its results, PDCA, running controlled experiments, and so on.
- About the specific type of process being improved, for example, cycle-time reduction.

Several important elements of cycle-time reduction process wisdom were discussed (pages 485-491).

Phase 2. Definition

The top management of an organization needs to be sure Phase 2 elements are in place. Otherwise, cycle-time reduction efforts are likely to fail.

2A. BUSINESS INITIATIVE

For sufficient business reasons, a company or other organization should undertake a business initiative. What the initiative will be is driven by business objectives and customer requirements.

An "initiative" is different from a project. An initiative is a broad effort to improve either in a certain way or the company's overall capability in a certain area. For instance, a company might undertake a companywide initiative to listen to customers better, decrease product defects, or decrease cycle-times.

Initiatives serve to help create alignment in an organization. They are, in essence, the clearly stated strategies by which an organization achieves its business objectives. Initiatives provide the impetus for process improvement projects and help order priority among an organization's alternative improvement projects.

Communication of the initiative around the organization helps ensure that resources will be aligned in support of the process improvement effort. Complete alignment of the management team in support of the initiative is essential.

As mentioned under subphases 1a and 1b, it is important this initiative be appropriate. Cycle-time reduction is not automatically the initiative an organization needs.

2B. PROCESS IMPROVEMENT CAPABILITY

One needs a capable team of people to carry out the improvement. A capable team consists of people who are sufficiently engaged to get the job done, have the skill and wisdom to do the job, and have the authority to do the job. (This is our definition of being "empowered.")

A process owner needs to ensure the team has the above characteristics.

2C. IMPROVEMENT OR CYCLE-TIME PROJECT

Once the elements of Phase 1 (business objectives, customer requirements, process ownership, and process wisdom) have been addressed and in turn the Business Initiative (2a) and Process Improvement Capability (2b) elements are in place, we are ready to define the project (or projects) required to improve something, and that something may be cycle-time.

For instance, we might decide to improve the cycle time of our new product development process, or we might decide to improve the cycle time of our order acquisition process. The definition of the project would likely include: schedule, staffing, metrics, current values of metrics (if available), expected improvements, budget, customer requirements, outline of approach, etc.

The improvement effort is going to result in a changed process design, for example for new product development; and that process design needs to deal with several sub-elements, such as those enumerated in Phase three.

Phase 3. Process Design

The CQM cycle-time study group initially concluded that the relevant sub-components of a good process were the four elements shown at the sides of the hexagon in Figure 23-14: metrics (3b), process method (3c), tools (3d), and organization (3e). However, from the study and his own work Rasmussen has concluded that two other important elements were missing from the study group's first formulation and he added these to the APC model: starts control (3a) and process knowledge (3f).

3A. STARTS CONTROL

Starts control refers to methods to prevent starting more projects than the organization has resources for, or can coordinate and manage efficiently. This is probably the most important design element. See page 491 for more on this topic.

3B. METRICS

The benefit of process changes, tools, organizational changes, and so on, cannot be accurately assessed without metrics. Obviously, we need metrics, and many people start improvement efforts there. However, we must not stop with metrics—they alone will not make improvements. Thus, the model being described in this paper treats metrics as only one of several components.

Also, we must find relevant metrics that help us actually *improve* in ways that actually *help* our business.

When one starts looking at improving a process such as the new product development process, it is shocking how few metrics one has and how poorly defined they are. People are not able to agree on things as simple as when a project started or when it was initially scheduled to be complete. One needs appropriate and well-defined metrics. One may be able to do some retroactive construction, but first one needs to begin to keep them.

Reinertsen recommends creating explicit quantitative models that we can use to make trade-offs, for the process (e.g., cost of work in process or engineering change orders) and across the whole business (e.g., cost of development versus time-to-market) [237, chapter 2 and pages 201-202].

As consultant Brad Goldense noted in his presentation to the study group, such models allow predictions to be made which can be compared with actuals to improve the model (and its dynamics), so the predictions will better match reality going forward. Goldense also emphasizes looking at predictive as well as reactive metrics— "fundamental laws" which can be found by looking at trends across many projects.

As already noted, the metrics need to address systemwide effects, not just local optimizations. The metrics also have to be monitored and used often enough to actually operate the system. For instance, Cisco monitors many new product development metrics on a weekly basis.

3C. PROCESS METHOD

The process method is the process to be followed, for instance, the product development process. This needs to be made explicit and will vary depending on the type of business one is in: some companies (e.g., a drug company with massive investment in each step of developing a new product) may find traditional phase review processes (such as were promoted heavily as best practice in the early 1990s) as appropriate. Other companies may find other process methods more appropriate.

The first step is to make the process visible. This involves thinking about and documenting the actual process and, at least generally, whether it is an existing process or a proposed new process. Improving something intangible is virtually impossible.

The process method can be documented at many different levels. The level of documentation needs to be in touch with the way the people undertaking the process actually do their work. Finally, one can have different perspectives when thinking about and documenting a process. One can look at the process in terms of material flow, the information flow, the dependencies of the process, or in terms of who is making commitments to whom.

At the most basic level, a process must be partitioned into phases. Give serious thought to having greater granularity of steps within phases you typically use in processes. Greater granularity provides increased visibility (and, thus, increased understanding) of the process, which allows earlier feedback of problems or other process improving information. Greater granularity also dumps smaller chunks into queues. For instance, the typical new product development phase review process has four or five phases, each of which is months long, and has a phase review at the end of each. Such very ungranular phase review processes tend to increase cycle times.

Some steps will vary widely from cycle to cycle of a process. For instance, Cisco has different versions of their new product development process for different classes of customers. The metrics for these situations need to be categorized appropriately.

3D. TOOLS

The real benefit of tools cannot be assessed unless a process and metrics are in place. We also need to run controlled experiments while collecting metrics data to understand which tools matter most, if at all.

Many tools might be used. Some tools are generally relevant to cycle-time reduction (or are even more broadly applicable), such as automated data and metric collection, project scheduling tools, resource allocation aids, methods of doing cost versus speed trade-offs, tools from system dynamics, and the dependency structure matrix [83]. Some tools are relevant to specific application areas, for instance, for new product development: voice of the customer methods, computer-aided design tools, simulators, test configurations, quality function deployment, design for manufacturing, and design for assembly. The trick is to choose tools that will genuinely help increase effectiveness and efficiency in a given situation.

A corollary to choosing the right tools is to avoid using inappropriate but available tools that can lead you astray. Two common examples of available but often counter-productive tools are:

- Traditional cost accounting, which often drives people to optimize irrelevant metrics (such a subprocess utilization) at the expense of the overall system throughput—this is a substantial part of the message Goldratt conveys in [116].
- Some process scheduling and Gantt charting tools make scheduling necessary slack times at the correct points in a process difficult. They also make calculating the probabilities of various combinations of events and thus total project results difficult.

3E. ORGANIZATION

Organization includes reporting, roles, how teams are set up, whether they are "heavyweight" (teams that have the necessary people and authority to make wide-ranging changes, as appropriate), and so forth. Unfortunately, the first step most companies take when they are dissatisfied with results is to reorganize, since reorganization is easier than doing what needs to be changed. However, this is a case of changing the process around before understanding the problem, what Deming called "tampering." Consequently, reorganizing typically doesn't improve things and may make them worse (since at minimum it is disruptive and may result in key talent being reorganized away). Rummler and Brache report that by the time they get called to consult, the company has often already reorganized a couple of times with no effect.

Organization should be derived from the process: form follows function. First one should work on the process and then reorganize to match the process. Organization should probably be the last of the six sub-elements of process design to be worked on.

Many organizational issues need to be considered:

- The organization needs to reduce paralleling of both people and projects, and the organization must stop running at over 100 percent capacity.
- The organization needs to take care about putting safety factors into tasks and to avoid incentive systems that encourage people to put safety factors into tasks.
- Management needs to avoid rewarding getting a task done on time because this often lengthens the time estimates people give for a task and, thus, ultimately the time to do the task since all slack inevitably is used.
- Management needs to be appropriately involved—making sure teams have appropriate staffing, removing obstacles to success, and so on.
- Management must make sure methods are available for sharing knowledge, both explicit and tacit.
- The organization needs to sort out how customers and users will be involved early in projects.
- The organization needs to understand the alternatives to heavyweight teams, which is the assumed answer these days by many companies.

Brad Goldense in his presentation to the study group supported the viewpoint stated above that the organization should be derived from the process and other design elements. Specifically, he noted many people talk about various kinds of teams, but process is more important. He continued, saying that an appropriate process is necessary for teams to operate in a stable way.

3F. PROCESS KNOWLEDGE

Once a new or improved process (for instance, for new product development) has been designed, it will not be perfect and may have some severe glitches that seemed like a good idea at design time but are not in practice. Each time the process is used, new things are learned about what does and does not work well and about various possible improvements. The process design needs to include a mechanism for capturing this new insight and making it accessible to future process users.

Some learning from executing the process is folded back into the design of the process through continuous improvement. However some knowledge from past cycles of a process will not affect the design of the process but will be useful to future cycles of the process. This can include hints, known pitfalls, or work that can be reused in a future similar cycle of the process. This information must be made available in an organized way to future process users.

This mechanism might be written product design standards (such as APC uses). It might be a database (such as what Cisco creates for each project to go with its design process). It might be some other mechanism to "socialize" improved practice. APC has created templates of the records that need to be kept for each project, so that people know the format well enough to access the process knowledge.

Phase 4. Implementation

4A. TRAINING AND DEPLOYMENT

Once a new or improved process has been created (for instance, for new product development), then people have to be trained in the method, which must be deployed throughout the primary organization concerned with it (R&D, in the case of new product development) as well as throughout the rest of the organization as appropriate (e.g., manufacturing, sales, and customer support).

4B. EXECUTION

Finally, one is ready to use the process, for instance, to develop the next new product.

Phase 5. Continuous Improvement

Phases 1 and 2 of this model assure that the company is designing an improved process in an area that actually matters to the company and that improving the process is feasible. In addition, the parts of these phases relating to having a process improvement capability should also enable the ongoing continuous improvement work. Phase 3 is about the design of the new or improved process, and Phase 4 brings the new or improved process into use. These phases also should have been designed to enable ongoing improvements and deployment.

Phase 5, continuous improvement, recognizes that no process is ever right the first time and typically applies to the stage 3 process design and the phase 4 training and deployment system. Even if the process was right when designed, circumstances change. The initial process design, in fact, is just a theory about what should work. The real learning about what does work comes from trying the process and then adapting it.

Every company that undertakes improvement of a key business process reports that it should have deployed it sooner, gotten real world feedback sooner, and thus improved the process sooner. However, the natural human tendency is to try to be sure that such an important process is really right before deployment.

Another natural human tendency is to put many controls on change of such an important business process, so that it cannot be changed casually. This inhibits PDCA of the process. It also convinces the people we want to use the process that the process exists in some sort of dream world that doesn't match real life issues (since the process won't be perfect upon first release and what was right will change), and they will repeatedly dismiss the process as irrelevant.

APC has a set of "process coordinators" who are responsible for the design and deployment of their new product development process. Each of these individuals has the authority to change the process immediately. This helps convince the users that the process is relevant because when a user points out a problem and the coordinator sees the validity of the user's point, the coordinator can say "You're right; let me change it." These process coordinators report to the senior engineering managers (who aren't authorized to change the process). Incidentally, the APC engineers spontaneously started a "users group" for their new product development process as a forum to discuss the process and provide feedback.

More global application of the APC model

Element 2c of the model could be parameterized to apply to "Improvement of <any capability> in <any business process>," and the rest of the model would still apply. For instance, oval 2c could be written "Improvement of Cost in Acquisition of Orders" or "Improvement of Quality in Production of Product."

NOTES

1. Benchmarking was developed by Xerox and six sigma and cycle-time reduction by Motorola.
2. There are newer books [34, 50, 272], but this was the first thorough treatment of this contemporary definition of benchmarking. A brief introduction to benchmarking was also provided in [25, pages 19–24].
3. Benchmarking evolved separately from proactive problem solving, "voice of the customer," and quality function deployment, so the vocabulary differs. Critical success factors can be described as important unmet quality requirements of the internal (or external) customers of the function being benchmarked. Enablers are the means for satisfying quality requirements at world-class levels. Benchmarking customer satisfaction directly as well as operationally defined quality variables is a standard part of full-blown quality function deployment, as taught by the American Supplier Institute, for example.
4. Recall that, generally speaking, a matrix diagram is used to identify the least number of means to accomplish the requirements. Across the top are options for means of accomplishing organizational change and improvement activities and infrastructure. Only benchmarking is shown; to use such a matrix to make choices about a companywide organizational change and improvement program, one would include 7 QC steps and 7 QC tools, proactive improvement and the 7 tools for management and planning, customer visitation, and the other elements described throughout this book. Along the left side are requirements that a company might have for an organizational change and improvement program to succeed. These issues will vary from company to company.
5. We start with this summary of Motorola's six sigma program in 1990, because it was first. In the years since, six sigma has been widely deployed in other companies. This spread of the method will be sketched in a later subsection.
6. Six sigma was developed by the late Bill Smith, whom we met in 1990, and others at Motorola. Bill Smith was a driving force for six sigma at Motorola.
7. See, e.g., [131]. These defect ratios are different from the ratios for various multiples of 1 standard deviation because Motorola's definition for six sigma includes the possibility of a shift in the mean of the distribution (this is also briefly explained in the first subsection below). See also [129]. Mikel Harry, also at

Motorola and its Six Sigma Research Institute and later a participant in ABB's six sigma program, is now at the Six Sigma Academy, along with Rich Schroeder who followed the same path from Motorola to ABB to the Six Sigma Academy.

8. However, the theoretical calculations must be done at a low level, not centrally; the staff will reject centrally determined goals. Thus, six sigma at Motorola involved an improvement process that was operated locally.

9. See the example of baggage handling in [33].

10. GE's 1998 annual report gives a cost of six sigma of $500M and benefit of six sigma of $1.3B; the 1999 annual report gives a cost of $500M and benefit of $2.1B.

11. A longer summary of the history of six sigma and Harry and Schroeder's involvement may be found in [192]. Their current book on six sigma is [130]. A short introduction to the modern practice of six sigma is [33].

12. In 1999, AlliedSignal merged with Honeywell and now operates under the Honeywell name.

13. We were told the story of six sigma at AlliedSignal and Honeywell by Chris Mastro. Chris took our class at MIT while on leave from AlliedSignal, returned to AlliedSignal to be a "black belt," and is now Director of Six Sigma Plus for Performance Polymers. He is responsible for increasing deployment of "Six Sigma Plus" across all functional areas of his business and representing his business on the corporate Six Sigma Plus Executive Council, the senior steering team that drives quality and productivity for Honeywell.

14. We see certain parallels between DMAIC and the 7 steps: approximately, D=step 1, M=some of step 2, A=the rest of step 2 and step 3, I=steps 4, 5, and some of 6, C=the rest of step 6 and step 7.

15. From the beginning, Motorola had facilitators known as "black belts."

16. People become master black belts, black belts, and green belts by completing the training and getting certified upon completion of an improvement project with business impact. Certification is a requirement for everyone. All "belts" are expected to complete at least one project per year after becoming certified.

17. Quality, like safety, is the responsibility of all employees, not just people in a formal quality role. Six sigma is driven by each of AlliedSignal's functional leaders.

18. Thus, it appears that six sigma at AlliedSignal correlates well to the methods of customer focus, continuous improvement, and total participation described in this book, with more emphasis on the use of sophisticated statistical tools than we provide, although we support their use by appropriately trained people.

19. In October 2000, GE announced an offer to buy Honeywell.

20. All but the first sentence of this paragraph are according to [33].

21. In Shoji Shiba's experience, Toyota calls its activities TQM, not Lean Production as we have been told in the United States.

22. We have always assumed use of more sophisticated statistical tools by those who knew them.

23. See [266], Shigeo Shingo's seminal work on setup reduction theory and methods.

24. Yogesh Parikh, for many years with CQM founding member Digital and now with CQM member Mercury Computer Systems, introduced CQM to the AΔT method about 1991 or 1992; he also briefed us on AΔT's history.

25. Thus, when actually using this method, companies should perhaps find a different name for "non-value-added" work.

26. The participants in all or part of this study group were the following: Bob Abramson, Open Market; Mark Braun, Boston University; Anthony Carroccio, Health Alliance; Stephen Denker, GTE Internetworking; Stephen Graves, MIT; Tom Hennings, Plastic Moldings; Robert Herrick, Health Alliance; John Hillerich, III, Hillerich & Bradsby; Verne Johnson, Portman Equipment; Scott Jones, Servend; Thomas Lee, CQM; Brad Nelson, Teradyne; Richard Paynting, CTI-Cryogenics; Neil Rasmussen, APC; Richard Rodriguez, Zaring National; Carl Roos, Franciscan Health System; Steve Rosenthal, Boston University; Ed Starr, GTE Internetworking; David Walden, CQM; and Toby Woll, CQM.

27. We define "process wisdom" more fully below (1d, page 414). A more detailed discussion of the process wisdom topics below can be found in [235].

28. This curve is calculated by dividing total fixed costs of the plant by the fraction of utilization.

29. Curves such as shown in the figure may be found in any book on queuing theory, for example, [169, page 98].

30. This example was suggested to us by [237, page 46].

31. Reinertsen draws a similar figure [237, page 48] and provides additional discussion of it.

32. There are methods of controlling the queues. Reinertson's book lists (and any queuing theory book will list) increasing capacity, managing demand, reducing variation in the components of the system, and putting in place control systems of various types.

33. See also [117, page 126] for Goldratt's version of this figure.

34. A more general version of Goldratt's argument sketched here may be found in [269, page 200 of 1991 first edition]. It argues that any time you dilute resources you cause economic damage. This dilution of resources can come from multi-tasking the same resources or from simultaneously supporting too many projects even when they are fully staffed.

35. Note, we are not arguing against doing projects or subprojects in parallel as in concurrent engineering. We are worried about time-sharing the same resources across several projects. Each project or subproject needs its resources to be available when needed and not to be switched away from it at inappropriate times.

36. See the comment from Reinertsen on page 19 of [235] for an important exception.

24

Hoshin Management

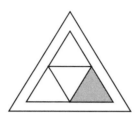

Hoshin management aligns the activities of people throughout the company so the company can achieve key goals and react quickly to a changing environment. Hoshin management involves all of the managers in a coordinated way in the annual planning cycle of the company. Thus, it provides an important strategy for total participation as well as fulfilling its obvious purpose of company alignment.

In this chapter we describe one form of how hoshin management works, relate hoshin management to other management methods, and conclude with a case study of the use of hoshin management at Analog Devices.

24.1 HOSHIN MANAGEMENT AND ITS PARTS

Aspects of what has become hoshin management were tested by a number of Japanese companies in the second half of the 1960s. Among these companies were Toyota, Komatsu, and Bridgestone Tire Company. By the late 1960s and early 1970s, hoshin management had taken shape. It spread rapidly and became one of the major components of TQM in Japan.

Hoshin management was the first attempt at business breakthrough rather than process breakthrough which dealt systematically with process improvement across a company to produce desired business results. Management by objectives (MBO)—also an attempt at business breakthrough—was not connected to the processes.

Hewlett-Packard (HP), which knew about hoshin management through its Japanese Yokogawa HP (YHP) activity, was perhaps the first U.S. company to employ hoshin management as a key part of its ongoing management system. Over many years of use, HP revised the methods of hoshin management and adapted them to U.S. company culture. In particular, HP developed a set of forms, process, and overall structure for hoshin management that a number of other U.S. companies have learned. This transfer of the "technology" of hoshin management happened through HP leaders moving to other companies and taking the methods with them and by leaders from HP graciously teaching the methods to leaders from other companies. Several CQM companies have gotten important insights about hoshin management from HP; its hoshin management system is discussed in detail in [270], and the HP case study in Chapter 26 (starting on page 577) also touches on it.

What we call hoshin management the Japanese call hoshin kanri. Other English speaking authors have called it management by policy or policy deployment, probably following a Japanese translation of policy deployment. However, "policy" as used in "policy deployment" means something different than what is meant in a typical U.S. company when one talks of policy. We will follow the current convention of calling it hoshin management.[1]

Hoshin Management for Alignment

Hoshin management has three alignment purposes:

- It aims to align all the people throughout the company toward the key company goals, using indirect rather than direct enforcement, creating a sense of urgency; thus, even hourly employees are influenced to choose activities with strategically important objectives.
- It aims to align all jobs and tasks, whether routine work or improvement work, focusing and coordinating efforts and resources toward the key company goals in order to create breakthroughs.
- It aims to bring the company's goals and activities quickly and effectively into alignment with rapid societal or environmental changes.

Figure 24-1 illustrates the power of alignment. In part A of the figure, the people and jobs are poorly aligned; the result is a total force that is limited and possibly ill-coordinated with key company goals. In part B, people and jobs are properly aligned; the result is a strong force aimed toward company goals. Part C shows that as environmental changes occur, company goals must change quickly and people and jobs realign to these new goals.

Hoshin management also has another purpose (discussed in greater detail in Chapter 25): to force managers to run the PDCA cycle themselves as part of their routine job and, therefore, to develop themselves as managers.

Components, Phases, and Elements of Hoshin Management

The main components of hoshin management are shown in Figure 24-2.[2]

As shown at top left of the model, the company's long-term and mid-term vision and plans must be adjusted in consideration of environmental changes. From the mid-term plan, annual hoshins are developed.[3,4] Hoshins are statements of the desired outcome for the year, plus the means of accomplishing the desired outcomes and measuring the accomplishment. Each hoshin ideally will include the five elements shown in Figure 24-3[5] on page 506. An example of a complete hoshin is shown in Figure 24-4 on page 506.

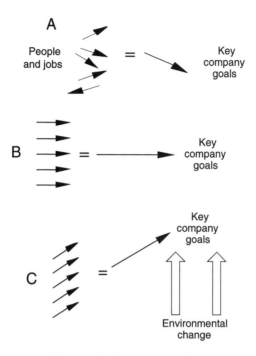

Figure 24-1. Power of Alignment

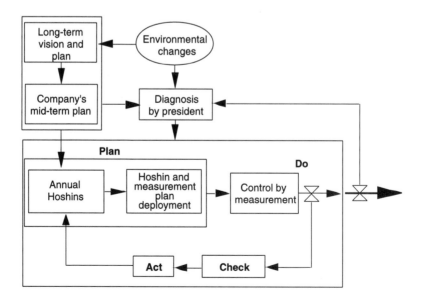

Figure 24-2. Hoshin Management

Hoshin = statement of desired outcome for next year
  + focused means
  + metrics to measure progress
  + target values for metrics
  + deadline date

Figure 24-3. Five Elements of a Hoshin

The primary, or top-level, annual hoshins are then deployed (or cascaded) throughout the organization. In other words, a hierarchy of subgoals and means for accomplishing and measuring them is developed, all in alignment with the top-level hoshins. At each lower level, the hoshins have the same format but are more specific.

Next, a hoshin monitoring (or control by measurement) plan is made for monthly monitoring of whether the goals and subgoals are being accomplished and the planned means for accomplishing them are being executed; corrective action if they are not. Once the hoshins are deployed and the control by measurement plan is in place, these plans are executed. When it is time to plan for the next year, the data on which means were carried out and what was accomplished are analyzed to discover what needs to be improved for the next cycle, and decisions are made on appropriate actions. This information is fed into the planning for the next year. Also on a yearly basis, the president diagnoses the hoshin management system and suggests improvements relating to the system's effectiveness, any environmental changes that have occurred, and the company's long-term and mid-term plans.

Statement of desired   Daily practice of
outcome for next year = market-in concept

Focused means = Create attractive product by
                  improving market research;

                  Increase customer satisfaction of
                  our product by using quality tables;

                  Assume on-time delivery by improving
                  processes;

                  Improve quality of production proces
                  by using statistical process control (SPC).

Metric to measure progress = On-time delivery rate

Target value for metric = 100 percent

Deadline date = March 1999

Figure 24-4. Example Hoshin

Proactive, Reactive, and Control Phases in Hoshin Management

Hoshin management includes the problem-solving approaches enumerated in the WV model—proactive, reactive, and control—as described below.

In the proactive phase, the long-term and mid-term vision and plans are adjusted in consideration of environmental changes, and the hoshin management system is itself managed, diagnosed, and improved.

The reactive phase is best thought of as a year-long PDCA cycle:

- Plan: Develop annual top-level hoshins, deploy the hoshins down the organization, and develop the control by measurement plan.
- Do: Carry out the hoshins over the course of the year.
- Check: Analyze why hoshins were not accomplished. Did the planned means not work, or were the planned means not carried out?
- Act: Decide what to improve for next year.

The control phase is carried out over the course of the year. The company uses the control by measurement plan to monitor the results and controls the results and the means so that the planned means are, in fact, carried out and corrective action is taken when the means and results are not as planned.

As Figure 24-5 shows, the proactive, reactive, and control phases of hoshin management overlap each other. Proactive and reactive overlap at the top-level annual hoshins. Reactive and control overlap where the control by measurement plan is used to monitor things over the course of the year, and the control phase is the Do part of the reactive phase.

Thus, PDCA cycles exist in hoshin management. First, an inner PDCA cycle exists in the control portion of hoshin management. Second, an annual reactive PDCA

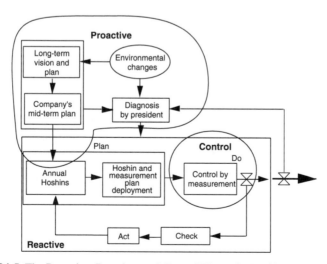

Figure 24-5. The Proactive, Reactive, and Control Phases in Hoshin Management

cycle is used. Third, an outer PDCA cycle starts from the long-term and mid-term plan, goes through the annual deployment and execution (do), and then does the diagnostic check and act to improve in the hoshin management system. These three PDCA cycles are consistent with the overall goal of the company.

Figure 24-5 also illustrates the following five phases of hoshin management, which we'll describe in turn:

1. Strategic planning and setting the hoshin (proactive)
2. Hoshin deployment
3. Monitoring the hoshin; controlling with metrics (control)
4. Check and act (reactive)
5. President's diagnosis

Phase 1—Strategic Planning and Setting the Hoshin (Proactive)

The current operational management system of a company and the way people are currently doing their work should ideally provide a continuing degree of improvement in, for example, customer satisfaction (see top left of Figure 24-6).[6] However, analysis of circumstances may reveal that greater rates of improvement are needed. In such cases, companies must analyze the difference between what the existing management system can provide and what they need. They can pinpoint the root factors that prevent the current system from improving fast enough and plan a solution. Solutions will employ standard tools and analogues of the 7 steps (numbered 1–7 in Figure 9-1, page 123 of Chapter 9). The 7 management and planning tools (described in Chapter 13, page 213) will also be used. When the solution is deployed, it may have two parts. First, it may be necessary to improve what people are currently doing; second, it may be necessary for people to do new things. In either case, a revised system of routine work should provide the needed rate of improvement of customer satisfaction.

Hoshin management provides a systematic mechanism for calculating the difference between what a company can do and what it must do. It determines what improvements are necessary, and insures that solutions cascade through the organization so that people's routine work actually changes. Consider the schematic representation of the annual hoshin planning process in Figure 24-7 on page 508.

The past (what it has been doing), the environment, and the vision of the future dictate what a company must do. To address the past, a company has the facts (what is), if it has the discipline to use them. The reactive, PDCA, portion of the hoshin management model deals with what is. The proactive portion of the hoshin management model addresses the environment (a given which the company needs to discover and address) and future vision (what is wished to be or will be). Once a company knows what is needed, it must focus people and jobs throughout the company according to what they can contribute to those needs. The hoshin plan and its deployment does this—it gives people the tools they need to change the way they work.

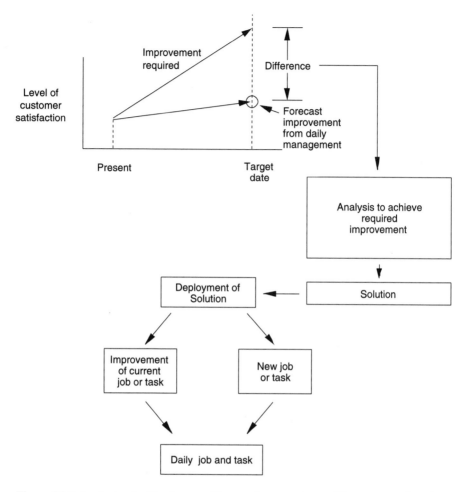

Figure 24-6. Analyzing the Gap between Forecast Improvement and Improvement Required

The part of the hoshin planning process that deals with the past will be discussed later in this chapter. Dealing with the future is an essential phase in strategic planning, and a substantial component of leadership is planning for change. There is a large body of existing theory and practice of planning for change. For the purposes of this chapter, we will assume the reader is familiar with some method of strategic planning and can imagine using that method for constructing the mid-term plan required by hoshin management. In Chapter 29, we describe one specific method for creating the mid-term plan (see the section beginning on page 680).

Here is an example of a hierarchy of goals we heard about in a presentation given in 1991 by Michio Ikawa, president of NEC Shizuoka [140]. NEC Shizuoka is a part of NEC, and all NEC companies have the same corporate identity: "Computers & Communication" [229]. Based on the NEC corporate identity, NEC Shizuoka developed its

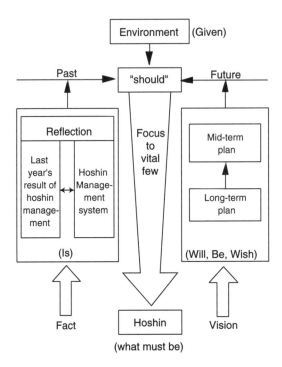

Figure 24-7. The Annual Hoshin Planning Process

company philosophy. From its company philosophy, NEC Shizuoka developed its Vision 2001, or mid-term plan. Vision 2001 is the basis of the annual plan. All of this goal setting can be charted as shown in Table 24-1, which includes the annual goals derived from the longer-term goals.

Another example of a hierarchy of goals can be found in the case study of hoshin management at Analog Devices, see Table 24-6 (page 535) and the description that surrounds the table. Analog Devices' method of strategic analysis and hoshin setting is also described in the first two steps of their case study (pages 534–537).

Phase 2—Hoshin Deployment

Once a company has obtained the annual hoshin through analysis of the future and past, it is time to deploy the hoshin throughout the organization (see left half of middle of Figure 24-5, page 507).

Hoshin deployment has three fundamental aspects: moving down and up the ladder of abstraction, basing the deployment on facts and analysis, and deploying metrics to measure how well the means have been carried out and the targets achieved. (Steps 2–5, pages 536–540, of the Analog Devices case study illustrate its way of deploying the president's hoshin.)

Table 24-1. NEC Shizuoka's Goal-Setting Process

Corporate Identity	Computers & Communication
⇓	
Company Philosophy	1. quality first 2. customer first 3. development of employee capabilities
⇓	
Vision 2001 (mid-term plan)	1. total sales $1.4 billion • company to focus on office automation • convey quality-first attitude to all employees • accelerate new product development and factory automation 2. etc. 3. etc.
⇓	

Annual Plan (1990)	1. most important policy
	• full implementation of quality-first attitude
	• quick introduction and adaptation toward small volume and large variety production system
	• etc.
	2. target (goal)
	• cost down
	  – implementation of factory automation requires pre-analysis
	  – with no-people production system
	• etc.
	3. guideline for management's behavior
	• role was production only
	• role should be planning design and production

Moving Down and Up the Ladder of Abstraction

Hoshin management moves down and up the ladder of abstraction in several ways. For instance, you can move from a long-term vision to an annual plan and deploy the management hierarchy (see Figure 24-8).

You can also first move down and then up the hierarchy of processes to understand the targets and to analyze the root causes of worse-than-expected performance [174]. For instance, Professor Kogure illustrated the machine as a higher-level process that is in turn set up by a lower-level process, consisting of operators, materials, machines, and methods (see Figure 24-9).

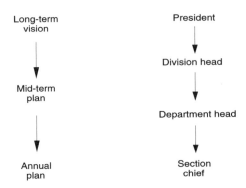

Figure 24-8. Deployment Down the Hierarchy

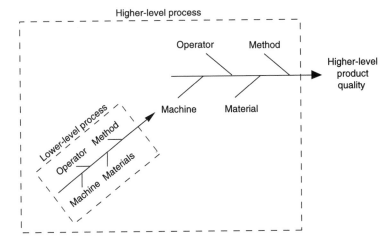

Figure 24-9. Deployment from Lower-level to Higher-level Process

Basing the Deployment on Facts and Analysis

A simple example of the deployment of hoshins from the president to the functional organizations will follow. Each of the hoshins has the standard form

Outcome by Means: Metric: Target: Deadline

The units of the metrics typically change at every level in the deployment and may differ from one hoshin to the next at the same level. Deployment will descend many levels in the organization, perhaps to the section level.[7]

Suppose, through analysis of the past, the environment, and the vision for the future, the president concludes that an annual hoshin should be "reduce costs 20 percent by decreasing the length of business cycles." Thus, the outcome by means is *reduce costs by decreasing length of business cycles*, the metric is *percent decrease*, and the target percentage is *20* (for this example we'll exclude the deadline).

The next step is to deploy relevant hoshins to each of the functional divisions below the president (see Figure 24-10).

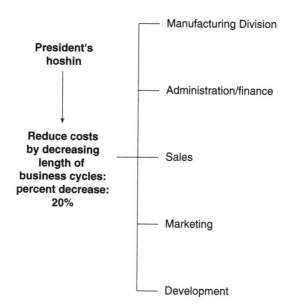

Figure 24-10. Deploying Hoshins to the Functional Divisions

Facts and analysis are essential to the deployment of a hoshin from one level down to the next. Analysis of the facts about key goals focuses hoshin deployment on the vital few.

The president and division heads must determine what prevents the company from achieving the key goals, and the president's subordinates must do the same. In other words, to deploy the targets and means sensibly, you must stratify the market, customers, products, sources of possible cost reduction, and so on. For example, you analyze which products have the biggest sales, which products grew most last year, and where cycle time can be reduced (see Figure 24-11).

The president and the division heads gather and stratify the data and then select the biggest problem at the next level for hoshin deployment (see Figure 24-12).

At the lower levels, this analysis begins with the question, "What in our division prevents us from addressing our superior's proposed hoshin?" For instance, in the above example, the manufacturing division leader might ask, "What prevents us from decreasing the length of our business cycles?" Once again, a systematic, fact-based analysis is done, using, for example, Pareto diagrams, Ishikawa diagrams, and a 7 steps PDCA process. As a result of this analysis, the manufacturing director might conclude that the root cause of manufacturing's inability to achieve the president's hoshin is

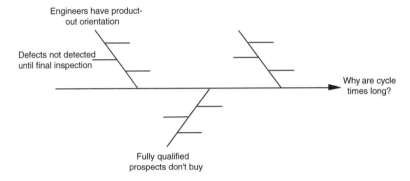

Figure 24-11. Analysis of Facts about Key Goals

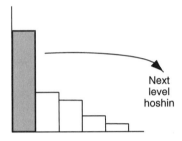

Figure 24-12. Stratifying to Select Problems for the Next Level Hoshin

"unresponsive procurement and inventory system." Similarly, each functional area would determine what prevents its own achievement of the president's hoshin.

Figure 24-13 shows what might result from each function's analysis of what prevents achievement of the president's hoshin.

From this analysis, each functional manager can draft appropriate hoshins deploying the president's hoshin to the functional area. Facts and analysis are also used to develop the hoshins, as well as the means and targets. Table 24-2 shows hoshins that might be developed on the basis of data given in Figure 24-13.

The system of hoshin deployment described here focuses on finding the process to achieve the desired outcome. In this sense, it is very powerful. However, it has a weakness in that it fails to make clear what each means contributes to the higher-level outcome. Hoshin management, as it has developed in Japan, has a remedy for this weakness. We will return to this issue later in the chapter.

Let's take this deployment down another level, for instance, in the sales function. The sales hoshin in the example we've been following is "Decrease average sales cycle 30 percent by decreasing qualified prospects who don't buy." The sales division contains the direct sales and sales support departments. Each of these departments must gather the facts and analyze what prevents them from achieving the sales hoshin. Their analysis might resemble Figure 24-14.

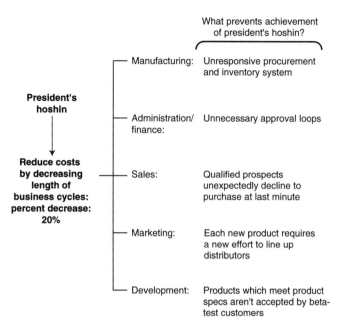

Figure 24-13. Function-Level Analysis of Barriers to Achieving President's Hoshin

You also use facts to align the deployment process. At a given level in the deployment, the manager's hoshins indicate a desired outcome and the means deemed appropriate to achieve the desired outcome. These hoshins are passed to the manager's reports, who draft hoshins supportive of those received from above. However, they may have disagreements. Between levels, managers use facts to verify the validity and

Table 24-2. Development of Functional Division Hoshins

Function	What prevents achievement of President's Hoshin	Functional Division Hoshin
Manufacturing	Unresponsive procurement and inventory system	Decrease manufacturing cycle time by implementing JIT: percent decrease: 50%
Admin/finance	Unnecessary approval loops	Decrease key admin and finance cycles by flowcharting processes and eliminating NVA work: percent decrease: 40%
Sales	Qualified prospects unexpectedly decline to purchase at last minute	Decrease average sales cycle by decreasing qualified prospects who don't buy: percent decrease: 30%
Marketing	Each new product requires a new effort to line up distributors	Decrease average time to release a new product by creating strategic alliances: percent decrease: 50%
Development	Products which meet product spec aren't accepted by beta-test customers	Decrease average time to successful product release by increasing engineers' understanding of customer context: percent decrease: 30%

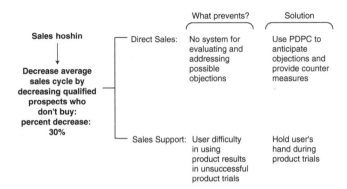

Figure 24-14. Analysis of Barriers to Achieving Sales Hoshin

feasibility of hoshins or to adjust them. These facts are conveyed back and forth on standard data sheets and through face-to-face discussions. This process of aligning the hoshins through the use of factual analysis is known as "catchball" in Japan. Catchball is indicated by the following symbol: ⓧ. Catchball is not a negotiation of conflicting desires; catchball reconciles the plan with facts. The catchball occurs throughout the hierarchy (as shown in Figure 24-15). Analog Devices has provided an excellent example of fact-based catchball (see the figures and tables of steps 2 and 3 of the Analog Devices case study, pages 535–539).

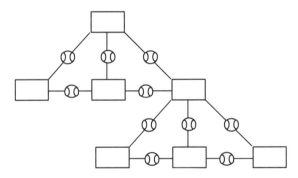

Figure 24-15. Aligning Hoshins through Catchball

Once the analysis of facts and catchball is complete at all levels, a deployment results (see Figure 24-16).

How much guidance should a manager provide to subordinates in deploying hoshins? In his book [216], Masao Nemoto gives the following guidelines for managers deploying hoshins:

- Targets should be challenging but persuasive.
- Local issues need not be included as hoshins.
- Include as hoshins the few issues that will get special attention.

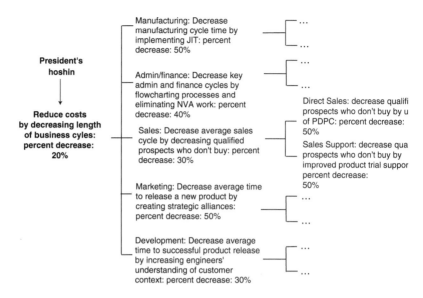

Figure 24-16. Deployment to the Next Level

- The superior must provide implementation plans (means) for key hard items.
- The superior provides "points to consider" for a few items.
- Subordinates develop the rest of the means themselves.

While we have shown the deployment above as a tree, the deployment is typically documented in an alignment matrix (see Figure 24-17, page 518).

In the figure, the dotted circles indicate that hoshins a and b of the subordinate are aligned with hoshin B of the superior, and hoshin c of the subordinate is aligned with hoshin C of the superior. In this case, no subordinate has a hoshin related to the superior's hoshin A. Focusing on the vital few at every level may mean that subordinates do not address all of the superior's hoshin goals.

Such alignment charts can be easily extended to summarize the hoshins of all of the subordinates of a manager, as in Figure 24-18 on page 518. In this example all three subordinates have hoshins that are aligned with the superior's hoshin C, and subordinates 1 and 2 have hoshins that are aligned with the superior's hoshin B. Subordinate 1 does not have a hoshin related to the superior's hoshin A, but that may not be a concern because subordinates 2 and 3 do have hoshins that are aligned with A.

Deploying Metrics

A third critical element of the deployment phase (along with moving down and up the ladder of abstraction and using facts and analysis) is use of metrics on the plan execution and its results. The nature of these metrics can be made clear only through an examination of their use in the third (and next) phase of hoshin management.

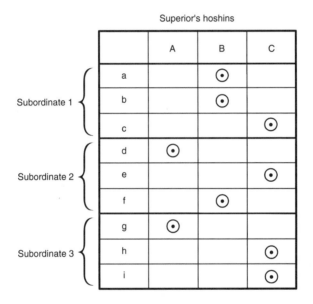

Figure 24-17. Hoshin Alignment Matrix

Figure 24-18. Extended Alignment Matrix

Phase 3—Monitoring the Hoshin; Controlling with Metrics (Control)

This phase of hoshin management is shown in the right middle of Figure 24-5 (page 507). Each of the hoshins deployed includes a metric and target (see Figure 24-19).

The metrics are monitored and compared against the target. Although the metrics and targets may also be shown in alignment matrices, Figure 24-19 shows them as little meters superimposed on the deployment tree. In addition to the meters representing metrics to monitor the outcome, the illustration also shows meters (metrics and targets) to help control execution of the means.

These metrics and targets permit the results and means to be monitored over the course of the year and corrective action to be taken as appropriate (see Figure 24-20). This is SDCA, where the "standard" is the planned means. Also, the metrics and targets tell you at year's end (or sooner) whether the failure to achieve the desired out-

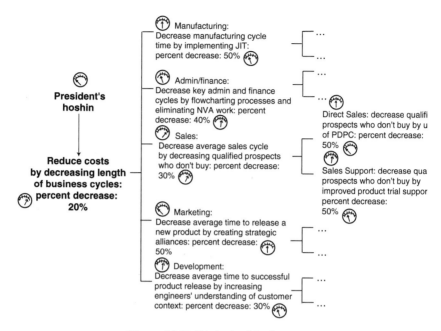

Figure 24-19. Deploying Metrics

come was due to malfunctioning of the planned means or to a failure to carry out the planned means. If the means were carried out, then the process capability (planned improvements to product results) is inadequate and discrepancies between planned and actual results should initiate PDCA. In other words, the metrics allow you to monitor and control processes, even the process of changing the processes themselves.

The measurements of means and targets are monitored monthly, and actions are taken if the measurements are outside prespecified limits. A document specifying which actions to take in the case of unexpected measurements is called a measurement implementation plan or control by measure plan.

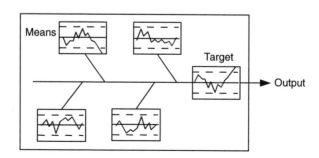

Figure 24-20. Using Metrics to Monitor Results and Means

An example of a measurement implementation plan from Analog Devices can be found in Table 24-10 (page 542).

Unifying Routine Work with Hoshin Management

The purpose of hoshin management is to align every person and every activity so they address the key company goals. If people's routine work is not in alignment with the top-level hoshins, assignments must be modified appropriately. Managers have considerable discretion over which activities they emphasize, and the "natural" balance of activities may or may not support the current hoshins well. Thus, a necessary and fundamental aspect of hoshin management is analysis of the routine work.

The components that support the objectives of each person's routine work need to be listed and organized. The result can be summarized in a tree (see Figure 24-21).

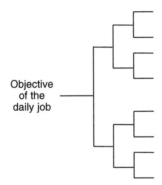

Objective
of the
daily job

Figure 24-21. Tree for Components Supporting the Daily Job Objectives

Next, the hoshins relevant to this person need to be correlated with the components which support his or her current routine job objectives, and new tasks must be added as necessary to accomplish the hoshins (see Figure 24-22).

From this correlation matrix it is possible to do the following:

- Understand which routine job tasks have higher priority, because they address hoshins
- Understand that new routine job tasks have to be added so that the person addresses previously unaddressed hoshins
- Everyone understands what each other is doing

You can then institute control by measurement methods (metrics and targets) that enable each person to monitor and control his or her own activities. Each must be sure to follow the process and accomplish the desired results. So, each person can run his or her own personal PDCA.

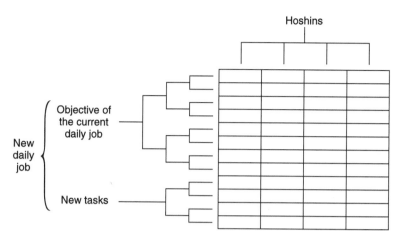

Figure 24-22. Correlating Hoshins with Components Supporting the Current Daily Job Objectives

Phase 4—Check and Act (Reactive)

Once the annual plan has been made (Plan) and deployed over the year (Do), it is time to check for weaknesses in the plan or the way it was carried out (Check) and to Act appropriately to influence the next year's plan or possibly the long-term or mid-term plans (see Figure 24-23, page 522).

The Check step entails discovering why the planned process didn't achieve the desired results. In other words, a process has been created that can be analyzed using reactive improvement methods, and you use the 7 steps to analyze the difference between the plan and reality and then determine the main causes of the difference. For instance, using the data taken as part of the measurement plan, you can discover whether parts of the plan weren't carried out or were carried out but didn't produce the planned result (see Figure 24-24, page 522). This provides feedback to the next planning cycle.

It is important to enforce such fact-based analysis through use of the 7 steps. For this purpose hoshin management dictates the use of analysis data sheets that the president or division head "diagnoses" to make sure they are done.

The Act step involves deciding on the key parts of the process to improve over the next cycle. This brings us back to Plan and Do as described previously.

Phase 5—President's Diagnosis

At the top of the hoshin management model is diagnosis by the president (see slightly above the middle of Figure 24-5, page 507). This is part of the proactive phase of hoshin management, the outside proactive PDCA loop of the model for hoshin management. Each year, the president assesses how each division or functional area carries out its hoshin management activities. During the first step, the group to be

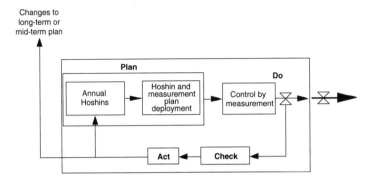

Figure 24-23. Checking and Acting to Modify the Plan

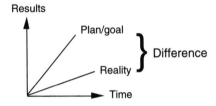

Figure 24-24. Analyzing the Difference between Plan and Reality

audited provides a status report document to the president and his or her change management staff.

Next the president, an external change agent, and the diagnosis team visit the site of the group being diagnosed. The second step consists of two parts, a presentation by the work group leader at the factory and a visit to the work group in its own environment. The first is formal; the second is personal and informal.

The third step begins while the president is still visiting the work group in its own environment. Still in a personal and informal manner, the external change agent accompanying the president summarizes the strengths and weaknesses seen, and the president provides appropriate oral reinforcement. In Japan, this summary step may end with a round of sake and continued informal discussion. The third step ends one month later when the diagnosis team sends a follow-up memo on what the work group should do to improve.

During the fourth step, the president and associated staff plan how to improve the diagnosis process for the next planning cycle. The site visits are typically one day in length. During that day, the president and the accompanying team may visit several groups at the site. These site visits are the president's main job as part of hoshin management—they cannot be delegated. Early in the implementation of hoshin management, the president should visit all the sites. Ideally, the president should continue to visit every site. Certainly, the most important should be visited each year. At one major Japanese construction company with many branch offices, the president visited 100 sites per year.

A detailed example of presidential diagnosis at Teradyne can be found in Chapter 26 beginning on page 582. An example of yearly hoshin diagnosis at the division level can be found in step 7 of the Analog Devices case study starting on page 531.

Purposes and Benefits

Presidential diagnosis has several purposes. First, it provides a deadline effect and thus indirect enforcement of the yearly PDCA cycle of the divisions or functional areas; the date is announced one year in advance, so improvements must be finished by that date. Second, the president's diagnosis will guide the divisions on how to strengthen their quality improvement systems. The diagnosis is not a check of the results, but a check of their analysis (PDCA) process. Third, the yearly diagnosis gives the president another opportunity to show personal leadership of change. Fourth, presidential diagnosis aids the president's own learning process.

- The president hears and sees what is really happening (e.g., changes, latent problems, environmental pressures). This is important because subordinates hesitate to speak about problems, and some presidents are disinclined to hear about them.
- The president gets continuing education about quality: the accompanying change agent, an outside quality expert, asks questions that enlighten the president.
- The president personally participates in a PDCA cycle and becomes more adept in using proactive PDCA.
- The president is able to compare divisions and identify strong and weak models.

Hoshin Management as "Systems Engineering" for Alignment

Hoshin management is intended to systematize alignment (within the company and between the company and the environment), i.e., to make it a form of engineering, like process engineering for manufacturing. Therefore, the same infrastructure elements are necessary for hoshin management as are needed for process engineering.

In the case of process engineering, the elements of the system consist of physical elements such as the building or jigs; however, in the case of hoshin management, the elements of the system are invisible and influence the organization indirectly. "Soft" rather than "hard" elements must play key roles.

Table 24-3 shows the correspondence between the elements of process engineering and those of hoshin management.

HP has done a particularly good job of implementing the components of hoshin management listed in Table 24-3. They have a strong overall structure or system, they have a strong process flow, and they have excellent manuals and training in use of hoshin management. In particular, HP has developed the forms or data sheets of hoshin management to an excellent level. Data sheet formats are a tool leading to effectiveness and efficiency like any good tool should do. HP's

Table 24-3. Process Engineering Compared with Hoshin Management

	System	Process	Tools	Operation
Production process engineering	Building	Machines	Jigs	Manuals
Hoshin management	Hoshin management system	Flow	Datasheets	Manuals

hoshin management forms are clear and usable and enable a strong form of monitoring and checking. The explicit system, manual, and forms that Analog Devices uses are also noteworthy.

Still, hoshin management needs improvement. The methods of setting the hoshins need to be improved as do the methods of monitoring. Stronger sets of tools are needed in both cases. The methods need to be even more scientific.

We have shown how hoshin management aligns the organization. In Chapter 25, we show how hoshin management enforces the use of PDCA by all managers.

24.2 MANAGEMENT BY OBJECTIVES AND CONVENTIONAL BUSINESS PLANNING

Hoshin management has obvious parallels with management by objectives and clearly must be related to conventional business planning.

Hoshin Management versus Management by Objectives

In the Japanese view, the United States may not have felt the need for hoshin management as strongly as Japan does. As shown in Figure 24-25, in Japan, the CEO is felt to have less authority relative to vice presidents and division directors than do CEOs in the United States.[8]

Kogure quotes a 1980 survey of U.S. and Japanese companies which revealed that U.S. companies were superior in formalization, concentration of authority in the upper levels, and systemization of management planning systems; U.S. companies were also

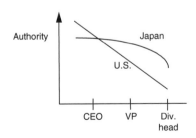

Figure 24-25. Comparison of Authority Levels

strong in various aspects of cross-functional management (small business units) and in production management systems [173]. Therefore, Japanese companies felt it necessary to institute a formal system of deployment of policy from higher to lower levels in the company. They assumed that in the U.S. context, where top-down management prevails, top management directives may penetrate more easily to the bottom than theirs did.

Japanese companies don't have clear lines of authority—it is part of the Japanese culture to appreciate "softness" in such issues. Japanese companies prefer a bottom-up to a top-down system, and their hoshin management methods have developed accordingly. For instance, as mentioned earlier, the hoshin management system includes the explicit interlevel negotiation system of "catchball." Thus, hoshin management evolved to include a significant bottom-up component to modify the initial top-down policies.

In his book, Professor Kogure emphasizes the difference between hoshin management and MBO. Hoshin management puts stress on achieving results by controlling the process. MBO as typically practiced puts stress on achieving objectives by managing people.

MBO and hoshin management do the same job with regard to deploying company goals into individual goals and letting people try to achieve them. Even though Japanese hoshin management focuses on process, management does pay attention to results; emphasis on process is not permission to fail to achieve the results. Since hoshin management controls the process to produce results, you can analyze the process for the causes of failure and change the process until it does produce the desired results (see Figure 24-26).

With its emphasis on making people responsible for results, MBO all too often abdicates responsibility for understanding the process used to meet the objectives. For example, it may not take into account whether the process is capable of achieving the objectives. Practiced this way, not only does MBO gamble on individuals and their own processes, which may or may not be capable, but MBO also has no way to learn how to improve if the individual or process is not capable—MBO typically does not even learn from an individual who is capable. If only the targets and not the means are deployed, as frequently happens with MBO, the deployment shown in Figure 24-16 (page 517) looks more like that shown in Figure 24-27 on page 526.

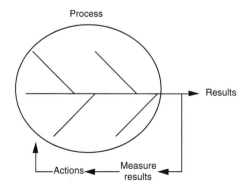

Figure 24-26. Analyzing and Changing the Process to Get Results

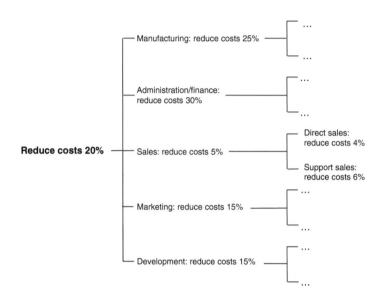

Figure 24-27. Management by Objectives

Note that the units of the metrics stay the same from level to level of the deployment. This is really a system of partitioning or dispersion of objectives rather than deployment.

Table 24-4 compares MBO and hoshin management based on our observations of actual use in U.S. companies.

Sales management often exemplifies the extremes of MBO. The cycle shown in Figure 24-28 will be familiar to many U.S. managers. In the MBO cycle illustrated in the figure, the effort is to achieve sales performance by controlling the investment in salespeople and motivating their output, with little direct effort to understand, teach, and improve the sales skill of the organization. Managers and salespeople conspire to present sales as an individual skill that depends on the company's ability to attract successful salespeople. The company makes no effort to control its destiny directly by learning to sell its product and to develop salespeople who can do so.

While companies using MBO may perceive less need for a system to deploy and manage policy than Japanese companies, the purposes of hoshin management (page 504) are equally important to both. The system has proved useful to U.S. companies, as demonstrated by Hewlett-Packard, Analog Devices, and others.

Sarv Singh Soin of Hewlett-Packard gives the following view of hoshin management (which he calls Hoshin planning):

> You may ask the question, "Why adopt Hoshin planning? After all it is very similar to MBO and we have been successful with MBO." While MBO has many strengths, it has also many weaknesses. For example, there is a weak linkage between strategy and implementation; there is no detailed planning

Table 24-4. Comparison of Management by Objectives and Hoshin Management

Management by Objectives	Hoshin Management
Deploy a portion of the top-level target to each segment at each level (no change of units of measure)	Deploy targets with different metrics to each segment at each level (change of units of measure)
Lower-level management is responsible for providing the means	Higher-level management suggests plausible means for key targets
Some negotiation of targets (considerable pressure for lower-level management to accept targets proposed by higher-level management)	Catchball of targets and means based on facts and analysis
Little monitoring of the means (if it works, it's ok)	Some targets and metrics are aimed at controlling adherence to the means
	Analysis of causes and failure of the means of the last planning cycle is used to improve methods proposed in next planning cycle
Presidential recriminations for missing targets and sometimes replacement of the responsible manager	Presidential diagnosis of the CAPD cycle and suggestions on how to improve next time
New manager blames predecessor's system for past problems and begins to plan a new system	Old manager learns from past to do a better job next time
Dependence on undocumented skill in heads of hopefully capable individual managers	**Attempt to document needed skill and institutionalize it in the company**

Figure 24-28. An MBO Cycle for Sales Management

process; there is an insufficient consensus approach; a hierarchy of objectives, although apparent in theory, may not exist in reality; finally, and most important, there is no framework for a formalized review procedure to monitor and ensure success.

Hoshin planning on the other hand has all the strengths of MBO and more to boot but none of its weaknesses. The strength of Hoshin planning is that it is a systematic and tightly coupled process. It does, however, require much more effort and consensus than MBO; but it helps provide a focus, a single-minded approach by the entire management team. The entire process is designed to ensure success. In the final analysis, Hoshin planning can be considered a more mature MBO process [270, page 58].

Soin's view that hoshin management is a more mature form of MBO is consistent with our view of hoshin management as being complementary to the conventional business planning process, as discussed in the next section.

Hoshin Management and Conventional Business Planning

The conventional business planning process has many parallels to the hoshin management process we have described in this chapter (see Figure 24-29). In Chapter 26, we will describe how HP (beginning on page 588) and Analog Devices (beginning on page 593) use hoshin management and their forms of conventional business planning as parallel and complementary systems. Teradyne provides another example, of a customized mix of aspects of hoshin management and conventional business planning [37, page 14].

The conventional business process is substantially focused on results. In fact, MBO as it is often practiced can be viewed as a system to deploy desired results. However, process is necessary to achieve results, and providing the means to produce the results is the domain of hoshin management.

Hoshin management also takes a longer term view than the conventional annual business plan often takes. The actual goal of the company is not its annual results, but to achieve the company's vision and mid-term plan. The annual business plan is but a step toward the mid-term plan and vision. Hoshin management takes into account that some of the means necessary to achieve the mid-term plan and company vision may take more than one year. (It, therefore, builds into annual plans the means for achieving longer-term objectives.) For instance, for a U.S. company to sell products in Japan takes more than a first-year sales target. It takes a multi-year effort to understand the Japanese market and develop a capability to address that market. In this example, hoshin management will address the higher (longer-term) objective of selling products in Japan, while the annual business plan may specify only the Japanese sales expected for the next year.

As shown in Figure 24-29 (and discussed in detail earlier in this chapter), hoshin management begins by analysis of the environment, the vision, the mid-term plan, and last year's weaknesses to discover the top-level (company or CEO) hoshins. These top-level hoshins address the means necessary to achieve both the mid-term plan and

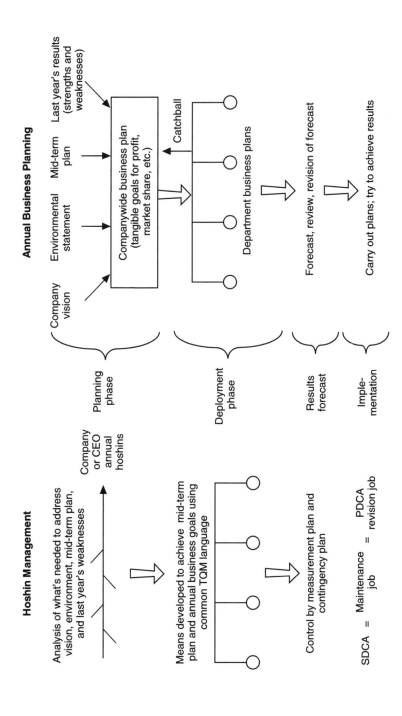

Figure 24-29. Hoshin Management Compared with Conventional Business Planning

the annual business goals. They are deployed downward through the organization using a common language of effective change:

- Facts: using measurable data
- Process: using Ishikawa diagrams to understand what's really happening
- Focus: using Pareto diagrams to be sure to address the vital few

In the deployment of hoshins, the outcome at each higher level is the target of the means of the next lower level, as shown in the figure below:

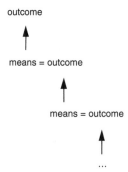

Let's put a 7 steps slant on this. In step 1, we state the theme, that is, the desired outcome.

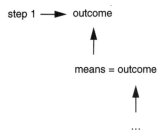

What is the means then? It is step 4, the solution.

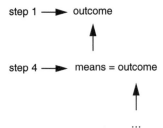

It is clear from this figure that we are missing something—steps 2 and 3, data collection and causal analysis. This makes it clear that creation of the means at the next lower level in hoshin management should not be a speculative exercise. Rather, the means is derived from data collection and causal analysis.

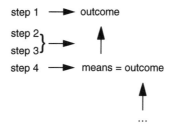

Then, control by measurement is used to develop the basis of the interleaved SDCA (maintenance) and PDCA (incremental improvement) cycles through which the deployed plan is implemented. As was stated earlier in this chapter, metrics are needed to measure the results and the means.

Hoshin management is a vehicle to integrate the entire organization to achieve the company goals. Kansai Electric showed that to integrate the entire organization, two types of PDCA were necessary: $PDCA_1$ and $PDCA_2$. $PDCA_2$ is hoshin management (see Figure 24-30 on page 532).[9] This is discussed in more detail in Chapter 25.

An Alternate Hoshin Deployment System

Earlier in the chapter, we mentioned that the hoshin deployment system has a weakness in that it fails to clarify the connection between the means and its effect on the higher-level outcome. MBO does not have this weakness since it specifies to what degree each lower unit affects the result; however, MBO doesn't specify the means of accomplishing objectives. Akao describes a method of addressing this weakness [5, page 9].

In this alternative deployment method, the top-level goal is stated and then guidelines are stated for the subdepartments. This first stage of deployment might look very much like the MBO deployment shown earlier (Figure 24-31 on page 532).

Once the top-level outcome and guidelines for the next level are deployed, means are deployed (see Figure 24-32 on page 532). The means are developed further on the basis of facts and 7 steps analysis of obstacles to the goal (see Figure 24-33 on page 533).

Hybrid systems of deployment are also possible, where guidelines toward the top-level outcome are deployed and the alternating target and means system of deployment described earlier in the chapter is used to develop the means and process metrics and targets.

24.3 HOSHIN MANAGEMENT AT ANALOG DEVICES

The discussion and example of this section are drawn from [9, 265], with particular help from Bob Stasey, chief quality officer of Analog Devices, Inc. (ADI).

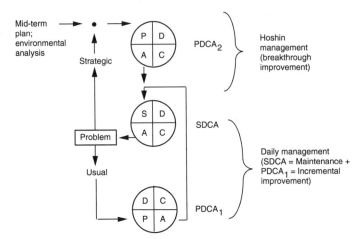

Figure 24-30. Two Types of PDCA for Organization Integration

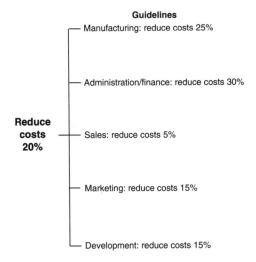

Figure 24-31. Guidelines from Top-level Goal

ADI sees hoshin management[10] as a systematic planning and execution approach for managing and reviewing issues requiring breakthrough or continuous improvement, which it does by:

- Identifying key business issues
- Planning to ensure these issues are addressed
- Measuring progress
- Reviewing results
- Aligning the organization

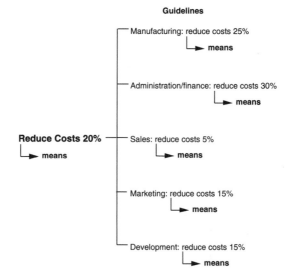

Figure 24-32. Means for Achieving Second-Level Guidelines

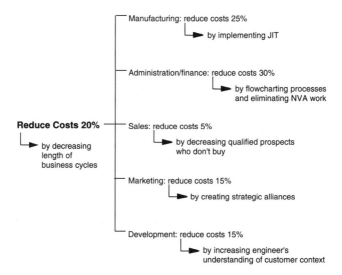

Figure 24-33. Top Management and Functional Means

At ADI, hoshin management has two aspects. The first focuses on the few critical issues for the organization that will have the biggest impact on customer satisfaction and business competitiveness. These require breakthrough improvement. Hoshin management's other focus is on key business processes known as "business fundamentals." Business fundamentals require continuous improvement.[11]

In addition, hoshin management focuses on both the results of the plan and the planning process. The PDCA cycle is used to check for weaknesses or flaws in the plan as well as deviations from expected results. This is a means for learning from and improving the planning process itself.

Using hoshin management at ADI provides a clear focus on the vital few goals for everyone. It involves coordination across business strategies, foundries, and corporate functions to direct action and assure alignment. The process starts with the identification of key areas for breakthrough and continuous improvement by the CEO. Once this is done, cascading of objectives throughout the organization can begin. Hoshin harnesses the capability, focus, and commitment available from the entire organization to achieve breakthrough results on critical business concerns.

ADI has codified hoshin management as a seven-step process (not to be confused with the 7 steps of reactive improvement), as shown in Figure 24-34.[12]

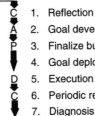

1. Reflection & explore essentials
2. Goal development
3. Finalize business goals
4. Goal deployment
5. Execution of hoshin
6. Periodic review
7. Diagnosis

Figure 24-34. ADI's 7 Step Hoshin Management Process

The rest of this subsection provides a step-by-step example of the use of hoshin management at ADI which applies it both reactively and proactively. The following is a reactive hoshin example.

Step 1: Reflection & Explore Essentials

ADI views Reflection & Explore Essentials as the most important step in hoshin management. It is carried out at the corporate and division levels. Reflection considers the past performance of the company, and explores the essential elements necessary to meet long-term goals while operating in the projected environment. The output of this step is an identification of the vital few issues or hoshins that must be addressed in the coming year or years.

The CEO, in concert with the vice presidents, conducts a corporatewide reflection. Division vice presidents may also conduct a division-specific reflection. Reflection, done properly, identifies key objectives correctly and increases the likelihood of meeting customer and business goals.

The identification of key issues came from three main areas: past performance which is a reflection of the current state of the business; future vision which is a reflection of the direction the company is moving toward; and environmental factors which is an assessment of the constraints under which the organization must function. Table 24-5 shows the kinds of data obtained from each of the three sources.

Reflection on the future state is a review of the mid-term goals (two to three years) and the long-term goals (more than three years). An example of these is shown in Table 24-6.

Table 24-5. Detailed Kinds of Data from Three Sources

Past Data	Future Data	Environmental Data
- Reflections on what has been done in the past - Strength/weakness analysis of prior year's plan - Analysis of prior year's Hoshin - Diagnosis of the Hoshin system	- Mid-term goals - Long-term goals - Noble goals - Company vision - Company mission	- Economic issues - Political issues - Social issues - Regulatory issues - Technology issues - Customer's environment - Competitive environment

Table 24-6. Long-term and Mid-term Goals

Long-term goals	Mid-term goals	Performance measure
Customer satisfaction	To be rated #1 vendor of choice by our customers	Best place to buy
Stockholder satisfaction	Sales growth ≥25% OPBT ≥25% Return on equity ≥25%	Best place to invest
Employee satisfaction	Quality work environment: Feeling secure and important, having fun, being proud	Best place to work

Step 2: Goal Development

In step 2, the CEO prioritizes the key issues that come out of step 1. The key issues are sorted into those which should be hoshins and those which will be business fundamentals (see Figure 24-35). Then, the CEO starts the catchball process with the senior management team of the company.

As part of the step 1 reflection by the CEO, it was noted that on-time delivery had become a major initiative in 1986 and during the period 1986–1990 performance had improved to approximately 95 percent. However, by 1993, with ADI entering major, high-volume markets where world-class delivery performance was expected, lack of additional improvement from 1991–1993 was of concern and could place ADI in a position of competitive weakness. Thus, one of the hoshins put foward in 1994 concerned on-time delivery.

ADI uses a hoshin planning table to list the five elements of a hoshin:[13]

- Statement of objectives: what needs to be achieved
- Goal: quantitative target of progress toward meeting the objectives
- Strategies with owners: how will the objective be met and who is responsible for making sure the strategy is completed

- Performance measure: metric and target of progress on strategies
- Deadline date: deadline for each strategy

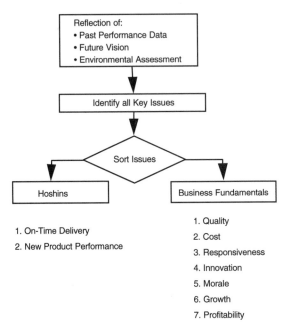

Figure 24-35. Sorting Key Issues

Table 24-7 is the partially complete planning table the CEO put forward to begin the catchball regarding the on time delivery hoshin.

After receiving this planning table, each division conducts data collection, data analysis, and root cause analysis to determine which strategies will enable them to meet the objective (each division applies the techniques of steps 2–4 of the 7 steps). The following examples came from one of ADI's divisions.

Employees analyzed the collected data to identify the major contributors to late delivery. Part A of Figure 24-36 on page 538 shows the top four bars of a late delivery Pareto diagram. The largest bar (performance to schedule) was split into another Pareto diagram for further analysis (part B of the figure). The largest bar (back end) of this Pareto diagram was in turn split into another Pareto diagram for further analysis (part C of the figure). The largest bar (warehouse) of this Pareto diagram was again split into another Pareto diagram for further analysis (Figure 24-37 on page 537). From this last Pareto diagram, an Ishikawa diagram was developed to determine the root causes of the late delivery problem (Figure 24-38 on page 540).

After completing the above pattern of analysis for each of the strategies for each department, the division finalized its first-level hoshin planning table (see Table 24-8 on page 537). The strategies in the table came from the highest level Pareto diagram.

Table 24-7. Annual Hoshin Planning Table from OCE

Prepared By: OCE	Date: 9/15/94	Fiscal Year: 94	Division:	Location/ Department:
SITUATION: Reliability of delivery commitments and flexibility to respond to rapidly changing demand are high priorities of customers. ADI's capabilities to satisfy these requirements are fragile and variable across the company, thus sapping large resources and costs to meet minimum standards. While delivery performance has improved, late deliveries remain at 6%.				

OBJECTIVE	#	STRATEGY/OWNER DEADLINE	PERFORMANCE MEASURE	
Meet factory commitments on delivery dates.			On-time deliver to Factory Commit Date On-time delivery to critical customers	
GOAL				
2% late deliveries				

The lower-level Pareto diagrams and the Ishikawa diagram were used in step 4 of the hoshin process as part of cascading the hoshin down into the division.

Step 3: Finalize Business Goals

In this step, the division management examines its hoshin planning table (Table 24-8, page 537) to validate whether implementing the year's hoshins and business fundamentals will bring the desired results for ADI's three main classes of stakeholders:

- Shareholders
  - sales
  - profitability
  - return on equity
- Customers
  - on-time delivery
  - shortened lead times
  - high level of responsiveness
- Employees
  - quality of work environment
  - employee satisfaction

Figure 24-39 on page 540 shows how ADI expects the five elements from the hoshin planning table should be linked before step 3 is completed. In this particular example, the question is, "Will implementing the strategies in the lower center of Table 24-8 and achieving the performance measures in the lower right of the table be sufficient to meet the objective in the middle left of the table?" The answer to both parts of the question must be yes; otherwise, adjustments or additions have to be made to either the strategies or performance measures.

A. Pareto of Reasons For Late Deliveries

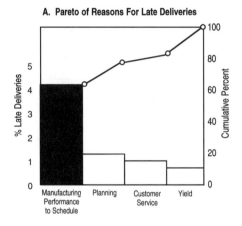

B. Pareto of Manufacturing Late Deliveries

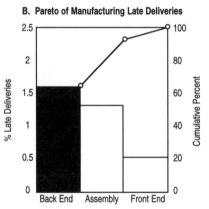

C. Pareto of Back-End Manufacturing Component of Late Delivery

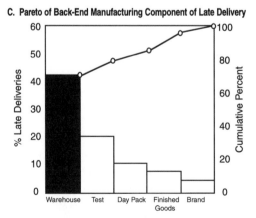

Figure 24-36. Pareto Analysis

Table 24-8. Annual Hoshin Planning Table Augmented by Division

Prepared By: *Richard Fitzpatrick*	Date: *11/10/93*	Fiscal Year: *94*	Division: *ADBV*	Location/ Department: *Limerick*
SITUATION: Feedback from our customers indicates that they are dissatisfied with our delivery performace to Factory Commit Date (5% late).				

OBJECTIVE	#	STRATEGY/OWNER DEADLINE	PERFORMANCE MEASURE
To fully satisfy customer expectations for reliably meeting factory commitments on delivery.	1	Reduce performance to schedule misses (Rob Marshall) 10/29/94	Reduce schedule misses from 2.7% to <1% Review weekly.
	2	Reduce errors in planning (Richard Fitzpatrick) 10/29/94	Reduce schedule error from 1.1% to <.3%. Review weekly
	3	Reduce customer service late deliveries (Declan McDaid) 10/29/94	Reduce customer type late deliveries from .6% to <.3%. Review weekly
GOAL			
Reduce line items late from 5% to 2% by 10/29/94.	4	Reduce yield problems as a cause of late deliveries (Frank Poucher) 10/29/94	Reduce late deliveries caused by yield problems from .6% to <.3%. Review weekly

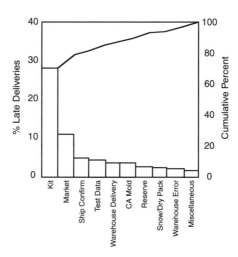

Figure 24-37. Pareto of Warehouse Component of Back-End Manufacturing Contribution to Late Deliery

Step 4: Goal Deployment

Figure 24-40 shows how the division cascaded the highest divisional level hoshin down through the division by turning strategies and performance measures at one level into objectives and goals at the next level. This cascading also made use of the Pareto and Ishikawa analysis from step 2.

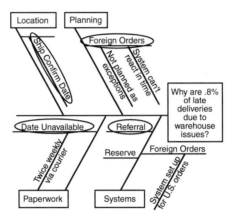

Figure 24-38. Root Cause Analysis for Late Deliveries Due to Warehouse Causes

WHAT		HOW		WHEN
Objectives	Goal	Strategies	Performance Measures	Deadline Date
What Analog needs to achieve	Quantitative target of progress toward meeting the objective	How will the objective be met	Numeric target for each strategy that will help reach the goal	Deadline for each strategy

Successfully implementing the strategies equates to achieving the objectives.

Achieving the target for each performance measures equates to achieving the goal.

Figure 24-39. Confirming the Plan

Step 5: Execution of Hoshin

As a hoshin is cascaded through a division, plans have to be made for implementing each element of the now distributed hoshin. ADI uses an "implementation table" to record the detailed implementation plan for each element. One of the strategies at the third level down in the cascade of the on-time delivery hoshin in the division was to reduce warehouse errors. Table 24-9 shows the implementation table for this.

Step 6: Periodic Review

For each hoshin, a plan for periodic review must be prepared. The following table (Table 24-10) is an example of ADI's "review table," in this case the review plan for

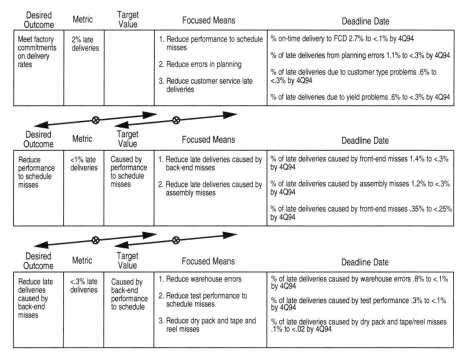

Figure 24-40. Cascading Hoshins

Table 24-9. Example Implementation Table

Department: Back End Manager: Tony																FY: 94 Dave: Jan 94		
Reference Number and Strategy:				1.1.1. Reduce Warehouse														
Ref #	TACTICS		Resp Person	Q1			Q2				Q3			Q4			Review Date & Remarks		
				N	D	J	F	M	A	M	J	J	A	S	O			
1.1.1.1	Pareto reasons for warehouses misses		T. Donnelly S. Kelly			x─x												
1.1.1.2	Identify root causes		T. Donnelly S. Kelly			x─x												
1.1.1.3	Plan international orders as exceptions		R. Fitzpartick				x──────x											
1.1.1.4	Daily transfer of C. of C. data		M. Ronan				x──────x											
1.1.1.5	Ship confirm Norwood time		C. Sullivan				x──────x											
1.1.1.6	Referral issues		B. Casey				x──────x											

the top-level division hoshin from Table 24-8. Hoshin performance is reviewed monthly at the corporate level. Within divisions and departments, the relevant performance measures may be reviewed weekly, or daily when circumstances demand it.

Table 24-10. Example Review Table

Legend:
Trend (T): ⇑ ⇓ Change since last
Concern (C): H High M Moderate L Low
Status (S): ○ On target   ○ Behind Plan   ● Far Below
               ◗ Metrics or strategy

Prepared By: Rich Fitzpatrick	Date: 5/1/94	Fiscal Year: 1994	Entity: ADBV	Location/ Department: Limerick		
Objective/Strategy (P)	Actual Performance & Limits (D)	T/C/S	Summary of Analysis of Deviations (C)	Implication for Future (A)	Review Date Planned	Actual
Reduce performance to scientific misses	Reduction from 2.7% to 1.5%	⇑ L ○			6/1/94	6/1/94
Reduce errors in planning	Reduction from 1.1% to .7%	⇑ L ○			5/1/94	5/1/94
Reduce customer service deliveries	Reduction from .5% to .1%	⇑ L ○			5/1/94	5/1/94
Reduce yield problems and causes of late deliveries	Reduction from .8% to .6%	⇑ L ○			5/1/94	5/1/94

Step 7: Diagnosis

At year end, a diagnosis of the content and quality of the hoshin process is done by the divisional leader, i.e., the hoshin owner. Table 24-11 came out of one such analysis. The benefits of diagnosing the hoshin system are:

1. Focuses on the hoshin system, not the hoshin achievement
2. Uncovers unknown issues
3. Goes to the source
4. Provides "deadline effect"

Overall Assessment of Hoshin Management at Analog Devices

Bob Stasey provided the following assessment. A complementary assessment is embedded in [265].

ADI's experience in hoshin management resulted in several important lessons. The first lesson was that hoshins are identified and deployed more effectively when they are linked to an annual business planning process. The second lesson was that the entire organization must be sufficiently skilled in quality improvement practices before attempting to implement hoshin management. The importance of these lessons is magnified when implementing proactive hoshins.

Table 24-11. Example of Hoshin Owner Diagnosis

WEAKNESS	WHAT	WHO	WHEN	WHERE	HOW
Data collection and root cause analysis completed for cycle time, not lines late Goals are in cycle time, not lines late	Revise strategies based upon data collection and root cause analysis of lines late	Planning Manager	1Q	Site	• Analyze data collection system • Restratify data based upon lines late • Establish root causality of lines late and determine strategies to effect solutions
Catchball was one way only, with no closure on time or resource requirements	Improve implementation planning to allow time for closure	Site VP	2Q	Site	• Start strategy planning 3 months earlier • Monitor bi-weekly at staff meeting

Business Planning

ADI employs an annual business planning process whose participants include every division and the product lines within each division. Each product line analyzes its customers, competitors and product offerings and then sets objectives for the coming year based upon its findings. The product line business plans are rolled up to the division level where common objectives across the product lines are identified. This "roll-up" of business plans continues at the corporate level where a team of senior-level managers reviews the divisional business plans paying particular attention to the objectives of each division. This team then selects the top one or two objectives for companywide focus, thus becoming the basis for the hoshin.

For example, product lines in one division may, during the course of their analysis of customer needs, determine that the availability of sample products early in a customer's design cycle is critical to the success of their respective businesses. They would include improving the availability of samples as an objective for their respective product lines. At the divisional level, this common objective would be identified as a divisional objective. At the corporate level, if other divisions had also identified improving sample availability as a key objective, then this would become a corporate hoshin.

The advantage of linking the business planning process to hoshin management has been apparent not just in the identification of corporate wide objectives. It has also been an important way to create alignment among the Analog Devices' divisions and product lines. Although hoshins are set at the corporate level and implemented in a top-down manner, they are developed from the bottom up, thereby creating buy-in from the very start of hoshin deployment.

Preparedness

Another of ADI's lesson was that reactive and proactive hoshins have different difficulty levels, and that proactive hoshin management should wait until the organization has developed sufficient skill in reactive problem solving. Measuring the adequate skill level in reactive problem solving can be as simple as measuring the performance, over time, of how quickly teams execute the 7 steps. It is then important to assure that all divisions or entities are skilled, not just a select few. The entire organization must be skilled because hoshin management requires deployment throughout an organization.

There are four reasons why proactive hoshins can be more difficult to deploy than reactive hoshins. First, reactive problem solving, as represented by the 7 steps, are typically replete with data whereas proactive activities begin with less data, and that data tends to be difficult to collect. For example, consider a proactive hoshin to better meet customer needs. The data comes from customers who are outside the organization making collection difficult. Even with the appropriate data collection methods, the qualitative nature of the data makes analysis difficult compared with standard reactive data (e.g., defects, days late) that can be transcribed into Pareto charts and analyzed with Ishikawa diagrams.

Second, decisions for proactive improvements are not as clear as they tend to be for reactive improvements. Often, reactive analysis leads to clear conclusions and outcomes, whereas proactive analysis leads to many strategy options. Picking the right strategy, even when rooted in data, can be difficult.

Third, reactive improvements tend to be tactical while proactive improvements tend to be strategic. Tactical activities are largely within one's control, whereas strategic activities rely on exogenous factors such as customers and competitors. That lack of control makes for little predictability in the success of implementing solutions.

Fourth, reactive improvements tend to be completed over shorter timeframes as compared to proactive improvements. The longer timeframes for proactive improvements make it more difficult to monitor improvements because of fewer cycles of learning. Sustaining organizational focus over improvement activities that can last years is more difficult. While reducing defects can happen quickly, improving customer relationships can take years. Keeping the organization aligned and focused on proactive goals is a considerable challenge.

Timing

ADI's experience suggests that timing is critical to the hoshin setting, deploying, and monitoring phases. Delaying determining the hoshin results in delayed hoshin execution and jeopardizes the planned breakthrough.

Deploying hoshin requires adequate time for execution. Developing the plan during the year runs the risks of finding you need more resources after having made a commitment and finding that you have too little time for implementation.

In the monitoring phase, adequate documentation is critical to uncovering any issue causing a target shortfall. Documenting the deviations and future implications proves useful when diagnosing the hoshin management system. The diagnosis will require going to the source. It is vital that you have the information on why the deviations occurred so that you can uncover hidden issues.

NOTES

1. For our discussion of hoshin management, we are grateful to JSQC and its Research Committee on the Case Study of Hoshin Management [152]. We have also been instructed by Masao Kogure, an expert on the theoretical foundations of hoshin management; see [175].

2. There is no one correct version of hoshin management. Each company adapts the basic concepts to its needs. The version we describe here is meant to be representative. It is based on a 1991 presentation by the president of NEC Shizuoka (Michio Ikawa), a 1991 presentation by Masao Kogure, a 1992 presentation by the president of NEC Kansai, and a 1992 presentation by Mitsuru Nitta of Tokyo Electric Power Company. Akao's book [5] provides an extensive description of hoshin management. See also [55].

3. Some companies use a semiannual planning cycle because it allows more accurate prediction and, thus, more relevant planning and a more frequently improvement cycle.

4. The Japanese translation of what we are here calling hoshins is "policies." We are not using the latter term because hoshin management is describing something different from "policies" in the usual American sense of the word.

5. Many companies use variations from this ideal.

6. The material here draws on [289].

7. It usually stops short of the individual.

8. This figure is derived from [154].

9. Figure 24-30 is adapted from a diagram in [182, page 171].

10. Which they call hoshin planning.

11. "Business fundamentals" is a phrase the ADI got from Hewlett-Packard, from which ADI also learned much about the practice of hoshin management. HP's version of combining hoshin management and business fundamentals is described in the HP case study beginning on page 588. We also discussed the relationship between hoshin management and conventional business planning earlier in this chapter (see page 524).

12. We explain in Chapter 25 about the CAPDC cycle that is shown on the left side of Figure 24-34.

13. Here is the correspondence between ADI's vocabulary for a hoshin and our vocabulary from earlier in this chapter: statement of objective = statement of desired outcome; strategy = focused means; goal = target (and implicit metric) for desired outcome; performance measure = metric and target for means; and deadline date = deadline date.

25
Leading Process Improvement

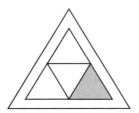

A difficult aspect of total participation is getting managers to practice the methods of business improvement and organizational learning. Managers initially don't understand their role in business improvement. Simply put, it is to teach and practice PDCA. Even when managers do understand their role, they find it difficult to practice. Developing managers so they can undertake their necessary role in business improvement is the subject of this chapter.

Note to reader: This chapter, on how individuals can learn to lead process improvement, in some sense logically fits the part of the book on the individual level of practice (Chapters 16–18). However, many of the methods discussed and the examples given depend on content that we did not have until now.

25.1 MODELING PERSONAL IMPROVEMENT

In Chapter 16 (page 324), we described Personal Quality Checklists as a tool to help an individual or small teams of individuals focus on specific areas where they wanted to improve. This method is a central tool in [240] by Roberts and Sergesketter. That book was partially motivated by the efforts of Sergesketter to figure out how to personally apply TQM in his organization.

In April 1992 at the CQM's annual conference, Bob Galvin, then CEO of Motorola, told a story about his friend Bernie Sergesketter, a senior executive with the Illinois telephone company, making the important point about improvement methods that a good first place to start is with oneself.[1]

It seems that the Illinois telephone company was implementing TQM, and Bernie Sergesketter was trying to provide leadership for this effort. He decided that fundamental to TQM was people personally practicing TQM, and therefore he decided that he must personally practice TQM. He chose a couple of simple things that he wanted to improve. These were (1) answering his own telephone before it rolled over to the answering service, and (2) getting to meetings on time. So he began keeping records of how often he managed to answer his own phone when he was in his office and how often he got to meetings on time. He kept his records on a folded piece of paper that he kept in his inside suit coat pocket, and he began to do little statistical process control calculations on this data.

Of course, if one's phone rings four times and then rolls over to someplace else, and if there is some variation in how many rings it takes one to answer (e.g., 2 rings variation), then one has to shoot for getting the phone before the third ring if one is to guarantee that one always answers before it rolls over after the fourth ring. Based on his data, Bernie began to always try to answer the phone after the first or second ring.

When people would bump into Bernie at a meeting or in the hall and ask him how he thought their TQM program was going, he would take his little data sheet out of his pocket and show them his data for answering his phone and for getting to meetings on time, and show them how SPC helped him see the mean and variance of his "response time." In effect, he would give them a little lesson in SPC as well as providing a personal example of "walking the talk."

Bernie's other improvement effort was getting to meetings on time, and he kept his data and began telling those people that he was meeting with about his project to improve his on-time arrival for meetings and asked them to help him. For instance, his colleagues could help him by pointing out that the current meeting needed to break up before it ran overtime so he could get to his next meeting on time.

Because Bernie himself began to get to meetings on time, and began to finish previous meetings with enough time so he could get to next meetings on time, those he worked with (mostly who worked in the organization he ran) began to try to follow Bernie's example about getting to meetings on time. And because, if one wants to assure that one almost always gets to meetings on time, one must aim to get there early with sufficient leeway to allow for one's mean time and variance between meetings, everyone began aiming to get to meetings early enough so that each would be there on time. However, since all processes have variance, if everyone aims early enough to account for their variance and to still be there on time, inevitably some days everyone will be there before the meeting is supposed to start. This happened with Bernie and his team. One day 10 minutes before the appointed start time, everyone was there. So they started the meeting early, and they discovered they only needed eight or nine minutes to finish their business. Thus, they finished the meeting before it was supposed to start (and there was some joking that finishing meetings before they were scheduled to start should be their new standard).

That's the end of the story. Now think for a moment about the ramifications for a business if everyone took the necessary steps to personally improve the way they performed in the business. At the very least, consider the career prospects for a person who worked so hard to improve himself or herself.

25.2 EMPLOYEE DEVELOPMENT AT NIMS

Although the case of the NIMS division of NEC took place in the 1980s in Japan, we include it here because it is an excellent example of managerial and individual development. Also, this rich case study provides excellent examples of several other dimensions of business improvement useful to companies everywhere today (in the year 2001). The story came from Kiyoshi Uchimaru whom we were privileged to talk with at length on several occasions. With his colleagues, Mr. Uchimaru wrote the book [288] describing the efforts of NEC Integrated-circuit and Microcomputer Systems (NIMS) to implement TQM. This is an unusual and important book that should be read by anyone thinking seriously about how to improve the management or a company, particularly someone trying to improve the performance of a new product development organization. Mr. Uchimaru died in the mid-1990s, a profound loss to modern management thought.

Here then is the story of NIMS.

NIMS is a 1,000-person design subsidiary of NEC. It started as a contract engineering shop with little capability for managing development. Later, deciding that it needed to develop the highest level of self-sufficiency, it embarked on a path of TQM implementation and, in 1987, won the Deming Prize. This effort was led by the then president, Kiyoshi Uchimaru, who himself had decades of engineering management experience.

There are three ways to look at the NIMS story reported here. First, it can be seen as a story of phase-in of a business improvement system—in terms of the three phases defined in Chapter 22 (pages 453): orientation, empowerment, and alignment.

The management at NIMS began with orientation, but it became captivated by the concept of hoshin management as a companywide method of aligning activities. Therefore, from the orientation phase, managers attempted to move directly to hoshin management and the alignment phase. Finding, however, that the NIMS staff did not have the necessary skill to work on companywide activities, they were forced to go back to the empowerment phase to teach the basics of TQM. With a little empowerment, they tried alignment again and were again forced to go back for more empowering skills. This cycle repeated several times until they had reached truly extraordinary levels of individual empowerment, after which they finally succeeded in alignment. In effect, hoshin management became the tool NIMS used to deploy each year's improvement ideas and to systematize successful ideas.

Second, the NIMS story is one of the systematic development of skill in a creative engineering environment (which is why we referred readers to it in Chapter 2, page 22). We have all heard statements such as "These improvement methods might be applicable to manufacturing, but it cannot be applied to a creative task such as engineering." The feeling at NIMS was no different. The NIMS technical staff cited all the usual reasons why systematic improvement could not apply to them. However,

Uchimaru makes the point that the history of science is itself a quality improvement story: develop a theory and Plan how to test it, Do an empirical experiment, Check the result to see if the experiment confirmed the theory, and Act to publish (standardize) the result. This PDCA cycle continues with each new theory being built on—or correcting—a previously held theory.

As Uchimaru sees things, an engineer who thinks systematic improvement methods do not apply to technical activities must not understand either engineering or systematic improvement or both. Systematic improvement is the application of the scientific method to business (pick an important problem, get the facts, analyze the facts, find the underlying truth, plan a method of improvement based on the underlying truth, systematically test it to verify that it works, standardize the new method, and then cycle around again). Uchimaru also explains why the complexity of modern business and technology requires a teamwork approach rather than each engineer "doing his own thing." In the case of NIMS, Uchimaru applied TQM both to the business of the company and to engineering methods.

Third, the NIMS story is one of managerial development (the subject of this chapter) arrived at through hoshin management (the subject of Chapter 24). When the methods of this book are taught or explained, the first question from most managers is, "How will I have to change what I am doing?" The NIMS case illustrates the evolution and development of the role of technical managers.

Uchimaru and his colleagues didn't see a clear path to successful TQM implementation for a technical group when they started. They applied continuous improvement over a period of many years, incrementally discovering methods that worked to improve NIMS design quality dramatically. During these repeated cycles, Uchimaru and his colleagues focused on two fundamental issues: making the development process ever more visible and inserting quality ever further upstream (that is, earlier in the design and development process). These two fundamental issues are represented by the horizontal and vertical axes of Figure 25-1.

Hoshin management cycles are often referred to as CAPD rather than PDCA cycles [106, page 96] to emphasize the control and feedback aspects of hoshin and to focus on the manager's primary role of planning the next phase of the improvement process. A later section in this chapter (page 561) describes the distinction between CAPD and PDCA more fully.[2]

Like most companies, NIMS started in the lower left corner of the figure with a nearly invisible development process and with quality insertion relatively far downstream (e.g., catching defects after they have been shipped to customers). By the time NIMS won the Deming Prize, it had evolved a highly visible development process with quality inserted as far upstream as possible, as the upper right of the figure shows. This didn't happen overnight. It took many years of what Uchimaru calls "trial and error." The shaded curving loops (CAPD cycles) indicate the trial-and-error cycle repeated over many years; the tight loops represent analyzing the results of the last trial, deciding on what to try next and planning the next trial. The long arches represent actually carrying out the next trial. The labeled dots between the straight line segments show successive areas of improvement activity. The fol-

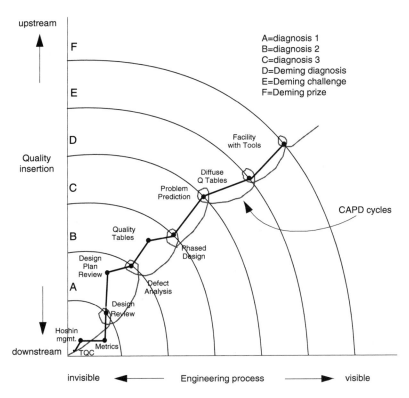

Figure 25-1. Stages in TQM Implementation at NIMS

lowing paragraphs briefly describe the successive improvement activities shown in the figure.

Because hoshin management is regarded as a pillar of TQM in Japan,[3] NIMS immediately tried to implement such a system (see slanting line segment nearest to the origin of the figure).[4] However, hoshin management did not immediately produce results as good as NIMS had sought, and they were forced first to develop some other skills.

The next step in NIMS's implementation was to install some quality metrics. By doing this, it was making the development process more visible. It discovered first that getting technical people to agree on a set of metrics, or even agree that there should be metrics, took many months. Once the technical people had agreed on a small set of metrics, NIMS discovered that metrics alone didn't provide much improvement. In other words, it began to realize the need for focusing on process instead of results.

NIMS then tried to improve its development processes by initiating design reviews. We all know about design reviews, meetings in which experienced and skilled designers from around the company review a proposed design. This was an attempt to insert the quality further upstream, that is, to find the bugs while still in the design stage rather than implement poor designs. This activity helped some, but not as much as NIMS hoped it would.

NIMS next figured out that if finding problems in the design further upstream was good, then finding problems in the design plan would be even better. Thus, the company initiated design plan reviews in which experienced managers and technologists from various areas reviewed development plans, looking for potential problems that could be corrected before the project got under way. Design plan reviews proved to be quite beneficial.

While the design and design plan reviews were proactive efforts to eliminate defects and other forms of waste, NIMS soon realized that it was not making good use of all of the data on defects—it was not using this data to eliminate root causes of defects, that is, to do reactive improvement. Thus, it changed its operating methods so that if defects were found, investigations would be undertaken to figure out at what earlier time the problem should have been detected and when the problem was actually created.

This process was called defect analysis (see Figure 25-2). By doing this analysis and shortening the two time intervals shown in the figure, NIMS made the development process clearer and also learned how to insert quality (or at least detect lack of quality) further upstream.

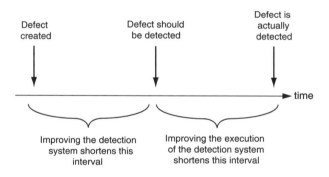

Figure 25-2. Defect Analysis

Having concentrated early improvement activities on various quality assurance activities, NIMS attempted to begin work on improving its product designs. First they began to use quality tables to capture customer-defined quality better. For a chosen project, NIMS determined product requirements and built a big quality table[5] to show how to achieve the requirements, but it took so long and was so big that it was not useful. So, NIMS reconsidered the customer requirements in light of which ones needed innovation (a small fraction) and which could be handled routinely (a large fraction). In other words, it learned to separate a development activity into parts requiring breakthrough improvement (e.g., invention of a new technology) and incremental improvement (e.g., a small change to an existing module). NIMS's activities requiring breakthrough were called bottlenecks, and the necessary innovative activity became known as bottleneck engineering. Then, it used quality tables to plan how to do the bottleneck engineering. This proved to be effective.

So far, the chronology of NIMS improvement activities described illustrates an important aspect of CAPD. NIMS didn't limit itself to reacting only to measured weaknesses of the previous cycle. The Plan part of CAPD also includes an often qualitative assessment of the next important direction. Therefore, we see NIMS's improvement targets moving through several cycles of defect detection and elimination and then changing direction to focus on effective deployment of customer requirements. The successful parts of each improvement effort were added to NIMS's overall product development system.

Once the customer requirements deployment system was made explicit, NIMS realized its design process was not very explicit. Thus, NIMS embarked on what it called phased hierarchical design. Of course, we all know about phase review systems for product development in which the development process is divided into five or six phases, each of which is several to many months long. NIMS divided these phases into much shorter subphases. This subdivision served two purposes. First, it provided many more instances of process visibility (e.g., clear interfaces, clear test procedures); second, it permitted earlier feedback about problems. Making the process more visible allowed NIMS to understand which methods did and didn't work, helped teams of engineers to work together efficiently, provided standard models for successive steps in the process for which standard tools could be built, and enabled greater reuse of modules. NIMS's phased hierarchical design method also included a detailed mapping between elements of the design and how each element was to be accomplished.

By this point NIMS had progressed significantly in making the process visible and in moving the quality insertion upstream. However, it had not progressed far enough. In particular, the ultimate source of defects is mistakes by engineers, and it was unclear how engineering managers should help engineers to improve their skill—"to become more professional" (in Uchimaru's words). By "professional," Uchimaru did not mean someone who gets paid for doing something each day; rather, he meant the equivalent of a golf pro—someone who shoots par.

Uchimaru says that any professional (at golf, the game of go, or VLSI design) has three characteristics:[6]

- A strong grounding in theory and the ability to apply the theory practically
- A large set of tools he or she knows how to use in different situations, acquired through experience (many turns of the improvement cycle mentioned above)
- A strong capability for analyzing failure (the professional understands why he or she made a mistake and learns from it)

The traditional way professionals are developed is by having a student study with a master. However, in the engineering field, the method often used to teach engineers is the school of hard knocks. Companies hire engineering graduates from good schools and assign them to projects without much guidance on how to do good engineering. In fact, many engineering managers think their only jobs are to allocate staff and tasks and monitor results, and they don't have any explicit system to develop better engineers. Uchimaru makes the point that engineering managers frequently use the notion that engineering is an individual art, learned through personal experience, as an excuse for why they can't do much to improve their engineers' abilities. However, Uchimaru says that if companies are to develop engineers who create fewer defects, engineering managers must become coaches who teach the young engineers professional skills.

This recognition led to a system called problem prediction. The subphases of phased hierarchical design are divided into still shorter phases, each a few days long. The engineering manager's job is to sit down regularly with each engineer and ask what the engineer is going to do in the next few days. Having heard the engineer's design plans, the manager asks the engineer to predict what might go wrong. Then, the manager tells the engineer to go about his work. A few days later, the manager again sits down with the engineer and asks him to describe his recent design work—what went wrong that the engineer did and didn't predict. The manager then helps the engineer evaluate the quality of the design because a junior engineer often is incapable of judging whether a design is good. Through this problem prediction and coaching process, the engineering manager teaches other engineers to be professionals. Uchimaru says that a good manager must know the capabilities of his or her engineers well enough to accurately predict the areas in which they will have problems; then, the manager can subtly guide the engineer to enable maximum learning from the engineer's process of prediction and reflection.

Figure 25-3 is a more detailed summary than shown in Figure 25-1 of the key CAPD cycles in the NIMS story.[7]

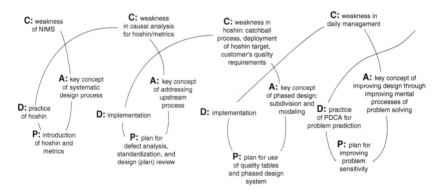

Figure 25-3. CAPD Cycles at NIMS

In the last two phases of the NIMS story, managers spread the techniques (such as quality tables) and facility of tool use throughout the company. Each of the concentric circles (labeled A, B, etc., in Figure 25-1) represents roughly a year's time. By iteratively improving and controlling its development process, NIMS used TQM as a learning system that eventually taught it how to bring its development processes to the point where it had far better results than industry averages and won the Deming Prize. With each CAPD cycle, it made another quality improvement. Starting with relatively superficial changes, NIMS gained skill to recognize and efficiently correct defects until eventually it was working at the profound level of improving the professionalism of its engineers. Uchimaru describes this as the "spiral up of craftsmanship."

Portability of the NIMS System

In 1993 a group of CQM CEOs, chief quality officers, and development VPs visited NIMS and heard Mr. Uchimaru first hand describe the NIMS system described immediately above. Mr. Uchimaru described a very impressive system of product development and very impressive results. At the end of his presentation, one of the CEOs noted how impressive the NIMS system was and asked Mr. Uchimaru how the CEO's company could adopt the NIMS methods. Mr. Uchimaru answered to the effect that

> I do not believe you can transport the NIMS system to your own company. I believe that you must develop your own system that addresses your company culture and business situation. I believe that you must start with some basic principles—such as the two with which NIMS started of finding defects earlier and making processes more visible—and then use a systematic process of trial and error to develop a system that works for you.

This was a surprising response at the time, especially since we all were thinking in terms of adopting best practices of others wherever we found them. However, in retrospect, Mr. Uchimaru was making an important point central to the methods described in this book: while one should look for best practices wherever one can find them, each company has to create its own overall system of best practices; in so doing, the company will create its own best practices that in turn can be shared with others. Each company needs to design its own integrated management system.

25.3 COMPANY STRATEGIES

Having obtained an overview of hoshin management (Chapter 24) and seen how NIMS used it incrementally to improve its development process (previous section), we now address the question of management development in organizational change and improvement. Improvement of managers' skills and managers' job processes is more complex than improvement for lower-level employees; company improvement strategies and systems typically must be augmented for managers. The necessary skills and processes for managers are more complex in three ways, and thus require extended improvement strategies.

First, managers are responsible for more complex processes. Managers are responsible not only for low-cost incremental improvements, but also for making larger-scale breakthroughs and deciding issues of resource allocation. If a company's improvement system focuses only on quality improvement teams of lower-level employees, managers are likely to equate quality improvement teams with improvement, and therefore exclude major breakthrough processes from systematic improvement. In addition, if improvement strategy and systems focus improvement on high-level or low-level teams, managers can lose sight of available improvements they can make to their own daily jobs. Also, long cycle-time processes tend to require a variation from PDCA as applied to short cycle-time processes; this long cycle variation of PDCA is known as CAPD, where you Check and Act on last year's hoshin management cycle, Plan the next year's hoshin management cycle, and then Do the planned hoshin management for the year (hence CAPD). These issues are discussed more fully later in the chapter, as is the distinction between CAPD and PDCA.

Second, more than anyone else, managers must take responsibility for achieving results, whatever the difficulties. If they don't, who will? However, many company strategies focus only on the desirability of accomplishing objectives and not the means of accomplishing actual results. To improve the company's capability systematically to achieve results, managers must learn to improve processes in which both the improvement and the consequences take time to ascertain; they must also learn how to discover what part of a process prevents the desired results and how to fix it. These issues are discussed later in the chapter.

Third, a system must exist to mobilize managerial participation in improvement activity in the company hierarchy. If the company uses a system of voluntary participation in improvement activities, a manager might choose not to participate, a decision that can leave those below with no leadership or support in quality improvement. However, the activities of managers differ significantly according to their level in the organization. Therefore, different mobilization strategies are needed for each level of the organization. These strategies are also discussed later in the chapter.

Ubiquity of the Dual Function of Work

When managers first learn about organizational change and improvement, they often think quality improvement teams do all improvement work and that the teams will use the 7 steps, 7 QC tools, QFD, and so on for reactive improvement. The following two subsections extend this view.

Incremental and Breakthrough Improvement

Many managers recognize that the systematic improvement methods can make incremental continuous improvement to specific processes. They often don't recognize, however, that systematic methods exist for seeking breakthrough improvements.

The following figures illustrate the three improvement levels to which all systematic methods are applied.[8] To a considerable extent, these parallel the three types of problem solving from the WV model: process control, reactive improvement, and proactive improvement.

The first level of improvement comes from greater adherence to standards. This is SDCA, as shown in Figure 25-4.

The second level of improvement comes from incremental improvement by QC circles and quality improvement teams. This is one type of PDCA, which we call $PDCA_1$, as shown in Figure 25-5.

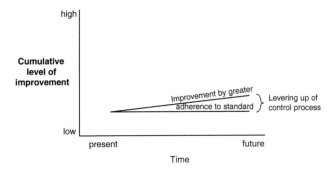

Figure 25-4. The SDCA Improvement Cycle

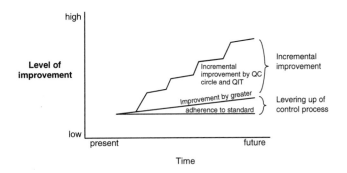

Figure 25-5. The $PDCA_1$ Improvement Cycle

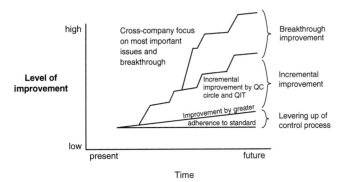

Figure 25-6. The $PDCA_2$ Improvement Cycle

The third level of improvement, another type of PDCA, comes from focusing on the most important issues across the company and on cross-company breakthroughs. Current information about the environment and company goals is needed for this; we call it PDCA$_2$, as shown in Figure 25-6. Hoshin management is a method of such breakthrough (PDCA$_2$) improvement.[9]

The relationship between different PDCA systems for continuous and breakthrough improvements is made explicit in Figure 25-7 which shows how Japanese companies apply appropriate improvement methods to both incremental and breakthrough improvement [179]. Coming out of the SDCA cycle near the bottom left of the figure are two types of problems that require improvement: (1) routine problems and accidents or acts of God, and (2) critical problems or profound problems (such as changing the company's quality culture). The first type of problem can be addressed by continuous improvement activities, while the second type of problem requires breakthrough activity and can be addressed by the company's system of hoshin management.

Routine Work and Improvement Work

Many managers think their daily job has no relation to the 7 steps or PDCA. However, the dual function of work also extends to managers' own work as well as their efforts to stimulate activities of improvement teams. Managers need to explicitly apply improvement methods to their own daily work.

Once managers understand the two types of PDCA, they must discover how these are relevant to their own routine work.

As shown in part A of Figure 25-8 on page 560 typical managers in companies not working on systematic improvement spend perhaps 70 to 95 percent of their time on routine work and firefighting. Unfortunately, the improvement methods for these problems are often intuition at best and guesswork at worst—not very efficient. This leaves the managers only 5 percent of their time, or frequently less, for critical problems and breakthrough improvements.

If managers are to have time to work on breakthrough improvements, they must reduce the time they spend on routine work and improvements, as in part A of the figure. This means they have to obtain the benefits of standardization and use an efficient improvement process (i.e., the 7 steps) on routine issues. Increasing use of explicit SDCA and PDCA$_1$ actually makes more time available for working on breakthrough improvements, as shown in part B of Figure 25-8 . Furthermore, the explicit improvement methods of SDCA and PDCA$_1$ produce more valid data, experience, and improvement skill. Not only do SDCA and PDCA$_1$ provide more time; they also develop intuition and innovation skill. In effect, they convert intuition from guesswork to mastery.

In companies practicing the methods of organizational change and improvement, managers do PDCA$_1$ themselves, as part of their daily jobs. There are three systems for getting managers to this level. In the first, quality improvement teams use the 7 steps, PDCA$_1$, and a little PDCA$_2$. They do this both to solve problems and to get on-the-job training in applying the 7 steps and PDCA. However, this first approach has two weaknesses: (1) diffusion of quality improvement teams is limited—that is, all managers can't participate in quality improvement teams; and (2) quality improvement teams move away from the idea that PDCA is a part of routine work.

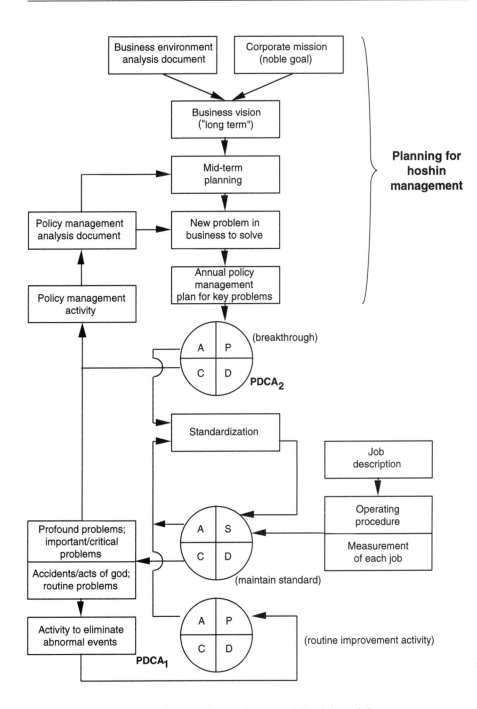

Figure 25-7. PDCA Systems for Continuous and Breakthrough Improvement

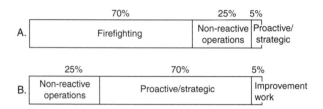

Figure 25-8. Usual and Desirable in Executive Time Management

Therefore, a second system is needed. This is hoshin management. Hoshin management forces all managers to use PDCA (in the form of CAPD) as part of their annual or semiannual plan for accomplishing key company objectives. In other words, hoshin management requires managers to practice $PDCA_2$.

Third, when managers have experience with $PDCA_2$, they are ready to tackle the hardest task, running $PDCA_1$ on their own routine work. Once a manager has experienced PDCA as a member of a quality improvement team or through hoshin management, the manager can begin to use systematic improvement in his or her own daily job.

Using the Concept of Hoshin Management in a Department

We mentioned that hoshin management provides an opportunity for managers to personally practice PDCA. However, hoshin management as normally practiced includes participation of managers from throughout the company, interlevel catchball, and a month or two to make the yearly plan. To many U.S. managers, hoshin management appears complex and documentation-intensive, making them reluctant to try it.

We have two observations on this. First, the empirical result, companywide improvement, is commensurate with the effort. Second, like so many models, the hoshin management model is applicable at many levels. A company's first experience with hoshin management doesn't have to be at a companywide level; a divisional or departmental team can apply the model to a planning task. Consider the hoshin management figure again (see Figure 25-9).

A department, for instance, has some longer-term (e.g., yearly) goals. As a result, they have decided that some specific "significant" task has to be accomplished, significant meaning a task with several independent subtasks to be performed by individuals or groups. Such a task might be a marketing communications plan (e.g., advertising or brochures) for the year. Rather than doing interdivisional and interlevel catchball, the entire department planning team might get together to deploy this task (i.e., plan the subtasks and perhaps subsubtasks) and to develop an appropriate plan to control the subtasks (monitor adherence to the plan for accomplishing the subtasks and monitoring results).

The departmental deployment of tasks and measurement parallels hoshin management as described in the previous section, except it is done on a more contained scale and with all of the managers participating. Thus, the deployment should be

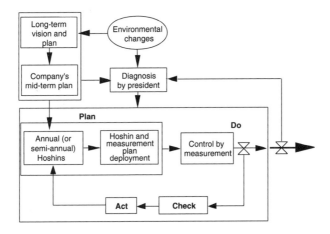

Figure 25-9. Hoshin Management

shorter and more straightforward, requiring, for example, a day or a few days of planning. Approaching the task planning in this way has the benefits of the hoshin management system, a plan that closely targets accomplishment of the task (rather than one based on guesswork), and a system for taking data to discover what actually happened with adherence to the plan and its results. This provides the necessary information to run the CAPD cycle, so each annual plan for this task benefits from the previous year's experience.[10]

CAPD versus PDCA

As stated earlier in this chapter, we write PDCA in the CAPD form to emphasize the control and feedback aspects of PDCA. The difference between PDCA and CAPD is to a considerable extent a point of view.[11]

PDCA applies well to manufacturing, administrative, or other processes where the past is repeated and the ultimate target remains more or less constant. For instance, consider the process of preparing a monthly financial schedule. The ultimate goal is to make the schedule more accurate, clearer and cheaper, and quickly done.[12]

As shown on the left of Figure 25-10, the process initially has considerable variation.

The first PDCA cycle is used to improve the process and its results, as follows:

P: Pick the problem most responsible for the variation in results, analyze the root causes of the problem, and plan countermeasures to fix the root causes.

D: Do the improvement.

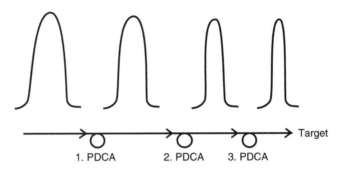

Figure 25-10. Repeating PDCA

C: Check that the improvement was effective.
A: Standardize it as appropriate, and go to the next improvement.

Under continuous improvement, the PDCA cycle is then run again (second cycle in the figure) to eliminate the next most important problem and further reduce the variance of the process and its results. Then PDCA is run again (third cycle), and so on. Every month the process is repeated, and the target remains the same—reduced variance to achieve a more improved and economically produced financial schedule.

CAPD applies well to planning situations, which take up the bulk of managers' time. In these situations, the past is unlikely to repeat, and emphasis must be on planning the future. Consider, for instance, the yearly sales plan. As with PDCA, the process initially has considerable variation, as shown at the left of Figure 25-11.

However, the target for the next planning cycle (target1) is likely to differ from the target for the previous planning cycle because times will have changed. Even so, you want less variance in the way you carry out the plan for the next year and the amount by which you miss objectives. So, you run the first CAPD cycle. The letters of CAPD have the following meanings.

CA: Discover what was wrong with the previous process that prevented achievement of the desired results; what are the key things to improve for the next cycle.
P: Determine what is desired for the future (e.g., what is the next target).
D: Carry out the plan for the year.
CA: Check whether target was achieved, and if not, why not (repeat CAPD).

The chronology of NIMS' CAPD improvement activities (pages 550–555) illustrates an important aspect of CAPD. NIMS didn't limit itself to reacting only to measured weaknesses of the previous cycle. The Plan part of CAPD also includes an often qualitative assessment of the next important direction. Thus, we see NIMS's improvement targets moving through several cycles of defect detection and elimination and then changing direction to focus on effective deployment of customer requirements. The successful parts of each improvement effort were added to NIMS's overall product development system.

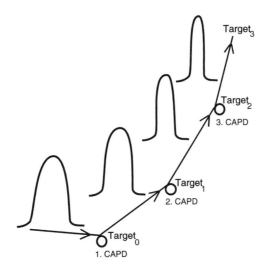

Figure 25-11. Repeating CAPD

The purpose of CAPD is to improve the process in the face of changing goals. Therefore, standardization in CAPD differs from standardization in PDCA in that you must standardize on improvements to the process but at the same time change the process to achieve changing goals.

PDCA is often compared to the scientific method: Plan an experiment to test a theory, Do the experiment, Check the results of the experiment, and Act appropriately to publish or revise the theory. In fact, PDCA is a great description of the scientific approach as applied, for instance, in an industrial, quality assurance situation where the target is known and relatively constant.[13] CAPD is more representative of the scientific method as applied by research scientists. Such scientists have to decide what theory to test next on the basis of previous results and events. They must plan an experiment, controlling variables that can be controlled, so they can accurately interpret the results. They analyze the results, extracting all possible information that will enhance their understanding, especially what did and didn't work, what parts of the experiment they were unable to carry out and why, and so on. Finally, they adopt and apply the validated parts of the theory and decide which key insights they should investigate in the next cycle.

CAPD differs from PDCA in degree and emphasis in three ways:

1. In CAPD, greater effort is required to conduct a controlled experiment or, at least, an experiment where it's clear what couldn't be controlled. In a typical manufacturing or administrative process to which PDCA would be applied, carrying out a controlled experiment is relatively easy.
2. Processes to which CAPD is applied are often so complex and interleaved with other processes or external events that the goals of the process change over the course of an improvement cycle.

3. In repetitive manufacturing and administrative processes, enough data can often be collected during the plan stage so that root causes can be identified. In the complex, evolving processes to which CAPD is applied, one often has to run the cycle several times to gain an understanding of the potential root causes—the NIMS case study at the beginning of this chapter is an example.

Using the CAPD Cycle in the Daily Job

One cliché is that Japanese managers take a long-term view of process while U.S. managers take a short-term view of results. The short-term versus long-term distinction is in many cases an illusion; the true distinction is between correcting the superficial and correcting that which endures. Results focus on the superficial. Process focuses on what creates enduring improvement.

Control of Process

Most people in a company act as if they don't understand that results come directly from the process. Figure 25-12 illustrates the process for baking a cake with the result coming from the process, which involves methods, operators, materials, equipment, and so on. The results of the baking process include the cake's quality characteristics: taste, texture, color, and so forth. (If you want a more high tech business example than a commercial bakery, think about baking an integrated circuit in a wafer fab.)

Many companies largely ignore the relationship between process and results and focus instead on objectives, hoping that by delegating aggressive objectives to capable people, they will somehow obtain the desired results.

You can control the process by monitoring it appropriately and taking appropriate actions to produce the results desired, for instance, a moist cake, as shown in Figure 25-13.

There are three levels of control of process in the concept of CAPD.

The process for making moist cakes requires an oven temperature of 350 degrees. The temperature can be monitored, and deviations from 350 degrees are used to adjust the oven temperature until it is on target. This is control of process by deviation of process from standard, *a* in Figure 25-13.

The moistness of the cake can be monitored, and deviations from the desired results used to adjust the process appropriately. This is control of process by deviation of result from standard, *b* in Figure 25-13.

Notice the emphasis on both results metrics and process metrics. If you don't look at results metrics, you won't know if the process is working. If you don't look at process metrics, you won't be able to determine what did or didn't work. You must monitor both kinds of metrics and pinpoint what must be done to improve the process and thus the results.

A third type of control is needed so that changes in the environment can be addressed. By monitoring the societal or cultural environment, you can use deviations

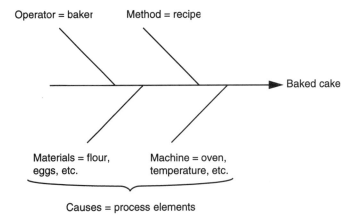

Figure 25-12. Process Elements of Cake Baking

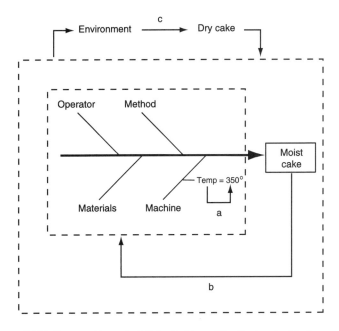

Figure 25-13. Process Control of Cake Baking—Monitoring the Environment

between current process goals and new cultural desires to adjust the total process and its goals to the new cultural norm. This is control of process by monitoring deviation of goals, *c* in Figure 25-13.

Assumption of Responsibility

The highly developed manager must become capable of controlling a company's destiny in an uncertain world. This requires taking responsibility for developing processes that address the real situation. It means applying CAPD at successively more difficult levels, as follows:

Level 0: *Watch results*—give little feedback beyond assigning blame to individuals to whom you assigned the task.

Level 1: *Take responsibility for the process*—control by monitoring deviation of process from standard. If you don't take responsibility for the process, you won't be able to maintain good results if they happen, and if they don't happen, you won't know why (that is, you won't know if the process didn't work or it wasn't followed).

Level 2: *Take responsibility for results*—control by monitoring deviation of results from standard. You rely not on opinion or intuition but on data leading to the real root causes of the results. Take responsibility for studying the process and then make the change necessary to achieve the desired results. Don't blame failure on individuals, the process, or circumstances.

Level 3: *Take responsibility for learning to survive in a changing environment*—control by monitoring deviation of goals. Take responsibility for helping the company survive in a changing world.

Institutionalizing the CAPD Cycle

Recall the domino theory described in Chapter 20, which is that the CEO or president must mobilize the change officer and senior managers before the middle managers can be mobilized (see Figure 25-14). Typically, a few unconvinced senior managers may also need further mobilization.

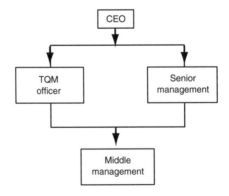

Figure 25-14. Domino Theory of Mobilization

Mobilize all levels of the organization to use the CAPD cycle. Work from the top down, from the bottom up, and in the middle, making a special effort to get the middle managers to do CAPD (see Figure 25-15). Since the nature of the job is different at each level, requiring different applications of CAPD, companies should use a different mobilization strategy at each level.

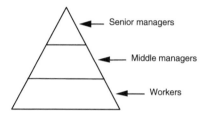

Figure 25-15. Mobilizing All Levels

Top-down Mobilization—President's Diagnosis

Diagnosis by the CEO or president and by the division head is an important tool to mobilize the company to CAPD.[14] These diagnoses have three purposes:

- To enforce the CAPD cycle in the organization and to communicate to all employees the concepts of systematic improvement and use of the 7 QC tools
- To bring about the company goals and to examine adherence to the planned means
- To give the president an understanding of the support subordinates need and give insight into the work environment of the lower third of the organization, particularly into employee attitudes

Achievement of these purposes yields clear benefits to the organization. The president's diagnosis has other benefits as well:

- Once doing periodic analysis, the company will have a vast amount of data about its organizational change and improvement activities and business activities; once this data is available, great opportunity for improvement exists.
- Diagnosis contributes to the education of a president. Whereas teaching is a first step to understanding the methods of organizational change and improvement, diagnosis is the next step, requiring study of what questions to ask and enough skill to give prescriptions for improvement.

Table 25-1 shows a typical plan for such a presidential diagnosis.[15] A detailed example of presidential diagnosis is provided starting on page 482.

Table 25-1. Plan for Presidential Diagnosis

1.	Decision about which division and who will be diagnosed	1 month ahead of diagnosis day
2.	Planning of diagnosis—main issues	1 month ahead
3.	Distribution of detailed schedule for diagnosis day	10 days ahead
4.	Submission of presentation transparencies and diagnosis document to the president	1 week ahead
5.	Logistics preparations	1 day ahead
6.	Diagnosis day	
7.	Reflection on weakness and comments by the diagnosis team	Within 1 week of diagnosis day
8.	President and executives make a formal document of their diagnosis	Within 15 days
9.	Division submits analysis of problems found by diagnosis and solutions	Within 1 month

Mobilizing the Middle—*Ochibo-hiroi* ("Gleaning")

The previous section described the presidential diagnosis as a top-down strategy for institutionalizing use of CAPD. This section deals with a strategy for the middle of the organization.

Since 1952, the Hitachi Corporation has used a system it calls *ochibo-hiroi*, the Japanese name of the painting by Jean-François Millet entitled *The Gleaners*, in which three women farmers are shown picking up wheat missed in the harvest. To Hitachi, *ochibo-hiroi*, or gleaning, means to pick up and use old experience.

Once a year in the Hitachi system, middle managers reflect on mistakes and complaints related to customers. Each section picks out its most serious or critical mistake of the past year and analyzes it in detail to see what can be learned.

Examples of symptoms to be gleaned from the year's experience are:

- Interacted poorly with a customer or another company
- Received a complaint that it didn't believe or accept
- Gave a customer excuses or an explanation for a problem rather than taking action on it

To understand and gain enduring benefit from the year's experience, middle managers must follow two guidelines:

- Take the viewpoint of the customer and assume responsibility for the problem.
- Focus on processes and root causes to find out why such a problem happened.

Figure 25-16 illustrates how the Hitachi group uses *ochibo-hiroi* to institutionalize CAPD in middle management. The people in the section do the ochibo-hiroi analysis under the leadership of the section head. The section head must learn about CAPD to lead the analysis and present its results. The section head has to give an explanation in front of middle managers. The division head diagnoses the section head's presentation. Thus, managers learn all the facts of what is going on in the division, as well as CAPD focused on the customer.

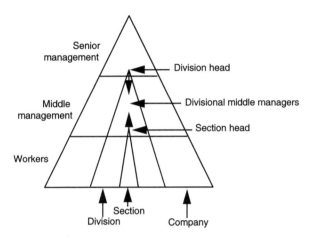

Figure 25-16. Institutionalizing CAPD in Middle Management

Bottom-up Mobilization—5S Activities

5S activities are very popular in many factories in Japan, where the 5S symbol is frequently seen. The 5Ss, as one Japanese company taught one U.S. supplier, are as follows [303]:

- *Seiri*: Keep only needed material at the job site; remove unnecessary items immediately.
- *Seiton*: Store materials in an orderly fashion.
- *Seiketsu*: Observe overall cleanliness; in neat and clean surroundings, something wrong is more obvious.
- *Seiso*: Clean tools, equipment, and job site whenever necessary; clean equipment works better.
- *Shitsuke*: Practice self-discipline.

Use of 5S has two purposes:

- To set CAPD in motion from the workers to the supervisors and their managers.
- To bring CAPD to the bottom of the organization, that is, to mobilize the workers to adhere to standards and see the benefits of standardization for long-term (not just immediate) improvement (see Figure 25-17). 5S activities find the implicit standard and highlight deviation from it.

25.4 INDIVIDUAL PRACTICE OF CAPD BY MANAGERS

We have given a number of examples of company strategies for developing management practice of CAPD: hoshin management, presidential diagnosis, ochibo-hiroi, and 5S. All of these can directly or indirectly force managers to practice CAPD. However, to practice CAPD most effectively, managers must also take personal

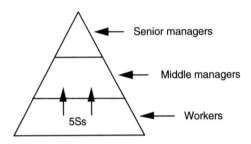

Figure 25-17. 5S from the Bottom Up

responsibility for understanding the full scope of application of CAPD and for developing their CAPD skills.

Suppose a manager sees a problem (N) in a certain process over the course of several months. As illustrated in Figure 25-18, problem N is the most serious problem in July, the second most serious in August, and again the most serious in September.[16]

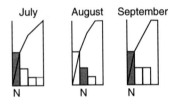

Figure 25-18. Data from a Process

Stages of Managerial Action

The manager's job is to take some action about this problem. The manager can take a variety of actions, each indicative of a further stage of development of individual practice of CAPD, as indicated in the second and third columns of Table 25-2.

Table 25-2. Stages of Managerial Action

Stage	Extent of managerial action	Managerial purpose	Means
0	Giving instructions		
1	Intuitive analysis	Dual function of work	Do own improvement work
2	Causal analysis	Prevention of recurrence	Use real information
3	Revision of standard	Adherence to process	Install system
4	Applying learning to other situations	Eliminating latent problems	Self-innovation
5	Integration of efforts	Business success	Focus

Stage 0: At this stage of managerial development, the manager does not understand the concept of dual function of work, thinks that quality improvement is "not my job," and assumes the manager's job is to give instructions. This is not an adequate level managerial responsibility.

Stage 1: At this stage, the manager shows understanding of the dual function of work—improvement is everyone's job and an important personal responsibility—but does not truly understand PDCA. The manager may think intuitively about the cause of the problem, devise a solution, and delegate implementation of the solution to a subordinate, but the manager has skipped data collection and causal analysis.

Stage 2: At this stage, the manager undertakes formal causal analysis of the problem and formal planning of a solution and only then delegates implementation to a subordinate (or perhaps even participates in the implementation), which may not result in an explicit SDCA system for the solution.

Stage 3: At this stage, the manager understands that a process or system must be created if an improvement is to be maintained. The manager undertakes formal causal analyses and solution planning, estimates the effect of the solution or evaluates the solution in an experimental way, and revises the standard if appropriate, including measurements to control the process.

Stage 4: At this stage, the manager examines other products and processes to see if they have the same problem and uses the analysis of the first product to improve the others. This is the expert level of managerial practice of organizational change and improvement.

Stage 5: At this stage, the manager understands stages 1–4; moreover, the manager understands that further improvement requires that these activities be used in concert, an integration of efforts to achieve business success.

Means Associated with Each Stage

The means of achieving each managerial purpose is listed in the right column of Table 25-2.

Stage 1 Means

To implement the dual function of work, the manager must not delegate all problems to a subordinate. Rather, the manager must personally do two things: provide a clear mission and goals and carry out the improvement work.

Regarding the first task, the manager must make clear two types of goals: noble goals and practical goals. The noble goal usually benefits the customer; the manager must constantly speak of personal belief in the primacy of the customer. Practical goals are what must be accomplished immediately by the manager and subordinates.[17]

However, the manager must do more than clearly state the mission and goal. The manager must demonstrate personal belief in improvement methods by using them in practice, for example, by running PDCA. Practicing improvement behaviors is hard for managers yet essential; if managers do not personally practice improvement activities in their own routine work, the staff will not believe in the methods and the manager will not gain skill in them. Managers should err on the side of not delegating improvement work. Hence, the important slogan "No delegation."

Stage 2 Means

Just fixing a problem is not sufficient. Future occurrences of the problem must be prevented. The key to prevention is to reveal what is really happening, that is, to get and use real information. The people with the true information are the people doing the job everyday. To get the true information from these people, the manager must adhere to two important practices: no criticism and active listening.

No criticism means that the manager must not ask who was at fault, why the problem wasn't found sooner, or how people could let this happen. Even when receiving a presentation of a plan, managers should encourage employees to speak openly, for example, by encouraging them to be candid about what should be done and why. Critiquing the plan seldom elicits as much real information as does encouraging employees to speak openly.

Critical questions, explicit laying of blame, or critical analysis will at the minimum stop employees from speaking and may make them falsify their information. Employees quickly learn what managers want and don't want to hear, and they give them what they want to hear. All managers have experienced this.

In fact, offering no criticism is not enough; approval is required. Divide the problem into small steps in which good points can be found and acknowledged immediately. Approval is more effective if directed at specifics ("it is good that you constructed a Pareto diagram") rather than generalities ("you are doing an excellent job"). We have heard of companies as impressive as Cisco applying this principle.

Stage 3 Means

Organizational change and improvement at the level we are describing is a mass movement. Everyone needs a system or process to follow; however, this system or process shouldn't be rigid. On page 333, we described the system at Disneyland, designed to launch visitors on an enjoyable visit, a process that happens automatically and without explicit discipline.

Another example of such a process is the theme selection matrix[18] used as step 1 of the 7 steps. This matrix guides quality improvement teams through the process of selecting appropriate tasks without imposing a rigid structure on the discussion.

Managers must learn to create business systems and processes that enforce work standards without rigid discipline. They must make the systems easy and enjoyable.

Stage 4 Means

The half-life of knowledge is getting shorter and shorter. Skills required for the job and society change rapidly. Managers must constantly renew their knowledge and themselves. We call this self-innovation, which has three keys:

1. Curiosity: Curiosity is critical because it provides natural motivation to find out what needs to be changed and how to change it.
2. Openness to learning from others: Curiosity is not enough. One doesn't learn quickly enough from personal investigation. One needs openness to learning from others. Thus, managers must listen empathetically, not critically. They must get rid of the I-already-know-it (IAKI) attitude (see page 25).
3. Fishbowl approach (going on site): Observing people in their own environment is often the most effective way to learn from others. The fishbowl principle is described in Chapter 13, page 231: one discovers more by observing things in their actual environment than from getting prestructured information, such as surveys or reports from subordinates. With regard to self-innovation, the fishbowl approach has three benefits:
   - It offers an alternative to the question/response model of learning, which leaves important questions unasked.
   - It enables triangulation, that is, one can look at things from several angles to discover what is actually happening.
   - The person with the most knowledge will learn the most from a visit; therefore, the manager should personally go on site.

Stage 5 Means

Companies have many problems and many capabilities, skills, and practices. We can apply the capabilities, skills, and practices to many problems simultaneously, as shown in Figure 25-19.

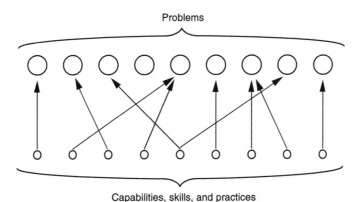

Figure 25-19. Attacking Many Problems at Once

This approach might be how the world would look to managers at Stage 4, when they have developed many skills but have not yet learned to integrate their efforts.

But such an approach is both time-consuming and self-defeating, diluting the effort necessary to conquer the problem. Practically speaking, you must integrate your efforts somehow. Focusing on a specific target puts sufficient capability on a problem to solve it; it provides the only feasible means of using many capabilities simultaneously and improving the way the capabilities are used together (see Figure 25-20).

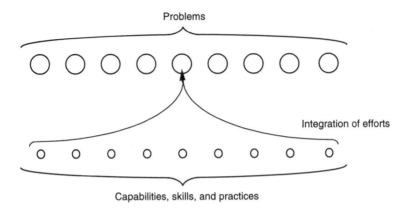

Figure 25-20. Focusing on a Specific Target

Actually succeeding in solving a problem is the most important component for future success. Integrating and focusing your capabilities so you can solve a problem is the first major step to this success. Initial success in the process gives one a sense of achievement, thereby reinforcing desire to know more, and so the cycle repeats itself. The enjoyment that comes from repeated success leads to more success. With success and enjoyment come ability and creativity (see Figure 25-21).

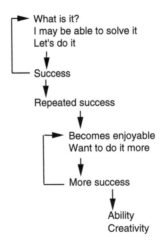

Figure 25-21. Reinforcing Ability and Creativity through Success

Ability in the figure means an integrated set of learning habits, attitudes, and skills that can be applied not only to college calculus but also to many other topics. The ability to deal skillfully with many new things is virtually a definition of creativity.

To summarize the details of the means for the five stages of managerial development, we add another column to the table (see Table 25-3).

Table 25-3. Managerial Action, Purpose, Means, and Components

Stage	Extent of managerial action	Managerial purpose	Means	Components of the Means
0	Giving instructions			Clear mission and goals Personal practice of improvement
1	Intuitive analysis	Dual function of work	Do own improvement work	No criticism Recognition of staff Active listening
2	Causal analysis	Prevention of recurrence	Use real information	Enjoyable, not rigid
3	Revision of standard	Adherence to process	Install system	Openness to learning Curiosity Swim in the fishbowl
4	Applying learning to other situations	Eliminating latent problems	Self-innovation	Narrow focus Repeated use
5	Integration of efforts	Leveraging for success	Focus	

NOTES

1. This story and more of Glavin's ideas on the personal practice of quality are found in [108].

2. Here is the short form: CAPDCAPDCAPD ... is like PDCAPDCAPDCA ... but with a different starting point.

3. Hoshin management is an advanced technique for focusing an entire organization each year on a small number of key improvement goals. We described it in Chapter 24.

4. This figure is our interpretation of the NIMS documentation, and the directions of the line segments are qualitative estimates.

5. See Figure 14-17, page 270, and Table 14-6, page 272, for examples of quality tables.

6. See the models of skill development mentioned in Chapter 2 (pages 22–28). In some sense, the steps listed here are Uchimaru's own model of skill development.

7. We will refer to this figure again in Chapter 27.

8. Based on a figure by Kozo Koura in [5, page 105] and a figure by Kaoru Ishikawa [148, page 170].

9. In Chapter 27, we will introduce skills for leading breakthrough of a more extreme form, resulting in a complete change of business. This might be called PDCA$_3$, although we call it SCMT.

10. For more details and essentially a step-by-step process on the idea of applying hoshin management at the department level, see [302].

11. Each company needs to decide whether to use both PDCA and CAPD in its vocabulary of change and improvement, or only to describe variations of PDCA. Having both PDCA and CAPD could cause confusion and debate—"Are we doing PDCA or CAPD now?" or "What exactly is the difference between PDCA and CAPD?"—which doesn't necessarily add value. On the other hand, in some companies managers or other professionals are loath to use the same tools that work in manufacturing and administration, that is, PDCA. In this case, it may be useful to emphasize the differences between PDCA and CAPD.

12. This statement can apply equally to the manufacturing of a steel cylinder, in which the ultimate goals are to make the cylinder ever more precisely, quickly, and cheaply.

13. Spear and Bowen provides a wonderful example [271] of the scientific method as used at Toyota.

14. We use the terms CEO or president to mean the top manager in the organization. In companies with a CEO and a president who reports to the CEO, the two officers should consider doing the diagnosis together.

15. This table is adapted slightly from [183]; see also [147, pages 161–169].

16. This case was developed from a case briefly mentioned in [152, page 172].

17. The benefit of hoshin management is that it breaks down these immediate targets, aligns them with the company goals, and provides a fact-based process for deciding which goals the managers should personally undertake and which should be delegated and to whom.

18. Defined on page 128.

26

Further Case Studies in Mobilization

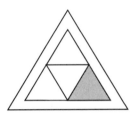

Throughout this book we have given examples and case studies illustrating specific activities such as reactive improvement, mobilization infrastructure, and so on. In this chapter, we will provide overviews of organizational change and improvement activities over many years in three companies.

The purpose of these long-term overviews is:

- To emphasize that successful organizational change and improvement is a long-term effort that requires many PDCA cycles.
- To illustrate that a long-term effort inevitably involves integrating many methods from many sources into the company's own new "best practices."
- To show some of the devices that companies use to move to the top-right corner of Figure 26-1 and the overall system they create to provide strong leadership toward strong empowerment—the way they change structures, systems, and processes to "force" participation.

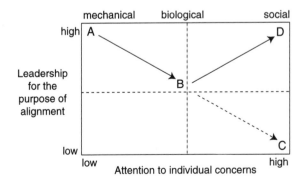

Figure 26-1. Strong Leadership and Strong Empowerment

26.1 TERADYNE STORY CONTINUED

We begin by finishing the Teradyne story we have been telling throughout the book. A list follows, in chronological order, of the parts of the Teradyne story we have been telling throughout this book:[1]

- CEO Involvement at Teradyne—page 410
- Teradyne Strategy for Introduction—page 415
- Process Management Mobilization at Teradyne—page 175
- 9 Steps Mobilization at Teradyne—page 185
- 9 Steps Case Study at Teradyne—page 186
- Monitoring Improvement Teams at Teradyne—page 445
- Teradyne story continued—immediately below
- Teradyne Aurora—page 630

Following is a summary of what was described in the earlier sections.

Teradyne's organizational change and improvement efforts (they think of them as TQM) have incrementally developed over years. They started with Crosby's methods without substantial CEO leadership. With their business crises in the late 1980s, CEO Alex d'Arbeloff got personally involved and led the top management team in a process of self-education about TQM. Alex D'Arbeloff then led a CEO crusade through all of the divisions telling them why change was necessary and what that change would be. Teradyne adopted the 7 infrastructures model as their method of mobilization and focused it on mobilizing 7 steps quality improvement teams throughout the company. Based on practical experience, top management with the help of a small number of TQM managers created the Teradyne standards and manual for 7 steps and provided impetus for many quality improvement teams to be established. In time they discovered that the 7 steps quality improvement teams were not performing as well as desired. With the help of the TQM managers, top management created the Teradyne standards and manual for better managing quality improvement teams, again based on practical experience. Next, needing to move beyond focusing only on reactive improvement, Teradyne helped created the 9 steps method of planning and executing new projects and deployed it throughout the organization.

The story continues

By the time Teradyne began to deploy the 9 steps in early 1992, a second TQM manager, Tom Pursch, was cycling through the corporate TQM office. Tom's previous position was as operations manager for Teradyne's connections systems division in Nashua, NH, and his appointment fit the Teradyne model of rotating line managers through the corporate and divisional TQM manager positions.

Spreading the common language

The top management team of Teradyne had taken the CQM's 6-day Course for Senior Managers taught by Shoji Shiba (upon which the first edition of this book was based) in the fall of 1990. By 1990, it had become clear that the TQM vocabulary Teradyne's top management had learned and was using needed to be spread throughout the company. Therefore, from July through September 1992, Shoji Shiba did a 6-Day course in Teradyne for 60 senior managers. By editing the videotapes of Shiba's presentations from that course, a six-hour course was developed to spread a common language. This let everyone know who "this Shiba guy" was. Approximately one year later, 5,000 people in the company had attended the six-hour course on "TQM Concepts," which included descriptions of market-in, PDCA, and so forth.

When manuals, courses, and the like are developed at Teradyne, they are developed by the companywide network of TQM managers (each of the 12 divisions has a TQM office, supporting the division similarly to how the companywide TQM office supports the company overall). This network of people meets monthly by phone and quarterly in person and establishes subcommittees, which go and do the work. In documenting principles and guidelines, they *always document the experience of line people* in using the various methods; their own contribution adds some organization and clarity.

Creating a planning process—hoshin management

Teradyne made its first attempt at a TQM planning process in late 1993. This was its first attempt to do formal companywide planning (along the lines of hoshin management). Out of this came the first annual plan for the "Teradyne Planning Process" in which every division signed up for levels of team participation, quality improvement team spin rate, and so on. This planning process used "five-element planning" tables (à la hoshin management), business plan review tables, a clear articulation of goals to be deployed and means of achieving them, and so forth; in general, the process was based on Teradyne's study of hoshin management. Also, as part of the divisions' plans, each was to use a voice of the customer process to get input for the goals of the company.

During 1993–1994, Jim Prestridge (a strategic thinker on the top management team) and George Chamilard (then general manager of Teradyne's connections systems division in Nashua, NH) began to document a planning process, including steps and flow. People then met to do a PDCA of this draft planning process; from this PDCA effort, detailed guidelines of what people were to do were developed.

Also, since Teradyne was nearing Motorola's deadline for applying for the Baldrige award, three teams were set up, each to address two of the seven Baldrige criteria. Alex d'Arbeloff addressed the seventh, leadership. They wrote and submitted the application, looking for feedback.

The customer data that divisions had collected and the data resulting from the Baldrige effort were integrated into the planning process for Teradyne's 1995 goals. Affinity diagrams were used to analyze the customer data and strengths and weaknesses from the Baldrige effort. From this analysis Teradyne, developed its TQM goals for 1995.

By this time, TQM was becoming part of the way work was done at Teradyne.

Beginning presidential diagnosis

Teradyne's key hoshin was changing the culture to TQM. As part of hoshin management, the president is supposed to visit the sites, the division management at each site, and the workers on the plant floor.

Presidential diagnosis in hoshin management is described in Chapter 24, starting on page 521. See particularly the subsection on Purpose and Benefits starting on page 523; review them now. A particularly important benefit of presidential diagnosis is that it provides another way for the divisions to learn from each other. Good ideas from one division are inevitably passed along to other divisions as the presidential diagnosis team moves from division to division. In their writings, TQM fathers Ishikawa, Juran, and Muzano make similar recommendations.

Therefore, in 1994, Teradyne started its presidential diagnosis activity, although it was initially not very well structured. Over time, Teradyne's presidential diagnosis has evolved to be similar to that described in Chapter 24.

By 1996, the presidential diagnosis had evolved to a focus on the 7 infrastructures (see Figure 26-2[2]). The diagnosis focused on how each division was implementing each of the 7 infrastructure elements and how the implementation could be improved. In 1996, for example, the divisions were instructed to concentrate on the Organizational Setting element and the Monitoring and Diagnosis element of the 7 infrastructures and told to choose two other elements of the 7 infrastructures also to address.[3]

Also, presidential diagnosis had become a major yearly reflection by the whole company and division management. Each of the 12 divisions is visited for four hours at which there are 20-minute presentations by the division and 40-minute tours related to the topic of the presentation. (For illustration purposes, the details of the presidential diagnosis cycle are described in a following subsection, starting on page 582).

In 1997, Teradyne completed its second 7 infrastructures-based presidential diagnosis, using the 7 infrastructures as the vehicle to examine how well it was using TQM methods. In 1998 and 1999, Teradyne used the company's vital few goals for the vehicle and expanded the number of executives who attended the sessions. Also, in 1999, it incorporated a new self-assessment component at the end of each visit in which the division and visitors did two LP diagrams answering the questions "What were the strengths (and weaknesses) of Division X's work?" In 2000, the vehicle was taking a better look, asking each division to reflect on how TQM has helped it manage through past business difficulties, what are some expected future challenges, and how will TQM be used to manage these challenges.

Skill development of the CQC

By 1995, Teradyne had spent five years in its "modern era" of TQM and had begun presidential diagnosis the year before. In that year, the Companywide Quality Committee (CQC)[4] asked itself if it was happy with what it had been doing for five years. For instance, some valuable things the CQC did early in its TQM implementation had

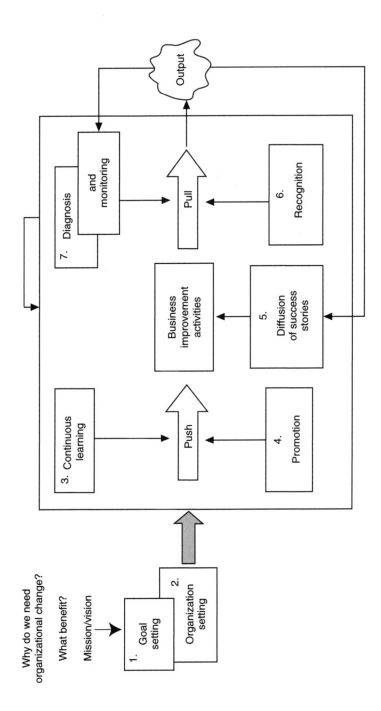

Figure 26-2. 7 Infrastructures for Mobilization at Teradyne

become more administrative over time and were no longer helpful. Many of these activities no longer needed CQC help.

As a consequence of thinking about what it should be doing to progress forward and its involvement in presidential diagnosis in terms of the 7 infrastructures, the CQC members decided their own skills weren't good enough and they should use CQC time to develop their skills in each area of the 7 infrastructures.

The CQC established a full-day TQM workshop every quarter, at which members set out to study the elements of the 7 infrastructures. In June 1996, they considered Organizational Setting, Goal Setting in August 1996, and were to consider Monitoring and Diagnosing in October 1996. However, they then changed the topic to Revolutionary Product Development (RPD) [310] because their analysis showed RPD was a key area the company needed to concentrate on.[5]

The CQC approached RPD in the same way Teradyne approaches most things. First, members looked at the division which (it happened) did development best and highlighted the division's best practices. They learned about effective practices, which provided a baseline to compare other divisions against. In the process of this comparison, the divisions learned from each other. (We provide more detail on this in a following section.)

In March 1997, the CQC held its delayed workshop on Monitoring and Diagnosis and its second workshop on Goal Setting in May 1997. At the same time as these CQC workshops, cross-company functional forums were also held.

The combination of presidential diagnosis in terms of the 7 infrastructure elements and CQC workshops on the same elements produced good results. At the first 7 infrastructures-based diagnosis in 1996, the Organizational Setting element was one of those diagnoses. The quality of divisional efforts with Organizational Setting was distributed like a normal distribution: a couple of divisions did especially well, a couple did badly, and most divisions were spread across the broad middle range, as shown in the "before" part of Figure 26-3. By 1997, the normal distribution narrowed its variance substantially and the mean had shifted up near where only the best performing divisions had been the first time around, as shown in the "after" part of the figure. Teradyne was led to expect a similar before-and-after effect as other elements were diagnosed and run through the PDCA cycle in succeeding years.

A Detailed Look at Diagnosis and Monitoring

As noted in an earlier subsection, Teradyne's TQM Annual Hoshin Plan includes each division's goals for how many teams, percentage of people on teams, and cycle time of teams. Each division reports on these visible metrics each month. However, this is not sufficient to understand what is really happening. Hoshin management's presidential diagnosis can provide much additional insight.[6]

Here is an example from the third year of presidential diagnosis at Teradyne. Each division was asked to report on:

1. Organizational Setting

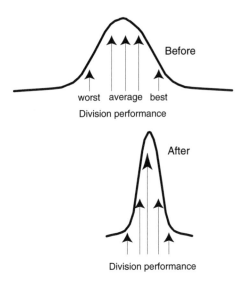

Figure 26-3. Teradyne Division Performance for Organizational Setting

2. Monitoring & Diagnosis
3. Two other elements of the 7 infrastructures where the division has a problem or something to demonstrate

The people who travel from division to division to do and support the presidential diagnosis are: George Chamilard, president; John Petrolini, corporate TQM manager; the other corporate TQM manager (the position through which line managers rotate); a division manager from a different division than the one being diagnosed; and another divisional TQM manager. The last two people participate to do mutual learning with the division being diagnosed. Often one participant in the diagnosis is a TQM manager from a division still to be assessed to give that division a "heads-up" about what to expect. Each of the 12 divisions is visited for four hours at which there are presentations by the division and plant tours relating to the topic of the presentation.

As is obvious, Teradyne manages presidential diagnosis just like anyone would manage anything important. Teradyne also manages it as a PDCA cycle, as can be seen below.

Plan

One needs to reduce variation, so every division is given a proposed agenda for the presidential visit to the division, covering the following:

I.   Opening (to put people at ease)—5 minutes
II. Presentation by division management—60 minutes
III. Tour of the floor—120 minutes
IV. Closing summary—55 minutes

The guidelines for the presidential visits are shown in Figure 26-4. The divisions were asked to provide some information in advance of the actual visits.

I. Desired outcomes
    . . .
    . . .
    . . .

II. Background (this is 3rd time)
    Process in year 1
    Goal determination in year 2
    . . .

III. Model
    Input from divisions

Presidential diagnosis

Feedback

Figure 26-4. Guidelines for Presidential Diagnosis

Do

Having planned the visits for presidential diagnosis, it is time to do them. The process of doing the visits takes three to four weeks and very specific times are scheduled for each division.

From previous years, Teradyne learned to schedule the presidential diagnosis visits at the best divisions first. This educates the traveling top management team and allows them to query other divisions in ways that lead to the spread of good practices.

Figure 26-5 is an example of the agenda for the presidential diagnosis visit from Teradyne's Nashua TCS plant.

At Nashua, the top management of the division pushed administration of teams "down a level" because aggregation of certain team management activities made sense. Therefore, instead of reporting on their management of quality improvement teams, the top management of TCS presented their norms and where they actually spent time. They also reported on other teams within the division involved in the planning of TQM.

The most beneficial learning from these visits may be what the divisions learn about themselves in preparing for their presentations.

Check

1. Process of presidential diagnosis. The check process for presidential diagnosis includes an LP diagram of strengths and weaknesses done by the president and a few others. This data is stratified into numbers of instances of each topic and is fed into the next year's diagnosis cycle. The presidential diagnosis was done at TCS and at every other visit.

```
┌─────────────────────────────────────────────────────┐
│              Presidential Diagnosis Agenda           │
│                 Teradyne Nashua Plant                │
│                                                       │
│  10:30 Opening remarks,  Alex/George                 │
│                                                       │
│  INFRASTRUCTURE PRESENTATIONS                         │
│  10:35 Organization Setting                          │
│          15 min. presentation/discussion             │
│  10:50 Continuous Learning                           │
│          15 min. presentation/discussion             │
│          5 min. walk to plant floor                  │
│          20 min. review of tools, etc., with supervisors │
│          15 min. discussion                          │
│  11:45 Incentives and Awards                         │
│          15 min. presentation/discussion             │
│                                                       │
│  LUNCH                                                │
│                                                       │
│  12:50 Diagnosis and Monitoring                      │
│          10 min. presentation                        │
│          10 min. presentation—Spin rate PDCA         │
│          15 min. tour/discussion with "Quick Spin" team │
│          20 min. discussion                          │
│   1:45  Closing Summary                              │
│   2:30  Adjourn                                      │
└─────────────────────────────────────────────────────┘
```

Figure 26-5. Example Presidential Diagnosis Agenda

2. Results. After all the visits were over, strengths and weaknesses were analyzed across divisions (500 labels in all) and used to refocus the CQC. From these observations, hypotheses were generated:

- Recognition
- Deployment
- Diagnosis
- Metrics

The last three of these suggested senior management was not involved enough in TQM. This led to a discussion of senior management involvement.

Act

The corporate TQM office had also taken copious notes, coded them, put them in an Excel database, and summarized them by organizational setting, monitoring and diagnosis, goal setting, continuous learning, and the other categories of the 7 infrastructures.

This led to the suggestion by CEO Chamilard for a workshop where managers would learn from each other. Workshops were held. Three were on elements of the 7 infrastructures: organizational setting, goal setting and deployment, and monitoring and diagnosis. The fourth workshop was on RPD. The workshops were from 8 A.M. to 6 P.M. and included homework.

Function, structure, process, and the manager's role as leader were considered by each person attending for each of the categories, to generate insight. The goal was to understand and share. At the meeting, sharing is done, guidelines are drafted, etc. The TQM office then turned these into more formal guidelines with justifications based on people's labels.

Deploying Revolutionary Product Development (RPD)

As mentioned above, Teradyne's CQC concluded that Teradyne's product development process needed improvement. Therefore, the CQC members looked around for best practice and zeroed in on Clark and Wheelwright's ideas on Revolutionary Product Development [310].[7]

RPD is a framework, not a process. The method has two parts:

Path 1:   How to pick products to develop, i.e., doing the right things
Path 2:   How to implement projects rapidly, i.e., doing the right things well

Teradyne decided to focus on Path 1 first, because Alex d'Arbeloff and others thought more of their problems were there.

In August 1995, a high-level, top management team was formed, led by Ed Ragas.[8] In October 1995, the team members read Wheelwright and Clarks's book. In June 1996 they visited HBS. In July 1996, RPD work began with two days of team training. Later in 1996, an RPD pilot was begun in each division with senior management participating on each team. All divisions completed Path 1 by June 1997, and a CQC workshop on RPD was held in August 1997. As a result of the "lessons learned" shared at this meeting, Path 1 guidelines were developed and completed by the end of 1996.

Once again Teradyne's top management developed the "Teradyne way" for a method introduced to the company. In this case, since RPD was presented by Wheelwright and Clark as a framework and not as a process, Teradyne was perhaps the first company to operationalize RPD.

A similar process began for Path 2 in October 1997. This included developing metrics to measure Paths 1 and 2, a model for a phase gate development system, a process project assessment, and a project execution strategy matrix (which is revised based on the assessments).

Management transition

By 1997, a significant management transition was taking place at Teradyne. Founder Alex d'Arbeloff was phasing out as CEO. (He remained as Chairman of the Board, taking a particular interest in several of Teradyne's new ventures, and took a half-time position as Chairman of the Board of MIT.) Jim Prestridge, who had been a key strategic thinker on the top management team for many years, phased out. Owen Robbins, who had been chief financial officer and led the general and administrative staff (and originally told us the story of TQM mobilization that we recounted in Chapter 20) retired.

George Chamilard, who had been instrumental in beginning Teradyne's quality effort in the late 1980s, became CEO. Mike Bradley, the first TQM Officer in 1990 and later VP of Worldwide Sales, took Owen Robbins' position leading the financial and G&A activities of the company. Ron Butler, who was leading operations for Teradyne in California and, with John Petrolini and us, had been a member of the CQM Design Team in 1990, became VP of human resources.

You will also remember that Teradyne rotates up-and-coming line managers through the corporate and divisional TQM manager positions for tours of 18 months to two years. However, as Alex d'Arbeloff told us, it is hard to keep people in these positions for their full intended tour of duty. There is pressure for these highly capable people to be rotated to new opportunities in line management in the divisions. Thus, today approximately 75 line managers—in perhaps two-thirds of the key divisional and corporate management positions—have served a tour as a divisional or corporate TQM manager.

Unlike so many companies that lose their organizational change and improvement program when new management takes over, Teradyne has used its management transitions to solidify its TQM program and bring people with TQM extensive experience into key management positions throughout the company.

In Teradyne, new methods are usually introduced to address a specific weakness. Teradyne doesn't try many things simultaneously, and it doesn't try things because it is supposed to be the way one does something. This approach goes all the way back to the formation of the company by Nick DeWolf and Alex d'Arbeloff, when they decided to specialize on diode testing and get good and big at doing that before addressing transistor testing. Year after year, Teradyne PDCAs its TQM program, further developing its management team, its business practices and its people with each PDCA cycle.

Teradyne has achieved a fair degree of maturity with regard to organizational change and improvement (at least compared to many other companies). At least three aspects of their system are particularly noteworthy:

- Their relentless practice of the PDCA cycle
- The way they involve people and share excellent practice
- The system they have created to obtain synergy—using 7 infrastructures and cross-organizational

Through all this, our friend John Petrolini, has served in the corporate TQM office as TQM manager. Shoji Shiba said, when introducing John to one of our classes at MIT, "John has studied a new kind of TQM and practiced it in Teradyne. He is the best person to describe the theory and practice and its subtleties. He will discuss how TQM was introduced into Teradyne and what they have done as the company got more mature. Each year, a company's way of practice has to evolve."

John's presentation to our class finished with a question and answer session. Two of the questions and answers were particularly revealing.

Question: Do people at Teradyne really want to participate? Answer: Life is a bell-shaped curve, with people at all positions on the curve in terms of their desire to participate. Teradyne is no different. However, I don't see how you can successfully work at Teradyne for very long and not participate. This is the way Teradyne does business. You won't have any way to communicate. Someone without a continuous improvement mentality begins to be someone who cannot succeed in the company.

Question: Does Teradyne still learn a lot after several years of practice of these methods? Answer: There are periods of improvement, then plateaus. We need to work more on the vital few. TQM is about fundamentals. We are now working on the product development process.

We appreciate the time John has taken to share the Teradyne story with us for this book.

26.2 HP STORY

The outline of Hewlett-Packard's story of mobilization of organizational change and improvement is based on what we learned from Brad Harrington's presentations to our MIT course.[9] Because HP allows considerable autonomy in how its business groups and divisions operate, probably no single "correct" story of HP mobilization exists. The story we got from Brad is how things have looked from his perspective.[10] Nonetheless, for the purposes of this book, this version of the story is representative enough of the essence of HP mobilization over the years.

TQC starts at HP

HP had always been concerned with quality; it was a key value of its founders from its founding in 1939. However, HP first learned about "total quality" in the sense we use it in this book from its Japanese subsidiary, Yokogawa Hewlett-Packard (YHP). In the late 1970s YHP, had suffered from quality, cost, and other problems in the very competitive Japanese business environment. To reverse this problem, YHP initiated a Total Quality Control (TQC) program (TQC is what TQM was originally called in Japan). The TQC efforts helped YHP turn its business performance around, and in 1982, YHP was awarded Japan's Deming Prize.[11] YHP's TQC program and performance so impressed HP CEO John Young, that he set very aggressive (e.g., a factor of 10 improvement) quality objectives for HP for the 1980s; in particular, John Young's challenge was to improve hardware reliability by a factor of 10 within a decade or sooner. These aggressive goals led to people from throughout HP studying the TQC methods being used by YHP. Soon, business groups and divisions throughout HP were using TQC methods, such as statistical quality control methods like the 7 QC tools and Just-In-Time manufacturing.

Thus, TQC has been practiced at HP for almost 25 years, which shows "constancy of purpose," to use Deming's famous phrase. Also, from the time of John Young's demand for "stretch goals," HP has also been CEO led, with a quite explicit organizational and management structure. TQC at HP has explicitly included customer focus, process improvement [107], and people participation."[12]

Quality Maturity System

While HP did companywide TQC, the HP way was to allow the operating units of the company considerable autonomy. In the earlier years of HP's companywide TQC program, various parts of the company learned and used many different quality improvement and customer focus methods. Thus, HP had trouble knowing how well the various parts of the company were doing. They didn't have a single set of process metrics to drive TQC such as Teradyne's number of teams trained, spin rate of teams, participation on teams, and so on. Therefore, according to [209],

> In the 1980s, HP started an effort to objectively measure how well HP businesses were institutionalizing TQC. At HP, progress is made by following a "measure, then manage" approach. In 1988, under CEO John Young's leadership, the corporation created the Quality Maturity System (QMS). Its purpose was to:
>
> 1. Define HP's Quality System and put into a context all the quality and management techniques in use; and
> 2. Provide an audit that management could use to benchmark where any part of Hewlett-Packard stood in its efforts to implement TQC.
>
> Each HP division was to receive a QMS review by 1991 and to achieve a QMS score of 3.0 (on a 5 point scale) by 1995.[13] A QMS review schedule was developed. HP Quality Managers were trained as QMS reviewers and this highly visible process was started.
>
> QMS version 1.0 focused on reviewing five areas of quality practice: planning, customer focus, improvement cycle, process management, and total participation. A QMS review also assessed the Quality department's contribution to improving the entity's quality maturity.
>
> Management teams benefited in several ways from undertaking QMS reviews. They understood how HP's many quality initiatives fit into a coordinated system of management. They were able to assess the "quality maturity" of their business more objectively. Recommendations and review scores highlighted areas where improvement would be beneficial. Finally, the reviewers were able to share practices that were getting good results elsewhere within HP. From 1991 to 1995, average QMS scores improved about 10 percent from one review to the next. This was clearly a sign that HP entities were "bootstrapping" their own success.

In the early 1990s, in response to the desire of the management teams of HP business groups and divisions to link quality work and strategic business success directly, a second version of QMS, QMS 2.0, was developed. This moved QMS beyond only quality elements to the inclusion of a management system model covering internal and external best practices for management and improvement. In the early 1990s, HP management teams wanted QMS to incorporate a direct link to strategic business success "strategic focus, business planning, process management, improvement projects, and leadership and participation" [209]. Assessments under QMS 2.0 increasingly took advantage of having division reviews be done by skilled reviewers (including senior managers) from other divisions. Thus, much cross-fertilization of best practices among divisions resulted. (See also [1].)

In the late 1990s, pressure built in HP to change QMS to align it to current business needs and to take even greater advantage of skilled assessors throughout the company. So, QMS 3.0 was created. QMS 3.0 would "leverage collective knowledge and wisdom from across HP to help entities improve performance now, while better preparing for sustained success in the future," and "be applied to a broad range of HP field, product, and support entities" [209].

Several aspects of the QMS system seem noteworthy to us:

- QMS has evolved over time. HP has continued to develop its own best practice monitoring mobilization of business improvement.
- QMS has increasingly viewed business management and management of quality and improvement as a single integrated system.
- QMS provides an "objective" measure to drive business groups and divisions to continue working to improve their improvement methods.
- QMS's interdivisional assessment teams provide a way to institutionalize mutual learning across the company.
- In the HP way, to use QMS is a decision each division makes for itself; corporate encouragement exists but using QMS is not a requirement. However, many divisions have adopted QMS because it helps them monitor themselves and gain useful insights from other experienced people from other divisions. It helps them, so they use it.

Yearly Business Planning Elements

HP has an annual planning cycle that includes the three elements described in the preceding three subsections that operate together in an integrated and coordinated way:

- Hoshin plan for breakthrough objectives
- Business fundamentals plan to monitor routine operation of core business processes
- Key project plans

The hoshin plan, business fundamentals, and key projects for the year are chosen based on a strategic plan. The strategic plan results from HP's 10-step planning process which deals with markets, customers, products and services, competitors, and financials.[14]

Hoshin Management

From about 1986 on, HP used a version of hoshin management. In fact, HP helped popularize hoshin management in this country, having helped many companies learn it and "sending" executives who knew it from HP to various start-ups. HP has also done an excellent job of adapting the forms of hoshin management to non-Japanese culture and making these forms be highly effective business management tools.

Of course, as described in Chapter 24, hoshin management is used to address the one or two especially important cross-functional or cross-organizational issues. Typically in a given year, each HP business unit addresses one corporationwide and one business unit hoshin. It aligns these (no more than two) key goals and means of accomplishing the goals throughout the organization. It gives everyone in the organization explicit goals, means, deadlines and so on, for these key activities.

HP states that its hoshin (or breakthrough) objectives:

- Aim to achieve a few stretch numerical goals or to resolve serious problems and deficiencies
- Involve multiple functions and departments
- Create large changes for the organization

Brad Harrington makes an interesting point about how hoshin management helps. We all know how much pressure there is in business to deal with urgent day-to-day issues, to make the monthly and quarterly financial goals, and so on. In the face of these urgent issues, we find no time for the important but less urgent issues such as making fundamental cross-organization changes in the way business is done that may take a year or more to accomplish. Hoshin management, says Brad, "Makes the important urgent." By having specific goals, plans, deadlines, and monitoring one or two important changes the organization is going to try to make over the course of a year and reviewing everyone for their performance against those goals, these important activities come into balance with and share the available time with the urgent day-to-day issues. Once again, HP is using structure and processes to motivate a desired behavior change.

Unlike most methods used in HP (for instance, QMS), for many years hoshin management was mandatory for all divisions. However, recently, in response to the *very* rapidly changing business environments faced by some of its division, HP has made hoshin management optional. Still many business groups and divisions are using it.

Business Fundamentals

Business fundamentals is the name HP gives for planning and monitoring typical yearly operational financial and other goals that:

- Are needed to meet day-to-day obligations
- Involve only direct reports
- Are incremental improvements of existing processes

The chart of business fundamentals includes a review of a business's key processes, reporting the status of metrics for each process. Examples include:

- Customers (e.g., customer satisfaction)
- Products (e.g., product generation slip rate and product failure rate)
- Order fulfillment (e.g., on-time delivery)
- Quality (e.g., quality maturity score)
- People (e.g., employee survey results)
- Financials (e.g., orders, revenue, and profits)

In effect, business fundamentals is a balanced scorecard that spans the domains of customer satisfaction, financial results, and so on. These areas of the yearly operating plan are monitored by exception using green, yellow, and red light symbols on the monthly and other periodic summaries to indicate areas that are going according to plan, may be at risk, or are in trouble.

Project Management Process

One of the major activities of a high-tech company like HP is executing projects: development projects, plant and equipment projects, marketing projects, and so on. Clearly, if people could improve the way they managed projects, it would help the company. Thus, HP organized a project to "benchmark" the best practices of people throughout the company who were seen as successful project managers. What was learned from these best practices throughout the company was aggregated into an explicit process for project management.

The project management process can be used to accomplish tasks under both hoshin management and business fundamentals (described in the next two subsections) as well as other projects.

Continuing Evolution

The organizational change and improvement methods at HP continue to evolve. As already mentioned, QMS 3.0 has been developed recently. Since 1995, HP has pushed for "Quality 1-on-1" [188] methods to see the customer point of view better and to build empathetic relationships with customers. HP has numerous other processes and models it has developed over the years, such as its 10-step business planning process and its new product development process.

Some people see the evolving use of methods (especially when methods are first introduced with lots of visibility and then fade in use) as evidence of something being wrong, as indicating "faddishness." Brad Harrington has another take on this. Brad notes that when a new idea is introduced people normally test it to see if it fits their situation and personality. How would they know whether the method is for them without trying it? Without a little experimentation with a new method, people will not understand whether to keep using it (to varying degrees), to modify it, or integrate it with other methods. Thus, a few years after a new method is introduced, one is likely to find it used in various places throughout the organization—the places for which it was appropriate. Going forward, not much emphasis will be placed on the (once new) method. Going forward, the method will have become "just the way we do business" for the groups using it.[15]

Before leaving the HP story, we want to mention one specific method that the top management team of HP's Medical Products Group used during the time Brad Harrington was chief quality officer.[16] Each member of the top management team had two job assignments. For instance, each of the executive committee line managers reporting to the general manager of the business group was also a member of the business group steering committee. Each had responsibility for leading an area of the business group's quality program, areas such as market focus, customer feedback, process management, improvement cycle, planning, participation, business measures, and quality maturity. Brad Harrington reports that this dual structure, of using line managers to lead one aspect of the quality infrastructure, worked well.[17]

After the HP-Agilent Split

We have learned the following about what has happened after the separation of Agilent from HP in 1999 and the arrival at HP of a new CEO from outside the company.

In the new HP, the businesses have been given increased freedom to choose their planning and implementation tools. Many managers continue to use hoshin management, business fundamentals, 10-step planning, etc. Some managers have developed custom tools to fit their business models, and some are experimenting with iterative, discovery-driven planning [200]. HP has changed QMS's name to BLS (Business Leadership System), and it is more than ever a model for an integrated management system in the sense we use the term in this book. The new CEO's focus is "Total Customer Experience," and HP is rolling out methods to support this, building on the Quality 1-on-1 thrust begun in 1995 and mentioned above.

Many of the HP methods described here also continue to be used in Agilent. Managers continue to find them useful.

It seems clear that the long HP history of evolution of business improvement methods continues in both companies.

26.3 ANALOG DEVICES STORY

Analog Devices Inc. (ADI) was a founding member company of CQM. Ray Stata, ADI founder, CEO until 1997 and still chairman, was co-founder and has always been chairman of CQM. Goodloe Suttler was, for many years, a senior executive at ADI who served in marketing and general management positions and until he left the company in 2000 was VP for planning, quality, and marketing. We first met Ray Stata and Goodloe Suttler in 1989 and 1990 when Ray was co-founding the CQM with Tom Lee and Shoji Shiba and Goodloe was a member of the CQM Design Team with us. This story of Analog Devices' quality journey comes from various presentations we have heard over the years from Goodloe and Ray.

Five case studies from Analog Devices were already presented in earlier chapters:

- Broken Pellicle 7 Steps at Analog in Chapter 9 (beginning on page 133)
- Efforbusters 7 Steps at Analog in Chapter 10 (beginning on page 163)
- Core Teams at Analog Devices in Chapter 19 (beginning on page 385)
- Self-Directed Work Teams at Analog Devices in Chapter 19 (beginning on page 388)
- Hoshin Management at Analog Devices in Chapter 24 (beginning on page 531).

The Business of ADI

ADI's customer mission statement is:

> To provide OEM customers with signal processing solutions in analog, digital, and mixed signal IC form that increases their products' performance and functionality, while decreasing their products's cost, size, weight, and power dissipation.

ADI has chosen to work in a sophisticated technology area, selling to the most demanding customers—other electronics companies that use ADI's components in their own (often very complicated) electronic devices. Furthermore, ADI has chosen to compete in the domain of providing more for less, a domain where quality and quality improvement methods are of paramount importance.

ADI has a dispersed customer base requiring 20 design centers around the world, a worldwide sales organization, and manufacturing in locations in the U.S. and overseas. Their major customers include many of the best companies in the world. For much of the 1990s, ADI expanded rapidly with dramatically increased business performance—four-fold increases in many areas over a decade. ADI produces state-of-the-art electronics devices using state-of-the-art fabrication systems and has been doing very well against its competition.

As ADI has passed the turn of the century, it faces many challenges: how to remain the leading supplier to many industry segments, developing an organization and system to manage an expanding business, further reducing development times for new devices built for customers, maintaining high levels of customer service, and developing and keeping the human talent to do all of the above. In particular, in 1997, Goodloe Suttler spoke of:

- Remaining strong in signal processing
- Operating a $5B organization
- Doing new product development in less than nine months
- Delivering what and when they promise
- Recruiting and retaining the best people

These challenges continue to keep ADI working on organizational change and improvement; they have to remain leaders.

Background

ADI has been explicitly pursuing organizational change and improvement since 1983, an effort which (like the others in this chapter) meets Deming's definition of "constancy of purpose." These companies didn't give up when an initiative failed to work as they hoped. They changed emphasis in what they were doing to do it better, adapted to current circumstances, and pushed ahead.

From Goodloe Suttler's point of view, ADI's efforts fall into four distinct eras.

Self-learning—1983–1986

The first era began with the realization "We know we can do better." They adopted Crosby's "cost of quality" orientation, as so many companies did in the mid-1980s, and they facilitated improvement themselves. It was a time of novices in the company teaching other novices in the company. The business results from these efforts were not significant.

Staff specialist as facilitator—1986–1989

The second era was motivated by growing concern with slowing growth. Something new had to be done. During this period, ADI hired a person who was well acquainted with Juran's ideas, and this staff expert drove their change efforts. The focus was on process instead of results. "Low hanging fruit" was picked in a number of areas, and ADI clearly made progress and improved. However, the journey was not smooth.

CEO as Leader—1989–1994

The third era was motivated by uncompetitive business results leading to fear of a takeover. Goodloe Suttler describes the motivation as "fear and possible humiliation." At this point Ray Stata met Shoji Shiba and ADI became a founding member of CQM. ADI was greatly influenced by Shoji Shiba's ideas (the ideas presented in the first edition of this book), particularly the emphasis on CEO and top management leadership and mutual learning (within the company and with other companies). During this period for the first time the organization seriously embraced improvement, and an improvement culture began to develop.

Senior managers as champions—1995–1999[18]

The fourth era was motivated by the desire to have improved quality be more than just a way of incrementally decreasing costs or increasing customer satisfaction. ADI wanted its efforts at organizational change and improvement to be a source of clear competitive advantage. During this time, ADI brought in the methods of other experts to complement what they had learned from Shoji Shiba and integrated the methods into a single coherent system. Top-level corporate strategy began to drive a quest for improvements in key areas, rather than relying on widespread local incremental improvements taken in the aggregate being enough to improve the performance of the

entire company. The entire senior management team took an increased role in mobilizing the company with an eye to selecting key strategic problems and crushing them.
Goodloe Suttler talked of the hunt for big game with rapid PDCA cycles.

Components of the ADI System

Hoshin Management

For some years ADI, has been using hoshin management. ADI learned about hoshin
management from Shoji Shiba and the CQM, used tips from HP, and did mutual learning with Teradyne. For a description of ADI's use of hoshin management, see Chapter
24, beginning on page 531.

Balance Scorecard

In the late 1980s, the top management team often argued about whether process or
results came first. Art Schneiderman, chief quality officer at that time, proposed what
he called, and what has now become famous as, the "balanced scorecard"—a set of
quarterly and annual metrics which combined financial goals, such as sales and profits, on equal footing with nonfinancial metrics, such as on-time delivery, quality, and
time-to-market. With consistent emphasis and review of balance scorecard performance by the CEO, both results and process came to be viewed as equally important by
senior management.

The evolution of the balanced scorecard is roughly as follows:

1986 The five-year plan, TQM, and nonfinancial goals were integrated
1987 Scorecard emerges
1988 Scorecard deployed to the divisions
1989 Harvard Business School case study published on ADI scorecard [160]
1991 Nolan Norton multi-client study cited ADI's method as best practice

As in so many other examples we have seen in this book, we see a company not waiting to copy someone else's best practice, but rather inventing a new best practice that
others have copied.

Today, the typical division "balanced scorecard" will be something like that
shown in Figure 26-6. The division will have items in the balanced scorecard for its
hoshin objectives, in this case a major increase in new product sales and very reliable
on-time delivery. The division will also have a typical balanced scorecard of financial, customer, employee, and innovation operating metrics it tracks and drives the
business against (in this case, copying HP, ADI calls these operating metrics "business fundamentals").[19]

For each item on the balanced scorecard, ADI will monitor one or more metrics.
For instance, a metric for "On-time delivery" in the figure might be "days late from
factory commit date." Every quarter ADI looks at plan versus actual for all of the items
on the balanced scorecard to understand any variances from the annual plan.

Figure 26-6. Dimensions of a Typical ADI Balanced Scorecard

Four Revolutions in Management Thinking

In the third era—CEO as Leader era—ADI adopted a close variation of the methods described in the first edition of this book (and also included in this edition). ADI's version of TQM included the four revolutions in management thinking (see Figure 26-7). ADI practiced learning at the four levels of practice or learning we have described in this book (see Figure 26-8).[20]

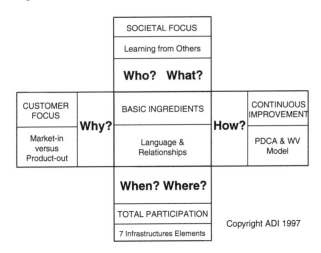

Figure 26-7. ADI Essential TQM Concepts

7 infrastructures. ADI notes that the elements of the 7 infrastructures (see Figure 21-3 or Figure 26-2) are part of the systems used by most or all Baldrige award winners. Therefore, ADI also uses the 7 infrastructures. ADI PDCAs this organizational infrastructure each year and uses its balanced scorecard each year as one way to drive improvement of practice of each element of the 7 infrastructures.

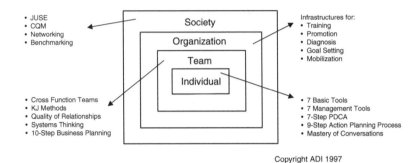

Figure 26-8. Learning Entities

WV, PDCA, and Learn Through Action. ADI correctly tracks WV and PDCA all the way back to John Dewey's principle of learning through action (see Figure 26-9). The relationship between the cycle in the figure and the WV model and PDCA cycle is obvious. Through repeated use of the model and cycles one moves from knowledge to understanding to skill. ADI uses the WV model and PDCA cycle to get many people learning. Goodloe Suttler notes one important reason to continue iterating between thought and practice in the WV model is that whatever you plan never works out as planned. One needs to keep iterating between theory and practice to adjust.

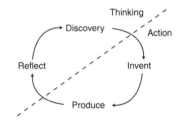

Figure 26-9. John Dewey's Cycle for Learning

Half-Life Model and Process Quality Improvement

Another innovation from ADI is the half-life model for driving the rate of process improvement.

Art Schneidermann of ADI noted [248, 249, 250] that if you are doing continuous improvement on a process you can calculate the rate of improvement over time. For instance, as in Figure 26-10, you can show time (in months) on the x-axis and the reduction in failure rate of parts produced by a process on a log scale on the y-axis. From the rate of improvement in the earlier months, one can predict a target improvement rate that you hope will apply in the later months. ADI uses such rates to set improvement goals and drive a faster rate of improvement than if improvement projects didn't have "objective" targets. For instance, if defective parts per million went from 20,000 to 50 over seven years, then the observed half-life is nine months. From this, ADI might select a target of less than 12 parts per million to be achieved 18 months later.

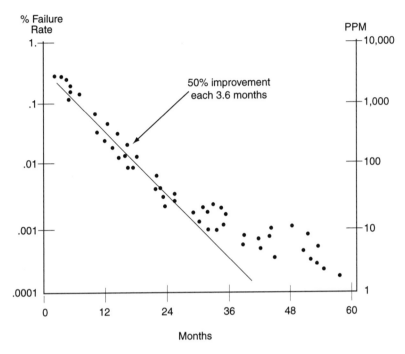

Figure 26-10. Example Half-life Rate

ADI has selected a variety of standardized processes for undertaking improvement projects, for instance:

- 7-step reactive improvement (Chapter 9)
- 8-step problem containment ("8D")
- 9-step project planning (Chapter 12)
- 10-step business planning (à la HP, page 605, note 14)

To each type of improvement activity, ADI applies the half-life model.

Using the half-life model and its variety of improvement types, ADI has seen astonishing improvements in a variety of business processes.

Segmenting Problem Complexity

In recent years, ADI has attempted to systematize more than basic reactive problem solving. ADI has attempted to understand the time scales of problems of various complexity levels and how to handle problems of different complexity levels. Figure 26-11 shows typical time scales for dealing with problems of different complexity

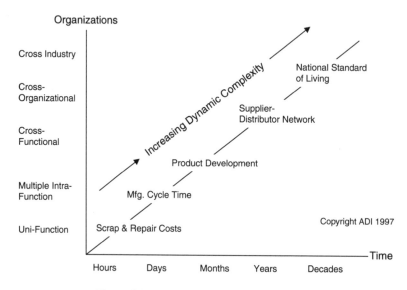

Figure 26-11. Dynamic Complexity of Messes

levels. Figure 26-12 shows two dimensions of complexity—human complexity and dynamic complexity—and the methods that seem appropriate for different mixes of these two complexity types.[21] Looking at this figure, the first thing that jumps out is that there are explicit methods for dealing with problems with low human complexity, regardless of their level of dynamic complexity. This is in keeping with the quote from

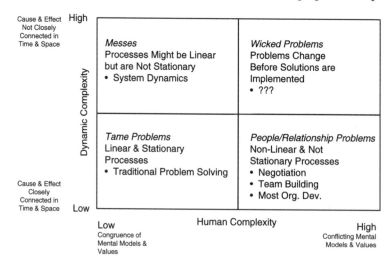

Figure 26-12. Problems of Different Complexities

Tom Malone, president of Milliken & Company, which we heard through ADI and quoted earlier in the book:

The Hard Stuff is Easy.
The Soft Stuff is Hard.
The Soft Stuff is More Important than the Hard Stuff.

Goodloe Suttler suggests that if you find yourself with a "wicked problem," it may be easier to tame it by first reducing the dynamic complexity rather than first trying to reduce the human complexity.

Regardless of the problem complexity, ADI believes the way to change behavior to provide the desired culture is to change the structures, systems, and processes (see Figure 21-2, page 425, which Goodloe Suttler reminded us the CQM Design Team had seen in 1990). Toward this end, ADI lists the *practices* (not tools) in Table 26-1 for engaging, empowering, and mobilizing the people of an organization.

Table 26-1. Practices, Provisions, and Purposes

Practice	Provides	Purpose
Process focused on improvement	Common methods and language to adapt to changes in environment	Enables teamwork
Entire company involvement	Competitive advantage	Uses full potential
Action based on facts	Priorities well grounded in reality	Gets results
Respect for people	Means fo continuing contributions	Keeps it going
Learning from others	Avoidance of reinvention and rediscovery	Saves time
Satisfying a customer	Common orientation and goals	Aligns priorities

Summary from Goodloe Suttler

TQM provides:

- Focus on customers (common goals)
- Quality tools (common language and common methods)
- Use of facts (common understanding)

Also needed are:

- Common vision
- Common values
- Uncommon people

26.4 TOM POWELL'S RESEARCH

We conclude this chapter with some theory from Professor Thomas Powell of Bryant College in Rhode Island [227].

Powell's research suggests that there is a three-level hierarchy (Figure 26-13) of implementation of TQM (and we assume that there would be parallel findings for implementation of other organizational change and improvement systems):

    a. Instruments: Quality themes and slogans, benchmarking, quality training, statistical measurement, etc.

    b. Improvements: Closer to customers, closer to suppliers, zero-defects goal, process improvement, etc.

    c. Intangibles: Executive commitment, open culture, employee empowerment, etc.

Some firms only implement the bottom level a, some implement levels a and b, and some implement all three levels.

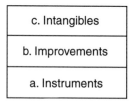

Figure 26-13. Three-level Hierarchy of TQM Implementation

Powell's research shows that firms that are only instrument-driven perform worse financially than non-TQM firms. Basically, these companies incur lots of the costs of implementation and few of the benefits.

His research further shows that firms that add the improvement-driven component perform slightly better financially than non-TQM firms. The additional improvement focus may make a measurable difference but is insufficient to achieve the dramatic levels of improvement most companies seek when beginning such an implementation.

Finally, Powell's research shows that firms that also add the intangibles component to drive their implementation perform significantly better than non-TQM firms. Engaging, empowering, and committing make a big difference.

Tom Powell concludes from his research that a list of practices typically need to be in place if all three levels are to be addressed and to get significant results. These practices from Powell's research are the titles of the following paragraphs, to which we have added our commentary on each of the practices.[22]

Study TQM first. We saw this in the Teradyne case study.

Know your strategic vision. ADI drives its organizational change and improvement strategically.

Fix the culture first. Our observations disagree with this. We believe you have to articulate the culture change you want first, but it will be difficult if not impossible to change it first.

Fix the structure, too. In all our examples, the company changed the structures, systems, processes, and roles to drive the desired culture change. David Lowe (CEO of ADAC when it won the Baldrige award) reports that the people in his engineering department couldn't seem to find time to work on improving their processes. Therefore, ADAC declared that all engineering stopped on Tuesday afternoons from 2 P.M. on, and that time would be dedicated to improvement work. Focusing on relatively short (13 weeks or less) improvement efforts, a great amount of improvement can be done if everyone participates for two or three hours a week. This is an example of changing the structure to force a desired behavior change.

Communicate. We see this is all aspects of the Teradyne approach.

Empower. We see this in all of our case studies.

Clear out ambivalence. John Petrolini mentioned a bell-shaped curve of participation, and David Lowe reports using Shiba's *2-6-2 rule*. Even in the best companies, perhaps 20 percent of the employees are leaders of change, perhaps 60 percent are willing or grudging followers, and 20 percent actively resist. One needs to give everyone a chance (perhaps two or three chances) to participate. Ultimately, however, you have to ignore those fighting what you want to do, and in many cases they will leave the company. This is what happens in every other field of endeavor. People who won't buy into the team's mission are dropped from the team.

Train executives first. All companies try to do this. Teradyne does it exceptionally well, with top management getting first training and learning the new methods well enough to develop the "Teradyne way" for the new methods.

Insist on results. The balanced scorecard that ADI invented and HP's implicit use of a balanced scorecard for business fundamentals drives a balance between improving processes and getting results. The Teradyne and ADI approaches of explicitly connecting improvement work to business goals also is a method of insisting that work on processes produce results.

Cascade training down. Again, Teradyne provides an excellent example. At ADAC, David Lowe only had an administrative person in the "training department" to schedule classes; all teaching was done by managers. When asked, "What if a manager is not a good teacher," David answered, "Then they are not good managers because teaching is part of the job."

Use Just-In-Time training. The big rollout of training to the entire company has not proved to be as effective as training people in parallel with them working on actual problems. Many companies have seen this. ADI has produced some explicit data that support this observation.

Set priorities. No company can do everything that appears could help. Priorities must be set. Some of the mechanisms we have seen for setting priorities are hoshin management ("to make the important urgent"), driving improvement work from the business strategy, and listening to customers to get priorities.

Proceed in phases. Teradyne, HP, and ADI have all gone through a variety of phases, as what they were doing didn't work and they needed to do something different, or as their practice in one area matured and they had the capacity to address their next priority. You can see from these case studies that implementing a "complete" organizational change and improvement system in a short time is an impossible task.

Reinforce. The companies we have described have built systems with reinforcing elements, and they all have methods of periodically PDCAing and reinvigorating the elements of their system and their employees.

NOTES

1. For another view of the Teradyne story, see [186, pages 29–51].

2. Compare this figure to Figure 21-3 (page 426), and you will see that Teradyne has changed "training and education" to "continuous learning" and "awards and incentives" to "recognition."

3. John Petrolini makes the point that the 7 infrastructures model for mobilization includes both push and pull, and that knowing how to do pull well is harder.

4. The top management of the company in its forum for improving the way the company was managed.

5. In essence, whatever the presidential diagnosis uncovers as a weakness becomes a topic for a future workshop. The presidential diagnosis is typically conducted from January through March and the lessons learned from it are used as topics for the four CQC workshops held in April, June, August, and October.

6. This presidential diagnosis from hoshin management also provides an important component of Diagnosis and Monitoring from the 7 infrastructures model since so much complementarity exits in how Teradyne uses the two tools to advance its TQM implementation.

7. The description in this subsection was provided by Brad Nelson, who was the line manager rotated into the corporate TQM office at the time.

8. Ragas is a Teradyne senior vice president, who served as mentor to two divisions and who had been declared owner of the RPD process.

9. In 1999, HP spun off a significant fraction of its business under the name of Agilent and brought in a new CEO from outside to lead the much larger remaining portion of the company which still operates under the HP name. Brad Harrington is a long-term HP employee who, when we first met him, was chief quality officer of HP's Medical Products Group. At the time this is being written, he is manager of human resource development for Agilent Europe.

10. We also drew on various HP documents and presentations we have seen over the years, and two papers [128, 209].

11. See page 613 for more on the YHP story.

12. It also implicitly has included the fourth of our four revolutions, societal networking or mutual learning, as will be seen momentarily in the description of HP's Quality Maturity System.

13. Brad Harrington remembers that the President's Quality Award was made, beginning in 1993, to the internal organizations with high maturity according to QMS and which met financial, customer satisfaction and employee satisfaction milestones. QMS was also emphasized as an important business criterion. The goal of this was to mobilize the parts of HP's decentralized company into action. Seven of 200 internal organization's received the award.

14. The 10 steps: 1. Statement of purpose, 2. Specific objective to achieve over a five-year period, 3. Description of customers and channels of distribution, 4. Description of competition, 5. Description of necessary products, 6. Plan for development or purchase and introduction of products and services, 7. Financial analysis of costs and returns, 8. Potential problem analysis, 9. Recommendations, and 10. First-year tactical plan.

15. Another noteworthy example is HP's use of software metrics and methods of software process improvement [121, 119, 120].

16. For more of the HP's Medical Products Group story, see [186, pages 51–66].

17. We speculate that by having line managers support each other in staff quality roles, they might also have gotten more accustomed to supporting each other in their line management roles.

18. This era was continuing through the time this section was drafted in 1999.

19. Note that the balanced scorecard items in the example shown in the figure span the four areas most commonly associated with a balanced scorecard: customer satisfaction, innovation, employee satisfaction, and financial performance.

20. In fact, our description of the four levels of practice (see page 47 of Chapter 3) is a paraphrase of how Ray Stata describes the four levels.

21. Goodloe Suttler states that this figure comes from Peter Senge.

22. We only focus on a few companies in the our discussion. Many other examples from this book and elsewhere could have been included.

27

The Practice of Breakthrough

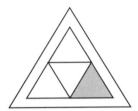

27.1 PROCESS VERSUS BUSINESS BREAKTHROUGH

We start with a brief review of the evolution of breakthrough in business perform-ance. It has had two major phases: taking advantage of processes and viewing the whole business as an integrated system (see Figure 27-1). The first "breakthrough" came in the 1930s: the move from ignoring the concept of process to realizing the benefits of recognizing processes and controlling them (Chapters 7 and 8). The sec-ond breakthrough was in the 1960s and 1970s: realizing the benefits of ongoing incre-mental improvement of processes (Chapters 9–14). The third breakthrough was begun in the late 1960s and was widespread by the 1980s: integrating improvement or reengineering of processes across the company, what is called hoshin management (Chapter 24). The fourth breakthrough came in the 1980s and 1990s: creation of general models such as the Baldrige, EFQM, and HP QMS models that sum up best practice and against which companies can benchmark themselves and, therefore,

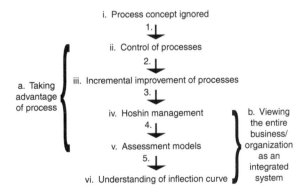

Figure 27-1. Evolution of Breakthrough

focus their improvement efforts (see "Diagnosis by External Assessment" beginning on page 446). In the late 1990s, we saw a fifth breakthrough: understanding the "inflection curve" and complete and necessary changing of businesses or business paradigms.

Figure 27-2 provides a way to look at things (using the vocabulary developed in this book) from the point of view of a particular company in an existing business. The company controls its processes (box A in the figure) and tries to improve business performance either by incremental improvement of processes (box B) or breakthrough improvement (box C) using methods such as steps iv and v in Figure 27-1.[1]

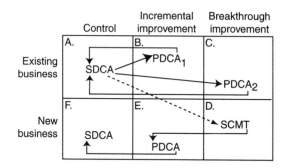

Figure 27-2. Improvement Cycles versus Stage of Business

However, sometimes a company cannot improve enough (either with incremental or breakthrough improvement) in its existing business to stay ahead of competition or is unable to deal with novel forms of competition. In this case, a company finds it necessary to jump to box D (Figure 27-2) to determine what the new paradigm will be (the SCMT breakthrough cycle is explained on pages 615 and 617). If the company cannot figure out a new paradigm, it is forced to go back to box A and possibly go out of business. If the company *can* figure out a new paradigm for the business, then it probably should go to box E to refine the new paradigm so it works in practice (what Geoffrey Moore is talking about when he describes crossing the chasm [211]), and then this becomes the standard (box F) for the new business. At this point, the cycle proceeds from box A with the new business becoming the existing business.

Understanding the inflection curve (step vi in Figure 27-1) and methods for successfully making the jump from box A to D in Figure 27-2 is the subject of this chapter. Based on Shoji Shiba's studies with a number of organizations and his awareness of Russell Ackoff's ideas on idealized design,[2] he has summarized a set of skills for leading breakthrough (see Chapter 17) and has derived a model for breaking through into a new business that are described below.[3]

In Chapter 17 (page 333), we introduced the idea of "conceptual skill." Looking at conceptual skill more broadly, we can divide its application into three stages; Chapter 17 dealt with the first stages and this chapter deals with the second and third stages:

Stage A: Exploration and formulation of a new concept (a primary subject of Chapter 17)

Stage B: Moving from the past business to a new business (this is the primary subject of this chapter)

Stage C: Recreating organizational integrity (see page 638)

The Inflection Curve

Once a leader has done the necessary exploration (Stage A of conceptual skill), then he or she needs to decide where to go next (Stage B). Such a juncture is represented graphically by what Professor Shiba has called "Andy Grove's inflection curve" (as illustrated by the portion of Figure 27-3 within the dotted box). A company can either stay on the arch AC that rises and then declines or, at the top of the arc (point B), it can begin a new upward turn into a new business and go on to new heights. (Inflection point F is a good place to begin to notice that something has changed and something has to be done.) Having chosen the new direction, one needs to focus mobilization on breakthrough in the new direction.

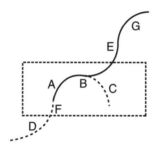

Figure 27-3. The Inflection Point for Business

Shoji Shiba, for reasons that will become clear later, likes to think about these inflection points in terms of the three questions shown in Figure 27-4, which are clearly quite applicable.

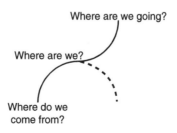

Figure 27-4. Timeless Questions

Alternative vocabulary. The inflection curve is essentially what many people have called the S-curve (for example, see Foster's well-known book [104]). A technology expands in the market (D to F in Figure 27-3) and then diminishes (F to B), to be replaced by a new technology that expands in the market (B to E) before it too diminishes (E to G). A discontinuity can often occur at point B—a gap while the new technology makes itself known and catches up to the existing technology.

Mathematicians often call the S-curve a "logistic curve," a name apparently given to such curves in the early part of the 1900s having nothing to do with logistics in the sense of trucks and warehouses. Cesare Marchetti of the International Institute for Applied Systems Analysis (IIASA) in Laxenburg, Austria, explains:

> [A logistic function] is a non-linear object appearing as an S-curve with a base and an asymptote. The quintessence of its importance is ... the fact [that] it represents diffusion processes, e.g., it is excellent in describing the diffusion of an epidemics ... From the about 3,000 applications [investigated] by my colleagues and myself, it comes out empirically that diffusion processes in the area of economics and social behaviour have a long-term stability so that the equation that fits them for a certain period of time can be used for forecasting [see, for example, [194, 195]]. It is here where the usefulness for managers comes to light. Also, the ... formal quantification of processes clarifies causes and effects in an objective way that often contradicts intuition and literature.

While business people are often aware of the concept of the inflection-curve or S-curve, they seldom take advantage of what they might deduce from the mathematics of such curves applied to their own businesses.

Furthermore, various families of logistics curves can be described by a couple of parameters [203]. Such parameters can be derived for different situations, such as, national populations. Thus, it is possible to estimate how steep the curves might be for different national populations, for instance, how fast a new technology will be adopted in The Netherlands versus in Japan [204].

Free software to analyze data in terms of logistics curves is available from the Program for the Human Environment of The Rockefeller University [205, 315].

27.2 CASE STUDIES AND A MODEL OF BUSINESS BREAKTHROUGH

As the issue of breakthrough has become more important in contemporary business, Shoji Shiba began to search for companies that managed to accomplish breakthrough. Two companies he found were Seiko and Yokogawa HP (YHP). YHP began the transition to a new way of operating somewhere between points B and C in Figure 27-3; Seiko began the transition to a product paradigm at point C.

Seiko

In 1989, Mr. Nobuyoshi Kambe was appointed Head of Seiko's Sports and Leisure Products Division. At the time of his appointment, the division was in dire straits:

sales were low ($30M/year), the division was running a deficit ($3M/year), and it had high inventories and high costs. Mr. Kambe was told by Seiko's CEO to recover the division's profitability within three years.

Mr. Kambe got permission from the CEO to do something drastic to turn the business around, even a change of business. In the end, the business turn-around involved developing one of the most popular golf clubs in Japan (the "S-Yard"). Between 1993 and 1996, the reinvented division sold half a million of these clubs with sales revenue in 1996 of $120M.

The division's journey to recovery involved the following three steps:

• Reducing personnel
• Setting an ideal future
• Swimming with the fishes

Mr. Kambe began by shaking up the division personnel. As shown in Figure 27-5, one-third of the division's people were transferred to other divisions of the company, one-third of the people were encouraged to take early retirement, and that same number of people were newly recruited into the division.

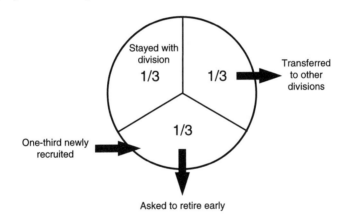

Figure 27-5. Change of Personnel

When the personnel transition was done, two-thirds as many people were employed in the division overall and only half of these had previously been in the division.

Next, Mr. Kambe and his people decided that their ideal future was to develop original and attractive new products, breaking with their traditional business of selling imported sporting goods, particularly sports-related clocks and watches. In other words, they decided that their ideal future involved freedom from traditional Seiko products (see Figure 27-6).

In breaking with traditional Seiko products, they looked at high-volume markets, such as fishing, skiing, and golf. They chose golf as their focus. They finally jumped into the fishbowl using voice of the customer methods to invent a special new type of golf driver from which they obtained the great business success already mentioned.

Figure 27-6. Freedom from Traditional Seiko Products

As seen in Table 27-1, from their swimming with the fishes, they learned that the market could be divided into two important segments: golfers under 50 years of age and golfers 50 years of age or older. The top three priorities of these two market segments are shown in Table 27-1. Japanese golfers under 50 cared about straight shots, distance and having a brand name club, while older golfers wanted the distance and accuracy that would let them compete with younger golfers but didn't care about brand name.

Table 27-1. Voice of the Customer Using the Fishbowl Principle

Popularity	Younger than 50	50 or older
1st	No hook, no slice!	
2nd	More distance!	No hook, no slice!
3rd	I want to have a golf club with a famous brand name	I don't care for any brand name

This data from the fishbowl provided an opportunity for Mr. Kambe's division and a development team, without significant golf experience, to design a new type of golf club for 50 and older golfers. The characteristics of this club are shown in Figure 27-7.

The key factors in Seiko's breakthrough to a new business as Shoji Shiba sees them are shown in Figure 27-8.

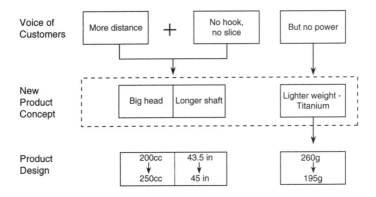

Figure 27-7. New Golf Club Concept

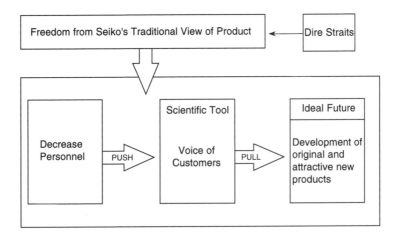

Figure 27-8. Key Factors in Seiko's Breakthrough

First, Mr. Kambe's group was in dire straits. They had a crisis that required them to make a real change. Next, the group broke free from Seiko's traditional approaches. They stirred things up with a massive personnel change and envisioned an ideal future involving original and attractive new products. With this motivation and ability to separate from the past (unfreezing prior conceptions) and a vision of a new future, they had the discipline to use specific voice of the customer methods to discover a route to new business success.

Yokogawa HP

In the past, YHP, the Japanese subsidiary of HP, had mediocre performance. Mr. Ken Sasaoka, Japanese Manager, said to the parent company, "Why don't you let me run

YHP? We really think we can do a better job." Bill Hewlett and Dave Packard agreed [221, pages 124–125]. What followed at YHP is illustrated in Figure 27-9.

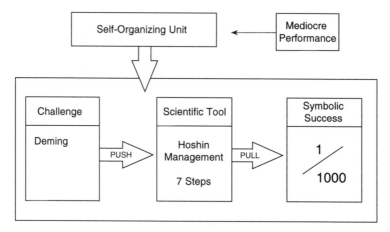

Figure 27-9. Key Factors in YHP's Breakthrough

After becoming a self-operated unit, YHP challenged the Deming Prize. In his past business career, Mr. Sasaoka had been involved in a dip-soldering improvement effort where incomplete soldering was reduced from .4 percent to three ppm, more than a 1,000 times improvement. For Mr. Sasaoka, this experience with massive improvement of dip soldering was a symbolic case that gave him an image of how much improvement could be made.

With push and pull, challenging for the Deming Prize and knowing that improvement methods worked (from the dip soldering experience), YHP had the motivation to use the scientific methods of hoshin management and 7 steps to do the improvement. A few years later, YHP won the Deming Prize.

A Model for Breakthrough

A similar pattern of key factors can be seen in the Seiko and YHP cases, shown in Figure 27-10:[4]

Five Key Factors for Breakthrough

1. Some event brings about a commitment to breakthrough.
2. Past tradition or practices must be unlearned.
3. Creative chaos is created to push mobilization.
4. A symbolic mental model (of success) is available to pull the mobilization
5. The scientific method and tools are used to make the change. (The scientific method is capable of great change. It is the most effective and efficient method of understanding what is going on in real life and transforming it, if we can

enable ourselves to use it. Steps 1 to 4 of this model provide the motivation and unfreezing of previous methods that enable the discipline of the scientific method.)

And then you have the breakthrough.

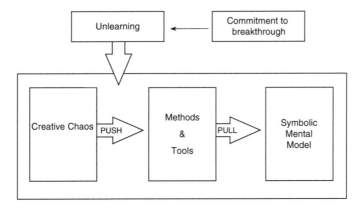

Figure 27-10. Five Key Factors for Breakthrough

Table 27-2 is a comparison of the two case studies given above for each of the five key factors.

Table 27-2. Key Factors in Breakthrough

Key Factors	YHP	Seiko
1. Commitment to breakthrough	Mediocre performance and quality problems	Dire straits
2. Unlearning	More autonomy for YHP	Freedom from traditional brand
3. Create creative chaos	Challenge for Deming Prize	Decrease personnel
4. Symbolic success	1000x improvement (by 7 Steps)	Ideal future of original and attractive new products
5. Scientific method and tools	Hoshin management	Voice of the customer

The combination of the five key factors and awareness of E. Nishibori's "process for creativity"[5] (Figure 27-11) suggested a three-phase model for breakthrough: commitment, a mental breakthrough, and a technical breakthrough (see Figure 27-12).

A new improvement cycle—for breakthrough

The components of Figure 27-12 suggest a new improvement cycle, this one for breakthrough—the SCMT cycle (Sense need or opportunity for breakthrough, Commit

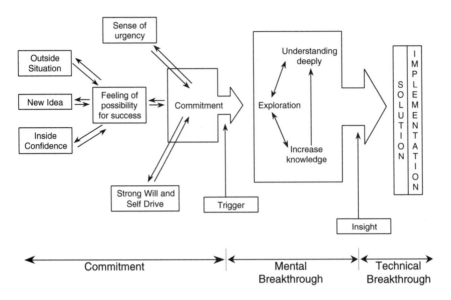

Figure 27-11. E. Nishibori's Process toward Creativity

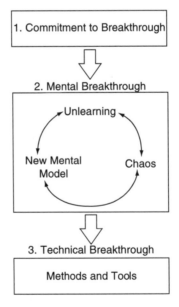

Figure 27-12. Three Phases of Breakthrough

to breakthrough effort, Mental breakthrough, Technical breakthrough), as shown in Figure 27-13.

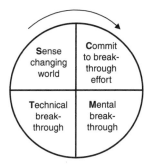

Figure 27-13. The SCMT Cycle

Mental breakthrough precedes technical breakthrough. You can't use the methodology of breakthrough if you are hung up in a non-breakthrough mentality. For instance, Teradyne's division in Nashua, NH, is world class in applying the 7 steps to typical processes. However, because of their focus on typical processes, they have a hard time seeing how to apply the 7 steps to big problems in the organization.

In the 1930s, the business need was for control (SDCA). In the 1960s and 1970s, the business need was for continuous improvement (PDCA), which began with ongoing incremental improvement (using the 7 steps) and, in 1970s, expanded to include ongoing breakthrough improvements of the existing business (using hoshin management). In the 1990s, the business need in a number of cases was for breakthrough into a new business area. Table 27-3 summarizes evolution of the business improvement paradigm. The SCMT cycle can take a place alongside the SDCA and PDCA cycles in an evolution from control through incremental improvement to breakthrough, as shown in Table 27-3 and Figure 27-14. (Theories X, Y, and W are defined on page 639.)

Table 27-3. Evolution of the Business Improvement Paradigm

	Control in the 30s	Continuous improvement in the 1960s and 1970s	Breakthrough to new business in the 1990s
Cycle:	SDCA	PDCA	SCMT
To create:	Product	Function	Competence
Fitness:	Standard	Use; cost	Latent requirements; changing paradigm
To serve:	Supplier/buyer	Customer	Stakeholder
New concept:	Variance/deviation	Process improvement	Unlearning
Human aspect:	Theory X	Theory Y	Theory W
Societal change:	Mass production	Consumer revolution	Continuous change of society

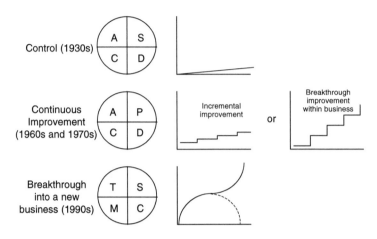

Figure 27-14. From Control to Breakthrough

Yokogawa Electric and Fuji Xerox

Having derived the three-phase breakthrough model of Figure 27-12, Shoji Shiba sought additional cases studies that support the validity of the model. Yokogawa Electric and Fuji Xerox provide such examples. Each of these is a case study of breakthrough with regard to the management elements within an existing business and, in fact, within a particular business function.

Yokogawa Electric

The story of Yokogawa Electric is the story of their development of a new approach to small group activity, that they called LETS.

Yokogawa Electric previously sold hardware products. To remain competitive in the changing world, it had to provide what it called "enterprise technology solutions" (ETS) which were substantially software based. Simultaneously, Yokogawa was faced with pressure from its employees to move away from its use of QC circles: in a company survey regarding what the company did *not* need, QC circles came in first, second, and third. These two pressures provided Yokogawa Electric with commitment to change (phase 1 of the three-phrase breakthrough model, see Figure 27-12) and led Yokogawa Electric to develop its LETS approach sketched below (the "L" in LETS stands for Lead, Learn, and Live; "let's practice ETS" is the implication of LETS).

At Yokogawa Electric, the unlearning component, phase 2, of the breakthrough model involved parting from use of QC circles and the rigid approach to problem solving traditionally used by QC circles which tended to control selection of themes and only allowed use of the 7 steps. As part of its unlearning, Yokogawa Electric emphasized the use of a good problem-solving method (e.g., 7 steps) rather than emphasizing control of theme selection, and it allowed alternative problem-solving methods (e.g., 9 steps). The other two components of Yokogawa Electric's mental breakthrough are illustrated in the left column of Table 27-4.

At Yokogawa Electric, the technical breakthrough (phase 3) portion of the breakthrough model involved new problem-solving steps and tools and focus on use of information technology (see the left column of Table 27-5).

Table 27-4. Mental Breakthrough at Yokogawa Electric and Fuji Xerox

	Yokogawa	Fuji Xerox
New Mental Model	• Enterprise Technology Solution Solution = Problem solving	Job = role Competency Salary and wage
Unlearning	• Part from QCC concept • Get rid of fixed (rigid) problem solving steps and tools	• Part from traditional Japanese way of personnel management
Chaos	• One-to-one communication	• Intensive survey of individual competency • Evaluation of degree of self-transformation by boss and direct report

Table 27-5. Technical Breakthrough at Yokogawa Electric and Fuji Xerox

Yokogawa	Fuji Xerox

• To create new problem solving steps and tools to fit ETS
 	
• Full use of information technology
	• To create competency model to fit Fuji Xerox's business.
	  - specific
	  - common
	  - primary
	
	• Competency dictionary

Fuji Xerox

Like Yokogawa Electric, Fuji Xerox was faced with a business problem and a people problem. Fuji Xerox had been primarily a hardware maker. It found itself increasingly in the information technology business based on a combination of software, service, and hardware. Fuji Xerox had also used the traditional approach to personnel management. The traditional system was based on life-long employment, a strict hierarchical seniority system, and wages based on years of experience, not performance on the job. However, Fuji Xerox had a sharp increase in personnel expenses and difficulty "creating job in daily work" using the traditional Japanese personnel management system.

As a consequence of the new business environment and the old personnel approach, Fuji Xerox was faced with having to deal with four situations: a) a knowledge-based society; b) a change in necessary work skills; c) personnel who felt no excitement about their daily work; and d) a value change in society. This situation provided the necessary commitment to attempt breakthrough.

In the mental breakthrough phase, unlearning consisted of abandoning the traditional Japanese way of personnel management. The creative chaos involved an intensive survey of individual competencies and evaluation of degree of self-transformation. The new mental model was to move from a system where the job and the role were synonymous to a system where roles depended on competencies with compensation related to performance. This is summarized in Table 27-4.

The implementation or technical breakthrough involved creating a competency model that integrated with Fuji Xerox's business (Table 27-5).

In summary, Fuji Xerox moved from a seniority-based system to a role-based system, from having vague definitions of roles to having clear definitions of each role (competency), from having rigid career paths to having flexible career paths, and from having a weak incentive system to having a system with a strong relationship between results and salary.

Strategies for Mental Breakthrough

Having found support for the three-phase model of breakthrough (Figure 27-12) in the case studies of Yokogawa Electric and Fuji Xerox, the next step was to try to find strategies or practices to support the phases of breakthrough. Of the three phases of the breakthrough model, mental breakthrough is the key process. Commitment only provides the necessary sense of urgency to search for mental breakthrough. Technical breakthrough cannot begin until there is mental breakthrough. Therefore, Shoji Shiba continued to look at the Yokogawa Electric and Fuji Xerox case studies for supporting practices focused on creating the mental breakthrough.

Strategies for finding a new mental model

Two strategies emerged for finding a new mental model: for top managers to have face-to-face discussions with real change leaders and for project team leaders to seek out best practices.

Fuji Xerox institutionalized face-to-face discussion between top managers and real change leaders. It called this "talk-nard,"[6] It might be described as a Japanese version of the GE Workout process [284, chapter 15]. A specific issue is announced. People from within the company nominate themselves to participate by submitting a comment on the issue. About 100 people are selected to participate in a face-to-face discussion with top managers. This happens between one and four times a year. Then top management thinks about what it learned and selects a *direction* of change (not a specific solution).

At Yokogawa Electric, project team members benchmarked the best practices of six sigma and QMS (see page 489). At Fuji Xerox, project team members benchmarked the best practices of a flat organizational structure at Seibu Department Store and the job-role-price approach at Benesse Corporation.

Strategies for unlearning

A couple of approaches were seen for unlearning. One approach is appointing project team members from outside the area of problem. For instance, at Fuji Xerox, the project team addressing the need for a new personnel management system included people from project development, sales, research, and production. No one on the team came from human resources.[7] Another approach is having a small number of team members focus on the same noble goal. Fuji Xerox and Yokogawa Electric used this approach.[8]

Strategies for creative chaos

Three approaches were seen for creating the necessary creative chaos:

- An individual touch—one-to-one communication and the talk-nard
- Time pressure—the project had to be done in nine months or a year
- Delving into individual characteristics—an intensive survey of individual characteristics and evaluations of degree of self-transformation by individual and supervisor (a sort of 360-degree review about transformation of skill and behavior)

Synergy of Methods

Shoji Shiba's search for strategies focused on mental breakthrough uncovered synergies with the first and third phases of the breakthrough model for some of the methods (Figure 27-15). The possibility of a more comprehensive model of practice that supports the three phases of breakthrough also came to mind, resulting in the model shown in Figure 27-16.

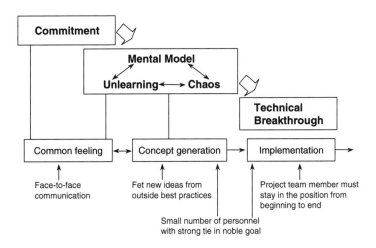

Figure 27-15. Supporting Strategies Synergies

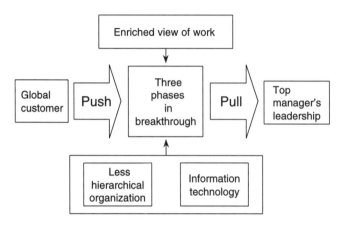

Figure 27-16. Common Practices to Support the Phases of Breakthrough

Push from global customer

If you see your situation only from the inside, a breakthrough is nearly impossible. You need the outside perspective. Furthermore, reacting to direct business pressure is often too late. You need to anticipate future crisis.

The "global customer" provides a source of latent pressure (not reaction to direct pressure). You need to pay attention to this hypothetical customer that may not be your customer today but may be a customer another company is beginning to serve. Furthermore, you need to pay attention to a hypothetical "global company"—that set of companies that is beginning to serve the global customer you are not serving—and what it is doing and how.

Pull of top manager's leadership

We have already discussed the difficulty the top manager has mobilizing business improvement through the traditional top-down hierarchy (beginning of Chapter 21). In this chapter, we discuss how the problem is even harder when a disruptive technology is involved. An alternative to traditional hierarchical leadership methods is required, for instance, using the "water ring principle" (Figure 27-17). The water ring principle refers to the CEO dropping a pebble in the water and creating a ripple effect that extends broadly and ultimately reflects in many directions.

One approach to stimulating the organization indirectly is enabling or empowering people. The chairman at Fuji Xerox told project team members redesigning the personnel management system, "You can do anything which makes people's daily job more enjoyable." The CEO of Fuji Xerox said, "Create a system which allows employees to do what they really want to do." The chief operating officer of Yokogawa Electric told the director in charge of QC circles, "It is possible to redirect QC circle activity toward ETS."

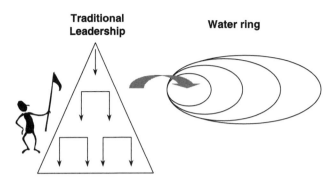

Figure 27-17. Traditional Leadership versus the Water Ring Principle

Another approach to stimulating the organization lies in the top manager's symbolic behavior.

- Hajime Sasaki had followed three principles while leading NEC's semiconductor division: aim a half step ahead (not a full step), make 100 site visits a year, and communicate face-to-face. When he became chairman of NEC, Mr. Sasaki tried to diffuse these principles to the whole organization. For instance, he personally visited 120 end users, 80 suppliers, and 75 group companies, and participated in committee work outside the company 75 times.

- At Honda, the top executives work together in a single room sitting at round tables, each of which has several seating positions without fixed seats at the tables in the room. Thus each executive can hear what the other executives are doing and talking about. This open behavior diffuses throughout the organization.

- Toyota is the number one company in Japan, and Shoichiro Toyota, chairman of Toyota, tries to exhibit powerful symbolic behavior. For instance, if he says, "Quality is important," few will listen. However, on December 3, 1998, Mr. Toyota was scheduled to attend one of the most important quality symposiums in Japan involving 100 quality leaders and 20 or 30 top managers, who were coming together for three days at a location high on the side of Mt. Fuji. Mr. Toyota was scheduled to give the keynote address. However, unexpectedly, the President of Argentina came to Japan and was scheduled to visit a Toyota factory on December 3. Mr. Toyota had no choice: he had to be at the factory on December 3 to receive the President of Argentina and had to cancel giving the keynote speech at the quality symposium on December 3. However, rather than canceling entirely, on the night of December 2, Mr. Toyota drove for several hours in falling snow to the symposium location, arriving at 11 p.m. He spoke to the symposium attendees for 30 minutes, and then drove on to the Toyota factory to meet the President of Argentina the next day. (A high-ranking quality person from Toyota remained to participate in all of the symposium.) This symbolic behavior had great influence *within Toyota* about the importance of quality.

A third approach to top management leadership is face-to-face communication. We have already mentioned Fuji Xerox's talk-nard. Konica has a "one-hour meeting technique" in which employees with a strong desire to change the organization talk directly with the top manager. The Sanden company uses "management study sessions" for the same purpose.

Less hierarchical organization and modern information technology

Another trend that supports the three phases of breakthrough is toward less hierarchical organization and full use of modern information technology. Once an organization becomes less hierarchical and flatter, the tendency for integration across the organization increases. The Baldrige, EFQM, or HP QMS criteria can be used to assess the flattened organization. The flatter organization requires and supports more openness, for instance, a Web page of improvement cases at Yokogawa Electric, the talk-nard at Fuji Xerox, and the competency dictionary at Fuji Xerox. Other electronic knowledge databases also support openness.

Enriched view of work

The historical view of why people work is changing. No longer sufficient is the explanation that they work for money in a paternalistic organization. For many people, nonmonetary incentives are stronger than financial incentives.[9] People want to be engaged and believe in the mission and vision, want a clear structure of the work process from where they can made their own contribution, and want to feel they are partners in the organization.

Fuji Xerox's motto was "new way of work" which was their companywide improvement activity after TQM. In order to enhance creativity which was the crucial factor for developing the future company, Fuji Xerox thought that employee satisfaction was the key. For Fuji Xerox, "new way of work" implied:

- Interesting place to work, great place to work
- Work because of what you really care about rather than money
- A great change in the mentality of people, such as no more seniority, no more life-long employment, etc.
- Flatter organization, people like more direct contact rather than communication through a hierarchy, people want more openness, information, and transparency

In Figure 27-16, we give the label "enriched view of work" to what Fuji Xerox calls "new way of work."

New view of teamwork

Reviewing the model in Figure 27-16, we can summarize the various practices into three categories (with considerable overlap among the practices), as shown at the bottom of Figure 27-18.

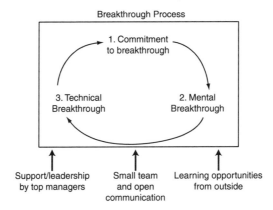

Figure 27-18. Styles of Operation to Support Breakthrough

Notice the parallel between the breakthrough process within the box in Figure 27-18 and the trust loop of Figure 16-19 (page 323). Commitment to breakthrough is related to having a relationship for a common purpose in the trust loop. Mental breakthrough is related to exploring opportunities in the trust loop. Technical breakthrough is related to successful action in the trust loop. As with the trust loop, commitment to the breakthrough process is reinforced by successful action (technical breakthrough) which depends on finding an appropriate new mental model which depends on having the necessary initial commitment. Increasing trust among the components is a key enabler.

Breakthrough needs a new structure of teamwork, as shown in Figure 27-19. Top management, change leaders, and the project team need to work collaboratively. Each is a source of outside input. The old hierarchical and functional approach does not meet the needs of breakthrough.

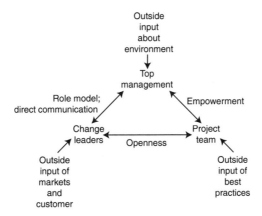

Figure 27-19. Team Structure for Breakthrough

27.3 BIGGEST OBSTACLE TO BUSINESS BREAKTHROUGH

There is a hypothesis that you can break through into a new business within the same organization. Seiko, Fuji Xerox, and YHP all purported to be examples of this. However, as explained in the next subsection, this hypothesis may not often be true. The subsection after next provides an example of the difficulty the founder and owner of a company had accomplishing a breakthrough within the existing business even with his personal involvement.

Innovator's Dilemma

We recommend you read *The Innovator's Dilemma* by Clayton Christensen of the Harvard Business School [62].[10] Professor Christensen tells the following (paraphrased) story.

Good business practice is to observe competitors carefully, listen emphathetically to customers, invest strongly in new technology, and focus investment and technology on the most profitable products. Such good business practice, unfortunately, ultimately can weaken a company, even a great company.

There is an important distinction between what Christensen calls "sustaining technologies" and what he calls "disruptive technologies." Sustaining technologies improve the performance of existing products or product families (see the middle row of Figure 27-14, page 618), often based on process improvement. Disruptive technologies can damage the demand for existing products or product families, by bringing to the market a different value proposition, typically cheaper, smaller, more convenient to use, and so on. One historical sequence of disruptive technologies is the mini-computer which seriously changed the market for the mainframe computer, the workstation which more or less wiped out the mini-computer market, and the PC which competes with important parts of the workstation market. Exploiting a disruptive technology tends to demand a change in business, as shown in the bottom row of Figure 27-14.

Unfortunately, a company has trouble making a bet on a disruptive technology:

- New technologies often outdistance market demand. Many of us have participated in new product development and introduction efforts that overshot their anticipated markets and made few sales. This is especially true for sales to the mainstream market.
- Betting on a disruptive technology flies in the face of "rational financial decision making." A cheaper product means lower margins. Going into a potential emerging market first is risky. The product based on the disruptive technology seems to ignore the voice of the most profitable customer segment which isn't interested in it. In general, betting on a disruptive technology seems to ignore the needs of customers and investors on which a company depends.
- Small, possibly emerging, markets don't deal with the growth needs of large companies. Many successful companies seek growth rates of 20 percent per year, which means a $5 billion company would need a new billion-dollar business the following year.

- Most successful business executives have learned to manage innovation in a context where analysis and planning were feasible, i.e., in a sustaining context. However, sound market research and good planning are not feasible when applied to disruptive technologies.

Consequently, most of the highest performing companies have well-developed systems that kill disruptive technologies (often explicitly and implicitly if not explicitly), making investing resources in disruptive technology difficult. And by the time the wisdom of having invested in a disruptive technology becomes apparent, it is too late—an upstart has disrupted or destroyed the market for a sustaining product line.

Dr. Maeda and Maeda Corporation

Shoji Shiba looked for instances of Japanese business executives trying to support disruptive technology within their organizations, and he found the case study of Maeda Corporation [191].

Dr. Matabe Maeda is the owner, chairman and CEO of Maeda Corporation. He does not have a technical background; he is a liberal arts graduate.

Dr. Maeda's hobby is making Japanese noodles, and he would serve guests noodles he had made himself. Noodle-making technique involves mixing the dough and rolling it in certain ways. One day Dr. Maeda thought,

> Excellent noodles come from excellent technique of kneading. Japanese noodle experts have applied their genius to developing masterful techniques of mixing. In our business of construction, concrete requires mixing. But the principle used in concrete mixing is limited to stirring; it does not involve a kneading action. The kneading technique used in making noodles in Japan since long ago can be applied to mixing concrete.

The noodle-making process involves a series of rolling in one direction, folding in half, rolling in the other direction, etc., as shown in Figure 27-20. No stirring is involved once the components of the dough have been initially mixed together. With support from only one other person, Dr. Yamada, Dr. Maeda built a prototype concrete mixing machine (A in Figure 27-21). This machine looked good to Dr. Maeda (see first SCMT cycle in Figure 27-22).

Next, Dr. Maeda thought he saw an opportunity for a joint project with two other companies to develop an operational machine (second cycle in Figure 27-22).

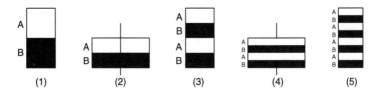

Figure 27-20. Japanese Noodle Kneading

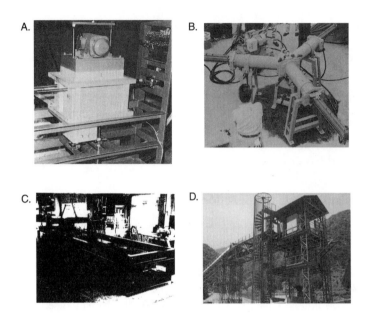

Figure 27-21. Series of Concrete Mixing Machines Using Japanese Noodle Kneading Principle

However, the prototypes they attempted to build failed, and they met strong resistance, especially from experts in concrete technology, i.e., people with PhDs in concrete material. They all tried to persuade Dr. Maeda not to develop a noodle-type concrete mixing machine.

Dr. Maeda did not give up even in the face of strong resistance. He was determined to go on without external partners. He did a laboratory experiment that

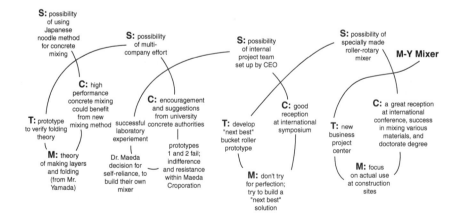

Figure 27-22. Breakthrough Cycles at Maeda Corporation

appeared to work, and he demanded that an internal team be created to work on the problem. Dr. Yamada was on the team as were three others who were against undertaking the effort (third cycle in figure). They built a series of prototypes, even though some of them didn't work (see B and C in Figure 27-21). Finally, they developed a new type of mixer (fourth cycle in Figure 27-22) and focused on actual use on construction sites with "development partners"; this resulted in developing an operational concrete mixing machine using the Japanese noodle principle (D in Figure 27-21). The final machine is in practical use and is known an M-Y Mixer (for Maeda-Yamada Mixer). In recognition of his innovation and his extraordinary documentation of the process of innovation, Dr. Maeda was awarded a doctorate in engineering from the University of Tokyo.

Dr. Maeda's work will not stop after the cycles shown in Figure 27-22. His next goal is to diffuse the new mixing technology for other uses, such as clay mixing or even noodle mixing. Each business sector will undoubtedly have its own resistance to disruptive technology; for instance, the Japanese noodle industry is committed to the traditional hand mixing method.

Dr. Maeda concludes, "Decisions in organizations tend to place their emphasis on feasibliity—possibility of realization. But there is no breakthrough if you just fulfill what seems feasible." Dr. Maeda suggests that a young engineer could never develop a good idea like the Japanese-noodle-principle concrete mixing machine in the face of organizational resistance. Even Dr. Maeda as chairman could barely push the idea through. Consequently, he established a small informal school within Maeda Corporation to develop the innovative ideas of young employees which the organization would typically kill. He calls this the "Maeda incubator of venture business."

Similar cases

Two other cases we know of illustrate the struggle of promoting a disruptive technology.

Micro-machining at Analog Devices. Ray Stata, founder and chairman of Analog Devices, told us a story similar to Dr. Maeda's. Analog Devices is primarily in the business of designing and fabricating integrated circuits. However, the possibility emerged of going into a business based on micro-machining technology. Ray says,

> At every step along the way from concept to planning to allocation of resources, the project would not have survived without strong sponsorship and support from the top, in this case from me as CEO. Ultimately, the new business was set up as a separate division, which continued to need my support as it fought its way to profitability.

Honda. Honda has an excellent culture of innovation. This is partly based on the following "Hondaism": "You cannot convince your boss only by talking; show your boss the product and then he will convince you." This is illustrated by the story of a solar car project at Honda. A solar car project was proposed. It was not accepted. Then an informal team continued the project, using some budget from the technical research department. After showing what they had already done, the project was given official recognition as a research project.

Dealing with the Innovator's Dilemma

The above case studies all show the difficulty of innovation within an existing organization, even though it sometimes happens. Typically, innovations are killed wherever they occur in the traditional hierarchical organization. The conclusion we draw is that innovative ideas must be protected in a separate or quasi-separate organization from the traditional hierarchical organization (see Figure 27-23). This new organization can operate in accordance with Figure 27-19.

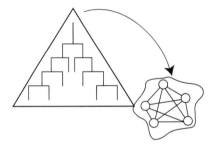

Figure 27-23. Spinout to Support Disruptive Technology

Case studies at Teradyne Aurora and ASKUL provide examples of spinning out a new organization.

Teradyne Aurora

This case study has been well documented in Harvard Business School case studies [36, 37]. We had the good fortune of having Alex d'Arbeloff, founder and chairman of Teradyne, tell us the story.

Two major lessons emerge from the Aurora case study: first, it is an example of setting up a separate organization to get around the innovator's dilemma; second, it is another example (as with the Maeda case study) of having to overcome a series of mental blocks and have a series of mental breakthroughs before a disruptive technology is fully deployed. Three breakthroughs occurred in the series (as shown in Figure 27-24): a breakthrough on the part of the initiator, Alex d'Arbeloff, about the need for a new product; a breakthrough by the entrepreneurial team that Alex set up to develop the product; and a breakthrough with development partners that helped bring the product to market.

The Aurora story. Teradyne makes equipment to test electronic devices. According to d'Arbeloff, in 1993, some people at Teradyne took a look into the future. They noted that they lived in the UNIX world but Windows NT was becoming a pervasive platform in the outside world with thousands of programmers writing new inexpensive

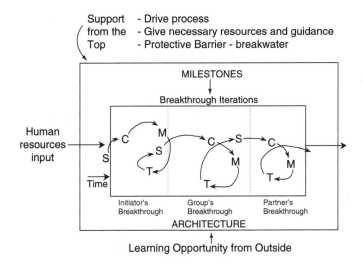

Figure 27-24. Series of Breakthroughs at Teradyne Aurora

applications software. They also noted that they were still using ECL technology while some competitors were using CMOS technology allowing all of the required functions to be put on one chip. Alex d'Arbeloff found that even as founder, chairmen, and at the time CEO, he could not get the existing organization to work on either NT (which people claimed was incompatible with their existing software) or CMOS (which people claimed could not work at a high performance level).

As time passed, some progress was made but not enough. One product line learned how to work with a hybrid of 90 percent CMOS and 10 percent time critical circuits in ECL. Test systems from the small vendor ASIX were studied; these systems were fully implemented in CMOS, albeit not always with high levels of performance. NT continued to be ignored.

Some years earlier, d'Arbeloff had met Rick Meuthing at a trade show. He had been at ASIX but had left and was teaching VLSI design at a Boston area university. Alex d'Arbeloff asked Meuthing if he wanted to help Teradyne invent an entirely new design for timing in CMOS. Meuthing had an idea he wanted to try and was hired as a consultant and demonstrated the feasibility of a new CMOS design.

Marc Levine was software engineering manager for Teradyne's Industrial Consumer Division until d'Arbeloff asked him to become the corporate TQM officer (another key player rotates through this Teradyne role). While visiting the VLSI division in California, d'Arbeloff and Levine discussed building a test system using CMOS and NT in a meeting with several company VPs and engineering managers. All agreed such a project was needed but no one felt able to take people off key existing projects. Thus, d'Arbeloff turned to Levine and asked if he could explore starting the CMOS/NT project within the company.

Levine prepared a short concept paper and discussed it with all the relevant VPs and all division technical leaders, getting widespread support. He then recruited one of Teradyne's most talented engineers, Hap Walker, with background in hardware, software, and tester design. When Hap left the project he was leading to join Levine in building the new test system, Levine accepted the job d'Arbeloff had asked him to do.

While Marc Levine's concept paper had suggested the project should report to the VLSI division head Ed Rogas, Alex d'Arbeloff and the top Teradyne management decided it would be set up as a separate start-up with its own board consisting of d'Arbeloff, Jim Prestridge, Rogas, Levine, and Walker, and that it would be at a separate location from Teradyne's Boston headquarters.

Levine and Walker created a product concept and visited non-Teradyne customers that used competitors' equipment. They confirmed the concept of medium performance at very low cost, use of CMOS and NT, and aggressive time to market. The board gave approval to hire six more people to develop a full business plan.

Alex d'Arbeloff next suggested that Levine, Walker, and Dan Proskauer (a software engineer) visit an application software manufacturer (for which d'Arbeloff was an investor and board member) where they discovered that the company only wrote its own software in its core competency area and acquired and assembled all other software at low cost from software catalogs of Windows applications in Excel, Visual Basic, and so on. Considering this approach, Proskauer concluded that Excel would be a flexible user interface, which they would not have to write from scratch and would support user-written applications in Visual Basic.

A 67-page business plan was written to bring out a new CMOS/NT product with breakthrough pricing, operating cost, etc., enabling Aurora to tap into a large market, although different development partners were required for different market segments. The organization was established at a separate location in suburban Boston with a simple organization and small staff.

By August 1996, the project was well underway and demonstrations to potential customers and senior management throughout Teradyne were possible. Aurora began to work closely with development partners. The Aurora team consulted with the development partners earlier than they would with many customers, and the development partners were allowed more influence. The partners provided detailed information on how they did testing and the capabilities they needed.

Getting the necessary staffing remained difficult because of a Teradyne-wide hiring freeze (in anticipation of a general turndown in the semiconductor industry) and other parts of Teradyne not wanting their best people taken. For this and other reasons, the Aurora people had to narrow their plans and focus on getting a prototype done able to persuade and get a lead user on board. Aurora also took advantage of the existing sales force of one division and of central engineering services.

Summary of the breakthroughs. Figure 27-24 illustrated the sequence of three breakthroughs implicit in the Teradyne Aurora case study. We summarized the details here:

1. The initiator, Alex d'Arbeloff, came to his mental breakthrough by sensing the symbolic phenomenon, studying and using benchmarking to further explore, conversing with groups of people who were looking ahead, and ultimately confirming in his own mind the direction he was considering.

2. The initiator, d'Arbeloff, achieved the necessary technical breakthrough by setting up a small separate entrepreneurial group, supported by the top management, and utilizing the key management processes of the parent company.
3. The members of the entrepreneurial group came to their mental breakthrough by conceiving a new product and plan, benchmarking it, gaining confidence in their conception, and ultimately creating a compelling new concept.
4. The entrepreneurial group came to its technical breakthrough (actually developing the product) by creating a detailed business plan and providing essential human resources along with physical and mental independence. They were open about the project with the rest of Teradyne, reducing possible threats from pieces of the parent.
5. The mental breakthrough in bringing the product to market included focusing on a limited target, creating development partnerships with a small number of companies, capturing the necessary information from these development partners, and focusing again on key features.
6. The technical breakthrough in bringing the product to market involved creating an architecture of development partnerships, a guide to using central resources, and a guide for trading off product and customer issues.

ASKUL

The Japanese stationary and office supplies market has been monopolized by the large company KOKUYO. In this environment, a small company promoting new products has little chance. In this environment, ASKUL was started and attempted continuous business breakthrough. From its first sale in 1994, the company grew to be a successful venture in 1999.

The parent company PLUS wanted a bigger foothold in the market dominated by KOKUYO. They initiated what in retrospect is a process with three key characteristics.

1. Blue sky committee. PLUS initiated a "blue sky committee" that operated from 1990–92 and investigated the future direction of a new business, i.e., defining the ideal customers and the ideal distribution system. They concluded they should not distribute to dealers or retail shows, channels that KOKUYO dominated, but rather should go directly to customers. They also decided they should avoid big and medium-sized companies demanding full service traditionally provided by customer service organizations in dealers and large retail shops. Rather, they focused on small companies which until then had to buy their office supplies in retail shops.

2. Started small. In 1992, Mr. S. Iwata (of the PLUS company) spun out with a two-person team and started the ASKUL venture. "ASKUL" meant "deliver tomorrow." Mr. Iwata believed that *time* could create new additional value. ASKUL offered next-day delivery of orders made by phone, fax, or the Internet from a 6,000-item catalog. Next-day delivery rate was 99.7 percent, with same day delivery for orders placed by 11 A.M. to locations within Tokyo and Osaka. Forty percent discounts from list price were offered to all customers.

ASKUL's business flow is shown in Figure 27-25. They created a virtual company with a minimal central ASKUL staff; a majority of the business functions were handled by out-source affiliates, temporary workers, and part-time workers. Reporting to the president of ASKUL were the financial and project innovation departments along with the organizations that handled their key business processes: customer support, efficient customer response, business planning, and back office. The ASKUL employees served in one of three roles: staff handling the core daily jobs, innovators improving the current business, and entrepreneurs looking five years into the future.

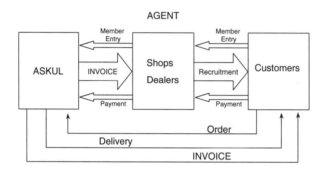

Figure 27-25. Business Flow of ASKUL

3. Innovation for customers. Rather than only offering products made by PLUS, ASKUL concluded that its real business purpose was to deliver all products regardless of manufacturer. Offering a 40 percent discount from list to all their customers drew criticism and resistance from the traditional stationary industry. However, ASKUL refused to compromise—its business purpose was to create the optimum system from a societal point of view. ASKUL concluded its job was not to sell office supplies but to create a system for how to sell office supplies. Using information technology, ASKUL made each day's orders immediately visible and undertook daily intensive analysis to enable quick action on new strategies or tactics with items and prices. The company worked jointly on this with suppliers and manufacturers (including those not traditionally part of the office supply industry). Such analysis and collaboration resulted in delivery of food and drink, foot warmers, etc., along with office supplies. ASKUL's approach became *continuous breakthrough.*

The elements of the ASKUL story fit into the three phases of breakthrough and the five success factor categories as shown in Table 27-6. The elements of the ASKUL story can be overlayed on the common practices model (Figure 27-16) as shown in Figure 27-26.

Table 27-6. Three Phases and Five Factors at ASKUL

Commitment	No channels to customer Little possibility to promote new product
New Mental Model	Time creates new value Optimum system in societal view Innovate for customer
Unlearning	Competitors products 40 percent discount Not to sell office supplies
Chaos	Spun out with two people
Technical Breakthrough	Virtual company Logistic center Digital picking Internet catalogue New tools for data analysis

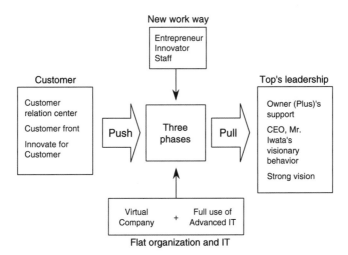

Figure 27-26. Common Practices at ASKUL

Parallels in the NIMS, Maeda, Teradyne, and ASKUL cases

We have now seen at least four examples that match the pattern shown in Figure 27-27. This pattern includes a breakthrough cycle, a series of iterations of that cycle, and an infrastructure involving milestones, an architecture, certain given inputs, support from the top, and learning from the outside.

The four examples are NIMS (Figure 25-3, page 554), Maeda Construction (Figure 27-22), Teradyne Aurora (Figure 27-24), and ASKUL. The details of the four cases are summarized in Table 27-7.

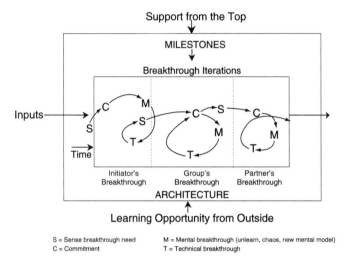

S = Sense breakthrough need   M = Mental breakthrough (unlearn, chaos, new mental model)
C = Commitment   T = Technical breakthrough

Figure 27-27. Infrastructure, Iterations, and Cycles of Breakthrough

27.4 INTEGRATION OF IDEAS

Organization and Paradigm Changes

An organization can attempt a breakthrough at several points on the inflection curve. Some organizations never attempt a change and simply decline out of existence (at D in Figure 27-28). Typically, organizations which attempt a change of direction wait until their existing business is on the downturn (point C in the figure) before changing. Some organizations are clever enough to attempt a change when at the top of their game (point B in the figure). Rarely does an organization anticipate the need to change while it is still on the upswing of current business (point A in the figure).

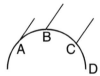

Figure 27-28. Early, Just-In-Time, Late Attempts to Jump from the Inflection Point

The cases studies of breakthrough we have described in this chapter and elsewhere in the book (Analog Devices in Chapter 24, NIMS in Chapter 25) fall in all the positions of Figure 27-28 as shown in Table 27-8 on page 638. In the Company col-

Table 27-7. Details of NIMS, Maeda, Teradyne Aurora, and ASKUL

	NIMS	Maeda Construction	Teradyne Aurora	ASKUL
Breakthrough cycle	CAPD	SCMT	SCMT	SCMT
Breakthrough iterations	New mgt. concept/ methods	Initator's	Initiator's	Initator's (CEO of PLUS and Blue Sky Committee)
	Development technology + new mgt.	Development team's	New business team's	Group's (Mr. Iawata and spin-out of ASKUL)
	Human skill + technology + new mgt.	Development partnership's	Development partners'	Development partner's
Milestones	Deming diagnoses		Concept paper; business plan	Twice yearly revision of catalog
Architecture	7 Infra- structures	Special project team	Separate company with corporate support	Spin-out, virtual company
Given inputs	People, resistence, time	People, resistence, time	Human resources, time	Time, outside resistance, Mr. Iwata and two others
Support from top	Mr. Uchimaru	Mr. Maeda	Alex d'Arbeloff	CEO of PLUS
Learning opporunities from outside	From Deming prize winners	From university experts, international conference	Non-Teradyne customers, application software manufacturer, development partners	Benchmarking U.S. methods of information networks, data mining, etc.

umn of the table, the letter in parentheses after the company name indicates the position in Figure 27-28 at which the company attempted breakthrough. The effort to begin ASKUL originally began when it was almost too late, but resulted in an organization continuously anticipating the need for and creating new breakthroughs—hence, the indications of C and A after its name.

The breakthrough case studies in this chapter and the rest of the book also span two other dimensions. As shown down the left side of Table 27-8, some of the breakthrough cases took place within a business function, some spanned the entire organization, and

Table 27-8. Organizational Structure and Paradigm Change

	Company	New operating paradigm	New product/ service paradigm
Within function	Yokagawa Electric (C)	LETS	Enterprise Technology Solution (ETS)
	Fuji Xerox (C)	Individual competency	
Whole organization	YHP (B-C)	TQM	
	NIMS (B-C)	TQM	Complete designs
	Analog Devices (B-C)	On-time delivery	
New organization	Seiko (C)		CMOS/NT tester
	Maeda (B)		Noodle style concrete mixing
	ASKUL (C; A)	Virtual organization; continuous breakthrough	Strong support of small business
	Teradyne Aurora (B)		Golf club

some took place in new organizations created specifically for the breakthrough business. As shown in the right two columns of the table, some of these breakthrough cases took the form of a new paradigm (disruptive technology) for how the business was operated, some took the form of a new paradigm of product or service, and others involved both a changed product or service and way of doing business.

Recreating Organizational Integrity

At the beginning of this chapter, we introduced three stages in the application of conceptual skill:

Stage A: Exploration and formulation of a new concept (a primary subject of Chapter 17)

Stage B: Moving from the past business to a new business (the subject of most of this chapter)

Stage C: Recreating organizational integrity

Once a leader has explored the situation broadly and formed a hypothesis of what must be done, once a leader has found the commitment to break with the past to make the mental breakthrough and follow on with the necessary technical breakthrough, once the organization has undergone breakthrough change and broken into the new business area, then the leader must see that a new organizational integrity is created.

Traditional methods such as described in the rest of this book can help with recreating organizational integrity—see the move from box D to box E in Figure 27-2 (page 608) and the reinforcing loop shown in Figure 27-18 (page 625).

The Real Meaning of Business Breakthrough

Leadership is about people, so a leader needs a theory about how people behave—about their human nature. Theories X, Y, and W are each the kind of hypothesis about human behavior to help to design an integrated management system.

Theory X says that people want stability and to be led. It suggests the power of standardization and control of workers in the pursuit of mass production. Theory Y says people seek self-determination and innovation [201]. It suggests the accrual of knowledge, continuous improvement, and worker development and empowerment in pursuit of creating something new.

Professor Shiba proposes a Theory W that embraces the duality of the nature of people: people want both a stable, controlled environment and to create something new (in many ways, these two are in conflict). We want strong, clear leadership to tell us what to do and make us secure. However, we also want to contribute to something new that changes our present existence and makes us feel uncomfortable.[11]

The new Theory W was suggested to Shoji Shiba by his study of the famous painting by Paul Gauguin entitled "Where do we come from? What are we? Where are we going?" (see Figure 27-29[12]). This masterpiece symbolically represents the questions

Figure 27-29. Shoji Shiba and Gauguin's Inspirational Painting

all leaders must answer to lead their organizations successfully to sustained ("eternal") existence. In Figure 27-30, we reproduce the inflection curve from the bottom row of Figure 27-14 (page 618) with Gauguin's three questions superimposed.

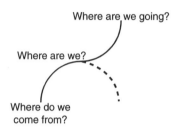

Figure 27-30. Eternal Questions

The painting is divided into three parts, and an arc of representative narrative flows from right to left. The right side of the painting illustrates a baby and maturation—this represents the question "Where do we come from?" The middle of the painting illustrates adults in the fullness of life—this represents the question "What are we?" The left side of the painting illustrates the decline of old age—this represents the question "Where are we going?"[13]

However, the top right and the top left corners of the painting are in a light color and have a shape that indicates a cycle from the top left back to the top right of the painting. It is as if the left side of the painting was connected back to the right side in a cylinder. This representation of a cycle is indicative of the possibility of "eternal life" of the human species. As the old generation passes, the possibility of a new generation exists. (See also [305, pages 96–103].)

Parallel to the theme of Gauguin's painting, business also needs "eternal life." The three questions of Gauguin are similar to the questions we must ask as we move along Grove's inflection curve (see Figure 27-4). We came from somewhere (Where did we come from?), we must decide what to do next (Who are we?), and we must figure out how to get there (Where are we going?).

We are all faced with the duality indicated by Gauguin in his painting. We know we cannot sustain ourselves if we allow no change, but we like working on clear goals and are uncomfortable with change. We recognize that to survive, our identity must evolve, but denying our existing identity temporarily leaves us without identity. Breakthrough requires unlearning and chaos before we settle into our new improved situation. Thus, to continue our existence, each organization and each individual in the organization (in their professional and personal existence) must grapple with the eternal questions: Where do we come from? What are we? Where are we going? Successfully answering these questions can bring enlightenment and transformation, and move both a corporation and the people within it through a threshold to a place where all kinds of masterpieces can be created. Leaders who can demonstrate and catalyze this will not only achieve breakthroughs but will also enable people to understand and become "Who they are."

This is a fundamental principle of business, leadership, and life. Each organization and person must find their unique place. We must listen carefully and respond honestly to what our emotions tell us. Throughout our lives we become no one else but who we are. You might say the sixth and overarching principle of effective leadership is:[14] "We only live once; let us be who we are."

NOTES

1. We have talked in this book about applying the scientific method to business. Boxes A, B, and C parallel the fact that most scientists spend most of their lives trying out smaller or larger changes within the existing general "paradigm" (to use the word of Thomas Kuhn who wrote a classic book on the structure of scientific revolution [180]). In the business analogy, companies mostly stay within the same basic paradigm for their business and the way they operate that business, while seeking small and large improvements within that business paradigm.

2. See Chapter 29, page 676.

3. Shoji Shiba's book with Tom Lee and Robert Wood [186] gives many case studies of the systems and processes leaders use. These case studies slightly overlap but substantially complement the case studies included in this book.

4. Shoji Shiba acknowledges that he developed this model for breakthrough as he worked to understand Ackoff's concept of Idealized Design; see Chapter 29, pages 676–680, and [2].

5. Mr. Nishibori was an engineer at NTT who studied quality deeply under Deming who introduced statistical process control to Japan. Mr. Nishibori also led the first expedition from Japan to the South Pole.

6. This is "Japanglish" for a talk promenade, [sic] talk-promenard.

7. Hill-Rom uses a similar approach in Kaizen Events where one-third of the people on the improvement team are from the process being improved, one-third are stakeholders in the process, and one-third know nothing about the process and may not even be from within the company [184].

8. A similar approach is used with Analog Devices core teams (see page 385).

9. Of course, this has been known since Hertzberg published his classic paper [135] but until recently has seldom sunk into mainstream management practice. The social model described in this book contains much of the same idea.

10. See also [63].

11. All three theories, X, Y, and W, must be present in different situations in a real company: Theory X is for control, Theory Y is for continuous improvement, and Theory W is for breakthrough. See Figure 27-14 and Table 27-3.

12. Courtesy, Museum of Fine Arts, Boston. Reproduced with permission, 2000. Museum of Fine Arts, Boston. All Rights Reserved. Photograph by Edward Nute, Plymouth, MA.

13. Notice the parallel with the left to right arc of business rise and fall in the above.

14. See Chapter 17, page 331, for a list of the first five principles.

The Fourth Revolution:
SOCIETAL NETWORKING

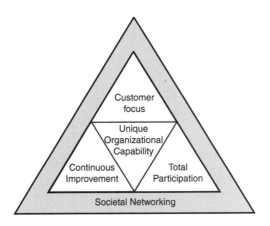

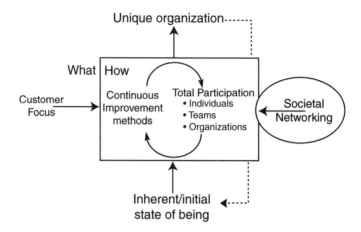

Societal Networking Provides Additional Support for the What and the How

This portion of the book describes the fourth of our management revolutions.

Chapter 28—Networking and Societal Diffusion

- Introduces an explicit system for networking about business improvement and organizational learning
- Provides a significant example of this
- Compares national methods
- Emphasizes the importance of indirect approaches to mobilization

Chapter 29—Ongoing Integration of Methods

- Provides case studies of integration of methods

28

Networking and Societal Diffusion–
Regional and National Networking

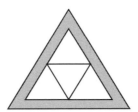

The fourth of our revolutions in management is societal learning. Societal learning can be thought of as network learning or learning from the network of companies, customers, suppliers, and others who are trying to improve the ways their companies function. Such mutual learning is necessary because the methods of organizational change and improvement are not a theory a company can simply learn and follow. Rather, our companies are continuing a vast societal and organizational experiment. They have developed new practices through trial and error. People learn how to do things by doing them and by learning what they must do. This changes as they learn more and as the world changes. Furthermore, it is too limiting for each company to discover the organizational means of developing its organizational change and improvement capability by itself. Reinventing the wheel consumes time and resources that even the largest and smartest company can't afford. Reinventing the wheel also risks developing an inferior version.

Reinventing wheel

If one company develops a method that works, that method should be diffused so other companies can also use it. For this reason, Japan has the tradition of "no secrets" about the methodology of quality improvements.

Japan has many such diffusion examples, such as guidelines for how QC circles meet and exchange factory visits. These were not theory. They evolved in QC circles, were a great success, and were then diffused throughout Japan. In the U.S., Milliken created "sharing rallies" to diffuse quality improvement success stories; this U.S. invention has been diffused to other companies.

One problem in implementing the methods of organizational change and improvement is a Catch-22 exists for some types of information and skill that makes internal development of methods difficult; so, societal diffusion becomes all the more important. For example, it is difficult for CEOs to be taught new methods of leadership by those below them in the company hierarchy; therefore, CEOs must get most of their information about improvement and mobilization methods from outside their company hierarchy.

At all corporate levels, the existence of success stories and experienced managers makes the methods easier to practice. But how does a company that is just beginning implementation find success stories on which to model its own activities or find experienced managers on whom to model its behavior? Executives should be looking outside their own companies or organizations for knowledge, training, and examples of practice of organizational change and improvement.

This chapter discussed the structure of organizational change and improvement beyond the individual corporation and the methods by which new understanding and skills are diffused from the broader quality and improvement culture into individual companies.

Companies need to participate in societal networking for reasons beyond the simple desire to gain efficiency in their organizational change and improvement implementations. A company will not like likely do high-quality work in a low-quality culture. If a company resides in a national or regional environment of poorly trained workers, customers tolerant of low-quality products, and weak competitors, the company will probably not find the will and the means for producing high-quality products. In particular, a company cannot stand on quality alone, without quality suppliers. The quality of the suppliers must be developed, and this is more possible within an industry or geographical quality culture. Participation in a widespread process of diffusion can be considered an investment in the creation of a regional or national quality culture, which in turn is an investment in a company's future ability to do business.

In brief, companies participate in regional and national efforts and organizations that diffuse methods of organizational change and improvement for three reasons: to avoid internally having to reinvent 40 to 50 years of improving practices; to create mutual learning and sharing of current discoveries among corporations; and to create a quality culture in which to do business. This chapter describes the elements of regional and national infrastructure, explaining how companies participate at each level.

28.1 THE JAPANESE MODEL

We start with a discussion about regional and national infrastructure for TQM diffusion in Japan because the Japanese have an explicit infrastructure for societal networking. In the U.S., things are less organized. We begin with a description of this Japanese infrastructure as it was in 1990. This allows us to describe in a later section some of the evolution of the infrastructure in Japan since the first edition.[1]

Japan has found three elements necessary for successful societal diffusion of TQM:[2]

- An infrastructure to support networking
- Openness with real cases
- Change agents (or catalysts)

These are described in the subsections starting, respectively, on this page, page 652, and page 653.

Infrastructure for Networking

The Japanese have identified six elements of the infrastructure for networking.[3] As shown in Figure 28-1, these elements are:

i. National promotional organization
ii. Training
iii. Knowledge dissemination
iv. Societal promotion activities
v. National standard certification
vi. Development of new methods

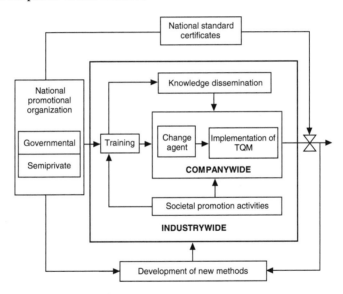

Figure 28-1. Infrastructure for Networking

Another element shown in the figure, the change agent, is considered to be in parallel with this six-element infrastructure. It is described in a later subsection.

National Promotional Organization

To support quality improvement, government and semiprivate national organizations developed in Japan. Each has a role to play.

One key in the development of TQM is to start from a standard. The national government organization is involved in standardization and sometimes in certification of quality. For instance, the government organization, Ministry of International Trade and

Industry (MITI), played an important role in providing an initial standard and establishing a certification process (Japanese Industrial Standards, or JIS). (Certification, which deals with quality standards for products and company practices, is the fifth element of the infrastructure for networking.)

Building on the activities of the government organization, which provide some of the basics, the semiprivate national promotional organizations do the follow-on work. Two non-profit national organizations for TQM exist in Japan: the Japanese Union of Scientists and Engineers (JUSE) and the Japanese Standards Association (JSA). The two organizations are complementary and serve the needs of large, medium, and small Japanese companies. JSA has a closer relationship with MITI, which has diffused standardization throughout Japanese industry. The primary roles of JUSE and JSA are training, knowledge dissemination, societal promotion activities, and development of new methods—the other four elements of the infrastructure for networking.

JUSE and JSA are highly effective organizations with a long-range perspective, and they tend to be neither as rigid as government organizations nor as shortsighted as commercial private consulting organizations.

JUSE and JSA also have an informal atmosphere, bringing together a variety of people interested in quality. In keeping with its name, JUSE brings together scientists and engineers from all disciplines, as well as managers. This is in contrast to the American Society for Quality Control (ASQC), which tends to be oriented toward a single discipline, that of quality specialists. JUSE also brings together people from different industries, the universities, and the national research institutions (e.g., agriculture, commerce). JUSE and JSA provide a place and opportunity for all these people to interact so they can draw on one another's knowledge and resources.

The participation of the national research institutions and universities is particularly valuable to industry, for several reasons: They are a source of intellectual capital, especially regarding statistics; workers there have more discretionary time than in industry; they tend to have a longer-term perspective; and university people, in particular, have another specialty and need not get their support from TQM activities.

Historically, JUSE and JSA didn't do consulting work (although that changed over time), which meant they weren't selling their collective wisdom. Therefore they have permitted great openness about information and know-how related to quality control.

JUSE is an influential quality organization in Japan.[4] When W. Edwards Deming visited Japan in 1950 and began teaching statistical quality control, JUSE embraced his teachings and spread them. It was JUSE that invited Joseph Juran to Japan to teach in 1954. JUSE promoted the quality circle movement [66, 67]. In 1951, JUSE instituted the Deming Prize, the prestigious award given to quality innovators in Japan and abroad, and JUSE organizes many of the conventions and events leading up to the awarding this prize each year. The Deming Prize has played a central role in the promotion of TQM.

Quality control education has also played a central role in the promotion of TQM. In 1949, JUSE started a 30-day basic quality control course for engineers. Over the next 10 years it programmed courses for middle and upper management and, in 1967, for foremen, so that every enterprise level was covered. A good deal of money was invested in training young engineers and managers, but it earned large returns for Japan. Ten or 20 years after beginning their quality education, people with solid quality control backgrounds sit on the boards of Japan's top corporations. Dr. Koji Kobayashi, the former president of NEC, is an example of this trend.

The JUSE organization proper is chiefly involved in arranging logistics for its activities rather than being the source of quality knowledge. For example, in 1989, the full-time staff of JUSE was 84, with 31 additional people employed by JUSE Press. By contrast, about 2,000 people from universities, corporations, and government collaborated to teach JUSE courses and served on the committees that created and improved JUSE courses. The "lean staff with extensive networking" structure is an interesting innovation, for it virtually guarantees that TQM knowledge is integrated and preserved within corporations and is not hoarded in JUSE or other external organizations such as consulting companies or universities. Also, members of JUSE are corporations rather than individuals, numbering about 1,850 in 1989. JUSE's aim is to increase knowledge within corporations, and its membership and staffing policies support this aim.

JUSE approaches corporate implementation from the top down as well as using middle-up, middle-down, and bottom-up approaches. JUSE's board of directors is made up of high-ranking industrialists; by tradition, the president of JUSE is the chairman or an ex-chairman of the Keidanren, the most prominent organization of Japanese CEOs [67, chapter 13, "The Building of a National Infrastructure in Japan"]. When Deming taught statistical quality control in the 1950s, he taught classes with presidents of corporations, not just engineers. Joseph Juran's focus in 1954 was top and middle management. As of 1991, nearly 5,000 top executives had gone through JUSE's five-day top executive's course, and another 9,000 had been participants in the JUSE five-day course for executives. Both courses had long waiting lists.[5]

Independent consulting organizations do not play a major role in implementing quality improvement in Japan, even though other areas of business are richly supplied with consulting companies, both Japanese and foreign-owned.

Training

Japan's national training infrastructure includes instruction in various skills for a variety of target students, from CEOs to line workers, from engineers to administrators. Training is a means of mutual learning among companies, in which knowledgeable instructors from one company teach people from many others.

One of the most important roles of the semiprivate national promotional organizations is education and training. JUSE's courses, for instance, are the source of quality instruction for many different organizations. This particularly helps the diffusion of TQM. Many companies find it less expensive to get training from JUSE, with its 2,000 collaborators (committees of people from industry and universities who develop course curricula and teach the courses), than to create their own training activities.

JUSE offers 270 courses to 33,500 people per year, but only in Tokyo and Osaka, whereas JSA offers 250 courses to 15,000 people per year in 58 smaller cities. Table 28-1 lists examples of JUSE courses for 1991. Notice when each course was established. Also noteworthy is that some of the courses in each subject area last as long as two to four weeks.

Table 28-1. Examples of 1991 JUSE Courses

Subject	Number of Offerings	First Course Established
Quality control	27	1949
Reliability	9	1960
Design of experiments	3	1955
Multivariate analysis	3	1970
Software production control	2	1980
Operations research	4	1962
Industrial engineering	2	1963
Marketing	1	1951
Sensory test	1	1957
Product liability	1	1973
Other management techniques	6	1972

Knowledge Dissemination

Knowledge dissemination includes publishing cases, instructional material, and research in books and periodicals for a variety of audiences. It also includes holding conventions and other events on quality. Within a quality culture where companies share information about their TQM successes and failures, such dissemination activities are an important means of mutual learning among companies.

Especially in the early years of the Japanese push for quality improvement (before quality became a popular subject), JUSE and JSA were a primary source of journals, magazines, and books related to quality. For example, JUSE publishes three monthly journals, including QC Circle, which has a monthly circulation of 170,000. Furthermore, between 1960 and 1985, about half of all quality control books published were publications of JUSE or JSA, as shown by the graph in Figure 28-2.

Since TQM in Japan began teaching that quality is everyone's job, the demand for books has increased. JUSE and JSA helped create a quality culture that provides an ongoing economic base for continuing dissemination of quality knowledge.

Knowledge dissemination includes more than just publishing activities. Each of the nine national districts for QC circles has a chapter that holds local conventions, mutual visits, study meetings, and discussions. Once every two days, there is a convention somewhere in Japan.[6]

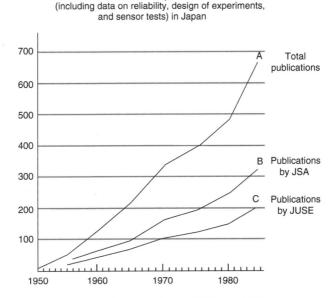

Figure 28-2. Publications of JUSA and JSA

Societal Promotion Activities

Japan has many types of societal promotion activities. These activities increase social awareness of quality, and they transfer quality techniques to different levels of company hierarchy and to different types and styles of industries (e.g., mass production, one-piece manufacturing, chemical industry). Examples of these activities are quality days, quality month (November), and quality awards. For instance, one of the major societal promotions in Japan is the Deming Prize for "Nationwide Promotion and Dissemination of TQC."

National Standard Certification

National Standard Certificates are issued by the government certifying that a given product meets certain quality specifications. Japanese Industrial Standards (JIS) are the province of the JIS Committee. To earn the right to display the JIS mark on its products, a company must standardize its manufacturing processes and allow its quality control levels to be examined and certified.[7] By 1993, about 11,000 plants in Japan have passed JIS inspection.

Development of New Methods

As quality concepts change, different methods are needed. The national infrastructure of societal networking provides a mechanism for the development of new methods, and JUSE and JSA have invested heavily in the development of new quality methods.

For instance, in the 1950s, JUSE invited Deming to Japan to teach statistical quality control, and JUSE invested in the development of statistical methods. More generally, JUSE set up the QC Research Group, and JSA set up the QC Research Committee. Meetings of these groups and less formal occasions provided the opportunities for debate among those who were taking the lead in developing new methods for total quality control. A participant recalls meetings normally lasted for one to two hours, and continued informally into the wee hours of the morning. These activities gradually built a consensus on how to adapt U.S. quality control methods to Japan.

The tradition of consensus building lives on. JUSE holds two three-day quality control residential symposia every year. Invited attendance is limited to about 100. The participants stay in the same hotel and are together from early in the morning until late at night. This proximity enables them to discuss the day's topics in formal and informal settings. A consensus emerges not from the forceful leadership of a few people but from face-to-face communication among the entire group.

JUSE follows a sequence of steps in the development of new methods. First, the JUSE Research Group regularly researches a new method. A symposium introduces the new method to a larger population. When the method has come into practical use with real case studies, a seminar is held. These steps were followed, for example, when the 7 management and planning tools were developed in the 1970s.

The 7 management and planning tools consist of six methods and tools for processing qualitative or linguistic information, and one tool for processing numerical data (in particular, for doing multivariate analysis). Methods and tools for processing linguistic information were necessary because of the continuing evolution of the quality concept. The quality concept moved beyond just statistical process control, and it became increasingly important to create a formulation process for problem solving. Also, quality activities had spread to a variety of industries, functions, and company positions—quality was no longer relevant only on the factory floor.

The history of the development of the 7 management tools proceeded as follows:

- A JUSE research committee for developing QC tools worked from 1972 to 1977.
- Professor Yoshinobu Nayatani and others proposed the 7 management and planning tools in 1977.
- A workshop on the 7 management and planning tools was started in 1978.
- A symposium on the 7 management and planning tools was started in 1978.
- The first book on the 7 management and planning tools was published in 1979.
- The 7 management and planning tools enjoyed great popularity in quality-related fields in Japan after 1979. [149]

Openness with Real Cases

The second of the three elements necessary for successful societal diffusion and networking is sharing actual cases. As stated at the beginning of this chapter, developing the methods of organizational change and improvement is a societal experiment. After one organization has success with a method, the method must be diffused. Therefore, companies must be open with real cases. Real cases means detailed processes of quality practices, such as improvement, or of quality assurance systems. This policy of openness applies not only to documents and presentations but also to demonstrations of their use in practice. For example, several CQM companies desired a system of diffusion of quality improvement success stories such as the system described in Chapter 21, page 373. However, even with the Japanese and Milliken models to study, it was difficult for a company to develop an efficient and effective presentation system. Therefore, within the CQM, companies have allowed representatives of other companies to attend their presentation days (QI story days), and the methods presented on such occasions have served as models for other companies.

In Japan, companies demonstrate they have no secrets in the know-how of quality improvement by distributing a wide range of information and success stories. For example, 33 books on quality were published by JUSE in 1988. Two-thirds of them dealt with concrete examples and case studies rather than with theoretical work.

Another mechanism for diffusion of real cases and success stories in Japan is Quality Month. For example, the schedule and activities for Quality Month in November 1988 were as follows:

Week 1

- Quality Conference for Foremen—92 case studies and 15 plant visits and on-site debates

Week 2

- Quality Conference for Managers—92 case studies and nine plant visits, debates, and panel discussions
- Top Management Conference
- Deming Prize Ceremony

Week 3

- Conference on TQC in the Service Industry

In all, 250 actual cases of implementation were presented during this period.

Change Agents (or Catalysts)

The third key factor for successful societal diffusion and networking is the use of change agents. Revolution from insiders is difficult because the revolution represents a paradigm change for the organization. Strong change agents from outside often play a necessary role in thought revolutions [242]. If they have sufficient knowledge and personality or prestige, and the necessary sense of mission, change agents serve as catalysts for change. From the Japanese point of view, some consultants have difficulty serving as change agents because they lack the necessary sense of mission.

Deming and Juran had the necessary qualifications, so in 1950 and 1954 they served as national change agents for quality in Japan.

28.2 TAKING A LESSON FROM JAPAN—CQM

Note to reader: We include the following history of the CQM partly to describe the organization so many of the methods and cases studies of this book come from and which is co-publisher of this book. However, we primarily provide this detailed case study because the CQM is the best model we know of societal networking of the sort we recommend and practices the ongoing development and integration of new methods we recommend.

In early 1990, seven Boston-area companies formed the Center for Quality Management to learn from and aid each other in their TQM implementations. The companies that formed the CQM had characteristics (described in Chapter 23) typical of companies that decide to implement TQM. With few exceptions, the seven companies that formed the CQM were all suffering from the economic slowdown that began in the late 1980s. Also, the CEOs of several of the companies had personally visited Japan and observed its business practices. At least one of the CEOs had lived in Japan, most had divisions in Japan and traveled to Japan frequently, and some had studied Japan's business practices through trade association committees on international competitiveness. Furthermore, several of these CEOs were regularly in contact with each other through existing business associations, such as the Massachusetts High Technology Council. Thus, business crisis and awareness of TQM as practiced in Japan motivated these CEOs to practice TQM.

In November 1989, Professor Shiba gave a seminar at MIT that several of the CEOs attended. Professor Tom Lee of MIT, who had been Shiba's colleague at the International Institute for the Application of Systems Analysis in Vienna in the 1980s, arranged for Professor Shiba to give the seminar.

As a result of whatever problems they were having at their companies, their knowledge of Japan and TQM, and Professor Shiba's introduction to TQM, the following seven Boston-area companies decided to form the Center for Quality Management:

- Analog Devices, Inc.
- Bolt Beranek and Newman Inc.
- Bose Corporation
- Digital Equipment Corporation
- GE Aircraft Engine Division
- Polaroid Corporation
- Teradyne, Inc.

Ray Stata of Analog Devices was chairman of the board, Professor Thomas Lee of MIT (on a part-time, pro bono basis) was president, and the board of directors consisted of the CEOs or other senior managers of the founding companies.[8]

The CQM was formed on the basis of the three-element model for societal diffusion, as expressed in its mission statement:

> The mission of the Center for Quality Management is to accelerate understanding and implementation of quality management concepts and methods by creating a network of like-minded organizations to share knowledge and experience. This will require a common language and a shared understanding of the basic methodologies to define problems and design solutions. In the broadest sense, the long-term objective of the Center is to promote organizational and societal learning about how to improve the performance of human systems.

Having decided to form the CQM, the founding CEOs needed a plan for the CQM's functions and operations, and they needed a joint understanding of what TQM was. To this end, they undertook a five-week design study in March and April of 1990. This design study, described in Chapter 19, was led by Shoji Shiba. All of the participants were senior line managers or senior quality staff members from the CQM companies, except three participants from MIT. The plan resulting from the CQM design study led to a committee structure, as shown in Figure 28-3. The intention was to have a lean staff and active committee structure (like JUSE), to put the know-how in the companies and not in the CQM staff.

After the design study ended, it took a few more weeks for the board to read the plan and approve it. Although a number of committees were proposed, not all of them became active in 1990. Activities that did take place in 1990 included the following:

- The seminar committee was active, sponsoring seminars by Florida Power & Light, Xerox, Motorola, and Corning.
- The research committee commissioned translation of the book *TQM for Technical Groups* [288].
- Shoji Shiba offered several one-day courses called CEO Introduction to TQM.
- The first CQM tool manual was developed.
- The six-day course, TQM for Senior Managers: Planning and Implementation, was offered in two parallel sessions in October, November, and December to 48 executives of CQM companies.
- The 1991 plan was prepared, its starting point being PDCA on 1990 activities.

The six-day course on TQM for senior managers was a particularly noteworthy achievement of 1990. The course was developed by Shoji Shiba with help from the CQM design team, and it was taught by Shoji Shiba. Several CEOs and their direct reports attended the course, which included much group work with TQM tools and a number of case studies presented by CEOs, senior managers, and members of the design team. The design team took notes on the entire six days and converted them into transparencies and draft text that could be used again by other presenters and as the basis for this book. A key concept of the course was "no delegation of improvement," which was demonstrated in many ways; for example, the CEOs themselves presented case studies.

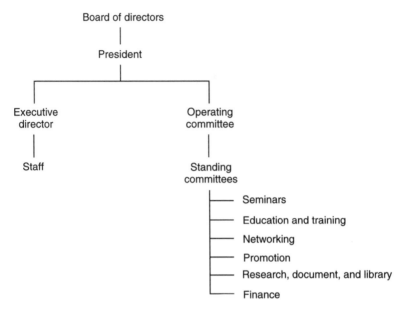

Figure 28-3. CQM Committee Structure

Key Elements of the CQM Approach

Organizations, not individuals, are members of the CQM. It is not a professional society. The first criterion for membership in the CQM is active participation of the most senior manager (CEO or CEO-equivalent) who is committed to leading the organizational change and improvement efforts in his or her organization. The other criterion for membership is that the CQM member is willing to share actual case studies, good and bad. Without top management leadership, organizational change will not happen; without efforts to change and improve and willingness to share the results, an organization will have nothing to share and, therefore, will not be able to participate in the CQM's mutual learning efforts.

Another key element of the CQM approach is that the CQM staff should be primarily for support and coordination of CQM members, and ideally the intellectual leadership of the CQM should reside in member companies. This is important because extensive organizational change and improvement methods we encourage in this book require a culture change. Thus, members must change how they think about and practice organizational improvement, and not primarily depend on outside consultants and outsourced training.

Two other key elements of the CQM approach are the adoption of a common language and baseline approach to facilitate shared learning opportunites (in particular, the vocabulary and methods of this book were selected), and members provide an "improvement culture" to each other and society at large. While using the common language for communication and comparison, many members do not use this common language within their own companies or may adapt it to their own organizations.

1991–1999 Activities

The first year, 1990, was a year of organization. The second year, 1991, was a year of orientation, deciding what was really important to do and getting it started.

As of 1991, the CQM had several long-term aspirations:

- To handle CQM company facilities outside of New England (California, Europe, Japan, and so forth)
- To participate in development of a national quality culture in the United States
- To expand the CQM model or help others copy the CQM methods
- To develop improved, advanced methods of TQM, moving beyond what was copied from Japan

By the third year, 1992, the challenge was to figure out how to address demands for growth: how to select new member companies who will actively participate; how to provide services to the expanded membership while still depending on the committee structure; and how to expand the staff without diminishing the intellectual leadership of the companies.

In the years between 1992 and now, each of these aspirations and challenges has been substantially met. The following subsections detail the path the CQM followed.

Expansion

The CQM started in the Boston-area with seven founding members. Already by 1991, other Boston area companies heard about the CQM and its approaches to mutual learning for the benefit of all and wanted to join, bringing the membership level to 24 by the end of 1991. In addition, some Boston-area members of the CQM were divisions of companies located in other locations (for example, a division of HP located near Boston), and other Boston-area members had divisions in other locations (for instance, Analog Devices had a division near Silicon Valley). Thus, by January 1994, a chapter of the CQM had been established in Silicon Valley, with its own chapter board of directors made up of member CEOs and a local chapter director (a member of the CQM staff located locally to facilitate local CQM activities). The Silicon Valley chapter had 10 or so initial members.

As CEOs in other geographic regions heard about the CQM, other groups of CEOs wanted their companies to be part of the CQM. In this way, CQM chapters were established in Louisville, Cincinnati, Western Europe, and Finland. By 1999, the CQM had over 115 members, 15 university affiliates, and 14 associate members. While the CQM does not actively seek expansion to other geographic regions, companies in new regions may become interested causing the CQM to expand further.

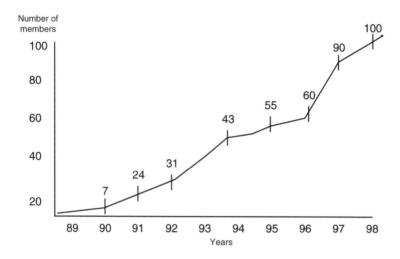

Figure 28-4. Growth of CQM Membership

Management

Within a couple of years of its founding, the committee system originally planned by the CQM Design Team (and used by each new chapter) ceased to be satisfactory for the CQM's daily management. Thus, a paid, full-time CQM executive director was hired to manage the CQM central office support staff. Over time, the CQM staff has grown to about 16 people, including the chapter directors. As of 1998, founding president (and pro-bono part-time employee) Tom Lee retired, and a new CQM president, Gary Burchill, was appointed to be a paid full-time president; he also handles the job of executive director.

Focus

From the beginning, one of the CQM's aspirations was to develop improved, advanced methods, moving beyond what was copied from Japanese TQM. This point was particularly important. The CQM companies initially copied Japan for efficiency's sake (of course, they had to adapt what they learned from Japan to the U.S. business culture). The CQM members were also reluctant to do too much at one time: learning and beginning to practice the Japanese version of TQM was enough effort for most.

However, the CQM board and staff always understood there was more to organizational change and improvement than the Japanese version of TQM as then practiced. In particular, the CQM companies had the opportunity (and often necessity) to learn and develop improved methods to integrate them with their existing practice of TQM.

In 1991 to 1993, CQM member companies worked with Gary Burchill to develop Concept Engineering (Chapter 14). By 1992, the CQM began an interchange with

Russell Ackoff and his colleagues to learn the methods of Idealized Design (to be described in Chapter 29). In the years that followed, other methods were integrated with the methods CQM members were already using (we'll elaborate on this in the research subsection below and in Chapter 29). Thus, in 1994, the CQM formally changed its name from Center for Quality Management to Center for Quality of Management. The name change clarified that the CQM and its members were interested in more than the narrow "management of quality" using TQM as the means—they were interested broadly in the "quality of management" in their companies.

From the beginning, the spectrum of CQM activities has fallen into three categories:

- Education
- Networking
- Research

Activities in these three areas are described in the following three subsections.

Education

In 1990, Shoji Shiba with assistance from members of the CQM Design Team offered two instances of a six-day course on TQM for senior managers. In 1991, the six-day course on TQM for senior managers was offered three more times to 72 more CEOs and senior managers. The courses were taught by CEOs and senior managers who had taken the course with Professor Shiba, to show executive leadership in TQM and to learn the material better. Companies also took the material into their own companies and based internal activities on it.

Also, in 1991, skill courses in the LP method (Chapter 13) and the 7 steps (see Chapter 9), based on initial versions developed in member companies (with Shoji Shiba's guidance).

Since 1991, a variety of other courses have been added to the CQM portfolio. Many of these were developed in member companies and contributed to the CQM. Some were based on the results of CQM research efforts, again primarily "staffed" by people from member companies. One or two have been jointly developed in alliances with other consortia.

The CQM "roadmap" of available courses as of 1999 is shown in Figure 28-5.[9]

Networking

The CQM and its chapters and member organizations do networking in many ways:

- Each year since 1991, the CQM has held a seminar series with speakers reporting on the change and improvement practices in world-class organizations.
- Chapters have regular roundtable meetings on specific topics, by functional areas, and so on. Most common are CEO roundtables and chief change or quality officer round tables.
- Members give courses they have developed to the CQM for use by other members.

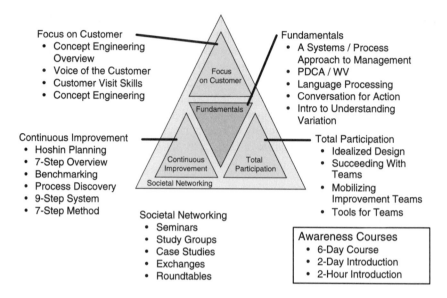

Focus on Customer
- Concept Engineering Overview
- Voice of the Customer
- Customer Visit Skills
- Concept Engineering

Fundamentals
- A Systems / Process Approach to Management
- PDCA / WV
- Language Processing
- Conversation for Action
- Intro to Understanding Variation

Continuous Improvement
- Hoshin Planning
- 7-Step Overview
- Benchmarking
- Process Discovery
- 9-Step System
- 7-Step Method

Total Participation
- Idealized Design
- Succeeding With Teams
- Mobilizing Improvement Teams
- Tools for Teams

Societal Networking
- Seminars
- Study Groups
- Case Studies
- Exchanges
- Roundtables

Awareness Courses
- 6-Day Course
- 2-Day Introduction
- 2-Hour Introduction

Figure 28-5. CQM Curriculum Roadmap

- Organizations exchange executive visits, executives teach in CQM courses offered locally, trainers and facilitators from one company attend train-the-trainer courses in another company, and upon occasion a delegation of visitors from one chapter visits companies in another chapter.
- People from one member company participate on improvement teams in another member company to see and learn a new method in practice, as is done for example within Kaizen Events in CQM's Cincinnati Chapter.
- Books, manuals, and the Journal of the CQM have been published to make methods and learning available in traditional printed format.
- Case studies, white papers, lists of resources, and notices of events are "published" either on the CQM's public Web site or on its member-only Web site.

Research

From the beginning the people from CQM member companies have worked together to learn, exchange, and develop new methods to add to the basic set of methods in the areas of the four revolutions from the first edition of this book. Guiding these efforts have been several principles:

- Look for weaknesses in their current management systems.
- Don't be bound to a single "school" or discipline.[10]
- Integrate and synthesize best methods into a system or step-by-step process (not just a set of tasks) that can be taught, practiced, and improved as more is learned.

- Do immediate field trials in member companies to get real-life experience.
- Keep repeating the improvement cycle, to recover from aspects of the initial process that didn't work the first time, to build on increased understanding, and to deal with new circumstances.

Since 1990, various combinations of CQM members have worked in a variety of areas. In each case, six to a dozen people periodically met, studied, and synthesized for periods ranging from a few months to a year or more. Areas of CQM research, synthesis, practice, and improvement since 1991 have included:

- Development of Concept Engineering for finding the latent needs of customers and users—described beginning on page 237
- A study of best practices of new product development—resulted in a seminar at which representatives of various CQM members presented their best practices
- Development, in collaboration with Russell Ackoff and his colleagues, of a step-by-step approach to Idealized Design—described in Chapter 29 (see page 680)
- A study of the methods of culture change—conclusions never published
- Study of how the methods of TQM can be applied in service organizations—resulted in a study report [15], and use of the vocabulary of three different types of processes described in section 6.3 (page 84)
- A survey of Cloutaire Rapaille's concepts of Cultural Archetypes—concluded with a seminar with presenters from four non-CQM companies describing their use of Rapaille's methods (see description on page 61)
- Development of Conversation for Action (or Personal PDCA)—methods to find shared concerns, make keepable commitments and build trusting relationships—described in section 16.1, page 299
- A survey of System Dynamics—concluded with an understanding of reasonable roles for system archetypes, causal loops, and simulation in the tool kit of methods of CQM members
- A tentative survey of Management of Innovation—never moved beyond the planning stages
- A survey of leadership—resulted in a seminar presentation, a set of working notes on CQM's member-only Web site, and a paper summarizing the survey is planned for the *Journal of the Center for Quality of Management*
- A survey of Strategic Planning—resulted in a seminar presentation and a set of working notes on CQM's member-only Web site
- A survey of Cycle-time Reduction—insights documented in a special issue of the CQM Journal [235]

In 1999, three of the CQM chapters were undertaking research efforts:

- Personal PDCA in the Louisville chapter
- Mobilization of entire organizations in the Cincinnati chapter
- Making good decisions rapidly with incomplete information in the Cambridge (Boston area) chapter

In general, many CQM members have followed the CQM recommended learning cycle: First, learn about the best practices of others. Second, individual companies integrate appropriate components into their own coherent management systems. Finally, share these new "best practices" with others. Learning best practices is not sufficient. A company has to make the best practices their own. In so doing, the company develops a new best practice it can share.

28.3 COMPARISON OF NATIONAL METHODS

Strong market pressure for innovation (and the need to do it efficiently) provides pull for societal learning. A nationwide quality promotion infrastructure provides push for societal learning. Change agents (particularly external change agents) with sufficient knowledge and prestige and the necessary sense of mission provide the catalyst for societal learning. Openness with real cases provides data for societal learning. (See Figure 28-6.) The Japanese model (presented in section 28.1, page 646) explicitly contains three of these learning elements (infrastructure to support networking, openness with real case, and change agents) and the fourth element is present implicitly.

Having an infratructure model also provides a baseline with which we can make comparisons. In the following subsections, we will use the Japanese model in two ways: to describe how the U.S. "system" differs from the way the Japanese implement the model and to suggest how activities within the model have evolved in Japan over the past few years. These two comparisons are summarized in Table 28-2.

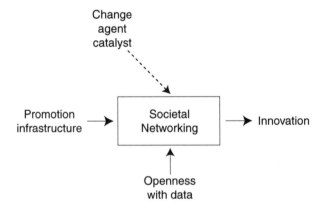

Figure 28-6. Forces for Societal Networking

The U.S. also has to deal with an issue that Japan doesn't, which is the multiculturalism that exists within companies, within markets, and within society at large. The many-headed U.S. "system" described below somehow accomodates such multiculturalism.

Table 28-2. Elements and Institutions of Societal Learning in Japan and the United States

Learning Element	Japan	United States
a. Infrastructure to support networking	Government and semi-private agencies (focused)	Government and non-profit agencies (fragmented)
i. National promotional organization	Semiprivate organizations > 40 years	Government jump-start Many societies and consortia Catch-up required
ii. Training	Substantially centralized Belief in authority	Decentralized Belief in references
iii. Knowledge dissemination	Centralized Unchanged	Many sources Seeking best practices
iv. Societal promotion activities	Traditional organizations Professionals Holy?	Government awards Celebrity leaders Comercialization
v. National standards certification	Addressing global markets Transition to ISO	Addressing global markets Transition to ISO
vi. Development of new methods	Centralized	Distributed
b. Openness with real cases	Industry ("no secrets in quality")	Industry (often wary of sharing quality methods)
c. Change agents	Universities, national research institutions (knowledge, prestige, sense of mission)	(Retired CEOs?)

Infrastructure for Networking

As described in section 28.1 (pages 647–649), in Japan, people from semiprivate agencies, primarily JUSE and JSA, provide the infrastructure for networking, with some government help.

In the United States, the situation is much more fragmented than in Japan. The federal and state governments and a variety of non-profit agencies, societies, and consortia provide the infrastructure of quality diffusion.

For instance, although the National Institute of Standards and Technology (NIST) gives its imprimatur to the Baldrige Award, the bulk of the effort to administer the Baldrige Award comes from individuals from industry and consultancies. Basically, the Baldrige Award organization is also a "semiprivate" organization. Furthermore, as in Japan, the major effort of addressing the need for a quality promotion infrastructure comes from industrial consortia. However, while only two major consortia exist in Japan (JUSE and JSA), such organizations have multiplied in the United States.

National Promotional Organization

As described above, Japanese national promotion is focused in JUSE and JSA. These semiprivate organizations have been promoting quality in Japan for over 40 years.

In comparison with their Japanese counterparts, American organizations that promote business improvement and quality are fragmented and numerous. A thorough survey of quality organizations would, therefore, be quite beside the point, at least for now, in understanding how a regional or national infrastructure works. However, a few brief descriptions should give the flavor of the membership, functioning, and curricula of quality organizations in the United States.

The American Society for Quality (ASQ) is a professional organization for quality specialists and is probably the largest quality organization in the United States. It has existed since 1946 when 17 smaller quality organizations joined together, their members all being practitioners of Walter Shewhart's methods. Some of these smaller organizations had existed since 1941. Shewhart and Deming were early participants in ASQ related activities.

In the 1980s, reacting to pressure on U.S. industry from Japan which had developed better methods of quality and improvement, a number of organizations and initiatives were undertaken. They were definitely playing catch-up, having vastly less commonality and coordination than the highly developed Japanese set of activities.

- The U.S. government attempted to jump-start the quality movement in the U.S. by establishing the Baldrige criteria for organizational excellence and the Baldrige award. A number of states created state quality awards that operated in a variety of ways.
- The American Supplier Institute (ASI) was spun off from Ford Motor Company's efforts to improve the quality of its supplier base.
- GOAL/QPC originated with a group of followers of W. Edwards Deming and has evolved into an independent training organization with both individual and corporate members. Its tools and practices have been adapted from the Japanese versions, observed on study trips. Instructors are both employees and free-lancers.
- Joseph Juran created his Juran Institute, which did consulting, while Juran himself wrote popular books and gave well-attended presentations.
- In addition to some of the biggest U.S. companies consulting Deming, he gave a highly visible course and made a well-known series of videotapes.
- Lloyd Dobyns and Clare Crawford-Mason produced an NBC-TV documentary called "If Japan Can...Why Can't We?" that was credited with bringing Deming and the quality movement to the attention of the American populace. Later, Dobyns and Crawford-Mason produced the series of videotapes distributed under Deming's name and featuring him.
- A number of big companies created their own quality standards and awards aimed at their suppliers' companies.
- The Center for Quality of Management (see section 28.2, page 654) was designed to be like JUSE in several respects. The membership comprises corporations rather than individuals, and the dual focus of the CQM is education and top management. Like JUSE, the CQM often uses instructors from member corporations rather than in-house staff. The CQM was modeled on JUSE because many of JUSE's features appeared to be what the member companies most needed.
- Innumerable independent consulting companies entered the arena of quality consulting, mostly from more traditional consulting arenas. Consulting companies

vary enormously in focus, ranging from specialty providers of everything from statistical software to mission- and vision-setting training, to "full-spectrum" companies whose services cover a range of TQM, six sigma, etc., methods.

- Many celebrity speakers and authors sell themselves as after-dinner speakers or through their own seminars, typically positioned as being for top management. Two examples are Michael Hammer of Business Process Reengineering fame, and Tom Peters who first became famous through the book he co-authored, *In Search of Excellence*, and now writes and speaks about "wow" and "liberation" management.
- In more recent years, a variety of other "institutes" and consortia (e.g., Society for Organizational Learning, Lean Enterprise Institute, and Six Sigma Academy) have been formed around certain topic areas.

The curious thing about the above history is that promotional activities started in the U.S. before they did in Japan (at ASQ and its predecessors). However, such promotional activites first became fully developed in a quite concentrated and coordinated way in Japan. The U.S. then began a fierce game of catch-up, and now probably has greater overall breadth than is available in Japan. Of course, in typical U.S. fashion, many autonomous groups are rushing in different directions, often claiming they are competing with each other, but in some sense providing a wave (or series of waves) of activity that relentlessly push U.S. businesses along. Unfortunately, these diverse U.S. groups do not usually show the relationships among the various methods and schools of thought and the possibilities for them complementing each other.

Training

In Japan training is concentrated in JUSE and JSA which are considered to be the authorities. This works in Japan where there is some acceptance of authority.

U.S. businesses and organizations don't believe in authority or the correct method. Rather, each U.S. organization feels the need to evaluate what offers are best in general and for them. Such evaluation is typically done based on sales presentations, arguments or dictates about which method or offering is best, and references (often quite informal references such as one CEO recommending a program to another CEO).

Also, a large number of sources of training can be found in the United States. Many companies have in-house training groups, sometimes large groups with many professional curriculum developers and trainers. In some companies, particularly smaller companies, executives and senior technical people do much of the training. In other companies, some or all of the training needs are out-sourced to consultants or commercial training organizations. Many organizations distribute packaged courses and train and certify people to teach their packaged courses.

One device that U.S. companies use to determine their own training needs is organizational assessments of strengths and weaknesses. Commercial training providers often use these (sometimes as a free "loss-leader") to "objectively ascertain" a potential customer's needs.

Knowledge Dissemination

The methods of organizational change and improvement are not a theory: they comprise a system for managing improvement that evolves according to the facts of success in practice. Experts from the United States introduced statistical quality control into Japan where it evolved into a set of practices that fit the Japanese culture and needs extraordinarily well. Out of statistical quality control, the Japanese created quality circles, kaizen, companywide quality control, and other concepts to develop what we know as TQM today and that continues to evolve.

For knowledge dissemination, the United States has the same variety and fragmentation as it has for promotional organizations and training. In addition, top business leaders are held in high regard and people in U.S. businesses have many opportunities to hear presentations by top business leaders on their methods. Also, many top business leaders have written books, some of them bestsellers.

In the United States, companies seek best practices, but they also seek a unique approach in many cases. This has pluses and minuses. On the plus side, companies *should* adapt best practices to their own situations, and the quest for uniqueness results in many experiments, which theoretically can quickly advance the overall state-of-the-art. On the minus side, many companies develop unique methods that don't work as well as "standard best practices" and, thus, don't lead to success or continued practice of the methods. Also, on the minus side, the U.S. environment for sharing results of experiments with new methods is as uncoordinated as the rest of the U.S. system we have been describing.

Arguably, the United States would benefit greatly from a more explicit and coordinated system for experimenting with quality methods in companies and diffusing the results of the experiments to evolve versions of the methods generally suitable for American culture and need, and adaptable to the culture and need of each company practicing the methods. However, such coordination on a broad scale seems unlikely. If anything, more competitive positioning is going on between the various U.S. organizations and methods than ever before.

The CQM has within its members, affiliates, and associates attempted to provide a coordinated approach to knowledge dissemination. No doubt other such organizations are coordinating approaches among their members, and many large companies are coordinating the dissemination of knowledge among their subsidiaries and divisions. In the CQM case, the CQM provides among it members the following elements of the Japanese model we are using in this chapter: promotional organization, training, knowledge dissemination, development of new methods, openness with real cases, and (to a limited extent) change agents. In particular, almost all of the CQM's courses, books, and manuals have resulted from joint development by member companies or development within one company which made the material available to the rest. CQM members may also draw on CQM for additional support in the areas CQM does support and must go to other sources in the areas the CQM does not support.

U.S. companies' interest in assessment mechanisms such as the Baldrige critera also has a plus and a minus. Outside or self-assessment against this standard criteria could hinder a company in finding its uniquely successful approach. However, assessment against such standard critera would more likely lead a company away from lots of counterproductive practices and increase its chances of building an excellent base system to which appropriate unique elements can be added.

Societal Promotion Activities

In Japan, a traditional collection of societal promotion activities are still in place, including JUSE, JSA, the Deming Prize, etc. As mentioned in section 28.1 (page 646), quality months and days traditionally receive considerable emphasis.

The U.S. version of Deming Prize is the Malcolm Baldrige National Quality Award (MBNQA or Baldrige Award).[11] An important benefit of the Baldrige Award is its promotion of quality in the United States. Companies advertise they have won the award; this practice forces prize-winning companies' competitors to focus on quality in addition to supporting the companies' own focus on quality. Companies are demanding their suppliers prepare themselves to apply for the Baldrige Award. Companies are undertaking full or superficial self-evaluations of their quality practices using the Baldrige criteria. Hundreds of thousands of copies of the Baldrige criteria have been distributed to companies and individuals requesting them. The press, trade, and academic journals have included many articles discussing the award. States and regions are establishing their own versions of the Baldrige Award, in some cases viewing them as an intermediate step on a company's path to the Baldrige Award.

In the early days of the Baldrige Award many in the United States discussed whether the Baldrige Award helped or hurt company quality practices [12]. However, its real or purported problems seem secondary compared with the benefit of national promotion of quality. Also, over time and with continuous improvement, the Baldrige Award has evolved as has the way companies use it. In particular, applying for the Baldrige award because it was the faddish thing to do seems over (and number of application forms requested has decreased somewhat in recent years). However, many companies are using the Baldrige critera for self-assessment to measure themselves against a base line of best practice and to guide or motivate their organizational change and improvement activities. At the same time, fewer business people are surprised when a company chooses to use the Baldrige criteria for self-assessment or to apply for the Baldrige award. Like any good idea, the Baldrige Award passed through a phase where it was too much of a fad, too often misused, and too often denigrated; today, it has settled into practical and productive use.[12]

As with knowledge dissemination, top business leaders also play a significant role in the United States in societal promotion. For instance, in our section on the spreading practice of six sigma (beginning on page 476), we described how the CEO of GE learned about six sigma from the CEO of Allied Signal.

Another important component of societal promotion in the United States is using company marketing and branding of products and services. Many advertisements state the company and its product or service have high quality and that its customers' satisfaction is a paramount concern to the company and its employees. Also, many companies, in fact, do compete in the quality and customer service domain—sometimes in a cutthroat manner. All this commercialized societal promotion creates a culture with increased customer expectations and businesses which presume they must meet increased customer expectations.

National Standard Certification

As described in section 28.1 (page 646), in the late 1980s, Japan had important national standards certificates. Today, the globalization of business has made international standards, such as ISO 9000, enormously important in Japan.

The United States has a variety of public and private standards that companies routinely adhere to for their products, such as the private UL and governmental FCC standards; often required by customers. The United States has never had an *important* national or state quality standard. Like Japan (and perhaps before Japan), globalization of business has resulted in widespread use of the ISO standards in the United States.

Development of New Methods

In section 28.1, we described the JUSE approach to development of new methods. No similar widespread U.S. system exists.

Again, many parallel (and to some extent competing) organizations work more or less together within a particular organization to develop new methods. Universities play a role, and many universities have industrial liaison programs. Organizations such as ASQ have working groups and sometimes sponsor codification of new methods. Many people, especially university professors and consultants, study a set of business cases, attempt to draw prescriptive conclusions from the cases, and publish step-by-step approaches. Consultancies often seek industry sponsorship to survey companies for their best practices which are summarized and perhaps codified and sold to other businesses.

Finally, in this chapter and in Chapter 14, we have described how CQM companies work together, similarly to the JUSE model, to synthesize new methods, quickly try them, and disseminate the methods through workshops and eventually courses.

Openness with Real Cases

In Japan, business or industry provides openness with real cases. "No secrets in quality," is the watchword in Japan.

Historically, U.S. industry has feared sharing process improvement methods with other companies, as if the process *improvement* methods were as secret as their processes themselves and product specifications. U.S. industry has become increasingly open with real cases (although many companies are still wary of sharing). The increased openness in the United States is partly a result of the spread of the idea of benchmarking: people have learned they can learn and share a lot without releasing significant secrets. Partly the increased openness in the United States is a result of the unavoidable need to form alliances with other organizations, which in many cases compete in some domains. Partly the increased openness is a result of increased management of suppliers by their customers. All three of these new behaviors have made sharing more commonplace and less shocking, and thus more an acceptable part of standard business practice.

Change Agents

In Japan, change agents primarily come from academia. Change agents in Japan have come from universities and national research institutions because they traditionally have had social prestige, especially popular universities such as Tokyo University, Tokyo Institute of Technology, Kyoto University, and others.

In the United States, we really haven't had change agents on a widespread basis. Plenty of famous individuals have helped a company or CEO see new possibilities, but few go into an organization and really catalyze its change process. Deming was an outsider who worked with some companies and may have helped catalyze change. Professor Kano and others served as change agents to Florida Power & Light, and Professor Shiba has served as a change agent for several of the CQM companies in the United States and Europe (and with non-CQM companies in other countries). Many consultancies claim to be or try to be change agents, and no doubt some succeed.

However, finding outside change agents remains an unsolved problem in the United States. Many in U.S. industry consider academics to be out of touch with real-world practices regardless of their prestige. American consultants have the same problem as Japanese consultants in acting as change agents; their short-term self-interest sometimes conflicts with their long-term sense of mission. Retired CEOs may be good candidates for change agents, since they have both prestige with industry and the necessary knowledge, but to fill the bill they must retain a vigorous sense of mission in their post-industry years.

Comparative Results

The Japanese model traditionally has worked well but has largely been applied to manufacturing companies. Also, over the past few years, the number of quality circles in Japan has decreased, despite the Japanese societal diffusion system. Shoji Shiba has also sensed a general weakening of the Japanese quality culture.

The U.S. "system" (and we use the term loosely) initially helped manufacturing companies. However, the methods of organizational change and improvement have also been spread first to service organizations and then to organizations of all types.

We may be seeing a new model of societal networking, suitable for the U.S. culture with its tendency to fragmentation and distrust of national authority (see Figure 28-7).

As shown in Figures 28-7 and 28-8, there are three forms of societal influence on U.S. companies. First (A in the figures), many sources try to influence anyone who will listen. Second, with modern forms communication and interaction, highly targeted influence exists (B in the figures): special interest groups, individuals easily

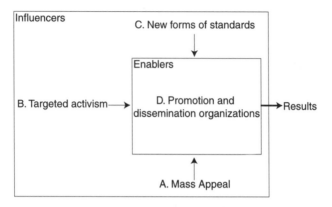

Figure 28-7. U.S. Forces in Societal Networking

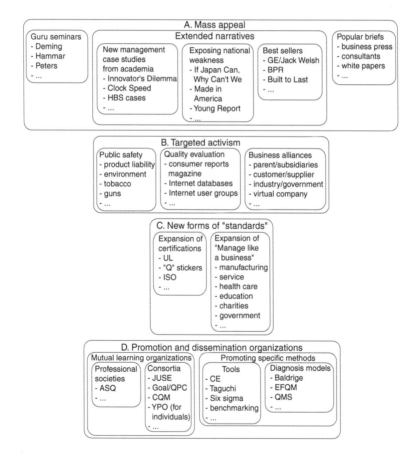

Figure 28-8. Components of Forces

obtaining information on products and services, and business alliances where one company influences specific other companies. Third (C in figures), business must live with new sorts of "standards" of operation, i.e., an expansion of traditional product standards, and pressure for organizations of all types to function in "more business-like ways."

In response to these three influences (A, B and C), a number of organizations exist (influence D) to enable companies to address the societal pressures (A, B, and C) and to use new methods. Enabling organizations aim to network among certain sets of companies or individuals, and aim to help people learn a specific method.

What conclusions should we draw? Possibly the advantage of the unfocused nature of the U.S. system, i.e., its lack of focus on only one application domain enables adapting to a changing environment. We recall Figure 6-16 (page 84)—too much of a system can be stultifying; too little of a system is inefficient. Somewhere in between is an optimal point. The U.S. system for promoting the methods of business change and improvement certainly has enough flexibility. It seems that a *little* more coordination could greatly increase the speed of improvement of all.

European Approach

We do not know enough of the European approach to speak about it at length. However, we can sketch what we know. The European Foundation for Quality Management (EFQM) is a semiprivate organization with member organizations throughout Europe (see page 447). It is a pan-European promotional organization with an assessment criteria and an award, somewhat like the Baldrige Award. In parallel, many European countries have their own national quality organizations with their own awards.

Our impression is that the rest of the European "system" is as amorphous and multi-headed as the U.S. system.

28.4 USE OF INDIRECT INFLUENCE

Change and improvement of the breadth we describe in this book require change throughout the company organization.

The traditional method of effecting change is from the top down, by order and enforcement of top-level managers, as in part A of Figure 28-9. Most top managers can testify to the difficulty of such an approach. Managers just below the top argue against changes, middle managers delay implementation, and much of the rest of the staff swears the changes can't work in the company. All three groups tend to continue doing whatever they have been doing.

The alternative is outside influence and outside power for change, as shown in part B of Figure 28-9 where the CEO from this company and other companies contribute to a societal or cultural movement for change and this reflects back throughout the company. A societal learning system provides an effective alternative to top-down

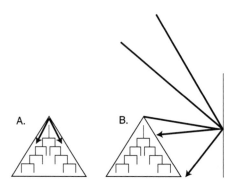

Figure 28-9. Alternative Approach to Influencing Entire Organization

change. The modern quality promotion program uses a regional or national organization or quality culture to exert outside influence for change.

This outside influence is beginning to emerge in the United States. The Baldrige Award has generated interest in quality from thousands of U.S. companies. Many companies are putting pressure on their suppliers to focus on quality. For example, in a

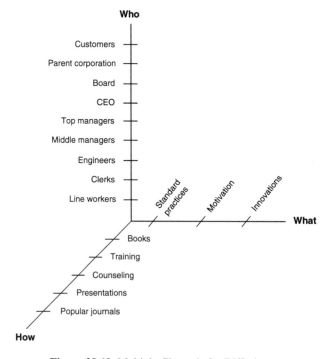

Figure 28-10. Multiple Channels for Diffusion

famous instance, Motorola has asked its suppliers to be ready to apply for the Baldrige Award. Ford's Q-1 quality rating has motivated many of its suppliers to improve.

Diffusion of QI stories is another example of outside influence. When workers in one company see workers in another effectively using improvement methodologies, they think in terms of application to their company. A manager is going to be more receptive to organizational change and improvement if all the other companies the manager might work for are also doing it. Young engineers would be more positive about using basic improvement methods if their universities required mastery of the methods for graduation.

Outside forces for quality infusion can be manifested in many ways, as shown in Figure 28-10. If the methods of organizational change/improvement and quality are to be spread throughout a society, it is not enough for parent corporations to require the methods and teach them to subsidiaries or for large customers to require the methods and teach them to suppliers. Moreover, the methods are a complex set of knowledge and practices, so that no single channel of diffusion is sufficient. A regional and national infrastructure requires several channels in several dimensions.

Indeed, Figure 28-10 implies 135 kinds of diffusion channels (this book of standards for top management is one example). All of the elements in each of the dimensions are opportunities for societal diffusion in an industry, region, or nation.

NOTES

1. A more extensive discussion of the Japanese infrastructure for networking circa 1990 was included in [264, Chapter 16].

2. You might substitute "business improvement" or "organizational change" for "TQM" while reading this section. Also, where appropriate, think of "quality" as "customer satisfaction."

3. Parts of this section were previously published in [261].

4. The information describing JUSE is primarily taken from JUSE's descriptive brochure, "JUSE: Organization and Activities."

5. Remarks by Mr. J. Noguchi in an informal lecture at JUSE headquarters, March 12, 1990.

6. Lecture by MIT professor Tom Lee on his visit to JUSE, November 7, 1989.

7. For a more detailed description, see [110, pages 185–186].

8. In essence, Tom Lee, Ray Stata, and Shoji Shiba were the *individual* co-founders of the CQM.

9. Often, CQM people and companies refer to societal networking as mutual learning.

10. At various times, the CQM has drawn on the following thinkers and methods: Russell Ackoff and Interactive Management, Chris Argyris and Action Science, Deming's version of TQM, Fernando Flores and the Language/Action Perspective,

Eli Goldratt and Theory of Constraints, Peter Senge and his Five Disciplines, and many other thinkers and experts from many other areas and methods.

11. John Petrolini of Teradyne provided us with a briefing on the Baldrige Award. See also [43].

12. See also [134, 267, 280, 291].

29

Ongoing Integration of Methods

From the beginning of this book,[1] we have admonished managers and business thinkers to stop viewing various organizational change and improvement systems as being in competition with each other and to spend their time figuring out how the methods complement each other and how parts of the various systems can be integrated into the appropriate system for their unique business situation. Many of the examples we have shown in this book illustrated instances of organizations integrating methods from various sources. In particular, the three case studies in Chapter 26—Teradyne, Hewlett-Packard, and Analog Devices—were very much stories of ongoing integration of methods into coherent systems for the unique organizational situation.

In this chapter, we will provide three more examples of integration of methods from various sources:

- The idealized design methods of Russell Ackoff and his Interactive Management with hoshin management and other methods taught by the Center for Quality of Management (CQM). This is an instance where a component from one domain is applied to improve a method from another domain.
- The integration by Gary Burchill of causal loops from the System Dynamics domain, the LP method from the TQM domain, and Ackoff's concept of "mess formulation" into the tool Gary calls Structural Process Improvement [46]. This is an example of combining several methods to create a new method (and to suggest an improvement to existing methods).
- The integration of methods from various sources into the management system at SerVend. This is an example of developing an overall integrated system for an organization.

Yet another example of integration, involving variations of many of the methods described in this book, may be found in [190].

Before, we go to the detailed examples, we will review some of the examples of integration given in the book or that we have seen in practice:

- Systems Thinking, which some people think of as its own set of methods, applies broadly to many things we have described in this book. Many situations may be so localized that you will not have to look at the bigger picture although, even then, it may pay off to take a look at the bigger picture to make sure you are working on the right local problem; instead, one can do local process control or reactive improvement. However, much of the time you need to be looking out for unintended consequences; in some cases, a much better solution is available by taking a systems viewpoint.
- System Dynamics methods such as causal loops are appropriate within the 7 steps, for instance, to help understand cause-and-effect relationships in situations too dynamic in terms of time delays and complexity of interrelationships for Ishikawa diagrams to be appropriate.
- We have shown how ADI, HP, and others use a balanced scorecard (or something close to it) to monitor TQM and other parts of their management systems. In particular, a balanced scorecard would seem to be relevant to a system dynamics approach.
- We suggested that the deployment methods developed for six sigma may be appropriate to apply to many other organizational change and improvement methods.
- The methods of Lean Production—Just-In-Time manufacturing—are used in many modern management systems. For instance, many CQM companies use it along with the methods described in this book.
- The methods of inventory minimization and time minimization from Theory of Constraints complement cycle-time reduction and other methods well.
- We describe in this book how the methods of Action Science from Argyris, the Language/Action perspective of Flores, and Semantics from Hayakawa work well together, and the combination begins to address the soft side of conventional business improvement.

We all *must* look for ways the various methods fit together, instead of focusing on how one is better than the other. The competitive approach will not maximize benefit to our organization and stakeholders. The competitive approach primarily benefits consultants selling the various methods and their services. We must learn to integrate across the boundaries of culture, philosophy, academic discipline, and schools of management thought.

29.1 APPLYING IDEALIZED DESIGN TO HOSHIN MANAGEMENT

As mentioned in Chapter 28, one of the first extensions the CQM took from our basic four revolutions of management thinking was to make use of some of Russell Ackoff's ideas on Interactive Management.[2] In particular, CQM studied Ackoff's methods to learn a more powerful method of strategic planning known as Idealized Design, to be used to create the mid-term strategic plan for hoshin management (see page 508 of Chapter 24) and for more general planning.

Problems with Common Forms of Strategic Planning

Ackoff takes a systems approach to business improvement in which he encourages a complete redo of an organization's management system—a breakthrough to a new management structure and system.

Ackoff motivates the need for aggressive redesign of business systems, structures and processes with an argument that goes something like the following:

> There are three typical approaches to strategic planning, which he calls "reactive," "inactive," and "preactive."
>
> The reactive approach that a few people take is based on the assumption that things used to work and somehow got broken and the organization needs to return to the way it used to do things.
>
> The inactive approach that a few people take is based on the assumption that things are working well now and the organization should work to keep doing these same things.
>
> The preactive approach is the approach that most companies use for strategic planning. Using this approach, organizations try to predict the business situation next year or five years from now and to modify their business system to address that business situation.
>
> The first two approaches are not particularly productive in most situations (especially in a rapidly changing world). The third approach depends on both successfully predicting the future (hard in the best of cases) and adapting the strategic plan to inevitable changes in the business environment (we have all seen that most strategic plans just sit on the shelf once done). In fact, this sort of strategic planning is usually messier yet. In addition to not having a good prediction of the future, most organizations do not have a clear picture of their current situation. Thus, they are trying to plan for a move between two undefined points—is it any wonder that the hypothetical quarter-by-quarter or month-by-month plan for the next year or two inevitably takes a lot longer or doesn't get done at all. Standing in the oasis of good enough current business situation, you may not know there is a vast desert between you and the objectives on the other side of the mountains in the distance, and this desert may be filled with unknown quicksand, the mountains may be unscaleable, there may be uncrossable chasms of which there is no view to the naked eye, and so on.

Vision, Environment, and Creating the Ideal Future

Thus, a new approach to planning is needed. This leads to Ackoff's concept of "interactive planning" and Idealized Design. As mentioned in the previous subsection, planning begins with a thorough analysis of the existing situation (so there is a well understood starting position). Next, an *idealized design* is created. This is the organizational structure and system you wish you had *now*, not in the future. This idealized design is created from a blank sheet of paper, with none of the constraints resulting from the existing system and structure—just the constraints of the existing business environment. In other words, Ackoff's approach to strategic planning goes from a weak existing system to a good system for the current situation; it goes between two knowable points. Thus, it is possible to develop a realistic plan for moving between these two points.

A Process for Creating a Mid-Term Plan

Russell Ackoff has proposed some interesting specific methods for developing a vision for the future. We describe one of them here. Ackoff calls it backward planning. Ackoff's methods are compatible with the mid-term plan in hoshin management.

Ackoff's planning method, which he outlines in his book [2], has five steps, three of which are described below.

Stage 1: Situation analysis. Situation analysis, or "formulating the mess," as Ackoff calls it, is identifying problems and opportunities. During this stage, all current aspects of the company and its people are analyzed, the sources of obstruction are listed, and past and current performance is extrapolated assuming things stay as they are.

Stage 2: Ends planning. Ends planning means designing the desirable future. This step includes designing organizational structure and management systems. But its most interesting aspect is what Ackoff calls *idealized design.*

Idealized design is a powerful method of stating the desired future and planning efficient and practical means of accomplishing it. Idealized design does not design the company for some future circumstance. Idealized design formulates the company you wish you had now.

Idealized design has the following properties:

- Work from the assumption that there is no system but the same environment.
- Design a technically feasible new system, considering the feasibility of the new system once it exists, not the feasibility or cost of bringing it into existence.
- Make sure that the new design is operationally viable in the current environment.
- The new system dissolves the mess.
- The new system allows for rapid learning and adaptation.

To do an idealized design, you need a mission statement saying what business the company wants to be in, how it wants to operate, and what it wants to accomplish. You also need to specify the desired properties of the design. Examples might include:

- What products or services the company should provide and what its distinguishing characteristics should be
- How the products should be sold (where, by whom, on what terms, pricing)
- How products should be serviced
- Where and how products should be manufactured
- Which support services should be provided internally and which externally
- How the company should be organized and managed

- Personnel policies
- Methods of financing company activities
- Environmental and regulatory responsibilities

The next step is to figure out a design with the desired properties. This design starts with a blank piece of paper. The designers assume the old system does not exist. This frees them from figuring out how to get from where they are to where they want to be, without constraints that usually impede change.

The key value of the idealized design is that the designers can see the differences and similarities between the existing system (analyzed in stage 1) and the ideal system (designed in stage 2). Once they understand those points of comparison, they can plan the means for getting from where they are to where they want to be.

Stage 3: Means planning. Means planning is creating the means by which one effects the desired future. With the information on what design (rather than just the market share, revenue, and profit goals) a company wants to have, the planners can approximate a path from the new to the old. One method Ackoff suggests for finding this path is to apply existing constraints successively on the new until the old is reached. This is illustrated in Figure 29-1.

Figure 29-1. Means Planning by Applying Constraints to the Idealized Design

At this point the designers have a map for undoing the constraints on the current system that prevent it from being the new system. They call this means planning.

Ackoff believes that the activities carried out in stages 1 through 3 will result in a plan that is much more feasible and focused than one created with the reverse strategy (starting from the present and moving toward future goals).

The typical company planning process goes something like this: The company decides on the goals it wants to achieve in 10 years and then plans toward them; the planners lay out a plan for achieving one-tenth of the goal per year (or project a hockey stick effect in which most advancement toward the goal is made in later years); the planners don't provide a detailed plan of the yearly changes to be made in the company to achieve the goals; the planners don't understand what the company will have to become in order to achieve the goals. Thus, the typical company planning process assumes a 10-year effort to reach goals without adequately understanding what those goals imply about the changes the company will have to make, and without making a plan for making those changes.[3]

In Ackoff's system of planning, the planners do situation analysis to make explicit where the company is, where the company will stay unless it changes, and what is preventing change. Then the planners create an idealized design describing what they would want their company to be like now if they could create an ideal company for competing in today's world. Then the planners figure out a path from the ideal company to the current company. By simply reversing this path, they have a demonstrable path from the current company to the future company, and one likely to be shorter than 10 years.

Ackoff's methods fit nicely into the hoshin management methods of TQM (see Figure 29-2).

Operationalizing Idealized Design

In collaboration with Russell Ackoff and his partner Jamshid Gharajedghi of Interact, the CQM has developed a process for applying the methods of idealized design and interactive planning as part of the overall set of methods described in this book [294]. This special issue is introduced by Russell Ackoff and includes four papers giving examples of the use of these methods. Toby Woll's paper [313] describes in part the effort to create a specific process for idealized design. In particular, the results of such interactive planning have often fed into hoshin management as suggested in Chapter 24.

The CQM collaboration with Ackoff and Gharajedghi began with an exchange of documentation between Gharajedghi, CQM president Tom Lee, and David Walden, then a senior executive at a CQM company. That meeting led to a two-day meeting at which a high-level delegation of six from CQM (including Lee, future CQM president Gary Burchill, CQM chairman Ray Stata, Steve Levy who was CEO of CQM-founding-member BBN, and the two authors of this book) compared methods with Ackoff, Gharajedghi, and several of their top consultants. Then Gharajedghi led a two-day workshop in their methods for the CQM president Tom Lee, executive director Toby

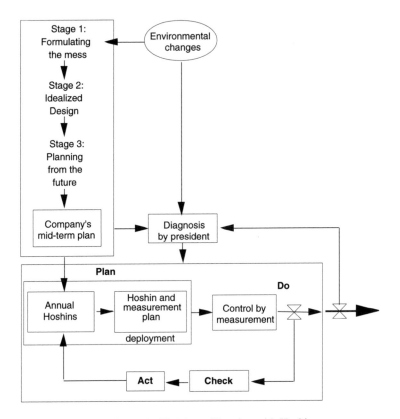

Figure 29-2. Meshing Ackoff's Means Planning with Hoshin

Woll, Shoji Shiba, several CEOs and senior managers of CQM companies, and Gary Burchill. Next, Lee and Woll watched Gharajedghi facilitate the method at a company. This was followed by joint facilitation work, and finally Woll (sometimes with the help of Lee) facilitated the method alone at a number of CQM and other companies. Along the way, Woll and Burchill documented more or less step-by-step processes for Idealized Design (Burchill's approach is described in the next section).

Figure 29-3 shows how one CQM member company, SerVend, integrated idealized design, hoshin management, annual planning, and everyday business planning into a coherent system.

29.2 STRUCTURAL PROCESS IMPROVEMENT CASE STUDY

In the mid-1990s, Gary Burchill was responsible for a substantial Navy procurement effort at the Naval Inventory Control Point. At the time, pressure existed to cut costs and do the same work through greater efficiency. As part of efforts to improve business processes, Gary developed what he calls Structural Process Improvement. The goal of Structural Process Improvement is to understand the current situation as a net-

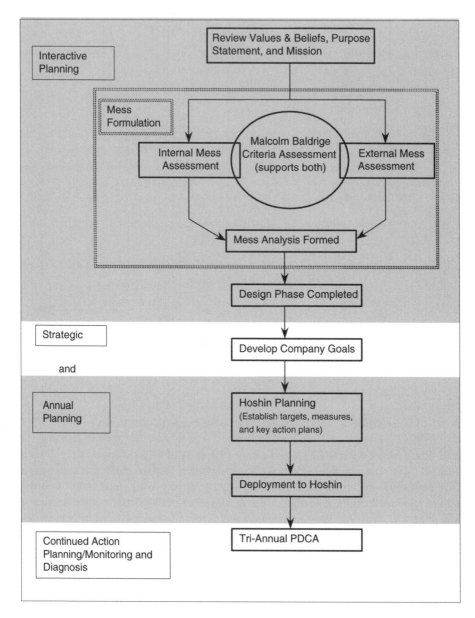

Figure 29-3. SerVend Planning Process

work of causes and effects, to find the high leverage points in the current system that can be changed to improve the system operation, and to implement the indicated changes. The steps of the process are:[4]

- Structure mapping, including language processing and system diagramming
- Environmental assessment
- Structural alignment, including obstruction analysis, gap analysis, and hoshin management

Structure Mapping

As mentioned in the previous section, Russell Ackoff recommends a systems approach and aggressive reengineering of business systems—he calls it idealized design. As a first step in this process, Ackoff recommends what he calls "mess formulation," documenting the current situation with all its messiness. Ackoff recommends looking at the mess from five points of view: authority (power), emotion (beauty), physical processes or method (knowledge), measurement systems (wealth), and conflict resolution (values). Gary decided that he and his staff would do mess formulation to understand their current situation.

Since the mid-1990s, people have looked into how to use the methods of system dynamics to help document the mess accurately. Ackoff's partner, Jamshid Gharajedghi, had investigated the use of system dynamics. Gary decided to use causal loops from system dynamics to document the mess his organization dealt with. For instance, Figure 29-4 shows a small part of the mess using the system dynamics technique of causal loop diagramming. Causal loops, such as this one, show what influences what in a situation. The arcs in causal loops are marked with **S**s or **O**s to indicate that as the variable at the beginning end of an arc goes up or down, the variable at the other end goes up or down in the same or opposite direction. In this example, as management focus on specific support components increases, discrete versus complete reviews increase. An **O** would indicate that as one end goes up, the other end would go down.

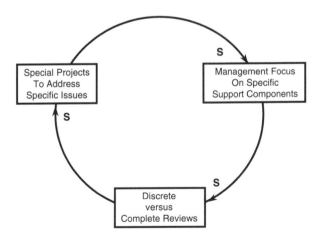

Figure 29-4. Example Causal Loop

As with his Concept Engineering method, Gary and his team started analysis of their situation by creating an image LP diagram of how employees saw their operating environment. Then Gary and his team further analyzed the mess from each of Ackoff's five points of view. They did this in a structured way by creating LP diagrams analyzing obstructions as seen from *each* of the five points of view. (The LP method is an excellent way to develop grounded data and to abstract those to high-level concepts.) The first-level titles from each of these six LP diagrams were then pulled together into a seventh, summary LP diagram, as shown in Figure 29-5. Thus, Burchill integrated methods by using the LP method to investigate Ackoff's five dimensions.

Traditionally, part of the "art" of drawing causal loops is deciding what the variables should be. Gary also applied the LP method to causal loop drawing to find appropriate variables. As Gary describes it

> We rigorously applied the rules of semantics in each [of the seven] LP diagrams. We scrubbed [the LP] cards to the maximum extent possible, to ensure that the facts reported on the labels were verifiable; even data cards regarding the themes of emotion were scrubbed into the language of reports. Additionally, we placed particular emphasis on first-level grouping and title making, because the first-level titles from the five obstruction diagrams were to serve as the data cards in the summary diagram and as the basis for variable development in our causal loop diagram.
>
> [Figure 29-6 on page 684] shows how we created names for relevant variables from LP group title headings.
>
> Once the variables were developed for each one of the LP titles, we began our analysis by identifying pairwise relationships between variables that related to the title in the selected group. We used a directed arc to show the causal direction from each variable to the next. [The arcs were labeled with Ss and Os as described above.]
>
> It was our experience that this process took many iterations and that different people created different relationships for each group. Ultimately though, we created one main story line loop related to the main theme and connected the various subplots to this main loop. The main causal loop diagram . . . is shown in [Figure 29-7 on page 684].

Thus, Burchill integrated LP methods with system dynamics methods to provide a structured method of causal loop variable creation.

Environmental Assessment

Having understood the current situation (the "mess"), Gary Burchill and his team did an environmental assessment for stakeholders, market trends, and business opportunities.

For instance, relating to stakeholders, they listed internal and external stakeholders and evaluated each in terms of the amount of influence each stakeholder could exert on the organization's policies and procedures and the amount of leverage the organization had on each stakeholder. This let them sort their stakeholder relationships

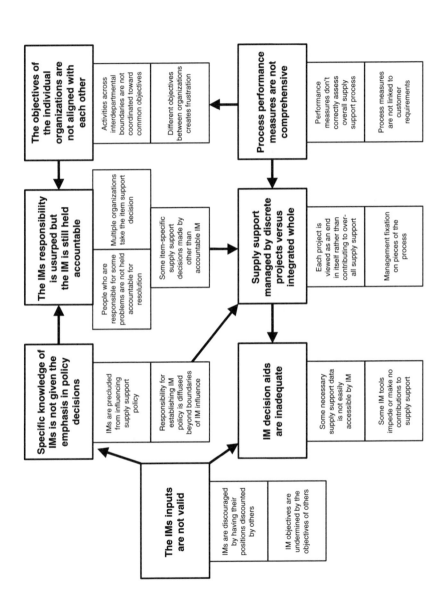

Figure 29-5. Summary LP Diagram

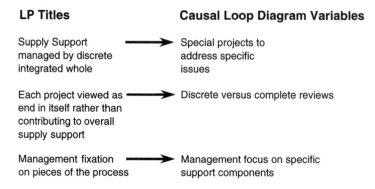

LP Titles   **Causal Loop Diagram Variables**

Supply Support   Special projects to
managed by discrete   address specific
integrated whole   issues

Each project viewed as   Discrete versus complete reviews
end in itself rather than
contributing to overall
supply support

Management fixation   Management focus on specific
on pieces of the process   support components

Figure 29-6. Variable Development

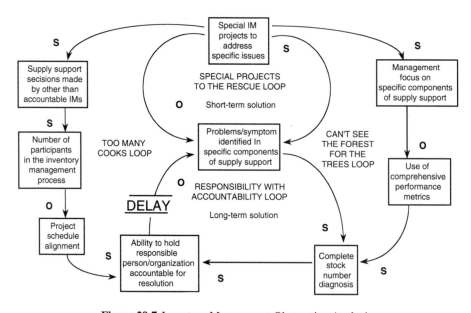

Figure 29-7. Inventory Management Obstruction Analysis

into those which were marginal, where they were dependent on a stakeholder, where they were independent of a stakeholder (a stakeholder was dependent on them), and where they had partnerships.

For market trends, an analysis was done to sort out the degree of impact versus the rate of change. They considered market trends from three points of view: technology, customers, and competition.

The business opportunity analysis used the stakeholder and market trends analyses to develop the *vital* few answers to three questions:

- What conditions must be met in order for the organization to be viable in the environment?
- What problems or needs should the organization try to meet?
- What capabilities does the organization have to be good at to deliver the necessary products or services?

Structure Alignment

Having done the detailed obstruction analysis (see Figure 29-7) and the detailed environmental assessment, Gary and his team were able to see the gap between where they were and needed to be.

In particular, the obstruction analysis provided indications of the high leverage points that could best drive the changes necessary to achieve the "ideal state" organization for the environment in which the organization resides. For each selected leverage point, the current state was known and the desired state was defined.

With the current and target state for each intervention point available, traditional hoshin management practices were used to deploy the improvements. One example from this hoshin deployment is shown in Figure 29-8. Thus, Burchill integrated aspects of the LP method, idealized design, system dynamics, and hoshin management.

Statement of Desired Outcome (May show different owner than basic tactical goal.)	Focused Means Sub Goal	Metrics to Measure Progress	Target Value	Deadline Date	Status
	Owner (if different from goal)		Actual Value	Actual Date if Different	
Develop Weapon System Team Performance Indicators (PIs)	1. Identify metric team members. Owener: div. heads. (PI team).	# of people	8	1 AUG 94	
	2. Identify 6 process Input metrics for each functional area. Owner: PI team.	# of metrics	24	8 AUG 94	
	3. Create tree diagam of metrics. Owner: PI team.	Tree diagram	1	15 AUG 94	
	4. Operationally define selected metrics. Owner PI team.	# of operational definitions	12-24	29 AUG 94	
	5. Prototype metric operational definitions. Owner: PI team.	# of prototypes	12-24	1 OCT 94	
	6. Operationally review and select process/result performance indicator set. Owner: div. heads.	process/result perf. indicator set	1	1 OCT 94	
STATUS LEGEND: << = SLIPPED A LOT < = SLIPPED A LITTLE @ = ON TRACK > = A LITTLE AHEAD >> = A LOT AHEAD V = COMPLETED					

Figure 29-8. Hoshin Template for Development of Performance Indicators

Actual implementations of the various changes took from three to 18 months depending on the complexity of the process being changed.

29.3 SERVEND CASE STUDY

We already introduced SerVend, specifically in Chapter 21 in the discussion goal setting as part of the 7 infrastructures. There we mentioned SerVend's purpose: "SerVend exists to create value and opportunities that change people's lives for the better." You might reread that section now. We also showed an illustration of SerVend's planning process earlier in this chapter (Figure 29-3, page 682).

More generally, SerVend provides a story of integration of methods to create the unique business system appropriate to SerVend. Like all stories of integration of methods, it is also a story of societal networking and mutual learning—SerVend drew on many sources and people who helped SerVend learn the new methods. But SerVend also improved these methods and combined them in new ways to make them their own, creating new best practices from which the rest of us may learn.[5]

SerVend International is a leading manufacturer of ice and beverage dispensers. It was founded in 1980 by Greg Fischer, his brother Mark, and father George, literally in a garage. Even then they called it SerVend *International*—they had a vision for their future.

SerVend grew and its management team developed their unique "SerVend Business System" to sustain that growth. In 1997, SerVend merged with The Manitowoc Company because the two companies together spanned the potential market well. The SerVend founding team stayed with SerVend for a transitional period through early 1999 during which time SerVend received the following national recognition:

- In October 1998, SerVend was one of three companies in the U.S. in the small business category to be honored with a site visit by the Malcolm Baldrige National Quality Award examiners.
- In November 1998, Flomatic International, SerVend's valve manufacturing division, received the Oregon Quality Award.
- SerVend was awarded the 1999 USA Today Quality Cup in the small business category.

More tangibly, from 1993 to 1999, SerVend produced the remarkable "hat trick" of increasing employee wages (almost double on the assembly line), increasing company profits, and decreasing prices to customers (by an average of 15 percent).

In 1999, after the transition of the SerVend business to Manitowoc, Greg retired from SerVend. Under the name Iceberg Ventures, Greg and a number of colleagues began to invest in emerging and hypergrowth companies. They bring to these companies both financial investment and the business system ideas we describe here.[6] In the "new economy" of the Internet era, the need for alignment, mobility, and speed has increased. Iceberg Venture's thought is that achieving this alignment, mobility, and speed should be easier by having a systematic management process from the beginning instead of adding it later when the company runs into problems from lack of process.

Evolution of SerVend's Business System

SerVend displays the components of its business system graphically in Figure 29-9. Notice that they modified our Four Revolutions graphic to include the leadership components of their business system.

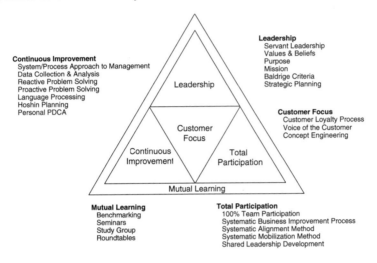

Figure 29-9. SerVend Business System

This subsection primarily consists of an edited version of an internal presentation given in SerVend in the later stages of implementation of its business system. In retrospect, it looks quite organized. However, basically they were on what they thought was a noble mission of business improvement; while Greg Fischer and his team had the insight that they needed a theory of management as well as a practice of management, this full business system evolved over a number of years. As Greg jokes, "everything 'collapsed' into this system."

The SerVend Business System is divided into seven parts, shown in Figure 29-10. This is a retroactive organization that Greg Fischer created in 1997 after considerable thought about what they had been doing and how to categorize their activities.

Components of the SerVend Business System

1. Prepare

2. Align

3. Measure

4. Deploy

5. Do IT!

6. Improve

7. Reflect

Figure 29-10. Components of the SerVend Business System

Study the outlines of the seven parts of the SerVend business system (Tables 29-1 to 29-7). You will see that the system integrates methods from many sources, including methods described in this book (roughly indicated by *s). The dates in square brackets are the years over which SerVend developed its skill in an element of its management system.

When they presented this outline of a business system to the SerVend employees, Greg states that mental light bulbs went on all over the room. Before the presentation of this outline there was much activity, but the average employee didn't understand how everything fit together. Obviously such an outline is useful to those leading change to help them sort out in their own minds what they have been doing.

A summary of Greg's story begins on page 694.

Table 29-1. Prepare

A. What are you doing? What is your goal?

    1. What's wrong?

    2. Yesterday's success may be today's opportunity (problem)
        a) SerVend's "go-go" to "adolescence"

B. How will you organize?

    1. Your company structure

    2. Your TQM/Business Improvement Model

C. Essential background work

    1. Choose a TQM theory ... all TQM theories are customer based and continuous improvement oriented*
        a) PDCA or process focus—where to start*
        b) Understanding Deming's System of Profound Knowledge8

    2. Define and live the cultural direction
        a) Situational management9
        b) "Servant leaders" [70] are most effective

    3. Provide the training
        a) The teaming direction: self-directed and managed teams*; cross-functional teams*
        b) Soft skills: Covey's "head, hands, and heart," 7 Habits, and Quadrant II10 [1993]
        c) Hard skills: problem identification*; problem solving (7 steps)*; 7 QC Tools*; 7 Management and Planning Tools*; 9 Steps* [1995–97]
        d) Knowledge of best-in-class: process capability and knowing the variation a process will consistently deliver*; six sigma (3.4 defects per million)* [1996–97]
        e) Baldrige direction: financial performance of Baldrige* winners11 [1997]

D. Cultural leadership requirements

    1. President and senior management commitment*

    2. Building your team [1995–96]
        a) Understanding behavior*/emotional intelligence
        b) How fast can your team change?
        c) How much stress will you put on your organization

Table 29-2. Align [1991]

A. Clarify/define the mission

B. *Values and beliefs* updated [1998]
    • We exist to develop our customers' loyalty
    • Respect for individuals guides our actions
    • We build trust through integrity and honest communication
    • Continuous learning is the cornerstone of our personal development
    • Everyone works to continuously improve our business systems
    • Proud, enthusiastic team members build a great company
    • All enjoy wealth from our activities

C. Align compensation and appraisal system with TQM effort [1993–94]
    1. Cultural compatibility appraisal system
    2. Skill-based compensation (SBC)
      a) Stabilize the workforce
    3. Non-SBC
      a) First area of team formation

D. Strategic planning is the ultimate TQM activity*
    1. Market-in focus*: **The Customer Rules**
    2. Work against best-in-class gaps [1996]
    3. Use Baldrige criteria for external assessment*: leadership, strategic planning, customer and market focus, information and analysis, human resource focus, process management, and business results [1998]
    4. Use CQM Interactive Planning Process* [1998]

E. Importance of the "vital few" goals—hoshin planning*

F. Regardless of the number of goals, align with customer; use the Voice of the Customer to establish corporate goals* [1996–97]
    1. Process quality
    2. Product quality
    3. Lower cost
    4. Workplace excellence
    5. Increase sales

G. Make sure your system changes endure—SDCA*

H. Cultural acceptance of a "weakness orientation"* [1995–96]
    1. Celebrate success
    2. Establish the "gestalt" to success
    3. Sugar works better than whips!

I. Share [1996]   1. Implement a defined profit sharing plan

Table 29-3. Measure

A. Key Performance Indicator (KPI) [1994–95] development[12]
1. Each team measures their KPIs
2. Measures are aligned company-wide [1995-96]   a) Driven off company goals

3. Phase II—measure and compare to best-in-class* [1997]
       a) Understand process capability
       b) Use quality tools to continuously improve

Table 29-4. Deploy

A. How to deploy your programs*
1. Team linkage/hierarchy [1993–94]   a) Systematic team process

2. Team skills [1994–95]
       a) Strategic Change Plan linkage to team improvement goals
       b) Common meeting formats
       c) Common decision making process

Table 29-5. Do IT!

A. Be proactive—habit number 1!
B. Follow the "60 percent is Okay" rule*

C. Use PDCA and quality tools in daily work*
    1. Quality is personal*
    2. Quality cannot be delegated*

D. Turn the PDCA wheel rapidly*
    1. Manage by process*
    2. "Jump-Up"*
    3. Get in the fishbowl*

E. Always be "market-in"*—focus on the customer

Table 29-6. Improve

A. PDCA wheel must be turning at all levels of your organization*
    1. Individually
    2. Teams
    3. Leadership team
    4. Your business system

B. Problem identification skills*
    1. CQM tools

C. Problem solving skills*
    1. CQM tools

D. The dual nature of work*

E. Build a workplace of
    1. Trust*
        a) Credible management
        b) All team members respected
        c)Sense of fairness exists
        d) Financial results are shared
    2. Pride in jobs and company
    3. Enjoy the people you work with
    4. Everyone works as a team

F. Reinforce/recognize/promote values and beliefs* [1998]

Table 29-7. Reflect

A. SerVend Reection of October 1998
    1. Get cross-functional teams to competency of natural work teams
        a) Personal PDCA
        b) Quarterly frequency of PDCA
    2. Improve Voice of the Customer process
    3. Quicken time to market
    4. Improve process capability—continue six sigma
    5. Use Baldrige criteria to assess business system

Greg Fischer on the SerVend Story

Greg has shared the following thoughts with us that we recount in the rest of this section.

Every company has a "mess," to use Ackoff's language. The question is what to do about it. A good first step is to apply SDCA to understand and standardize what you are doing. ISO 9000 is useful for this. Next, one needs to apply PDCA to improve the standard. If you are going to get this done in a practical amount of time, you need to turn through these cycles fast. You need to think in terms of the 60 percent rule. You need a culture that accepts risk taking, that accepts trying new things. From its formation, SerVend had an entrepreneurial culture and was change oriented.

Natural Work Teams

In 1992, a change in the organizational structure was desired so that "total participation" could be realized. SerVend had the analogy of a sports team in mind where all the players knew the plays and could apply them as appropriate. In some ways, this was the beginning of SerVend's formal efforts at business improvement.

SerVend faced two issues. First, what would the new initiative be; second, how would it change the organizational structure to support the new initiative. SerVend decided that "natural work teams"[7] would be the method, and from 1993 to 1994, they began forming natural work teams. Part of the concept was that natural work teams would serve as a method of involvement, alignment, and mobilization, as summarized and anticipated in Table 29-8.

The natural work teams are organized around functional work areas. Through training and systematic reinforcement, the people on each team all know the jobs in their areas, process for involvement and improvement, and the common corporate language. With this knowledge, when a plan is communicated to the people of a work team, they are able to quickly and efficiently execute [the plan]. [The SerVend] experience is that it takes years to get total participation and to "really do" teams well; however, once one has it, the teaming process provides tremendous speed advantage, [because of the ability to align and mobilize the company quickly through its natural work teams.]

[They] also rotated team member roles on natural work teams every 90 days. Team members are responsible for items such as customer representations, six sigma quality, safety, employee interests, etc. The knowledge gained from these roles accelerates [an understanding of the business as a system and heightens the output of] collective improvement. To ensure everyone understands their accountability for contributing to the success of the company's plan, everyone's role in [their] systematic business improvement is defined [93].

Reinforcing this team system are plans and checks ranging from a three-year to five-year plan to a daily action list and everything in between.

Table 29-8. Benefits of Teaming

Benefit to Team Member	Benefit to Company	Benefit to Customer
More interesting work	More flexible workforce	Products faster
Higher skill levels	Improved productivity	Lower cost
Higher job satisfaction	Improved workmanship	Higher quality
Uses "hands, head, and heart"	Able, involved, aligned work force	Ever-improving qualitiy

Important to making this change was to get top management team members to do what they were expecting others to do. Thus, SerVend started two top management teams: the SerVend (top) leadership team, and a cross-functional communications team.

The idea behind the communications team was that attempts at change often have problems because communication of what is happening and why is insufficient. Thus, SerVend set up a team representing 12 different areas of the company to identify critical communications issues and methods for addressing them. The goal was to find and fix communications problems within the month. For instance, they set up a rumor versus fact bulletin board. Rumors were immediately posted along with the actual facts. This corrected erroneous rumors and, in time, the frequency of counterproductive rumors died down.

SerVend also had a robust quarterly PDCA process.

A culture of openness is important for such teams to work. (Greg makes the point no secrets exist anyway.)

Aligning Leadership, Policies, and Vision

From 1993, SerVend increasingly tried to align the leadership and policies to be consistent with a world-class vision for how the company operated and the business results it produced.

Greg Fischer provides a test:

"Can people in the organization state the company's purpose and values and beliefs?"[13] The purpose and values and beliefs have to represent a system that employees believe in. If the employees believe, their loyalty to the company will increase. Certainly there cannot be a lack of integrity between the company values and the personal values of the employees. Fortunately, one can have integrity between company and individual values and beliefs, and we believe we have this consistency in the case of SerVend...

[Deming said] "transformation is everyone's job." [Transformation won't happen well without the engaged participation of the employees.]

Our people believe in having continuity between their personal and business lives. Furthermore, by all employees living these values and beliefs, they can focus on value-added work and avoid the politics and personal agendas...

Greg tells the story from a few years ago of bumping into a long-time well-producing employee just after she had had her annual performance review. She was told in the review that she had an attitude problem. When Greg bumped into her he innocently asked her how she was; and she told him that now she was feeling terrible and had lost her motivation. Greg asks, "What kind of system is it that takes away an employee's motivation?" At a meeting soon after that, they burned the performance review form in front of employees and for a couple of years after that didn't have a formal performance review system. Greg says you have to destroy the parts of your existing system that are at odds with a world-class vision.

CQM Involvement

In 1995, SerVend got involved with CQM as one of the charter members of CQM's Louisville chapter. CQM provided SerVend with teachings, tools, and a learning network for methods to achieve systematic improvement toward world-class business results. Until then, SerVend had natural work teams but not explicit methods for reactive and proactive improvement. SerVend's goal in adopting these methods was to improve their performance systematically so they could perform reliably and wouldn't have to depend on heroic actions to fix problems temporarily. If a company can perform reliably, it has a tremendous advantage over competition that cannot.

Over several years, SerVend adopted large parts of the CQM-taught methodology, that we describe in this book. Many of these methods they learned from other CQM companies, such as a version of hoshin management called DASH learned from ADAC.

Using the Baldrige Criteria

In 1997, SerVend began utilizing the Baldrige criteria based on their belief that the Baldrige criteria provides a comprehensive business system template that ensures that all stakeholder needs are met.

At the beginning of this case study, we noted that SerVend obtained external recognition as a result of its Baldrige work. However, like most companies applying, SerVend said the main benefits were internal though some of the benefits were personal. As part of preparing for the Baldrige application, employees were asked to write why the company was deserving. Some of these statements included descriptions of dysfunctional personal histories partially addressed by applying at home skills they learned at work.

Greg says that with such a match between personal, company, and customer purposes, values, and beliefs, world-class business results happen.

An Iterative, Incremental Process Leads to Breakthrough Results

SerVend did not create its unique business system (including methods from many sources) overnight. The SerVend business system was created one day at a time. First, they imitated; then, they innovated.

You need a theory, not just activity. Applying PDCA to your theory allows the system to learn and improve. The CQM Four Revolutions diagram (see Figure 3-1, page 42) is a theory. SerVend tried this theory, and improved it (see Figure 29-9, page 689) to address SerVend's unique situation.

Teams become great on the practice field. They have to keep refining and perfecting their plays (processes). They need to apply a theory and reflect on how to improve the theory. This iterative process builds skill.

Leadership drives change, and this needs to be in alignment with stakeholders' concerns. This is not a quality department function. This is how you run the company.

It is one thing to say something must be done. It is another thing to have a way how to do it. Without a theory and methods, systematic improvement efforts will be stymied.

The SerVend story demonstrates that starting with a noble goal at the beginning, and incrementally moving toward that goal, can lead to a unique and powerful management system.

Improvement can't be done all at once. It has to be done incrementally (but still aggressively pursuing progress) so the organization is not swamped by change. It also has to be done incrementally because it takes iteration to discover what works and how to make it work best. Constancy of purpose toward the noble goal of improvement provides the environment for the iterative process to take place.

The benefit of this ongoing iterative, incremental development of a unique business system is achievement of the business purpose: to create value and opportunities that change people's lives—all stakeholders' lives—for the better.

NOTES

1. And in [187, 186].

2. Ackoff apparently means management of how people interact with each other. His full system is described in [2].

3. In Watts Humphrey's discussion of the software development process, his definition of insanity was "doing the same thing over and over and expecting things to change."

4. This process is described in more detail in [48]. All quotes and figures in this section are taken from that paper. The method has also been integrated into the FOCUS process as the "Systems Path"—see [47].

5. We got the information about SerVend from personal communications with Greg Fischer and from [124, 94, 95, 93]. In particular, reading [124] will strongly complement this section.

6. Hence the name Iceberg—the investment is the tip of the iceberg, and the management help is the big part below the tip.

7. We described Analog Device's experience with such teams beginning on page 334; see also [97].

8. The elements of Deming's system of profound knowledge are appreciation for a system, knowledge about variation, theory of knowledge, and psychology.

9. You can have high and low manager involvement and high and low team member maturity and experience: low-low is the domain of the manager telling the team member what to do, low-high is the domain of the manager delegating to the team member, high-low is the domain of the manager trying to sell the team member on participation, and high-high is the domain of the manager and team member both participating.

10. Activities can be divided into those which are urgent and not urgent and those which are important and not important. Even if people can avoid unimportant activities, they tend to be driven to spend all of their time on important urgent activities. As Brad Harrington pointed out in the HP case study in Chapter 26, people can't seem to get to the quadrant of important but long-term ("not urgent") activities. SerVend's system works to allocate some effort to the important but not urgent quadrant—Covey's Quadrant II—which includes such activities as recognizing new opportunities, planning, and relationship building.

11. Greg quotes the famous "three"-times-S&P500 data from [218].

12. Greg Fischer says one component of the SerVend continuous improvement system is "measure like crazy." A series of 85 key performance indicators drive improvement.

13. SerVend's purpose was listed at the beginning of this case study, and the top-level statement of its values and beliefs is listed as II.B of the SerVend Business System outline in the previous section.

Afterword

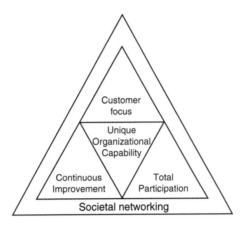

In the afterword of the first edition, *A New American TQM* published in 1993, we stated:

> TQM [our four revolutions in management] may be thought of as a system for changing demands of the environment—TQM is a system for learning. Continuous improvement, customer focus, total participation, and societal networking are concepts that support and focus the learning system.
>
> By applying the principles of TQM to itself, TQM will invent or acquire those quality concepts and practices necessary to meet the changing demands of the modern world.

This edition, *Four Practical Revolutions in Management*, updates the practice of business improvement and organizational learning through 1999. We have included new methods for each of our revolutions in management:

1. Customer focus
2. Continuous improvement
3. Total participation
4. Societal networking

We have emphasized methods of continuous improvement and total participation (22 of 29 chapters)—areas over which you have more control with which to develop your unique organizational capability. For each of the four revolutions, we also have described three approaches to breakthrough—the initial breakthrough of controlling processes, breakthrough by reengineering processes and products, and breakthrough into new businesses—as summarized in the figure captioned Four Revolutions and Approaches to Breakthrough.

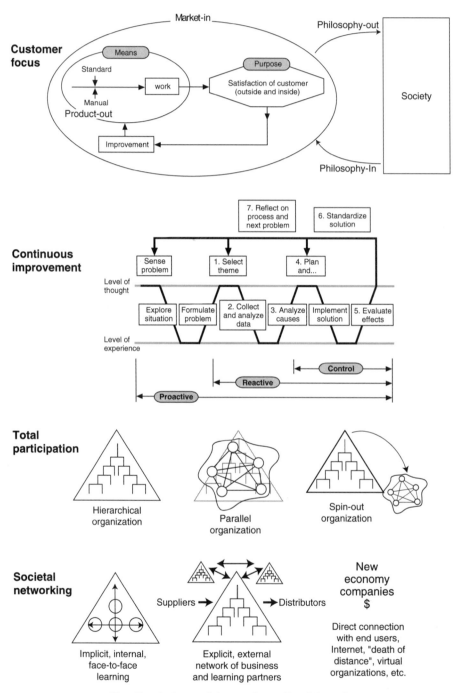

Four Revolutions and Approaches to Breakthrough

In parallel with describing the four revolutions and the methods of each, we have repeatedly touched on four themes for how one goes about learning new skill in an organization:

- Practice systematic development of skill
- Treat management as a coherent system
- Focus on people and their purposes
- Integrate best practices

As we write this afterword in early 2000, we see the evolution of management practice continuing. Our four practical revolutions in management and our four themes provide an organizational learning system and the topics that must be addressed by it. Applying these principles to the learning system itself will continue to result in the concepts and practices necessary to meet the changing demands of the modern world.

We are not sure what will be next in the evolution. However, at the beginning of 2000, from our interactions with CQM member organizations, we see emerging developments in several areas.

First, we see ongoing efforts to further improve existing methods, such as those in the shaded circles on the main diagonal of the figure captioned Problem Complexity versus Organizational Level.[1] For instance,

- High performance use of conversation in business—a CQM chapter is investigating more step-by-step methods for the concepts and models of Chapter 16 (page 297).
- Mobilizing for change—a CQM chapter is developing more step-by-step methods to augment the model of Chapter 21 (page 423) for mobilization of organizational change and business improvement [58].

However, the world is becoming a more complex place. As shown in the figure, increasingly complex problems must be handled at lower levels of an organization, increased organizational complexity means that even relatively simple problems require effort from high in the organization, and new methods and old methods involving more people more often must be aligned in pursuit of business purposes.

- Problem complexity: Increasing globalization, information technology, data availability, and time pressures are rapidly escalating decision complexity. As a result, the time to reach a decision often extends beyond the window of opportunity to take efficient action. Therefore, many complex decisions are based on the "gut feel" of senior decision makers. Unfortunately, research shows "intuition" is usually not applied consistently, which leads to second-guessing and half-hearted support within the organization. Organizations need pragmatic, visible, decision support processes. Individuals responsible for making, ratifying, or executing a given decision need to be able to trace the entire process from problem framing to alternative generation and selection.

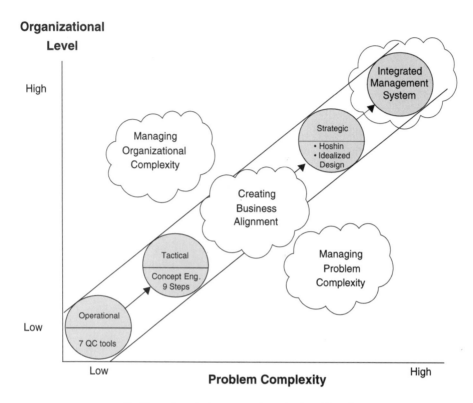

Problem Complexity versus Organizational Level

- Organizational complexity: Downsizing and decentralized decision making trends have significantly increased the span of control of many key positions within an organization. Concurrently, the moves toward cross-functional teams and supply chain management have decreased the sphere of direct control of the people who are accountable for managing the organization. As a result, the effort required to coordinate the actions of diverse participants significantly hampers the realization of business objectives. Models and step-by-step processes are needed that span from recognizing a need to collaborate through the final stage of obtaining commitments to action. People need skills that enable them to concentrate their efforts to address business concerns while capturing the value of diverse perspectives.
- Business alignment: The escalation in organizational and problem complexity are like black holes, drawing time and effort away from the short-term activities that are necessary to achieve longer-term objectives. Maintaining focus and alignment is important in the best of times, but critical during periods of high growth and dynamic conditions. Approaches need to be defined for building alignment between technology and market opportunities, long-term

strategy, and the operational activities required to support a specific business cycle plan.

- Integrated management system: Integrating the elements and methods of business improvement and organizational change into an integrated system has long been part of the four revolutions we have described in this book. As companies must increasingly address issues of managing problem and organizational complexities, business alignment, and developing new methods to do so, each organization must continue to integrate the new methods into its unique management system.

Finally, there is tremendous pressure for improvement methods, such as we have described in this book to be operated at so-called "net speed," the speed at which many businesses perceive they must operate today.

As we write this, the CQM and its chapters are investigating and creating new methods and beginning to teach them for each of the above mentioned topics. We look forward to those methods which develop and prove themselves in practice joining and modifying the methods we provide here to continue to provide high performance integrated management systems for organizations of all types, so each organization and its people can find their unique capabilities and prosper.

NOTES

1. As the figure indicates, as problem complexity increases the organizational level at which the problem must be addressed tends also to increase. A basic version of this figure, without the three big clouds, was sketched by Art Schneidermann in the early days of the CQM.

About the Authors

Shoji and Dave on a street in Cambridge, MA, after practicing Shoji's eating and drinking methodology

Shoji Shiba is currently a Visiting Professor at MIT, where he teaches graduate courses at the Sloan School of Management and in the Leaders for Manufacturing Program. Until 2000, he also was Professor of Business Administration and Dean of the School of Applied International Studies of Tokiwa University in Japan. Shoji Shiba also is Professor Emeritus of Tsukuba University in Japan, and also was an Adjunct Professor during an earlier stay at MIT.

As an international expert in TQM, Dr. Shiba is responsible for disseminating the practices and methodologies of TQM to the industries and governments of many countries, including Chile, China, France, Hungary, India, Ireland, Italy, Malaysia, Norway, Portugal, Spain, Sweden, Switzerland, Thailand, the United Kingdom, and the former USSR.

In honor of his work in Hungary, that country established the IIASA-Shiba Award, presented annually to groups and individuals who make significant contributions to TQM. Also, the president of the Hungarian Republic has bestowed the Hungarian Republic's Small Cross of Order of Merit upon Dr. Shiba, for the high value and generous activity which Dr. Shiba has accomplished in the field of quality improvement and management in Hungary.

In 1989 Dr. Shiba helped establish the Center for Quality of Management.

David Walden earned an undergraduate degree in mathematics at San Francisco State College and did graduate study in computer science at MIT. After college, he worked at MIT Lincoln Laboratory, Norsk Data (Oslo, Norway), and Bolt Beranek and Newman Inc. (Cambridge, Massachusetts).

At Bolt Beranek and Newman Inc., he was an original member of the team that developed the ARPANET, precursor of the Internet. In his over 30-year business career he held a succession of technical, technical management, and general management positions.

Since retiring from business, Mr. Walden has served in part-time positions with the non-profit Center for Quality of Management (CQM) and at the MIT Sloan School of Business where he was a Senior Lecturer. Mr. Walden is a frequent author, speaker, and editor on various technical and management topics.

In 1990, Mr. Walden was a member of the team of executives from Boston area companies that designed the operation of the CQM.

References

[1] Thomas E. Abell and Dawn Dougherty Fitzgerald. HP's quality management system: CEO roundtable report. *The Center for Quality of Management Journal*, 2(3):3–4, Summer 1993.

[2] Russell Ackoff. *Creating the Corporate Future*. John Wiley & Sons, New York, 1981.

[3] Yoji Akao. QFD Manual 1: *Hinshitsu Tenkai Niumon* (*Introduction to Quality Deployment*). JUSE, Tokyo, 1990.

[4] Yoji Akao. *Quality Function Deployment*. Productivity Press, Cambridge, MA, 1990.

[5] Yoji Akao. *Hoshin Kanri: Policy Deployment for Successful TQM*. Productivity Press, Cambridge, MA, 1991.

[6] Donald J. Albers and G.L. Alexanderson, editors. *Mathematical People: Profiles and Interviews*. Birkhauser, Boston, 1985.

[7] Scott Allen. Article on Roger Tory Peterson. *Boston Globe*, pages 25, 28, and 29, October 10, 1994.

[8] David Amsden, Howard Butler, and Robert Amsden. *SPC Simplified for Services*. Quality Resources, White Plains, NY, 1991.

[9] Analog Devices, Inc. Hoshin planning manual, May 1995. Section 4, *Analog Devices Planning Guidebook ... Planning for Competitive Advantage*, company confidential planning guide.

[10] Deborah Ancona and Chee-Leong Chong. Cycles and synchrony: The temporal role of context in team behavior. In E. Mannix and M. Neale, editors, *Research on Managing in Groups and Teams*, volume 2, pages 33–48. JAI Press Inc., Greenwich, CT, 1999.

[11] Deborah G. Ancona and David F. Caldwell. Bridging the boundary: External activity and performance in organizational teams. *Administrative Science Quarterly*, 37:634–665, 1992.

[12] David Garvin and various authors. Does the Baldrige award really work? *Harvard Business Review*, pages 126–147, January–February 1992.

[13] Erik Anderson and Jim Sanchez. Application of Concept Engineering on the Bose Enchilada project. *The Center for Quality of Management Journal*, 3(2):42–51, 1994.

[14] Walter Truett Anderson. *Reality Isn't What It Used To Be: Theatrical Politics, Ready-to-Wear Religion, Global Myths, Primitive Chic, and Other Wonders of the Postmodern World*. Harper & Row, San Francisco, 1990.

[15] Victor Aramati and Toby Woll. TQM in services: A report by the CQM study group. *Journal of the Center for Quality of Management*, 6(2):5–25, Fall 1997.

[16] Chris Argyris. *Overcoming Organizational Defenses*. Prentice Hall, Englewood Cliffs, NJ, 1990.

[17] Chris Argyris, Robert Putnam, and Diana McLain Smith. *Action Science*. Jossey-Bass Inc., San Francisco, 1985.

[18] Chris Argyris and Donald Schön. *Theory in Practice: Increasing Professional Effectiveness*. Jossey-Bass, San Francisco, 1974.

[19] Tetsuichi Asaku and Kazuo Ozeki. *Handbook of Quality Tools: The Japanese Approach*. Productivity Press, Cambridge, MA, 1990.

[20] Total Quality Management: A business process perspective. A.T. Kearney, Inc., Management Report No. 35, 1992.

[21] ATT. *Statistical Quality Control Handbook*. ATT Customer Information Center, Indianapolis, 2nd edition, 1958. ATT doc. no. 700–744.

[22] ATT. *Achieving Customer Satisfaction*. ATT Customer Information Center, Indianapolis, 1990. ATT doc. no. 500–443.

[23] James Bakken. Oral presentation, Annual Conference, Center for Quality Management, Cambridge, MA, April 1992.

[24] John Bartlett. *Familiar Quotations: A Collection of Passages, Phrases, and Proverbs Traced to their Sources in Ancient and Modern Literature*. Little, Brown and Company, Boston, 16th edition, 1992.

[25] Karen Bemowski. The benchmarking bandwagon. *Quality Progress*, 24(1), January 1991.

[26] Karen Bemowski. Quality, American style. *Quality Progress*, 26(2):65–68, February 1993.

[27] Karen Bemowski. Codes, cultural archetypes, and the collective cultural unconscious. *Quality Progress*, 28(1):33–36, January 1995.

[28] Karen Bemowski. What makes American teams tick? *Quality Progress*, 28(1):39–43, January 1995.

[29] Karen Bemowski. Americans' nostaligic affair with loyalty. *Quality Progress*, 29(2):33–36, February 1996.

[30] Warren Bennis and Burt Nanus. *Leaders*. Harper & Row, New York, 1985.

[31] Hugh Beyer and Karen Holtzblatt. *Contextual Design: Defining Customer-Centered Systems*, chapters 3–5. Morgan Kaufmann, San Francisco, 1997.

[32] Hugh R. Beyer and Karen Holtzblatt. Apprenticing with the customer: A collaborative approach to requirements definition. *Communications of the ACM*, 38(5):45–52, May 1995.

[33] Jerome A. Blakeslee, Jr. Implementing the six sigma solution: How to achieve quantum leaps in quality and competitiveness. *Quality Progress*, 32(7):77–85, June 1999.

[34] Christopher E. Bogan and Michael J. English. *Benchmarking for Best Practices: Winning through Innovative Adaptation*. McGraw-Hill, New York, 1994.

[35] David Bohm. *On Dialogue*. David Bohm Seminars, Ojai, CA, 1990.

[36] Joseph L. Bower. Teradyne: The Aurora project. Harvard Business School Case, revised March 29, 1999, 1997.

[37] Joseph L. Bower. Teradyne: Corporate management of distruptive change. Harvard Business School Case, revised March 25, 1999, 1998.

[38] George Box. Scientific method: The generation of knowledge and quality (the concept of continuous improvement as a fundamental part of the scientific process). *Quality Progress*, 30(1):47–50, January 1997.

[39] G.E.P. Box, J.S. Hunter, and W.G. Hunter. *Statistics for Experimenters*. John Wiley & Sons, New York, 1978.

[40] Vic Braden and Bill Burns. *Vic Braden's Tennis for the Future*. Little, Brown and Company, Boston, 1997.

[41] Mike Bradley and John Petrolini. How a 7-step process reduced roadblocks impeding quality improvement teams at Teradyne. *The Center for Quality of Management Journal*, 2(1):7–17, Winter 1993.

[42] Michael Brassard. *The Memory Jogger Plus+: Featuring the Seven Management and Planning Tools*. GOAL/QPC, Methuen, MA, 1989.

[43] Mark G. Brown. *Baldrige Award Winning Quality: How to Intrepret the Malcolm Baldrige Award Criteria*. Quality Resources/ASQC Quality Press, White Plains, NY/Milwaukee, WI, 1992.

[44] Nelson Bryant, September 1, 1993. Sunday New York Times "Outdoors" column with an annual list on best new product introductions for outdoor enthusiasts.

[45] Gary Burchill. *Concept Engineering: An Investigation of TIME vs. MARKET Orientation in Product Concept Development.* PhD thesis, Massachusetts Institute of Technology, 1993. Sloan School of Management.

[46] Gary Burchill. Structural process improvement at the Naval Inventory Control Point. *Center for Quality of Management Journal*, 5(1):22–31, Spring 1996. Special issue on Design and Planning in Organizations.

[47] Gary Burchill and Christina Hepner Brodie. *Voices into Choices—Acting on the Voice of the Customer.* Joiner Associates, Madison, WI, 1997. Copyright 1997 Center for Quality of Management, A Joiner Publication.

[48] Gary Burchill and David Walden. Revised Day 4 of CQM 6-Day Course with detailed speaking notes. Presented widely within the Center for Quality of Management, January 1996.

[49] Robert C. Camp. Benchmarking: *The Search for Industry Best Practices that Lead to Superior Performance.* ASQC Quality Press, Madison, WI, 1989.

[50] Robert C. Camp. *Business Process Benchmarking: Finding and Implementing Best Practices.* Productivity Inc., Portland, OR, 1995.

[51] Center for Quality of Management, Cambridge, MA. *The 7-Step Problem-Solving Method.* Revised October 1997.

[52] Center for Quality of Management, Cambridge, MA. *9-Step Project Planning System.* Revised June 1998.

[53] Center for Quality of Management, Cambridge, MA. *Concept Engineering.* Revised May 1997.

[54] Center for Quality of Management, Cambridge, MA. *Diagnosing Teamwork through the Quality Improvement (QI) Story.* Revised January 1998.

[55] Center for Quality of Management, Cambridge, MA. *Hoshin Planning.* To be published in 2001.

[56] Center for Quality of Management, Cambridge, *MA. Managing Teams.* Revised January 1998.

[57] Center for Quality of Management, Cambridge, MA. *Method for Priority Marking (MPM).* Revised August 1997.

[58] Center for Quality of Management, Cambridge, MA. *Mobilizing Change Using the 7 Infrastructures.* Draft manual 2.5, May 2, 2000; to be published formally in 2001.

[59] Center for Quality of Management, Cambridge, MA. *Tree Diagrams.* Revised April 1997.

[60] Edward Chapin. Reengineering in health care: Chain hand-offs and the four-phase work cycle. *Quality Progress*, 29(10):105–109, October 1996.

[61] Gay Cheney. *Basic Concepts in Modern Dance: A Creative Approach*. Princeton Book Company, Princeton, NJ, 1989.

[62] Clayton M. Christensen. *The Innovator's Dilemma: When New Technologies Cause Great Firms to Fail*. Harvard Business School Press, Boston, 1997.

[63] Clayton M. Christensen and Michael Overdorf. Meeting the challenge of disruptive change. *Harvard Business Review*, 78(2):66–76, March-April 2000.

[64] Dan Ciampa. *Manufacturing's New Mandate: The Tools for Leadership*. John Wiley & Sons, New York, 1988.

[65] Dan Ciampa. The CEO's role in time-based competition. In Joseph D. Blackburn, editor, *Time-Based Competition: The Next Battleground in American Manufacturing*. Business One-Irwin, Homewood, IL, 1991.

[66] Robert E. Cole. The macropolitics of organizational change: A comparative analysis of the spread of small-group activities. *Administrative Science Quarterly*, 30:560–87, December 1985.

[67] Robert E. Cole. *Strategies for Learning*. University of California Press, Berkeley, 1989.

[68] Dennis Conner with John Rousmaniere. *No Excuse to Lose*. W. W. Norton & Company, New York, 1987.

[69] Corning Company. Principles, structure, and strategies. *Corning Total Quality Digest*, (2), 1990.

[70] Stephen R. Covey. *The 7 Habits of Highly Effective People: Restoring the Character Ethic*. Simon & Schuster, New York, 1989.

[71] *The Language Processing Method*. Cambridge, MA. Revised November 1997.

[72] A special issue on Kano's methods for understanding customer-defined quality. *The Center for Quality of Management Journal*, 2(4), Fall 1993.

[73] A special issue on Concept Engineering. *The Center for Quality of Management Journal*, 3(2), 1994.

[74] CQM Design Team. The CQM design study. CQM Report No. 1, Center for Quality of Management, April 1990.

[75] CQM Journal Editors. An issue relating to Kano's method. *The Center for Quality of Management Journal*, 3(2), 1994.

[76] Report of the CQM study group on conversation. Conversation study group document 46, August 15, 1995.

[77] Philip Crosby. *Let's Talk Quality*. McGraw-Hill, New York, 1989.

[78] Matthew J. Culligan, C. Suzanne Deakins, and Arthur H. Young. *Back to Basics Management*. Facts on File, Inc., New York, 1983.

[79] Robert D. Buzzell and Bradley T. Gale. *The PIMS Principles—Linking Strategy to Performance*. The Free Press, New York, 1987.

[80] William R. Daniels and John G. Mathers. *Change-Able Organization: Key Management Practices for Speed and Flexibility*. Jossey-Bass Publishers, San Francisco, 1997.

[81] Alex d'Arbeloff. Changing for the 1990s. *The Center for Quality of Management Journal*, 2(1):3–6, Winter 1993.

[82] W. Edwards Deming. *Out of Crisis*. Massachusettes Institute of Technology Center for Advanced Engineering Study, Cambridge, MA, 1986.

[83] Stephen Denker, Donald Steward, and Tyson Browning. Planning concurrency and managing iteration in projects. *Center for Quality of Management Journal*, 8(2):55–62, Autumn 1999. Special Issues on Cycle-time Reduction.

[84] Augustus Donnell and Margaret Dellinger. *Analyzing Business Process Data: The Looking Glass*. ATT Customer Information Center, Indianapolis, 1990. ATT doc. no. 500-445.

[85] Larry R. Donnithorne. *The West Point Way of Leadership*. Currancy Doubleday, New York, 1993.

[86] Hubert L. Dreyfus and Stuart E. Dreyfus. *Mind Over Machine*. The Free Press, New York, paperback edition, 1988.

[87] Robin Dunbar. *The Trouble With Science*. Faber and Faber, London, 1995.

[88] Rafael Echeverria. *Ontologia Del Lenguaje*. Dolmen Ediciones, Santa Magdalena 187, Santiago, Chile, 1994.

[89] Jay S. Efran, Michael D. Lukens, and Robert J. Lukens. *Language, Structure, and Change—Frameworks of Meaning in Psycholotherapy*. W.W. Norton & Co., New York, 1990.

[90] Anders K. Ericsson and Neil Charness. Expert performance: Its structure and acquisition. *American Psychologist*, 49(8):725–747, August 1994.

[91] R. Gnanad Esikan. *Methods for Statistical Analysis of Multivariate Observations*. John Wiley & Sons, New York, 1977.

[92] Charles H. Fine. *Clock Speed: Winning Industry Control in the Age of Temporary Advantage*. Perseus Books, Reading, MA, 1998.

[93] Greg Fischer. Leadership and cycle-time reduction: Sustained cycle-time reduction efforts require top management leadership. *Center for Quality of Management Journal*, 8(2):43–48, Autumn 1999. Special Issue on Cycle-time Reduction.

[94] Greg Fischer and Keith Williams. Swimming with the fish: 7-steps at SerVend International. *CQM Voice*, 8(2):5–6, Fall 1997.

[95] Paul Fischer. Can we shamelessly steal your best practices? *CQM Voice*, 9(2), Fall 1998. Published on-line at www.cqm.org.

[96] George Fisher. Bedford, MA, presentation to the executives of Center for Quality Management member organizations, July 10, 1990.

[97] Kimball Fisher. *Leading Self-Directed Work Teams: A Guide to Developing New Team Leadership*. McGraw-Hill, New York, revised and expanded edition, 2000.

[98] Fernando Flores. *Management and Communications in the Office of the Future*. PhD thesis, University of California at Berkeley, 1982.

[99] Fernando Flores. Innovation by listening carefully to customers. Long Range Planning, 26:95–102, June 1993.

[100] Fernando Flores. *Creando Organizaciones Para El Futuro*. Dolmen Ediciones, Cirunajo Guzmán 194, Providencia, Chile, segunda edition, 1995.

[101] Fernando Flores. The leaders of the future. In Peter J. Denning and Robert M. Metcalfe, editors, *Beyond Calculation—The Next Fifty Years of Computing*, pages 175–192. Copernicus—an imprint of Springer-Verlag, New York, 1997.

[102] Richard Florida and Martin Kenney. *The Breakthrough Illusion*. Basic Books, 1990.

[103] Douglas Fong. Using the self-stated importance questionnaire to interpret Kano questionnaire results. *The Center for Quality of Management Journal*, 5(3):21–23, Winter 1996.

[104] Richard N. Foster. *Innovation: The Attacker's Advantage*. Summit Books, New York, 1986.

[105] Yoshiko Fujino and Kimiko Kimura. QC circle activities which were put up by the iron will of part-time oba-chan (aged ladies). *FQC* no. 265, 1984. The case was presented in English at the IC QCC convention, Toyko, 1985.

[106] Shirou Fujita. *A Strategy for Corporate Innovation*. Asian Productivity Organization, 8-4-14, Alkasaka 8-Chrome, Minato-ku, Tokyo 107, Japan, 1997.

[107] Stanley Gage. The management of key enterprise processes. *The Center for Quality of Management Journal*, 2(2):13–18, Spring 1993.

[108] Robert Galvin. Quality: A personal responsibility for executives. *The Center for Quality of Management Journal*, 2(2):3–7, Spring 1993.

[109] Redesigning product/service development: Working smarter. Video tape, Harvard Business School Publishing, 1997. Narrated by David Garvin.

[110] David A. Garvin. *Managing Quality*. The Free Press, New York, 1988.

[111] David A. Garvin. How the Baldrige award works. *Harvard Business Review*, pages 80–93, November–December 1991.

[112] Bill Gates and Collins Hemingway. *Business @ the Speed of Thought*. Warner Books, New York, 1999.

[113] Bill Gates, Nathan Myhrvold, and Peter M. Rinearson. *The Road Ahead*. Penguin USA, paperback edition, 1996.

[114] Jamshid Gharajedaghi. *Systems Thinking: Managing Chaos and Complexity, A Platform for Designing Business Architecture*. Butterworth Heinemann, Boston, 1999.

[115] Barney G. Glazer and Anselm L. Strauss. *The Discovery of Grounded Theory: Strategies for Qualitative Research*. Aldine de Gruyter, 1967.

[116] Eliyahu Goldratt. *The Goal*. North River Press, Croton-on-Hudson, NY, 2nd revised edition, 1992.

[117] Eliyahu Goldratt. *Critical Chain*. North River Press, Croton-on-Hudson, NY, 1997.

[118] Daniel P. Goleman. *Emotional Intelligence*. Bantam Books, New York, paperback reprint edition, 1997.

[119] Robert B. Grady. *Practical Software Metrics for Project Management and Process Improvement*. Prentice-Hall, Inc., Englewood Cliffs, NJ, 1992.

[120] Robert B. Grady. *Successful Software Process Improvement*. Prentice-Hall PTR, Upper Saddle River, NJ, 1997.

[121] Robert B. Grady and Deborah Caswell. *Software Metrics: Establishing a Computer-Wide Program*. Prentice-Hall, Englewood Cliffs, NJ, 1987.

[122] E.L. Grant and R.S. Leavenworth. *Statistical Quality Control*. McGraw-Hill, New York, 5th edition, 1980.

[123] Sherwin Greenblatt. How total quality took root at Bose. *The Center for Quality Management Journal*, 4(1):3–13, Winter 1995.

[124] Keith Williams Greg Fischer and Elaine Monson. Using CQM tools and the Baldrige application process to foster competitive success. *The Center for Quality of Management Journal*, 8(1):17–34, 1999.

[125] Abbie Griffin and John Hauser. The voice of the customer. Working Paper 91-2, MIT Marketing Center, Cambridge, MA, January 1991.

[126] Andrew Grove. *Only the Paranoid Survive*. Bantam Books, New York, paperback edition, 1999.

[127] Stephan H. Haeckel. *Adaptive Enterprise: Creating and Leading Sense-and-Respond Organizations*. Harvard Business School Press, Boston, 1999.

[128] Brad Harrington. Hewlett-Packard's Quality Maturity System. *The Center for Quality of Management Journal*, 2(1), Winter 1993.

[129] Mikel J. Harry. *The Nature of Six Sigma Quality*. Motorola University Press, Rolling Meadows, IL, 1988.

[130] Mikel J. Harry and Richard Schroeder. *Six Sigma, The Breakthrough Management Strategy Revolutionizing The World's Top Corporations*. Doubleday, New York, 1999.

[131] Mikel J. Harry and Reigle Stewart. Six sigma mechanical design tolerancing. Technical report, Motorola Government Electronics Group, Scottsdale, AZ, 1988. Publication no. 6u-2-10/88.

[132] John R. Hauser and Don Clausing. The house of quality. *Harvard Business Review*, 66(3), May-June 1988.

[133] S.I. Hayakawa and Alan R. Hayakawa. *Language in Thought and Action*. Harcourt Brace & Company, New York, fifth edition, 1990.

[134] Kevin B. Hendricks and Vinog R. Singhal. Don't count TQM out—evidence shows implementation pays off in a big way. *Quality Progress*, pages 35–42, April 1999.

[135] Frederick Herzberg. One more time: How do you motivate employees. *Harvard Business Review*, January-February 1968.

[136] Jack Hitt. Does the smell of coffee brewing remind you of your mothers'. *The New York Times Magazine*, pages 71–74, May 7, 2000. A description of Rapaille and his work by a *New York Times* writer who interviewed him.

[137] Karen Holtzblatt and Sandy Jones. Contextual inquiry: A participatory technique for system design. In Aki Namioka and Doug Schuler, editors, *Participatory Design: Principles and Practice*. Lawrence Earlbaum Pub., Hillsdale, NJ, 1993.

[138] Glenn House. Real life stranger than fiction. *The Center for Quality of Management Journal*, 8(2), Winter 1999.

[139] Spencer Hutchens, Jr. Strategic design: Key to profit in the 21st century. In Ross E. Robson, editor, *The Quality and Productivity Equation*. Productivity Press, Cambridge, MA, 1990.

[140] Michio Ikawa. TQC activities at NEC Shizuoka. *Reports of Statistical Application Research*, 37(1–2):67–68, 1990–1991. Union of Japanese Scientists and Engineers.

[141] Masaaki Imai. Kaizen, 7.

[142] Masaaki Imai. *Kaizen*. Random House, New York, 1986.

[143] Leonardo Inghilleri. Cultural Archetypes Seminar. Oral presentation, May 5, 1998. Center for Quality of Management, Cambridge, MA.

[144] Kaoru Ishikawa, editor. *QC Circle Koryo: General Principles of the QC Circle*. QC Circle Headquarters, JUSE, Tokyo, 1980.

[145] Kaoru Ishikawa. *Guide to Quality Control*. Asian Productivity Organization, Tokyo, 1982.

[146] Kaoru Ishikawa, editor. *How to Operate QC Circle Activities*. QC Circle Headquarters, JUSE, Toyko, 1985.

[147] Kaoru Ishikawa. *What Is Total Quality Control? The Japanese Way*. Prentice-Hall, Englewood Cliffs, NJ, 1985.

[148] Kaoru Ishikawa. *Introduction to Quality Control*. 3A Corporation, 1990.

[149] Kaoru Ishikawa, editor. Special Issue: Seven Management Tools. *Reports of Statistical Application Research*, 33(2), June 1986.

[150] Gary Jacobson and John Hillkirk. *American Samurai*. Macmillan, New York, 1986.

[151] Capers Jones. *Applied Software Measurement: Assuring Productivity and Quality*. McGraw-Hill, New York, 1991.

[152] JSQC Research Committee on the Case Study of Hoshin Management. *Hoshin Kanri unei-no tebiki (Guide for Hoshin Management)*. JSQC, 1989.

[153] Joseph M. Juran. Management interface—Taylor system and quality control. *Quality Progress*, 6(5):42, May 1973.

[154] Tadao Kagano, Yujiro Nonaka, Kiyonori Sakakibara, and Akihiro Okumura. *Ni-chi-Bei Kigyo no Keiei Hikaku (Comparison of Management Practices between U.S. and Japan)*. Nihon-Keizai-Shinbunsha, Tokyo, 1983.

[155] Roger Kahn. *The Boys of Summer*. Harper & Row, New York, 1972.

[156] Noriaki Kano and Kozo Koura. Development of quality control seen through the companies awarded the Deming Prize. *Reports of Statistical Application Research*, 37(1–2), 1990–1991. Union of Japanese Scientists and Engineers.

[157] Noriaki Kano and Fumio Takahashi. Hinshitsu no m-h sei ni tsuite (Motivator and hygiene factor in quality). *Quality, JSQC*, 14(2), 1984. Presentation given at Japanese Society for Quality Control Annual Meeting, October 1979.

[158] Noriaki Kano, Shinichi Tsuji, Nobuhiko Seraku, and Fumio Takahashi. Miryokuteki hinshitsu to atarimae hinshitsu (1), (2) (Attractive quality and must-be quality (1), (2). *Quality, JSQC*, 14(2), 1984. Presentation given at Japanese Society for Quality Control Annual Meeting, October 1982.

[159] Rosabeth Moss Kanter. *The Change Masters*. Simon & Schuster, New York, 1983.

[160] Robert S. Kaplan. Analog Devices, Inc.: The half-life system, June 29, 1993.

[161] Jon R. Katzenbach and Douglas K. Smith. *The Wisdom of Teams: Creating High-Performance Organizations*. HarperBusiness, New York, paperback edition, 1994.

[162] Jon R. Katzenbach and Frederick Beckett and Steven Dichter and Marc Feigen and Christopher Gagnon and Quentin Hope and Timothy Ling. *Real Change Leaders: How You Can Create Growth and High Performance at Your Company*. Times Business, a division of Random House, New York, paperback edition, 1995.

[163] Jiro Kawakita. *A Scientific Exploration of Intellect ("Chi" no Tankengaku)*. Kodansha, 1977.

[164] Jiro Kawakita. *The KJ Method: Chaos Speaks for Itself*. Chuo Koron-sha, Tokyo, 1991.

[165] Jiro Kawakita. *The Original KJ Method*. Kawakita Research Institute, Tokyo, 1991.

[166] Robert Kelley and Janet Caplan. How Bell Labs creates star performers. *Harvard Business Review*, 71(4):128–139, July-August 1993.

[167] Stephen P. Kelner. Human motivation and organizational mobilization. *The Center for Quality of Management Journal*, 9(1):25–42, Summer 2000.

[168] Bob King. *Better Designs in Half the Time*. Goal/QPC, Methuen, MA, 1989.

[169] Leonard Kleinrock. *Queuing Systems—Volume I: Theory*. John Wiley & Sons, New York, 1975.

[170] Donald E. Knuth. <<*Literate Programming*>>. Center for the Study of Language and Information, Leland Stanford Junior University, 1992. Chapter 10, "The Errors of TEX (1989)," pp. 243–291, and Chapter 11, "The Error Log of TEX (1978-1991)," pp. 293–339.

[171] Koji Kobayashi. *Computers and Communications: A Vision of C&C*. MIT Press, Cambridge, MA, 1986.

[172] Koji Kobayashi. *The Rise of NEC: How the World's Greatest Company Is Managed*. Blackwell Publishers, Cambridge, MA, 1991.

[173] Masao Kogure. *Japanese TQC: Its Review and New Evolution*. JUSE, Tokyo, 1988.

[174] Masao Kogure. Some fundamental problems on hoshin kanri in Japanese TQC. In *Transactions of the 44th Annual Quality Congress of the American Society for Quality Control*, page 5, San Francisco, CA, May 14-16, 1990.

[175] Masao Kogure. The principles and practice of hoshin management (part 1). *The Center for Quality of Management Journal*, 3(4):3–11, Fall 1994.

[176] Seiji Kojima. Analysis of the factors disturbing promotion of QC Circle activities. Master's thesis, University of Tsukuba, Tsukuba, Japan, 1989. Management and Policy Science Program.

[177] Robert J. Kokurka, Gary L. Stading, and Jason Brazeal. A comparative analysis of national and regional quality awards. *Quality Progress*, 33(8):41–49, August 2000.

[178] Kozo Koura. From Deming cycle to management cycle. *Quality, JSQC*, 20(1), 1990.

[179] Koura Kozo. Title unavailable. *Total Quality Control*, 42(3):273, March 1991.

[180] Thomas S. Kuhn. *The Structure of Scientific Revolutions*. University of Chicago Press, 3rd edition, 1996.

[181] Hitoshi Kume. *Statistical Methods for Quality Improvement*. AOTS Press, Tokyo, 1985.

[182] Kenji Kurogane, editor. *Effective Use of Control Items in TQC Activities*. Japanese Standards Association, Tokyo, 1990.

[183] Atsushi Kuwabara and Kouji Matsuzawa. QC audits by top management. *Quality, JSQC*, 17:163, April 1987.

[184] Gary LeBlanc. Kaizen at Hill-Rom. *The Center for Quality of Management Journal*, 8(2):49–53, Autumn 1999. Special Issue on Cycle-time Reduction.

[185] Mark C. Lee and John Newcomb. Applying the Kano methodology in managing NASA's science research program. *The Center for Quality of Management Journal*, 5(3), Winter 1996.

[186] Thomas H. Lee, Shoji Shiba, and Robert Chapman Wood. *Integrated Management Systems: A Practical Approach to Transforming Organizations*. John Wiley & Sons, New York, 1999.

[187] Thomas H. Lee and David Walden. Designing integrated management systems. *The Center for Quality of Management Journal*, 7(1):3–18, Summer 1998.

[188] Richard LeVitt. Quality 1 on 1. *The Center for Quality of Management Journal*, 6(2):29–40, Fall 1997.

[189] Paul Lillrank and Noriaki Kano. Continuous improvement: Quality control circles in Japanese industry. Technical report, Center for Japanese Studies, The University of Michigan, Ann Arbor, MI, 1989.

[190] David L. Lowe et al. ADAC Laboratories: Malcolm Baldrige national quality award winner, 1996. *Journal of Innovative Management*, Winter 1997–1998.

[191] Matabe Maeda. *Matabe Ha Tonnda*. Asuka-Shinsha Publishing Co., Tokyo, 1998.

[192] Miles Maguire. Cowboy quality: Mikel Harry's riding tall in the saddle as six sigma makes its mark. *Quality Progress*, 32(10):27–34, October 1999.

[193] Thomas J. Malone. On-line letter to "Fellow Associates," www.milliken.com, September 15, 1998.

[194] Cesare Marchetti. Branching out into the universe. In N. Nakicenovic and A. Grübler, editors, *Diffusion of Technologies and Social Behavior*. Springer-Verlag, New York, 1991.

[195] Cesare Marchetti, Perrin S. Meyer, and Jesse H. Ausubel. Human population dynamics revisited with the logistic model: How much can be modeled and predicted? *Technological Forecasting and Social Change*, 52(1):1–30, May 1996.

[196] Humberto R. Maturana and Francisco J. Varela. *The Tree of Knowledge: The Biological Roots of Human Understanding*. Shambhala Publications, Boston, paperback revised edition, 1992.

[197] Philip McArthur, Robert Putnam, and Diana McLain Smith. Climbing out of the muck. In Peter Senge et al., editor, *The Dance of Change: The Challenges to Sustaining Momentum in Learning Organizations*, pages 120–128. Currency Doubleday, New York, 1999.

[198] Steve McConnell. *Rapid Development*. Microsoft Press, Redmond, WA, 1996.

[199] Michael E. McGrath, Michael T. Anthony, and Amram R. Shapiro. *Product Development: Success Through Product and Cycle-time Excellence*. Butterworth-Heinemann, Stoneham, MA, 1992.

[200] R.G. McGrath and I.C. MacMillan. Discovery-driven planning. *Harvard Business Review*, 72(1):44–54, January-February 1995.

[201] Douglas McGregor. *The Human Side of Enterprise*. McGraw-Hill, New York, 25th anniversary printing edition, 1985.

[202] Christopher Meyer. *Fast Cycle Time: How to Align Purpose, Strategy, and Structure for Speed*. Free Press, 1993.

[203] Perrin S. Meyer. Bi-logistic growth. *Technological Forecasting and Social Change*, 47(1):89–102, September 1994.

[204] Perrin S. Meyer and Jesse H. Ausubel. Carrying capacity: A model with logistically varying limits. *Technological Forecasting and Social Change*, 61(3):209–214, September 1999.

[205] Perrin S. Meyer, Jason W. Yung, and Jesse H. Ausubel. A primer on logistic growth and substitution: The mathematics of the Loglet Lab software. *Technological Forecasting and Social Change*, 61(3):247–271, September 1999.

[206] Page on coroprate Web site, www.milliken.com, February 26, 2000.

[207] *MIT Management*. Cover story, pages 6–9. Fall 1991.

[208] Shigeru Mizuno, editor. *Management for Quality Improvement: The Seven New QC Tools*. Productivity Press, Cambridge, MA, 1988.

[209] John Monroe. Hewlett-Packard's QMS 3.0: Supporting changing priorities of HP businesses in a dynamic, competitive marketplace. *The Center for Quality of Management Journal*, 8(1):42–50, Spring 1999.

[210] Douglas C. Montgomery. *Introduction to Statistical Quality Control*. John Wiley & Sons, New York, 1985.

[211] Geoffrey A. Moore. *Crossing the Chasm: Marketing and Selling Technology Products to Mainstream Customers*. HarperBusiness, New York, 1991.

[212] Desmond Morris. *Manwatching: A Field Guide to Human Behavior*. Harry Abrams, New York, 1977.

[213] Ira Moscowitz and Ken Bethea. Self-directed work teams at Analog Devices. *The Center for Quality of Management Journal*, 9(1), 2000.

[214] David A. Nadler and Michael L. Tushman. Beyond the charismatic leader: Leadership and organizational change. *California Management Review*, 32(2):77–97, Winter 1990.

[215] Ichiro Nakajima. Analysis of development process of QC circles. Master's thesis, Management and Policy Science Program, University of Tsukuba, Tsukuba, Japan, 1983.

[216] Masao Nemoto. *Total Quality Control for Management*. Prentice-Hall, Englewood Cliffs, NJ, 1987.

[217] Jack Nicklaus with Ken Bowden. *Golf My Way*. Simon and Schuster, New York, 1974.

[218] Baldrige index outperforms S&P 500 for fifth year. National Institute of Standards and Technology press release NIST 99-02, February 4, 1999.

[219] Tadashi Ofuji, Michiteru Ono, and Yoji Akao. *QFD Manual 2: Hinshitsu Tenkai-Ho (1) (Quality Deployment Method (1))*. JUSE, Tokyo, 1990.

[220] Patrick O'Neill. Mutual learning in practice: Integration of ICBE, EFQM, and CQM practices. *The Center for Quality of Management Journal*, 8(1):35–41, 1999.

[221] David Packard. *The HP Way: How Bill Hewlett and I Built Our Company*. HarperBusiness, New York, 1995.

[222] Don Peppers and Martha Rogers. *The One To One Future: Building Relationships One Customer at a Time*. Currency Doubleday, 1993.

[223] Houston Peterson, editor. *A Treasury of the World's Great Speeches*. Simon & Schuster, New York, 1954.

[224] John Petrolini. Personal communication, March 1, 2000.

[225] B. Joseph Pine. *Mass Customization: The New Frontier in Business Competition*. Harvard Business School Press, 1992.

[226] Michael Polanyi. *Personal Knowledge: Towards a Post-Critical Philosophy*. University of Chicago Press, Chicago, paperback edition, 1974.

[227] Thomas Powell. When lemmings learn to sail: Turning TQM to competitive advantage. In B. Voss and D. Willey, editors, 1995 *Handbook of Business Strategy*, pages 42–54. Faulkner & Gray, New York, 1995.

[228] Dave Powlison. Psyching for sailing. *Sailing World*, July 1994. Sailing Medalist Section, pages 14–18.

[229] C.K. Prahalad and G. Hamel. The core competence of the corporation. *Harvard Business Review*, 68(3):79–91, May-June 1990.

[230] Robert W. Putnam. Transforming social practice: An Action Science perspective. *Management Learning*, 30(2):177–187, June 1999.

[231] All Japan QC Circle Conference Proceedings. Annual.

[232] G. Clotaire Rapaille. The stuff Americans are made of: An American strategy for quality improvement. Privately circulated undated videotape.

[233] G. Clotaire Rapaille. Keynote presentation. Center for Quality of Management Annual Meeting, June 4, 1996. Colonial Hilton Hotel, Reading, MA.

[234] G. Clotaire Rapaille. Private presentation. Center for Quality of Management Board of Directors Meeting, January 28, 1997. Cambridge, MA.

[235] Neil Rasmussen and David Walden. Observations from the 1997–98 CQM study group on cycle time reduction. *The Center for Quality of Management Journal*, 8(2):3–34, Autumn 1999. Special Issue on Cycle-time Reduction.

[236] Jack Reilly. Using the methods of Fernando Flores—An interview with Jack Reilly. *The Center for Quality of Management Journal*, 6(1):15–19, Spring 1997.

[237] Donald Reinertsen. *Managing the Design Factory: A Product Developers Toolkit*. The Free Press, New York, 1997.

[238] Research Committee on the 7 Management and Planning Tools. *Introduction to Seven Management and Planning Tools (Yasashi-shin QC7 Dougu)*. JUSE, Tokyo, 1984.

[239] Harvey Robbins and Michael Finley. *Why Teams Don't Work: What Went Wrong and How to Make It Right*. Peterson's/Pacesetter Books, Princeton, NJ, 1995.

[240] Harry V. Roberts and Bernard F. Sergesketter. *Quality is Personal: A Foundation for Total Quality Management*. Free Press, New York, 1993.

[241] Beth Robinson. Key findings on cycle-time reduction from the Cincinnati chapter's research committee. *The Center for Quality of Management Journal*, 8(2):35–42, Autumn 1999. Special Issue on Cycle-time Reduction.

[242] Everett M. Rogers. *Diffusion of Innovations*. Free Press, New York, 1962.

[243] Geary Rummler and Alan Brache. *Improving Performance: How to Manage the White Space on the Organization Chart*. Jossey-Bass, San Francisco, second edition, 1995.

[244] Mark Samuel with Barbara Novak. *The Accountability Revolution: Achieve Breakthrough Results in Half the Time!* IMPAQ Publishing, 1744 W. Katella Avenue, Suite 3, Orange, CA 92867, 2000.

[245] Edgar H. Schein. *Process Consultation: Its Role in Organization Development, Volume I*. Addison-Wesley Publishing, Reading, MA, 1987.

[246] Edgar H. Schein. *Process Consultation: Lessons for Managers and Consultants, Volume II*. Addison-Wesley Publishing, Reading, MA, 1988.

[247] Edgar H. Schein. Three cultures of management: The key to organizational learning. *Sloan Management Review*, 38(1):9–20, Fall 1996.

[248] Art Schneidermann. Setting quality goals. *Quality Progress*, 24(4):51–57, April 1988.

[249] Art Schneidermann. Metrics for the order fulfillment process, part 1. *Journal of Cost Management*, 10(2):30–42, Summer 1996.

[250] Art Schneidermann. Metrics for the order fulfillment process, part 2. *Journal of Cost Management*, 10(3):6–17, Fall 1996.

[251] Sidney Schoeffler, Robert D. Buzzell, and Donald F. Heany. Impact of strategic planning on profit performance. *Harvard Business Review*, March-April 1974.

[252] Peter R. Scholtes. *Team Handbook*. Joiner Associates, Inc., Madison, WI, 1988.

[253] Peter R. Scholtes. *The Leader's Handbook*. McGraw–Hill, New York, 1998.

[254] Donald A. Schön. *The Reflective Practitioner*. Basic Books, New York, 1983.

[255] John R. Searle. *Speech Acts: An Essay in the Philosophy of Language*. Cambridge University Press, Cambridge, England, 1969.

[256] John R. Searle. *The Construction of Social Reality*. The Free Press, New York, 1995.

[257] Peter Senge. *The Fifth Discipline: The Art and Practice of the Learning Organization*. Doubleday, New York, 1990.

[258] Peter Senge et al. *The Fifth Discipline Fieldbook: Strategies and Tools for Building a Learning Organization*. Currency Doubleday, New York, 1994.

[259] W.A. Shewhart. *Economic Control of Quality of Manufactured Product*. Van Nostrand Reinhold, New York, 1931. Republished Milwaukee: ASQC, 1980.

[260] Shoji Shiba. How I have observed quality management in European countries. In *Proceedings of the 6th EOQC European Seminar on Education and Training*, 1988.

[261] Shoji Shiba. Quality knows no bounds. *Look Japan*, pages 30–31, May 1989.

[262] Shoji Shiba. A New American TQM: Revolutions in Management. Twelve-tape video tape series developed by Shoji Shiba and produced by MIT Center for Advanced Engineering Study; now available from Center for Quality of Management, Cambridge, MA, 1994.

[263] Shoji Shiba and Masanobu Abe. TQM as a strategy for societal learning process. *Quality, JSQC*, 20(1), 1990.

[264] Shoji Shiba, Alan Graham, and David Walden. *A New American TQM: Four Practical Revolutions in Management*. Productivity Press and Center for Quality of Management, Portland, OR, and Cambridge, MA, 1993. The first edition of this book.

[265] Shoji Shiba, Tom Pursch, and Robert Stasey. Introduction to hoshin management: Achieving alignment at Analog Devices and Teradyne. *The Center for Quality of Management Journal*, 4(3):22–33, Fall 1995. Special Issue on Employee Involvement.

[266] Shigeo Shingo. *A Revolution in Manufacturing: The SMED System*. Productivity Press, Cambridge, MA, 1985.

[267] Vinod R. Singhal and Kevin B. Hendricks. The financial justification of TQM. *The Center for Quality of Management Journal*, 8(1):3–16, Spring 1999.

[268] Douglas K. Smith. *Taking Charge of Change: 10 Principles for Managing People and Performance*. Addison-Wesley Publishing Company, Reading, MA, 1996.

[269] Preston G. Smith and Donald G. Reinertsen. *Developing Products in Half the Time*. Van Nostrand Reinhold, New York, 2nd edition, 1998.

[270] Sarv Singh Soin. *Total Quality Control Essentials*. McGraw-Hill, Inc., New York, 1992.

[271] Steven Spear and H. Kent Bowen. Decoding the DNA of the Toyota production system. *Harvard Business Review*, 77(5):97–106, September-October 1999.

[272] Michael J. Spendolini. *The Benchmarking Book*. AMACOM, New York, paperback reprint edition, 1994. Scheduled in May 2000 for publication in hardcover second edition.

[273] Charles Spinosa, Fernando Flores, and Hubert L. Dreyfus. *Disclosing New Worlds*. The MIT Press, Cambridge, MA, 1997.

[274] Ray Stata. A conversation about conversations. *The Center for Quality of Management Journal*, 4(4):15–20, Winter 1995.

[275] Ray Stata. Presentation to course 15.766, Leader's for Manufacturing Program, Summer 1999.

[276] Thomas A. Stewart. A new way to wake up a giant. *Fortune*, pages 90–103, October 22, 1990.

[277] William Strunk and E. B. White. *The Elements of Style*. Allyn & Bacon, Boston, third edition, 1995.

[278] Jeff Swift. Core teams success at Analog Devices. *CQM Voice*, 8(2):12–13, Fall 1997.

[279] John Szarkowski. *Photography Until Now*, page 11. The Museum of Modern Art, New York, 1989.

[280] Lawrence S. Tai and Zbigniew H. Przasnyski. Baldrige award winners beat the S&P 500. *Quality Progress*, 32(4):45–51, April 1999.

[281] Sheridan M. Tatsuno. *Created in Japan*. Harper Business, New York, 1990.

[282] Robert J. Thomas. *What Machines Can't Do: Politics and Technology in the Industrial Enterprise*. University of California Press, paperback edition, 1994.

[283] Lester C. Thurow. Building wealth. *The Atlantic Monthly*, 283(6):63–64, June 1999.

[284] Noel M. Tichy and Stratford Sherman. *Control Your Destiny or Someone Else Will: How Jack Welch is Making General Electric the World's Most Competitive Company*. Currency Doubleday, New York, 1993.

[285] Bruce W. Tuckman. Developing sequence in small groups. *Psychological Bulletin*, 1955.

[286] Eric Twiname. *Sail, Race and Win*. Sail Books, Boston, 1983.

[287] Eric Twiname. *Sail, Race and Win*. Sheridan House Inc., 146 Palisade Street, Dobbs Ferry, NY 10522, second edition, 1993. Revised by Cathy Foster.

[288] Kiyoshi Uchimaru, Susumu Okamoto, and Bunteru Kurahara. *TQM for Technical Groups: Total Quality Principles for Product Development*. Productivity Press, Portland, Oregon, 1993.

[289] Hidemi Ueda, Yoshio Mitsufi, and Susumu Yamada. Case study of hoshin management, daily management, and cross-functional management (2). *Total Quality Control*, 38(11):79–89, 1987.

[290] Karl T. Ulrich and Steven D. Eppinger. *Product Design and Development*. McGraw-Hill, New York, 1995.

[291] Unattributed. Baldrige award winners beat the S&P 500. *Quality Progress*, page 51, April 1999.

[292] Glen L. Urban and John R. Hauser. *Design and Marketing of New Products*. Prentice-Hall, Inc., Englewood Cliffs, NJ, second edition, 1993.

[293] Abbott Payson Usher. *A History of Mechanical Inventions,* pages 65–68. Harvard University Press, 1929.

[294] Various authors. Special issue on design and planning in organizations. *The Center for Quality of Management Journal*, 5(1), Spring 1996.

[295] Eric von Hippel. Lead user analyses for the development of new industrial products. *Management Science*, 34:569–582, May 1988.

[296] Eric von Hippel. *The Sources of Innovation*. Oxford University Press, New York, 1988.

[297] H.M. Wadsworth, K.S. Stephens, and A.B. Godfrey. *Modern Methods for Quality Control and Improvement*. John Wiley & Sons, New York, 1986.

[298] Designing effective and efficient action: Conversations for commitment. Video tape, *Center for Quality of Management*, 1996. Developed and narrated by David Walden with support from Belinda Grosskopf.

[299] David Walden. Thoughts on goals and metrics. *The Center for Quality Management Journal*, 3(1):33–38, Winter 1994.

[300] David Walden. The systematic development of skill as a basis for competitive product development. *The Center for Quality of Management Journal*, 4(1):3–41, Winter 1995. This paper has an extensive bibliography of papers related to acquiring mastery, primarily in non-management areas.

[301] David Walden. Designing effective and efficient action. Circulated widely within Center for Quality of Management and without, June 22, 1996, slightly revised Spring 1997.

[302] David Walden. Task deployment management. *The Center for Quality of Management Journal*, 6(1):27–33, Spring 1997.

[303] James P. Walker. A disciplined approach to continuous improvement. Packard Electric monograph, 1988.

[304] Ted Walls and David Walden. Understanding unclear situations and each other using the Language Processing Method. *Journal of the Center for Quality of Management*, 4(4):29–37, Winter 1995.

[305] John C. Welchman. Invisible colors: *A Visual History of Titles*. Yale University Press, New Haven, CT, 1997.

[306] Donald J. Wheeler. *Understanding Variation—The Key to Managing Chaos*. SPC Press, Knoxville, TN, 1993.

[307] Donald J. Wheeler. *Advanced Topics in Statistical Process Control—The Power of Shewhart's Charts*. SPC Press, Knoxville, TN, 1995.

[308] Donald J. Wheeler and David S. Chambers. *Understanding Statistical Process Control*. SPC Press, Knoxville, TN, second edition, 1992.

[309] Donald J. Wheeler and Sheila R. Poling. *Building Continual Improvement—A Guide for Business*. SPC Press, Knoxville, TN, 1998.

[310] Steven C. Wheelwright and Kim B. Clark. *Revolutionizing Product Development: Quantum Leaps in Speed, Efficiency, and Quality*. The Free Press, New York, 1992.

[311] Edward O. Wilson. *Consilience*. Alfred A. Knopf, New York, 1998.

[312] Terry Winograd and Fernando Flores. *Understanding Computers and Cognition: A New Foundation for Design*. Addison-Wesley, Wakefield, MA, paperback edition, 1987.

[313] Toby Woll. Idealized design and TQM: Planning by practitioners. *The Center for Quality of Management Journal*, 5(1):4–21, Spring 1996. Special issue on Design and Planning in Organizations.

[314] James Womack, Daniel T. Jones, and Daniel Roos. *The Machine that Changed the World: The Story of Lean Production*. Harper Collins, New York, paperback reprint edition, 1991. Shows how focusing on cycle time changed an entire industry.

[315] Jason W. Yung, Perrin S. Meyer, and Jesse H. Ausubel. The loglet lab software: A tutorial. *Technological Forecasting and Social Change*, 61(3):273–295, September 1999.

Index

0-1 requirements, 251
0-1 term, 455
0-1 thinking, 210
1H. See 4Ws/1H, 5Ws/1H
2-6-2 rule. *See* Shiba
4Ms. *See* Man machine method material
4Ps. *See* People plant policies procedures
4Ws/1H, 194
5 Disciplines. *See* Five Disciplines
5 Evils, 185, 200
5 Principles, 200–204
5S activities, 569
5Ws/1H, 209, 228
6-3-3-4 model, 16
7 Infrastructures, 332, 425–450,
    597–598, 604
  monitoring, 446
7 Management and Planning Tools, 213–215,
    280, 508
  methods/tools, combination, 215–217
7 QC steps, 8
7 QC tools, 8, 11, 77, 145–147, 200, 420
  combination, 216
  de-emphasis, 459
  usage, 124, 131, 132, 152, 567
7 Steps format, 442
7 Steps improvement cycles, 430
7 Steps method (7 Steps), 8, 123, 124, 170,
    175–185
9 Steps, contrast, 184–185
  application, 419, 420
  case study, 133–145
  combination, 216
  diagnosis, case study, 163–173
  format, 152
  introduction, 175–177
  management diagnosis. *See* Reactive
    improvement
  QITs, 177, 178, 181, 355
  repetition, 185
  steps, 131–133

tools, 131–133
  format, 156–157
  usage, 152, 153
  experience, 177–178
7 Steps PDCA process, 513
7 Steps training, 438
7-step improvement process, 11
9 Steps
  contrast. *See* 7 Steps method
  method relationship, 196–197
  mobilization. *See* Teradyne
  usage. *See* Teradyne
60 percent rule, 82
70/30 rule, 163, 186
360-degree view, 202, 217

A

ABB, 476, 501
Abe, Masanobu, 453, 723
Abell, Thomas E., 707
ABM. *See* Activity base management
Abramson, Bob, 502
Abstract words, avoidance, 251
Abstractionists, 335
Accident/injury, 185, 200
Accountability, 401. *See also* Interlocking
  accountability; Personal
  responsibility/accountability
Achievement, sense, 128
Ackoff, Russell, 38, 39, 641, 673, 707
  axiom, 458
  design methods, 675
  idealized design, introduction, 680
  ideas, 608
  language, 694
  recommendations, 683
  strategic planning, approach, 678
  systems approach, 677
Act, 184, 225–226, 289–290, 507, 585–586.
  See also Plan Do Check Act; Standard
  Do Check Act

Action. *See* Coordinated action
  conversations, 308–315
  course, 115–117
  facts usage, 79–81
  learning, 598
  plans, 469
  usage, 56
Action Design, 300, 327
Action Science, 300, 676
Activity base management (ABM), 478
Actual-delta-theoretical (AÄT), example,
  480–484
ADAC, 359, 437, 455, 696
  awards, 603
ADI. *See* Analog Devices
AΔT. *See* Actual-delta-theoretical
Affective language, 206
  minimization, 208
Affinity diagram, 213
After-action review, 350
Aggressive learning, 28
Agilent, split. *See* Hewlett-Packard
Akao, Yoji, 248, 459, 707
Albers, Donald J., 707
Alcoa Aluminum, 467
Alexanderson, G.L., 707
Alignment, 455. *See also* Business; Cycle-
  time reduction; Leadership;
  Organizations; Policies; Structure;
  Vision
  creation, 543
  Hoshin management, usage, 504, 523–524
  phase, 458–459
  strategies, 463–464
Allen, Scott, 707
AlliedSignal, 477–478, 501, 667
  metrics, 477
  Six Sigma
    focus, 462
    implementation, 476
All-Japan QC Circle Conferences, 375
Alternatives, identification/selection, 190–191
Ambiguous/unambiguous statements,
  248–256
Ambivalence, deletion, 603
American Power Conversion (APC), 409
  model, 468, 492–500
  product design standards, 498
American Society for Quality (ASQ), 664,
  665, 668
American Society for Quality Control
  (ASQC), 648

American Supplie Institute (ASI), 664
Amsden, David, 707
Analog Devices (ADI), 38, 55, 133, 163,
  292, 379, 593–601, 707
  background, 595–596
  business, 594
  Cambridge Fab, self-directed work teams,
    388–395
  CE, interaction, 236
  core teams, 385–388
  Hoshin management, usage, 524, 531–544
    assessment, 542–544
  micro-machining, 629
  participants, 300
  review table, 540
  system, components, 596–601
Analysis
  phase, 469
  process, 523
  usage. *See* Hoshin deployment
Ancona, Deborah G., 707
Anderson, Erik, 708
Anderson, Walter Truett, 708
Annual goals, 428
Annual targets, 428
Anthony, Michael T., 719
Anthropologists, 227, 243
APC. *See* American Power Conversion
Approval/disapproval, 207
Aramati, Victor, 708
Argyris, Chris, 300, 301, 327, 676, 708
Artz, Edwin, 415
Asahi, 229
Asaku, Tetsuichi, 708
ASI. *See* American Supplier Institute
ASIX, 631
ASKUL, 630, 633–636
  breakthrough parallels, 635–636
ASQ. *See* American Society for Quality
ASQC. *See* American Society for Quality
  Control
Assessment, 327. *See also* Atom of work;
  Baldrige assessment; Environmental
  assessment; Self-assessment
  criteria, 452
  deferring, 317
  diagnosis. *See* External assessment
Associated means, stages. *See* Managerial
  action
Atom of work, 308–315, 323
  assessment, 313–314

negotiation, 310–311
performance, 311–313
preparation, 309–310
AT&T, 708
Audience
    solution implementation, explanation, 159
    theme explanation, 153–154
Aurora. *See* Teradyne
Ausubel, Jesse H., 720, 727
Auxillary verbs (should/must), avoidance,
    252
Awards, 444–445

B

Bakken, James, 120, 708
Balanced scorecard, 596–597
    usage, 676
Baldrige assessment, 468
Baldrige award. *See* Malcolm Baldrige
    National Quality Award
Baldrige criteria, 382, 478, 664
    usage, 696
Baldrige effort, 579
Baldrige index, 721
Baldrige model, 607
Bankruptcy, 409
Banks, 103, 105
Bannister, Roger, 53
Barlett, John, 708
BBN. *See* Bolt Beranek and Newman
Beckett, Frederick, 717
Before-and-after Pareto diagrams, 160
Behavior chart. *See* Process
Behavior, coordination, 297
Bemowski, Karen, 708, 709
Benchmark analysis, 271
Benchmarking, 468–472
    requirements, 472
    usage. *See* Motorola; Xerox
Bennis, Warren, 709
Best practices, 577. *See also* Standard best
    practices
    integration, 35–36, 701
Best-in-class companies, 468
Bethea, Ken, 389, 391–393, 403, 720
Beyer, Hugh R., 709
Biological model, 31–33
Blakeslee, Jr., Jerome A., 709
BLS. *See* Business Leadership System
Blue sky committee. *See* PLUS
Bogan, Christopher E., 709
Bohm, David, 301, 709

Bolt Beranek and Newman (BBN), 229, 233,
    379, 403, 441, 654
    CE interaction, 236
    customer visitation program (case study),
        221–226, 240–242, 257, 271, 280
Bootstrapping. *See* Success
Bose Corporation, 379, 409, 654
    CE interaction, 236
    study group, 301
Bossidy, Larry, 477, 478
Boston College, School of Business, 300
Bottlenecks, 215, 552
Bottom-to-top communication, 414
Bottom-up hierarchy, 286
Bowden, Ken, 720
Bowen, H. Kent, 576, 724
Bower, Joseph L., 709
Box, George E.P., 709
Brache, Alan, 492, 722
Braden, Vic, 709
Bradley, Michael, 177, 180, 432, 587, 709
Braun, Mark, 502
Breakdown. *See* Organizations
    conversation, 307
    declaration, 314, 315
Breakthrough, 84, 90, 338, 555. *See also*
    Continuous breakthrough; Cross-
    company breakthroughs; Teradyne
    attempt, 637
    case studies. *See* Business breakthrough
    change, 638
    continuous improvement, usage, 350–351
    contrast. *See* Continuous improvement;
        Process
    cycle. *See* Sense Commit Mental
        breakthrough Technical breakthrough
    factors, 614
    goals, 286
    improvement, 556–558
    cycle, usage, 615–617
    methods, synergy, 621–624
    model, 614–620. *See also* Business
        breakthrough
    objectives, Hoshin plan, 590
    parallels. *See* ASKUL; Maeda
        Corporation; NIMS; Teradyne
    practice, 607
    process, 625
    results, 696–697
    strategies. *See* Mental breakthrough
Breakthrough-only approach, 89
Bridgestone Tire Company, 503

Brodie, Christina Hepner, 280, 282, 710
Broken Pellicle QIT, 133
Brown, Mark G., 709
Bryant College, 602
Bryant, Nelson, 709
Burchill, Gary, 70, 236, 252, 277, 323, 675,
    680–681, 710
  codification, 301
  dissertation, 279
  LP method, integration, 687
  Navy experience, 323–325
  team, 326, 327
Burns, Bill, 709
Business
  alignment, 702–703
  complexity, 362
  concerns, 534
  conversations (classes), tangible models,
    299
  cycles, 512
  decreasing, 513
  fundamentals, 590–592
  globalization, 668
  goals
  drivers, 475
  finalizing, 537–539
  initiative, 494
  movement, 609
  objectives, 492
  planning, 524–531, 543
  elements, 590–592
  Hoshin management, usage, 528–531
  plans, roll-up, 543
  success, 358, 571
  system, evolution. See SerVend
    International
  units, 377
  value equation, 87
Business breakthrough
  case studies, 610–625
  contrast. See Process
  meaning, 639–641
  model, 610–625
  obstacle, 626–636
Business Excellence Model. See European
    Foundation for Quality Management
Business improvement, 362
  course, 437
  efforts, 85
  financial benefit, 36–37
  methods, 209
Business Leadership System (BLS), 593

Business Process Reengineering, 493, 665
Buss, Dennis, 94
Buzzell, Robert D., 712, 723

C
CAD. See Computer-aided design
Caldwell, David F., 707
Cambridge Fab. See Analog Devices
Camp, Robert C., 468, 710
Capability. See Intuitive capability
CAPD. See Check Act Plan Do
CAPDC, 545
Caplan, Janet, 717
Carlzon, Jan, 94
Carroccio, Anthony, 502
Caswell, Deborah, 714
Catalysts, 653–654
Catchball, 516, 525. See also Interdivisional
    catchball; Interlevel catchball
Cattleya Gold Prize, 373
Causal analysis, 530
  solution consistency, 159
Causal loops, integration, 675
Cause-and-effect diagram, 132, 139, 146,
    156–158, 477
  usage, 187, 201, 214
Cause-and-effect relations, 147, 213
Cause-and-effect relationships, 187
Causes
  analysis, 139–140, 157–158, 165–167
  investigation, 157–158
CE. See Concept engineering
Center for Quality Management, 659
Center for Quality of Management (CQM),
    218, 236, 434, 710
  companies, 370, 387, 653
  Design Study, 280
  design study team, 379
  Design Team, 379–385, 403, 450, 453, 711
  establishment, 48
  formation, 654–655
  history, 654–662
  Journal Editors, 711
  member companies, 297
  study, 85–86
  Study Group, 299, 301–302, 305–307, 711.
    See also Conversation; Cycle-time
    reduction
  first learnings, 324
CEO. See Chief Executive Officer
Certification. See National standard
    certification

Chambers, David S., 120, 726
Chamilard, George, 415, 421, 579, 583, 585
Chance, 203
Change. *See* Organizational change
    agents, 646, 653–654, 662, 669
    leading, 329
    officer, 432, 433
    program, 427
    systems, 478–479
Chaos, strategies. *See* Creative chaos
Chapin, Edward, 711
Charness, Neil, 359, 712
Check, 184, 211, 224–225, 289–290, 507,
    521, 584–585. *See also* Plan Do Check
    Act; Standard Do Check Act
Check Act Plan Do (CAPD)
    application, 566
    aspects, 553
    concept, 564
    cycle, 550, 554
    institutionalization, 566–569
    usage, 564–566
    form, 560
    PDCA contrast, 561–564
    practice, manager usage, 569–575
    skills, 570
    usage, institutionalization, 568
Check sheet, 132, 145, 442
Cheney, Gay, 711
Chief Executive Officer (CEO)
    crusades, patterns, 413–414
    involvement, 405–414
    case study. *See* Teradyne
    leadership, 405, 424, 595
Chong, Chee-Leong, 707
Christensen, Clayton M., 626, 711
Ciampa, Dan, 711
Cisco, 572
    monitors, 496, 497
Clark, Kim B., 726
Class work, linking, 439
CMOS, 631, 632
CMOS/NT, 631, 632
Coaches, 399–400
Coaching roles, 353–354
Cole, Robert E., 711
Commentary, 24
Commit. *See* Sense Commit Mental
    breakthrough Technical breakthrough
Commitment, 298, 310–312
    building, 449
    micro-demonstration, 28

Common causes, 113
Communication, 298, 375, 494, 603. *See
    also* Bottom-to-top communication;
    Top-to-bottom communication
    channels, 414
    facilitation, 436
    skill, 332. *See also* Teams
Company
    activities, financing methods, 679
    exchange/networking, 444
    integration, evolution, 13–15
    optimization system, 20
    strategies, 555–569
    survival, 19
Companywide program, PDCA usage, 456
Companywide Quality Committee (CQC),
    175, 189–190, 419, 654–662
    activities (1991-1999), 657–662
    approach, elements, 656–657
    approval, 195
    education, 659
    expansion, 657–658
    focus, 658–659
    involvement, 696
    management, 658
    networking, 659–660
    research, 660–662
    skill development, 580–582
    usage. *See* Teradyne
Competitive product data, 269–271
Competitors, knowledge, 224
Complexity. *See* Organizational complexity;
    Problem complexity
    levels, 599
    segmentation. *See* Problems
    types, 600
Computer-aided design (CAD), 386
    tools, 88
Concept, 173
Concept engineering (CE), 211, 236–237,
    278, 711
    approach, 245
    development, 281, 661
    interaction. *See* Analog Devices; Bolt
        Beranek and Newman; Bose; Genrad;
        Polaroid
    method, 684
    outline, 237–239
    usage. *See* Stripping basket
Concepts. *See* Products
    avoidance. *See* Intangible concepts
    generation, 272–277

selection, 272–277
Conceptual skill, 333–338, 608
Concerns. *See* Customers
   integration, 66–68
   variation. *See* Shared concerns
Conclusions, understanding, 158
Conner, Dennis, 711
Conscious incompetence, 23
Consequent effects, evaluation, 161
Constraints
   determination, 189–190
   theory, 93, 674, 676
Contextual inquiry. *See* Digital Equipment
   Corporation
   methods, 245
   performing, 245
Continuous breakthrough, 634
Continuous improvement, 42, 71, 323, 449,
   499–500
   activities, 285
   breakthrough, contrast, 88–92
   scientific method, contrast, 92–93
   usage, 416. *See also* Breakthrough;
      Processes; Work
   WV model, 74–83
Continuous quality improvement, 73
Control, 491, 518–521. *See also* Process;
   Starts control
   method, 111–112
   phase. *See* Hoshin management
Control chart, 132, 147
Control plans, 477
Controller's office, 103
Conversation. *See* Action; Breakdown; Face-
   to-face conversations; Possibilities;
   Relationships; Two-way conversation
   classes, tangible models. *See* Business
   CQM study group, 299–302
   importance/difficulty, 297–299
   types/models, 305–323
Conviction, 413–414
Conway, Earl, 415
Coopers & Lybrand, 120
Coordinated action, 402
Core, Craig, 389
Core teams, 225, 367. *See also* Analog
   Devices
   benefits, 386–387
Corning Glass Company, 464, 655, 711
Corporate culture. *See* Fitness of corporate
   culture
Corporate strategy, 595

Cost, 189
Cost of quality approach, 595
Cost/price contrast, formulas, 8–9
Countermeasures, development, 191–193
Covey, Stephen R., 698, 711
CPM charts, 215
CQC. *See* Companywide Quality Committee
CQM. *See* Center for Quality of
   Management
Crawford-Mason, Clare, 664
Creative chaos, strategies, 621
Creativity, 352, 364
   enhancement, 624
Critical paths, 215
Crosby 14-point process, 415
Crosby, Philip, 182, 421, 451, 595, 712
Cross-company breakthroughs, 557
Cross-company efforts, 378
Cross-company functional forums, 582
Cross-company team, 367, 368
Cross-company teamwork, 379
Cross-disciplinary interactions, 36
Cross-functional activities, 457
Cross-functional committees, 460
Cross-functional systems, 459
Cross-functional teams, 362, 367–368,
   377–379, 382, 402
Cross-organization changes, 591
Cross-organizational issues, 591
Cross-training, 391
CRs. *See* Customer requirements
Culligan, Matthew J., 712
Cultural archetypes (Rapaille), 61–62
Cultural desires, 565
Culture, 669. *See also* Improvement; Low-
   quality culture
   repair, 603
Cunningham, Fred, 300, 301, 345
Curiosity, 352–353, 573
Customer concerns, 60–66
   discovery, 60–62
   reasoning sequence, 63–64
   viewpoints, 62–63
Customer Focus Day, 225
Customer requirements (CRs), 492–493. *See*
   also One-dimensional customer
   requirements
   characteristics, investigation, 260–268
   classification, questionnaire usage,
      261–263
   customer satisfaction, 260–261
   identification, 100–101

issues, 253–256
LP diagram, 257, 258
measures/targets, 101
metrics, generation, 269
operational definition, 270–271, 276–277
relationships, understanding, 257–260
selection, 256–257
statements, 277
understanding, 239
    integration, 269–271
    usage, 248–260
Customer satisfaction, 73, 285, 288, 416, 462
decay, 268
definition, 3–11
evolution, 3
methods, evolution, 11–13
Customer visitation, 201, 221–232
activities, institutionalization, 225
identification, 240–241
key points, 227–232
principles, 221
program, case study. See Bolt Beranek and
    Newman
purpose, clarification, 227
target, setting, 227
visits, training, 227–228
Customer-related performance, 153
Customer-related process, 291
Customers, 55–56, 592. See also Long-term
    opportunity customers; Voice of the
    customer
account, 310
base, 594
benefit, 427
contact, 353
context, collection, 242–247
data, 269–271
delivery, 129
    environment, 275
    image, development, 248
understanding, 239–248
focus, 42, 49, 286, 471, 601
evolution/challenges, 59
goals, 427
stages, 59–60
identification, 56, 100, 103–104
image LP, 246, 248
individualization, 69–70
innovation. See PLUS
interviews, 245
listening. See Potential customers
loyalty, 428

meeting, necessity, 230
needs, 56, 244. See also Output
    understanding, 239–248
organizations, 356
push. See Global customer
respect, 228–229
support organization, 385
unhappiness, 222
Customization. See Mass customization
cycle, 83, 92, 117, 144, 288, 292
completion, 364
usage, 159, 237, 359
Cycle time, 143
Cycle-time measurement, 56
Cycle-time processes, 488, 556
Cycle-time project, improvement, 495
Cycle-time reduction, 429, 468,
    479–500, 676
alignment/orientation, 492–494
CQM Study Group, 484–485
definition, 494–495
execution, 499
focus. See High Voltage
implementation, 499
process
    design, 495–498
    wisdom, 485–491
purpose, 472
requirements, 492
usage, 475
Cycle-time results, 427

D

Daguerre, 91
Daniels, William R., 712
d'Arbeloff, Alex, 175, 185, 191, 335, 410, 712
CEO initiative, 425
involvement, 578
Japan, travels, 415
LP diagram, demonstration, 420
managers/supervisors, meeting, 417
recollection, 630–633
Shiba meeting, 416
video statement, 411, 414, 421, 455
Darwinian model, 437
DASH, 696
Data. See Competitive product data;
    Customers; Group similar data;
    Language data; Qualitative data
analysis, 136–139, 155–157, 164–165
stratification, 155–156, 384
understanding, 218

usage, 530. *See also* Process;
    Quantitative data
writing, 218
Data collection, 136–139, 155–157, 164–165.
    See also Proactive improvement
collector choice, 241
methods, 469
process, description, 155
usage, 530
Deadline
    date, 536
    effects, 443, 542
Deakins, Suzanne, 712
Decision making, 402
    basis, 81
Declarations, 304–305
Defects, 185, 200, 472
    reduction, 477
    scorecard, creation, 225
Define Measure Analyze Improve Control
    (DMAIC), 477, 478
Delay, 185, 200
    curves, 487
    elimination, 473
Delighters, 261
Delivery, 189
Dellinger, Margaret, 712
Deming criteria, 382
Deming Library, 120
Deming Prize, 48, 413, 445–446, 453, 549
    ceremony, 653
    challenge, 468, 614
    inception, 648
    Nationwide Promotion and Dissemination
        of TQC, 651
Deming, W. Edwards, 4, 82, 112–113, 465,
    497, 654, 712
    system, 698
Denker, Stephen, 502, 712
Deployment, 499, 585
    tree, 518
Design
    operationalizing. *See* Idealized design
    plan reviews, 552
Design Structure Matrices, 106
Detail, avoidance. *See* Premature detail
Detailed plan
    development, 193–194
    implementation/monitoring, 193–194
Development. *See* Self-development
Dewey, John, 598

Diagnosis, 333, 445–450, 542, 583–585.
    See also 7 Steps method; External
    assessment; President's diagnosis;
    Process; Quality improvement; Reactive
    improvement; Self-diagnosis
    examination, 582–586
    results. *See* Presidential diagnosis
Dichter, Steven, 717
Diffusion. *See* Quality Improvement;
    Societal diffusion; Success; Total
    Quality Management
    difficulty, 451
Digital Equipment Corporation (DEC), 281,
    379, 464, 476, 654
    contextual inquiry, 243–245
Direct reports, 591
Direct-selling activities, 229
Disapproval. *See* Approval/disapproval
Discovery. *See* Customers; Process discovery
    usage. *See* Management
Disneyland, 332, 572
Disruptive technologies, 626–627
Divorced spouses, 103
DMAIC. *See* Define Measure Analyze
    Improve Control
Do, 211, 224, 289, 381, 507, 521, 584. *See
    also* Plan Do Check Act; Standard Do
    Check Act
Dobyns, Lloyd, 664
Donnell, Augustus, 712
Donnithorne, Larry R., 712
Dow, 477
Downstream development, requirements
    definition, 260–272
Downstream use, 239
    documentation, 269–271
Downtime, 244
DRAM, 91, 92
Dreyfus, Hubert L., 712
Dreyfus, Stuart E., 712
Drucker, Peter, 57, 106, 148
Dual function. *See* Language; Work
Dunbar, Robin, 94, 712
Durer, Albrecht, 339
Dynamic/static implementation strategy, 46

E
Echeverria, Rafael, 300, 301
ECL technology, 631
Edison, Thomas, 124, 350
Education, 333, 414, 434–440. *See also*
    Companywide Quality Committee

management, PDCA usage, 435, 440
observations. *See* World-class education
professionals, usage, 435, 437–438
providing, 427
Effectiveness increase, process usage, 84–85
Effects, evaluation, 142–144, 160–162. *See also* Consequent effects
EFQM. *See* European Foundation for Quality Management
Efran, Jay S., 712
Elapsed time, 481
Electronic documents, Internet distribution, 68
Employees, 103
  development. *See* NIMS
  requirements, 104–105
    measures/targets, 105
  survey results, 592
  total participation, 42
  usage. *See* Engaged employees
Empowerment, 453, 603
  contrast. *See* Leadership
  phase, 456–457
Enablers, 448
Ends planning, 678–679
Engaged employees, usage, 285–287
Engineering process. *See* Quantitative engineering process
English, Michael J., 709
Enthusiasm/effectiveness, evolution, 374–375
Environment, 677–678. *See also* Customers; Fitness for societal/global environment; Local improvement; Physical environment; Team-oriented environment; Teradyne; Work
Environmental assessment, 684–687
Environmental responsibilities, 679
Eppinger, Steven D., 725
EPROM, 91
Ericsson, Anders K., 359, 712
Errors, 472
Esaki, Leo, 335
Esikan, R. Gnanad, 712
Essentials, exploration, 186–188, 534–535
Eternal life, 640
European Foundation for Quality Management (EFQM), 607, 624
  Business Excellence Model, 447–450, 452, 671
European Quality Award, 448
Event-driven principle, 416
Excel, 632

Exchange/networking. *See* Company
Excheverria, Rafael, 712
Executives, training, 603
Expansion. *See* Companywide Quality Committee
Explicit joining. *See* Improvement; Routine work
Explicit models. *See* Shared concerns
Explicit structures, creation. *See* Mobilization
Explicit theories, development/testing, 352
Exploration, planning, 239–242
Expression, clarity, 206–210
External assessment, diagnosis, 446–450

F
Face-to-face conversations, 374
Face-to-face selling time, optimization, 130
Facilitators, 163, 457
  staff specialists, 595
Facts. *See* Management by fact; Symbolic facts
  contrast. *See* Opinion
  evaluation, 168
  focus, 384
  grouping, 219
  statements. *See* Statements of fact
  usage, 601. *See also* Action; Hoshin deployment
Failure rate. *See* Products
Family cooperation, extent, 373
Fault tree analysis, 477
FCC. *See* Federal Communications Commission
Federal Communications Commission (FCC), 668
Federal Reserve Bank, 54
Feedback, 24, 32, 191, 499, 553. *See also* Plan Do Check Act cycle
Feigen, Marc, 717
Field social scientists, 227
Financial benefit. *See* Business improvement
Financials, 592
Fine, Charles H., 712
Finley, Michael, 722
Fischer, Greg, 395, 413, 450, 688–697, 713, 714
Fischer, Mark, 688
Fischer, Paul, 713
Fishbowl
  approach, 573
  entering, 334

exiting, 336
principle, application, 230–232
Fisher, George, 221, 222, 233, 474, 713
Fisher, Kimball, 713
Fitness for societal/global environment, 16
Fitness of corporate culture, 16
Fitness of cost, 4, 7–8, 11–13, 268
Fitness to latent requirement, 4, 9, 11–13
Fitness to standard, 4, 11
Fitness to use, 4, 5, 11
Fitnesses. See Four fitnesses
    company awareness, 10–11
Fitzgerald, Dawn Dougherty, 707
Five Disciplines, 674
Flomatic International, 688
Flores, Fernando, 38, 300–301, 305, 327,
    676, 713, 726
Florida Power & Light, 655, 669
Florida, Richard, 713
Flowcharting, 313. See also Process
FOCUS, 211, 213, 281
    method, 280
    process, 697
    variation, 237
Focus, 462–463. See also Companywide
    Quality Committee; Customers
    groups, 243
    narrowing, 186, 188–189
    narrowness, 154
Focused pickup, 220
Fong, Douglas, 713
Ford, Henry, 31
Ford Motor Company, 115, 120
    Q-1 quality rating, 673
Foremen, Quality Conference, 653
Forming, 396
Foster, Richard N., 713
Four fitnesses, 4, 60
Fuji Xerox, 409, 619–622, 624, 626
Fujino, Yoshiko, 371, 375, 713
Fujita, Shirou, 713
Full-time data analysis, 279
Functional group, 369–377
Functions, applicability, 475
Fundamentals, searching, 348
Future, creation, 677–678

G
Gage, Stanley, 713
Gagnon, Christopher, 717
Gale, Bradley T., 712
Galvin, Robert, 547, 575, 714

Gantt chart, 154, 193, 215
Garbage in, garbage out, 205
Garvin, David A., 452, 707, 714
Gauge capability studies, 477
Gaugin, Paul, 639, 640
GE Jet Engine Division, 379
General Electric (GE), 478, 501
    Aircraft Engine Division, 654
    Six Sigma, focus, 462
    Workout process, 620
General Motors (GM), 477
Genrad, CE interaction, 236
Gharajedaghi, Jamshid, 680, 683, 714
Girl Scouts, 57
Glazer, Barney G., 232, 714
Gleaning. See Ochibo-hiroi
Global company, 622
Global customer, 622
    push, 622
Global environment. See Fitness for
    societal/global environment
Global leadership, 428
Global market, competing, 362
Global Positioning System (GPS), 61
GOAL/QPC, 664
Goals. See Annual goals; Breakthrough;
    Intermediate goals; Noble goals;
    Personal goals; Process; Unit goals
    deployment, 539–540
    simplicity, 475
    development, 535–537
    drivers. See Business
    examples. See SerVend International
    setting, 333, 425, 427–430, 471
Godfrey, A.B., 725
Goldense, Brad, 496
Goldratt, Eliyahu, 93, 490, 497, 502,
    674, 714
Goleman, Daniel P., 714
Goodhue, John, 491
GPS. See Global Positioning System
Grady, Robert B., 714
Graham, Alan, 345, 451, 723
Graham, Martha, 352
Grant, E.L., 714
Graphs, 132, 146
Graves, Stephen, 502
Greenblatt, Sherwin, 409, 714
Griffin, Abbie, 715
Group similar data, 219
Group work, 363–364
    leader, 365

Groups. *See* Functional group; Title groups; Work groups
   dynamics. *See* Small group dynamics
   layout, 219
   relationship, 219
Grove, Andrew, 333, 425, 715
GTE, 233

H
Hacking, 349
Haeckel, Stephan H., 715
Half-life model, 598–599
Hallmark Cards, 470, 471
Hamel, G., 721
Hammer, Michael, 493, 665
Hands-on capability, 432
Hard-side issues, 292
Harrington, Brad, 286, 592, 593, 604, 698, 715
Harris Semiconductor, 394
Harry, Midel J., 715
Harvard Business School, 596, 626, 630
Hauser, John R., 715, 725
Hayakawa, Alan R., 208, 232, 715
Hayakawa, S.I., 208, 232, 301, 321, 676, 715
Health care providers, 59
Heany, Donald F., 723
Hemingway, Collins, 714
Hendricks, Kevin B., 715, 724
Hennings, Tom, 502
Herrick, Robert, 502
Herzberg, Frederick, 715
Hewlett, Bill, 614
Hewlett-Packard (HP), 238, 286, 447, 503, 588–593. *See also* Yokogawa HP
   Agilent, split, 593
   evolution, 592–593
   Hoshin implementation, 523
   Medical Products Group, 593
   Palo Alto training center, 338
   study group, 301
   TQC, usage, 588–589
Hierarchical organization, 362
   reduction, 624
Hierarchical relationships, 395
High Voltage, cycle-time reduction focus, 462
High-performance team, 397
High-quality work, 385, 646
Hillebrand, Gus, 413
Hillerich, John, 502
Hillkirk, John, 717

Hill-rom, 641
Hill-Rom managers, 413
Histogram, 132, 147, 477
Hitachi, 441, 568
Hitt, Jack, 715
Holtzblatt, Karen, 281, 709, 715
Honda, 623, 629–630
Honeywell, 465
Honeywell quality value (HQV), 478
Hope, Quentin, 717
Horton, 345
Hoshin deployment, 510–518
   alternate system, 531
   facts/analysis, usage, 512–517
   system, 514
Hoshin management, 286, 503, 569, 579, 591
   case study, 594
   components, 503–524
   control phase, 507–508
   elements, 504–506
   execution, 540
   focus. *See* NTT Data Corporation
   idealized design, application, 676–681
   management by objectives, contrast, 524–528
   methods, 680
   monitoring, 518–521
   phases, 504–506
   proactive phase, 507–510
   purpose, 520
   reactive phase, 507–508
   setting, 508–510
   strategic planning, 508–510
   usage, 596. *See also* Alignment; Analog Devices; Business; Routine work concept, 560–564
Hoshin monitoring, 506
Hoshin performance, review, 541
Hoshin plan. *See* Breakthrough
Hoshin planning, 526–528
Hoshin results, determination delay, 544
Hoshins, 528
House, Glenn, 715
How? questions, 214
HP. *See* Hewlett-Packard
HQV. *See* Honeywell quality value
Human interaction skill, 332
Human performance laboratories, 243
Human resources department, 103
Human skill, 332–333
Humphrey, Watts, 697
Hunter, J.S., 709

Hunter, W.G., 709
Hutchens, Jr., Spencer, 715
Hybrid parallel organization, 465

I

I Already Know It (IAKI), 25, 573
IAKI. *See* I Already Know It
IBM, 447, 476
Idealized design, 677, 678
  introduction. *See* Ackoff
  operationalizing, 680–681
Ideas, integration, 636–641
IIASA. *See* International Institute for
  Applied Systems Analysis
Ikawa, Michio, 428, 509, 545, 716
Image activities, 441
Image LP, 256. *See also* Customers
Implementation, 455
  table, 540
Impressionists, 334
Improvement, 96–98, 346–347, 602. *See also*
  Breakthrough; Business improvement;
  Continuous improvement; Incremental
  improvement; Iterative improvement;
  Local improvement; Proactive
  improvement; Process improvement;
  Quality improvement; Reactive
  improvement; Systematic improvement
case study. *See* Structural process
  improvement
confirmation, 160–161
continuation, 150
culture, 656
cycle, 563. *See also* Plan Do Check Act
  usage. *See* Breakthrough
efforts, 118
  time allotment, 356–357
financial benefit. *See* Business
goals, 56
level, 555–558
methods, 668
modeling. *See* Personal improvement
needs, 352
organization, 461
process
  emphasis, 161–162
  presentation, 442
skill, 123, 149
suggestions, 373
support, 341–342
teams, monitoring. *See* Teradyne
triggers, 375–376

types, 76–79
usage, 73
work, 357, 558–560
  explicit joining, 287–291
improvement
cycle, 290
  engine, 331
Incentives, 444–445
Incremental improvement, 412, 556–558
Indirect influence, usage, 671–673
Individual learning, 22
Individual skills, 401–402
Individual work, 363–364
Individualization. *See* Customers
Inflection curve, 609–610
Inflection points, 609
Influence, usage. *See* Indirect influence
Information, 24
Information Technology (IT), reduction, 624
Infrastructure, 332, 635. *See also*
  Mobilization; Networking;
  Organizational infrastructure
elements, 427–450
model, 652
Inghilleri, Leonardo, 61, 716
Initiation strategies, 405
Inktomi, 465
Innovation. *See* PLUS
Innovative processes, 86–88
Innovators, dilemma, 626–627
  resolution, 630–636
Input-process-output models, 313
Inspection, usage problems, 111–112
Institutional support structures, creation,
  435, 440
Institutional support systems, 434
Instruments, 602
Insurance companies, 103
Intangible concepts, avoidance, 252
Intangibles, 602
Integration, 68
  phase, 469
Intel, 300, 425
Interactive planning, 677
Interdivisional catchball, 560
Interlevel catchball, 560
Interlocking accountability, 401
Intermediate goals, 427
International Institute for Applied Systems
  Analysis (IIASA), 610, 654
Internet, 16
  distribution. *See* Electronic documents

Interpretation, 68
Interview, 75. *See also* Customers
  script, 246–247
Intuitive capability, 203–204
  usage, 241
Isaacs, Bill, 301
Ishikawa analysis, 539
Ishikawa diagrams, 157, 178, 214, 365
  usage, 530, 537
Ishikawa, Kaoru, 94, 580, 716
ISO 1400, 16
ISO 9000, 668
IT. *See* Information Technology
Iterative improvement, 82–83
Iwata, S., 633

J
Jacobson, Gary, 716
Japanese companies, 367
Japanese Industrial Standards (JIS), 651
Japanese lessons, 654–662
Japanese model. *See* Societal networking
  comparative results, 669–671
Japanese presentation system, benefits,
  442–444
Japanese QC circle activities, 133
Japanese QC team, evolution, 371–374
Japanese Standards Association (JSA), 48,
  648, 650, 663
  training, 665
Japanese Union of Scientists and Engineers
  (JUSE), 48, 232, 402, 648–653, 663
  approach, 668
  Research Committee, 213
  training, 665
Japanglish, 641
JIS. *See* Japanese Industrial Standards
JIT. *See* Just-In-Time
Johnson, Verne, 502
Jones, Capers, 355, 717
Jones, Daniel T., 727
Jones, Sandy, 715
Jones, Scott, 502
JSA. *See* Japanese Standards Association
JSQC Research Committee, 545, 716
Judgments, 207, 304, 306
Junguzza, Joe, 428, 450
Juran, Joseph M., 464, 580, 654, 716
JUSE. *See* Japanese Union of Scientists and
  Engineers
Just-In-Time (JIT)
  manufacturing, 120, 480, 588

meetings, 168
training, usage, 603

K
Kagano, Tadao, 716
Kahn, Roger, 347, 716
Kaizen, 666
  events, 660
Kambe, Nobuyoshi, 610–613
Kano analysis, 262
Kano diagram, 263–265
Kano matrix, 263–265
Kano method, 262, 711
Kano, Noriaki, 60, 260, 421, 716, 717, 719.
  See also Requirements dimensions
Kano questionnaire, 263–265
Kano surveys, e-mail distribution, 280
Kanter, Rosabeth Moss, 717
Kaplan, Robert S., 717
Katzenbach and Smith model, 396–397
Katzenbach, Jon R., 395–398, 403, 717
Kawakita, Jiro, 93, 717
  principles, 200–201, 233, 241
Keane Associates, 300, 301
Kearns, 409
Keidanren, 649
Kelley, Robert, 717
Kelner, Stephen P., 450, 717
Kenney, Martin, 713
Kimura, Kimiko, 371, 713
King, Bob, 717
Kirin, 229
KJ method, 201, 218, 232
Kleinrock, Leonard, 717
Knowledge, 24. *See also* Process
  dissemination, 647, 650–651, 666–667
  workers, 362
Knuth, Donald E., 350, 717
Kobayashi, Koji, 333, 339, 450,
  649, 718
Kobayashi Kosei, 371
Kodak, 476, 477
Kogure, Masao, 511, 524, 525, 545, 718
Kojima, Seiji, 718
Kokurka, Robert J., 718
KOKUYO, 633
Komatsu, 503
Konica, 624
Koura, Kozo, 94, 575, 716, 718
Kuhn, Thomas S., 641, 718
Kume, Hitoshi, 718
Kurahara, Bunteru, 725

Kurogane, Kenji, 718
Kuwabara, Atsushi, 718
Kyoto University, 669

L
Labor division, theory, 52, 53
Ladder of abstraction, 208–209, 338, 517
   movement, 511–512
Ladybug Circle, 371, 374–376
LAN. *See* Local Area Network
Language, 343. *See also* Affective language;
   Image LP; Qualitative language; Report
   language
   data, 204–210
   dual function, semantics usage, 205–206
   usage, 578–579
Language Processing (LP), 209. *See also*
   Customers
   demonstration. *See* d'Arbeloff
   development. *See* Requirements LP
   diagram, 258, 363, 379. *See also*
   Customer requirements
   method, 127, 178, 201, 213, 338, 659
   integration. *See* Burchill
   low-level issues, voting, 219
   overview, 217–219
   usage, 218, 233, 382
   titles, 684
LaRosa's, 462
LaVigna, Michael, 233
Leaders, 399–400. *See also* Teams
   personality, 424
Leaders for Manufacturing program. *See*
   Massachusetts Institute of Technology
Leadership, 342, 414. *See also* Chief
   Executive Officer; Global leadership
   alignment, 695–696
   empowerment, contrast, 33–35
   personality, force, 424
   pull. *See* Managers
   skills, 329–331, 330–338
      types, 331
   thinking. *See* Shiba
Leading learner, 431
Lean Enterprise Institute, 665
Lean Production, 479, 501
   methods, 676
Learn Use Teach Inspect (LUTI), 437
Learning, 471. *See also* Action; Aggressive
   learning; Organizational learning; Self-
   learning; Uniform learning; Individual
   learning

commitment. *See* Mutual learning
environmental influences, creation,
   435, 439
openness, commitment, 25–27
opportunity, creation, 435, 438–439
process, following, 26–27
setting, 24–28
strategies. *See* Unlearning
   learning, 229–230
Leavenworth, R.S., 714
LeBlanc, Gary, 413, 718
Lee, Mark C., 718
Lee, Thomas H., 421, 502, 641, 654, 673,
   680, 718, 719
Lessons. *See* Positive lessons
   learning, 162–163, 350
Levine, Marc, 631–632
LeVitt, Richard, 719
Levy, Steven, 222, 233, 421, 680
LFM. *See* Massachusetts Institute of
   Technology
Lienholders, 103
Life-long employment, 624
Lillrank, Paul, 719
Lincoln Laboratory. *See* Massachusetts
   Institute of Technology
Line managers, rotation, 433
Ling, Timothy, 717
Listeners, 153
Listening, 68. *See also* People
L.L. Bean, 54, 470, 471
LNPL. *See* Lower natural process limit
Local Area Network (LAN), 101
Local improvement, supportive environment,
   347–358
Log scale, 598
Logic, 156
Logical consistency, 156
Logistics curves, 610
Long-term opportunity customers, 130
Lowe, David, 359, 437, 455, 603
Lower Control Limit, 121
Lower natural process limit (LNPL), 111,
   114–115, 118, 121
Lower specification limit (LSL), 110
Lower-level Pareto diagram, 537
Low-level issues. *See* LP method
Low-quality culture, 646
LP. *See* Language Processing
LSL. *See* Lower specification limit
LUTI. *See* Learn Use Teach Inspect

M

MacGregor, 33, 39
MacMillan, I.C., 719
Maeda Corporation, 627–630
  breakthrough parallels, 635–636
  case study, 630
Maeda, Matabe, 627–629, 719
Maguire, Miles, 719
MAIC. *See* Measure Analyze Improve
  Control
Malcolm Baldrige National Quality Award
  (MBNQA), 37, 48, 413–415, 437,
  445–447
  examiners, 688
  quality, interest, 672
  value, 359, 663, 667
  winners, 597
Malone, Thomas J., 414, 601, 719
Man machine method material (4Ms), 157
Management. *See* Companywide Quality
  Committee; Middle management;
  Quality; Teams; Total Quality
  Management
  acceptance. *See* Solutions
  attendance. *See* Senior management
  coherent system, approach, 28–30, 701
  diagnosis. *See* Reactive improvement
  guidance, 152
  interest, 150–151
  involvement, 407
  level, increase, 330
  methods, 299
  mobilization, case study. *See* Process
  practice, evolution, 30–33
  process. *See* Projects
    discovery, usage, 95
  quality, 43
  revolutions, 41–42
  system, 293
  teams, 367–369, 395–396
  thinking
    principles, 21
    revolutions, 597–598
  tools, 12. *See also* 7 Management and
    Planning Tools
  transition, 586–588
Management by fact, 412, 427
Management by objectives (MBO), 524–531
  contrast. *See* Hoshin management
Management by process, 73–74
Managerial action, stages, 570–571
  associated means, stages, 571–575

Managerial participation, 556
Managers, 399–400. *See also* Senior
  managers; Total Quality Management
  leadership, pull, 622–624
  Quality Conference, 653
  rotation. *See* Line managers
  usage. *See* Check Act Plan Do
Manet, Edouard, 336
Manufacturing. *See* Just-In-Time
Manufacturing Technicians (MTs), 391
Mapping. *See* Structure
Marchetti, Cesare, 610, 719
Market research, 201, 278
Market-in, 51–55, 476
  concept, 52, 73, 153, 377
  necessity, 52–55
  results, 153
Masaaki, Imai, 716
Mask fabrication, 144
Mask holder, 139, 140
Mass customization, 69
Mass movement, 149
Massachusetts High Technology Council,
  654
Massachusetts Institute of Technology
  (MIT), 203, 237, 325, 654, 720
  Leaders for Manufacturing (LFM)
    program, 27, 336, 337
  Lincoln Laboratory, 354
  research, 230
  Sloan School of Management, 236, 336
Master. *See* Non-master
Mastery. *See* Personal mastery
  achievement, 358–359
    common element, 343–345
  techniques, 347
Mastro, Chris, 501
Mathers, John G., 712
Matrix. *See* Kano matrix
Matrix data analysis, 215
Matrix diagram, 214, 221
  usage, 216
Matsuzawa, Kouji, 718
Maturana, Humberto R., 300, 301, 719
May, Jerry, 351
MBNQA. *See* Malcolm Baldrige National
  Quality Award
MBO. *See* Management by objectives
McArthur, Philip, 719
McConnell, Steve, 719
McGrath, Michael E., 719
McGrath, R.G., 719

McGregor, Douglas, 719
Means planning, 471, 679–680
Means, stages. *See* Managerial action
Measure Analyze Improve Control (MAIC),
   478. *See also* Define Measure Analyze
   Improve Control
Measurement plans, 269
Mechanical model, 31
Meetings. *See* Just-In-Time; Presentation
   meetings; Self-directed work teams
   conduct, 373
   setup, 365
Melvin, Rick, 389
Members, engagement/alignment. *See*
   Organizations
Mental breakthrough, 632. *See also* Sense
   Commit Mental breakthrough Technical
   breakthrough
   strategies, 620–621
Mental model, 327
   discovery strategies, 620
Metrics, 102, 198, 495–496, 585. *See also*
   AlliedSignal; Process; Quality metrics;
   Quantitative metrics; Results
   choice, 271
   control, 518–521
   deployment, 510, 517–518
   establishment, 189–190
   generation, 239, 269. *See also* Customer
   requirements
   scores, 180
   selection, 269–271
   targets, 269–271
   units, 512
   usage, 551
Meuthing, Rick, 631
Meyer, Christopher, 720
Meyer, Perrin S., 720, 727
Michelangelo, 334
Micromachine Products Division (MPD), 403
Micro-machining. *See* Analog Devices
Microprocessor, 91
Middle ground, 154
Middle management, 414
Mid-term plan, creation process, 678–680
Millet, Jean-Francois, 568
Millikan, Roger, 292
Milliken & Company, 414, 601, 645
Ministry of International Trade and Industry
   (MITI), 647–648
MIS department, 302
Mission, 427–431, 624

examples. *See* SerVend International
   statements, 428. *See also* U.S. company
   value/mission statements
Mistake-proofing techniques, 480
Mistakes, 185, 200
MIT. *See* Massachusetts Institute of
   Technology
MITI. *See* Ministry of International Trade
   and Industry
Mitsufi, Yoshio, 725
Mizuno, Shigeru, 720
Mobilization, 369, 443. *See also*
   Organizations; Process; Quality
   Improvement Team; Teradyne; Top-
   down mobilization
   case studies, 577
   explicit structures, creation, 423–425
   general model, 425–450
   improvement, 178–181
   infrastructure, 423
   results, 180–181
   strategy, 227, 405
Models. *See* Biological model; Mechanical
   model; Social model
Moment-of-truth processes, 86
Monitoring, 333, 445–450, 583. *See also* 7
   Infrastructures; Detailed plan; Hoshin
   management; Teams; Teradyne
   examination, 582–586
Monroe, John, 720
Monson, Elaine, 714
Montgomery, Douglas C., 720
Moore, Geoffrey A., 720
Morris, Desmond, 720
Moscowitz, Ira, 148, 174, 388, 392, 394,
   403, 720
Motivation, 357–358, 376–377, 443–444. *See*
   also Self-motivation
   talent, 347
Motorola, 53, 221, 415, 455, 655
   benchmarking, usage, 473
   Six Sigma
      focus, 462
      goals, 475
      slogan, 472
      support structure, 440
      waste, 474
MPD. *See* Micromachine Products
   Division
MPM. *See* Multipriority method
MTs. *See* Manufacturing Technicians
Multiple thoughts, 256

Multipriority method (MPM), 220–221, 225, 233
method, 382
usage, 256–258
Multi-tasking, avoidance, 490–491
Multivalued attributes, usage, 251
Multi-valued thinking, 384
Multi-valued thought, two-valued thought (contrast), 210
Multiview
creation process, 316–321
grid, 323
Murphy's Law, 30
Murray, George, 105
Mutual learning, 47, 294, 435
commitment, 28
usage, 438
Muzano, 580
Myhrvold, Nathan, 714

N
Nadler, David A., 720
Nakajima, Ichiro, 720
Nanus, Burt, 709
National Bureau of Standards, 452
National Institute of Standards and Technology (NIST), 452, 663
National networking, 645
National promotion organization, 647–649, 663–665
National Public Radio, 59
National standard certification, 647, 651, 668
Natural work teams, 694–695
Naval Inventory Control Point (NAVICP), 323–324, 681
NAVICP. *See* Naval Inventory Control Point
Navratilova, Martina, 345
Navy. *See* U.S. Navy
Nayatani, Yoshinobu, 213, 652
NEC, 16, 38, 55, 333, 339, 427–428, 450
semiconductor division, 623
NEC Integrated-circuit and Microcomputer Systems (NIMS), 22, 463, 465
breakthrough parallels, 635–636
case study, 286, 350, 359, 564
documentation, 575
employee development, 549–555
system, portability, 555
NEC Kansai, 545
NEC Shizuoka, 428, 509–510
Negative statements, avoidance, 251
Negotiation. *See* Atom of work

Nelson, Beebe, 300
Nelson, Brad, 502
Nemoto, Masao, 451, 516, 720
Networking. *See* Company; Companywide Quality Committee; National networking; Regional networking; Societal networking
infrastructure, 647–652, 663–668
usage. *See* Societal diffusion
Newcomb, John, 718
Newfield Group, 300
Nicklaus, Jack, 345, 720
NIH. *See* Not Invented Here
NIMS. *See* NEC Integrated-circuit and Microcomputer Systems
Nishibori, E., 615, 641
NIST. *See* National Institute of Standards and Technology
NMJ. *See* Not My Job
Noble goals, 427
Nolan Norton multi-client study, 596
Nonaka, Yujiro, 716
Non-business fields, 342
Non-business world, lessons, 342–347
Non-master, 343
Nonmonetary awards, 444
Non-TQM companies, 42
Non-value-added activities, 102, 483, 484
Non-value-added work, 481
Nonverbal signs, 150–151
Norming, 396
Not Invented Here (NIH), 25
Not My Job (NMJ), 26, 288
Novak, Barbara, 722
NTT Data Corporation, 465
Hoshin management focus, 462

O
Objectives. *See* Management by objectives
statement, 535
Observations, 68, 275–276. *See also* World-class education
Observer. *See* Open observers
Observers-That-We-Are, 65
Observer-That-One-Is, 64, 65, 286
Obstacles, usage, 191–192
Ochibo-hiroi (gleaning), 568–569
OEM customers, 594
Offers, 315
Ofugi, Tadashi, 248, 721
Okamoto, Susumu, 725
Okumura, Akihiro, 716

One, Michiteru, 248, 721
One-dimensional customer requirements, 261–263
O'Neill, Patrick, 721
One-to-one marketing, 69
Ongoing process, working, 152–153
On-time delivery, 129, 592, 596
Open enrollment, 436
Open observers, 316, 352–354
Open-ended inquiry, 241, 242
Open-ended questions, 227, 245–246
Openness, 573, 646, 662. *See also* Societal networking
Operational processes, 86
Operational success stories, 427
Opinion, fact (contrast), 206–208
Optimistic plans, development, 191
Order fulfillment, 592
Oregon Quality Award, 688
Organizational capability, development, 41
Organizational change, 441
Organizational complexity, 701, 702
Organizational infrastructure, 425
Organizational integrity, re-creation, 609, 638–639
Organizational learning, 22
  system, 20
Organizational setting, 582
Organizations, 107, 497–498, 660. *See also* Customers; Sub-organization
  alignment, 532
  bottom, mobilization, 569
  breakdown, 314
  changes, 636–638
  evolution. *See* Parallel organization
  members, engagement/alignment, 285
  middle, mobilization, 568–569
  mobilization, 661
  reduction. *See* Hierarchical organization
  setting, 431–434
  transformation, 45
Orientation, 453. *See also* Cylcle-time reduction; Results
  phase, 455–456
Outer PDCA cycle, starting, 508
Out-of-context inquiry methods, 243
Output
  determination
    customer needs, 110
    process usage, 110–111
  specification, meeting, 112
  variance, 436–437

reduction, 112
Ownership. *See* Process
Ozeki, Kazuo, 708

P
Packard, David, 614, 721
Paradigm, changes, 636–638
Parallel organization. *See* Hybrid parallel organization
  evolution, 459–461
Pareto creation, 170
Pareto diagram, 132, 146, 156, 164, 477. *See also* Before-and-after Pareto diagrams; Lower-level Pareto diagram
  construction, 572
  data, 178
  derivation, 157
  usage, 137, 530, 536
Pareto items, 169
Parikh, Yogesh, 281, 502
Participant observation, 241, 242
Participation, 376
  bell curve, 603
Pasteur, Louis, 350
Paynting, Richard, 502
Payroll service bureau, 103
PDCA. *See* Plan Do Check Act
PDPC. *See* Process decision program chart
Pedagogic skills, 353–354
People, 592, 601, 660
  focus, 30–35, 701
  listening, 414
  purposes, 701
  relationship. *See* Processes
People plant policies procedures (4Ps), 157
Peppers, Don, 721
Performance, 344, 348. *See also* Atom of work; Customer-related performance
  improvement, 349
  laboratories. *See* Human performance laboratories
  levels, 469
  management, tackling, 387–388
  measure, 536, 539
  relationship. *See* Personal mastery
  review cycles, 392
  standards, usage, 355
  time, allotment, 349
Performing, 396
Periodic analysis, 567
Periodic review, 540–542
Personal contact, making, 413

Personal goals, 378
Personal improvement, modeling, 547–549
Personal mastery, performanc relationship,
    343
Personal PDCA, 661
Personal quality checklists, 324–325, 547
    methods
        personal use, 325–326
        team use, 326–327
Personal responsibility/accountability, 401
Personality. *See* Leaders; Leadership
Personnel policies, 679
PERT chart, 215
Peters, Tom, 665
Peterson, Houston, 721
Peterson, Roger Tory, 347
Petrolini, John, 175, 177, 180–186, 193, 721
    briefing, 674
    contributions, 421
    observation, 418, 459, 587, 603
    selection, 415
Phase review process, 225
Phase-in, 453
    patterns, 461–464
    U.S. focused strategies, 467
Phases. *See* Alignment; Empowerment;
    Orientation
Philosophy-in, 56–57, 68
Philosophy-out, 56–57, 68
Physical arrangement. *See* Teamwork
Physical environment, 245
Picasso, Pablo, 335
Pickup. *See* Focused pickup; Unconstrained
    pickup
PIMS. *See* Profit impact of market strategies
Pine, B. Joseph, 721
Pipp, Frank, 424
PITM. *See* Prove It To Me
Plan, 184, 222–224, 507, 583–584. *See also*
    Plan Do Check Act
    creation process. *See* Mid-term plan
Plan Do Check Act (PDCA), 82, 88–89,
    222–226, 366, 427. *See also* Personal
    PDCA
    concept, 173
    contrast. *See* Check Act Plan Do
    improvement cycle, 459
    incorporation, 458
    incremental improvement, 531
    inhibiting, 499
    initiation, 519
    learning, 229–230

loop. *See* Proactive PDCA loop
    practicing, 560
    process. *See* 7 Steps PDCA process
    running, 173–174, 571
    understanding, 108
    usage, 174, 181, 190, 216, 389, 598. *See
    also* Companywide program; Education
Plan Do Check Act (PDCA) cycle, 83, 92,
    117, 144, 464, 577
    continuation, 550
    conversion, 385
    feedback, 418
    practice, 587
    running, 417–418, 504
    starting. *See* Outer PDCA cycle
    usage, 159, 237, 382, 428, 534
Planning, 75. *See also* Ends planning;
    Hoshing planning; Means planning
    cycle, 522, 562
    phase, 469
    process, creation, 579
    tools. *See* 7 Management and Planning
    Tools
Plans
    development. *See* Detailed plan;
        Optimistic plans
    implementation/monitoring. *See*
        Detailed plan
Platinum accounts, 387
PLUS
    blue sky committee, 633
    customers, innovation, 634
    size, beginning, 633–634
Polanyi, Michael, 285, 721
Polaroid Corporation, 379, 428, 477, 654
    CE interaction, 236
    Land camera, 9
Policies, alignment, 695–696
Poling, Sheila R., 121, 726
Positive lessons, comments, 150
Possibilities, conversations, 316–322
Potential customers, listening, 242–247
Potential team, 397
Powell, Thomas, 295, 602, 721
    (research), 602–604
Powlison, Dave, 721
Practices, 344, 469, 491. *See also* Reflective
    practice
    levels, 47–48. *See also* Total participation
    time, allotment, 349
Practicing methods, 349
Practitioners, rotation, 353–354

Prahalad, C.K., 721
Premature detail, avoidance, 252
Preparation, 220
Preparedness, 543–544
Presentation format, 442
Presentation meetings, 438
Presidential diagnosis, 567–569, 580
    process, 584–585
    results, 585
President's diagnosis, 521–523, 567–568
    purposes/benefits, 523
Prestridge, Jim, 579, 586
Price
    competition, 416
    contrast. See Cost/price contrast
Pricing requirement, 129
Prior tradition, 348
Priorities, setting, 603
Proactive improvement, 79, 196, 199
    application, range expansion, 280–281
    data collection, 201–204
    expansion, 278–281
    process, 211
    standard tools, 211–221
    steps, 211–221
    usage. See Products
Proactive methods, 471–472
    balance, 476
Proactive PDCA loop, 521
Proactive phase. See Hoshin management
Proactive stage, 79
Problem complexity, 701
Problem solving, 370, 402
Problems
    complexity, segmentation, 599–601
    exploration, 125, 127
    identification, 125–131
    process detection, 162
    reflecting, 169–170
Problem-solving cycle, 163
Problem-solving method, 196
Problem-solving process, 73, 75, 123–125,
    142, 402
Problem-solving skills, 161, 162
Problem-solving steps, 377
Problem-solving training, 378
Procedures, usage, 162
Process. See Customer-related process;
    Management by process; Proactive
    improvement; Work
    balance, 467–468, 475
    behavior chart, 110, 114–117

business breakthrough, contrast, 607–610
control, 76–77, 107–109, 117–118, 181,
    564–565
data, usage, 156
design, 495. See also Cycle-time reduction
    tools, 497
detection. See Problems
development. See Teradyne
diagnosis, 379
documentation, 181
emphasis. See Improvement
engineers, 332
flowcharting, 477
focus, 351, 472
goals, 427
identification, 56, 100–102
knowledge, 495, 498
management mobilization. See Teradyne
    case study, 175
mapping, 56
method, 496–497
metrics, 564
model. See Quality Improvement Team
observation, 241
output, 110, 112–117
ownership, 493
participation, 242
QI, 598–599
quality, 430
reflection, 144–145, 162–163,
    169–170, 274
standardization, 430
thinking, 95–98
usage. See Effectiveness increase; Output
variation, 107
wisdom, 494. See also Cycle-time
    reduction
Process decision program chart (PDPC),
    214–215
Process discovery, 98–105, 181
    benefits, 102
    examples, 103–105
    steps, 99–102
    usage. See Management
Process for results, 351–352
Process improvement, 117–118
    capability, 495
    case study. See Structural process
    improvement
    leading, 547
Process-driven principle, 416

Processes. *See* Innovative processes;
    Moment-of-truth processes; Operational
    processes
    continuous improvement, usage, 84–92
    explicitness, 351–352
    incremental improvements, 591
    people, relationship, 291–295
    types, 85–88
Process-oriented intermediate goals, 429
Procter and Gamble, 415
Product-out, 51
Products, 469, 592
    competitive analysis, 470
    complexity, 362
    concept, 276–277
    data. *See* Competitive product data
    delivery requirements, 102
    development. *See* Revolutionary Product
    Development
    proactive improvement usage, 235
    failure rate, 592
    generation slip rate, 592
    identification, 56, 100, 104
    introduction, 337
    providing, 100
    requirements, exceeding, 102
    review board, 225
    weaknesses, 224
Projects
    plans, 590
Profit impact of market strategies
    (PIMS), 39
Projects
    description, 186
    management process, 592
    planning, 183
    progress, 193
    tasks, arrival, 488–490
Promotion, 333, 471
    activities. *See* Societal promotion
    activities
    organization. *See* National promotion
    organization
Promotional activities, 441
Prove It To Me (PITM), 26
Przasnyski, Zbigniew H., 724
Pseudo-team, 397
Purpose, focuse, 30–35
Pursch, Tom, 578, 723
Pushing power, 453
Putnam, Robert W., 39, 300, 301, 327,
    719, 721

Q
QC. *See* Quality Control
QC Research Group, 652
QCD. *See* Quality cost delivery
QFD. *See* Quality Function Deployment
QI. *See* Quality Improvement
QIP team, 148
QIT. *See* Quality Improvement Team
QMS. *See* Quality Maturity System
QMs. *See* Quality metrics
Qualitative data, 204, 335
    gathering, 355
Qualitative language, 331
Quality, 129, 189, 592. *See also*
    Management; Process; Total quality
    analysis, 477
    building, 6
    checklists. *See* Personal quality checklists
    concepts, 9–11. *See also* Fitness of cost;
    Fitness to latent requirement; Fitness to
    standard; Fitness to use
    example, 10
    continuing evolution, 15–16
    control, education, 648
    cost, approach. *See* Cost of quality
    approach
    goals, 56
    importance, 623
    inspection, 6
    invisible ideas, 260
    management, 43, 76, 659
    results, 427
    satisfaction decay, 265–268
    table, usage, 270–271
    tools, 601
Quality Control (QC), 124
    circles, 11, 13, 197, 367–377, 650
    activities, 373, 375–377. *See also*
    Japanese QC circle activities
    implementation, 406
    team, evolution. *See* Japanese QC team
    theme, 373
Quality cost delivery (QCD), 54, 60, 100–104
    categories, 105
Quality Function Deployment (QFD), 11,
    211, 276–277, 459, 477
Quality Improvement (QI). *See* Continuous
    quality improvement; Process
    general guidelines, 149–152
    history, 415
    practices, 542
    sample diagnosis, 170–173

step-by-step guidelines, 152–163
story, 149, 150, 154, 409, 442
    diagnosis, 439
    diffusion, 457, 673
    presentation, 151, 152
    representation, 443
Quality Improvement Team (QIT), 96, 126,
    176, 367, 443. *See also* 7 Steps method;
    Broken Pellicle QIT
    cycle, 178
    metrics, 186
    mobilization, 180
    process model, 179
Quality Maturity System (QMS), 589–590,
    604, 607, 620
Quality metrics (QMs), 269–272
Quantitative data, 335
    usage, 354–355
Quantitative engineering process, 277
Quantitative metrics, 269
Quantitative results, 354–355
Questionnaire. *See* Kano questionnaire
    usage. *See* Customer requirements
Questions. *See* Open-ended questions
Queuing theory, 486

R
Radar graph, 146
Ragas, Ed, 586, 604
Rallies, sharing. *See* Sharing rallies
Ramaswamy, Ranjan, 238
Rapaille, Clautaire, 61. *See also* Cultural
    archetypes
Rapaille, Clotaire, G., 286, 721
Raskin, Larry, 301
Rasmussen, Neil, 502, 722
R&D. *See* Research and development
Reactive improvement, 77–79, 123, 124, 156,
    521
    7 steps, 402
    management diagnosis, 149
    standardization, 132
    steps/tools, 131–133
    usage, 196, 200
Reactive methods, 471–472
    balance, 476
Reactive phase. *See* Hoshin management
ReadRite Corporation, 338
Real team, 397
Reasoning
    cycle, 65–66
    sequence. *See* Customers

Recognition, 585
Recreational activities, 373
Recruiting, 348
Red Cross, 57, 59
Reflected practices, 425
Reflection, 443, 534–535. *See* Process
Reflective practice, 24, 36, 349–351
Regional networking, 645
Regression analysis, 477
Regulatory responsibilities, 679
Reilly, Jack, 58, 300, 722
Reinertsen, Donald, 489, 722, 724
Reinforcement, 604
Relations diagram, 213–214, 382
Relationships, conversations, 322–323
Renoir, Pierre-August, 337
Report language, 205
Requirements dimensions (Kano), 60–61
Requirements LP, development, 258–260
Research. *See* Companywide Quality
    Committee
Research and development (R&D), 348, 459,
    465, 499
Respect, lack, 378
Response time, 548
Responsibility. *See* Personal
    responsibility/accountability
    assumption, 566
Results, 376–377, 445, 448. *See also* Cycle-
    time results; Process for results;
    Quality; Quantitative results
    balance, 467–468
    focus, 472
    getting, 603
    goals, 351
    metrics, 564
    orientation, 475
Retirement trusts, 103
Review. *See* Periodic review
    board. *See* Products
    process. *See* Phase review process
    table. *See* Analog Devices
Revolution, 378, 653
Revolutionary Product Development (RPD),
    582, 604
    deployment, 586
Rinearson, Peter M., 714
RISC processors, 91
Ritz-Carlton Hotel Company, 61
Robbins, Harvey, 722
Robbins, Owen, 587
Roberts, Harry V., 324–326, 547, 722

Robinson, Beth, 722
Rockefeller University, 610
Rodriguez, Richard, 502
Rogas, Ed, 632
Rogers, Everett M., 722
Rogers, Martha, 721
Role playing, 345
Roos, Carl, 502
Roos, Daniel, 727
Root cause, 159, 165, 167
Root cause reversal, solution usage, 159
Rosenthal, Steve, 502
Rousmaniere, John, 711
Routine operations, execution, 463
Routine work, 289, 438–439, 558–560
  delegation, 366
  explicit joining, 287–291
  unification, Hoshin management usage,
    520–521
RPD. *See* Revolutionary Product
  Development
Rummler, Geary, 492, 722
Running, 173–174
Running chart, 389

S

Sakakibara, Kiyonori, 716
Samuel, Mark, 401, 722
Sanden company, 624
Sasaki, Hajime, 623
Sasaoka, Ken, 613–614
Scatter diagram, 132, 147
Schedule, inclusion, 154
Schein, Edgar H., 295, 325, 357, 401, 722
Schneidermann, Art, 703, 722, 723
Schoeffler, Sidney, 723
Scholtes, Peter R., 723
Schon, Donald, 708
Schools/colleges, 59
Schroeder, Richard, 501, 715
Schwettmann, Fred, 329
Scientific method, contrast. *See* Continuous
  improvement
SCMT. *See* Sense Commit Mental
  breakthrough Technical breakthrough
Scorecards, 596
Script. *See* Interview
S-curve, 610
SDCA. *See* Standard Do Check Act
SDWTs. *See* Self-directed work teams
Searle, John R., 327, 723
Seiketsu, 569

Seiko, 610–613, 614, 626
  approaches, 613
  products, 611
Seiri, 569
Seiso, 569
Seiton, 569
Self-assessment, 447
Self-development, 341
  form, testing, 349–350
Self-diagnosis, 162
Self-directed work teams (SDWTs), 198, 367,
  389, 391. *See also* Analog Devices
  benefits/problems, 393–394
  case study, 594
  meeting, 392
Self-improvement, 357
Self-learning, 595
Self-motivation, 357
Semantics
  principles, expansion, 302–305
  usage, 204–210. *See also* Language
Senge, Peter, 674, 723
Senior management, attendance, 149–150
Senior managers, 176, 437, 566, 595–596
Seniority, 624
Sense Commit Mental breakthrough
  Technical breakthrough (SCMT), 576,
    615–616
  breakthrough cycle, 608
Seraku, Nobuhiko, 717
Sergesketter, Bernard F., 326, 547–548, 722
SerVend International, 395, 413, 450
  Business System, 689
  business system, evolution, 689–693
  case study, 688–697
  examination, 694–697
  goals/values/mission examples, 429–431
  issues, 694
  management system, 675
  opportunities/rewards, 430
  work teams, focus, 462
Services, 469
  delivery requirements, 102
  identification, 56, 100, 104
  providing, 100
  requirements, exceeding, 102
Shapiro, Amram R., 719
Shared commitment, 400–401
Shared concerns, 308, 314–315
  aligning/coordination, explicit models, 323
  discovery, 316–322
  process, 321–322

variations, 66–68
Sharing rallies, 645
Sherman, Stratford, 725
Shewhart, Walter A., 94, 112, 664, 723
Shiba, Shoji, 4, 93, 154, 185–186, 403, 673,
    718, 723
    2-6-2 rule, 603
    advice, 203, 219, 230, 336
    business experience, 188
    concept, 337
    courses, 655
    data collection, 406, 420
    experience, 501
    guidance, 222, 379
    instruction, 224, 596, 655
    knowledge, 197
    leadership thinking, 330
    meeting. *See* d'Arbeloff
    presentations, 579
    recollection, 202–204, 587
    recommendations, 228
    research, 627
    sequence, 464
    Stata meeting, 595
    steps, 218
    strategies, search, 621
    students, 375
    studies, 608
    study, 329, 330
    survey, 409
    theories, 639
    translations, 381
    visits, 451
Shingo, Shigeo, 480, 502, 724
Shipment, delay, 130–131
Shitsuke, 569
Shizuoka. *See* NEC Shizuoka
Shriver, Pam, 345
Shuba, George, 347
Singhal, Vinog R., 715, 724
Sisyphus model, 456
Situation analysis, 678
Six Sigma, 206, 232, 429, 468, 472–479,
    667
    Academy, 476, 501, 665
    application, 474–476
    focus. *See* AlliedSignal; General Electric;
      Motorola
    name, reason, 473–474
    positioning, 478–479
    practice, spreading, 476–479
Six Sigma Plus, 478

Skill development, 22–28, 173–174. *See also*
    Companywide Quality Committee
    application, commitment, 27–28
    phases, 22–24
    practice, 701
Skills, 344, 353. *See also* Conceptual skill;
    Human skill; Improvement; Leadership;
    Pedagogic skills; Problem-solving
    skills; Soft-side skills; Teamwork;
    Technical skill; Individual skills
    degree, 23
    erosion, 358
Skunk works organizations, 349
Slack time, 488, 489
Slip rate. *See* Products
Sloan School of Management. *See*
    Massachusetts Institute of Technology
Small group dynamics, 374–375
Smith, Bill, 53, 456, 473, 500
Smith, Diana McLain, 719
Smith, Douglas K., 395–398, 403, 717, 724
Smith, Preston G., 724
Social model, 33
Social sciences, 36
Societal diffusion. *See* Total Quality
    Management
    networking usage, 645
Societal environment. *See* Fitness for
    societal/global environment
Societal learning, 405
    cases, 444
Societal networking, 42, 236–237, 643
    case study, 299–302
    Japanese model, 646–654
      cases, openness, 652–653, 668–669
      methods, development, 651–652, 668
    methods, 45
      integration, 675
    national methods, comparison, 662–671
Societal promotion activities, 647, 651,
    667–668
Societies, advancement, 427
Society for Organizational Learning, 665
Soft-side skills, 292
Software development/test, 385
Soin, Sarv Singh, 526, 724
Solutions
    consistency. *See* Causal analysis
    implementation, 140–142, 159–160,
      167–168
      facts, 160
    management acceptance, 160

planning, 140–142, 159–160, 167–168
  explanation. *See* Audience
screening, 274
standardization, 162, 168–169
statements, avoidance, 251–252
usage. *See* Root cause reversal
Sony, Walkman, 9, 265
SPC, 548
Spear, Steven, 576, 724
Spendolini, Michael J., 724
Spinosa, Charles, 724
SQC. *See* Statistical Quality Control
Stading, Gary L., 718
Staff specialists. *See* Facilitators
Stakeholder, 686
Standard, 289–290. *See also* Standard Do
  Check Act
Standard best practices, 666
Standard Do Check Act (SDCA), 77, 198,
  211
  achievement, 463
  action, 518
  activity, 181, 182
  adherence, 556
  application, 694
  cycle, 78, 107, 230, 288–289, 292
    usage, 117, 558
  maintenance, 531
  process, 290
  system, 571
Standardization. *See* Solutions
  facts, 162
Starr, Ed, 502
Starts control, 491, 495
Stasey, Robert, 531, 723
Stata, Ray, 292, 300, 324, 415, 673, 724
  Ackoff quote, 458
  descriptions, 605
  history, 593
  recollections, 421, 629
  report, 460
  Shiba meeting, 595
State/local governments, 59
Statements. *See* Ambiguous/unambiguous
    statements; U.S. company value/mission
    statements
  avoidance. *See* Negative statements;
    Solutions
Statements of fact, 302–303
Statistical Quality Control (SQC), 4
  usage. *See* Toyota
Stephens, K.S., 725

Stepping stones, 202–203
Stewart, Reigle, 715
Stewart, Thomas A., 724
Storming, 396
Strategic planning, 677. *See* Hoshin
    management
  forms, problems, 677
  survey, 661
Strategic vision, knowledge, 602
Stratification, 132, 147. *See also* Data
Strauss, Anselm L., 232, 714
Stripping basket (case study), 248, 250–277
  concept engineering usage, 237–239, 245
Structural process improvement, 675
  case study, 681–687
Structure
  alignment, 687
  mapping, 683–684
  repair, 603
Strunk, William, 281, 724
Sub-organization, 333
Success, 375. *See also* Business
  bootstrapping, 589
  responsibility, 358
  stories. *See* Operational success stories
    diffusion, 333, 441–444, 471
Support structure. *See* Motorola
  creation. *See* Institutional support
    structures
Supportive environment. *See* Local
    improvement
Surveys, 243
  data, 263
  e-mail distribution. *See* Kano surveys
Suttler, Goodloe, 593–595, 598
  (summary), 423, 601
Swift, Jeff, 386, 724
Symbolic cases, 336
Symbolic facts, 232
Synergy. *See* Breakthrough
System Dynamics, 675, 676
System QA, 385
Systematic improvement, 75–76
Systems engineering, 523–524
Systems Path, 697
Systems Thinking, 676
Szarkowski, John, 91, 724

T
Taguchi experiments, 477
Tai, Lawrence S., 724
Takahashi, Fumio, 717

Talk-nard, 620, 624
Tampering, 497
Tangible models. *See* Business
Tasks, planning, 183
Tatsuno, Sheridan M., 724
Taylor, 52, 53
TCS. *See* Teradyne
Teacher-student roles, 435, 438
Teaching
assignment, 439
usage, 352
Team-oriented environment, 388
Teams. *See* Analog Devices; CQM
    Design Team; Cross-functional
    teams; High-performance team;
    Management; Natural work teams;
    Potential team; Pseudo-team;
    Real team
  activities, 369–379
  benefits. *See* Core teams
  case studies, 363
  comments, 394–395
  communication skill, 332
  development model, 363, 396–402
  effectiveness, 363
  focus, 363
  fundamentals, 361–367
  leader, 392
  management, 392–393
  maturity model, 389–390
  members, 366
  monitoring, 392–393. *See also* Teradyne
  operations, 391–392
  performance, 356
  role, 356
  setup, 378
  system, improvement, 392–393
  types, 367–396
  work, 414
Teamwork, 412, 477. *See also* Cross-
    company teamwork
  case study, 371–374, 379–385
  development, 399
    models, 363
  environment, 364–366
  focus, 363
  necessary conditions, 400–402
  physical arrangement, 365–366
  plan, 365
  skill, 361
  view, 624–625

Technical breakthrough, 625, 633. *See also*
    Sense Commit Mental breakthrough
    Technical breakthrough
Technical skill, 331–332
Teradyne, 379
  9 Steps
    case study, 578
    mobilization, 185–186, 578
    usage, illustration, 186–196
  Aurora, 578, 630–633, 636
    breakthroughs, summary, 632–633
  breakthrough parallels, 635–636
  CEO involvement (case study), 410–413,
    578
  CQC usage, 586
  improvement teams, monitoring, 445, 578
  introduction strategy, 415
  mobilization, 175, 335, 578–588
  process development, 399
  process management mobilization, 578
  QI teams, focus, 462
  strategy (case study), 415–420
  TCS plant, 584
  TQM
    Annual Hoshin Plan, 582
    companywide introduction, 415–420
    office, 440
  Values, 417
TEX math typesetting program, 355
Texas Instruments, 412, 476
Theme
  completion, 373
  explanation. *See* Audience
  selection, 125, 128, 133–136, 152–154, 164
    matrix, 128
  statement, examples, 125, 129–131
Theory of Constraints. *See* Constraints
Theory W, 639, 641
Theory X, 639, 641
Theory Y, 639, 641
Thinking. *See* 0-1 thinking; Multi-valued
    thinking; Shiba; Two-valued thinking
Thomas, Robert J., 295, 724
Thomson, Lord Kelvin, 354
Thought. *See* Multiple thoughts; Two-value
    thought
  contrast. *See* Multi-valued thought
Throughput, incompatibility. *See*
    Utilization
Thurow, Lester C., 94, 725
Tichy, Noel M., 725
Time pressure, 621

Time scale, 337
Timing, 544
TIPD. *See* Transportation and Industrial
    Products Division
Title groups, 219
Tokyo Institute of Technology, 669
Tokyo rika University, 260
Tokyo University, 669
Top-down mobilization, 567–568
Topics
    advancing, 160
    agreement, 218
Top-to-bottom communication, 414
Total participation, 42, 283. *See* Employees
    practice levels, 293–295
Total productive maintenance (TPM), 478
Total quality, 588
Total Quality Control (TQC), 588
    usage. *See* Hewlett-Packard
Total Quality Management (TQM), 16, 17,
    382, 412, 708
    background, 329
    committee, 431
    companies. *See* Non-TQM companies
    companywide introduction. *See* Teradyne
    concepts/practices, 42
    development, 41
    diffusion, 649
    managers, 433
    positioning, 478–479
    presentation, 192
    societal diffusion, 646
    studying, 602
    usage, 46–47, 85
Toyota, 503, 623
    SQC, usage, 479
    TQM program, 478
TPM. *See* Total productive maintenance
TQC. *See* Total Quality Control
TQM. *See* Total Quality Management
Tradition. *See* Prior tradition
Training, 412–413, 434–440, 499, 647,
    649–650, 665. *See also* 7 Steps training;
    Cross-training; Customer visitation;
    Executives; Problem-solving training
    cascading, 603
    inputs, planning, 435–437
    providing, 426
    usage, 333, 348. *See also* Just-In-Time
Translation. *See* Customers
    guidelines, 250
    usage, 250–252

Transportation and Industrial Products
    Division (TIPD), 386–388
Tree analysis. *See* Fault tree analysis
Tree diagram, 214, 270
Trial/error, usage, 349
Triggers, 399. *See also* Improvement
Trust loop, 323
    model, 398–402
Trusting relationships, building, 322–323
Tsuji, Shinichi, 717
Tuckman, Bruce W., 396, 725
Tuckman model, 396
Turing Award, 350
Tushman, Michael L., 720
Twiname, Eric, 342, 359, 725
Two-value thought, contrast. *See* Multi-
    valued thought
Two-valued concepts, avoidance, 251
Two-valued thinking, 251
Two-way conversation, 317

U
Uchimaru, Kiyoshi, 549, 553–555, 725
Ueda, Hidemi, 725
Ulrich, Karl T., 236, 725
Unconstrained pickup, 220
Understanding, 24
    evolution, 43–47
    usage. *See* Customers
        understanding, 108
Uniform learning, 436
Unions, 103
Unit goals, 377
Universal truth, 36
University of Chicago, 324
University of Lille, 232
Uniview, 322
    grid, 323
UNIX, 630
Unlearning, strategies, 621
UNPL. *See* Upper natural process limit
Upper Control Limit, 121
Upper natural process limit (UNPL), 111,
    114–115, 118, 121
Upper specification limit (USL), 110
Urban, Glen L., 725
U.S. company value/mission statements,
    428–429
U.S. Declaration of Independence, 302
U.S. focused strategies. *See* Phase-in
U.S. invented methods, 467–468
U.S. Navy (case study), 323–327

U.S. Olympic Sailing Team, 351
USA Today Quality Cup, 688
   usage, 174, 181, 190, 216, 379, 598. *See
      also* Education
User requirements, 214
Usher, Abbott Payson, 91, 725
USL. *See* Upper specification limit
Utilization
   curves, 487
   throughput incompatibility, 485–488

V
Value
   equation. *See* Business
   examples. *See* SerVend International
   statements. *See* U.S. company
      value/mission statements
Values, 601
Varela, Francisco J., 719
Variance
   analysis, 477
   reduction. *See* Output
   usage, 112–113
Variation. *See* Process
   example, continuation, 118–120
   mishandling, 108–109
   sources, determination/removal, 112
   stability/unstability, 113–114
   types, 114–115
   usage, 109–117
Velazquez, Diego, 336
Vision, 223, 427–431, 601, 624, 677–678.
   See also World-class vision
   alignment, 695–696
   statements, 428
Visitation. *See* Customer visitation
   process, 241–242
   program (case study). *See* Bolt Beranek
      and Newman
Visual Basic, 632
Vital few, 170, 427, 686
   focus, 217
   issues, 81–82
VLSI, 631
VOC. *See* Voice of the customer
Vocabulary, 610
Voehl, Frank, 423
Voice. *See* Customers
   multiple interpretations, 256
Voice of the customer (VOC), 37, 110, 198,
   440, 500
   collection, 242–247

   initiative, 243
   transformation, 248–256
   translation, 250, 253–256
Voluntarism, 376–377
von Hippel, Eric, 58, 203, 240–241, 725

W
W model, 93
Wadsworth, H.M., 725
Wafer fabrication, 134–145, 165
Walden, David, 70, 502, 680, 710, 719, 722,
   723, 725, 726
   case study, 403
   codification, 301
   experience, 354
   rereading, 342
   research, 343
Walker, Hap, 632
Walker, James P., 726
Walkman. *See* Sony
Walls, Ted, 70, 726
Waste, 185, 200
Water ring principle, 622
WCNDT. *See* We Could Never Do That
We Could Never Do That (WCNDT), 26
Weakness orientation, 125–127, 152
Webspective, 462
Welchman, John C., 726
What if? questions, 214
Wheeler, Donald J., 120, 121, 359, 726
Wheelwright, Steven C., 726
Which? questions, 214
White, E.B., 281, 724
Why? questions, 213, 457
Williams, Keith, 713, 714
Wilson, Edward O., 726
Winograd, Terry, 726
Winslow, Peter, 238
Woll, Toby, 502, 680–681, 708, 726
Womack, James, 727
Wood, Chapman Robert, 641, 718
Work. *See* Atom of work; Group work;
     High-quality work; Improvement; Non-
     value-added work; Teams; Individual
     work
   concept, changes, 51
   continuous improvement, usage, 84–92
   dual function, 288, 571
      ubiquity, 556–560
   enriched view, 624
   environment, 243
   explicit joining. *See* Improvement

identification, 56
process, 412
teams. *See* Analog Devices; Natural work
   teams
   focus. *See* SerVend International
Work groups, 47, 397
Work-arounds, 182
Worker presentations, 442
World War II, 3
World Wide Web (WWW / Web) site, 19
World-class education, 434
   observations, 435–440
World-class performance, 438
World-class training, 434
World-class vision, 695
W.R. Grace, 300
WV model, 75, 93, 107, 123–125, 278, 402.
   See also Continuous improvement
   components, 200
   expansion, 211, 278–281
   extension, 238
   usage, 152, 199, 368, 598

X
Xerox, 409, 410, 424, 437, 655. *See also* Fuji
   Xerox
   benchmarking, 500
   focus, 462
   usage, 455
   cost reduction strategy, 465

Y
Yamada, Susumu, 627, 629, 725
YHP. *See* Yokogawa HP
Yokogawa Electric, 610, 619–622
   web page, 624
Yokogawa HP (YHP), 456, 503, 588, 603,
   613–614, 626
Yo-one ceremony, 27–28
Young, Arthur H., 712
Young, John, 588
Yung, Jason W., 720, 727

Colophon

The text and draft layout of this book were created using LaTeX2E. Illustrations were created and saved in EPS format using Adobe Illustrator. The source text was transformed into a PostScript file using components of the "free" MiKTeX TeX distribution including the **dvips** driver, which also embeds EPS figures in the PostScript file. For editing iterations, the PostScript output was transformed to the PDF format using Adobe Distiller 3.01.

The final electronic version of the manuscript was produced by compiling the LaTeX2E (files into HTML using the VTeX LaTeX processor and cutting and pasting from HTML to text-only files. The text files were formatted and "typeset," including illustrations, using QuarkXpress, which also produced final Postscript output from which printing was done.

Type composition of this book was in Times Roman and Helvetica. Various weights of these typefaces were used for style.